CERTIFICATE IN ESG INVESTING CURRICULUM 2023

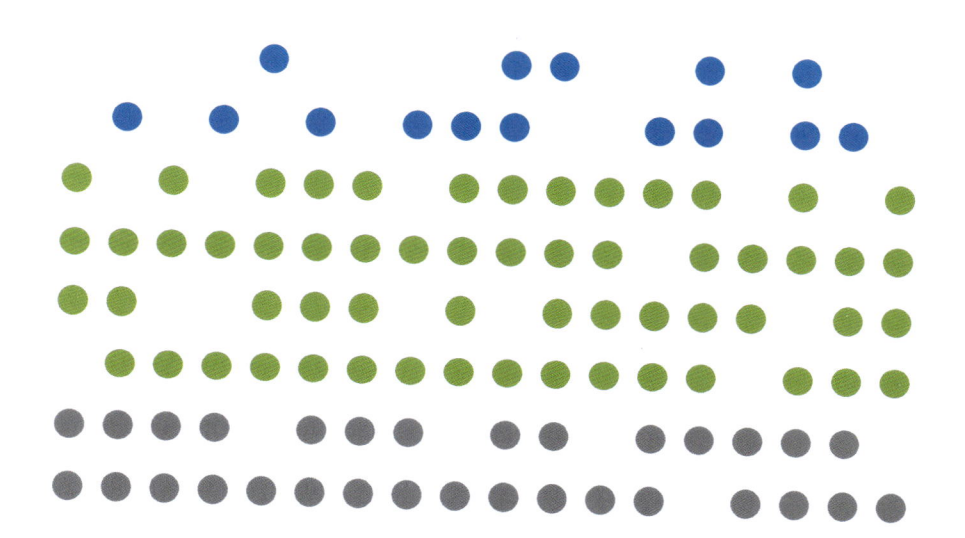

CFA Institute
Certificate in ESG Investing

COPYRIGHT

© 2022 CFA Institute. All rights reserved.

No part of this publication may be reproduced or transmitted in any form or by any means, electronic or mechanical, including photocopy, recording, or any information storage and retrieval system, without permission of the copyright holder.

To view a list of CFA Institute trademarks and the Guide for the Use of CFA Institute Marks, please visit our website at www.cfainstitute.org.

ISBN: 978-1-953337-80-1

Authors

Chapters 1 and 2
Clarisse Simonek, CFA , WeESG
Thomas Verhagen, WeESG

Chapter 3
Shuen Chan, Legal & General Investment Management (LGIM), Real Assets
Iancu Daramus, Fulcrum Asset Management

Chapter 4
Vincent van Bijleveld, Finance Ideas Sustainable Investment Consultants
Rudy Verstappen, Altera Vastgoed

Chapters 5, 6 and 9
Paul Lee, Redington

Chapter 7
Ben Yeoh, CFA, RBC Global Asset Management

Chapter 8
J. Jason Mitchell, Man Group plc

CFA Institute would also like to sincerely thank the following contributors:

Sylvia Solomon, ASIP
Brishni Mukhopadhyay, CFA
Monica Filkova, CFA
Claudia Gollmeier, CFA, CIPM
Matyas Horak, CFA, FRM
Fionnuala O'Grady, MSc
Vincent Piscaer
Maxine Wille, CFA
Hardik Shah, CFA
William Moomaw, PhD
David Sanders, CFA
Nick Bartlett, CFA

CONTENTS

Copyright		ii
Authors		ii
Unit Aims		xi
Introduction		xiii
ESG Update		xiii
Foreword by Marg Franklin		xv

Chapter 1 — Introduction to ESG Investing — 17

Introduction	17
What Is ESG Investing?	18
Long-Termism and ESG Investing	18
The Definition and Scope of ESG Issues	19
Types of Responsible Investment	20
Responsible Investment	21
Macro-Level Debate on ESG Integration	27
Macro-Level Debate on Integrating ESG Considerations	28
Financial Materiality of ESG Integration	37
Efficiency and Productivity	37
Reduced Risk of Fines and State Intervention	38
Improved Ability to Benefit from Sustainability Megatrends	43
Challenges in Integrating ESG Factors	46
ESG Factors' Influence on Financial Performance	49
Putting ESG Investing into Practice	51
Investment Decisions	51
Shareholder Engagement	52
Policy Engagement	52
Key Initiatives	52
United Nations Initiatives	53
Reporting Initiatives	58
Key Facts	*62*
Further Reading	*64*
Self Practice and Self Assessment	*65*
Solutions	*69*

Chapter 2 — The ESG Market — 71

Introduction	71
History of ESG Investing, Including Modern Responsible Investment	72
A Brief History of Sustainability	72
Early Phase of ESG Investing	72
Modern Responsible Investment	73
ESG Investing in Numbers	74
Market Drivers of ESG and Challenges in ESG Integration	79
Asset Owners	81
Pension Funds	84
Insurance	88
Sovereign Wealth	89

	Individual (Retail) Investors and Wealth Management	90
	Asset Managers, Fund Promoters, and Financial Services	91
	Investment Consultants and Retail Financial Advisers	93
	Investment Platforms	94
	Fund Labelers	94
	Policymakers, Regulators, Investees, Governments, Civil Society, and Academia	95
	Examples of Policy and Regulatory Developments across the Globe	97
	Investees	103
	Governments	104
	Civil society	104
	Academia	104
	Key Facts	*105*
	Further Reading	*108*
	Self Practice and Self Assessment	*109*
	Solutions	*113*
Chapter 3	**Environmental Factors**	**115**
	Introduction	116
	Key Environmental Issues	117
	Climate Change	121
	Pressures on Natural Resources	139
	Pollution, Waste, and a Circular economy	146
	Systemic Relationships between Business Activities and Environmental Issues	150
	Systemic Risks to the Financial System: Physical and Transitional Risks	151
	The Relationship between Natural Resources and Business	153
	Supply, Operational, and Resource Management Issues	154
	Supply Chain Transparency and Traceability	156
	Key "Megatrends" and Drivers Influencing Environmental Change in Terms of Potential Impact on Companies and Their Environmental Practices	161
	Growth of Environmental and Climate Policies	161
	International Climate and Environmental Agreements and Conventions	161
	Assessment of Materiality of Environmental Issues	178
	Corporate and Project Finance	179
	Public Finance Initiatives	180
	Asset Management	183
	Approaches to Account for Material Environmental Analysis and Risk Management Strategies	185
	Levels of Environmental Analysis	186
	Analyzing Environmental Risks	188
	Applying Material Environmental Factors to Financial Modeling, Ratio Analysis, and Risk Assessment	196
	Opportunities Relating to Climate Change and Environmental Issues	200
	Circular Economy	201
	Clean and Technological Innovation	202
	Green and ESG-Related Products	208
	Blue Economy	214

Contents

Key Facts	*217*
Further Reading	*219*
Self Practice and Self Assessment	*220*
Solutions	*224*

Chapter 4 Social Factors — 227

Introduction to Social Factors	228
Social and Environmental Megatrends	228
What Are Social Megatrends?	228
Globalization	229
Automation and Artificial Intelligence (AI)	229
Inequality and Wealth Creation	230
Digital Disruption, Social Media, and Access to Electronic Devices	231
Changes to Work, Leisure Time, and Education	231
Changes to Individual Rights and Responsibilities and Family Structures	232
Changing Demographics, Including Health and Longevity	232
Investor Initiatives: Equitable Circulation of COVID-19 Vaccines	233
Urbanization	234
Religion	234
Environmental Megatrends with Social Impact	235
Key Social Issues and Business Activities	236
Internal Social Factors	237
Human Capital Development	237
Working Conditions, Health, and Safety	238
Human Rights	239
Labor Rights	241
External Social Factors	244
Stakeholder Opposition and Controversial Sourcing	244
Product Liability and Consumer Protection	245
Social Opportunities	246
Animal Welfare and Antimicrobial Resistance	246
Identifying Material Social Factors for Investors	247
Country	247
Sector	249
Company Level	249
Application of Social Factors in Investments	249
Materiality or Risk Assessment	250
Quality of Management	253
Ratio Analysis and Financial Modeling	253
Key Facts	*255*
Megatrends	255
Further Reading	*257*
Self Practice and Self Assessment	*258*
Solutions	*262*

Chapter 5 Governance Factors — 265

Corporate Governance: Accountability and Alignment	266

What is Governance? Why Does It Matter?	266
Formalized Corporate Governance Frameworks	270
Corporate Governance Codes	270
Shareholder Engagement and Alignment	275
Characteristics of Effective Corporate Governance: Board Structure and Executive Remuneration	277
Board Structure, Diversity, Effectiveness, and Independence	278
Executive Remuneration	283
Characteristics of Effective Corporate Governance: Transparency, Capital Allocation, and Business Ethics	285
Reporting and Transparency	285
Financial Integrity and Capital Allocation	287
Business Ethics	288
Structural Corporate Governance Differences in Major World Markets	290
Corporate Governance in Australia	290
Corporate Governance in France	291
Corporate Governance in Germany	292
Corporate Governance in Italy	293
Corporate Governance in Japan	294
Corporate Governance in the Netherlands	295
Corporate Governance in Sweden	295
Corporate Governance in the UK	296
Corporate Governance in the USA	297
Corporate Governance and the Independent Audit Function	299
Reviewing Financial Statements, Annual Reports, and Wider Reporting (Including Sustainability Reports)	299
The Independence of Audit Firms and Conflicts of Interest	301
Auditor Rotation	301
Sampling and Audit Work	302
Enhanced Auditor Reports	302
Auditor Liability	303
Internal Audit	304
Corporate Governance and the Investment Decision-Making Process	304
Integrating Governance into Investment and Stewardship Processes	308
Key Facts	*310*
Further Reading	*311*
Recommended Books on Individual Scandals	311
Self Practice and Self Assessment	*312*
Solutions	*316*

Chapter 6   Engagement and Stewardship   319

Stewardship & Engagement: What's Involved and Why It's Important	319
What Is Stewardship? What Is Engagement?	320
Why Engagement?	323
Engagement in Practice	326
Codes/Standards & Engagement Styles	327
Code Revisions 2020	329
Code Provisions	331
Engagement Styles	332

Contents

Styles: Top-Down and Bottom-Up	333
Styles: Issue-Based and Company-Focused	333
Effective Engagement: Forms, Goal Setting	334
Forms of Engagement	334
Strategy and Tactics: Goal-Setting	336
Effective Engagement: Objectives, Practicalities, Escalation, Collective Strategies	340
Setting Engagement Objectives	340
Practicalities of Engagement	341
Escalation of Engagement	342
Collective Engagement	344
Special Considerations: Proxy Voting, Asset Classes	347
Voting	347
Asset Classes	350
Corporate Fixed Income	350
Sovereign Debt	351
Private Equity	352
Infrastructure	352
Property	353
Fund Investments	354
Key Facts	*355*
Further Reading	*357*
Self Practice and Self Assessment	*358*
Solutions	*363*

Chapter 7 ESG Analysis, Valuation, and Integration — 365

Why Investors Integrate ESG	366
Why Investors Integrate ESG	366
Meeting Requirements under Fiduciary Duty or Regulations, or Meeting Client and Beneficiary Demands	367
Lowering Investment Risk and Increasing Investment Returns	367
More Tools and Techniques to Use in Analysis and Improving the Quality of Engagement and Stewardship Activities	369
Reputational Risk at a Firm Level	369
The Different Approaches to Integrating ESG	370
Qualitative ESG Analysis	371
Quantitative ESG Analysis	371
Highlights between the Quantitative Approaches and Qualitative Approaches and Terminology Confusion	373
Tools and Elements of ESG Analysis	374
Elements of ESG Integration	375
Differences between Company or Business Analysis and Security Analysis	376
Typical Stages of Integrated ESG Assessment (Research and Idea Generation Stage)	377
Research and Idea Generation Stage	377
Typical Stages of Integrated ESG Assessment (Scorecards Can Be Used to Assess ESG Risk and Opportunity, and Materiality Assessments and Risk Mapping)	381

Materiality Assessments and Risk Mapping	382
Using the SASB as a Baseline Framework in a Materiality Assessment	388
Valuation and Company Integrated Assessment Stage and the Challenge of Company Disclosure on ESG Topics	391
Model Adjustments Based on ESG Assessment	391
Investment Decision and Portfolio Construction and ESG Integration Techniques in Practice (Seven Cases)	395
Discussion of Private Markets, Real Estate, and Infrastructure; Discussion of ESG in Fixed Income and Differences to Equity; and Challenges to ESG Integration	404
Discussion of ESG in Fixed Income and Differences to Equity	405
Challenges to ESG Integration	406
Challenges from Incomplete Datasets and Identifying and Assessing ESG Data	407
Investment Firm Culture Challenge	408
Criticism for ESG Integration	409
Range of ESG Integration Databases and Software Available	409
Areas of Focus for Investors Compared to Rating Agencies	416
Mutual Fund and Fund Manager ESG Assessment, Company ESG Assessment and Rating, Primary and Secondary ESG Data Sources, and Other Uses of ESG and Sustainability Systems Data	416
Company ESG Assessment and Rating	418
ESG Index Providers	419
Primary and Secondary ESG Data Sources	419
Other Uses of ESG and Sustainability Systems Data	420
"Big Data" Analysis of Multiple ESG Factors	420
Resource, Supply, and Operational Risk Mitigation	420
Modeling Future Sustainability Scenarios, Including Climate Change, Wage Growth, and Social Effects	421
Fixed Income, Credit Rating Agencies, and ESG Credit Scoring	424
Different Levels at Which ESG Factors Can Affect Bond Price Performance and Credit Risk	424
Continuing Evolution for Credit and ESG Since PRI Releases	425
Global and Regional Credit Rating Agencies	425
Corporate Credit Risk Assessments	426
Certain Fixed-Income Investors Use QESGs	427
Green Bonds Considered a Different Class of Credit	427
Sovereign Credit Risk Assessment	428
ESG and Credit Ratings: Discussion over Relationship	428
Potential Bias in Ratings	430
Key Facts	*431*
Conclusion	431
Further Reading	*432*
Appendix	*433*
Sustainalytics and Its ESG Products	433
The Sustainalytics' ESG Risk Rating	433
Unmanaged Risk: How Sustainalytics Arrives at the Scores	434
Calculating the Final Unmanaged Risk Score	434
MSCI ESG Research	435

Contents

MSCI ESG Risk Score	437
MSCI ESG Opportunity Score	437
MSCI Controversy Assessment	438
MSCI Data Sources	438
MSCI Final Letter Rating Summary	438
MSCI ESG Research	438
Self Practice and Self Assessment	*439*
Solutions	*444*

Chapter 8 — Integrated Portfolio Construction and Management — 447

Introduction to Integrated Portfolio Construction and Management	448
Integrating ESG: Strategic Asset Allocation Models	448
Integrating ESG: Asset Manager Selection	458
Approaches to Integrating ESG: Portfolio Level Framework	461
Approaches to Integrating ESG: Role of Analysts, Portfolio Managers, and Internal and External Research	465
Role of Analysts	465
Role of Portfolio Managers	465
Complementing Internal Research with External ESG Resources	467
Approaches to Integrating ESG: Quantitative Research Developments in ESG Investing	470
The Evolution of ESG Integration: Exclusionary Preferences and Their Application	474
Universal Exclusions	475
Conduct-Related Exclusions	476
Faith-Based Exclusions	476
Idiosyncratic Exclusions	476
Applying Exclusionary Preferences	476
ESG Screening within Portfolios and across Asset Classes: Fixed Income, Corporate Debt, and ESG Bonds	478
Fixed Income (Government, Sovereign, Corporate, and Other)	480
ESG Screening within Portfolios and across Asset Classes: Green Securitization and Sovereign Debt	484
Green Securitization	484
Sovereign Debt	484
ESG Screening within Portfolios and across Asset Classes: Listed and Private Equity	488
Listed Equity	489
Private Equity	491
ESG Screening within Portfolios and across Asset Classes: Real Assets – Real Estate and Infrastructure	493
Integrating ESG Screens within Portfolios to Manage Risk and Generate Returns	496
Integrating ESG to Manage Portfolio Risk	496
Integrating ESG to Generate Investment Returns	499
Quantitative Approaches That Embed ESG Factors	499
Efforts to Develop Standards for ESG Investing: EU Regulatory Implications	502
Other Efforts to Develop Standards for ESG Investing	509

Applying ESG Screenings to Individual Listed and Unlisted Companies and Collective Investment Funds	510
Listed Companies and Collective Investment Funds	510
Unlisted Companies and Collective Investment Funds	514
Managing the Risk and Return Dynamics of an ESG Integrated Portfolio: Optimizing Portfolios for ESG Criteria, Strategies, Objectives, Investment Considerations, and Risks	515
ESG Strategies, Objectives, Investment Considerations, and Risks: Full ESG Integration, Exclusionary Screening, and Positive Alignment	518
Full ESG Integration	518
Exclusionary Screening	520
Positive Alignment or Best-in-Class	521
ESG Strategies, Objectives, Investment Considerations, and Risks: Thematic and Impact Investing	521
Thematic Investing	521
Impact Investing	522
Integrating ESG in Passive Portfolios and Established Datasets	526
Relying on Established Datasets	529
Key Facts	*532*
Further Reading	*534*
Self Practice and Self Assessment	*537*
Solutions	*541*

Chapter 9 Investment Mandates, Portfolio Analytics, and Client Reporting — 543

Introduction: Accountability to Clients and Alignment with Them	543
Accountability to Clients and Alignment with Them	544
Clarifying Client Needs: Defining the ESG Investment Strategy	546
Fully Aligning Investment with Client ESG Beliefs	549
Developing Client-Relevant ESG-Aware Investment Mandates	552
The RFP Process	555
Investment Integration	558
Engagement and Voting	559
Outsourcing	560
Collective Action	561
Assessing the Quality of Engagement and Voting	561
Tailoring the ESG Investment Approach to Client Expectations	562
Holding Managers to Account: Monitoring Delivery	565
Holding Managers to Account: Measurement and Reporting	573
Key Facts	*577*
Further Reading	*578*
Appendix: SFDR Disclosures and CFA Institute Disclosure Standards	*579*
Global ESG Disclosure Standards for Investment Products	579
SFDR Disclosures	580
Self Practice and Self Assessment	*582*
Solutions	*586*

CERTIFICATE IN ESG INVESTING 2023

Unit Aims

By the end of this unit, learners should be able to demonstrate:

- An understanding of the context for different approaches to responsible investment and specifically, consideration of environmental, social and governance (ESG) factors.
- An understanding of the underlying issues that constitute factors within each of the environmental, social and governance areas.
- An understanding of the broader sustainability context and global initiatives.
- An understanding of the ESG market: relevance, size, scope, key drivers and challenges, and risks and opportunities.
- An understanding of environmental factors, systemic relationships, material impacts, megatrends and approaches to environmental analysis at country, sector and company levels.
- An understanding of social factors, systemic relationships, material impacts and approaches to social analysis at country, sector and company levels.
- An understanding of governance factors, key characteristics, main models and material impacts.
- An understanding of engagement and stewardship.
- An understanding of ESG analysis, valuation and integration.
- An ability to analyse how ESG factors may affect industry and company performance, and security valuation across a range of asset classes.
- An understanding of ESG integrated portfolio construction and management.
- An ability to apply a range of approaches to ESG analysis and integration across a range of asset classes.
- An understanding of investment mandates, portfolio analytics and client reporting.

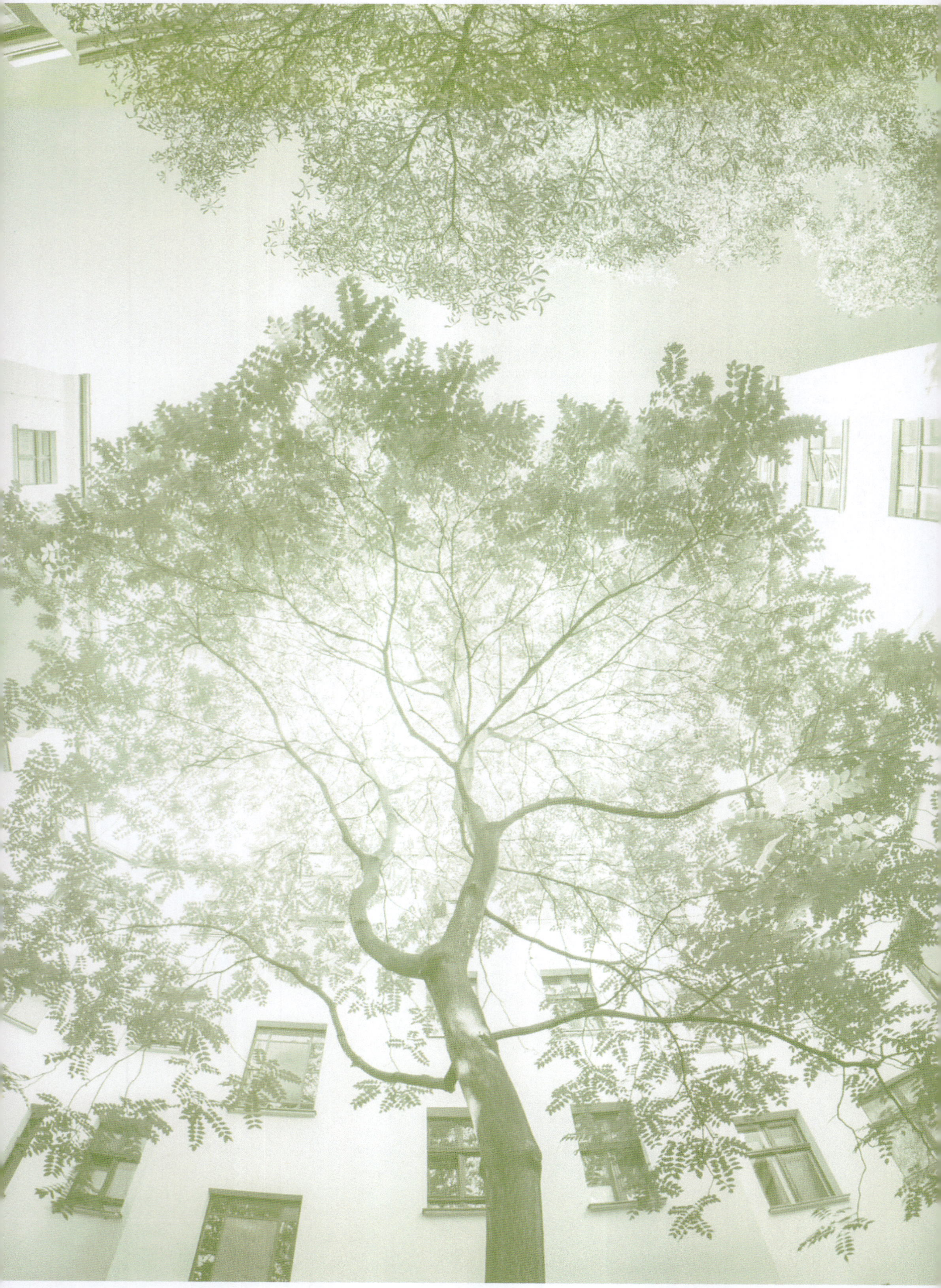

INTRODUCTION

This curriculum provides essential reading for candidates of the Certificate in ESG Investing, including examples, key facts and self-assessment questions.

Content is valid for examinations taken beginning 1 February 2023. Candidates must confirm that the version of the curriculum they are preparing from corresponds to and is valid for the period when they intend to take the examination.

ESG Update

Changes will be made as necessary to keep the curriculum up to date.

Details of the date of the latest change and of any outstanding corrections or amendments can be found at CFAInstitute.org.

Candidates should check the website on a regular basis to ensure their study material is up to date.

The exam is made up of one unit, covering the following topic areas:

1. Introduction to ESG
2. The ESG market
3. Environmental factors
4. Social factors
5. Governance factors
6. Engagement and stewardship
7. ESG analysis, valuation and integration
8. ESG integrated portfolio construction and management
9. Investment mandates, portfolio analytics and client reporting

The curriculum provides broad coverage and excellent preparation for the examinations.

The Certificate in ESG Investing is developed, administered and awarded by CFA Institute.

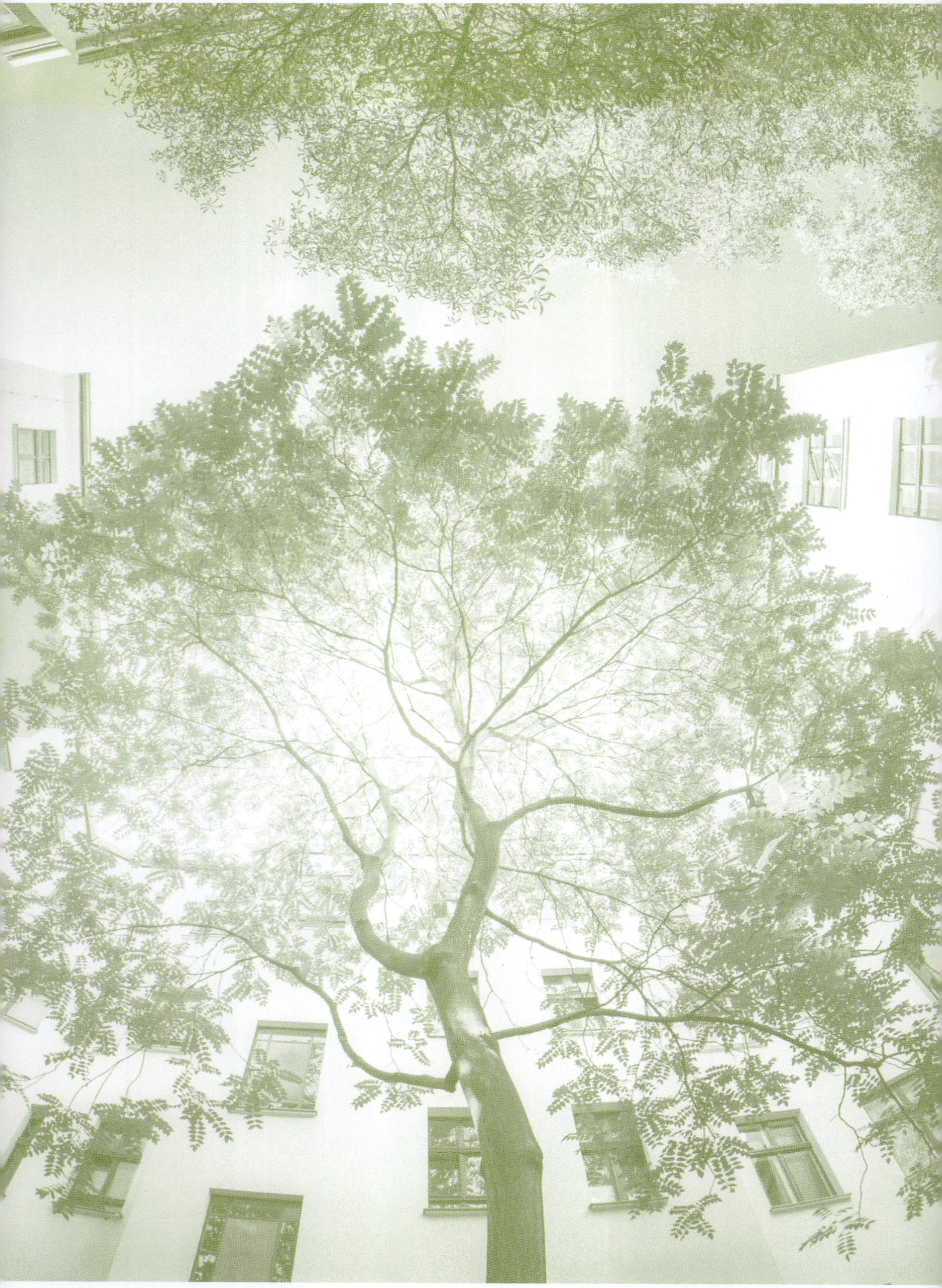

FOREWORD BY MARG FRANKLIN

Since our establishment in 1947, we have never wavered from our commitment to develop highly educated, ethical professionals who pledge to put their clients' interests first. Our founders started us down this path more than seven decades ago, and the CFA Institute we know today is a testament to their vision.

As the industry has evolved since our founding, we too have adapted to the needs of new generations of learners and professionals. We believe we are uniquely positioned to address some of the financial industry's greatest challenges as we build on the legacy of our first 75 years.

The recent pandemic brought to the fore the need to reset long-term priorities and for the industry to focus and articulate its impact, particularly within the context of environmental, social, and governance (ESG) factors. As we diversify our product portfolio and expand our impact through our ESG offerings to our candidates, members, societies, and other stakeholders, the concept of relevance underpins our efforts in this area.

In 2021, for example, concerns over potential ESG product greenwashing and a demand from investors for products and skills to support sustainable investing led CFA Institute to launch the first voluntary Global ESG Disclosure Standards for Investment Products. As the global leader in standards for the investment management profession, we used our widely adopted GIPS® model to create the standards to provide transparency, reliability, and comparability, thereby enabling investors, consultants, advisors, and distributors to better understand, compare, and evaluate ESG investment products.

Setting global industry standards to ensure transparency and safeguard trust remains integral to our mission, and we are harnessing our capabilities to educate and support investment professionals so that they can lead the industry in the critical initiatives that will shape the future of our profession. The Certificate in ESG Investing, developed in concert with CFA Society of the UK and launched globally in 2021, was the first of its kind to be introduced on this scale.

This certificate stands as a prime example of the relevance of our offerings, as well as the importance of broadening our product portfolio to meet the educational needs of today's professionals. Demand has been strong for the certificate—not only from individuals but also from global employers who want their workforce to be equipped with this knowledge for the benefit of their business and, ultimately, end investors.

A number of prominent asset managers, asset owners, wealth managers, and other firms have lent their support to the certificate, showcasing the value of this program to employers, and candidates have enrolled in promising numbers. We are proud of this achievement, and we continue to work tirelessly with our extensive society networkto set the educational standards for our industry.

Thank you again to everyone who has helped to nurture, develop, and promote these initiatives to the industry.

Marg Franklin, CFA
President and CEO, CFA Institute

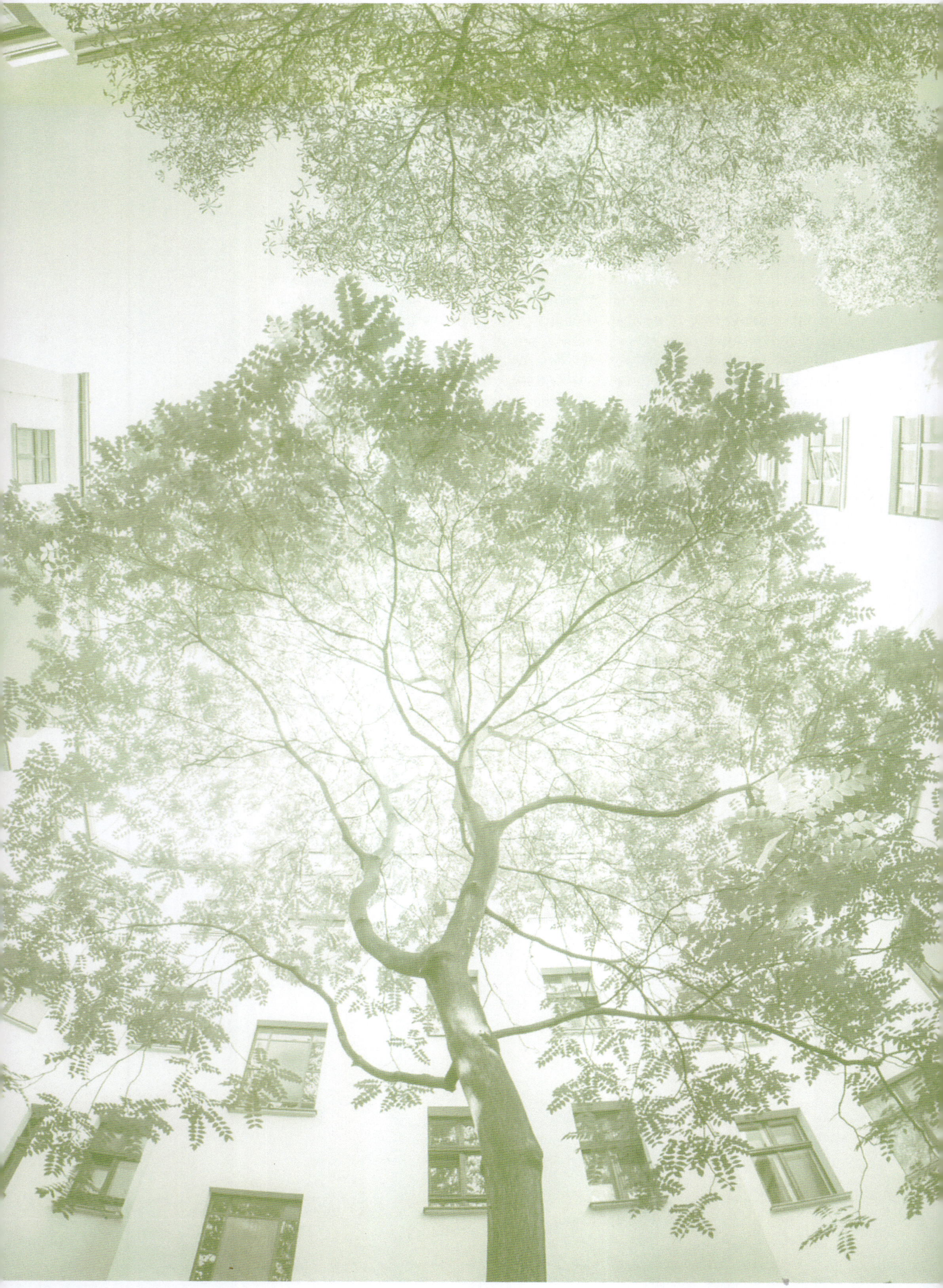

CHAPTER 1

Introduction to ESG Investing

LEARNING OUTCOMES

Mastery	The candidate should be able to:
☐	1.1.1 define ESG investment and different approaches to ESG investing: responsible investment, socially responsible investment, sustainable investment, best-in-class investment, ethical/values-driven investment, thematic investment, green investment, social investment, shareholder engagement
☐	1.1.2 define the following sustainability-based concepts in terms of their strengths and limitations: corporate social responsibility and triple bottom line (TBL) accounting
☐	1.1.3 describe the benefits and challenges of incorporating ESG in decision making, and the linkages between responsible investment and financial system stability
☐	1.1.4 explain the concepts of the financial materiality of ESG integration, double materiality, and dynamic materiality and how they relate to ESG analysis, practices, and reporting
☐	1.1.5 explain different ESG megatrends, their systemic nature, and their potential impact on companies and company practices
☐	1.1.6 explain the three ways in which investors typically reflect ESG considerations in their investment process
☐	1.1.7 explain the aims of key supranational ESG initiatives and organizations and the progress achieved to date

INTRODUCTION

There was a time when environmental, social, and governance (ESG) issues were the niche concern of a select group of ethical or socially responsible investors. That time is long gone.

The consideration of ESG factors is becoming an integral part of investment management. Asset owners and investment managers are developing ways to incorporate ESG criteria into investment analysis and decision-making processes. The emergence of responsible investment proponents, such as the United Nations Principles for Responsible Investment (PRI), has encouraged a fundamental change in investment practices whereby investors explicitly employ ESG factor analysis to enhance returns and better manage risks. Societal and client pressure and the growing evidence of the direct financial benefits of incorporating ESG analysis have led integration to become more mainstream.

This chapter provides an overview of the concept of ESG investing, as well as the different types of responsible investment and their implications. It highlights the main benefits of integrating ESG factors and identifies ways in which ESG investing is implemented in practice.

ESG investing sits within a broader context of sustainability; this chapter also highlights a number of key initiatives in the business and investment communities that seek to assist all parties to navigate the associated challenges.

2 WHAT IS ESG INVESTING?

☐ 1.1.1 define ESG investment and different approaches to ESG investing: responsible investment, socially responsible investment, sustainable investment, best-in-class investment, ethical/values-driven investment, thematic investment, green investment, social investment, shareholder engagement

ESG investing is an approach to managing assets where investors explicitly incorporate **environmental, social, and governance (ESG)** factors in their investment decisions with the long-term return of an investment portfolio in mind.

Long-Termism and ESG Investing

Many stakeholders of investment, including finance regulators, have recognized the shortfalls of **short-termism** in investment practice and have sought to increase awareness of the value of **long-termism** and encourage this approach.

Short-termism covers a wide range of activities. For the purpose of this topic, the two most relevant ones are

- trading practices, where investors trade based on short-term momentum and price movements rather than long-term value, and
- investors engaging with investee companies in a way that prioritizes maximizing quarterly financials.

These short-term investing strategies might offer rewards but may have consequences for the long term. With its disproportionate focus on quarterly returns, short-termism may leave companies less willing to take on projects (such as research and development) that may take multiple years – and patient capital – to develop. This was indeed confirmed by a review conducted on the UK equity market and long-term decision-making by Professor John Kay for the UK Government in 2012.[1] Instead of productive investment in the real economy, short-termism may promote bubbles, financial instability, and general economic underperformance. Furthermore, short-term investment strategies tend to ignore factors that are generally considered more long term, such as ESG factors. Because of the adverse effects mentioned, regulators are

---

[1] John Kay, "The Kay Review of UK Equity Markets and Long-Term Decision Making: Final Report" (July 2012).

catching up and taking action. For example, the **Shareholder Rights Directive (SRD)** was issued by the European Union (EU) in September 2020, requiring investors to be active owners and to act with a more long-term focus.

In other words, ESG investing aims to correctly identify, evaluate, and price social, environmental, and economic risks and opportunities. ESG factors are defined in Exhibit 1.

Exhibit 1: ESG Factors Defined

	Environmental Factors	Social Factors	Governance Factors
Definition	Factors pertaining to the natural world. These include the use of and interaction with renewable and non-renewable resources (e.g., water, minerals, ecosystems, and biodiversity).	Factors that affect the lives of humans. The category includes the management of human capital, non-human animals, local communities, and clients.	Factors that involve issues tied to countries and/or jurisdictions or are common practice in an industry, as well as the interests of broader stakeholder groups.

The Definition and Scope of ESG Issues

There is currently no universal standard for assigning "E," "S," and "G" issues, and they may overlap with one another. The assignment of these issues depends on the specific properties of investors, businesses, and their stakeholders. **Stakeholders** are members of groups without whose support an organization would cease to exist,[2] as well as communities impacted by companies and regulators.

Examples of the definition and scope of ESG issues can be illustrated by the two widely referenced organizations in Exhibit 2 and Exhibit 3.

Exhibit 2: Examples of ESG Issues

Environmental	Social	Governance
▸ Climate change	▸ Human rights	▸ Bribery and corruption
▸ Resource depletion	▸ Modern slavery	▸ Executive pay
▸ Waste	▸ Child labor	▸ Board diversity and structure
▸ Pollution	▸ Working conditions	▸ Trade association, lobbying, and donations
▸ Deforestation	▸ Employee relations	
		▸ Tax strategy

Source: PRI, "What Is Responsible Investment? (2020). www.unpri.org/an-introduction-to-responsible-investment/what-is-responsible-investment/4780.article.

---

[2] R. Edward Freeman and David L. Reed, "Stockholders and Stakeholders: A New Perspective on Corporate Governance," *California Management Review* 25 (April 1983): 88–106. www.researchgate.net/publication/238325277_Stockholders_and_Stakeholders_A_New_Perspective_on_Corporate_Governance.

Exhibit 3: Your Guide to ESG Reporting

ESG Ratings

Environmental
- Biodiversity
- Climate Change
- Pollution and Resources
- Water Security

Supply Chain: Environmental

Social
- Labor Standards
- Human Rights
- Community
- Health and Safety
- Pollution and Resources
- Customer Responsibility

Supply Chain: Social

Governance
- Anti-Corruption
- Corporate Governance
- Risk Management
- Tax Transparency

Source: FTSE Russell, "FTSE Russell Stewardship, Transition and Engagement Program for Change: 2018 STEP Change Report" (2018). https://content.ftserussell.com/sites/default/files/research/ftse_russell_step_change_2018_report.pdf.

3. TYPES OF RESPONSIBLE INVESTMENT

> 1.1.2 define the following sustainability-based concepts in terms of their strengths and limitations: corporate social responsibility and triple bottom line (TBL) accounting

ESG investing is part of a group of approaches collectively referred to as **responsible investment**. ESG investing is concerned with how ESG issues can impact the long-term return of assets and securities, whereas other responsible investment approaches can also take into account non-financial value creation and reflect stakeholder values in an investment strategy. There is no standard set of criteria for identifying responsible investment. The main investment approaches are presented in this section to demonstrate the wide spectrum of different types of responsible investment.

Responsible investment is an umbrella term for the various ways in which investors can consider ESG factors within security selection and portfolio construction. As such, it may combine financial and non-financial outcomes and complements traditional financial analysis and portfolio construction techniques.

All forms of responsible investment except for engagement are ultimately related to portfolio construction (in other words, which securities a fund holds). Engagement, both by equity owners and bond holders, concerns whether and how an investor tries to encourage and influence an issuer's behavior on ESG matters. There is no standard classification in the industry; the types of responsible investment overlap and evolve over time.

Exhibit 4 illustrates some of the conceptual differences between these approaches and how they range from strictly "finance-only" investment, with no consideration of ESG factors, to the other end of the spectrum, where the investor may be prepared to accept below-market returns in exchange for the high positive impact the projects and

Types of Responsible Investment

companies in the portfolio deliver. As investors move toward the left-hand side of the spectrum, they are increasingly interested in aligning their capital with ESG-related investment opportunities, in order to capture associated financial returns and/or to have a positive impact by financing solutions to societal challenges.

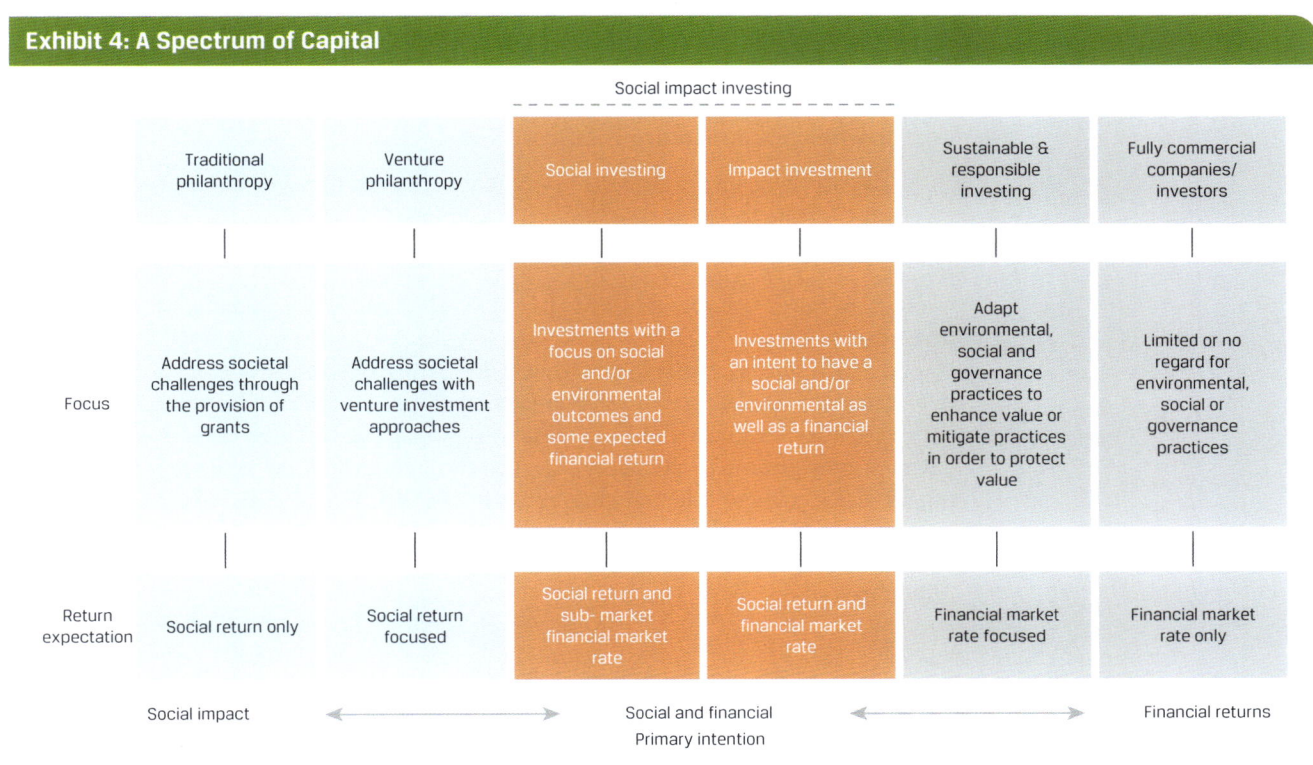

Exhibit 4: A Spectrum of Capital

	Traditional philanthropy	Venture philanthropy	Social investing	Impact investment	Sustainable & responsible investing	Fully commercial companies/investors
Focus	Address societal challenges through the provision of grants	Address societal challenges with venture investment approaches	Investments with a focus on social and/or environmental outcomes and some expected financial return	Investments with an intent to have a social and/or environmental as well as a financial return	Adapt environmental, social and governance practices to enhance value or mitigate practices in order to protect value	Limited or no regard for environmental, social or governance practices
Return expectation	Social return only	Social return focused	Social return and sub-market financial market rate	Social return and financial market rate	Financial market rate focused	Financial market rate only

Social impact investing spans Social investing and Impact investment.

Primary intention: Social impact ← → Social and financial ← → Financial returns

Source: Organisation for Economic Co-Operation and Development (OECD) (2019), *Social Impact Investment 2019: The Impact Imperative for Sustainable Development*, OECD Publishing, Paris, doi.org/10.1787/9789264311299-en. Used with permission of OECD; permission conveyed through Copyright Clearance Center, Inc.

Note: For illustrative purposes only.

Responsible Investment

Responsible investment is a strategy and practice to incorporate ESG factors into investment decisions and active ownership.[3] It is sometimes used as an umbrella term for some (or all) of the investment approaches mentioned in the following subsections.

At a minimum, responsible investment consists of mitigating risky ESG practices in order to protect value. To this end, it considers both how ESG might influence the risk-adjusted return of an asset and the stability of an economy and how investment in and engagement with assets and investees can impact society and the environment.

Socially Responsible Investment

Socially responsible investment (SRI) refers to approaches that apply social and environmental criteria in evaluating companies. Investors implementing SRI generally score companies using a chosen set of criteria, usually in conjunction with sector-specific

---

3 PRI, "What Is Responsible Investment?"

weightings. A **hurdle** is established for qualification within the investment universe, based either on the full universe or sector by sector. This information serves as a first screen to create a list of SRI-qualified companies.

SRI ranking can be used in combination with best-in-class investment, thematic funds, high-conviction funds, or quantitative investment strategies.

Best-in-Class Investment

Best-in-class investment (also known as "positive screening") involves selecting only the companies that overcome a **defined ranking hurdle**, established using ESG criteria within each sector or industry.

- ▸ Typically, companies are scored on a variety of factors that are weighted according to the sector.
- ▸ The portfolio is then assembled from the list of qualified companies.

Bear in mind, though, that not all best-in-class funds are considered "responsible investments."

Due to its all-sector approach, best-in-class investment is commonly used in investment strategies that try to maintain certain characteristics of an index. In these cases, security selection seeks to maintain regional and sectorial diversification along with a similar profile to the parent market-cap index while targeting companies with higher ESG ratings. The tracking error for **MSCI World SRI**, which is designed to represent the performance of companies with high ESG ratings and employs a best-in-class selection approach to target the top 25% companies in each sector, is only 1.79% (see Exhibit 5).

Exhibit 5: Characteristics of an SRI Index Using a Best-in-Class Approach (not tested; for illustration only)

Sector	Parent Index (%)	SRI Index (%)	Region	Parent Index (%)	SRI Index (%)	ESG Rating	Parent Index (%)	SRI Index (%)
Information technology	18.1	19.6	US	63.8	60.7	Leader	24	67
Financials	15.4	14.6		8.1	7.5	Average	65	33
Health care	12.9	13.4	Japan UK	5.3	—	Laggard	10	0
Industrials	11	11.1	Canada	3.4	3.8			
Consumer discretionary	10.3	10.9	France	3.7	4.3			
Consumer staples	8.3	10.0	Other	15.7	19.2			
Communication services	8.5	4.5						
Materials	4.2	4.9						
Energy	4.5	4.4						
Utilities	3.6	3.2						
Real estate	3.3	3.6						

Source: MSCI, "MSCI SRI Indexes" (2020). www.msci.com/msci-sri-indexes.

Types of Responsible Investment

Sustainable Investment

Sustainable investment refers to the selection of assets that contribute in some way to a sustainable economy—that is, an asset that minimizes natural and social resource depletion.

- It is a broad term, with a broad range of interpretations that may be used for the consideration of typical ESG issues.
- It may include best-in-class and/or **ESG integration**, which considers how ESG issues impact a security's risk and return profile.
- It is further used to describe companies with positive impact or companies that will benefit from sustainable macro-trends.

The term "sustainable investment" can also be used to mean a strategy that screens out activities considered contrary to long-term environmental and social sustainability, such as coal mining or exploring for oil in the Arctic regions.

Thematic Investment

Thematic investment is investment in themes or assets specifically related to ESG factors, such as clean energy, green technology, sustainable agriculture, gender diversity, or affordable housing. This approach is often based on needs arising from economic or social trends. Two common investment themes focus on increased demand for energy and water and the availability of alternative sources of each. Global economic development has raised the demand for energy at the same time as increased greenhouse gas emissions are widely believed to negatively affect the earth's climate. Similarly, rising global living standards and industrial needs have created a greater demand for water and the need to prevent drought or increase access to clean drinking water in certain regions of the world. While these themes are based on trends related to environmental issues (refer to the following subsection), social issues—such as access to affordable health care and nutrition, especially in the poorest countries in the world—are also of great interest to thematic investors (refer to the subsequent "Social Investment" section.

Bear in mind, though, that not all thematic funds are considered to be responsible investments or best-in-class. Becoming such a fund depends not only on the theme of the fund but also on the ESG characteristics of the investee companies.

Green Investment

Green investment refers to allocating capital to assets that mitigate

- climate change,
- biodiversity loss,
- resource inefficiency, and
- other environmental challenges.

These can include

- low-carbon power generation and vehicles,
- smart grids,
- energy efficiency,
- pollution control,
- recycling,
- waste management and waste of energy, and
- other technologies and processes that contribute to solving particular environmental problems.

Green investment can thus be considered a broad subcategory of thematic investing and/or impact investing. Green bonds, a type of fixed-income instrument that is specifically earmarked to raise money for climate and environmental projects, are commonly used in green investing.

Further details on green investing and green bonds can be found in Chapter 3.

Social Investment

Social investment refers to allocating capital to assets that address social challenges. These can be products that address the **bottom of the pyramid (BOP)**. "BOP" refers to the poorest two-thirds of the economic human pyramid, a group of more than four billion people living in poverty. More broadly, BOP refers to a market-based model of economic development that seeks to simultaneously alleviate poverty while providing growth and profits for businesses serving these communities. Examples include

- micro-finance and micro-insurance,
- access to basic telecommunication,
- access to improved nutrition and health care, and
- access to (clean) energy.

Social investing can also include social impact bonds, which are a mechanism to contract with the public sector. This sector pays for better social outcomes in certain services and passes on part of the savings achieved to investors.

Impact Investment

Impact investing refers to investments made with the specific intent of generating positive, measurable social or environmental impact alongside a financial return (which differentiates it from philanthropy). It is a relatively smaller segment of the broader responsible investing market. Impact investing is usually associated with direct investments, such as in private debt, private equity, and real estate. However, in recent years, impact investing has increasingly become mainstream in the public markets.

Impact investments can be made in both emerging and developed markets. They provide capital to address the world's most pressing challenges. An example is investing in products or services that help achieve one (or more) of the 17 Sustainable Development Goals (SDGs) launched by the United Nations in 2015, such as the following:

- "SDG 6: Clean Water and Sanitation—Ensure availability and sustainable management of water and sanitation for all"
- "SDG 11: Sustainable Cities and Communities—Make cities and human settlements inclusive, safe, resilient and sustainable" [4]

Measurement and tracking of the agreed-upon impact generally lie at the heart of the investment proposition.

Impact investors have diverse financial return expectations. Some intentionally invest for below-market-rate returns in line with their strategic objectives. Others pursue market-competitive and market-beating returns, sometimes required by fiduciary responsibility. The **Global Impact Investing Network (GIIN)** estimated the size of the global impact investing market to be US$502 billion (£361billion); its 2019 annual survey indicated that 66% of investors in impact investing pursue competitive, market-rate returns.[5]

---

[4] https://sdgs.un.org/goals.
[5] A. Mudaliar, R. Bass, H. Dithrich, and N. Nova, "2019 Annual Impact Investor Survey". Global Impact Investing Network (19 June 2019). https://thegiin.org/research/publication/impinv-survey-2019.

Types of Responsible Investment

Ethical (or Value-Driven) and Faith-Based Investment

Ethical and faith-based investment refers to investing in line with certain principles, often using negative screening to avoid investing in companies whose products and services are deemed morally objectionable by the investor or certain religions, international declarations, conventions, or voluntary agreements. Typical exclusions include

- tobacco,
- alcohol,
- pornography,
- weapons, and
- significant breach of agreements, such as the **Universal Declaration of Human Rights** or the **International Labour Organization's Declaration on Fundamental Principles and Rights at Work**.

From religious individuals to large religious organizations, faith-based investors have a history of shareholder activism to improve the conduct of investee companies. Another popular strategy is portfolio building with a focus on screening out the negative; in other words, avoiding "sin stocks" or other assets at odds with their beliefs.

In the following subsections, we cover a few examples of faith-based negative screening.

Christian

Investors wishing to put their money to work in a manner consistent with Christian values seek to avoid, in addition to the activities listed previously, investing in firms that

- facilitate abortion, contraceptives, or embryonic stem-cell research or
- are involved in the production and sale of weapons.

They often favor firms that support human rights, environmental responsibility, and fair employment practices via the support of labor unions.

Shari'a

Investors seeking to follow Islamic religious principles cannot do the following:

- invest in firms that profit from alcohol, pornography, or gambling;
- invest in companies that carry heavy debt loans (and therefore pay interest);
- own investments that pay interest;
- liaise with firms that earn a substantial part of their revenue from interest; or
- invest in pork-related businesses.

Exhibit 6 shows negative screening strategies for various types of funds.

Exhibit 6: Negative Screening Strategies

Negative Screening	Christian Funds	Islamic Funds	SRI Funds
Alcohol	X	X	X
Gambling	X	X	X
Tobacco	X		X
Pornography	X	X	
Pork products		X	
Interest-based financial services		X	

Negative Screening	Christian Funds	Islamic Funds	SRI Funds
High leverage companies		X	
Anti-family entertainment	X		
Marriage lifestyle	X		
Abortion	X		
Human rights	X		X
Workers' rights	X		X
Bioethics	X		
Weapons	X	X	X

Source: Adapted from Inspire Investing, "Faith-Based Investment and Sustainability" (2019). www.inspireinvesting.com/2019/03/26/faith-based-investment-and-sustainability/.

Shareholder Engagement

Shareholder engagement reflects active ownership by investors in which the investor seeks to influence a corporation's decisions on ESG matters, either through dialogue with corporate officers or votes at a shareholder assembly (in the case of equity). It is seen as complementary to the previously mentioned approaches to responsible investment as a way to encourage companies to act more responsibly. Its efficacy usually depends on

- the scale of ownership (of the individual investor or the collective initiative),
- the quality of the engagement dialogue and method used, and
- whether the company has been informed by the investor that divestment is a possible sanction.

For further details on the process of engagement, see Chapter 6.

ESG investing also recognizes that the generation of long-term sustainable returns is dependent on stable, well-functioning and well-governed social, environmental and economic systems. This is the so-called **triple bottom line** coined by business writer John Elkington. However, since its inception, the concept of TBL evolved from a holistic approach to sustainability and further into an accounting tool to narrowly manage trade-offs. Therefore, Elkington "recalled" the term in a 2018 *Harvard Business Review* article.[6]

Ultimately, ESG investing recognizes the dynamic interrelationship between social, environmental, and governance issues and investment. It acknowledges that

- social, environmental, and governance issues may impact the risk, volatility, and long-term return of securities (as well as markets) and
- investments can have both a positive and a negative impact on society and the environment.

Corporate Social Responsibility

The concept of ESG investing is closely related to the concept of investees' **corporate sustainability**. Corporate sustainability is an approach aiming to create long-term stakeholder value through the implementation of a business strategy that focuses on the ethical, social, environmental, cultural, and economic dimensions of doing

---

[6] J. Elkington, "25 Years Ago I Coined the Phrase 'Triple Bottom Line.' Here's Why It's Time to Rethink It," *Harvard Business Review* (25 June 2018). https://hbr.org/2018/06/25-years-ago-i-coined-the-phrase-triple-bottom-line-heres-why-im-giving-up-on-it.

business.[7] Related to this approach, **corporate social responsibility (CSR)** is a broad business concept that describes a company's commitment to conducting its business in an ethical way. Throughout the 20th century and until recently, many companies implemented CSR by contributing to society through philanthropy. While such philanthropy may indeed have a positive impact on communities, modern understanding of CSR recognizes that a principles-based behavior approach can play a strategic role in a firm's business model, which led to the theory of TBL.

The TBL accounting theory expands the traditional accounting framework focused only on profit to include two other performance areas: the social and environmental impacts of a company. These three bottom lines are often referred to as the **three P's**:

1. people,
2. planet, and
3. profit.

While the term and concept are useful to know, including for historical reasons, they have been replaced in the industry with a broader framework of sustainability that is not restricted to accounting.

Effective management of the company's sustainability can

- reaffirm the company's license to operate in the eyes of governments and civil society,
- increase efficiency,
- attend to increasing regulatory requirements,
- reduce the probability of fines,
- improve employee satisfaction and productivity, and
- drive innovation and introduce new product lines.

ESG investing recognizes these benefits and aims to consider them in the context of security/asset selection and portfolio construction.

There are many organizations and institutions contributing to the further exploration of interactions between society, environment, governance, and investment. This curriculum focuses on how professionals in the investment industry can better understand, assess, and integrate ESG issues when conducting stock selection, carrying out portfolio construction, and engaging with companies.

MACRO-LEVEL DEBATE ON ESG INTEGRATION

1.1.3 describe the benefits and challenges of incorporating ESG in decision making, and the linkages between responsible investment and financial system stability

There is a range of beliefs about the purpose and value, both to investors and to society more broadly, of integrating ESG considerations into investment decisions. Some of the main reasons for integrating ESG factors are detailed in this section. It starts

---

[7] M. Ashrafi, M. Acciaro, T. R. Walker, G. M. Magnan, and M. Adams, "Corporate Sustainability in Canadian and US Maritime Ports," *Journal of Cleaner Production* 220 (20 May 2019): 386–97. https://doi.org/10.1016/j.jclepro.2019.02.098.

with an overview of some important perspectives in the debate on integrating ESG considerations, financial materiality of integration, and challenges in integrating ESG issues and finishes with integration and financial performance.

Macro-Level Debate on Integrating ESG Considerations

This subsection describes various perspectives from which, over the years, the debate on the purpose and value of integrating ESG factors has been held. These include perspectives of risk, fiduciary duty, economics, impact and ethics, client demand, and regulation.

Risk Perspective

Evidence of the risks current megatrends carry is illustrated by the World Economic Forum's 2020 Global Risk Report, which for many years has highlighted the growing likelihood and impact of extreme weather events and the failure to address climate change.[8] Note that Exhibit 7 highlights how risks related to the environment have been significantly increasing in importance in recent years while classic economic risks have disappeared from the top five risks. Environmental risks are high on the radar. Among all global risks, climate now tops the agenda.

---

8 World Economic Forum, "The Global Risks Report 2020" (15 January 2020). www.weforum.org/reports/the-global-risks-report-2020.

Macro-Level Debate on ESG Integration

Exhibit 7: Top Global Risks

[Heatmap chart showing Likelihood and Impact of top global risks by year from 2007 to 2020, color-coded by risk category]

Economic
- Asset bubble
- Critical infrastructure failure
- Deflation
- Energy price shock
- Financial failure
- Fiscal crises
- Illicit trade
- Unemployment
- Unmanageable inflation

Environmental
- Biodiversity loss
- Climate action failure
- Extreme weather
- Human-made environmental disaster
- Natural disasters

Geopolitical
- Global governance failure
- Interstate conflict
- National governance failure
- State collapse
- Terrorist attacks
- Weapons of mass destruction

Societal
- Failure of urban planning
- Food crises
- Infectious diseases
- Involuntary migration
- Social instability
- Water crises

Technological
- Adverse technological advances
- Cyberattacks
- Data fraud or theft
- Information infrastructure breakdown

Source: World Economic Forum, "The Global Risks Report 2020" (2020). www.weforum.org/reports/the-global-risks-report-2020.

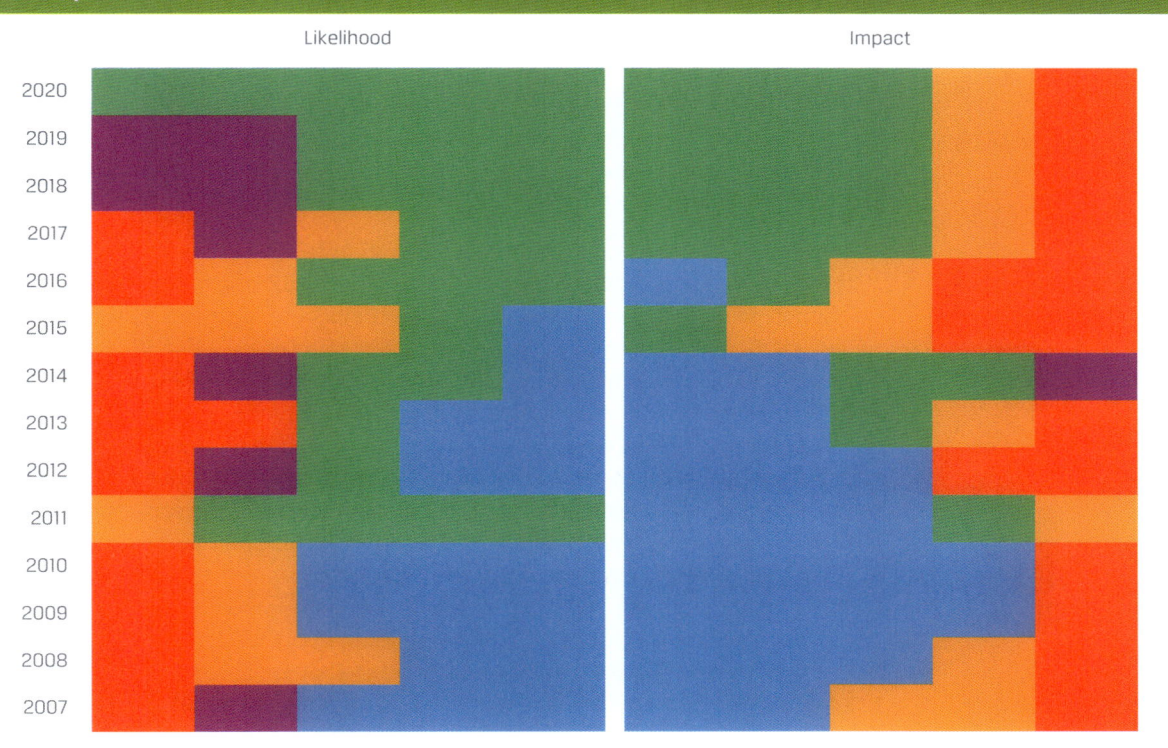

Recognizing the change in profile of key risks to the economy, in 2015, Mark Carney, then governor of the Bank of England and chairman of the Financial Stability Board (the international body set up by the G20 to monitor risks to the financial system), referred to this challenge in a speech that became a cornerstone for the integration of climate change to financial regulators:

Climate change is the tragedy of the horizon. We don't need an army of actuaries to tell us that the catastrophic impacts of climate change will be felt beyond the traditional horizons of most actors—imposing a cost on future generations that the current generation has no direct incentive to fix. . . . The horizon for monetary policy extends out to two to three years. For financial stability it is a bit longer, but typically only to the outer boundaries of the credit cycle—about a decade. In other words, once climate change becomes a defining issue for financial stability, it may already be too late.[9]

In line with Carney, in his annual letter to chief executives in 2020,[10] Larry Fink, the CEO of BlackRock, stated that the investment firm would step up its consideration of climate change in its investment considerations because it was reshaping the world's financial system. Concretely, in a parallel letter to its clients, BlackRock committed to divesting from companies that generate more than 25% of their revenues from coal production for its actively managed portfolios and required reporting from investee companies on their climate-related risks and plans for operating under the goals of the Paris Agreement to limit global warming to less than 2°C (3.6°F).[11] As the largest asset manager in the world, BlackRock's decision could represent a new paradigm in the investment industry in which the integration of material ESG factors is mainstream.

Prudent investors are engaging with companies to ask them to disclose not only what they are emitting today but also how they plan to achieve their transition to the net-zero world of the future. There is value in being able to spot winners and losers in a rapidly changing risk landscape. Investors that are attempting to take advantage of this usually operate over a longer time frame than the usual quarterly or one-year time horizon, with the objective of understanding emerging risks and new demands so that they can convert these into above-market performance.

> **CASE STUDIES**
>
> ### Water Depletion Due to Climate Change
>
> Companies are already experiencing risks in their manufacturing due to water depletion, which has been aggravated by acute impacts of climate change. Water has largely been considered a free raw material and therefore is used inefficiently, but many companies are now experiencing the higher costs of using the resource, as well as suffering an increasing frequency of extreme weather events.
>
> Pacific Gas and Electric Company (PG&E), a listed US utility, was driven to bankruptcy proceedings due to wildfire liabilities.[12] The company's equipment led to more than 1,500 fires between 2014 and 2017. As low humidity and strong winds worsen due to climate change, the fire hazard increases. In 2018, a problem with PG&E equipment was deemed to have led to fires that killed at least 85 people, forced about 180,000 to evacuate from their homes, and razed more than 18,800 structures.

---

9 M. Carney, "Breaking the Tragedy of the Horizon—Climate Change and Financial Stability," Bank of England, speech given at Lloyd's of London (29 September 2015). www.bankofengland.co.uk/speech/2015/breaking-the-tragedy-of-the-horizon-climate-change-and-financial-stability.
10 L. Fink, "A Fundamental Reshaping of Finance," BlackRock (2020). www.blackrock.com/corporate/investor-relations/2020-larry-fink-ceo-letter.
11 BlackRock, "Sustainability as BlackRock's New Standard for Investing" (2020). www.blackrock.com/au/individual/blackrock-client-letter.
12 M. McFall-Johnsen, "Over 1,500 California Fires in the Past 6 Years—Including the Deadliest Ever—Were Caused by One Company: PG&E. Here's What It Could Have Done but Didn't," *Business Insider* (3 November 2019). www.businessinsider.com/pge-caused-california-wildfires-safety-measures-2019-10?r=US&IR=T.

> Coca-Cola Company faced a water shortage in India that forced it to shut down one of its plants in 2004. The company has since invested US$2 billion (£1.4 billion) to reduce water use and improve water quality in the communities in which it operates. SABMiller, a multinational brewing and beverage company, has also invested heavily in water conservation, including US$6 million (£4.3 million) to improve equipment at a facility in Tanzania affected by deteriorating water quality.
>
> In extreme cases, assets can become stranded—in other words, obsolete due to regulatory, environmental, or market constraints. In Peru, for example, social conflict related to disruptions to water supplies resulted in the indefinite suspension of US$21.5 billion (£15.5 billion) in mining projects since 2010.

There are many ways in which ESG factors can impact a company's bottom line. Nonetheless, identifying those issues that are genuinely material to a sector and company is one of the most active challenges in ESG investment. Each company is unique and faces its own challenges related to its culture, particular business model, supply chain structure, and so on. So not only are there substantial differences between sectors, but there are also differences between what is most material to individual companies within a single sector.

For further details on how to assess materiality and what tools are available, refer to Chapters 7 and 8.

Fiduciary Duty Perspective

For many years, fiduciary duty was considered a barrier to considering ESG factors in investments. In the modern investment system, financial institutions or individuals, known as fiduciaries, manage money or other assets on behalf of beneficiaries and investors. Fiduciary duties exist to ensure that those who manage other people's money act in their beneficiaries' interests, rather than serving their own.

Beneficiaries and investors rely on these fiduciaries to act in their best interests, which are typically defined exclusively in financial terms. Due to the misconception that ESG factors are not financially material, some investors have used the concept of fiduciary duty as a reason not to incorporate ESG issues.

In 2005, the **United Nations Environment Programme Finance Initiative (UNEP FI)** commissioned the law firm Freshfields Bruckhaus Deringer to publish a report titled "A Legal Framework for the Integration of Environmental, Social and Governance Issues into Institutional Investment" (commonly referred to as **the Freshfields report**). The authors argued that "integrating ESG considerations into an investment analysis so as to more reliably predict financial performance is clearly permissible and is arguably required in all jurisdictions."[13] Despite the conclusions of the report, many investors continue to point to their fiduciary duties and the need to deliver financial returns to their beneficiaries as reasons why they cannot do more in terms of responsible investment.

However, an increasing number of academic studies and work undertaken over the last decade by progressive investment associations, including the UNEP FI and **Principles for Responsible Investment (PRI)**, on the topic have clarified that financially material ESG factors must be incorporated into investment decision making.

---

13 Freshfields Bruckhaus Deringer, "A Legal Framework for the Integration of Environmental, Social and Governance Issues into Institutional Investment," UNEP Finance Initiative (October 2005): p. 13. www.unepfi.org/publications/investment-publications/a-legal-framework-for-the-integration-of-environmental-social-and-governance-issues-into-institutional-investment.

The 2005 UNEP FI report[14] and the more recent report published by the PRI in 2019[15] both argue that failing to consider long-term investment value drivers—which include ESG issues—in investment practice is a failure of fiduciary duty. The 2019 PRI report concluded that modern fiduciary duties require investors to do the following:

- Incorporate financially material ESG factors into their investment decision making, consistent with the time frame of the obligation.
- Understand and incorporate into their decision making the sustainability preferences of beneficiaries or clients, regardless of whether these preferences are financially material.
- Be active owners, encouraging high standards of ESG performance in the companies or other entities in which they are invested.
- Support the stability and resilience of the financial system.
- Disclose their investment approach in a clear and understandable manner, including how preferences are incorporated into the scheme's investment approach.

For further details on fiduciary duty, see Chapter 2.

Economic Perspective

Another reason for implementing ESG stems from the recognition that negative megatrends will, over time, create a drag on economic prosperity as basic inputs (such as water, energy, and land) become increasingly scarce and expensive and that the prevalence of health and income inequalities increase instability both within countries and between the "global north and south." There is an understanding that unless these trends are reversed, economies will be weakened, exposed to sustainability-led bubbles and spikes. While this may not have a significant impact on asset managers whose performance is judged by their ability to provide alpha, it may considerably affect asset owners, who depend on total returns in the long term to pay out pensions and their liabilities.

As mentioned previously, the **Financial Stability Board (FSB)** has already identified climate change as a potential systemic risk, which may also be the case for other issues. The economic implications of these environmental issues (such as climate change, resource scarcity, biodiversity loss, and deforestation) and social challenges (such as poverty, income inequality, and human rights) are increasingly being recognized.

In fact, the **Stockholm Resilience Centre** identified nine "planetary boundaries" (see Exhibit 8) within which humanity can continue to develop and thrive for generations to come[16] and in 2015, it found that four of them—climate change, loss of biosphere integrity, land-system change, and altered biogeochemical cycles (phosphorus and nitrogen)—have been crossed. Two of these—climate change and biosphere integrity—are deemed "core boundaries," for which significant alteration would "drive the Earth System into a new state."

---

14 Freshfields Bruckhaus Deringer, "A Legal Framework for the Integration of Environmental, Social and Governance Issues into Institutional Investment."
15 PRI, "Fiduciary Duty in the 21st Century: Executive Summary" (2019). www.unpri.org/fiduciary-duty/fiduciary-duty-in-the-21st-century/244.article.
16 Stockholm Resilience Centre, "The Nine Planetary Boundaries" (2015). www.stockholmresilience.org/research/planetary-boundaries/planetary-boundaries/about-the-research/the-nine-planetary-boundaries.html.

Macro-Level Debate on ESG Integration 33

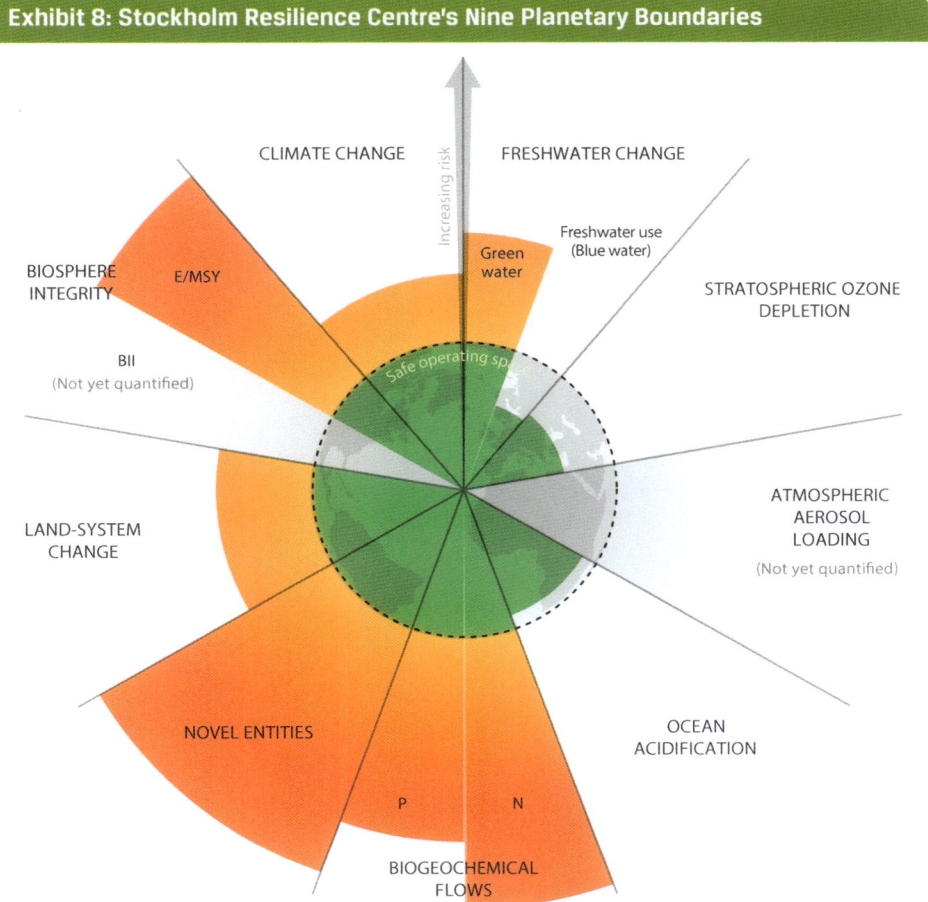

Exhibit 8: Stockholm Resilience Centre's Nine Planetary Boundaries

Source: Stockholm Resilience Centre, "New Assessment Reveals Dramatic Changes to the Global Water Cycle, with Parts of the Amazon Drying Out" (2022). www.stockholmresilience.org/research/research-news/2022-04-26-freshwater-boundary-exceeds-safe-limits.html.

A popular framework that builds on that of "planetary boundaries" is **doughnut economics**. Exhibit 9 shows this visual framework. It is a diagram developed by economist Kate Raworth that combines planetary boundaries with the complementary concept of social boundaries. The name comes from the shape of the diagram, a disc with a hole.

Exhibit 9: Doughnut Economics

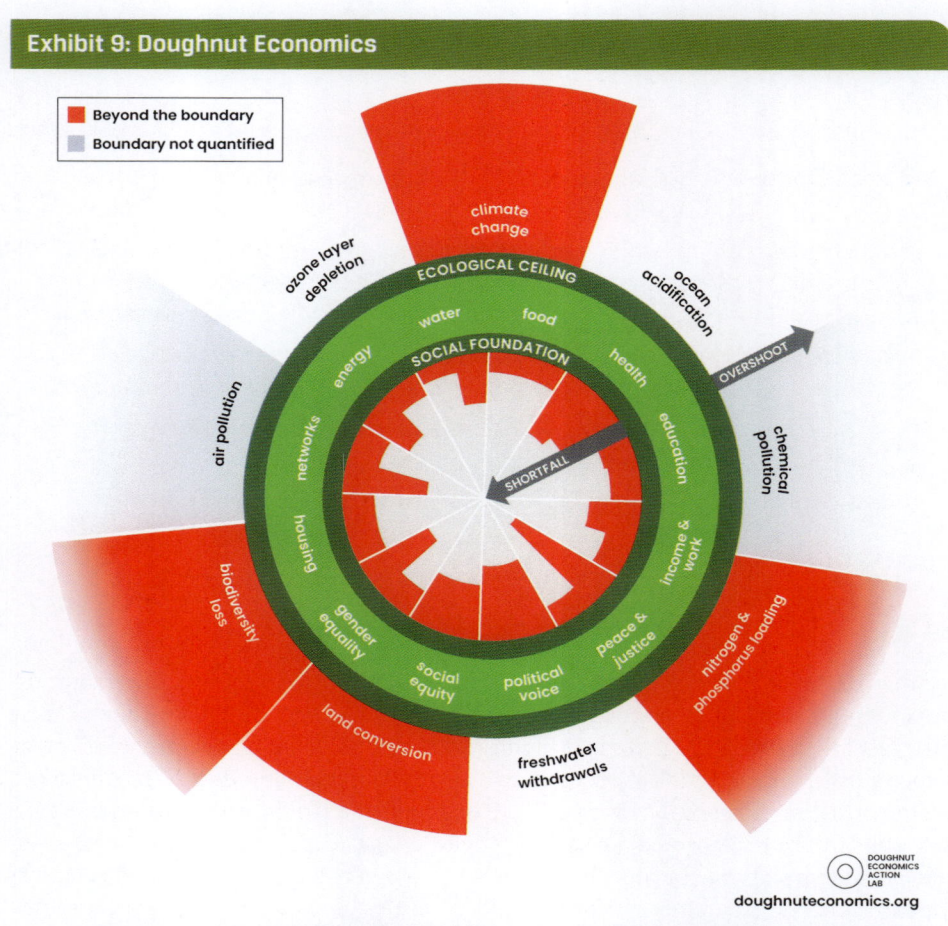

Source: K. Raworth, *Doughnut Economics: Seven Ways to Think Like a 21st Century Economist* (White River Junction, VT: Chelsea Green Publishing, 2017).

Social issues are also having a significant impact on the wider economy. Income inequality in OECD countries is at its highest level for 30 years, and Oxfam estimated that as of January 2022, the wealth of the 10 richest billionaires has doubled since the beginning of the COVID-19 pandemic; together, they own as many assets as the 3.8 billion people who make up the poorest half of the planet's population.[17] This significant level of income inequality is creating a number of social stresses, including security-related issues.[18] In 2014, the world spent 9.1% of its gross domestic product (GDP) on costs associated with violence. Undernutrition is also still common in developing economies and has severe economic consequences: The economic cost of undernutrition in Ethiopia alone is just under US$70 million (£50 million) a year. While the number of undernourished people in the world has declined sharply, one out of eight people suffers from chronic malnutrition.

Large institutional investors have holdings that, due to their size, are highly diversified across all sectors, asset classes, and regions. As a result, the portfolios of **universal owners**, as they are known, are sufficiently representative of global capital markets that they effectively hold a slice of the overall market. Their investment

---

[17] A. Ratcliff, "Billionaire Fortunes Grew by $2.5 Billion a Day Last Year As Poorest Saw Their Wealth Fall," Oxfam International (21 January 2019). www.oxfam.org/en/press-releases/billionaire-fortunes-grew-25-billion-day-last-year-poorest-saw-their-wealth-fall.

[18] PRI, "The SDG Investment Case—Macro Risks: Universal Ownership" (12 October 2017). www.unpri.org/sdgs/the-sdgs-are-an-unavoidable-consideration-for-universal-owners/306.article.

Macro-Level Debate on ESG Integration

returns are thus dependent on the continuing good health of the overall economy. Inefficiently allocating capital to companies with high negative externalities can damage the profitability of other portfolio companies and the overall market return. It is in their interests to act to reduce the economic risk presented by sustainability challenges to improve their total, long-term financial performance. There is therefore a growing school of thought that investors should integrate the price of externalities into the investment process and take into account the wider effects of investments by considering the impact on society and environment and in the economy as a whole.

For that reason, investors increasingly call for governments to set policies in line with the fundamental challenges to our future. The UN's **Sustainable Development Goals (SDGs)**,[19] an agreed framework for all UN member state governments to work toward in aligning with global priorities (such as the transition to a low-carbon economy and the elimination of human rights abuses in corporate supply chains), were welcomed by the investment community.

Impact and Ethics Perspective

Yet another reason for practicing responsible investment is some investors' belief that investments can or should serve society alongside providing financial return. This belief translates into focusing on investments with a positive impact and/or avoiding those with a negative impact.

- Those investing for **positive impact** see investment as a means of tackling the world's social and environmental problems through effective deployment of capital. The aim is to put beneficiaries' money to good use rather than to invest it in any activity that could be construed as doing harm—essentially a moral argument. This idea is giving rise to the growing area of impact investment, itself a response to the limits of philanthropy and a recognition of the potential to align returns with positive impacts.

- Those avoiding **negative impact**, at times for religious reasons, usually do not invest (negative screening) in securities from controversial sectors (such as arms, gambling, alcohol, tobacco, and pornography).

Client Demand Perspective

Clients and pension fund beneficiaries (defined in more detail in Chapter 2) are increasingly calling for greater transparency about how and where their money is invested. This effort is driven by the following:

- Growing awareness that ESG factors influence
  - Company value
  - Returns
  - Reputation
- Increasing focus on the environmental and social impacts of the companies they are invested in

Asset owners, such as pension funds and insurers (as defined in Chapter 2), are instrumental for responsible investment because they make the decisions about how their assets, representing on average around 34% of GDP in OECD countries, are

---

19 United Nations, "Take Action for the Sustainable Development Goals" (2020). www.un.org/sustainabledevelopment/sustainable-development-goals/.

managed.[20] The number of them that are integrating ESG considerations continues to grow. In 2020–2021, 88 asset owners signed on to the PRI for the first time. In 2020, a group of asset owners launched the Net-Zero Asset Owner Alliance under the auspices of the UN, committing to transition their investment portfolios to net-zero greenhouse gas (GHG) emissions by 2050.

Further details on the demand for, and supply of, responsible investment, as well as the market more broadly, are discussed in Chapter 2.

Regulatory Perspective

Finally, regardless of their views or beliefs, some investors are being required to increasingly consider ESG matters. Since the mid-1990s, responsible investment regulation has increased significantly, with a particular surge in policy interventions since the 2008 financial crisis. Regulatory change has also been driven by a realization among national and international regulators that the financial sector can play an important role in meeting global challenges, such as combating climate change, modern slavery, and tax avoidance.

Among the world's 50 largest economies, the PRI found that 48 have some form of policy designed to help investors consider sustainability risks, opportunities, or outcomes. In fact, among these economies, there have been over 730 hard and soft law policy revisions that encourage or require investors to consider long-term value drivers, including ESG factors. Hard laws are actual binding legal instruments and laws. Soft laws are quasi-legal instruments that do not have legally binding force or whose binding force is somewhat weaker than the binding force of traditional law. Soft law over time may become hard law.

For further details on how regulation has played a key role in increased demand for responsible investment, refer to Chapter 2.

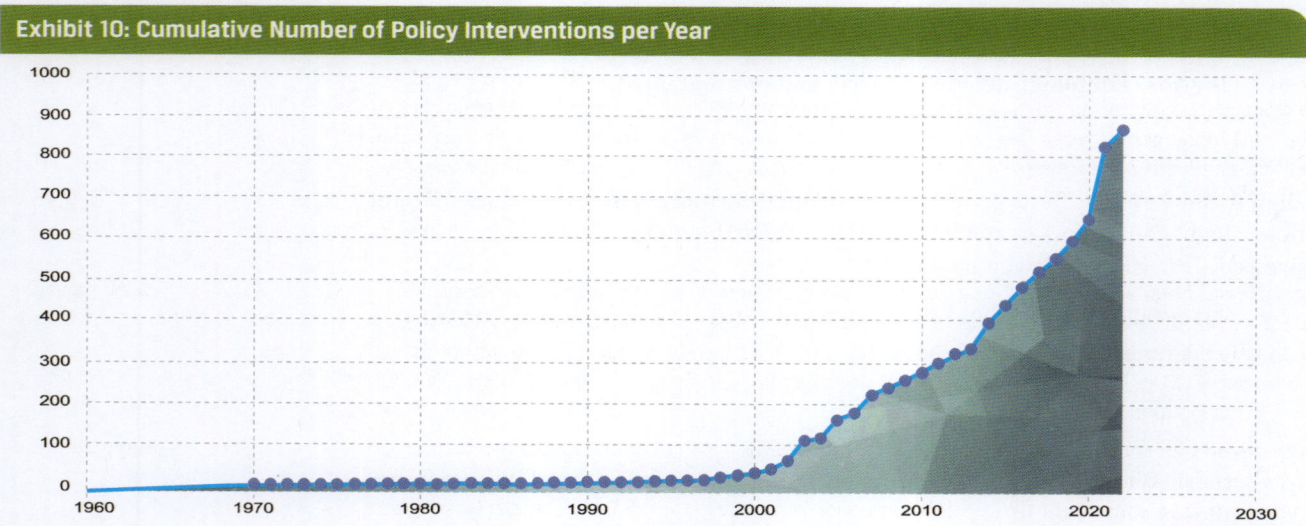

Exhibit 10: Cumulative Number of Policy Interventions per Year

Source: PRI, "Regulation Database" (updated April 2022). www.unpri.org/sustainable-markets/regulation-map.

---

20 R. Sievänen, H. Rita, and B. Scholtens, "The Drivers of Responsible Investment: The Case of European Pension Funds," *Journal of Business Ethics* 117 (September 2012): 137–51. www.researchgate.net/publication/236667333_The_Drivers_of_Responsible_Investment_The_Case_of_European_Pension_Funds.

FINANCIAL MATERIALITY OF ESG INTEGRATION

5

☐ 1.1.4 explain the concepts of the financial materiality of ESG integration, double materiality, and dynamic materiality and how they relate to ESG analysis, practices, and reporting

☐ 1.1.5 explain different ESG megatrends, their systemic nature, and their potential impact on companies and company practices

One of the main reasons for ESG integration is recognizing that ESG investing can reduce risk and enhance returns because it considers additional risks and injects new and forward-looking insights into the investment process. ESG integration may therefore lead to

1. reduced cost and increased efficiency,
2. reduced risk of fines and state intervention,
3. reduced negative externalities, and
4. improved ability to benefit from sustainability megatrends.

Each of these outcomes is described in greater detail in the following subsections

Efficiency and Productivity

Sustainable business practices build efficiencies by

- conserving resources,
- reducing costs, and
- enhancing productivity.

Sustainability was once perceived by businesses and investors as requiring sacrifices, but the perception today is very different. Significant cost reductions can result from improving operational efficiency through better management of natural resources, such as water and energy, as well as from minimizing waste.

Research conducted by McKinsey & Company found that resource efficiency can affect operating profits by as much as 60% and that more broadly, resource efficiency of companies across various sectors is significantly correlated with the companies' financial performance.[21] A study analyzing data from the global climate database provided by **CDP** (formerly, the Climate Disclosure Project) estimated that companies experience an average internal rate of return of 27%–80% on their low-carbon investments.[22]

A strong ESG proposition can help companies attract and retain quality employees and enhance employee motivation and productivity overall. Employee satisfaction is positively correlated with shareholder returns. The London Business School's Alex Edmans found that the companies that made Fortune's 100 Best Companies to Work For list generated 2.3%–3.8% higher stock returns a year than their peers over a horizon of longer than 25 years.[23]

---

21 W. Henisz, T. Koller, and R. Nuttall, "Five Ways That ESG Creates Value," *McKinsey Quarterly* (November 2019). www.mckinsey.com/business-functions/strategy-and-corporate-finance/our-insights/five-ways-that-esg-creates-value?cid=soc-web.
22 We Mean Business Coalition, "The Climate Has Changed," (21 September 2014). www.wemeanbusinesscoalition.org/blog/the-climate-has-changed/.
23 A. Edmans, "Does the Stock Market Fully Value Intangibles? Employee Satisfaction and Equity Prices," *Journal of Financial Economics* 101 (September 2011): 621–40. www.sciencedirect.com/science/article/abs/pii/S0304405X11000869.

CASE STUDIES

Savings from Efficiency Measures

The Dow Chemical Company

Between 1994 and 2010, The Dow Chemical Company invested nearly US$2 billion (£1.4 billion) in improving resource efficiency and saved US$9.8 billion (£7 billion) from reduced energy and wastewater consumption in manufacturing.[24] The company's long-established focus on resource efficiency cost reductions enabled it to achieve savings of US$31 million (£22.3 million) on its raw materials alone, compared to a net income of approximately US$4 billion (£2.9 billion), in 2018.

General Electric

In 2013, General Electric reduced its GHG emissions by 32% and water use by 45% compared to the 2004 and 2006 baselines, respectively. This resulted in savings of US$300 million (£215.7 million).[25]

Aeon Group

Between 2015 and 2018, the Japanese retail group Aeon achieved a decrease of 9.7% in food waste, which was equal to 32.14 kg or ¥1 million (£6,826) in net sales.[26]

Walmart

Within 10 years, Walmart improved the fuel efficiency of its fleet by approximately 87% through better routing, cargo loading, and driver training. In 2014 alone, these improvements resulted in avoiding 15,000 metric tons of CO_2 emissions and savings of nearly US$11 million (£7.9 million).[27]

Nike

Almost half (40%) of Nike's footwear manufacturing waste is generated by cutting scraps from materials such as textiles, leather, synthetic leather, and foams. In 2018, modern cutting equipment, which can achieve smaller gaps between cut parts than traditional die-cutting can, was deployed to various factories. The estimated value of savings was US$12 million (£8.6 million), compared to its net income of US$1.1 billion (£0.8 billion), and nearly 1.2 million kilograms of material for that fiscal year.[28]

Reduced Risk of Fines and State Intervention

With all the discussion regarding climate change, dwindling energy resources, and environmental impact, it is no surprise that state and federal government agencies are enacting regulations to protect the environment. Integrating sustainability into a business will position it to anticipate changing regulations in a timely manner. For

---

[24] T. Whelan and C. Fink, "The Comprehensive Business Case for Sustainability," *Harvard Business Review* (21 October 2016). https://hbr.org/2016/10/the-comprehensive-business-case-for-sustainability.
[25] GE, "GE Works: 2013 Annual Report," letter to shareowners (2014). www.ge.com/jp/sites/www.ge.com.jp/files/GE_AR13.pdf.
[26] Aeon, "Aeon Sustainability Data Book 2019" (2019). www.aeon.info/export/sites/default/common/images/en/environment/report/e_2019pdf/19_data_en_a4.pdf.
[27] T. Whelan and C. Fink, "The Comprehensive Business Case for Sustainability."
[28] M. Parker, "Letter to Shareholders," NIKE, Inc. (24 July 2018). https://s1.q4cdn.com/806093406/files/doc_financials/2018/ar/docs/nike-shareholders-letter-2018.pdf.

example, a 2019 UN Environment Programme report found that there has been a 38-fold increase in environmental laws put in place since 1972.[29] It also found that enforcement remains weak today but that significant events indeed result in fines. It concluded that the level of enforcement could quickly change with little notice to investors.

Analysis conducted by McKinsey & Company showed that, typically, one-third of corporate profits are at risk from state intervention (not only fines).[30] For pharmaceuticals, the profits at stake are about 25%–30%, and for the automotive, banking, and technology sectors, where government subsidies (among other forms of intervention) are prevalent, the value at stake can reach 60% (see Exhibit 11).

Exhibit 11: Estimated Share of EBITDA at Stake

Estimated Share of EBITDA at Stake		Examples
Banks	50%–60%	Capital requirements, systemic regulation ("too big to fail"), and consumer protection
Automotive, aerospace and defense, technology	50%–60%	Government subsidies, renewable regulation, and carbon-emissions regulation
Transport, logistics, infrastructure	45%–55%	Pricing regulation and liberalization of sector
Telecom and media	40%–50%	Tariff regulation, interconnection, fiber deployment, spectrum and data privacy
Energy and materials	35%–45%	Tariff regulation, renewables subsidies, interconnection, and access rights
Resources	30%–40%	Resource nationalism, mineral taxes, land-access rights, community reach and reputation
Consumer goods	25%–30%	Obesity, sustainability, food safety, health and wellness, and labeling
Pharmaceuticals and health care	25%–30%	Market access, regulation of generic drugs, pricing, innovation funding, and clinical trials

Source: W. Henisz, T. Koller, and R. Nuttall, "Five Ways That ESG Creates Value," *McKinsey Quarterly* (November 2019). www.mckinsey.com/business-functions/strategy-and-corporate-finance/our-insights/five-ways-that-esg-creates-value?cid=soc-web. Copyright (c) 2021 McKinsey & Company. All rights reserved. Reprinted by permission.

CASE STUDIES

Major Fines

BP and Deepwater Horizon

The biggest corporate fine to date was levied against BP in the wake of the 2010 Deepwater Horizon oil spill in the Gulf of Mexico, the largest in history. BP settled with the US Department of Justice for US$20.8 billion (£15 billion) in 2016;[31] total compensation ultimately paid out by the company reportedly exceeded US$65 billion (£46.7 billion).

---

29 UN Environment Programme, "Environmental Rule of Law: First Global Report" (24 January 2019). www.unenvironment.org/resources/assessment/environmental-rule-law-first-global-report.
30 W. Henisz, T. Koller, and R. Nuttall, "Five Ways That ESG Creates Value."
31 D. Rushe, "BP Set to Pay Largest Environmental Fine in US History for Gulf Oil Spill," *Guardian* (2 July 2015). www.theguardian.com/environment/2015/jul/02/bp-will-pay-largest-environmental-fine-in-us-history-for-gulf-oil-spill.

Financial Crisis and the Bank of America

Several of the largest fines have hit the financial services industry, a direct result of the scrutiny facing banks in the wake of the financial crisis. These include the second highest fine (US$16.65 billion, or £12 billion), which was paid by Bank of America in 2014 for its role in the subprime loan crisis.[32] Just two years before that, the bank agreed to a US$11.8 billion (£8.5 billion) settlement with the US federal government over foreclosure abuses.

Volkswagen's Emissions Scandal

The third largest fine was paid by Volkswagen, which, in 2016, faced US$14.7 billion (£11.5 billion) in civil and criminal penalties from the United States in the wake of its scandal over emissions cheating.[33] The scandal dampened the hype of diesel as a fuel for the future. Today, most major automotive companies are directing their current (and future) investments toward electric cars while striving to meet increasingly aggressive emission targets.

Reduced Negative Externalities

The term **externalities** refers to situations where the production or consumption of goods and services creates costs or benefits for others that are not reflected in the prices charged for them. In other words, externalities include the consumption, production, and investment decisions of firms (and individuals) that affect people not directly involved in the transactions. Externalities can be either negative or positive.

The concept of externality, though central to the concept of sustainability and responsible investment, dates back to 1920, having been introduced by Cambridge professor Arthur Pigou in his book *The Economics of Welfare*. Externalities often occur when the production or consumption of a product's or service's private price equilibrium cannot reflect the true costs or benefits of that product or service for society as a whole.

Example Pollution

In the case of pollution, a polluter makes decisions based only on the direct cost and profit opportunity associated with production and does not consider the indirect costs to those harmed by the pollution. These indirect costs—which are not borne by the producer or user—may include decreased quality of life, higher health care costs, and forgone production opportunities (for example, when pollution harms activities, such as tourism).

Professor William Nordhaus, who was recently awarded the Nobel Prize for his work on the externality of climate change, developed a model to measure the impact of environmental degradation on economic growth and thus created a price for carbon pollution. However, externalities can also be due to social factors—for example, when companies fail to pay a living wage or submit their employees to poor working conditions.

In short, when externalities are *negative*, private costs are lower than societal costs, resulting in market outcomes that may not be efficient or, in other words, leading to "market failures."

---

[32] "Bank of America and the Financial Crisis," *New York Times* (21 August 2014). www.nytimes.com/interactive/2014/06/10/business/dealbook/11bank-timelime.html.
[33] "VW in $14.7bn US Deal over Rigged Cars," *Financial Times* (27 June 2016).

For that reason, externalities are among the main reasons why governments intervene in the economic sphere.[34] As far back as the 1920s, British economist Arthur Pigou suggested that governments should tax polluters an amount equivalent to the cost of the harm incurred by others. Such a tax would yield the market outcome that would have prevailed with adequate **internalization** of all costs by polluters. Internalization refers to all measures (public or private) to ensure that externalities become reflected in the prices of commercial goods and services.[35] As environmental and social regulation and taxation become more common, it is expected that an increasing proportion of this cost might be forced into companies' accounts.

In the social sphere, recent developments in the interpretation of the **OECD Guidelines for Multinational Enterprises**[36] and the **UN Guiding Principles for Business and Human Rights**[37]—clarifying that these instruments apply to investors and give rise to responsibility for conducting human rights due diligence on investments—are in effect paving the way for more formal internalization of social costs in hard law.[38]

Internalization can happen in various ways. In regard to the transportation industry, for example, internalization can happen through

- market-based instruments (e.g., charges, taxes, and tradable permits);
- regulatory instruments (e.g., vehicle emission and safety standards, traffic restrictions); or
- voluntary instruments (e.g., agreements with the car industry to reduce CO_2 emissions from new passenger cars).

Understanding the risks posed by "externalized" environmental and social costs in the real economy is central to the practice of investment, because the internalization of these externalities could significantly impact the costs and profits of companies' products and services, affecting their bottom line. The uncertainty surrounding the timing and extent of internalization is a critical component of the overall risk landscape facing investors.

Beyond affecting companies' financial performance, these externalities can also have a drag on the wider economy, potentially affecting the total return investors may achieve in the long term. A study by an environmental consulting company found that the top 3,000 publicly traded companies were responsible for US$2.15 trillion (£1.6 trillion) worth of environmental damage in 2008 and that global environmental damage would cost an estimated US$28 trillion (£20 trillion) by 2050.[39] Environmental harm was found to be a material risk that could significantly affect the value of capital markets and global economic growth.

---

34 T. Helbling, "What Are Externalities?" *Finance & Development* 47 (December 2010). www.imf.org/external/pubs/ft/fandd/2010/12/basics.htm.
35 H. Ding, M. He, and C. Deng, "Lifecycle Approach to Assessing Environmental Friendly Product Project with Internalizing Environmental Externality," *Journal of Cleaner Production* 66 (1 March 2014): 128–38. www.sciencedirect.com/science/article/abs/pii/S0959652613006811.
36 OECD, "OECD Guidelines for Multinational Enterprises" (2018). www.oecd.org/corporate/mne/.
37 UNGC, "Guiding Principles Business on Human Rights: Implementing the United Nations 'Protect, Respect and Remedy' Framework" (2011). www.unglobalcompact.org/library/2
38 See, for example, F. Marotta, "Subject: Request from the Chair of the OECD Working Party on Responsible Business Conduct" (27 November 2013). www.ohchr.org/Documents/Issues/Business/LetterOECD.pdf.
See also Norwegian National Contact Point for the OECD Guidelines for Multinational Enterprises, "Final Statement: Complaint from Lok Shakti Abhiyan, Korean Transnational Corporations Watch, Fair Green and Global Alliance and Forum for Environment and Development vs. Posco (South Korea), ABP/ APG (Netherlands) and NBIM (Norway)" (27 May 2013). https://vdocuments.mx/final-statement-nettsteder-for-final-statement-complaint-from-lok-shakti-abhiyan.html?page=1.
39 S. Wainwright, "Putting a Price on Global Environmental Damage," *Trucost News* (5 October 2010).

CASE STUDIES

Air Travel and Carbon Emissions

Before the COVID-19 pandemic, air travel was the source of around 2.5% of global CO_2 emissions, but it is estimated to grow by 300% by 2050. For that reason, the European Commission (EC) has for many years been assessing and advocating for the internalization of externalities associated with transportation.

In 2010, the European Union (EU) expanded the scope of its **Emissions Trading System (ETS)** to include aviation.[40] The EU's ETS for aviation requires all non-commercial operators who travel into, out of, and between EU and European Economic Area (EEA) member states to monitor their CO_2 flight emissions and purchase carbon allowances equal to the emissions on intra-EU flights when emitting more than 1,000 tonnes of CO_2 under the full scope (in, out of, and within the EU).

In 2019, the ministers of finance of the Netherlands, Germany, France, Sweden, Italy, Belgium, Luxembourg, Denmark, and Bulgaria asked the EC to introduce a measure to offset the CO_2 emissions of planes.

A report from the independent research and consultancy organization CE Delft[41] showed that tax exemptions for the aviation sector lead to

- higher passenger demand,
- aviation sector growth (in terms of both jobs and value added), and
- more flights.

The report also shows that a tax could result in a 10% increase in average ticket price and an 11% decline in passenger demand but that CO_2 emissions would decrease by 11%.

Impacts in the aviation sector	Current Situation Value	Abolition of Ticket Tax Value	Change	Introducing VAT on All Tickets (19%) Value	Change	Introducing Fuel Excise Duty Value	Change
Passenger demand (millions)	691.5	718.5	+4%	570.4	−18%	616.0	−11%
Average ticket price (€)	304	293	−4%	358	+17%	333	+10%
Number of flights and connectivity			+4%		−18%		−11%
Employment (1,000 FTE)	362	376	+4%	296	−18%	321	−11%
Value added (€ billions)	43.4	45.1	+4%	35.6	−18%	38.5	−11%
CO_2 emissions (metric ton)	149.5	155.3	+4%	123.3	−18%	133.1	−11%
People affected by noise (thousands)	2,851.5	2,919.8	+2%	2,495.9	−12%	2,637.1	−8%
Aviation-related fiscal revenue (€ billions)	10.0	2.6	−74%	39.9	+297%	26.9	+168%

Sweden and France have acted unilaterally:[42] Sweden introduced a SEK60–SEK400 (£5–£34) carbon tax for all airline passengers in April 2018, and France introduced a levy of €1.50 (£1.31) to be charged on domestic and intra-European flights. In addition, France will charge €3 (£2.62) on flights outside the EU. Starting

---

40 European Commission, "Aircraft Operators and Their Administering Countries" (2019). https://ec.europa.eu/clima/policies/ets/monitoring/operators_en.
41 CE Delft and Directorate-General for Mobility and Transport, "Taxes in the Field of Aviation and Their Impact: Final Report" (2019). https://op.europa.eu/s/oarR.
42 C. Stokel-Walker, "Only Extreme Eco-taxes on Flights Will Change Our Flying Habits," *Wired* (12 July 2019). www.wired.co.uk/article/plane-tax-eco-france-sweden.

in 2020, a business class seat on a flight in the EU includes a €9 (£7.85) eco-charge, while a longer flight in business class includes a €18 (£15.70) eco-charge. The French government estimated that the "eco-tax" will raise €180 million (£151 million) a year from flights, which will be invested in other forms of transport, such as trains, according to the transport ministry.

Air France expects the eco-tax to cost the company an extra €60 million (£52 million) a year, which is believed to have encouraged it to buy more efficient planes in order to negotiate with the government.[43] Price sensitivity for passengers is relatively low, however, and the tax is deemed more of a symbolic first step. It is a practice used in the past by governments to start environment-related taxes low and get people used to the idea before increasing them. For example, the United Kingdom's landfill tax, introduced in 1996, started at £7 per tonne of waste deposited but now stands at £91.35 per tonne, an effective deterrent.[44]

In 2021, French lawmakers voted in favor of a bill to end routes where the same journey could be made by train in under two and a half hours. France is not the first country to replace flights with train rides. In 2020, Austrian Airlines replaced a flight route between Vienna and Salzburg with an increased train service, after receiving a government bailout with provisions to cut its carbon footprint.

Improved Ability to Benefit from Sustainability Megatrends

There is a multitude of implications from the so-called sustainability megatrends. Being able to integrate a response to these trends into business operations can be a success factor for an investee firm. From the investor perspective, these megatrends can be part of a successful portfolio construction strategy.

For this reason, business leaders, investors, economists, and governments are increasingly recognizing the economic implications of

- ► social challenges (such as increasing income inequality, poverty, and human and labor rights abuses) and
- ► environmental issues (such as climate change, biodiversity loss, and resource scarcity).

These factors have interacted with

- ► the aftermath of the 2007–08 financial crisis,
- ► aging populations,
- ► the rise of emerging economies, and
- ► rapid technological changes.

This interaction increases the complexity and the impact that social and environmental challenges have on the growth and profitability of sectors and businesses.

There is no agreement about what these megatrends are and how many of them exist. Four megatrends, which are widely recognized across governments and businesses, are discussed in the following subsections.

---

43 C. Stokel-Walker, "Only Extreme Eco-taxes on Flights Will Change Our Flying Habits."
44 C. Stokel-Walker, "Only Extreme Eco-taxes on Flights Will Change Our Flying Habits."

Emerging Markets and Urbanization

The locus of economic activity and dynamism is shifting to emerging markets and to cities within those markets, which are going through industrial and urban revolutions simultaneously. Until recently, 97% of the Fortune Global 500 were headquartered in developed economies, but nearly half of the world's large companies are expected to be headquartered in emerging markets by 2025. Nearly half of global GDP growth between 2010 and 2025 will come from 440 cities in emerging markets—95% of them small and medium-size cities.[45] This change will impact not only where headquarters are located but also supply chains, their workforces, and the expectation of the local communities, as well as where new consumers come from.

Technological Innovation

Technology has always had the power to change behavior and expectations. What is new is the speed of change. It took 76 years for the telephone to penetrate half of all US households. The smartphone has achieved the same in less than a decade.[46] Accelerated adoption invites accelerated innovation. By 2014, seven years after the iPhone's launch, the number of applications created had hit 1.2 million and users had downloaded more than 75 billion total apps, more than 10 for every person on the planet.[47]

Social media is the new social fabric and acts as a platform for both crowd intelligence and influence. Its influence stretches far beyond its initial use as a means to stay connected with people and now reaches into corporate risk management and geopolitics. Its capacity both to mobilize online crowds and to lead people into narrow filter bubbles has had major repercussions in recent years, including civil strife. Furthermore, issues around human rights, including free speech, and tensions between big social media companies and sovereign nation states have led to headlines and point in the direction of a possible new ordering of societal power, the outcome of which remains to be seen.

Artificial intelligence—namely, computer systems able to perform tasks normally requiring human intelligence—is poised to change and grow at an exponential speed beyond the power of human intuition to anticipate. It is being used by the health industry to track patients' data and medication intake, by businesses to automate customer service and robotize manufacturing, by energy companies' smart grids to forecast energy supply and demand, and by self-driving cars to optimize routes. Gartner (an IT research firm) estimated that one-third of jobs will soon be replaced by smart machines and robots, and Google estimated that robots will attain the level of the human intelligence by 2029. It has significantly impacted most sectors.

Demographic Changes and Wealth Inequality

By 2030, the world's population is projected to rise by more than 1 billion. At the same time, the population is getting older. Germany's population is expected to shrink by one-fifth, and the number of people of working age could fall from 54 million in 2010 to 36 million in 2060. China's labor force peaked in 2012. Today, about 60% of the world's population lives in countries with fertility rates below the replacement rate.[48]

---

45 McKinsey & Company, "McKinsey Special Collections: Trends and Global Forces" (April 2017). www.mckinsey.com/~/media/McKinsey/Business%20Functions/Strategy%20and%20Corporate%20Finance/Our%20Insights/Strategy%20and%20corporate%20finance%20special%20collection/Final%20PDFs/McKinsey-Special-Collections_Trends-and-global-forces.ashx.
46 PWC, "Technological Breakthroughs" (2020). www.pwc.co.uk/issues/megatrends/technological-breakthroughs.html.
47 McKinsey & Company, "McKinsey Special Collections."
48 McKinsey & Company, "McKinsey Special Collections."

A smaller workforce will place a greater onus on productivity for driving growth and may cause economists to rethink the economy's potential. Caring for large numbers of elderly people has already started to reshape industries and put severe pressure on government finances. At the same time, the rise in population overall will only increase the demand for and stress on renewable and non-renewable resources. A growing global population is expected to demand 35% more food by 2030. Finally, increasing concentration of wealth and rising inequality have already led to increasing social strain. This increase in inequality happens across and within countries, contributing to depressed economic growth, criminal behavior, and undermined educational opportunities.[49]

Climate Change and Resource Scarcity

As the world becomes more populous, urbanized, and prosperous, the demand for energy, food, and water will rise. But the Earth has a finite amount of natural resources to satisfy this demand. Without significant global action, average temperatures are predicted to increase by more than 1.5°C (2.7°F), a threshold at which scientists believe significant and potentially irreversible environmental changes will occur. The interconnectivity between trends in climate change and resource scarcity is amplifying the impact: climate change could reduce agricultural productivity by up to a third across large parts of Africa over the next 60 years. Globally, demand for water will increase by 40% and demand for energy by 50%.

In short, the world's current economic model is pushing beyond the limits of the planet's ability to cope.

Evolution of Materiality: From Static to Dynamic

Recent movements (such as #MeToo and Black Lives Matter), recent events (such as the COVID-19 pandemic), and their implications, including regulation, highlight that priority issues can suddenly present new, previously unaccounted for risks for corporations and their investors. These require agile responses not only from corporations but also from capital providers to mitigate the quickly emerging risks that can impact the financials of a business. This concept—that what is financially material to a company not only can but most likely does change—has been defined as *dynamic materiality*. For investors, it means that the understanding of what is financially material for a company must be constantly in review to reflect the quickly evolving nature of ESG factors.

Double Materiality

Double materiality is an extension of the accounting concept of financial materiality. Information on a company is material and should therefore be disclosed if a reasonable person would consider the information important. As illustrated in the previous section, because ESG factors, especially climate, can be material for a company, they have now been widely accepted in financial markets as potentially financially material, therefore requiring disclosure.

The concept of double materiality takes this notion one step further: It is not just climate-related impacts on the company that can be material but also impacts of a company on the climate—or any other ESG factor. For further detail, see Exhibit 12. In 2019, the European Commission was the first to formally describe the concept of double materiality in the context of sustainability reporting and the need to get a full picture of a company's impacts. This means in practice that both companies and investors are increasingly identifying, monitoring, and managing the most significant impact that companies and investment portfolios have on society and the environment.

---

49 Max Lawson, Anam Parvez Butt, Rowan Harvey, Diana Sarosi, Clare Coffey, Kim Piaget, and Julie Thekkudan, "Time to Care: Unpaid and Underpaid Care Work and the Global Inequality Crisis," Oxfam International (20 January 2020). www.oxfam.org/en/research/time-care.

Exhibit 12: The Concept of Double Materiality

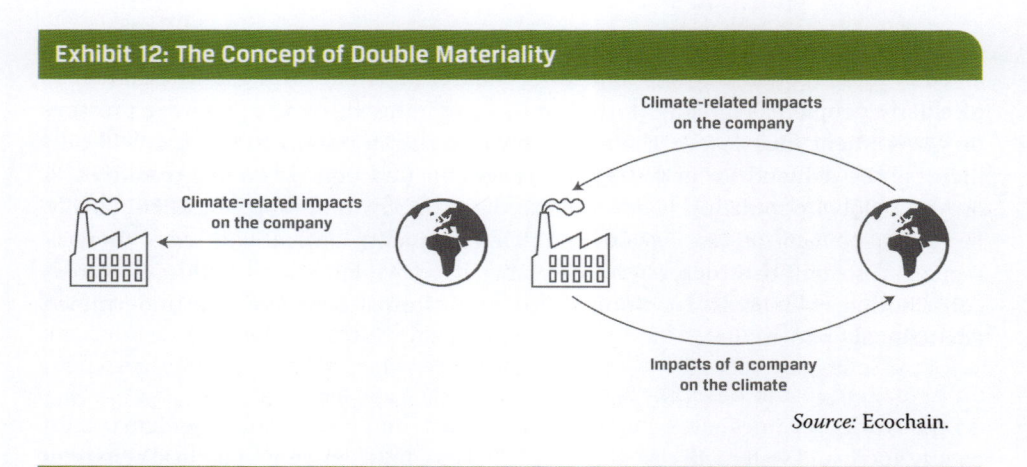

Source: Ecochain.

6 CHALLENGES IN INTEGRATING ESG FACTORS

ESG investing has seen rapid development in recent years, but challenges to its further growth remain. Challenges to taking a more proactive approach to ESG investing exist across the whole of the investment decision-making process.

Prior to wishing to implement ESG investing:

- The perception that implementing ESG investing may have a negative impact on investment performance
- The interpretation that fiduciary duty prevents investors from integrating ESG factors
- The advice given by investment consultants and retail financial advisers many times not having been supportive of products that integrate ESG factors

Once the decision has been made to implement ESG investing:

- The lack of understanding of how to build an investment mandate that effectively promotes ESG investing or lack of understanding of what are the needs of asset owners regarding ESG investing.
- The impression that significant resources, which may be lacking in the market or may be expensive, are needed—including human resources, technical capability, data, and tools.
- The gap between marketing, commitment, and delivery of funds regarding their ESG performance

Some investors still question whether considering ESG issues can add value to investment decision making despite wide dissemination of research that demonstrates that ESG integration can help limit volatility and enhance returns. Interviews conducted by the PRI show that investment professionals place a greater weight on experience from their own careers than they do on third-party evidence.[50] It can thus be helpful for an internal evidence base to be built or to engage with direct peers on ESG processes and investment benefits.

---

50 PRI, "How Asset Owners Can Drive Responsible Investment: Beliefs, Strategies and Mandates" (2016). www.unpri.org/download?ac=1398.

Interpretations of fiduciary duty are partially related to perception of the impact on ESG investing on risk-adjusted returns. Despite regulators in various jurisdictions clarifying a modern interpretation of fiduciary duty, contrasting views remain as to how ESG integration fits with institutional investors' duties. Some institutional investors remain reluctant to adapt their governance processes because they see a conflict between their responsibility to protect the financial interests of their beneficiaries and the consideration of ESG factors.

The challenge pertains not only to the impact of ESG investing on portfolio returns. Screening, divestment, and thematic investment strategies involve "tilting" the portfolio toward desired ESG characteristics by over- or underweighting sectors or companies that perform either well or poorly in those areas. Institutional investors may feel that this conflicts with their obligation to invest prudently, because it involves straying from established market benchmarks. This increases the tracking error, a key measure of active risk widely used in the industry that is due to active management decisions versus the benchmark made by the portfolio manager.

For further details on the challenges of portfolio construction, refer to Chapter 8.

The barriers mentioned earlier, together with other reasons, may explain why investment consultants and retail financial advisers have offered advice that is not seen as supportive of ESG investing. Consultants and advisers often base their advice on a very narrow interpretation of investment objectives. What they perceive as a lack of interest by asset owners in responsible investment has also contributed to them being less willing to integrate ESG investing into their mainstream offerings. Asset owners and individual retail investors can ensure ESG factors are standing items in meetings and ask how consultants and advisers integrate ESG factors into their advice. Investor-led initiatives can also increase engagement with these actors to enhance their understanding of ESG investing and address barriers to its consideration in investment advice.

Even once an investor has decided to consider ESG factors in investment decision making, various barriers remain. Some asset owners believe they do not have the scale or capacity to influence the products offered by fund managers. Others are unsure of how to integrate ESG factors in requests for proposals or mandates. The absence of clear signals from asset owners that they are interested in ESG investing means that investment managers have limited understanding of what asset owners expect on that matter and reduced incentive to develop such products. As a result, asset owners have fewer options for ESG investing products in the market to choose from. There are investor-led initiatives that hope to address this problem. The International Corporate Governance Network (ICGN) established a **Model Mandate Initiative**, the University of Cambridge Institute for Sustainability Leadership developed a toolkit for establishing long-term, sustainable mandates, and the PRI published numerous guidance documents to support asset owners in incorporating ESG investing into manager selection and investment mandates.

For further details on mandates, refer to Chapter 9.

The challenge of resources is especially prominent for asset owners who have funding constraints or investors who see ESG investing as separate from the core investment process (e.g., marketing or compliance). In addition to the costs of building or buying expertise in ESG investing, investors may face other costs for items, such as research, data, monitoring, and reporting. The European Fund and Asset Management Association estimated the average total price of external data for an investor to be €100,000 (£87,237).[51]

---

51 EFAMA, "EFAMA Reply to EC Consultation on Long-Term and Sustainable Investment" (23 March 2016). www.efama.org/newsroom/news/efama-reply-ec-consultation-long-term-and-sustainable-investment.

Even when financial resources are available, investors still have difficulty identifying or creating technical resources, such as high-quality, standardized datasets, modelling capability, and valuation techniques. Without such resources, it is not always straightforward to understand the effects of ESG risks and opportunities at the investee company level. This is because these risks and opportunities will be invisibly incorporated into the investee's overall financial performance and, therefore, before their materialization, will be invisible in the investor's (non-ESG) financial models.

- Data availability: Although ESG data from investees are increasingly available from specialized providers, disclosure is still a significant challenge, especially in asset classes other than listed equities. Investment analysis thus remains limited by corporate disclosure, which varies in quality and scope. It is also limited by investors' understanding of those data and which metrics are financially material. There is considerable effort by the private sector and policymakers to reach a consensus on what degree and type of corporate disclosure is needed, but no single standard is universally implemented.

- Modeling: It can be challenging to integrate ESG factors into traditional financial models, because they do not always have a short-term financial impact. Furthermore, most financial analysts' models extrapolate from historical data, which may be less relevant for forecasting future ESG-related outcomes. For example, measuring a company's past and current carbon footprint does not give as much information about its future valuation as understanding its strategy for reducing its carbon intensity. Similarly, it is hard to estimate the viability or impact of a breakthrough technological innovation based on historical patterns. Notably, a lot of ESG models focus on risks, and there are fewer tools for assessing positive ESG performance.

- Valuation techniques: Equity investors can adjust corporate valuations for ESG factors in a number of ways. Investors could vary the discount rate applied to future corporate cash flows, which raises the question of how much of a discount should be applied to various kinds of ESG risk. Alternatively, they could apply higher or lower multiples to valuation ratios (such as price-to-earnings or book value), which might lead to double-counting if ESG factors are already partially priced by the market.

As a result of these difficulties, ESG analysis often takes the form of a qualitative input that is used alongside traditional quantitative models. The portfolio manager might use the quality score just for information or might set a hurdle for a stock to be included in the portfolio. These types of risk metrics are less respected by portfolio managers than financial analysis because quantifying the input and its impact is generally a challenge.

For further details on financial materiality, data suppliers, and integrating ESG factors in valuation techniques, refer to Chapter 7.

A growing challenge for the industry is greenwashing. Greenwashing originally described misleading claims about environmental practices, performance, or products but has been used more widely to incorporate ESG factors more broadly. The phenomenon is not restricted to the investment industry, but with the rise of a plethora of new ESG-type funds, including impact funds, the challenge of how to spot and avoid greenwashing has become more prevalent. Asset owners, as well as individual retail investors, have questioned why certain stocks, either involved in significant controversies or with controversial activities, are part of the top holdings of ESG funds, which has at times impacted the credibility of responsible investment efforts. Part of the frustration comes from the lack of a better standard in the industry to differentiate between an investment lens based on ESG integration, which concerns the financial materiality of ESG matters, and those based on impact or ethics. While a fund can incorporate both lenses, some funds incorporate only one or the other; effective disclosure and education are required in order to properly manage investors' expectations regarding these different approaches to responsible investment.

The EU has recently launched various initiatives to standardize claims around the green and ESG credential of funds and indexes, which will contribute to a clampdown on greenwashing. Further advancements from the governments of other jurisdictions, as well as voluntary action and initiatives of investors themselves, would contribute to maintaining and enhancing the implementation and credibility of responsible investment.

ESG FACTORS' INFLUENCE ON FINANCIAL PERFORMANCE

There is growing recognition in the financial industry and in academia that ESG factors indeed influence financial performance. An analysis of over 2,000 academic studies on how ESG factors affect corporate financial performance found "an overwhelming share of positive results," with just 1 in 10 showing a negative relationship.[52] Various studies also indicate that engaging with companies on ESG issues can create value for both investors and companies, by encouraging better ESG risk management and more sustainable business practices.[53] These studies provide evidence that ESG issues can be financially material to companies' performance and potentially to alpha.

Mounting evidence shows that sustainable business practices deliver better financial performance. The topic has not only been the focus of various individual studies but also the subject of **meta-analysis**, which is a research process used to merge the findings of single, independent studies to reach an overall conclusion.

In summary, these **meta-studies** suggest that in most research papers, there was a positive correlation between ESG performance and corporate financial performance, including stock prices. These findings provide academic evidence for the financial materiality of ESG factors. This correlation, however, does not hold for fund performance, suggesting that the asset management industry in general has not been consistently able to translate ESG analysis into alpha.

CASE STUDIES

Meta-Data Studies

One of the first meta-data studies, in 2012, was conducted by Deutsche Bank,[54] assessing over 100 studies. The vast majority (89%) of studies showed that companies highly rated for ESG factors outperformed the market, while 85% demonstrated outperformance in terms of business performance. These results were strongest over the medium to long term. Deutsche Bank found weaker

---

52 Global Research Institute, "Digging Deeper into the ESG-Corporate Financial-Performance-Relationship" (September 2018). https://download.dws.com/download?elib-assetguid=714aed4c2e83471787d1ca0f1b559006.
53 PRI, "How ESG Engagement Creates Value for Investors and Companies: Executive Summary" (26 April 2018). www.unpri.org/academic-research/how-esg-engagement-creates-value-for-investors-and-companies/3054.article.
Elroy Dimson, Oğuzhan Karakaş, and Xi Li, "Local Leads, Backed by Global Scale: The Drivers of Successful Engagement," *RI Quarterly Vol. 12: Highlights from the Academic Network Conference and PRI in Person 2017* (19 September 2017). www.unpri.org/academic-research/local-leads-backed-by-global-scale-the-drivers-of-successful-engagement/537.article.
54 M. Fulton, B. Kahn, and C. Sharples, "Sustainable Investing: Establishing Long-Term Value and Performance," DB Climate Change Advisors (June 2012).

results with respect to the influence of ESG factors on investment funds. They concluded that companies with good ESG factors outperform but that investors were not always good at capturing that outperformance.

The University of Oxford and asset manager Arabesque in 2014 reviewed the academic literature on sustainability and corporate performance and found that out of the 200 studies analyzed,

- 90% concluded that good ESG standards lower the cost of capital,
- 88% showed that good ESG practices result in better operational performance, and
- 80% showed that stock price performance is positively correlated with good sustainability practices.[55]

Another study, conducted in 2015, combined the findings of around 2,200 individual studies (35 times larger than the average sample of previous meta-analyses) and thus claimed to be the most exhaustive overview of the academic evidence on ESG factors and performance.[56] In this case, about 90% of studies demonstrated a relationship between ESG factors and financial performance that was not negative (i.e., positive or neutral performance), with the large majority showing positive correlation between ESG factors and performance across equity, fixed income, and property, as well as in aggregate.

The meta-study showed a significant difference between the impact of ESG factors on corporate financial performance, at the asset-class level, and on investment fund performance:

- 15% of the studies on portfolio-level impact were positive and
- 11% were negative.

The authors suggested three reasons why the results differ:

1. The alpha from ESG factors might be captured elsewhere in factor studies (and thus is "drowned out by noise").
2. The impacts of different ESG approaches in the various studies might cancel each other out.
3. The costs of implementation consume the available alpha.

Finally, a February 2021 meta-study conducted by the NYU Stern Center for Sustainable Business and Rockefeller Asset Management examined the relationship between ESG factors and financial performance in more than 1,000 research papers from 2015 to 2020.[57] They conducted the research differently from previous meta-studies. They divided the articles into those focused on corporate financial performance (e.g., operating metrics, such as ROE, ROA, or stock performance for a company or group of companies) and those focused on investment performance (from the perspective of an investor, generally measures of alpha or such metrics as the Sharpe ratio on a portfolio of stocks).

---

55 G. L. Clark, A. Feiner, and M. Viehs, "From the Stockholder to the Stakeholder: How Sustainability Can Drive Financial Outperformance" (2015). https://ssrn.com/abstract=2508281.
56 G. Friede, T. Busch, and A. Bassen, "ESG and Financial Performance: Aggregated Evidence from More Than 2000 Empirical Studies," *Journal of Sustainable Finance & Investment* 5 (15 December 2015): 210–33. https://doi.org/10.1080/20430795.2015.1118917.
57 Tensie Whelan, Ulrich Atz, Tracy Van Holt, and Casey Clark, "ESG and Financial Performance: Uncovering the Relationship by Aggregating Evidence from 1,000 Plus Studies Published between 2015–2020" (10 February 2021). https://rcm.rockco.com/insights_item/esg-and-financial-performance.

They found a positive relationship between ESG and financial performance for 58% of the "corporate" studies focused on operational metrics, such as ROE, ROA, or stock price, with 13% showing neutral impact, 21% with mixed results (the same study finding a positive, neutral, or negative results), and only 8% showing a negative relationship. For investment studies typically focused on risk-adjusted attributes, such as alpha or the Sharpe ratio on a portfolio of stocks, 59% showed similar or better performance relative to conventional investment approaches, while only 14% found negative results. They also found positive results when they reviewed 59 climate change or low-carbon studies related to financial performance. On the corporate side, 57% arrived at a positive conclusion, 29% found a neutral impact, 9% had mixed results, and 6% were negative. Looking at investor studies, 65% showed positive or neutral performance compared to conventional investments, with only 13% indicating negative findings.

PUTTING ESG INVESTING INTO PRACTICE

1.1.6 explain the three ways in which investors typically reflect ESG considerations in their investment process

ESG investing is a strategy and practice related to incorporating ESG factors in investment decisions and active ownership. Institutional investors typically reflect ESG considerations in three ways:

1. incorporating ESG factors into investment decision-making,
2. through corporate engagement, and
3. through policy engagement.

Different institutions take different approaches and blend these elements differently, reflecting their culture and investment style.

Investment Decisions

Incorporating ESG factors into investment decision making can happen throughout the investment value chain:

- Asset owners
  - can include ESG factors in their requests for proposal and consider them in their appointment process,
  - are often supported by investment consultants, who can factor in asset managers' ESG policy, implementation, and outcomes in their selection process, and
  - can reassure themselves that their views on ESG issues are implemented by integrating them into investment mandates and monitoring processes.
- Asset owners and some asset managers can embed ESG considerations into **strategic asset allocation (SAA)**. SAA is the process in which an investor chooses to allocate capital across asset classes, sectors, and regions based on their need for return and income and their risk appetite.

- Asset managers and asset owners who invest directly can incorporate ESG issues into their security selection process. This can be done by
  - using ratings to apply a filter or threshold, which rules potential investments in or out of the investment universe,
  - integrating ESG issues in their financial and risk analysis, or
  - using ESG criteria to identify investment opportunities through a thematic approach (e.g., a water fund, impact investing).

For further details on this process, see Chapters 7 and 8.

Shareholder Engagement

Investors can encourage investees to improve their ESG practices via a company's annual general meeting (AGM) by formally expressing their views through voting on resolutions. Engagement can also happen outside this process (with an investment firm, individually, or through a collective initiative), discussing ESG issues with an investee company's board or management.

For further details on this process, see Chapter 6.

Policy Engagement

The proper functioning of the market and thus public policy, such as the EU's taxonomy for sustainable activities, critically affects the ability of institutional investors to generate sustainable returns and create value. Policy engagement by institutional investors is therefore a natural extension of an investor's responsibilities and fiduciary duties to the interests of beneficiaries.

Investors can work with regulators, standard setters, and other parties (e.g., consultants and stock exchanges) to design a financial system that

- is more sound and stable,
- levels the playing field, and
- brings ESG factors more effectively into financial decision making.

Investors can

- respond to policy consultations,
- participate in collective initiatives, and
- make recommendations to policymakers.

Further details on this process are discussed in Chapter 6.

9 KEY INITIATIVES

> 1.1.7 explain the aims of key supranational ESG initiatives and organizations and the progress achieved to date

Various initiatives have contributed to increasing the investment industry's awareness of ESG issues, as well as enhancing its ability and capacity to integrate ESG factors into the investment process.

United Nations Initiatives

The United Nations (UN) has played a critical role in the advancement of sustainability and specifically responsible investment in the past 30 years. Three of its initiatives are of particular interest to investors.

United Nations Global Compact

Chief among the supranational initiatives, the **United Nations Global Compact (UNGC)** was launched in 2000 as a collaboration between leading companies and the UN. It has since gained remarkable traction and now claims to be the largest corporate sustainability initiative in the world, with over 8,000 corporate signatories spanning the globe. These signatories agree to adhere to the 10 principles, derived from broader global standards, such as the **Universal Declaration of Human Rights** and the **International Labour Organization's Declaration on Fundamental Principles and Rights at Work**. The 10 principles of the UNGC cover the areas of human rights, labor, environment, and anti-corruption. It has provided investors with a helpful set of principles to assess and engage with companies, as well as directly aided companies in becoming more sustainable.

United Nations Environment Programme Finance Initiative (UNEP FI)

UNEP FI is a partnership between UNEP and the global financial sector to mobilize private sector finance for sustainable development.

UNEP FI started in 1992 with a few banking institutions, and today it works with over 300 members—banks, insurers, and investors—to catalyze integration of sustainability into financial market practice. The frameworks UNEP FI has established or cocreated include the following:

- The Principles for Responsible Investment, established in 2006 by UNEP FI and the UN Global Compact, now applied by more than half the world's institutional investors (US$103.4 trillion, or £74 trillion)
- The Principles for Sustainable Insurance (PSI), established in 2012 by UNEP FI and today applied by more than one-quarter of the world's insurers (more than 25% of world premium volume)
- The Principles for Responsible Banking (PRB): As of April 2021, more than 220 banks have signed up to the PRB, representing US$57 trillion (£41 trillion) in total assets, or more than one-third of the global banking sector.

Principles for Responsible Investment

The PRI comprises a UN-supported international network of investors—signatories working together toward a common goal to understand the implications of ESG factors for investment and ownership decisions and ownership practices.

The PRI provides support in four main areas:

1. The PRI provides a broad range of tools and reports on best practices for asset owners, asset managers, consultants, and data suppliers, supporting the implementation of the principles across all asset classes and providing insights into ESG issues.
2. It hosts a collaborative engagement platform, by which it leads engagements and also enables like-minded institutions to coordinate and take forward engagement with individual companies and sectors.

3. The PRI reviews, analyzes, and responds to responsible investment-related policies and consultations. It also provides a policy map to investors and facilitates communication between investors and their regulators on the topic of responsible investment.
4. The PRI Academy develops, aggregates, and disseminates academic studies on responsible investment-related themes.

The PRI developed six voluntary principles that provide overarching guidance on actions members can take to incorporate ESG issues into investment practice. The six principles are as follows:[58]

1. We will incorporate ESG issues into investment analysis and decision-making processes.
2. We will be active owners and incorporate ESG issues into our ownership policies and practices.
3. We will seek appropriate disclosure on ESG issues by the entities in which we invest.
4. We will promote acceptance and implementation of the principles within the investment industry.
5. We will work together to enhance our effectiveness in implementing the principles.
6. We will each report on our activities and progress towards implementing the principles.

The PRI also leads or establishes partnerships with other organizations to develop initiatives, such as a review of fiduciary duty around the world and the establishment and implementation of the **Sustainable Stock Exchanges Initiative**. Many of its workstreams and initiatives are supported by committees made of members, which is a key way for investors to gain further insight and contribute to the development of knowledge and the further implementation of responsible investment across the industry.

For some in the investment industry, membership in the PRI has become a badge for being a responsible investor. The PRI does require members to report annually on their responsible investment practices, which are assessed by the PRI. The report is made available to the public, while the assessment is private to the member, which can then decide whether and with whom it shares the assessment (e.g., asset managers share the report with an existing or prospective client asset owner). Amid criticism that despite the assessment, there were no minimum requirements to become a member beyond payment of the membership fees, the PRI implemented minimum requirements in 2018. The three requirements are as follows:

1. Investment policy that covers the firm's responsible investment approach, covering >50% of assets under management (AUM)
2. Internal or external staff responsibility for implementing responsible investment policy
3. Senior-level commitment and accountability mechanisms for responsible investment implementation

In recent years, the growth of the ESG market and the increased use of the term "ESG" has been highly correlated to the growth in PRI membership. This relationship may be linked to the fact that the principles are designed to be compatible with a wide

---

58 www.unpri.org/about-us/what-are-the-principles-for-responsible-investment.

Key Initiatives

range of investment styles that operate within a traditional fiduciary framework. PRI signatories have grown about 30% a year since 2006. This growth rate demonstrates the overall market opportunity for ESG investing.

Exhibit 13 shows the growth in PRI signatories, in terms of both membership numbers and assets under management, for the period April 2006 to March 2020, inclusive. Exhibit 14 shows the number of signatories worldwide in 2019.

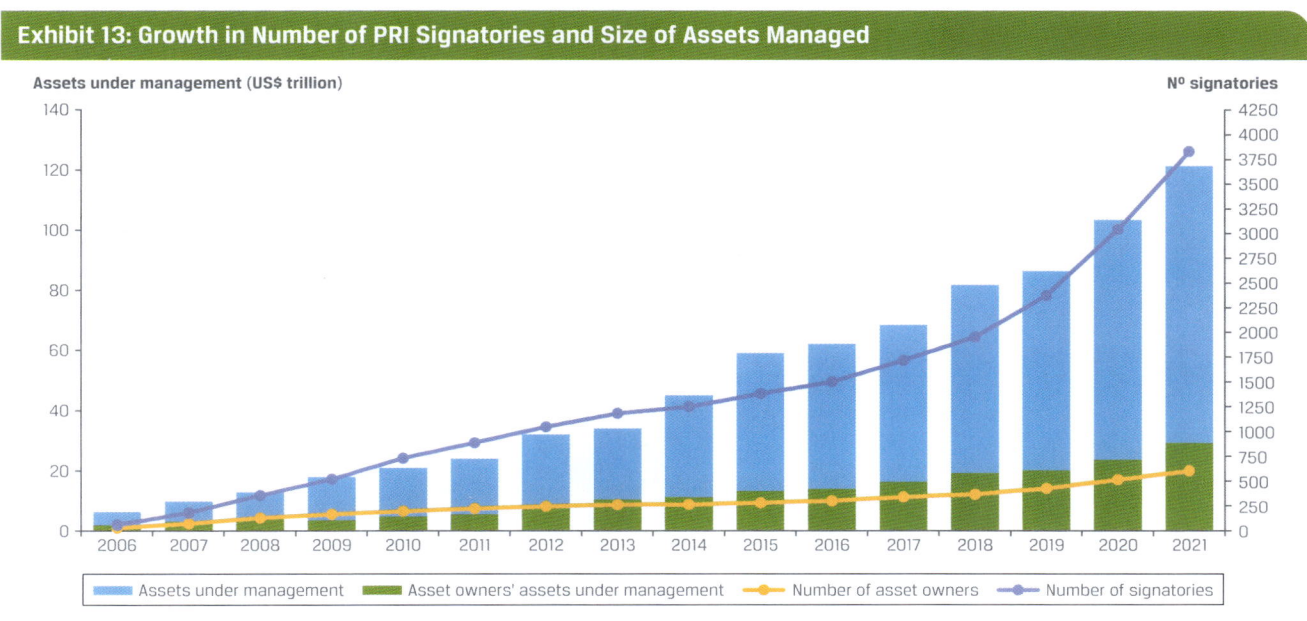

Exhibit 13: Growth in Number of PRI Signatories and Size of Assets Managed

Source: PRI, "About the PRI" (2020). www.unpri.org/pri/about-the-pri.

Exhibit 14: PRI Signatories Worldwide, 2019

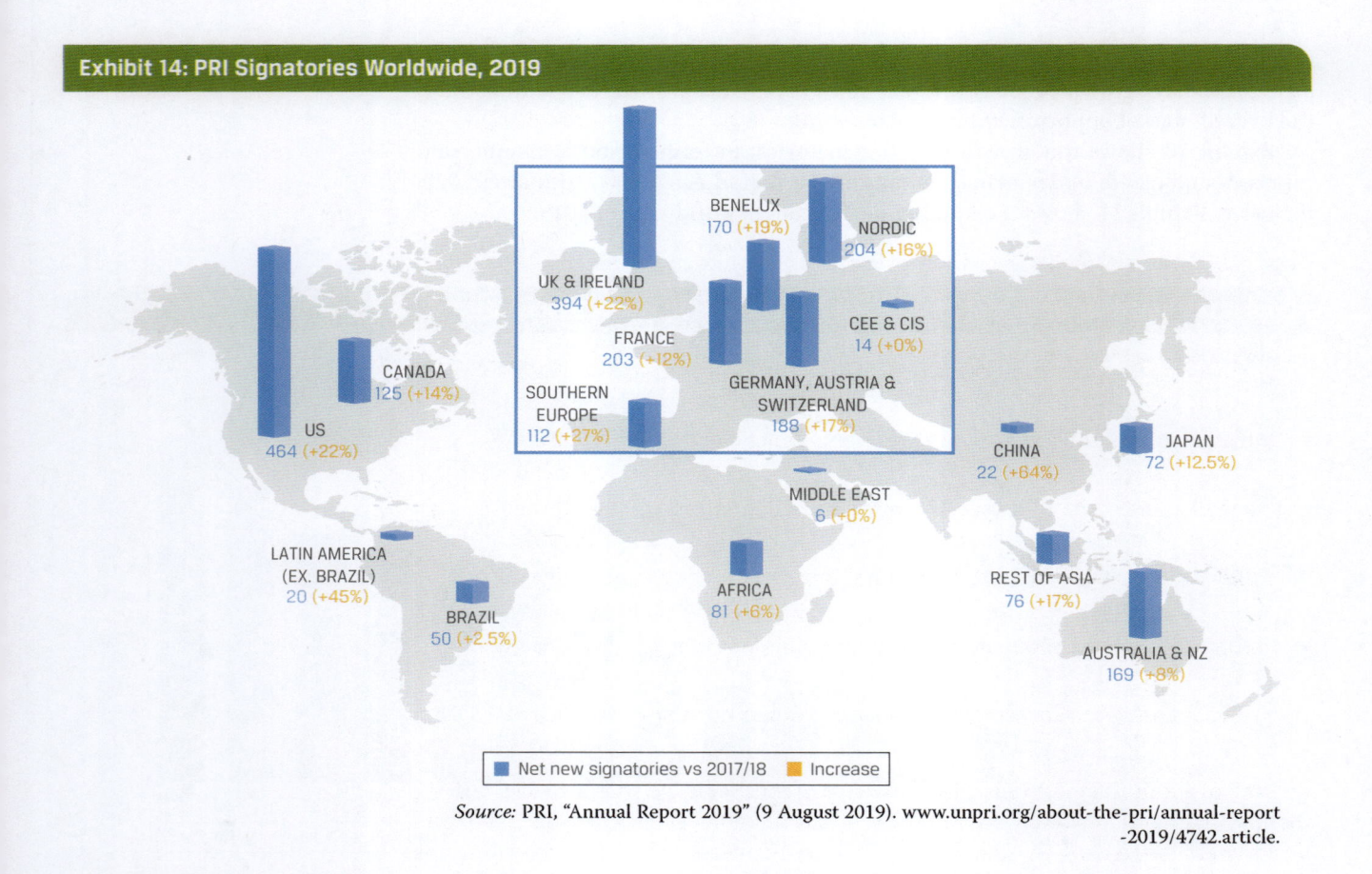

- UK & IRELAND: 394 (+22%)
- BENELUX: 170 (+19%)
- NORDIC: 204 (+16%)
- FRANCE: 203 (+12%)
- CEE & CIS: 14 (+0%)
- SOUTHERN EUROPE: 112 (+27%)
- GERMANY, AUSTRIA & SWITZERLAND: 188 (+17%)
- US: 464 (+22%)
- CANADA: 125 (+14%)
- CHINA: 22 (+64%)
- JAPAN: 72 (+12.5%)
- LATIN AMERICA (EX. BRAZIL): 20 (+45%)
- BRAZIL: 50 (+2.5%)
- MIDDLE EAST: 6 (+0%)
- AFRICA: 81 (+6%)
- REST OF ASIA: 76 (+17%)
- AUSTRALIA & NZ: 169 (+8%)

Legend: Net new signatories vs 2017/18 — Increase

Source: PRI, "Annual Report 2019" (9 August 2019). www.unpri.org/about-the-pri/annual-report-2019/4742.article.

In April 2021, PRI asset owner signatories numbered 606 and managed aggregate assets of over US$31.2 trillion (£22.4 trillion). The total number of signatories was 3,811, with assets of about US$110 trillion (£79.1 trillion).

United Nations Framework Convention on Climate Change

Climate change has been a focus to the UN and more recently, of investors as well. The **United Nations Framework Convention on Climate Change (UNFCCC)**, launched at the Rio de Janeiro Earth Summit in 1992, aims to stabilize GHG emissions to limit man-made climate change.

The UNFCCC hosts annual Conference of the Parties (COP) meetings, which seek to advance member states' voluntary agreements on limiting climate change.

The following are the two COPs of particular importance:

1. The COP3 meeting in Kyoto in 1997, which created the **Kyoto Protocol**. This commits industrialized countries to limit and reduce their GHG emissions in accordance with agreed individual targets.
2. The COP21 meeting in Paris in 2015, which led to the **Paris Agreement**. This commits developed and emerging economies to strengthen the response to the threat of climate change by keeping a global temperature rise this century well below 2°C (3.6°F) above pre-industrial levels.

The Paris Agreement had a significant impact on investors, including government and civil societies' expectations of them. This has led to investor-led initiatives to understand how to become aligned with the Paris Agreement, as well as various organizations engaging with investors on the topic.

Key Initiatives 57

UN Sustainable Development Goals

The Sustainable Development Goals (SDGs), agreed to by all UN members in 2015 in replacement of the **UN Millennial Goals**, are the UN's blueprint to address key global challenges, including those related to poverty, inequality, climate change, environmental degradation, peace, and justice. The 17 goals are interconnected and particularly aimed at governments. The Paris Agreement, though negotiated in parallel to the SDGs, became one of its goals.

Despite the goals and subsequent targets not being directly applicable to businesses and investors, the SDGs have become a powerful framework for these groups, with some investors already reporting against their impact on the SDGs and allocating capital to contribute to their achievement. Exhibit 15 provides an illustration of the SDGs.

Exhibit 15: UN Sustainable Development Goals

Note from UN: The content of this publication has not been approved by the United Nations and does not reflect the views of the United Nations or its officials or Member States.

Source: United Nations, "Take Action for the Sustainable Development Goals" (2020). www.un.org/sustainabledevelopment/sustainable-development-goals/.

Glasgow Financial Alliance for Net Zero (GFANZ)

GFANZ brings together existing and new net-zero finance initiatives across banking, insurance, and asset management in one sector-wide coalition. It provides a forum for its 450 members responsible for assets of over $130 trillion to accelerate the transition to a net-zero global economy. GFANZ was launched in 2021 by Mark Carney, UN Special Envoy for Climate Action and Finance and UK Prime Minister Johnson's

Finance Adviser for COP26, and the COP26 Private Finance Hub in partnership with the UNFCCC Climate Action Champions, the Race to Zero campaign, and the COP26 Presidency.

Race to Zero is the UN-backed global campaign rallying non-state actors—including companies, cities, regions, and financial and educational institutions—to take rigorous and immediate action to halve global GHG emissions by 2030. All members are committed to the same overarching goal: reducing GHG emissions across all scopes swiftly and fairly in line with the Paris Agreement, with transparent action plans and robust near-term targets.

Reporting Initiatives

Currently, there is a lack of standardization in sustainability reporting because there are multiple competing frameworks and methodologies. This situation has repercussions for the integrity of ESG data.

ESG-Related Initiatives

Global Reporting Initiative

The **Global Reporting Initiative (GRI)** publishes the GRI Standards, which provide guidance on disclosure across environmental, social, and economic factors for all stakeholders, including investors, whereas the other major frameworks are primarily investor focused. Several thousand organizations worldwide use the GRI framework, which is among the most well known and is the standard for the United Nations Global Compact. The framework covers the most categories of sustainability activity and encourages anecdotes and further prose to help contextualization.

Value Reporting Foundation

The Value Reporting Foundation (VRF) was formed upon the merger of the **International Integrated Reporting Council (IIRC)** and the **Sustainability Accounting Standards Board (SASB)**, two well-known global reporting initiatives. The objective of the VRF is to provide investors and corporations with a comprehensive corporate reporting framework across the full range of enterprise value drivers and standards. Before the merger, the IIRC developed the **Integrated Reporting Framework (IRF)** and the SASB issued the SASB Standards. IRF encouraged companies to integrate sustainability into their strategy and risk assessment by integrating it into the traditional annual report. The aim of the integrated report was to make it easier for investors to review such information as part of normal research processes and thus increase the likelihood that sustainability information is material to investment decisions. The SASB Standards were focused on key material sustainability issues, which affect 70-plus industry categories and were developed along with the SASB materiality maps. The SASB products were particularly helpful for investors determining what is material for reporting, and they aid more standardized benchmarking. The product suites of the two merging organizations are expected to be combined into one portfolio of offerings.

International Business Council ESG Disclosure Framework

The **ESG Disclosure Framework (EDF)** of the **International Business Council (IBC)** aims to bring greater consistency and comparability to sustainability reporting by establishing common metrics for company disclosure. The framework encourages disclosure on a "comply or explain" basis, with materiality, confidentiality, and legal constraints listed as acceptable reasons for not disclosing to a particular disclosure metric. Reporting is encouraged via annual reports or proxy statements to help ensure board oversight and participation of sustainability disclosure.

Key Initiatives

International Sustainability Standards Board (ISSB)

In 2021, the IFRS Foundation Trustees announced the creation of a new standard-setting board—the ISSB. The intention is for the ISSB to deliver a comprehensive global baseline of sustainability-related disclosure standards that provide investors and other capital market participants with information about companies' sustainability-related risks and opportunities to help them make informed decisions. The ISSB's proposals build on the work of the Climate Disclosure Standards Board, the International Accounting Standards Board, the Value Reporting Foundation (which houses Integrated Reporting and SASB Standards), the TCFD, and the World Economic Forum.

Corporate Sustainability Reporting Directive (CSRD)

Due to go live in 2023, the CSRD will replace the Non-Financial Reporting Directive (NFRD), the previous regulation that required many EU corporations to report against the ESG metrics. The CSRD will cover nearly five times more corporations (50,000) and will be more prescriptive on the format and standards.

Climate-Related Initiatives

Task Force on Climate-Related Financial Disclosures

The Financial Stability Board **Task Force on Climate-Related Financial Disclosures (TCFD)** takes the Paris Agreement's target of staying well under 2°C (3.6°F), with the ambition of staying under 1.5°C (2.7°F), and tries to operationalize it for the business world. Its June 2017 Final Report urges companies to disclose against the following:

- *Governance*—the organization's governance around climate-related risks and opportunities
- *Strategy*—the actual and potential impacts of climate-related risks and opportunities on the organization's businesses, strategy, and financial planning
- *Risk management*—the processes used by the organization to identify, assess, and manage climate-related risks
- *Metrics and targets*—the metrics and targets used to assess and manage relevant climate-related risks and opportunities

The TCFD recommends that these disclosures are provided as part of the mainstream financial filings. For many, the emphasis that the TCFD puts on climate change as a board-level issue is its greatest contribution, both in terms of enhancing disclosure and in helping to ensure that this crucial issue is actively considered at the top of organizations. It should also drive a substantial advance in disclosures by seeking transparency about realistic scenario planning, particularly around the physical impacts of climate change.

CDP (Formerly, the Carbon Disclosure Project)

CDP is a non-governmental organization (NGO) that supports companies, financial institutions, and cities to disclose and manage their environmental impact. It runs a global environmental disclosure system in which nearly 10,000 companies, cities, states, and regions report on their risks and opportunities on climate change, water security, and deforestation.

Climate Disclosure Standards Board

The **Climate Disclosure Standards Board (CDSB)** is an international consortium of business and environmental NGOs with the mission to create the enabling conditions for material climate change and natural capital information to be integrated into mainstream reporting.

Other Initiatives

Asia Investor Group on Climate Change

The Asia Investor Group on Climate Change (AIGCC) is an initiative to create awareness among Asia's asset owners and financial institutions about the risks and opportunities associated with climate change and low-carbon investing. AIGCC provides capacity for investors to share best practices and to collaborate on investment activity, credit analysis, risk management, engagement, and policy.

AIGCC was founded to represent the Asian investor perspective in the evolving global discussions on climate change and the transition to a greener economy.

Global Impact Investing Network

The **Global Impact Investing Network (GIIN)** focuses on reducing barriers to impact investment by building critical infrastructure and developing activities, education, and research that help accelerate the development of a coherent impact investing industry. It does the following:

- facilitates knowledge exchange,
- highlights innovative investment approaches,
- builds the evidence base for impact investing, and
- produces tools and resources.

Of note are its databases IRIS+ (of metrics for measuring and managing impact) and ImpactBase (of impact investing funds).

Global Sustainable Investment Alliance

Many countries have a national forum for responsible investment. The **Global Sustainable Investment Alliance (GSIA)** is an international collaboration of these membership-based sustainable investment organizations. It is a forum itself for advancing ESG investing across all regions and asset classes.

Core members of the GSIA include representatives from the regional responsible investment forums of Europe, the United States, Canada, Japan, Australia, and New Zealand. The GSIA reports draw on in-depth regional and national reports and work from GSIA members.

International Corporate Governance Network

The **International Corporate Governance Network (ICGN)** is an investor-led organization established in 1995 to promote effective standards of corporate governance and investor stewardship to advance efficient markets. Of note, the ICGN developed two key guidance documents for investors: one on stewardship and another on investment mandates.

The EU's Sustainable Finance Disclosure Regulation

In 2021, the European Union's Sustainable Finance Disclosure Regulation (SFDR) came into force. The SFDR is designed to support institutional asset owners and retail clients to compare, select, and monitor the sustainability characteristics of investment funds by standardizing sustainability disclosures. The disclosures are about the integration of sustainability risks, the consideration of adverse sustainability impacts, the promotion of environmental or social factors, and sustainable investment objectives. The SFDR is one of the building blocks of the EU's Sustainable Finance Action Plan. It applies to all financial advisers and financial market participants that construct financial products and/or provide investment advice or insurance advice in the European Economic Area (the EU member states plus Iceland, Liechtenstein, and Norway). The SFDR stipulates areas of mandatory disclosure at two levels: that of the investment firm and that of the product. Further, it introduces a new concept into the EU's regulatory environment:

Key Initiatives

Principal Adverse Impacts (PAIs). PAIs are the negative effects from an investment on sustainability factors. These PAIs go into great detail and consist of 18 indicators for which disclosure is obligatory and 46 voluntary disclosure indicators. Further, the SFDR defines two categories of sustainable financial products: Article 8 products that *promote sustainability characteristics* and the more strictly defined Article 9 products that have stringent primary objectives for positive sustainability outcomes.

CFA Institute Global ESG Disclosure Standards for Investment Products

In 2021, CFA Institute published the Global ESG Disclosure Standards for Investment Products, the first global voluntary standards for disclosing how an investment product considers ESG issues in its objectives, investment process, and stewardship activities.

KEY FACTS

1. ESG investing is an approach to managing assets where investors explicitly acknowledge the relevance of environmental, social, and governance (ESG) factors in their investment decisions, as well as their own role as owners and creditors. ESG investing also recognizes that the generation of long-term sustainable returns is dependent on stable, well-functioning and well-governed social, environmental, and economic systems.

2. The concept of ESG investing is closely related to the concept of investees' corporate sustainability. Related to this, corporate social responsibility (CSR) is a broad business concept that describes a company's commitment to conducting its business in an ethical way.

3. All forms of responsible investment except for engagement are ultimately related to portfolio construction (in other words, which securities a fund holds). Some focus more on improving financial returns using financially material ESG factors, while others combine robust returns with optimizing the impact the investment has on society and the environment. Engagement, both by equity owners and bond holders, concerns whether and how a fund tries to encourage and influence an issuer's behavior on ESG matters.

4. One of the main reasons for ESG integration is that responsible investment can reduce risk and enhance returns. Financial materiality can be due to
   a. reduced cost and increased efficiency,
   b. reduced risk of fines,
   c. reduced externalities, and
   d. improved adaptability to sustainability megatrends.

5. Evidence of the risks that ESG megatrends carry is illustrated by the World Economic Forum's Global Risks Report,[59] which for many years now has highlighted the growing likelihood and impact of extreme weather events and the failure to address climate change.

6. For many years, fiduciary duty was considered a barrier to considering ESG factors in investments. The modern interpretation of fiduciary duty, put forward in the Freshfields report,[60] recognizes that failing to consider long-term investment value drivers—which include ESG issues—in investment practice is a failure of fiduciary duty.

7. Large institutional investors, known as universal owners, have holdings that are highly diversified across all sectors, asset classes, and regions. Their investment returns are thus dependent on the overall economy. A reason for implementing ESG stems from the recognition that negative megatrends will, over time, create a drag on economic prosperity and may increase instability both within countries and between the "global north and south."

8. A reason for practicing responsible investment is the belief that some investors have that investments can or even should serve society alongside providing financial return. The UN Sustainable Development Goals (SDGs), a framework agreed by all UN member state governments to work toward aligning with global priorities, has been adapted by some of the investment community to manage and improve the impact of their investments.

---

[59] World Economic Forum, "The Global Risks Report 2020."
[60] Freshfields Bruckhaus Deringer, "A Legal Framework for the Integration of Environmental, Social and Governance Issues into Institutional Investment."

Key Facts

9. Client demand is instrumental for responsible investment because clients make the decisions about how their assets, representing on average 34% of GDP in OECD countries, are managed. The number of them that are integrating ESG considerations continues to grow.

10. Institutional investors typically reflect ESG considerations by incorporating ESG factors into investment decision making, through corporate and policy engagement. These factors can be included
    a. in their investment mandates,
    b. in their strategic asset allocation process,
    c. by applying a filter based on ratings,
    d. by integrating ESG issues into financial models, or
    e. by using ESG factors to identify investment opportunities.

11. The financial materiality of ESG investment is driven by its ability to reduce risk and enhance returns, because it considers additional risks and injects new and forward-looking insights into the investment process.

12. The ability to integrate a response to sustainability megatrends into business operations can be a success factor for an investee firm.

13. ESG investing has seen rapid development in recent years, but challenges to its further growth remain. These challenges manifest themselves prior to a firm wishing to implement ESG investing (perceptions about performance, old fiduciary duty interpretations, or non-supportive advice) and also once the decision has been made to implement ESG investing (a lack of understanding, the impression of resource intensity, or a gap between marketing-commitment-delivery).

14. There is a growing recognition in the financial industry and in academia that ESG factors influence financial performance. Various studies indicate that engaging with companies on ESG issues can create value for both investors and companies by encouraging better ESG risk management and more sustainable business practices.

15. The UN hosts or sponsors various initiatives that drive sustainability and ESG investing. Of note is the Principles for Responsible Investment (PRI), which comprises an international network of investors working together to understand the implications of ESG factors for investment and ownership decisions and ownership practices. The PRI provides a broad range of tools and reports on best practice for the various actors in the investment value chain. Recently, the growth of the ESG market and the increased use of the term "ESG" has been highly correlated with the growth in PRI membership.

16. The Financial Stability Board Task Force on Climate-Related Financial Disclosures (TCFD) takes the Paris Agreement's 2°C (3.6°F) target and tries to operationalize it for the business world. It should also drive a substantial advance in disclosures by seeking transparency about realistic scenario planning, particularly around the physical impacts of climate change, including for investors.

FURTHER READING

Eccles, R., I. Ioannou, G. Serafeim. 2012. "The Impact of Corporate Sustainability on Organizational Processes and Performance." National Bureau of Economic Research Working Paper 17950. www.nber.org/papers/w17950. doi:10.3386/w1795010.3386/w17950

International Corporate Governance Network 2012. "ICGN Global Stewardship Principles – ICGN Global Stewardship Principles & Endorsers."

International Corporate Governance Network 2016. "ICGN Global Stewardship Principles."

International Corporate Governance Network 2017. "ICGN Global Governance Principles."

Law Commission 2013. "Fiduciary Duties of Investment Intermediaries."www.lawcom.gov.uk/project/fiduciary-duties-of-investment-intermediaries.

PRI 2016. "From Principles to Performance."http://10.unpri.org/wp-content/uploads/2016/04/PRI-final-report_-single-pages.pdf.

SELF PRACTICE AND SELF ASSESSMENT

1. Which of the following investment approaches focuses on enhancing the long-term value of an investment portfolio?

   a. ESG investing
   b. Impact investing
   c. Conventional financial investing

2. Which of the following ESG investments addresses the bottom of the pyramid (BOP)?

   a. Green bonds
   b. Micro-finance bonds
   c. Fund investing in smart grid technology

3. The "core planetary boundaries" identified by the Stockholm Resilience Centre are:

   a. biosphere integrity and climate change.
   b. climate change and land-system change.
   c. biosphere integrity and land-system change.

4. ESG integration can have a material financial impact on a company, resulting in:

   a. reduced costs.
   b. reduced efficiency.
   c. increased negative externalities.

5. Which of the following statements regarding externalities is *most* accurate?

   a. Externalities can be due to environmental or social factors.
   b. When externalities are positive, private costs are lower than societal costs.
   c. Internalization of externalities does not affect companies' financial performance.

6. Which of the following is a minimum requirement for signatories to the Principles of Responsible Investment (PRI)? Members must:

   a. be active owners in the companies in which they are invested.
   b. seek appropriate disclosure on ESG issues by the investee companies.
   c. have senior-level commitment and accountability mechanisms for responsible investment implementation.

7. Which of the following organizations developed a toolkit for establishing long-term, sustainable investment mandates?

   a. Principles of Responsible Investment (PRI)
   b. International Corporate Governance Network (ICGN)
   c. University of Cambridge Institute for Sustainability Leadership

8. Which of the following statements is *most* accurate? The majority of studies suggest that:

   a. good ESG standards increase the cost of capital for a company.
   b. ESG performance and investment fund performance are positively correlated.

c. ESG performance and corporate financial performance are positively correlated.

9. Greenwashing refers to:
   a. countries exporting hazardous waste to other countries.
   b. companies making misleading claims about their environmental practices.
   c. companies introducing substances into the environment that are harmful.

10. The ESG reporting framework used by the United Nations Global Compact signatories is published by the:
    a. Global Reporting Initiative (GRI).
    b. Value Reporting Foundation (VRF).
    c. International Business Council (IBC).

The following information relates to questions 11-25
Self Assessment Questions

These questions are provided only to enable you to test your understanding of the chapter content. They are not indicative of the types and standard of questions you may see in the examination. The Self-Assessment questions do not include an explanation of the correct answer.

11. What is ESG investing?
    a. An approach to managing companies that explicitly acknowledges the relevance of *environmental, social,* and *governance* factors in corporate decision making
    b. An approach to managing assets where investors explicitly acknowledge the relevance of *environmental, social,* and *economic* factors in investment decision making
    c. An approach to managing assets where investors explicitly acknowledge the relevance of *environmental, social,* and *governance* factors in their investment decisions
    d. An approach to managing assets where investors explicitly acknowledge the relevance of *environmental, social,* and *economic* factors in corporate engagement

12. Which of the following is not an example of a social factor?
    a. Labor rights
    b. Local communities
    c. Product safety
    d. Biodiversity

13. What is not one of the three P's in the triple bottom line concept?
    a. People
    b. Planet
    c. Profit
    d. Principle

14. Which of the following sectors is *not* typically excluded by ethical and faith-based

Self Practice and Self Assessment

investments?
- a. Tobacco
- b. Alcohol
- c. Controversial weapons
- d. Technology

15. The efficiency of shareholder engagement does *not* depend on:
    - a. the scale of ownership of the individual investor or the collective initiative.
    - b. the quality of the engagement dialogue and the method used.
    - c. whether divestment is known to be a possible sanction.
    - d. the amount of security in free float.

16. In what sense are ESG considerations non-financial?
    - a. They are difficult to value precisely and difficult to time.
    - b. They are issues that will never turn into financials.
    - c. They reside in a different category of performance.
    - d. They can only ever be measured qualitatively.

17. For which of the following sectors will the management of greenhouse gas emissions be most material?
    - a. Software
    - b. Recruitment
    - c. Power generation
    - d. Fund management

18. Which of the following is not a form of ESG investment?
    - a. Valuation investment
    - b. Ethical investment
    - c. Thematic investment
    - d. Impact investment

19. Which of the following statements is true about best-in-class investment?
    - a. It involves selecting only the companies that overcome a defined ranking hurdle.
    - b. It cannot be used to maintain key characteristics, such as regional and sectoral diversification of an index.
    - c. It refers to selecting companies that fall under a sustainability-related theme.
    - d. It refers to allocating capital to assets that best mitigate climate change.

20. In which way can ESG matters become financially material for a company and contribute to reduced risk and enhanced return?
    - a. Increased cost and reduced efficiency
    - b. Increased externality
    - c. Increased risk of fines
    - d. Increased adaptability to sustainability megatrends

21. What kinds of situations does the term "negative externality" best describe?
    - a. Situations where the production of goods induces costs to others that are not reflected in the prices charged for them

b. Situations where the consumption of services induces benefits to others that are not reflected in the prices charged for them
   c. Situations where the production or consumption of a product or service's private price equilibrium cannot reflect the true costs of that product or service for society as a whole
   d. Situations where the production or consumption of a product or service's private price equilibrium cannot reflect the true benefits of that product or service for society as a whole

22. According to Oxfam, "reports show that the richest 1% in the world have more than double the wealth of 6.9 billion people."[1] Which megatrend does this refer to?
   a. Emerging and urban
   b. Technological disruption
   c. Demographic changes and wealth inequality
   d. Climate change and resource scarcity

23. What is the most probable reason why an investor would engage with policy makers on ESG issues?
   a. The consideration of ESG-related matters can contribute to the proper functioning of the financial markets.
   b. Asset owners need regulators to level the playing field in order to be able to increase their percentage of ESG investments.
   c. Policy consultations on ESG investing are mandatory in order to ensure that all perspectives are taken into consideration.
   d. ESG investors require a sound and stable financial system in order to create alpha from ESG megatrends.

24. Which of the following is not a typical method by which ESG factors are reflected in investment approaches?
   a. Integrating ESG factors into investment decision making
   b. Engaging actively with companies on ESG matters
   c. Engaging in public policy debates on ESG issues
   d. Disclosing the investor's corporate social responsibility activities

25. What are the four broad groupings of issues covered by the UN Global Compact?
   a. Environmental, social, governance, and impact
   b. Human rights, labor, environment, and anti-corruption
   c. Poverty, diversity, sustainability, and transparency
   d. Education, development, fairness, and independence

---

1 A. Ratcliff, "Billionaire Fortunes Grew by $2.5 Billion a Day Last Year As Poorest Saw Their Wealth Fall."

SOLUTIONS

1. A is correct. ESG investing is focused on enhancing long-term value by using ESG factors to mitigate risks and identify growth opportunities.

2. B is correct. Social investments (not green investments) allocate capital to assets that address the bottom of the pyramid—that is, the poorest two-thirds of the economic human pyramid. Micro-finance is an example of such social investment.

3. A is correct. The Stockholm Resilience Centre has identified nine "planetary boundaries" within which humanity can continue to develop and thrive for generations to come. Two of these—climate change and biosphere integrity—are deemed "core boundaries," for which significant alteration would "drive the Earth system into a new state."

4. A is correct. ESG investing can reduce risk and enhance returns, because it considers additional risks and injects new and forward-looking insights into the investment process. ESG integration may therefore lead to reduced cost and increased efficiency, reduced risk of fines and state intervention, reduced negative externalities, and improved ability to benefit from sustainability megatrends.

5. A is correct. Externalities can occur due to environmental factors, such as pollution or social factors, for example, when companies fail to pay a minimum wage. When externalities are negative, private costs are lower than societal costs. Internalization of these externalities could significantly impact the costs and profits of companies' products and services, affecting their bottom line.

6. C is correct. The PRI implemented three minimum requirements, one of which is the senior-level commitment and accountability mechanisms for responsible investment implementation.

7. C is correct. The University of Cambridge Institute for Sustainability Leadership developed a toolkit for establishing long-term, sustainable mandates.

8. C is correct. Most studies suggest that there is a positive correlation between ESG performance and corporate financial performance.

9. B is correct. Greenwashing is the overrepresentation or misrepresentation—either intentionally or unintentionally—of the qualifications and credibility of an investment portfolio that promotes itself as green, sustainable, responsible, or ESG.

10. A is correct. The Global Reporting Initiative (GRI) publishes the GRI Standards, which provide guidance on disclosure across environmental, social, and economic factors for all stakeholders, including investors, whereas the other major frameworks are primarily investor focused. Several thousand organizations worldwide use the GRI framework, which is among the most well known and is the standard for the United Nations Global Compact.

11. C is correct.

12. D is correct.

13. D is correct.

14. D is correct.

15. D is correct.
16. A is correct.
17. C is correct.
18. A is correct.
19. A is correct.
20. D is correct.
21. C is correct.
22. C is correct.
23. A is correct.
24. D is correct.
25. B is correct.

CHAPTER 2

The ESG Market

LEARNING OUTCOMES

Mastery	The candidate should be able to:
☐	2.1.1 explain the history of ESG investing
☐	2.1.2 explain the size and scope of ESG investing in relation to geography, strategy, investor type, and asset class
☐	2.1.3 explain key market drivers of ESG integration: investor demand/intergenerational wealth transfer, regulation and policy, public awareness, and data sourcing and processing improvements
☐	2.1.4 explain the key drivers and challenges for ESG integration among key stakeholders: asset owners, asset managers, fund promoters, financial services, policymakers and regulators, investees, government, civil society, and academia

INTRODUCTION

The environmental, social, and governance (ESG) investing market has become mainstream. A growing number of institutions assert that they integrate ESG considerations into their investment decisions and into their ownership activity. ESG investing commands a sizable share of professionally managed assets across all regions and constitutes a major force across global financial markets.

This chapter traces the roots of ESG investing back to the 16th century and presents its transformation to its modern interpretation and implementation, which is still evolving. The size and scope of ESG investing, as well as its characteristics, have been developing quickly, and this chapter highlights some of the numbers regarding the ESG market.

The drivers for the growth in assets managed under an ESG approach in recent years are both intrinsic and extrinsic to the investment industry. The growing demand from institutional asset owners and individual retail investors is a driving force, providing direct commercial incentives for asset managers to engage. Government policy and regulation have been proliferating across various regions, while information from non-governmental organizations (NGOs) and other members of civil society has also stimulated the market's growth.

Finally, this chapter discusses the challenges to further growth and enhanced quality of ESG investing, as well as some of the ways these barriers can be overcome.

2 HISTORY OF ESG INVESTING, INCLUDING MODERN RESPONSIBLE INVESTMENT

☐ 2.1.1 explain the history of ESG investing

In this section, we will look at the history of environmental, social, and governance investing, covering its roots and development into what ESG investing is today.

A Brief History of Sustainability

In 1983, in response to mounting concern surrounding ozone depletion, global warming, and other environmental problems associated with raising the living standards of the world's population, the United Nations (UN) General Assembly convened the **World Commission on Environment and Development (WCED)**, an international group of environmental experts, politicians, and civil servants. The WCED (also called the Brundtland Commission) was charged with proposing long-term solutions for bringing about sustainable development. In 1987, the commission issued the Brundtland Report, also called *Our Common Future*, which introduced the concept of sustainable development: "meeting the needs of the present without compromising the ability of future generations to meet their own needs." The Brundtland Report also described how sustainable development could be achieved.

The report laid the foundations for the **Rio de Janeiro Earth Summit**, also known as the **Rio Summit** or the **UN Conference on Environment and Development (UNCED)**, held in 1992, which ultimately led to the creation of the UN Commission on Sustainable Development that same year. The summit spelled out the role of business and industry in the sustainable development agenda. Its Rio Declaration on Environment and Development states that businesses have a responsibility to ensure that activities within their own operations do not cause harm to the environment because businesses gain their legitimacy through meeting the needs of society.

Early Phase of ESG Investing

The concept of ESG investing is not a recent phenomenon: responsible investing dates back as far as investing itself. In the 17th and 18th centuries, religious groups, such as the Quakers and Methodists, already laid out guidelines to their followers about the types of activities in which they should or should not invest. Negative screening (in other words, deliberately opting not to invest in companies or industries that do not align with values) was the most popular form of **socially responsible investment (SRI)**, or ethical investing, in the early days. Because of these historical roots of ESG investing, with it initially being grounded in ethical issues of a societal nature and environmental issues coming to the fore in a later period, the term *SRI* came into use.

One of the first ethical mutual funds that moved to screens based on religious traditions was the Pioneer Fund, which was launched in 1928.[1] The modern institutionalization of ethical exclusions arguably began at the height of the Vietnam War in 1971 with the establishment of the Pax World Fund (now IMPAX Asset Management).[2] At the time, the fund offered an alternative investment option for those opposed to the production of nuclear and military arms.

In the late 1970s, the divestment movement became increasingly globalized through the divestment campaign in protest of South Africa's system of apartheid. **The Sullivan Principles**, used by investors to engage and divest, required that a condition for investment for the investee company was to ensure that all employees, regardless of race, are treated equally and in an integrated environment as a condition for investment. The disinvestment campaign, which was implemented not only by investors but also by governments and corporates, was credited by some as pressuring the South African government to embark on the negotiations ultimately leading to the dismantling of the apartheid system, resulting in real-world change. This form of SRI, referred to as value-based or exclusionary SRI, primarily considered ethical behavior.

Mainstream popular and political support for sustainable development gained further momentum following the 1992 Rio Summit.

Modern Responsible Investment

The key developments between early and modern SRI have been (1) the growth in shareholder activism, (2) the more widespread consideration of environmental factors, and (3) the introduction of positive-screening investing, which seeks to maximize financial return within a socially aligned investment strategy. In this way, SRI ultimately integrates ESG factors into the traditional investing framework focused only on profit and risk-adjusted return. This situation paved the way for *responsible investment*, which considers financial and ESG factors when valuing companies.

In the early 2000s, a renewed interest and desire for a more concrete definition of SRI (including corporate governance) emerged, in addition to financial, social, and environmental factors. The widespread fraud at Enron Corporation and other companies resulted in an increasing emphasis on the importance of good corporate governance and in specific regulations, such as the **Sarbanes–Oxley Act of 2002** in the United States.

The modern form of ESG investing began with a letter and call to action. In January 2004, UN secretary-general Kofi Annan wrote to the CEOs of significant financial institutions to take part in an initiative, under the authority of the UN Global Compact and with the support of the International Finance Corporation (IFC), to integrate ESG factors into capital markets. The initiative produced a report titled "Who Cares Wins — Connecting Financial Markets to a Changing World," which effectively coined the term "ESG."

The report made the case that embedding ESG factors in capital markets makes good business sense and leads to more sustainable markets and better outcomes for societies. At the same time, the UN Environment Programme Finance Initiative (UNEP FI) produced the so-called Freshfields Report, which showed that ESG issues are relevant for financial valuation and, thus, fiduciary duty. These two reports formed the backbone for the launch of the **Principles for Responsible Investment (PRI)** at the New York Stock Exchange in 2006 and the launch of the **Sustainable Stock Exchange Initiative (SSEI)** the following year.

---

1 L. Renneboog, J. Ter Horst, and C. Zhang, "Socially Responsible Investments: Institutional Aspects, Performance, and Investor Behavior," *Journal of Banking & Finance* 32 (September 2008): 1723–42. www.sciencedirect.com/science/article/abs/pii/S0378426607004220.

2 IMPAX Asset Management, "History" (2021). https://impaxam.com/about-us/history/.

Of the many issues concerning ESG considerations, climate change has gained particular attention in the eyes of governments, regulators, businesses, and investors. The Stern Review on the Economics of Climate Change, known simply as the Stern Review, was a particular influence on the investment industry. At the request of the UK government, economist Sir Nicholas Stern led a major review of the economics of climate change to understand the nature of the economic challenges and how they can be met. The report, published in 2006, concluded that climate change is the greatest and widest-ranging market failure ever seen, presenting a unique challenge for economics, and that early action far outweighs the costs of not acting. According to the report, without action, the overall costs of climate change would be equivalent to losing at least 5% of global gross domestic product (GDP) each year, now and forever. Including a wider range of risks and impacts could increase this number to 20% of GDP or more. Although not the first economic report on climate change, it had an important influence on how investors understand climate change, in the United Kingdom and globally.

The Global Financial Crisis of 2008, the COVID-19 pandemic beginning in 2020, and increased geopolitical tensions leading to war in Ukraine in 2022 provided stark reminders of the interdependence between societies, economies, and financial markets. They also provided clear illustrations that market pressures do not always result in ideal outcomes for the wider good.

These situations reignited institutional investors' interest in the risks and opportunities presented by the extra-financial performance of a company, enhanced by the growing perception of large asset owners as "universal owners"—that is, owners that are tied to the performance of markets and economics as a whole.

3 ESG INVESTING IN NUMBERS

> 2.1.2 explain the size and scope of ESG investing in relation to geography, strategy, investor type, and asset class

Given the many definitions of responsible investment, there is a range of data regarding the responsible investment market. One of the most comprehensive market reviews is conducted by the Global Sustainable Investment Alliance (GSIA), which conducts research in the five major markets for responsible investment (Europe, the United States, Japan, Canada, and Australia/New Zealand) every two years. Its most recent report[3] showed sustainable investing assets in the five major markets stood at US$35.3 trillion (£2781 trillion) at the start of 2020, a 15% increase in two years. In all the regions except Europe, the market share of sustainable investing has grown, as seen in Exhibit 1. In terms of where sustainable and responsible investing assets are domiciled globally, the United States (48%) and Europe (34%) continue to manage the highest proportions.

---

3 Global Sustainable Investment Alliance, "Global Sustainable Investment Review 2020" (2021). www.gsi-alliance.org/wp-content/uploads/2021/08/GSIR-20201.pdf.

ESG Investing in Numbers

Exhibit 1: Growth of ESG Assets by Region

Region	2012 (US$ bn)	2014 (US$ bn)	2016 (US$ bn)	2018 (US$ bn)	2020 (US$ bn)
Europe	8,758	10,775	12,040	14,075	12,017
United States	3,740	6,572	8,723	11,995	17,081
Japan		7	474	2,180	2,974
Asia excl. Japan		45	52		
Asia incl. Japan	40				
Canada	589	729	1,086	1,699	2,423
Australia/New Zealand	134	148	516	734	906
Total	13,261	18,276	22,891	30,683	35,301

Notes: Asia excluding Japan 2014 assets are represented in US dollars based on the exchange rates at year-end 2013. All other 2014 assets, as well as all 2016 assets, were converted to US dollars based on exchange rates at year-end 2015. All 2018 assets were converted to US dollars at the exchange rates at the time of reporting. Assets for 2020 were reported as of 31 December 2019 for all regions except Japan, which reported as of 31 March 2020.
Source: GSIA, "Global Sustainable Investment Review 2020," "Global Sustainable Investment Review 2018," "Global Sustainable Investment Review 2012."

Responsible investment directs a sizable share of managed assets in each region, as can be seen in Exhibit 2. This share of assets ranges from 24% in Japan to 62% in Canada. Clearly, sustainable investing constitutes a major force across global financial markets. The proportion of sustainable investing relative to total managed assets grew in most regions, and in Canada, responsible investing assets now make up most of the total assets under professional management. The exceptions to this trend are Europe and Australia/New Zealand, where sustainable investing assets have declined relative to total managed assets since 2018. At least part of the market share decline in Europe and Australia/New Zealand stems from a shift to stricter standards and definitions for sustainable investing in those markets.

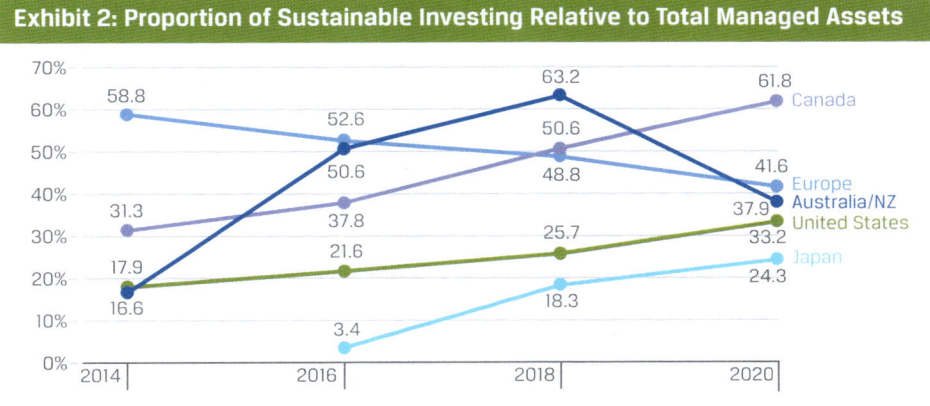

Exhibit 2: Proportion of Sustainable Investing Relative to Total Managed Assets

Region	2014	2016	2018	2020
Canada	31.3	37.8	50.6	61.8
Europe	58.8	52.6	48.8	41.6
Australia/NZ	16.6	50.6	63.2	37.9
United States	17.9	21.6	25.7	33.2
Japan		3.4	18.3	24.3

Source: GSIA, "Global Sustainable Investment Review 2020."

As of 2020, the largest sustainable investment strategy globally was ESG integration, as shown in Exhibit 3, with a combined US$25.1 trillion (£19.2 trillion) in assets under management (AUM). This is followed by negative, or exclusionary, screening, which had remained roughly stable in terms of AUM over the prior four years at US$15.0 trillion in assets.

- Norms-based and negative/exclusionary screening is the largest strategy in Europe.
- Sustainability thematic investing, impact/community investing, positive/best-in-class investing, and ESG integration command most assets in the United States.
- Corporate engagement and shareholder action constitute the predominant strategy in Japan.

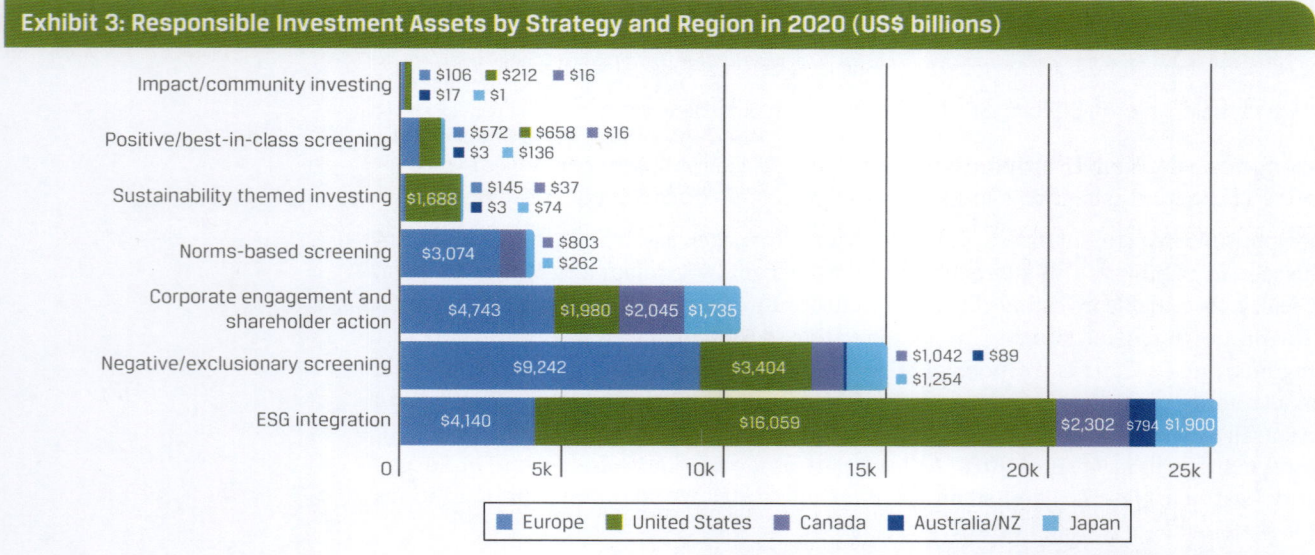

Exhibit 3: Responsible Investment Assets by Strategy and Region in 2020 (US$ billions)

Strategy	Europe	United States	Canada	Australia/NZ	Japan
Impact/community investing	$106	$212	$16	$17	$1
Positive/best-in-class screening	$572	$658	$16	$3	$136
Sustainability themed investing	$1,688	$145	$37	$3	$74
Norms-based screening	$3,074		$803	$262	
Corporate engagement and shareholder action	$4,743	$1,980	$2,045		$1,735
Negative/exclusionary screening	$9,242	$3,404	$1,042	$89	$1,254
ESG integration	$4,140	$16,059	$2,302	$794	$1,900

Source: GSIA, "Global Sustainable Investment Review 2020."

Over the 2016–20 period, as shown in Exhibit 4, the ESG integration strategy had the largest growth, which was mostly driven by the US market. Anecdotally, this growth is attributable to "relabeling" or "recycling" of already-existing funds by fund managers, with an open debate as to what extent such relabelings lead to increased greenwashing.

ESG Investing in Numbers

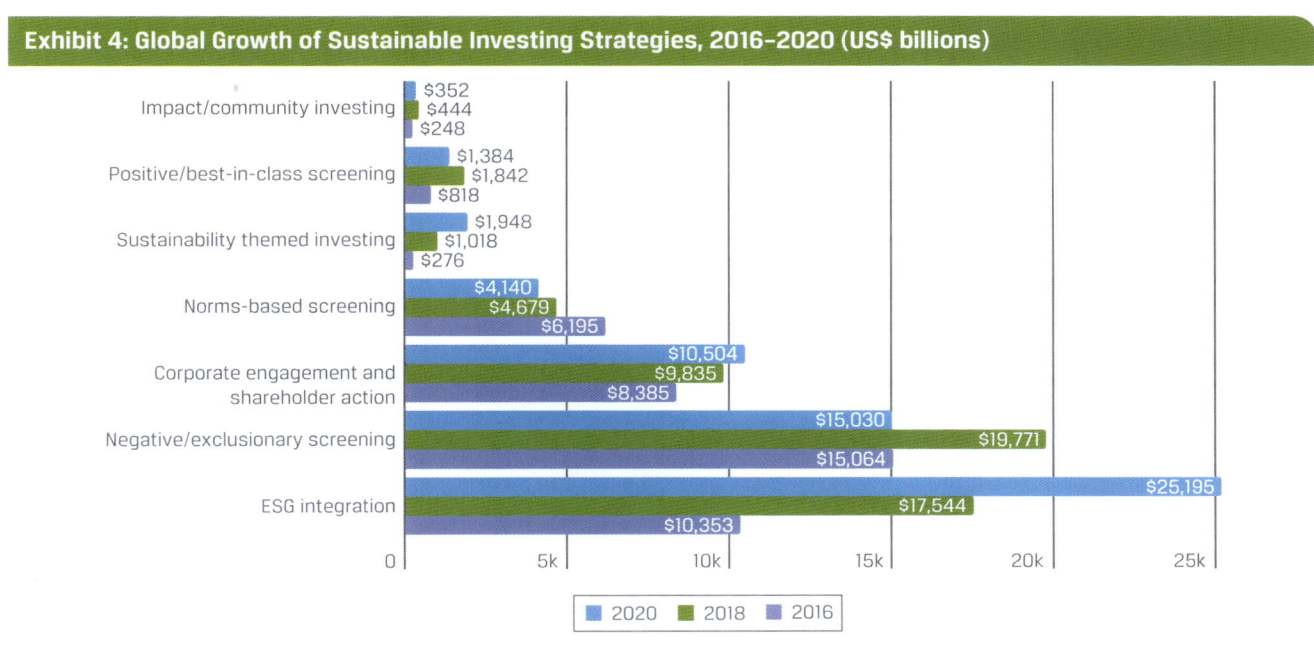

Exhibit 4: Global Growth of Sustainable Investing Strategies, 2016–2020 (US$ billions)

Strategy	2020	2018	2016
Impact/community investing	$352	$444	$248
Positive/best-in-class screening	$1,384	$1,842	$818
Sustainability themed investing	$1,948	$1,018	$276
Norms-based screening	$4,140	$4,679	$6,195
Corporate engagement and shareholder action	$10,504	$9,835	$8,385
Negative/exclusionary screening	$15,030	$19,771	$15,064
ESG integration	$25,195	$17,544	$10,353

Source: GSIA, "Global Sustainable Investment Review 2020."

Investments managed by professional asset managers are often classified as either

- retail (investment by individuals) or
- institutional (investment firms).

Although institutional investors tend to dominate the financial market, interest by retail investors in responsible investing has been steadily growing:

- In 2012, institutional investors held 89% of assets, compared with 11% held by retail investors.
- In 2018, the retail portion had grown to one quarter, as seen in Exhibit 5.

Exhibit 5: Global Shares of Institutional and Retail Sustainable Investing Assets, 2016–2018

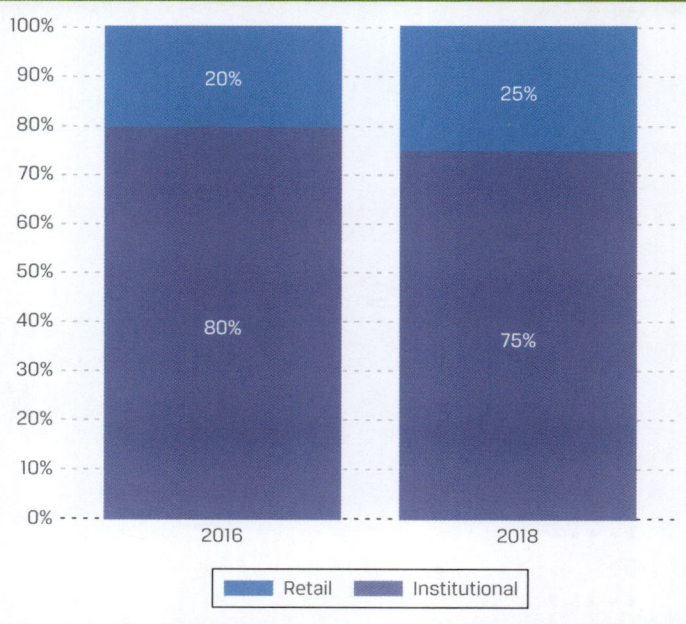

Year	Retail	Institutional
2016	20%	80%
2018	25%	75%

Note: Institutional and retail investor data were not collected in Australia or New Zealand.

Source: Global Sustainable Investment Alliance (2018). *2018 Global Sustainable Investment Review*. Available at: www.gsi-alliance.org/wp-content/uploads/2019/06/GSIR_Review2018F.pdf

Responsible investment extends across the range of asset classes commonly found in diversified investment portfolios, as shown in Exhibit 6 which shows the asset class allocation reported in Europe, the United States, Japan, and Canada in 2018. In that year, collectively in these regions,

- most assets were allocated to public equities (51% at the start of 2018), whereas
- the next largest asset allocation was in fixed income (36%).

In 2018, real estate/property and private equity/venture capital each held 3% of global sustainable investing assets. Sustainable investments could also be found in hedge funds, cash or depository vehicles, commodities, and infrastructure. These assets are reflected in the "other" assets category; for further details, see Exhibit 6.

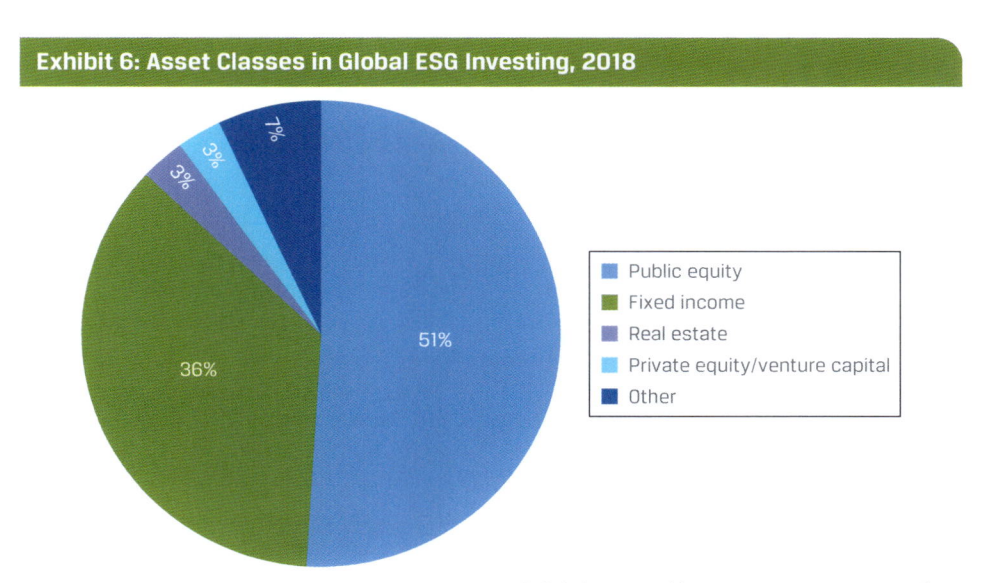

Exhibit 6: Asset Classes in Global ESG Investing, 2018

- Public equity: 51%
- Fixed income: 36%
- Real estate: 3%
- Private equity/venture capital: 3%
- Other: 7%

Source: GSIA, "Global Sustainable Investment Review 2018."

MARKET DRIVERS OF ESG AND CHALLENGES IN ESG INTEGRATION

4

☐ 2.1.3 explain key market drivers of ESG integration: investor demand/intergenerational wealth transfer, regulation and policy, public awareness, and data sourcing and processing improvements

Various stakeholders shape the push and pull for responsible investment, steering its demand and supply. There are a significant number of actors involved. This section presents the main stakeholders, focusing on the actors that influence investment decisions more directly, either by

- ▶ the choices they make or
- ▶ the services and/or information they provide.

The main stakeholders are as follows:

A. Asset owners
   1. Pension funds
   2. Insurance
   3. Sovereign wealth funds, endowment funds and foundations
   4. Individual (retail) investors and wealth management

B. Asset managers

C. Fund promoters
   1. Investment consultants and retail investment advisers

2. Investment platforms
3. Fund labelers

D. Financial services (investment banks, investment research and advisory firms, stock exchanges, financial and ESG rating agencies)
E. Policymakers and regulators
F. Investees
G. Government
H. Civil society and academia

All these stakeholders are covered in detail later in this chapter.

There is no standard way of dividing up the investment value chain; the main actors were aggregated in this manner for the purpose of discussing their role within responsible investment. Exhibit 7 provides an example of the investment value chain for listed equities. The value chain for other asset classes may differ slightly, with more or fewer intermediaries between the assets and the final owner of capital.

It is, however, worthwhile to generally clarify the roles of shareholders, investors, and investment managers.

▶ **Shareholders** hold a direct equity position in a firm, and both individual persons and financial institutions can be shareholders. The term comes from the individual or investment firm literally having a share of the company. It is most commonly used when talking about the rights and responsibilities that come with being an "owner" of a company, such as stewardship, voting, and engagement. This differentiates it from a situation where an individual or an investment firm lends money or invests in a bond (in other words, they are not an equity holder of a company). Because bond investors do not have a share and are not owners of a company, they cannot vote. Nonetheless, expectations around engagement are increasing for those who invest in loans and bonds as well, making the difference between the two terms more subtle.

▶ **Investors** is a very generic term that refers to parties—both retail investors and institutional investors—that hold a financial stake in an asset. Investors can invest in any type of asset class, be it debt or equity, and an investor can be an asset owner or an asset manager.

▶ **Investment managers** refers to people or organizations that invest on behalf of their clients under an investment mandate that those clients have agreed to.

Asset Owners 81

Exhibit 7: Financial System Value Chain

BEST PRACTICE

FINANCIAL SYSTEM

1. ASSET OWNERS	2. INVESTMENT CONSULTANTS	3. INVESTMENT MANAGERS	4. INVESTMENT BROKERS	5. STOCK EXCHANGES	6. POLICY MAKERS
Advanced sustainability commitments are widely implemented throughout the asset owners, including board, trustees, CIO, portfolio managers, research analysts and legal counsel, and across asset classes and investment strategies. Sustainability factors are integrated in the selection process for investment consultants, investment managers and embedded in investment mandates.	As asset owners signal their commitment to sustainability considerations, investment consultants will be incentivised to better assess investment managers on ESG performance, and make recommendations accordingly. Investment consultants will offer a wide range of ESG investment products and services to markets, in line with trustees needs, including explanations of how these products align with fiduciary duties.	As market signals grow, investment managers will offer advanced ESG investment products, in order to maintain their market share. This will include meaningful shareholder engagement, consistent with the investment beliefs of their clients, with advanced reporting to asset owners on implementation and the outcomes that have resulted.	Investment brokers and independent research providers will integrate research on ESG performance in company buy, hold and sell recommendations, requiring companies to provide robust, credible and detailed accounts of their management of ESG issues, and of the financial significance of these issues. Investment brokers and independent research providers will engage ratings agencies, data providers and policy makers on issues relevant to responsible investment.	Sitting at the heart of the investment chain, stock exchanges will strengthen listing requirements for companies and offer advanced sustainability indices on a range of ESG metrics.	With sustainability embedded through the investment chain, policy makers will be more inclined to support regulatory initiatives which reinforce responsible investment practice, engaging pension funds on issues beyond capital allocation, such as climate change, including policy formulation and policy implementations.

REAL ECONOMY

Source: PRI.[4]

ASSET OWNERS 5

☐ 2.1.3 explain key market drivers of ESG integration: investor demand/intergenerational wealth transfer, regulation and policy, public awareness, and data sourcing and processing improvements

☐ 2.1.4 explain the key drivers and challenges for ESG integration among key stakeholders: asset owners, asset managers, fund promoters, financial services, policymakers and regulators, investees, government, civil society, and academia

Asset owners include pension funds, insurance companies, sovereign wealth funds, foundations, and endowments. They generally invest their assets in an investment vehicle with the goal of getting returns from the invested capital. They seek to maximize returns at a given level of risk, and some derive utility from non-financial impacts as well. In practice, asset owners have legal ownership of their assets and make asset allocation decisions. Many asset owners manage their money directly, while others outsource the management of all or a portion of their assets to external managers. Exhibit 8 presents the differences between asset owners, asset managers, and intermediaries. In 2019, institutional asset owners accounted for US$54 trillion (£38.8 trillion), of which 35%—around US$19 trillion (£13.7tn)—was concentrated in the 100 largest asset owners.[5]

---

4 PRI, "How Asset Owners Can Drive Responsible Investment: Beliefs, Strategies and Mandates" (2016). www.unpri.org/download?ac=1398.
5 Willis Towers Watson, "Largest Asset Owners Are Critical to Aiding Society's Biggest Issues," press release (14 November 2019). www.willistowerswatson.com/en-SG/News/2019/11/largest-asset-owners-are-critical-to-aiding-societys-biggest-issues.

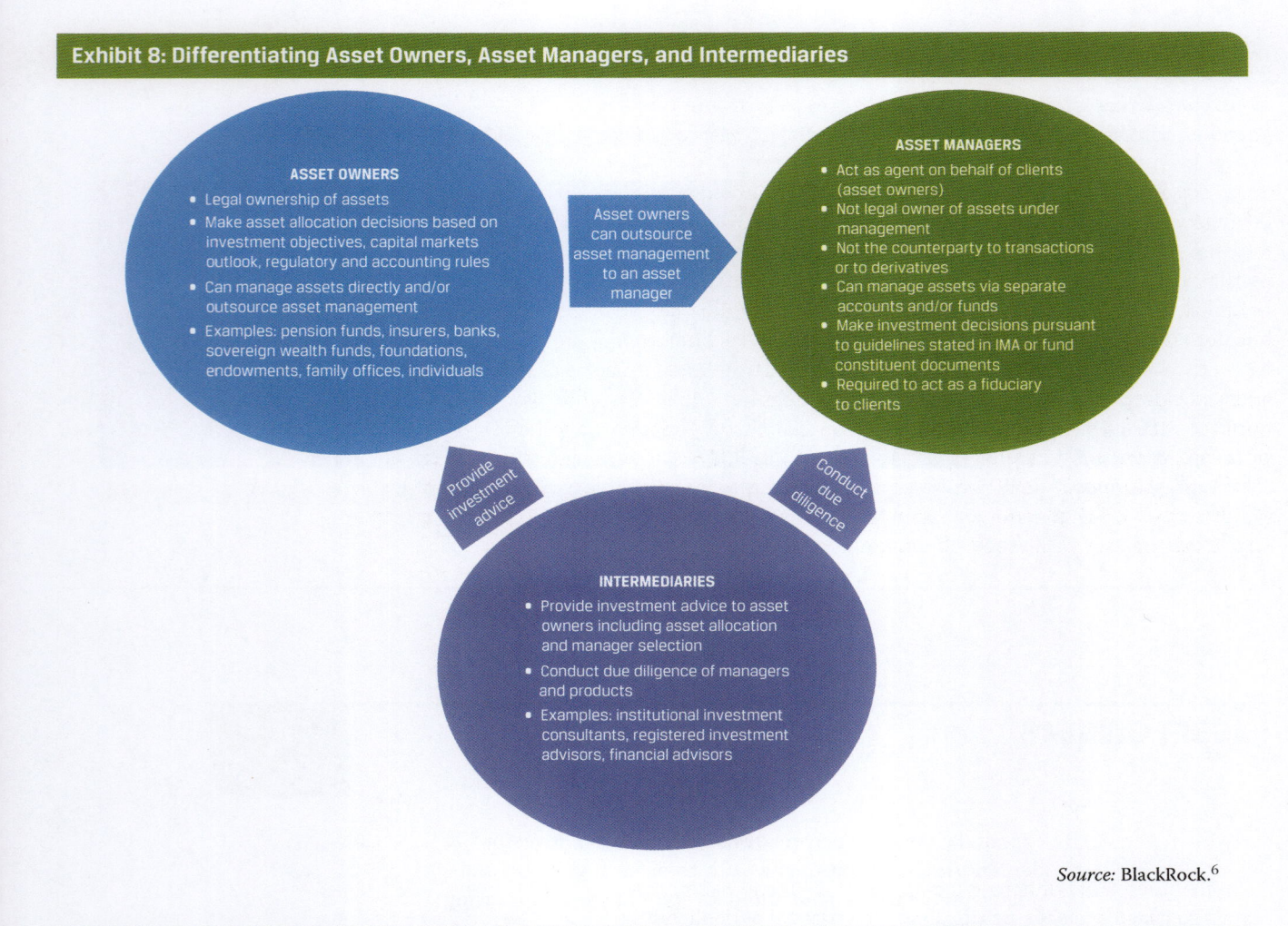

Exhibit 8: Differentiating Asset Owners, Asset Managers, and Intermediaries

ASSET OWNERS
- Legal ownership of assets
- Make asset allocation decisions based on investment objectives, capital markets outlook, regulatory and accounting rules
- Can manage assets directly and/or outsource asset management
- Examples: pension funds, insurers, banks, sovereign wealth funds, foundations, endowments, family offices, individuals

Asset owners can outsource asset management to an asset manager

ASSET MANAGERS
- Act as agent on behalf of clients (asset owners)
- Not legal owner of assets under management
- Not the counterparty to transactions or to derivatives
- Can manage assets via separate accounts and/or funds
- Make investment decisions pursuant to guidelines stated in IMA or fund constituent documents
- Required to act as a fiduciary to clients

Provide investment advice | *Conduct due diligence*

INTERMEDIARIES
- Provide investment advice to asset owners including asset allocation and manager selection
- Conduct due diligence of managers and products
- Examples: institutional investment consultants, registered investment advisors, financial advisors

Source: BlackRock.[6]

Asset owners set the tone for the investment value chain. Their understanding of how ESG factors influence financial returns and how their capital affects the real economy can significantly drive the amount and quality of ESG investing from the investment value chain.

The approach that owners take to ESG investing and how meaningful they are in steering the investment value chain are influenced by the type of investor they are. This includes, in particular, whether they are investing

▶ directly or via external asset managers or
▶ out of their own account or acting on behalf of (or in trust for) beneficiaries.

The effectiveness of asset owners in steering the investment value chain toward an increased integration of ESG depends on

▶ the number of asset owners implementing responsible investment,
▶ the total AUM of these assets, and
▶ the quality of implementation across the different asset classes.

---

6 BlackRock, "Who Owns the Assets? Developing a Better Understanding of the Flow of Assets and the Implications for Financial Regulation" (May 2014). www.blackrock.com/corporate/literature/whitepaper/viewpoint-who-owns-the-assets-may-2014.pdf.

Asset Owners

This situation creates a multiplier effect throughout the investment market. Effective implementation of responsible investment by individual asset owners signifies to the market that responsible investment is a priority for asset owners. In turn, this influences the willingness of investment consultants and investment managers to focus on responsible investment and ESG issues in their products and advice. By implementing their commitments to responsible investment with enough scale and depth, asset owners can accelerate the development of responsible investment through the investment chain.

Institutional asset owners establish contracts, known as **investment mandates**, with asset managers. These are important because they define the expectations around the investment product and, at times, even aspects around the manager's processes and resources more broadly.

Exhibit 9 shows the outcomes of an older (from 2015) survey by PRI of its asset owners' signatories about explicit expectations they have included within clauses of investment mandates. The majority had made some form of expectations explicit, and given the increasing voluntary and mandatory guidance around stewardship, it is reasonable to expect that asset owners' requirements around engagement have since increased.

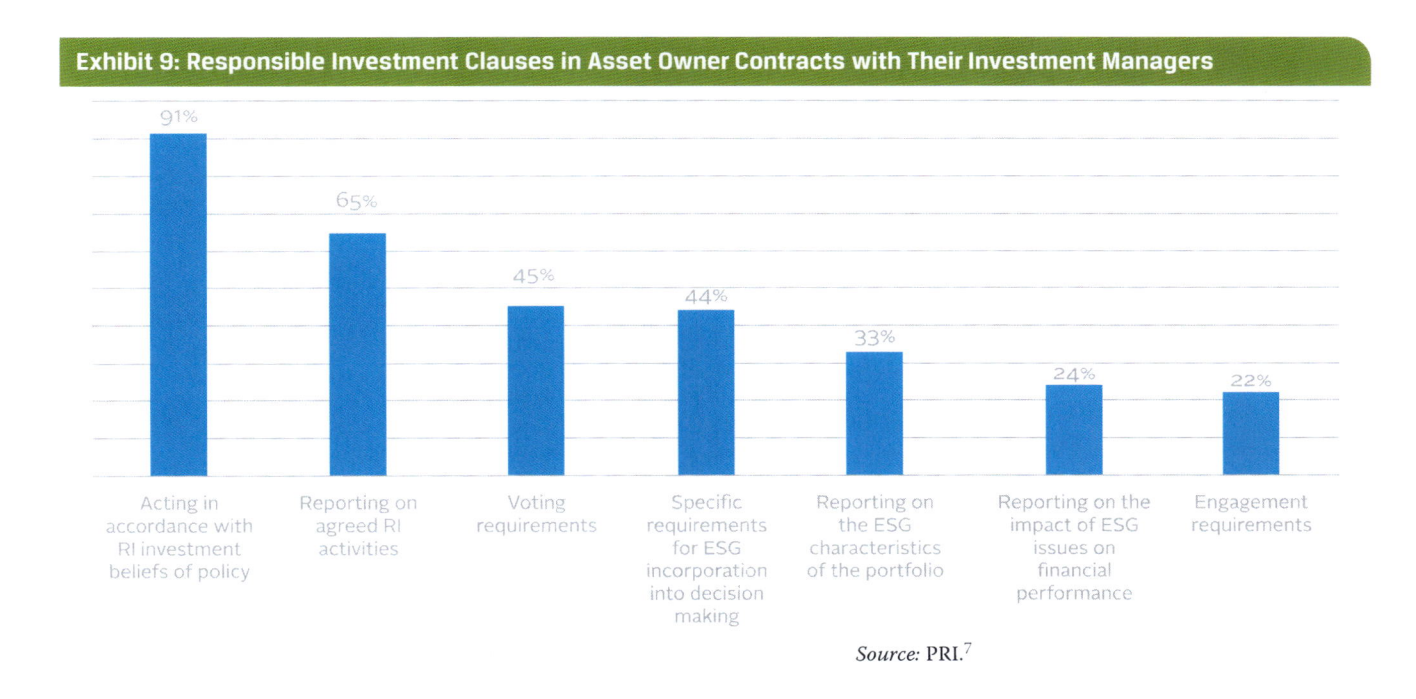

Exhibit 9: Responsible Investment Clauses in Asset Owner Contracts with Their Investment Managers

Clause	Percentage
Acting in accordance with RI investment beliefs of policy	91%
Reporting on agreed RI activities	65%
Voting requirements	45%
Specific requirements for ESG incorporation into decision making	44%
Reporting on the ESG characteristics of the portfolio	33%
Reporting on the impact of ESG issues on financial performance	24%
Engagement requirements	22%

Source: PRI.[7]

One of the challenges asset owners occasionally face in integrating ESG considerations is a hesitancy on the part of consultants and retail financial advisers to integrate ESG investing into their offerings or to assess the ESG characteristics of funds, leading to fewer options for the asset owners to choose from in the market. Related to this issue is that some asset owners also believe they do not have the scale or capacity to influence the products offered by fund managers or these managers' interpretation of fiduciary duty. Other asset owners are unsure of how to integrate ESG considerations

---

7 PRI, *How Asset Owners Can Drive Responsible Investment: Beliefs, Strategies and Mandates* (2016). https://www.unpri.org/download?ac=1398

within requests for proposals or mandates. Finally, there can be challenges for smaller asset owners who have limited resources to conduct their own ESG assessment of managers and their funds.

Pension Funds

Of the 100 largest asset owners, 59% are pension funds.[8] For their size, as well as the long-term nature of their investment, pension funds play a key role in influencing the investment market.

Pension funds are responsible for the management of pension savings and pay-outs to individuals. Given the long-term nature of their liabilities, ESG factors—more long term in nature—are particularly relevant to their investments.

Pension funds as institutions are driven by three internal players:

1. *Executives*, who manage the fund's day-to-day functioning
2. *Trustees*, who hold the ultimate fiduciary responsibility, act separately from the employer, and hold the assets in the trust for the beneficiaries of the scheme
3. *Beneficiaries* (or *members*), who pay into the fund or are pensioners benefiting from the assets

Similar to the board of a company, the board of trustees is responsible for ensuring that the pension scheme is run properly and that members' benefits are secure. The level of delegation between trustees and executives (on such matters as policy and asset manager selection) varies depending on the governance of the pension fund. The level of alignment between them also varies significantly across pension funds.

Beneficiaries are generally not aware of the details of investment decisions but may enquire why their pension funds are invested in a company that is violating human rights or engage with their pensions to divest from nuclear weapons. As a result, these actors have different roles and, at times, different interests but may all help advance pensions' fund policy and implementation of responsible investment.

Federal and state governments are also often among the largest institutional investors—typically through pension schemes or sovereign wealth funds. When governments align their policy intent with their own direct investment influence, there is scope for significant impetus to be added toward ESG integration. Some governments and investment funds have recognized this fact.

In theory, asset owners with long-term liabilities (such as pension funds) are well aligned with long-term investing and are due to benefit from it. In practice, they at times help create the problem by rewarding managers and companies for short-term behavior.

Pension funds can, however, integrate long-termism into their investment belief statements. They can, for example, set up investment mandates that place value on long-termism and demand long-term metrics from asset managers and underlying assets. The requirement to consider ESG factors within investment mandates also reinforces the asset owners' appreciation for the link between ESG factors and long-term returns.

---

8 Willis Towers Watson, "Largest Asset Owners Are Critical to Aiding Society's Biggest Issues."

Asset Owners

> **CASE STUDIES**
>
> ### ABP Pension Fund
>
> In September 2021, ABP, the Dutch pension fund for educational workers and civil servants, announced that it will divest its entire EUR15 billion worth of investments in fossil fuel producers by 2023. ABP is the fifth largest pension fund in the world and stated that "radical change" is needed because global temperatures are projected to rise beyond 1.5°C in the next seven years.
>
> At the time of the statement, the holdings in about 80 companies accounted for almost 3% of ABP's total assets.[9] The fund stated that it did not expect the divestment to have a negative effect on its long-term returns.
>
> "We [will exit] our investments in fossil fuel producers because we see insufficient opportunity for us as a shareholder to push for the necessary significant acceleration of the energy transition at these companies," said Corien Wortmann-Kool, ABP's chair.
>
> ABP was facing the risk of legal action in the Netherlands over its earlier refusal to divest from fossil fuels.

> **CASE STUDIES**
>
> ### HSBC Bank UK Pension Scheme
>
> In 2016, the HSBC Bank UK pension schemes transitioned the equity component of its defined contribution (DC) default investment strategy to a passive smart-beta fund that integrates ESG factors by embedding climate tilts.
>
> An HSBC comment piece on the product noted, "Investment performance does not need to be negatively impacted. . . . This is critical, because although investors are increasingly demanding that funds are allocated responsibly, they are not necessarily prepared to compromise on performance."
>
> In fact, the scheme aims to provide a better risk-adjusted return than is available from a conventional market cap–weighted index. The inclusion of the climate tilts gives scheme members greater relative exposure to firms less at risk from climate change.

> **CASE STUDIES**
>
> ### Government Pension Investment Fund
>
> Between 2017 and 2020, the Government Pension Investment Fund (GPIF), an influential universal owner from Japan with investments worldwide, invested in nine different ESG-themed indexes. GPIF promotes ESG investment for the purpose of improving the long-term return of the whole asset by reducing the negative externality to the environment and society.
>
> GPIF holds the view that among important ESG issues, environmental concerns, such as climate change, represent a cross-border, global challenge. Therefore, it has embarked on investment that incorporates all elements of ESG investing in both their domestic and foreign portfolios. In choosing the ESG indexes, GPIF emphasized the following:

---

9 Chris Flood, Josephine Cumbo, "Dutch Pension Giant ABP to Dump €15bn in Fossil Fuel Holdings," *Financial Times* (26 October 2021).

1. "positive screening" that determines constituent companies based on their ESG evaluation should be adopted;
2. the evaluation should be based on public information, and its method and results should be publicly disclosed; and
3. ESG evaluators and index providers should be properly governed, and their conflicts of interest should be properly managed.[10]

> **CASE STUDIES**
>
> ### UK Environment Agency Pension Fund
>
> In 2014, the £2.4 billion UK Environment Agency Pension Fund (EAPF) launched a formal search for investment managers to manage a portfolio of sustainable, global listed equities, with a specific focus on the long-term contract with the appointed manager. Candidates were expected to
>
> - have a long-term strategic approach to sustainability,
> - integrate ESG considerations broadly, and
> - have a strong commitment to non-financial research, which should go beyond short-term considerations of ESG risk factors and "standard" corporate governance.
>
> The request for proposal (RFP), known at the time as the "RFP for a long-term mandate," sent a strong signal to the market of the link between long-termism, with regard to both the contract itself and the investment horizon, and ESG investing.
>
> In 2018, the EAPF investment pool became a part of Brunel Pension Partnership and published the Asset Management Accord, which sets out expectations for long-term manager relationships.[11] Of note, the accord highlights long-term value creation and stewardship and clarifies that frequent communication should not lead to short-term pressure.

Pension Fund Trustees

Pension fund trustees, as fiduciaries of the pension fund members, have a responsibility to act in the best interests of the beneficiaries. Regulation regarding fiduciary duty defines a significant part of their role and responsibilities, and thus, its interpretation can have a significant impact on whether trustees believe they can, must, or must not integrate ESG considerations into their fund policies and processes.

Litigation

Pension fund trustees may face fiduciary legal risks from financial losses caused by climate change. Lawyers have been commissioned in Australia and the United Kingdom to assess the matter. They have found that pension fund trustees may be failing to take sufficient steps to address climate risk and, therefore, may be failing to manage the scheme's investments in a manner consistent with members' best interests. This situation could result in trustees exposing themselves to the possibility of legal challenges for breach of their fiduciary duties.

---

10 Government Pension Investment Fund: www.gpif.go.jp/en/investment/esg/.
11 Brunel Pension Partnership, "Brunel Launches Pioneering Asset Management Accord," press release (29 November 2018). www.brunelpensionpartnership.org/2018/11/29/brunel-launches-pioneering-asset-management-accord.

Asset Owners

The risk of legal action is highlighted by a 2019 case in Australia where a member of the Retail Employees Superannuation Trust took his pension fund to court for failing to disclose information on the impact of climate change on his investments and how they were addressing the issue.[12] Also in 2019, 14 of the United Kingdom's biggest pension funds were warned by lawyers that they risk legal action if they fail to consider the effects of climate change on their portfolios. As a result, fiduciary duty is a driver for trustees and their pensions to act on ESG issues. In a survey that was conducted among more than 300 global institutional investors, 46% of respondents cited the need to meet fiduciary duty and regulations as a key driver for adopting ESG principles.[13]

Pension Fund Members

Although pension fund members are not investment professionals, they can influence pension fund decisions because they are the ultimate beneficiaries. Interpretation of fiduciary duty in some jurisdictions recognizes that "acting in the interest" of pension fund beneficiaries is not necessarily restricted to financial outcomes and may incorporate their other interests, such as ethical preferences. Though still rare in the industry, some pension funds have started to use feedback from members to fine-tune their sustainable investment policies.

CASE STUDIES

Surveys by Dutch Pension Funds

The €26.2 billion (£22.9 billion) Dutch multi-sector pension fund PGB conducts an annual survey on responsible investment among its participants.[14] In order to make decisions based on its members' input, the fund conducted a mandatory survey on members' risk appetite and included an additional questionnaire that related to ESG issues.

Of the 3,500 respondents, 90% indicated a preference for investments in sustainable energy, whereas just 14% supported investments in arms and only 17% supported investments in tobacco. As a result of the input from the respondents, PGB excluded tobacco firms and companies selling firearms to civilians from its investment universe. In 2020, PGB transitioned to a fully integrated ESG strategy, with all of its AUM falling in the scope of a new ESG policy.[15]

The €9.9 billion (£8.6 billion) Dutch hospitality pension fund Horeca & Catering conducted its most recent survey at the end of 2017, generating a response from 9,500 members and 526 employers. Its participants indicated that labor conditions, environment, fraud, and corruption mattered the most to them. As a result of the consultation, the scheme excluded companies that violate the UN's Global Compact Principles and aimed to reduce carbon emissions from its investment portfolio by 20% in the next two years. And in 2021, Horeca & Catering divested from companies with more than 50% of revenue coming from fossil fuel production.[16]

---

12 Jennifer Thompson, "Pension Funds Warned of Legal Action over Climate Risk," *Financial Times* (12 August 2018).
13 James Comtois, "Institutional Investors See ESG as Part of Their Fiduciary Duty – Survey," *Pensions & Investments* (12 November 2019). www.pionline.com/esg/institutional-investors-see-esg-part-their-fiduciary-duty-survey.
14 Sameer Van Alfen, "Dutch Schemes Fine-Tune ESG Investments Following Member Feedback," *IPE* (7 November 2018). www.ipe.com/dutch-schemes-fine-tune-esg-investments-following-member-feedback/10027711.article.
15 See www.pensioenfondspgb.nl/en/about-pensioenfonds-pgb/investing/SRI/.
16 See www.phenc.nl/over-ons/nieuws/PensioenfondsHoreca&Catering-stapt-uit-fossiel.

Insurance

Insurance is divided into the following categories:

- **Property and casualty (P&C).** This category includes insurance from liabilities and damages to property (due to calamities or from legal liabilities in the home, vehicle, etc.).
- **Life.** This category covers financial losses resulting from loss of life of the insured, as well as offering retirement solutions.
- **Re-insurance.** In other words, a reinsurer provides insurance to an insurer, sharing a portion of an insurer's risk against payment of some premium.

Insurers are by nature sensitive to certain ESG issues due to factors affecting insurance products, such as

- the frequency and strength of extreme weather events (P&C) and
- demographic changes (life insurance).

This sensitivity has contributed to insurers having developed a very advanced understanding of these issues. Many insurers have an (internal) asset management business that invests the insurance premiums. The interactions between the insurance business and the internal asset management business within insurance companies led to these asset managers advancing rapidly in their understanding of ESG issues.

Importantly, in terms of climate risks, insurers are double exposed because both sides of their balance sheet can be hit by climate risks: the asset side via transition risks and the liability side via physical risks.

CASE STUDIES

Insurers and ESG Issues

Munich Re, a re-insurer, felt the repercussions of climate change on its business model. Research suggests that climate change is shifting the probability distributions of natural catastrophes, such as hurricanes and blizzards, increasing the cost for re-insurers.

An example of the dire impact of even the slightest change in weather patterns for hurricanes highlights the challenges climate change imposes on this industry: a change of 5%–10% in wind speed during hurricane season will lead to damages amounting to roughly 0.13% of total US GDP.[17]

Similarly, in a worst-case scenario assuming a change in average temperature by 3°C–4°C (5.4°F–7.2°F), damages caused by natural catastrophes (e.g., flooding) would quadruple in the United Kingdom.

Pricing for re-insurance is thus heavily reliant on knowledge of these exact probabilities. As a result, Munich Re has

- invested significantly in climate change research and modeling,
- built a climate change research center, and
- established an extensive natural catastrophe database.

---

[17] N. Stern, *The Economics of Climate Change: The Stern Review* (Cambridge, UK: Cambridge University Press, 2007).

> In 2016, Axa, valued at the time at €1.8 billion (£1.3 billion), was one of the global insurers and investors that divested from tobacco. At the launch of the Tobacco Free Finance Pledge,[18] Axa's CEO noted that "as a health insurer, we see every day the impact of smoking on people's health and wellbeing," recognizing the influence that Axa's life insurance business was having on its investment arm.[19]

Sovereign Wealth

Sovereign wealth is wealth managed through a state-owned investment fund—a **sovereign wealth fund (SWF)**. The amount of investment capital is usually large and is held by a sovereign state. The global volume of assets under management by sovereign wealth funds was estimated to be US$8 trillion (£5.8 trillion) in 2020.[20] Often the wealth comes from a sovereign state's capital surpluses.

Sovereign wealth funds are often mandated in line with the mid- to long-term objectives of their state, which might go beyond optimizing financial return and include broader policy objectives, such as

- economic stabilization,
- securing wealth for future generations, and
- strategic development of the state's territory.

These objectives can but don't necessarily have to align with ESG concerns. There is some evidence that SWFs take ESG issues into account in asset selection and investor engagement in listed equities, but this evidence is mainly driven by observation of the practices of some of the more transparent SWFs.[21]

Endowment Funds

Endowment funds are funds set up in a foundation by institutions (universities or hospitals, for example) that wish to fund their ongoing operations through withdrawals from the fund. Given the often societal purpose of endowments, there is an active debate on how to align the ongoing operational funding with such topics as divestment. Examples of this debate can be found in the United Kingdom, where universities are pressured by their students to have more sustainable investments in their endowments.[22]

Foundations and Public Charities

In such countries as the United States, private foundations and public charities are charitable organizations that invest their capital to fund charitable causes. Usually for both, the legal form of organization (LFO) is a "foundation," but the difference between the two is that

- private foundations originate their capital through one funder (typically a family or a business), whereas
- public charities originate their capital through publicly collected funds.

---

18 Principles for Sustainable Insurance, "The Tobacco-Free Finance Pledge." www.unepfi.org/psi/tobacco-free-finance-pledge/.
19 AXA, "AXA Signs the Tobacco Free Finance Pledge" (26 September 2018). www.axa.com/en/magazine/axa-signs-the-tobacco-free-finance-pledge.
20 H. Liang and L. Renneboog, "The Global Sustainability Footprint of Sovereign Wealth Funds," European Corporate Governance Institute Finance Working Paper No. 647/2019 (10 January 2020).
21 H. Liang and L. Renneboog, "The Global Sustainability Footprint of Sovereign Wealth Funds."
22 A. Mooney and S. Riding, "Students Call on UK University Endowments to Invest Responsibly," *Financial Times* (3 October 2020).

Foundations can have ESG exposures through their investment, as well as ESG objectives through their charitable work.

Individual (Retail) Investors and Wealth Management

The adoption of ESG investing by retail investors has been generally slower than for institutional investors.

At the end of 2018 in the United States, only US$161 billion (£115.7 billion) of the total US$22.1 trillion (£15.9 trillion) in assets have gone to those referencing ESG considerations. This percentage is much smaller than for institutional investors.[23]

However, inflows in open-ended and exchange-traded funds (ETFs) have been increasing: In 2020, they attracted a record US$51.1 billion (£36.7 billion) in net flows. This amount is more than twice the previous record set in 2019, when they were at a record US$18 billion (£12.9 billion); inflows in 2018, then at a record high as well, amounted to US$5.5 billion (£4 billion). Moreover, in 2020, sustainable fund flows accounted for nearly one-fourth of overall flows into funds in the United States. Morningstar, a research firm that offers an investment platform for retail investors, reported that in 2020, 71 sustainable funds were launched in the US market, easily topping the previous high-water mark of 44 set in 2017, with at least 30 funds launched each year from 2016 to 2020.[24]

Generational Differences

Millennials are usually defined as those born between 1981 to 1996. Studies and surveys have generally found that millennials are quite interested in ESG investing:

- A 2017 study of high-net-worth investors stated that 90% of millennials want to direct their allocations to responsible investments in the next five years.[25]

- Another study found that 75% of individual investors in the United States were interested in sustainable investment; the percentage of millennials was higher, at 86%.[26]

- Younger high-net-worth investors are most likely to review the ESG impact of their investment holdings, including 88% of millennials and 70% of Generation X; 82% of high-net-worth investors who make investment decisions based on ESG factors see investing as one way of expressing their personal values.[27]

Millennials are a large demographic, representing 75 million people in the United States alone, and are the future recipients of an expected US$30 trillion (£21.6 trillion) intergenerational wealth transfer through inheritance from baby boomers.

---

23 GSIA, "Global Sustainable Investment Review 2018" (2019).
24 Morningstar, "Sustainable Funds U.S. Landscape Report" (2021). www.morningstar.com/lp/sustainable-funds-landscape-report.
25 Bank of America Corporation, "2016 Environmental, Social & Governance Report" (2016). https://about.bankofamerica.com/assets/pdf/Bank-of-America-2016-ESG-Summary-Report.pdf.
26 Morgan Stanley Institute for Sustainable Investing, "Sustainable Signals: New Data from the Individual Investor" (2017). www.morganstanley.com/pub/content/dam/msdotcom/ideas/sustainable-signals/pdf/Sustainable_Signals_Whitepaper.pdf.
27 Bank of America, "Putting Wealth into Action: Competing Priorities and Lack of Time to Comprehensively Plan Are Top Reasons Why Good Intentions Fall Short" (26 June 2018). https://newsroom.bankofamerica.com/press-releases/global-wealth-and-investment-management/putting-wealth-action-competing-priorities.

Bank of America Merrill Lynch has predicted that over the next two or three decades, millennials could put between US$15 trillion (£10.8 trillion) and US$20 trillion (£14.4 trillion) into US-domiciled ESG investments, which would roughly double the size of the entire US equity market.[28]

ASSET MANAGERS, FUND PROMOTERS, AND FINANCIAL SERVICES

6

- ☐ 2.1.3 explain key market drivers of ESG integration: investor demand/intergenerational wealth transfer, regulation and policy, public awareness, and data sourcing and processing improvements
- ☐ 2.1.4 explain the key drivers and challenges for ESG integration among key stakeholders: asset owners, asset managers, fund promoters, financial services, policymakers and regulators, investees, government, civil society, and academia

Asset managers select securities and offer a portfolio consisting of those securities to asset owners. They influence the ESG characteristics of the portfolio through selection, as well as engaging with investee companies to improve their ESG performance. While they react to asset owners' interest in ESG issues, they can also play a key role in proposing new products and approaches to considering ESG factors. Asset managers are central in the investment value chain.

ESG offerings by asset managers generally began with active-listed equities but recently evolved to other asset classes. The knowledge gained by integrating ESG considerations in the equity valuation of companies was, to a certain extent, transferred to that of corporate bonds. Because fixed-income funds also include non-corporate issuers (such as supranationals, governments, and municipalities), methodologies to integrate ESG considerations expanded to enable the ESG analysis to incorporate all the issuers of the fund.

Over the past 10 years, the rise of green bonds has further propelled fixed-income as an asset class of interest to responsible investors. Funds of infrastructure, real estate, private equity, and private credit have been slower to systematically and explicitly conduct ESG integration. Nonetheless, real estate, private equity, and private credit have been instrumental in the structuring of impact investing funds.

The offering of indexes and passive funds with ESG integration by asset managers started 20 years after that of active investments. The use of indexes is nonetheless critical for the investment industry: They are performance benchmarks and serve as the basis for passive investment funds, such as ETFs. The first ESG index, the Domini 400 Social Index (now called MSCI KLD 400 Social Index), was launched by KLD Research & Analytics in 1990. In recent years, the trend toward passive investment and, particularly, investors' preferences for ETFs, together with the increased availability of ESG data and research, have spurred the market's development of ESG indexes (see Exhibit 10 for further detail).

---

28 Bank of America Corporation, "2016 Environmental, Social & Governance Report."

As of 2021, there were over 1,000 ESG indexes (of the 3.3 million indexes that were globally available according to the Index Industry Association, or IIA),[29] reflecting the growing appetite of investors for ESG products and the need for measurement tools that accurately represent the objectives of sustainable investors. ESG factors have also been successfully integrated into factor investing, smart beta funds, and derivatives, reflecting the penetration of ESG within a much more complex product offering by asset managers. IIA reported in the 2021 edition of its annual survey that the number of ESG-themed indexes grew by 43%, surpassing the 2020 growth figure of 40%.[30]

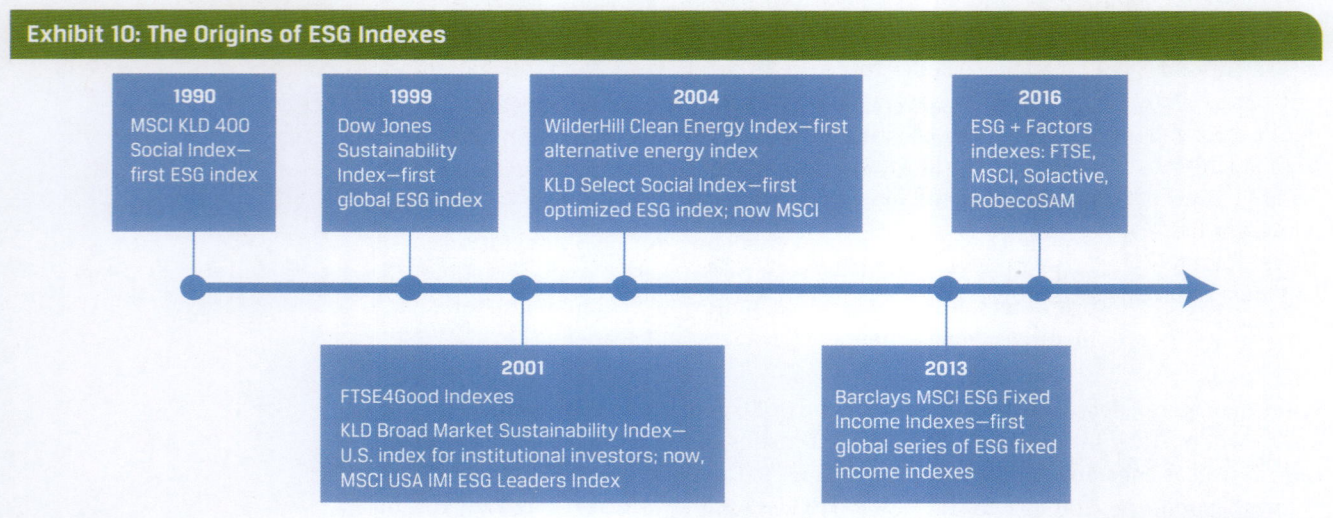

Exhibit 10: The Origins of ESG Indexes

- **1990** — MSCI KLD 400 Social Index—first ESG index
- **1999** — Dow Jones Sustainability Index—first global ESG index
- **2001** — FTSE4Good Indexes; KLD Broad Market Sustainability Index—U.S. index for institutional investors; now, MSCI USA IMI ESG Leaders Index
- **2004** — WilderHill Clean Energy Index—first alternative energy index; KLD Select Social Index—first optimized ESG index; now MSCI
- **2013** — Barclays MSCI ESG Fixed Income Indexes—first global series of ESG fixed income indexes
- **2016** — ESG + Factors indexes: FTSE, MSCI, Solactive, RobecoSAM

Source: iShares by BlackRock, "An Evolution in ESG Indexing" (2019).

Asset managers who wish to differentiate themselves have been investing significantly in ESG-related resources. Some have merged with or acquired asset managers specializing in ESG or impact investing; others have invested significant amounts in technology, using data science to develop their in-house scoring systems and dashboards. One global investor, for example, has built a proprietary system to measure the progress of fixed-income issuers against specific ESG-related objectives. Asset managers have also expanded their human resources, with some responsible investment teams increasing to over 20 people.

Some of the challenges faced by asset managers in integrating ESG issues include

- ▸ a lack of clear signals from asset owners that they are interested in ESG investing,
- ▸ a very narrow interpretation of investment objectives on which consultants and advisers base their advice for owners, and
- ▸ resource challenges, especially for investors who see ESG investing as separate from the core investment process (e.g., engagement, marketing, or compliance).

---

29 C. Svaluto Moreolo, "The Origin of ESG Indices," *IPE* (magazine, June 2019). www.ipe.com/the-origin-of-esg-indices/10031442.article.
30 IIA, "Fifth Annual Benchmark Survey Shows Record Growth in Number of ESG Indices, Alongside Broadening of Fixed Income Indices." www.indexindustry.org/2021/10/25/fifth-annual-iia-benchmark-survey-reveals-significant-growth-in-esg-continued-multi-asset-innovation-heightened-competition/.

Asset Managers, Fund Promoters, and Financial Services

For this purpose, the **fund promoter** is defined as including:

- investment consultants and retail financial advisers,
- investment platforms, and
- fund labelers.

Investment consultants and retail financial advisers are investment professionals who help institutions and individuals, respectively, set and meet long-term financial goals, usually through the proposal of investment funds. They can consider ESG characteristics of the funds in their screening and short-listing of funds to clients. Fund labelers can set standards to award labels to investment vehicles after the assessment of their ESG processes and performance.

Investment Consultants and Retail Financial Advisers

Ensuring that **investment consultants** and **retail financial adviser**s incorporate ESG factors into their core service provision is crucial for the next wave of responsible investment. These two groups are considered the gatekeepers for the expansion of ESG investing, since they advise asset owners and individual investors, respectively. As a trusted source of knowledge to trustees (particularly for small and medium-sized asset owners) and retail investors, the PRI's aim is for consultants and advisers to understand the investment implications of ESG issues and turn them into investment recommendations, because their advice is often accepted with little hesitation.

This focus of the PRI was prompted by a its review in 2017 concluding that most consultants were failing to consider ESG issues in investment practice.[31] The PRI found that often the advice it gives to investors did not support products that integrate ESG factors. To address this issue, the PRI published guidance in 2019 for asset owners to request ESG information from consultants.[32] Further challenges could emerge because consultants and financial advisers often base their advice on a narrow interpretation of investment objectives. What they perceive as a lack of appetite by asset owners in responsible investment has also led historically to them being less keen to integrate ESG investing into their mainstream offerings. some jurisdictions, such as the EU, are sidestepping this conundrum by introducing mandatory regulation for investment funds and rating agencies to explicitly consider ESG issues (Sustainable Finance Disclosure Regulation, or SFDR, and EU Credit Rating Guidelines) and for financial service providers to explicitly take stock of investors' ESG preferences across various investor categories and asset classes (Markets in Financial Instruments Directive, or MiFID, Undertakings for the Collective Investment of Transferable Securities, or UCITS; Alternative Investment Fund Managers Directive, or AIFMD).

There is much that consultants can do. With regard to investment strategy, they can

- aid trustees in understanding their fiduciary obligations,
- formulate a strategy inclusive of ESG considerations, and
- draft investment principles and policies in line with the strategy and fiduciary obligations.

Within their manager selection role, consultants can help asset owners design a proposal and formulate a mandate that integrates their investment beliefs on ESG issues and expectations on implementation.

---

31 PRI, "Investment Consultants Services Review" (2017). www.unpri.org/sustainable-financial-system/investment-consultants-services-review/571.article.
32 PRI, "Investment Consultants and ESG: An Asset Owner Guide" (2019). www.unpri.org/asset-owner-resources/investment-consultants-and-esg-an-asset-owner-guide/4577.article.

Finally, consultants can include asset managers' capabilities and processes related to ESG investing within their research, screening, selection, and appointment processes. Advisers can play a similar role with individual investors, proactively providing relevant ESG information and including ESG investments in their offerings and advice.

Investment Platforms

The research and recommendations of **investment platforms** can be highly influential in the asset management industry and can be a positive or negative recommendation driving a significant amount of capital into or away from any given fund.

Morningstar, one of the main investment platforms, offers a service that rates asset managers and their funds. In 2016, the platform started integrating ESG ratings in its offerings. Investment platforms can integrate the extent and depth that funds integrate ESG investing to

- increase awareness of ESG funds for both retail and institutional investors and
- enable easier identification of and information on these funds.

However, in February 2022, Morningstar reclassified almost 1,700 funds, worth US$1.2 trillion, away from its list of sustainable funds. It cited its own research analyzing additional criteria provided by funds following the implementation of new EU disclosure rules called "SFDR."

Fund Labelers

Labels provide benchmarks and quality guarantees for both practitioners and clients. In just over a decade, sustainable finance has led to the creation of eight specialized labels in Europe alone. Labels are usually either general, looking at ESG investing as a whole, or thematic, usually focused on environment or climate. Few labels have been applied to multiple countries, creating challenges for global investors seeking to offer certified ESG funds across multiple jurisdictions. Certifications have been perceived as a marketing tool by some actors. Nonetheless, in practice, it is not necessarily associated with a marketing strategy in line with the fund's promises. A quarter of the funds certified on ESG criteria in Europe do not have a name reflecting a sustainable approach, and around 30 are thematic environmental funds.[33]

Financial services are defined as including

- investment banks,
- custodial banks,
- investment research and advisory firms,
- stock exchanges, and
- financial and ESG rating agencies.

Financial service companies are important enablers of responsible investment because they make significant contributions to the availability of securities with higher ESG quality and increase the quality of information about ESG characteristics of securities and assets in general. For example:

- Investment banks can support a company issuing a green bond (a bond where proceeds are specifically earmarked to be used for climate and environmental projects).

---

33 Novethic, "Overview of European Sustainable Finance Labels" (2019). www.novethic.com/sustainable-finance-trends/detail/overview-of-european-sustainable-finance-labels.html.

- Sell-side analysts and rating agencies can consider ESG factors within their analysis, recommendations, and ratings.
- Stock exchanges can increase disclosure requirements on ESG data by listed companies (as encouraged by the Sustainable Stock Exchange Initiative).
- Proxy voting service providers—those who vote on behalf of shareholders at companies' annual general meetings—can integrate ESG considerations in their voting and voting recommendations.

Improvements in ESG data sourcing and analysis have contributed to the growth of the ESG market. Analysis and ratings of investees from an ESG perspective have been dominated by traditional credit rating companies, as well as a handful of specialist firms. One-theme consultants, such as those specializing in helping investors understand and quantify the risk posed by climate change to their portfolios, are also well established, though many new ones continue to enter the market. The growth of the industry and its consolidation (through partnerships, mergers, and acquisitions) has increased investors' ability to further implement ESG investing. It has also helped policymakers and regulators reassure themselves that requirements to assess ESG risk and reporting on it are increasingly possible.

Further details on ESG rating agencies and suppliers can be found in Chapter 7.

POLICYMAKERS, REGULATORS, INVESTEES, GOVERNMENTS, CIVIL SOCIETY, AND ACADEMIA

7

☐ 2.1.3 explain key market drivers of ESG integration: investor demand/intergenerational wealth transfer, regulation and policy, public awareness, and data sourcing and processing improvements

☐ 2.1.4 explain the key drivers and challenges for ESG integration among key stakeholders: asset owners, asset managers, fund promoters, financial services, policymakers and regulators, investees, government, civil society, and academia

Financial regulation is downstream from policy choices. Financial supervision is downstream from financial regulation. This section highlights the various roles of policymakers and regulators and provides some examples of sustainable finance regulation from across the globe.

Policymakers are responding to the growing urgency of sustainability topics. Some issues can have a profound impact on:

- the stability of the financial system (for example, climate change and emerging issues, such as biodiversity and resource scarcity) and
- the risks to an individual investor's portfolio.

The objectives of **financial regulator**s are to:

- maintain orderly financial markets,
- safeguard investments in financial instruments, savings/pensions, and investment vehicles, and
- bring about an orderly expansion of activities of the financial sector.

Financial regulators consider how ESG factors might impact the stability of economies and the financial markets and how these factors might influence the long-term risk–return profile of financial instruments. They also encourage and enable the growth of certain ESG products, such as green bonds, and require disclosure on ESG characteristics.

Other regulators can influence the ESG characteristics of companies by strengthening matters regarding environment, labor, communities, and governance and can require further disclosure on those issues.

Regulations generally involve three themes:

1. **Corporate disclosure**. Guidelines on corporate disclosure typically come from government or stock exchanges to encourage or require investee companies to disclose information on material ESG risks. While this does not impose any requirement on investors themselves, it improves their ability to consider these risks in their investment decisions.
2. **Stewardship**. Regulation on stewardship governs the interactions between investors and investee companies and seeks to protect shareholders and beneficiaries as well as the health and stability of the market. In most jurisdictions, stewardship codes remain voluntary, though mandatory regulation has been approved in Europe.
3. **Asset owners**. Regulation on asset owners typically focuses on pension funds, requiring them to integrate ESG factors and disclose their process and outcome. Some regulators, such as those in the United Kingdom, Australia, and Singapore, are also beginning to consider climate risk for the insurance market and the financial industry more widely.

Exhibit 11 illustrates how policymakers and regulators tie together varies sustainability policy objectives with regulatory interventions.

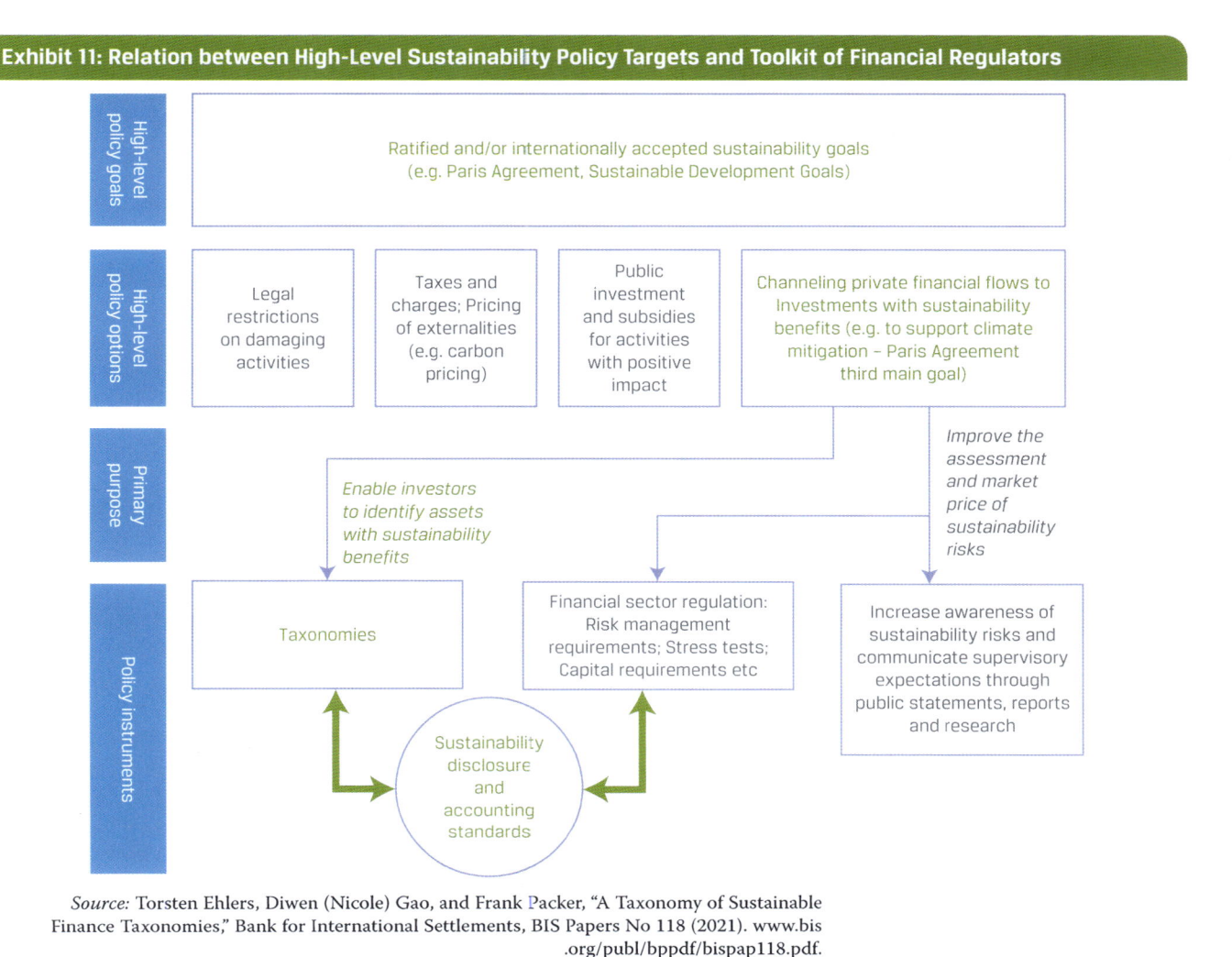

Exhibit 11: Relation between High-Level Sustainability Policy Targets and Toolkit of Financial Regulators

High-level policy goals: Ratified and/or internationally accepted sustainability goals (e.g. Paris Agreement, Sustainable Development Goals)

High-level policy options:
- Legal restrictions on damaging activities
- Taxes and charges; Pricing of externalities (e.g. carbon pricing)
- Public investment and subsidies for activities with positive impact
- Channeling private financial flows to Investments with sustainability benefits (e.g. to support climate mitigation – Paris Agreement third main goal)

Primary purpose:
- Enable investors to identify assets with sustainability benefits
- Improve the assessment and market price of sustainability risks

Policy instruments:
- Taxonomies
- Financial sector regulation: Risk management requirements; Stress tests; Capital requirements etc
- Increase awareness of sustainability risks and communicate supervisory expectations through public statements, reports and research
- Sustainability disclosure and accounting standards

Source: Torsten Ehlers, Diwen (Nicole) Gao, and Frank Packer, "A Taxonomy of Sustainable Finance Taxonomies," Bank for International Settlements, BIS Papers No 118 (2021). www.bis.org/publ/bppdf/bispap118.pdf.

Examples of Policy and Regulatory Developments across the Globe

In a review conducted by the PRI on sustainable finance policy in 2019, 97% of the new or revised policies were developed after 2000. The continued acceleration has been driven by the rapid development in Europe (with many initiatives being developed under the EU Action Plan on Financing Sustainable Growth) and Asia (where markets have seen significant updates to reporting requirements and corporate governance expectations). Another significant factor has been periodic revisions of stewardship and corporate governance codes, with national authorities introducing or periodically strengthening ESG expectations. Stewardship is closely linked to shareholder engagement. Further details can be found in Chapter 6.

Global—Task Force on Climate-Related Financial Disclosures

In 2017, the **Task Force on Climate-Related Financial Disclosures (TCFD)** released climate-related financial disclosure recommendations to help firms voluntarily disclose information to support capital allocation. Since its launch, the TCFD recommendations have been made mandatory in various jurisdictions, including New Zealand,

Switzerland, Hong Kong SAR, Japan, Singapore, and the United Kingdom. In the EU, SFDR, which has a broader scope than TCFD in terms of sustainability topics, effectively made TCFD mandatory. In the near future, wider TCFD implementation is expected, with all of the G–7 countries backing mandatory reporting, meaning that Canada and the United States will also move to mandatory TCFD reporting.

The TCFD recommendations center on four key areas:

1. Governance
2. Strategy
3. Risk management
4. Metrics and targets

Europe–EU Taxonomy Regulation

The EU Taxonomy Regulation, published on 22 June 2020, established a framework that states conditions for an economic activity to be considered environmentally sustainable. These include

- contributing substantially to at least one of the six environmental objectives listed in the next paragraph,
- "doing no significant harm" to any of the other environmental objectives, and
- complying with minimum, EU-specified, social and governance safeguards.

The Taxonomy Regulation establishes six environmental objectives:

1. Climate change mitigation
2. Climate change adaptation
3. The sustainable use and protection of water and marine resources
4. The transition to a circular economy
5. Pollution prevention and control
6. The protection and restoration of biodiversity and ecosystems

Europe–EU Sustainable Finance Disclosure Regulation

SFDR, published in December 2019, created requirements to promote consideration of environmental and social risks that may affect investments. These disclosures aim to enhance transparency of sustainably invested products to prevent green washing. It identifies so-called *principal adverse impacts* that have a negative impact on the environmental and social issues stemming from investment decisions.

China–Guidelines for Green Financial System, Green Asset Taxonomy, and PBOC 2021–25 Strategy

In 2016, the People's Bank of China (PBOC), in collaboration with six other government agencies, issued guidelines establishing the green financial system. These guidelines marked a turning point for China's sustainable finance policy. Previous policy reforms tended to be reactive to financial crises. The new generation of policy recognizes that to be effective, reforms need to tackle multiple aspects of interconnected and complex capital markets. In addition, in 2021, China launched the Common Ground Taxonomy with the EU, and in that year, the PBOC announced a new, five-year strategy with strong support for the origination of green loans, bonds, insurance, and derivatives.

The United States—2022 SEC proposal

In the United States policies have long remained voluntary or based on a "comply or explain" expectation, which led some investors to continue to challenge the assertion that ESG integration is a requirement. However, in April 2022, the US SEC proposed far-ranging disclosure requirements for climate risks. This proposal was open to a 60-day consultation process, but in its initial version, it governs how a regulated firm is to report on the following:[34]

- How climate related risks are governed by a firm's board and management
- The firm's climate-related impacts, goals, targets, and transition plans
- The firm's Scope 1 (direct operational emissions) and Scope 2 (emissions from energy used by the firm) greenhouse gas emissions
- The firm's Scope 3 emissions if material—that is, the emissions in its upstream and downstream supply chains

Combined Effect of Regional Strategies

Combined, these regional strategies have been a significant driver in the overall policy growth in in this space—in particular, the EU Action Plan on Financing Sustainable Growth. Moreover, it is anticipated that as policies on ESG issues and financial regulation reach maturity, an increasing number of governments will recognize the importance of moving to stronger requirements in the following ways:

- moving away from "comply or explain" regulation and to "comply and explain" regulation,
- changing from voluntary to mandatory disclosures, and
- moving from policy to implementation and reporting.

For example, the Network for Greening the Financial System, a group of 127 central banks and supervisors established in 2017, explicitly recognizes climate risks as relevant to a supervisory mandate, and it has challenged policymakers, other central banks, and supervisors to act to limit the catastrophic impacts of runaway climate change.

Challenges to ESG investing can emerge if regulators hold a narrow interpretation of fiduciary duty, such as with the US Department of Labor's (DOL's) 2020 ruling on fiduciary duty and non-financial objectives (see the following case studies).

CASE STUDIES

The United States

In the United States, private sector retirement plans are subject to the provisions of the **Employee Retirement Income Security Act (ERISA)**. ERISA sets standards for fiduciaries of defined benefit and defined contribution plans based on the principle of a prudent-person standard.

The DOL is responsible for issuing regulation and guidance on fiduciary responsibility provisions. While only pension plans in the private sector are under the jurisdiction of the DOL, it is of great influence because the public sector often looks to ERISA principles as a benchmark for best practice in meeting common law fiduciary standards in their governance.

---

34 SEC, "Fact Sheet: Enhancement and Standardization of Climate-Related Disclosures." www.sec.gov/files/33-11042-fact-sheet.pdf.

ERISA defines the responsibilities of institutional investors entrusted with retirement assets. Chief among these is the obligation to always act to protect the interests of plan participants and beneficiaries. Under ERISA, plan sponsors and other fiduciaries generally must do the following:

1. Act solely in the interest of plan participants and beneficiaries.
2. Invest with the care, skill, and diligence of a prudent person with knowledge of such matters.
3. Diversify plan investments to minimize the risk of large losses.

Plan sponsors that breach any of these fiduciary duties may be held personally liable.

To some extent, the DOL started addressing ESG matters within ERISA in the 1990s.[35] In its Interpretive Bulletin (IB) 1994-1, issued under the Clinton administration, it corrected a popular misperception at the time by establishing that economically targeted investments (ETIs), which generate societal benefits in addition to financial return, are compatible with ERISA's fiduciary obligations as long as their expected rate of return is commensurate with the rates of return offered by alternative investments with similar risk characteristics. This was referred to as the "all things being equal" test.

In 2008, the DOL under the George W. Bush administration replaced IB 1994-1 with IB 2008-01, which stated that the fiduciary consideration of collateral, non-economic factors in selecting plan investments should be rare and, when considered, documented in a manner that demonstrates compliance with ERISA's rigorous fiduciary standards. This publication had the effect of discouraging fiduciaries from considering ETIs and ESG factors.

Thus, the responsible investment community welcomed the DOL's IB 2015-01 under the Obama administration, which significantly expanded the use of ESG investing principles under ERISA:

> *IB 2015-01 confirms the Department's longstanding view that plan fiduciaries may invest in ETIs based, in part, on their collateral benefits so long as the investment is appropriate for the plan and economically and financially equivalent with respect to the plan's investment objectives, return, risk, and other financial attributes as competing investment choices. The IB also acknowledges that in some cases ESG factors may have a direct relationship to the economic and financial value of the plan's investment. In such instances, the ESG issues are not merely collateral considerations or tie-breakers, but rather are proper components of the fiduciary's primary analysis of the economic merits of competing investment choices. When a fiduciary prudently concludes that such an investment is justified based solely on the economic merits of the investment, there is no need to evaluate collateral goals as tie-breakers."* [36]

---

35 US Department of Labor, "Economically Targeted Investments (ETIs) and Investment Strategies That Consider Environmental, Social and Governance (ESG) Factors" (2015). www.dol.gov/sites/dolgov/files/ebsa/about-ebsa/our-activities/resource-center/fact-sheets/etis-and-investment-strategies-that-consider-esg-factors.pdf.

36 US Department of Labor, "Economically Targeted Investments (ETIs) and Investment Strategies That Consider Environmental, Social and Governance (ESG) Factors."

Yet in 2020, the pendulum swung back, under the Trump administration, when the DOL issued the so-called final rule, 85 FR 72846. This ruling removed all mention of ESG concepts and replaced it with the words "non-financial objectives" on the basis that the term "ESG" lacks uniform usage and a precise definition. This rule included the following ideas:

- The DOL believed that "tie-breaker" scenarios permitting investment decisions based on non-financial factors are extremely rare, and therefore, as a practical matter, ERISA fiduciaries should continue to refrain from making investment decisions based on non-financial factors.
- Fiduciaries must evaluate investments based solely on financial factors that have a material effect on the return and risk of an investment, and ESG factors may be considered as financial factors in evaluating an investment only if they present material economic risks or opportunities.
- Specific obligations were further imposed, such as documentation requirements, on ERISA plan fiduciaries considering ESG-oriented investing.

The Biden administration directed the DOL to review the final rule in a fact sheet issued in January 2021.[37] In March 2021, the DOL released a statement of non-enforcement, and in October 2021, it issued a new rule to allow consideration of ESG criteria and proxy voting in private sector retirement plans.

CASE STUDIES

The United Kingdom

There has been an extensive discussion in the United Kingdom about the fiduciary duties of institutional investors. In the wake of the 2008 global financial crisis, Professor John Kay was commissioned by the UK government to conduct a review of the structure and operation of UK equity markets. His report, *The Kay Review of UK Equity Markets and Long-Term Decision Making: Final Report*, published in July 2012, emphasized the need for a culture of long-term decision making, trust, and stewardship to protect savers' interests.[38] The report recognized the essential role that fiduciary duties play in the promotion of such a culture but highlighted the damage being done by misinterpretations and misapplications of fiduciary duty in practice.

In response, the government asked the Law Commission to investigate the subject of fiduciary duty in more detail. In 2014, the Law Commission published its report, "Fiduciary Duties of Investment Intermediaries." On financial factors, the report concluded that "whilst it is clear that trustees may take into account environmental, social and governance factors in making investment decisions where they are financially material, we think the law goes further: Trustees should take into account financially material factors." [39]

On non-financial factors, the Law Commission's term for ESG factors, the report concluded,

---

37 White House, "Fact Sheet: List of Agency Actions for Review" (20 January 2021). www.whitehouse.gov/briefing-room/statements-releases/2021/01/20/fact-sheet-list-of-agency-actions-for-review.
38 John Kay, "The Kay Review of UK Equity Markets and Long-Term Decision Making: Final Report" (July 2012).
39 Law Commission, "Fiduciary Duties of Investment Intermediaries" (2014). www.lawcom.gov.uk/app/uploads/2015/03/lc350_fiduciary_duties.pdf.

> *By "non-financial" factors we mean factors which might influence investment decisions motivated by other (non-financial) concerns, such as improving members' quality of life or showing disapproval of certain industries. In broad terms, trustees should take into account financially relevant factors. However, the circumstances in which trustees may make non-financially related decisions are more limited. In general, non-financial factors may only be taken into account if two tests are met:*
>
> 1. *trustees should have good reason to think that scheme members would share the concern; and*
>
> 2. *the decision should not involve a risk of significant financial detriment to the fund.*

CASE STUDIES

The EU

The EU Action Plan on Financing Sustainable Growth, agreed on in 2019, requires the following:

- Mandatory disclosure of policies in relation to ESG risk (consistent with the PRI's fiduciary duty recommendations) for all firms and financial products
- Comply or explain disclosure of the principal adverse impacts of the investment on sustainability factors (mandatory for firms with more than 500 staff) at the firm and product level
- Enhanced disclosure obligations for firms promoting specific environmental or social objectives

The **Technical Expert Group (TEG)** was established to assist the European Commission in the technical development of various delegated aspects of sustainable finance regulation. In June 2019, the TEG issued reports on an EU Taxonomy, a voluntary EU Green Bond Standard, and voluntary low-carbon benchmarks. The "Taxonomy Technical Report" aimed to significantly advance a shared understanding among investors on activities and sectors that contribute to climate change mitigation and adaptation.[40] When the TEG concluded its work, it was succeeded by the Platform on Sustainable Finance, a permanent expert group of the European Commission that established, under Article 20 of the Taxonomy Regulation.

The EU's **Shareholder Rights Directive** II, which came into force in 2019, seeks to improve the level and quality of investors with their investee companies, better aligning executive pay with corporate performance and increasing disclosure on how an asset manager's investment decisions contribute to the

---

[40] EU Technical Expert Group on Sustainable Finance, "Financing a Sustainable European Economy: Taxonomy Technical Report" (June 2019). https://ec.europa.eu/info/sites/info/files/business_economy_euro/banking_and_finance/documents/190618-sustainable-finance-teg-report-taxonomy_en.pdf.

medium- and long-term performance of investee companies. In order to achieve that, it requires investors to have an engagement policy and annually report on the following:

- how this is integrated into their investment strategy,
- how the dialogue is carried out,
- how voting rights and shareholder rights are being executed,
- how the manager collaborates with other shareholders, and
- how potential conflicts of interest are dealt with.

Of note, Article 173 of the French Energy Transition Law, which came into force in 2016, strengthened mandatory carbon disclosure requirements for listed companies and introduced carbon reporting for fund managers and asset owners.

CASE STUDIES

China

In 2018, the Asset Management Association of China (AMAC) released the Guidelines for Green Investment. These guidelines state that "ESG is an emerging investment strategy in the asset management industry and an important initiative for the investment fund industry to implement the green development concept and establish a green financial system."

It is anticipated that the AMAC will make great efforts to facilitate the implementation of the guidelines.

In June 2021, the China Securities Regulatory Commission issued a set of ESG disclosure guidelines. The guidelines entail mostly voluntary reporting on climate risks; biodiversity risks; pollution of air, water, and soil; and waste management.

Investees

Investees include all entities in which investments can be made. These include

- companies,
- projects (such as infrastructure projects and joint ventures),
- agencies (including the World Bank and International Finance Corporation), and
- jurisdictions (for instance, countries/regions, provinces, and cities).

Decision makers in these entities can influence how they manage ESG risks and the impact they have on the environment and society. Furthermore, they decide on the level of disclosure of ESG factors to provide to existing and potential investors. In fact, one of the most pressing issues for ESG investing is a lack of access to reliable and consistent ESG data. Various reporting initiatives exist to try to address this issue.

Governments

Governments in general have recognized three main ways in which the investment industry and, more specifically, responsible investment play a significant role in achieving positive outcomes for society.

1. Social security systems and public pensions are in a predicament in many countries, and their citizens are thus turning to corporate or private pension plans for financial stability later in life.
2. Many countries, developed or developing, need to build or restore public infrastructure (such as water systems, transportation means, and energy distribution), which is usually costly for government treasuries.
3. Many governments have recognized that a transition to a low-carbon economy will require significant shifts in capital. These are all areas where governments can encourage the consideration of the financial materiality of ESG issues and the social and environmental impact of investments to advance national priorities.

Civil society

Civil society, including non-governmental organizations (NGOs), has played a major role in pushing for increased sustainability at company level and, more recently, in demanding increased transparency and consideration around the impact that investment has on society and the environment. Some partner with investment firms and regulators to help improve their understanding of specific ESG matters, while others bring to light actions that are deemed insufficient to address global challenges.

Academia

Academic research has been influential in validating the business case for integrating ESG factors into the investment process. Academia can continue to conduct studies focusing on the various aspects of ESG factors and their integration into investment decisions, as well as their impact on investment returns and the financial markets more broadly.

KEY FACTS

1. In 1987, a commission put together by the UN issued the Brundtland Report, also called *Our Common Future*, which introduced the concept of sustainable development and described how it could be achieved.

2. The concept of responsible investing dates back to the 17th century. One of the first ethical mutual funds that moved to screens based on religious traditions was the Pioneer Fund, which was launched in 1928. The modern institutionalization of ethical exclusions arguably began at the height of the Vietnam War in 1971, with the establishment of the Pax World Fund.

3. In the early 2000s, the UN Global Compact's report "Who Cares Wins" encouraged financial institutions to integrate ESG factors into capital markets. Concurrently, UNEP FI produced the so-called Freshfields Report, which showed that ESG issues are relevant for financial valuation and thus, fiduciary duty. These two reports formed the backbone for the launch of the Principles for Responsible Investment (PRI) in 2006.

4. The Global Sustainable Investment Alliance's most recent report shows sustainable investing assets in the five major markets stood at US$30.7 trillion (£22 trillion) at the start of 2018, a 34% increase from two years before. The proportion of sustainable investing relative to total managed assets grew in almost every region, and in Canada and Australia/New Zealand, responsible investing assets now make up most of the total assets under professional management.

5. Although institutional investors tend to dominate the financial market, interest by retail investors in responsible investing has been steadily growing; in 2018, the retail portion of total ESG assets totaled one quarter.

6. Most ESG assets are allocated to public equities (over 50% at the start of 2018). The next largest asset allocation is in fixed income (36%).

7. Asset owners set the direction of the investment value chain. Asset owners' understanding of how ESG factors influence financial returns and how their capital impacts the real economy can significantly drive the amount and quality of ESG investing from the investment value chain.

8. Institutional asset owners establish contracts, known as investment mandates, with asset managers. These are important because they define the expectations around the investment product and at times even aspects about the manager's processes and resources more broadly. The large majority (over 90%) of asset owner signatories of the PRI require in their investment mandate that asset managers act in accordance with the asset owner's responsible investment policy, and over half of the asset owners (65%) also require reporting.

9. Many actors in the investment value chain have recognized the shortfalls of short-termism in investment practice and have sought to increase awareness of the value of long-termism and encourage it. Short-termism may leave companies less willing to take on projects (such as research and development) that may take multiple years—and patient capital—to develop. Furthermore, short-term investment strategies tend to ignore factors that are considered more long term, such as ESG factors. This assertion was confirmed by a review conducted on the UK equity market and long-term decision making by Professor John Kay for the UK Government in 2012.

10. In theory, asset owners with long-term liabilities (such as pension funds) are well aligned with long-term investing and are due to benefit from it. In practice, they at times help create the problem by rewarding managers and companies for short-term behavior.

11. Insurers are by nature sensitive to certain ESG aspects due to factors impacting insurance products, such as the frequency and strength of extreme weather events (property and casualty) and demographic changes (life insurance).

12. The adoption of ESG investing by retail investors has been generally slower than that of institutional investors. Surveys have generally found that millennials are interested in ESG investing, which may increase ESG assets in retail investing in the near future.

13. Asset managers influence the ESG characteristics of the portfolio through selection, as well as by engaging with investee companies to improve their ESG performance. While they react to asset owners' interest in ESG issues, they can also play a key role in proposing new products and approaches to considering ESG factors.

14. ESG offerings by asset managers generally began with active-listed equities but recently evolved to other asset classes, especially fixed income. The offering of indexes and passive funds with ESG integration by asset managers started 20 years after that of active investments. The use of indexes is nonetheless critical for the investment industry: They are performance benchmarks and the basis for passive investment funds, such as ETFs.

15. Investment consultants and retail financial advisers are investment professionals who help institutions and individuals, respectively, set and meet long-term financial goals, usually through the proposal of investment funds. They can consider the ESG characteristics of the funds in their screening and short-listing of funds for clients.

16. Financial regulators consider how ESG factors might impact the stability of economies and the financial markets and how these factors might influence the long-term risk–return profile of financial instruments. They also encourage and enable the growth of certain ESG products, such as green bonds, and require disclosure on ESG characteristics.

17. Over 95% of new or revised policies were developed after 2000, driven by rapid development in Europe and Asia, as well as the rise of stewardship and corporate governance codes, with national authorities introducing or periodically strengthening ESG expectations.

18. Companies and other investees can contribute to the growth of ESG investing by how they manage ESG risks, the impact they have on the environment and society, and the level of disclosure they provide on these matters.

19. 19 Governments have recognized that responsible investment can play a role in funding both public infrastructure and the transition to a low-carbon society. They also recognize that responsible investment can play a role in the transition of pension systems, whereby citizens rely more heavily on private pension plans.

20. Civil society and NGOs can help increase the awareness of companies on their ESG risk. They can also help with improving disclosure. The outcomes of academic research can increase focus on various aspects of ESG factors and investment decision making.

21. Some investors still question whether considering ESG issues can add value to investment decision making despite wide dissemination of research that demonstrates that ESG integration can help limit volatility and enhance returns.

22. Some investors also still question whether their fiduciary duty allows them to implement ESG investing. Internal evidence on the impact of considering ESG factors and engaging with direct peers can help overcome these barriers.

Key Facts

23. The advice given by investment consultants and retail financial advisers has often not been supportive of products that integrate ESG factors. Investor-led initiatives that engage with these actors have contributed to this situation gradually changing.
24. A lack of understanding on how to implement ESG factors in the various phases of the investment process, as well as perceptions around the cost and availability of data and tools, can limit the growth of ESG investing.
25. The rise of ESG-labeled funds also increased the risk of "greenwashing." Further work by regulators combined with the development of voluntary market standards would make it easier for investors to understand the characteristics of responsible investments and the differences between various types of responsible investment, helping build trust in the market.

FURTHER READING

Amel-Zadeh, A., and G. Serafeim. 2018. "Why and How Investors Use ESG Information: Evidence from a Global Survey." Financial Analysts Journal 74 (3): 87–103. www.cfainstitute.org/research/financial-analysts-journal/2018/faj-v74-n3-2. doi:10.2469/faj.v74.n3.2

Bassen, A., T. Busch, and G. Friede. 2015. "ESG and Financial Performance: Aggregated Evidence from More than 2,000 Empirical Studies." Journal of Sustainable Finance & Investment 5 (4): 210–33. doi:10.1080/20430795.2015.1118917

Forum pour l'Investissement Responsable. 2016. "Understanding the French Regulation on Investor Climate Reporting." Article 173-VI. www.frenchsif.org/isr-esg/wp-content/uploads/Understanding_article173-French_SIF_Handbook.pdf.

Fulton, M., B. Kahn, and C. Sharples. 2012. "Sustainable Investing: Establishing Long-Term Value and Performance." Working paper 12 (June).

International Corporate Governance Network. 2012. "ICGN Global Stewardship Principles."

National Association Pension Funds. 2014. "What Do Pension Scheme Members Expect of How Their Savings Are Invested?"

SELF PRACTICE AND SELF ASSESSMENT

1. Which of the following asset classes has the lowest allocation of global sustainable investing assets?
   a. Real estate
   b. Public equity
   c. Fixed income

2. Asset managers:
   a. include pension funds and sovereign wealth funds.
   b. are not the counterparty to investment transactions.
   c. have legal ownership of the assets under management.

3. Which of the following parties holds the ultimate fiduciary responsibility in a pension fund? The pension fund:
   a. trustees
   b. auditors
   c. executives

4. Which of the following established a framework that states conditions for an economic activity to be considered environmentally sustainable?
   a. EU Taxonomy Regulation
   b. Climate Disclosure Standards Board
   c. Task Force on Climate-Related Financial Disclosures

5. Which role do insurance companies *most likely* undertake?
   a. Asset owners
   b. Intermediaries
   c. Asset managers

6. An ESG government policy with a "comply and explain" approach suggests that:
   a. the country is applying lighter ESG requirements.
   b. ESG integration for supervised entities is voluntary.
   c. ESG integration at a country level is at a mature stage.

7. Which of the following required investors to be active owners and to act with a more long-term focus?
   a. EU Taxonomy Regulation
   b. EU Shareholder Rights Directive (SRD)
   c. EU Sustainable Finance Disclosure Regulation

8. Which of the following is *most* accurate with respect to individual investors?
   a. Retail investors are often referred to as "universal owners."
   b. Retail investors have been faster in adopting ESG investing compared to institutional investors.
   c. Millennial high-net-worth investors are more likely to review the impact of their investment holdings than Generation X high-net-worth investors.

9. With regard to ESG investing, financial regulators:

   a. act as fiduciaries to asset owners.
   b. participate in collective engagements.
   c. consider how ESG factors might influence the long-term risk–return profile of financial instruments.

10. Which two reports formed the backbone for the launch of the Principles for Responsible Investment (PRI) in 2006?

    a. "Who Cares Wins" and the Freshfields Report
    b. "Who Cares Wins" and the Brundtland Report
    c. The Brundtland Report and the Freshfields Report

The following information relates to questions 11-25
Self Assessment Questions

These questions are provided only to enable you to test your understanding of the chapter content. They are not indicative of the types and standard of questions you may see in the examination. The Self-Assessment questions do not include an explanation of the correct answer.

11. Which regions manage the highest proportion of sustainable and responsible investment assets?

    a. Asia and North America
    b. Australia and the United States
    c. Canada and Europe
    d. Asia and Europe

12. What is the largest sustainable investment strategy globally?

    a. Impact investing
    b. Best-in-class
    c. ESG integration
    d. Negative screening

13. The largest and second largest asset classes that implement responsible investment are, respectively:

    a. public equities and fixed income.
    b. passive equities and active equities.
    c. fixed income and infrastructure.
    d. hedge funds and commodities.

14. Why is ESG investing a concern for investors who are cautious of high tracking error?

    a. The perception that exclusion resulting from ESG will distort the weight of sectors and countries in the portfolio in comparison to the benchmark
    b. The understanding that exclusion results in fewer available securities to invest in and thus a more limited investment universe
    c. The belief that high-performing stocks may be excluded due to negative ESG characteristics, resulting in underperformance in comparison to the benchmark

Self Practice and Self Assessment

    d. The awareness that ESG investing requires a redefinition of active risk

15. Why are investment mandates important for ESG investing?
    a. They define the expectations of asset owners who are signatories of the PRI.
    b. They are contracts that define the requirements of the asset manager with regard to ESG issues.
    c. They require asset managers to report on the ESG rating of their funds.
    d. They have limited the implementation of stewardship.

16. Which of the following is not an outcome of short-termism?
    a. Disproportionate focus on quarterly returns
    b. Companies are more willing to take on projects, such as research and development.
    c. "Patient capital" is less likely to develop.
    d. Less investment in long-term assets, such as infrastructure.

17. How are pension fund members most likely to influence responsible investment?
    a. Their formal investment advice to pension fund executives must be implemented.
    b. They monitor company controversy through social media and inform asset managers.
    c. They act in the interest of sustainable companies.
    d. Their ethical preferences may be taken into account.

18. Which of the following is not among the challenges limiting the development of ESG investing?
    a. Lack of regulation and voluntary initiatives
    b. The availability of expertise and skilled individuals
    c. The quality of data, research, and analysis
    d. Limited tools to assist with portfolio construction and management

19. What is the least likely reason why a pension fund trustee may consider ESG investing?
    a. Pension fund trustees should act in the interests, including non-financial interests, of pension fund members, and the members have voiced their interest in social and environmental impacts.
    b. Pension fund trustees have the fiduciary duty to consider factors that are financially material to the long-term returns of the pension fund.
    c. Pension fund trustees risk legal action by not managing climate change–related risks.
    d. Pension fund trustees are the ultimate beneficiaries of pension funds and, as a result, should act in their interest.

20. In what way can investment consultants be a barrier to the growth of the ESG investing market?
    a. By not considering ESG characteristics of the funds in their screening
    b. By setting poor standards for ESG fund labels
    c. By short-listing only ESG funds
    d. By helping trustees understand their fiduciary duties

21. In what way can stock exchanges support the advancement of ESG investing?
    a. By rating the ESG characteristics of a listed security
    b. By increasing the requirement on the disclosure of ESG data by listed securities
    c. By structuring and issuing green bonds
    d. By integrating ESG considerations within their voting recommendations

22. What is the main challenge with policies that are "comply or explain" regarding ESG issues?
    a. It is the sole indication that the policy has not reached maturity.
    b. It leads to investors challenging the assertion that ESG integration is a requirement.
    c. It allows investors to explain all kinds of behavior away.
    d. It completely excuses investors from reporting on ESG practices.

23. Which matters does the Technical Expert Group address?
    a. Green bonds and engagement
    b. Green bonds and low-carbon benchmarks
    c. Carbon disclosure and long-termism
    d. Climate risk and fiduciary duty

24. Why was the US Department of Labor's clarification of fiduciary duty in 2015 welcomed by the ESG investing industry?
    a. It allowed plans to invest in generating societal benefits in addition to financial return, as long as they were deemed appropriate for the plan's investment objectives, return, and risk.
    b. It provided a standard for economically targeted investments (ETIs).
    c. It specified that as long as the expected rate of return was commensurate with the rates of return offered by alternative investments with similar risk characteristics, ETIs were compatible with fiduciary duty.
    d. It incentivized pension funds subject to ERISA to invest in ETIs.

25. What is the highest risk to the industry regarding greenwashing?
    a. The overestimate of the ESG investing market
    b. The disappointment of clients with quarterly financial returns
    c. The negative impact on the industry's credibility
    d. The increased challenge to standardization

SOLUTIONS

1. A is correct. Real estate has the lowest allocation of global ESG investments (public equity has the highest allocation, followed by fixed income).

2. B is correct. Asset managers are not the counterparty to investment transactions (asset owners are the counterparty. Pension funds and SWFs are "asset owners," although they may manage some of their own assets while outsourcing some assets to asset managers.

3. A is correct. The pension fund trustees hold the ultimate fiduciary responsibility. They act separately from the employer and hold the assets in the trust for the beneficiaries of the scheme.

4. A is correct. The EU Taxonomy Regulation established a framework that states conditions for an economic activity to be considered environmentally sustainable.

5. A is correct. Insurance companies are asset owners; they have legal ownership of their assets and make asset allocation decisions.

6. C is correct. An ESG policy with a "comply and explain" approach suggests that the policy is mandatory and stronger ESG requirements apply to supervised entities. Hence, ESG integration is at a mature stage.

7. B is correct. The SRD was issued by the EU and requires investors to be active owners and to act with a more long-term focus.

8. C is correct. Studies and surveys have generally found that younger high-net-worth investors are most likely to review the ESG impact of their investment holdings, including 88% of millennials and 70% of Generation X.

9. C is correct. Financial regulators consider how ESG factors might impact the stability of economies and the financial markets and how these factors might influence the long-term risk–return profile of financial instruments.

10. A is correct. The report "Who Cares Wins" and the Freshfields Report formed the backbone for the launch of the PRI.

11. C is correct.

12. D is correct.

13. A is correct.

14. A is correct.

15. B is correct.

16. B is correct.

17. D is correct.

18. A is correct.

19. D is correct.

20. A is correct.

21. B is correct.
22. B is correct.
23. B is correct.
24. A is correct.
25. C is correct.

CHAPTER 3

Environmental Factors

LEARNING OUTCOMES

Mastery	The candidate should be able to:
☐	3.1.1 explain key concepts relating to climate change, including climate change mitigation, climate change adaptation, and resilience measures
☐	3.1.2 explain key concepts related to other environmental issues, including pressures on natural resources, including depletion of natural resources; water; biodiversity loss; land use and marine resources; pollution; waste; and a circular economy
☐	3.1.3 explain the systemic relationships between business activities and environmental issues, including systemic impact of climate risks on the financial system; climate-related physical and transition risks; the relationship between natural resources and business; supply, operational, and resource management issues; and supply chain transparency and traceability
☐	3.1.4 assess how megatrends influence environmental factors; environmental and climate policies; international climate and environmental agreements and conventions; international, regional, and country-level policy and initiatives; carbon pricing
☐	3.1.5 assess material impacts of environmental issues on potential investment opportunities, corporate and project finance, public finance initiatives, and asset management
☐	3.1.6 identify approaches to environmental analysis, including company-, project-, sector-, country-, and market-level analysis; environmental risks, including carbon footprinting and other carbon metrics; the natural capital approach; and climate scenario analysis
☐	3.1.7 apply material environmental factors to financial modeling, ratio analysis, and risk assessment
☐	3.1.8 explain how companies and the investment industry can benefit from opportunities relating to climate change and environmental issues: the circular economy, clean and technological innovation, green and ESG-related products, and the blue economy

1 INTRODUCTION

> 3.1.1 explain key concepts relating to climate change, including climate change mitigation, climate change adaptation, and resilience measures

The range of environmental factors that have a material financial impact on investments—the *E* in "ESG"—is broad and far reaching. Environmental risks have continued to gain prominence, generating heightened concern worldwide. The increased understanding of the mechanisms through which human actions impact the planet has led to growing public acceptance of the need to reduce pollution and global emissions of greenhouse gases, to preserve and improve biodiversity, and to use natural resources more efficiently. In addition to measures aimed at the *mitigation* of environmental impact, there is a growing need of *adaptation* to a changing environment, as advances in climate science have also cast light on processes that are already or may soon become irreversible: "The cumulative scientific evidence is unequivocal: Climate change is a threat to human well-being and planetary health. Any further delay in concerted anticipatory global action on adaptation and mitigation will miss a brief and rapidly closing window of opportunity to secure a liveable and sustainable future for all."[1]

Environmental decision making requires navigating both *factual* considerations (about what is likely to happen) and *normative* considerations (about what conditions of the world are desirable or acceptable). For investors, gaining an appreciation of the evolving policies, technologies, and consumer preferences regarding sustainability can support the pursuit of profitable investments and help prevent losses in investment value. Whether it is governments planning industrial policy, regulators deciding emissions accounting rules and securities regulation, executives setting out corporate strategy, or consumers weighing purchase options, we will illustrate in what follows how environmental factors are already affecting a wide and expanding share of behaviors, sectors, and institutions.

Other investors may see the support of projects and activities with a positive environmental impact as a standalone end, regardless of financial impact. More broadly, the nature of investment mandates, time horizons, ultimate beneficiaries, or personal values—all can play a role in defining the preferences of investors in terms of risk, return, and impact. Growing awareness of environmental and climate impacts is reflected in increasing levels and scope of corporate disclosure (e.g., the adoption of the recommendations of the Task Force on Climate-Related Financial Disclosures, or TCFD) and the introduction of policies (e.g., the European Green Deal) to accelerate sustainable finance.

This chapter identifies and describes some of the key environmental factors and major external drivers to help analysts, portfolio managers, and asset owners define investor beliefs and assess material environmental risks and opportunities in their portfolios.

The term *climate change* has come to mean the changes in the earth's systems that determine the climate, including the increase in heat-trapping gases in the atmosphere and the change in the reflectivity of some of the earth's surfaces. Climate change mitigation is the set of actions that reduce the added warming of the earth that is caused by human actions. Climate change adaptation is the set of actions taken to adapt

---

1 Intergovernmental Panel on Climate Change (IPCC), "Climate Change 2022: Impacts, Adaptation and Vulnerability: Summary for Policymakers" (2022).

human practices to function better in a warming world with rising seas and more frequent and intense droughts, precipitation, and storms. Climate resilience measures are adaptation actions that are able to function even though the climate is changing.

Economic activities from supplying fuels and raw materials to producing food are extractive in nature, usually leaving exploited planetary systems less capable of providing the next round of goods and services to meet society's and individuals' demands. For example, current metal ores often have less than one-tenth the concentration of metals as when these ores were first mined. This means that there is at least 10 times as much tailings, or crushed rock produced, and greater disturbance to the land. This increases the price of the metal being mined and increases pressure to find and exploit new sources. Increasing harvesting of trees for forest products is putting pressure on natural forest resources as harvest cycles are shortened to meet demand. As these resources are depleted, there is always a search for substitutes, but in many cases, as with water, there is no substitute. This is a growing problem, with increased water demand and decreased supply because of climate change–induced drought in the southwest and western parts of the United States, for example. Urban development is decreasing the amount of agricultural and forest land. Moreover, energy projects, including solar and wind farms, are resorting to taking over agricultural land and cutting down forests. This loss of important ecosystems has led to a dramatic decline in the number of species and the extinction of many species. A 2019 IPBES report predicted that 1 million species would go extinct by 2100.[2]

Our current economic system produces large amounts of waste, such as the vast amount of plastic waste that is making its way into oceans. All industrial processes release pollution, meaning unwanted harmful—sometimes toxic—chemicals, heat, or radiation. In the natural world, there is neither waste nor pollution. All materials not used by any organism become either building materials, food, or energy for a different organism. That is the idea behind the circular economy: It is an economy whereby all materials are used and reused multiple times—for example, turning waste paper into other forms of paper or into cellulose building insulation rather than burning it or putting it into a landfill.

KEY ENVIRONMENTAL ISSUES 2

☐ 3.1.2 explain key concepts related to other environmental issues, including pressures on natural resources, including depletion of natural resources; water; biodiversity loss; land use and marine resources; pollution; waste; and a circular economy

Economics and the environment are inextricably linked. Consider the similarities between one widely used definition of economics—the study of "the relationship between ends and scarce means which have alternative uses"[3]—and a widely used definition of environmental sustainability: seeking "to meet the needs and aspirations

---

2 IPBES, "Global Assessment Report on Biodiversity and Ecosystem Services of the Intergovernmental Science-Policy Platform on Biodiversity and Ecosystem Services," edited by E. S. Brondizio, J. Settele, S. Díaz, and H. T. Ngo (2019). https://ipbes.net/global-assessment.
3 L. Robbins, *An Essay on the Nature and Significance of Economic Science* (London: Macmillan, 1932): p. 15.

of the present without compromising the ability to meet those of the future."[4] The use and depletion of natural resources and the trade-offs between present costs and future benefits are topics that have been central to economics since its inception as a discipline.

Less appreciated, historically, has been the dependency of the successful conduct of economic activity on a stable, habitable planetary system. In recent decades, however, the scientific community has issued increasingly stark warnings that the consequences of economic activities—notably the burning of fossil fuels for energy, the conversion and degradation of ecosystems from resource extraction and land development, and other forms of pollution and environmental degradation—are jeopardizing the stability of what for over 10,000 years has been a relatively stable climate system, supportive of human society.[5] This instability could lead to dangerous, potentially catastrophic consequences for all life on earth.

The differing time horizons for the consequences of the range of human actions present a major challenge for policymakers and investors in this area. First, the *impacts* of environmental change unfold over different scales in time and space, from short-term, acute manifestations to longer-term, chronic patterns (e.g., the failure of a farmer's annual crop due to a flash flood compared to long-term reduced food productivity in an entire region due to the cumulative effects of erosion of fertile topsoil, drought, and a changing climate). Second, the *causes* of change also exhibit different dynamics. In some cases, the removal of a stressor removes the associated harm (e.g., if logging stops, a forest will likely regrow), but in other cases, the harm persists (e.g., if a factory stops emitting greenhouse gases, its past emissions continue to warm the atmosphere). Note that regrowing forests is a start, but it's mitigation, not a solution, until there is a forest capable of doing the same as the old growth forest; this can take 5–10 years or more. This is important to note in the context of carbon offsets.

The notion of "planetary boundaries" has been introduced as a way to highlight certain classes of risks and stressors. They describe boundaries to processes (such as global temperature and nitrogen limits, continued protection from damaging ultraviolet radiation provided by the stratospheric ozone layer, and biodiversity loss) that regulate the stability and resilience of the earth operating system, with concerns raised that certain economic activities are on track to breach the boundary or may have already done so. For example, it is estimated that human activities "now convert more atmospheric nitrogen into reactive forms than all of the earth's terrestrial processes combined." [6]

Beyond these boundaries lie domains of increased risk or uncertainty—including, at the extreme, planetary configurations never seen before in the history of our species. Yet, despite the growing sophistication and power of climate modeling, an element of irreducible uncertainty remains, stemming from the undetermined consequences of actions and policy measures not yet taken. One the one hand, investment techniques and practices developed to help investors navigate uncertainty (such as the assignment of probability to the costs and benefits of future scenarios, appropriately discounted) can be extended to certain areas of environmental decision making. On the other hand, the possibility of systematic, undiversifiable, and potentially catastrophic risks (as in some of the worst-case climate scenarios) highlights the importance of precautionary judgments that must be made in the absence of full evidence and perfect information.

---

4 United Nations, "Report of the World Commission on Environment and Development: Our Common Future" (1987). https://sustainabledevelopment.un.org/content/documents/5987our-common-future.pdf.
5 Most notably, the reports from the IPCC, an intergovernmental body of the United Nations.
6 Stockholm Resilience Centre, "Planetary Boundaries" (2017). www.stockholmresilience.org/research/planetary-boundaries.html.

Key Environmental Issues

"Better safe than sorry" and "no such thing as a free lunch" have both been used to illustrate aspects of rational decision making; the tension between the absolute and relative approaches to risk taking that they describe is also present for environmentally aware investing. What measures are worth enacting and financing (and at what cost), and what outcomes are worth avoiding (whatever the cost)? Such questions form the conceptual backdrop to much of this chapter.

Conversely, it has been suggested that bringing investment and economic activities back in line with planetary boundaries can not only help to address environmental risks but—through a more judicious and equitable use of natural resources—also protect and enhance important socioeconomic factors, such as employment and access to health.[7] Reconciling traditional notions of financial value with a more nuanced understanding of broader positive and negative impacts ("externalities") that are not easily quantifiable in monetary terms represents an area of ongoing innovation—not just in finance but also in policy and law. To choose a few examples that will be discussed in this chapter, the trade in such securities as carbon allowances uses market mechanisms as an incentive for companies to reduce their *future* pollution; the development of "natural capital" approaches aims to recognize the *present* value of ecosystems as a guide to policy making; and a growing wave of lawsuits seeks compensation for *past* contributions to environmental damages.

According to an update by the Stockholm Resilience Centre from 2022, six of nine planetary boundaries (see Exhibit 1) have already been crossed as a result of human activity:

- ▶ climate change,
- ▶ loss of biosphere integrity,
- ▶ land-system change,
- ▶ freshwater (green water boundary),
- ▶ novel entities (including plastic pollution), and
- ▶ altered biogeochemical cycles (phosphorus and nitrogen loading).[8]

---

7 K. Raworth, "Meet the Doughnut: The New Economic Model That Could Help End Inequality," World Economic Forum (28 April 2017). www.weforum.org/agenda/2017/04/the-new-economic-model-that-could-end-inequality-doughnut/.
8 Stockholm Resilience Centre, "Planetary Boundaries."

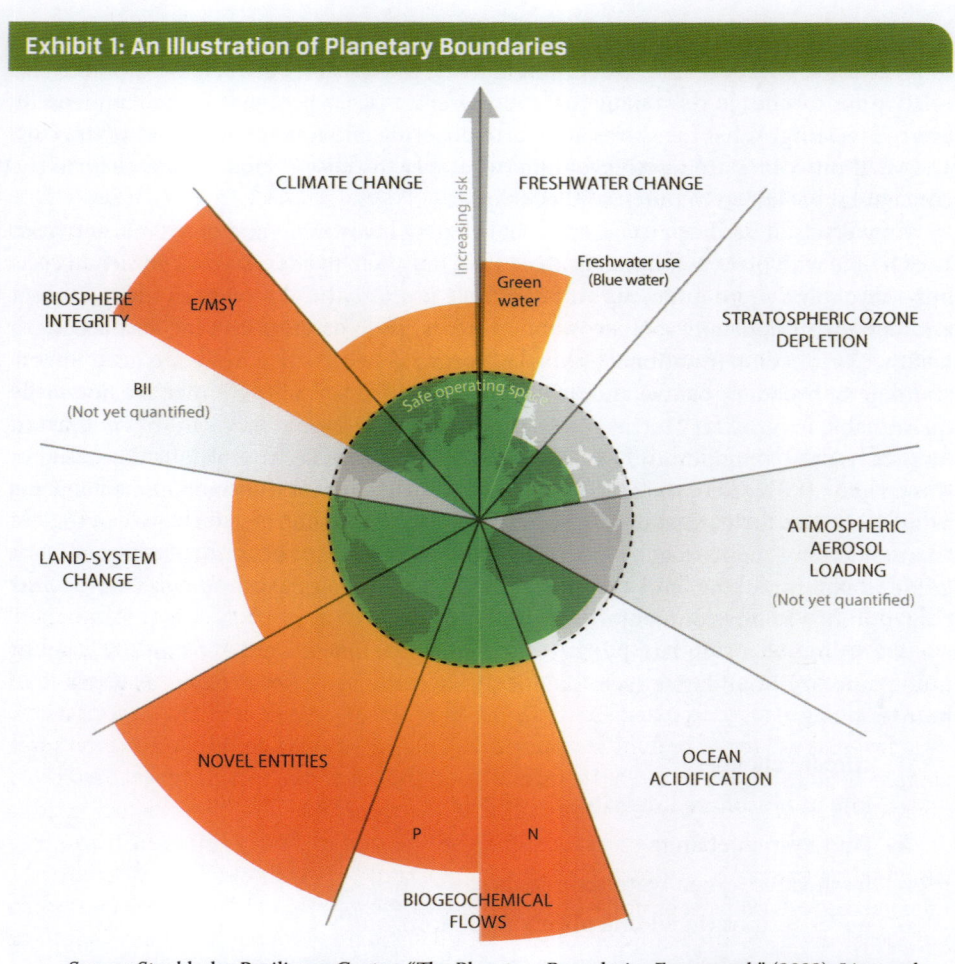

Exhibit 1: An Illustration of Planetary Boundaries

Source: Stockholm Resilience Centre, "The Planetary Boundaries Framework" (2022). Licensed under CC BY 4.0 Credit: "Azote for Stockholm Resilience Centre, based on analysis in Persson et al 2022 and Steffen et al 2015". https://www.stockholmresilience.org/research/planetary-boundaries.html

---

While it may be seen as a good in itself, the pursuit of environmental sustainability can also be justified because it benefits financial interests. Conversely, as societal preferences, regulation, and technology change, ongoing investments in environmentally damaging activities may carry unrewarded risks, which can lead to losses in revenues and falling asset values.

There are numerous studies and frameworks that identify a range of environmental factors that are relevant to how investors assess risks and opportunities in their decisions. This field of study is vast and constantly evolving.

In this section, the environmental issues covered will include

A. climate change,

B. pressures on natural resources and systems (including water, biodiversity, land use and forestry, and marine resources), and

C. pollution, waste, and a circular economy.

Although this section will cover each issue separately, it is important to note that these issues are linked and have systemic consequences for business activities and vice versa, as we will further explain.

Climate Change

Climate change is defined as a change of climate, directly or indirectly attributed to human activity, that alters the composition of the global atmosphere and that is, in addition to natural climate variability, observed over comparable time periods.[9] Climate change is one of the most complex issues facing us today and involves many different dimensions, including

- science,
- economics,
- society,
- politics, and
- moral and ethical questions.

It is an issue with local manifestations (e.g., extreme weather events, such as more frequent and/or more intense tropical cyclones) and global impacts (e.g., rising global average temperatures and sea levels), which are estimated to increase in severity over time. Because the planet does not warm uniformly—the Arctic is warming more than three times faster than the global average[10]—atmospheric and ocean circulation patterns are being altered in complex and not fully understood ways.

The main man-made driver of the warming of the planet is rising emissions of heat-trapping **greenhouse gases (GHGs)**. These gases are dispersed throughout the atmosphere and allow visible sunlight to reach the earth's surface, where it is absorbed, thereby warming the land, oceans, and atmosphere and evaporating water. And the warm earth radiates heat back toward space, but these gases absorb heat and reradiate some of it back to the earth's surface. The gases act in a similar manner to the glass windows of an automobile that allow visible light energy in but block the radiant heat from leaving. Few people have experienced this effect in a glass "greenhouse," which gives the extra heating its name, and today it is more descriptively referred to as the "hot car effect." Carbon dioxide (CO_2) is the most significant contributor to the warming effect, because of its higher concentration in the atmosphere, which is at levels not seen since long before Homo sapiens first appeared (see Exhibit 2).[11]

---

[9] Definition of climate change by the United Nations Framework Convention on Climate Change (UNFCCC).
[10] Arctic Monitoring and Assessment Programme, "Arctic Climate Change Update 2021: Key Trends and Impacts: Summary for Policy-Makers" (2021). www.amap.no/documents/download/6759/inline.
[11] NOAA, "Climate Change: Atmospheric Carbon Dioxide" (2020). www.climate.gov/news-features/understanding-climate/climate-change-atmospheric-carbon-dioxide.

Exhibit 2: CO₂ Levels in the Atmosphere for Past 800,000 Years

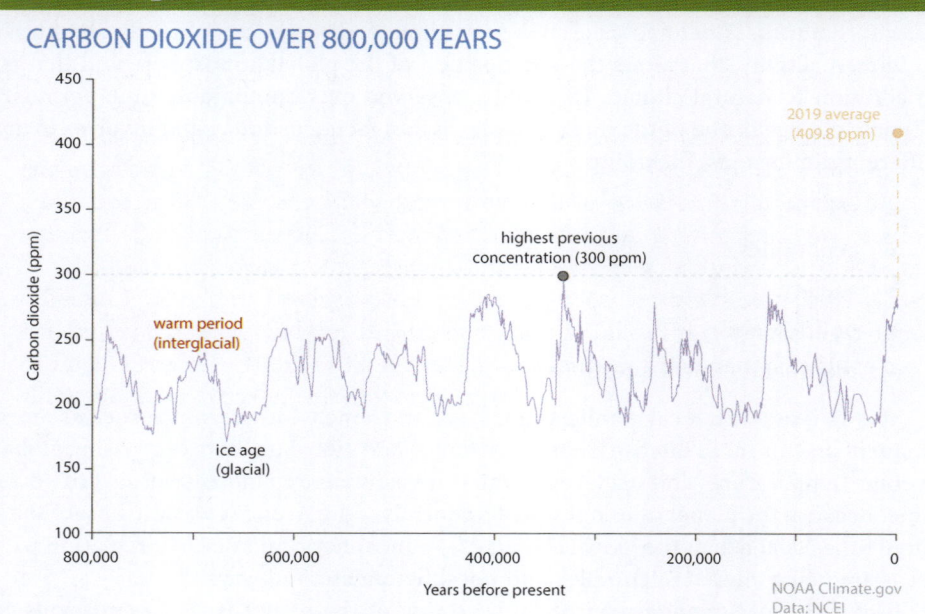

CARBON DIOXIDE OVER 800,000 YEARS

Source: NOAA, "Climate Change: Atmospheric Carbon Dioxide" (2020).

Much of this increase has occurred with the accelerated burning of fossil fuels since the industrial revolution, with more than half the CO_2 emissions from the late 17th century onward occurring in the last 30 years.[12]

Other important GHGs include methane, nitrous oxide, and other fluorinated gases. Although the average lifetime in the atmosphere of such gases is shorter than that of carbon dioxide, they have a much higher "global warming potential"—30 times stronger in the case of methane and over 23,000 times stronger for sulphur hexafluoride—that is the same weight of carbon dioxide when compared over a century.[13]

Emissions of GHGs primarily come from energy, industry, transport, agriculture and changes in land use (such as deforestation and the degradation of forests, grasslands, wetlands, and agricultural soils), with CO_2 resulting from the burning of fossil fuels (e.g., in power plants, gas boilers and vehicles) representing the highest share—around two-thirds—of all GHGs (see Exhibit 3).[14]

---

[12] Institute for European Environmental Policy, "More Than Half of All CO_2 Emissions since 1751 Emitted in the Last 30 Years" (29 April 2020). https://ieep.eu/news/more-than-half-of-all-co2-emissions-since-1751-emitted-in-the-last-30-years.

[13] United States Environmental Protection Agency, "Climate Change Indicators: Greenhouse Gases" (2021). www.epa.gov/climate-indicators/greenhouse-gases.

[14] UN Environment Programme (UNEP), "Cut Global Emissions by 7.6 Percent Every Year for Next Decade to Meet 1.5°C Paris Target—UN Report," press release (26 November 2019). www.unep.org/news-and-stories/press-release/cut-global-emissions-76-percent-every-year-next-decade-meet-15degc.

Key Environmental Issues

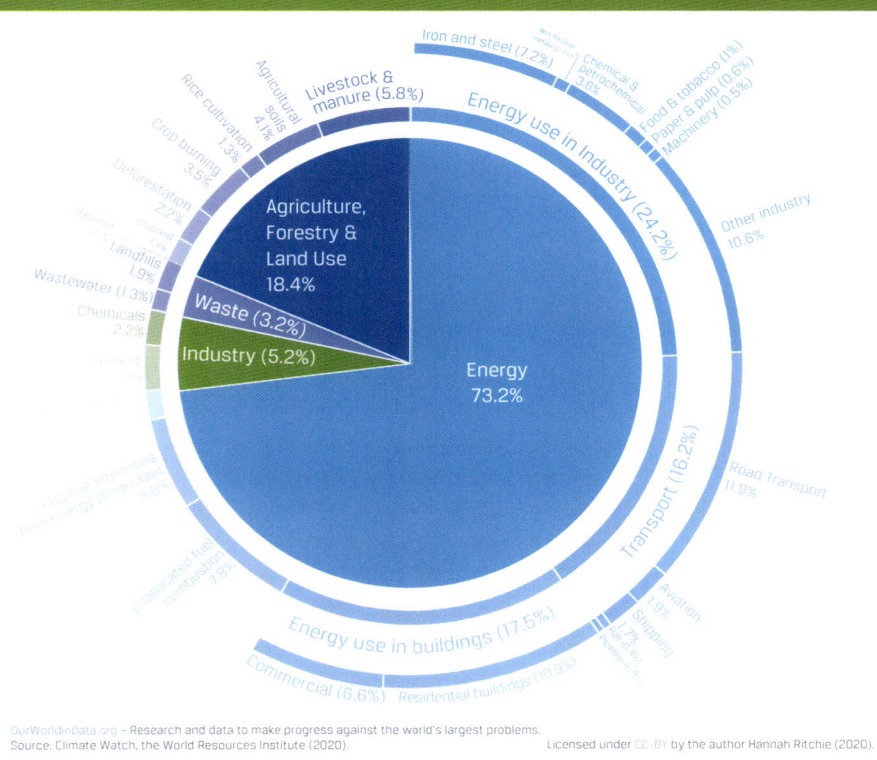

Exhibit 3: Global GHG Emissions by Economic Sector

Note: This is shown for the year 2016 — global greenhouse gas emissions were 49.4 billion tonnes CO$_2$eq.

Sources: Data from World Resources Institute; H. Ritchie and M. Roser, "Emissions by Sector" (2020). https://ourworldindata.org/emissions-by-sector#total-greenhouse-gas-emissions-by-sector.

Limiting global warming has been compared with avoiding overfilling a bathtub by simultaneously turning off the faucets and opening the drain—in other words, reducing both the **flow** of new emissions and removing the **stock** of existing GHGs in the atmosphere. When these rates of addition and removal are equal, the level stabilizes. In the case of the atmosphere, our activities are adding carbon dioxide and other GHGs, and it is the natural world that is removing carbon dioxide. However, it is the amount of GHGs remaining in the atmosphere that determines the extent of warming. To achieve the desired global average temperature requires adjusting atmospheric concentrations to specified levels.[15] That point is often overlooked when government and business leaders agree to become "zero net carbon by 2050." Preindustrial levels of atmospheric CO$_2$ were 278 ppm (parts per million) in the atmosphere, and along with other naturally occurring greenhouse gases, including water vapor and methane, these levels maintained a stable climate conducive to agriculture and the development of urban civilizations as we know them. In 2022, CO$_2$ levels had climbed to 417 ppm—an increase of 50%![16]

---

15 UN Framework Convention on Climate Change, "Article 2: Objective" (1992). https://unfccc.int/resource/ccsites/zimbab/conven/text/art02.htm.
16 R. Betts, "Met Office: Atmospheric CO$_2$ Now Hitting 50% Higher than Pre-Industrial Levels" (16 March 2021). www.carbonbrief.org/met-office-atmospheric-co2-now-hitting-50-higher-than-pre-industrial-levels/.

To achieve any specified temperature rise limitation, there is an additional complication. As the world warms from direct GHG additions, amplifying feedbacks cause additional warming from nature. A warming ocean adds more water vapor, thawing permafrost releases more methane—melting sea ice, ice caps in Greenland and Antarctica, and glaciers everywhere—and less snow cover reduces the amount of sunlight that is reflected back into space. Hence, the warming earth causes natural processes to create additional warming.

One concerning possibility is that these feedbacks might place the world on course to breach certain "tipping points." Like a sand pile toppling when just a few more grains are added, this notion is used to describe abrupt—and potentially irreversible—changes to the earth system in response to a relatively small change in warming.

Such potential tipping points include the following:

- The thawing of the permafrost—frozen ground in the Northern Hemisphere—which allows microbes to decompose previously frozen plant and animal material and release vast amounts of carbon dioxide and methane, thereby further accelerating climate change uncontrollably. This is similar to what happens when electric power is interrupted: Frozen foods thaw and are quickly decomposed by bacteria.
- The disintegration of the West Antarctic ice sheet, which holds enough ice to raise global sea levels by over three meters.
- The "dieback" of the Amazon rainforest—changes in temperature and deforestation that would render the forest unable to sustain itself, making one of the world's largest natural stores of carbon emit more carbon than it absorbs.
- Melting the Greenland ice cap, thereby reducing the salinity and density of North Atlantic waters, which could shut down the system of currents in the Atlantic Ocean that brings warm water and the air over it to Northern Europe. The ironic cooling of this region while the world is warming may lead to "widespread cessation of arable farming" in the United Kingdom and parts of Europe.[17]

Exhibit 4 illustrates some of the socioeconomic impacts resulting from climate change.

---

17 R. McSweeney, "Explainer: Nine 'Tipping Points' That Could Be Triggered by Climate Change," Carbon Brief (10 February 2020). www.carbonbrief.org/explainer-nine-tipping-points-that-could-be-triggered-by-climate-change.

Key Environmental Issues

Exhibit 4: Select Socioeconomic Impacts of Climate Change

Impacted Economic System	Area of Direct Risk	Socioeconomic Impact	How Climate Change Exacerbated Hazard
Liveability and Workability	2003 European heat wave	US$15 billion (£12 bn) in losses	2 × more likely
	2010 Russian heat wave	≈55,000 deaths attributable	3 × more likely
	2013–14 Australian heat wave	≈US$6 bn (£4.8 bn) in productivity loss	Up to 3 × more likely
	2017 East African drought	≈800,000 people displaced in Somalia	2 × more likely
	2019 European heat wave	≈1,500 deaths in France	≈10 × more likely
Food Systems	2015 Southern African drought	Agriculture outputs declined by 15%	3 × more likely
	Ocean warming	Up to 35% decline in North Atlantic fish yields	Ocean surface temperatures have risen by 0.7°C (1.3°F) globally
Physical Assets	2012 Hurricane Sandy	US$62 bn (£49.5 bn) in damage	3 × more likely
	2016 Fort McMurray Fire, Canada	US$10 bn (£8 bn) in damage, 1.5 million acres of forest burned	1.5–6 × more likely
	2017 Hurricane Harvey	US$125 bn (£99.8 bn) in damage	8%–20% more intense
Infrastructure Services	2017 flooding in China	US$3.55 bn (£2.8 bn) of direct economic loss, including severe infrastructure damage	2 × more likely
Natural Capital	30-year record low Arctic sea ice in 2012	Reduced albedo effect, amplifying warming	70%–95% attributable to human-induced climate change
	Decline of Himalayan glaciers	Potential reduction in water supply for more than 240 million people	70% of global glacier mass lost in past 20 years is due to human-induced climate change

Sources: Woods Hole Research Center (now Woodwell Climate Research Center); analysis by Jonathan Woetzel, Dickon Pinner, Hamid Samandari, Hauke Engel, Mekala Krishnan, Brodie Boland, and Carter Powis, "Climate Risk and Response: Physical Hazards and Socioeconomic Impacts," McKinsey Global Institute (16 January 2020). www.mckinsey.com/business-functions/sustainability/our-insights/climate-risk-and-response-physical-hazards-and-socioeconomic-impacts?sid=3046547320.

In 2021, the Intergovernmental Panel on Climate Change (IPCC) estimated that human activities have caused approximately 1.1°C (1.8°F) of global warming above pre-industrial levels, and global warming is likely to reach 1.5°C (2.7°F) by 2040 even under the very low emissions scenario.[18] Note that these numbers are global averages, so warming in different regions may be much higher: Warming over land has been twice that observed over oceans, for example.[19] The IPCC is mandated by 196 governments to synthesize climate science and publish reports. A 2018 report determined what needed to be done to meet the somewhat arbitrary goals set in Paris in 2015 and agreed to by all governments of limiting global warming–caused average temperature increases by 2.0°C by 2100 and to make every effort to limit the rise to 1.5°C. The IPCC's Sixth Assessment Report on the physical science of climate change, published in August 2021, was dubbed "code red for humanity" because of the irrevocable evidence that climate change is already having significant impacts and the 1.5°C goal will not be met without immediate and significant action. Specifically, scientists ran multiple scenarios and found that

> *under the five illustrative scenarios, in the near term (2021–2040), the 1.5°C global warming level is very likely to be exceeded under the very high GHG emissions scenario (SSP5-8.5), likely to be exceeded under the intermediate and high GHG emissions scenarios (SSP2-4.5 and SSP3-7.0), more likely than not to be exceeded under the low GHG emissions scenario (SSP1-2.6) and more likely than not to be reached under the very low GHG emissions scenario (SSP1-1.9).*[20]

These differences of a few fractions of a degree may seem small but are highly consequential. The IPCC further estimated that limiting warming to 1.5°C (2.7°F) instead of 2°C (3.6°F) by the end of this century could reduce "climate-related risks to health, livelihoods, food security, water supply, human security and economic growth": around 400 million fewer people frequently exposed to extreme heatwaves and around 10 million fewer people exposed to rising sea levels, in addition to reduced impacts on vulnerable ecosystems, such as the Arctic and warm water coral reefs (which "mostly disappear" at 2°C [3.6°F]).[21] See Exhibit 5 for various potential climate change impacts based on different warming scenarios.

---

18 IPCC, "Climate Change 2021: The Physical Science Basis: Summary for Policymakers" (2021): p. 15. www.ipcc.ch/report/ar6/wg1/downloads/report/IPCC_AR6_WGI_SPM_final.pdf.
19 M. Byrne, "Guest Post: Why Does Land Warm Up Faster Than the Oceans?" Carbon Brief (1 September 2020). www.carbonbrief.org/guest-post-why-does-land-warm-up-faster-than-the-oceans.
20 IPCC, "Climate Change 2021: The Physical Science Basis" (6 August 2021). www.ipcc.ch/report/sixth-assessment-report-working-group-i/.
21 IPCC, "Special Report: Global Warming of 1.5°C" (2018). www.ipcc.ch/report/sr15.

Key Environmental Issues

Exhibit 5: Selected Impacts of Climate Change under Different Warming Scenarios

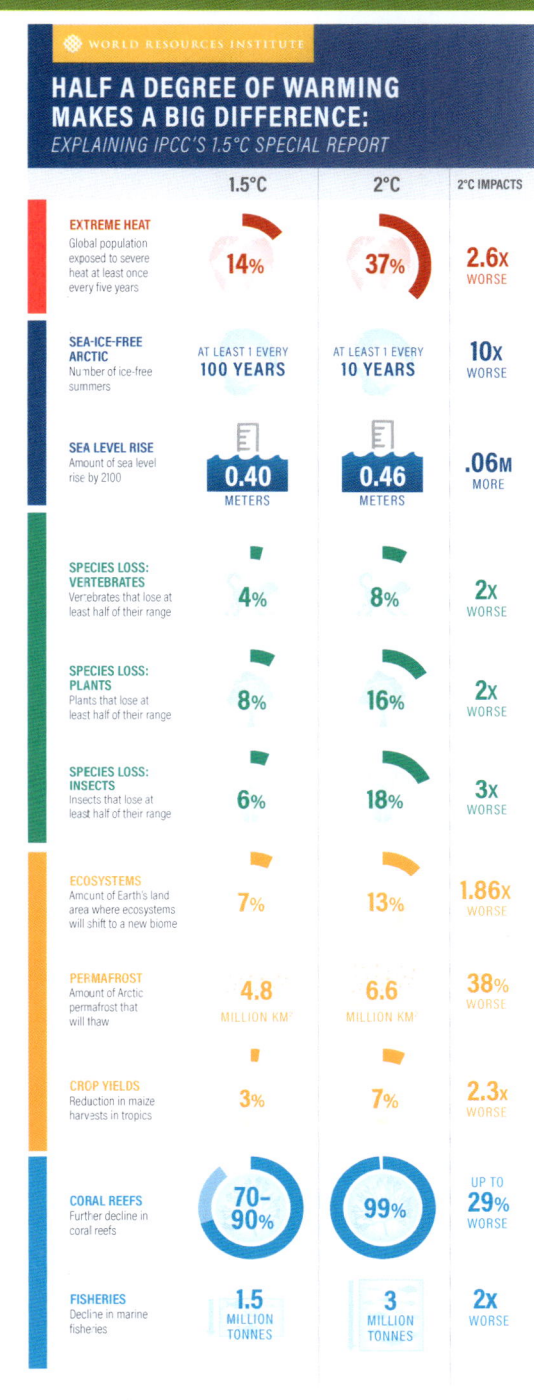

WORLD RESOURCES INSTITUTE

HALF A DEGREE OF WARMING MAKES A BIG DIFFERENCE:
EXPLAINING IPCC'S 1.5°C SPECIAL REPORT

	1.5°C	2°C	2°C IMPACTS
EXTREME HEAT Global population exposed to severe heat at least once every five years	14%	37%	2.6x WORSE
SEA-ICE-FREE ARCTIC Number of ice-free summers	AT LEAST 1 EVERY 100 YEARS	AT LEAST 1 EVERY 10 YEARS	10x WORSE
SEA LEVEL RISE Amount of sea level rise by 2100	0.40 METERS	0.46 METERS	.06M MORE
SPECIES LOSS: VERTEBRATES Vertebrates that lose at least half of their range	4%	8%	2x WORSE
SPECIES LOSS: PLANTS Plants that lose at least half of their range	8%	16%	2x WORSE
SPECIES LOSS: INSECTS Insects that lose at least half of their range	6%	18%	3x WORSE
ECOSYSTEMS Amount of Earth's land area where ecosystems will shift to a new biome	7%	13%	1.86x WORSE
PERMAFROST Amount of Arctic permafrost that will thaw	4.8 MILLION KM²	6.6 MILLION KM²	38% WORSE
CROP YIELDS Reduction in maize harvests in tropics	3%	7%	2.3x WORSE
CORAL REEFS Further decline in coral reefs	70–90%	99%	UP TO 29% WORSE
FISHERIES Decline in marine fisheries	1.5 MILLION TONNES	3 MILLION TONNES	2x WORSE

Source: Kelly Levin, Sophie Boehm, and Rebecca Carter, "6 Big Findings from the IPCC 2022 Report on Climate Impacts, Adaptation and Vulnerability," World Resources Institute (27 February 2022). www.wri.org/insights/ipcc-report-2022-climate-impacts-adaptation-vulnerability.

Estimates of the economic costs of climate change vary but suggest significant potential losses. A 2015 report suggested damages by 2100 equivalent to US$4 trillion (£2.9 trillion) in net present value,[22] and the IPCC has suggested costs of US$54 trillion (£38.8 trillion) and US$69 trillion (£49.6 trillion) for 1.5°C (2.7°F) and 2°C (3.6°F) scenarios, respectively.[23]

There are, however, important caveats when considering such results, which are highly dependent on assumptions and scenarios. First, under the standard economic practice of discounting, cash flows far into the future have very little present value. This perspective, however, may be under-representing the risks of potentially catastrophic outcomes that could severely affect economies and countless human lives. This argument has been put forth by climate economist Martin Weitzman, with his so-called **dismal theorem**, which suggests that standard cost–benefit analysis is inadequate to deal with the potential downside losses from climate change. However small their probability, as long as we cannot completely rule out scenarios of climate-induced civilizational collapse, their expected value must be properly understood as being equivalent to negative infinity, he has argued.[24]

On a different but related note, economist Nicholas Stern has argued that moral considerations warrant the use of a low discount rate when assessing future climate damages, in order to place adequate value on the lives and welfare of future generations.[25] The thrust of Stern's and Weitzman's arguments is that the issue of how much society should invest today in order to safeguard a livable climate in the future requires a different—mathematical and ethical—treatment from standard economic problems, such as, "Would you prefer to receive £10 today or £100 in one year?"

Second, many economic models used to calculate future climate damages usually share the limitation of assuming negative impacts that ramp up only gradually, and usually do not model sharp discontinuities and "tipping points." In other words, they model a society that "keeps warm and carries on," even though some of these scenarios approach the limits of adaptability and habitability.

For example, one widely used model estimates that 6°C (16.2°F) of warming would result in a sacrifice of only about 9% of global income by the end of the century.[26] However, it has been suggested that at global average warming of around 7°C (12.6°F), regions of the world would see persistent combinations of temperature and humidity where the average healthy adult overheats and dies after a few hours (even if they sit in the shade, are resting, and have access to water) because the human body can no longer cool itself through perspiration and breaks down.[27] (This "wet-bulb" temperature threshold has already been momentarily crossed on several occasions in South Asian

---

[22] B. Gardner, "The Cost of Inaction," Economist Intelligence Unit (24 July 2015). https://eiuperspectives.economist.com/sustainability/cost-inaction.
[23] IPCC, "Special Report: Global Warming of 1.5°C."
[24] M. L. Weitzman, "Fat-Tailed Uncertainty in the Economics of Catastrophic Climate Change" *Review of Environmental Economics and Policy* 5 (Summer 2011): 275–92. https://scholar.harvard.edu/files/weitzman/files/fattaileduncertaintyeconomics.pdf.
For a critical reply, see W. D. Nordhaus, "The Economics of Tail Events with an Application to Climate Change," *Review of Environmental Economics and Policy* 5 (Summer 2011): 240–57. www.journals.uchicago.edu/doi/10.1093/reep/rer004.
[25] N. H. Stern, *The Economics of Climate Change: The Stern Review* (Cambridge, UK: Cambridge University Press, 2006).
[26] B. Ward, "A Nobel Prize for the Creator of an Economic Model That Underestimates the Risks of Climate Change," Grantham Research Institute (2 January 2019). www.lse.ac.uk/granthaminstitute/news/a-nobel-prize-for-the-creator-of-an-economic-model-that-underestimates-the-risks-of-climate-change/.
[27] S. C. Sherwood and M. Huber, "An Adaptability Limit to Climate Change Due to Heat Stress," *Proceedings of the National Academy of Sciences* 107 (3 May 2010). www.pnas.org/content/107/21/9552.

Key Environmental Issues

cities.[28]) Almost inevitably, models are calibrated based on past economic outcomes, but this presents a potential tension when dealing with what may be radically different future outcomes.

Responding to climate change is usually presented in terms of two main approaches:

1. reducing and stabilizing the levels of heat-trapping GHGs in the atmosphere (**climate change mitigation**) or
2. adapting to the climate change already taking place (**climate change adaptation**) and increasing climate change resilience.

However, this is not a binary option: Climate change adaptation will always be required because we are already experiencing the effects of climate change, and some of the most effective climate policies pursue both objectives simultaneously. We will look at climate change mitigation and adaptation in the following subsections.

Climate Change Mitigation

Climate change mitigation is a human intervention that involves reducing the sources of GHG emissions (for example, the burning of fossil fuels and wood for electricity, heat, or transport) and simultaneously enhancing the sinks that store these gases (such as forests, oceans, and soil) in an attempt to slow down the process of climate change. The goal of mitigation is to

- "avoid dangerous interference with the climate system,"[29]
- stabilize GHG levels in a time frame sufficient to allow ecosystems to adapt naturally to climate change,
- ensure that food production is not threatened, and
- enable economic development to proceed in a sustainable manner.

While discussions of climate change policy usually call for adaptation to the warming that is irreversible, the overarching framing is usually that of mitigation—that is, trying to prevent what is not inevitable. The aim of the international Paris Agreement on climate change, for example, is to hold "the increase in the global average temperature to well below 2°C (3.6°F) above pre-industrial levels and pursuing efforts to limit the temperature increase to 1.5°C (2.7°F) above pre-industrial levels" by the end of the century.[30]

Examples of mitigation strategies include greater adoption and policies to promote sustainability across different areas, such as the following:

- **Energy.** Deploying renewable energy sources (such as wind, solar, geothermal, hydro, and some biofuels that are shown to be low carbon and produced sustainably). Unfortunately, not all biofuels are better than petroleum alternatives when life-cycle emissions, including nitrous oxide from fertilizing crops, and other production emissions are considered.[31] Burning wood

---

[28] "Explained: How Jacobabad in Pakistan crossed a temperature threshold too severe for human tolerance," *Indian Express* (8 July 2021). https://indianexpress.com/article/explained/explained-pakistan-jacobabad-crossed-a-temperature-threshold-too-severe-for-human-tolerance-7383104/.
[29] UN Framework Convention on Climate Change, "Article 2: Objective."
[30] United Nations, "Paris Agreement" (2015). https://unfccc.int/sites/default/files/english_paris_agreement.pdf.
[31] Harish K. Jeswani, Andrew Chilvers, and Adisa Azapagic, "Environmental Sustainability of Biofuels: A Review," *Proceedings of the Royal Society A: Mathematical, Physical and Engineering Sciences* 476 (November 2020). https://doi.org/10.1098/rspa.2020.0351.

to generate electricity or commercial-scale heat releases more CO_2 at the time of combustion and forgoes accumulation of carbon had the trees been allowed to continue growing.[32]

- **Buildings.** Retrofitting buildings to become more energy efficient and using building materials and equipment that reduce buildings' **carbon footprint**.
- **Transport.** Adopting more sustainable, low-carbon transportation and infrastructure (such as electric vehicles, rail and metro, and bus rapid transit), particularly in cities, but also decarbonizing shipping, road, and air transport.
- **Land use and forestry.** Improving forest management, reducing deforestation, and growing more of our existing forests to achieve their potential for biodiversity and carbon accumulation—a management process known as *proforestation*.[33]
- **Agriculture.** Improving crop and grazing land management to increase soil carbon storage.
- **Carbon pricing and other economic measures.** Implementing carbon reduction policies that penalize heavy emitters and promote GHG emission reductions in the form of either a carbon tax or cap-and-trade mechanism and direct payment for carbon accumulation by forests and soils.
- **Industry and manufacturing.** Developing more energy efficient processes and less carbon intensive products; reducing process emissions from cement and steel making and other greenhouse gases, including methane leaks from the fossil fuel industry and agriculture; and developing equipment and processes to facilitate carbon capture, energy storage (e.g., batteries, pump systems), recycling efficiency, and so on.

Industry, materials and manufacturing present particular challenges. Although deindustrialization or a reduction in consumption could, in theory, have mitigation effects (consider the significant drop in GHG emissions and in economic output accompanying the COVID-19 pandemic), due consideration must also be given to the associated negative societal impacts (e.g., recessions and unemployment). Alternatively, achieving green industrialization at scale (including the decommissioning and retrofitting of existing facilities) may, unless addressed through improved resource efficiency and circular design, be a *reforestation material-intensive process.*

The IPCC has noted the relatively uneven state of play with regard to technological innovation in several relevant areas:

For almost all basic materials—primary metals, building materials and chemicals—many low- to zero-GHG intensity production processes are at the pilot to near-commercial and in some cases commercial stage but not yet established industrial practice. Introducing new sustainable basic materials production processes could increase production costs but, given the small fraction of consumer cost based on materials, are expected to translate into minimal cost increases for final consumers. Hydrogen direct reduction for primary steelmaking is near-commercial in some regions. Until new chemistries are mastered, deep reduction of cement process emissions will rely on already commercialised cement material substitution and the

---

[32] John Sterman, William Moomaw, Juliette N. Rooney-Varga, and Lori Siegel, "Does Burning Wood Help or Harm the Climate?" *Bulletin of the Atomic Scientists* (10 May 2022). https://thebulletin.org/premium/2022-05/does-wood-bioenergy-help-or-harm-the-climate/.

[33] William R. Moomaw, Susan A. Masino, and Edward K. Faison, "Intact Forests in the United States: Proforestation Mitigates Climate Change and Serves the Greatest Good," *Frontiers in Forests and Global Change* (11 June 2019). www.frontiersin.org/articles/10.3389/ffgc.2019.00027/full.

availability of [carbon capture and storage]. Reducing emissions from the production and use of chemicals would need to rely on a life-cycle approach, including increased plastics recycling, fuel and feedstock switching, and carbon sourced through biogenic sources, and, depending on availability, [carbon capture and utilization], direct air CO_2 capture, as well as [carbon capture and storage]. Light industry, mining and manufacturing have the potential to be decarbonised through available abatement technologies (e.g., material efficiency, circularity), electrification (e.g., electrothermal heating, heat pumps) and low- or zero-GHG emitting fuels (e.g., hydrogen, ammonia, and bio-based & other synthetic fuels).[34]

CASE STUDIES

The Race to Net Zero

Stabilizing global average temperature rise at any level depends on achieving a balance between GHG sources going into and out of the atmosphere—that is, reaching "net-zero" emissions. The earlier this point is reached, the less warming the world is likely to experience. The current "net-zero GHG emissions" strategy endorsed by many governments and CEOs is intended to meet the Paris Agreement goal of keeping temperature from rising by more than 1.5°C.

The world's foremost assembly of climate scientists—the IPCC—found that to have a two in three chance of limiting global average temperature rises to 1.5°C (2.7°F) requires reducing emissions 45% below 2005 levels by 2030, net-zero CO_2 emissions around 2050, and continued net negative emissions until beyond 2100, coupled with deep reductions in emissions of other GHGs, such as methane.[35]

Net-zero targets are increasingly being adopted by governments (e.g., those of the United Kingdom, the EU, China, Japan, Canada, and South Korea), states and territories (e.g., Nevada in the United States and Victoria and Queensland in Australia), and companies (e.g., Amazon, ArcelorMittal, BT Group, BP, Ikea, Qantas, Sony, and Walmart).

As of April 2022, 88% of global emissions of greenhouse gases, 90% of GDP, and 85% of the world's population were in jurisdictions covered by net-zero targets.[36] These 2050 targets have also been adopted by many corporations.

Modeled net-zero pathways can therefore differ significantly in their emissions profile—with the role of interim targets (2025, 2030) and the assumed reliance on carbon capture and/or offsets (e.g., in emissions-intensive companies' net-zero commitments) coming under increased scrutiny. Many offsets simply transfer credit for emission reductions and do not change the amount of CO_2 in the atmosphere.

The higher the ambition of mitigation policies, the higher the required upfront investment. The IPCC has estimated that in the energy sector alone, between US$1 trillion and US$4 trillion (£0.7 trillion to £2.9 trillion) of additional annual investment in energy supply and around US$1 trillion (£0.7 trillion) in energy demand will be

---

34 IPCC, "Climate Change 2022: Mitigation of Climate Change: Summary for Policymakers" (2022). https://report.ipcc.ch/ar6wg3/pdf/IPCC_AR6_WGIII_SummaryForPolicymakers.pdf.
35 Note that this assumes the world will not significantly rely on what are currently speculative, expensive carbon capture technologies. It is technically possible to construct other temperature pathways, depending on modelling assumptions – the scale up of carbon capture, and the potential for reductions in non-CO_2 GHG emissions globally. However, given the risks of "tipping points" discussed in the previous section, caution is needed when considering the extent to which ongoing emissions will be compensated by future technological fixes.
36 Net Zero Tracker (2022). https://zerotracker.net/.

needed up to 2050 to limit warming to 1.5°C (2.7°F).[37] However, the IPCC has further noted that "how these investment needs compare to those in a policy baseline scenario is uncertain."[38] In other words, even scenarios without climate mitigation require investments—for example, in oil and gas extraction and transportation or in coal and gas power plants—and it is unclear how those costs may evolve alongside temperatures. For example, around half of the oil and gas fields in the Russian Arctic are estimated to be in areas where melting permafrost can cause severe damage to infrastructure, such as pipelines and shipping terminals;[39] in mid-2020, such melting under a diesel storage tank caused the largest environmental accident in the Russian Arctic region.[40] Given that the world is already investing approximately US$1 trillion (£0.7 trillion) yearly in the energy sector,[41] the important question is, What kind of energy system is being financed for new and expired capital replacement, and what is the extent to which today's investments risk locking in future emissions?

Looking more broadly across sectors, the IPCC has highlighted that many mitigation options exist today, many of which have lower economic costs compared to alternatives (see Exhibit 6).

---

37 IPCC, "Special Report: Global Warming of 1.5°C."
38 IPCC, "Special Report: Global Warming of 1.5°C."
39 Jan Hjort, Olli Karjalainen, Juha Aalto, Sebastian Westermann, Vladimir E. Romanovsky, Frederick E. Nelson, Bernd Etzelmüller, and Miska Luoto, "Degrading Permafrost Puts Arctic Infrastructure at Risk by Mid-Century," *Nature Communications* 9 (2018). www.nature.com/articles/s41467-018-07557-4.
40 BBC, "Russian Arctic Oil Spill Pollutes Big Lake Near Norilsk" (9 June 2020). www.bbc.co.uk/news/world-europe-52977740.
41 International Energy Agency, "Investment Estimates for 2020 Continue to Point to a Record Slump in Spending" (23 October 2020). www.iea.org/articles/investment-estimates-for-2020-continue-to-point-to-a-record-slump-in-spending.

Key Environmental Issues

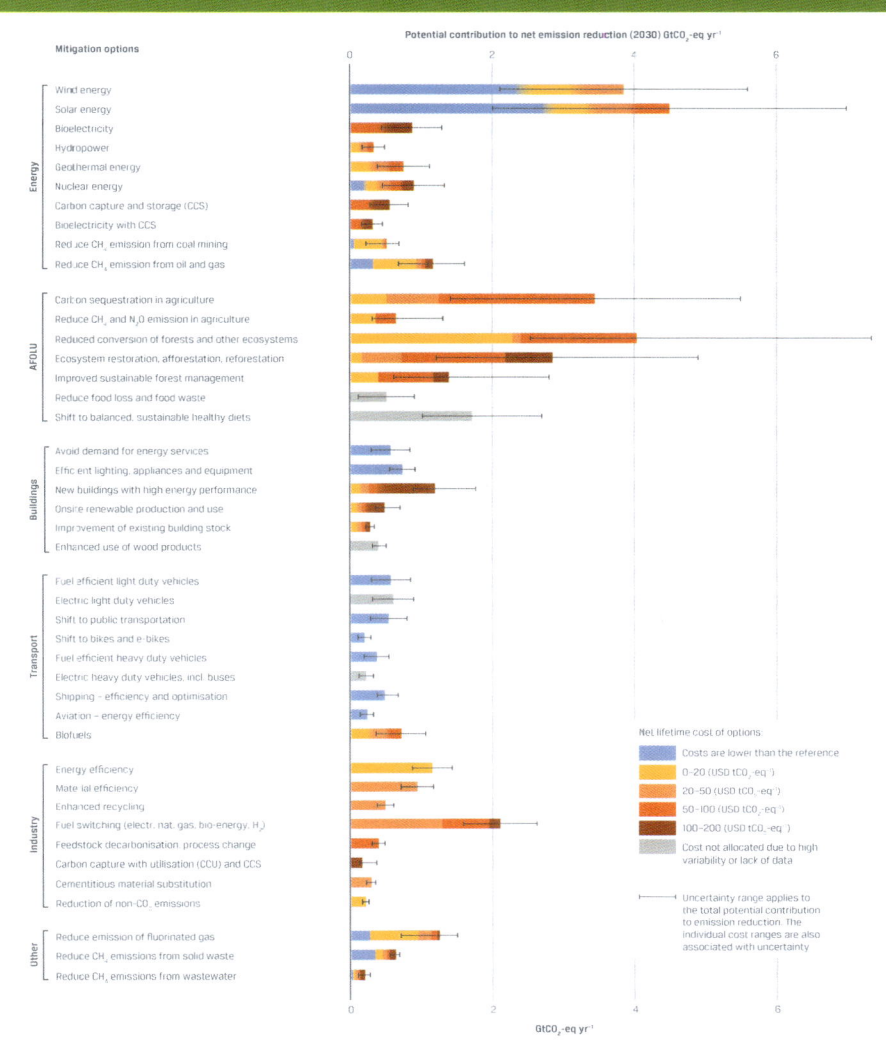

Exhibit 6: Overview of Mitigation Options and Their Estimated Range of Costs and Emission Reduction Potentials in 2030

Source: IPCC, "Climate Change 2022: Mitigation of Climate Change: Summary for Policymakers" (2022). https://report.ipcc.ch/ar6wg3/pdf/IPCC_AR6_WGIII_SummaryForPolicymakers.pdf .

However, despite the availability of options, the rate of deployment, set against the backdrop of the current rate of emissions and the insufficient strength of the policies so far announced by governments worldwide, may render certain mitigation goals increasingly unachievable. To illustrate the scale of the challenge, in 2020, the COVID-19 pandemic led to the largest recorded drop in yearly CO_2 emissions, approximately 7%. It is estimated that similar reductions would be needed *each year* until 2030 to meet the 1.5°C (2.7°F) goal.[42]

Despite a suite of policies introduced to foster a 'green recovery' after the pandemic (see the following box, "The 'Green Recovery'"), the UN has noted that given the global rebound in emissions, "the opportunity to use pandemic recovery spending to reduce emissions has been largely missed."[43]

---

42 UNEP, "Emissions Gap Report 2020" (2020). www.unep.org/emissions-gap-report-2020.
43 UNEP, "Emissions Gap Report 2021" (2021). www.unenvironment.org/emissions-gap-report-2021.

> **THE "GREEN RECOVERY"**
>
> The roster of policy measures announced by governments in the aftermath of the COVID-19 pandemic has created an opportunity to promote sustainability objectives, alongside economic development. A survey of economists has highlighted several policy areas perceived to have a high "multiplier" effect on economic activity and high potential to decrease GHG emissions: investments in "clean" physical infrastructure, renovations or retrofits to improve energy efficiency, natural capital investment, clean energy research and development (R&D), and investment in education and training.[44]
>
> The reality on the ground has been mixed, with capital and policy support continuing to flow to both "green" and "brown" sectors. For example, a review of country-level measures in the EU found that less than a third of the total €700 billion in analyzed recovery plans was assessed as likely to have a positive or very positive climate contribution.[45]
>
> At the global level, the International Energy Agency estimated that at the end of October 2021, US$470 billion have been earmarked by governments to support clean energy.[46]

As illustrated in Exhibit 7, a significant gap still remains between the shorter-term policy commitments of governments (known as nationally determined contributions, or NDCs) and the magnitude of emission cuts needed.

---

44 C. Hepburn, B. O'Callaghan, N. Stern, J. Stiglitz, and D. Zenghelis, "Will COVID-19 Fiscal Recovery Packages Accelerate or Retard Progress on Climate Change?" Smith School Working Paper 20-02 (2020).
45 Green Recovery Tracker, "Country Reports" (2022). www.greenrecoverytracker.org/country-reports-overview.
46 International Energy Agency, "Sustainable Recovery Tracker" (2021). www.iea.org/reports/sustainable-recovery-tracker.

Key Environmental Issues

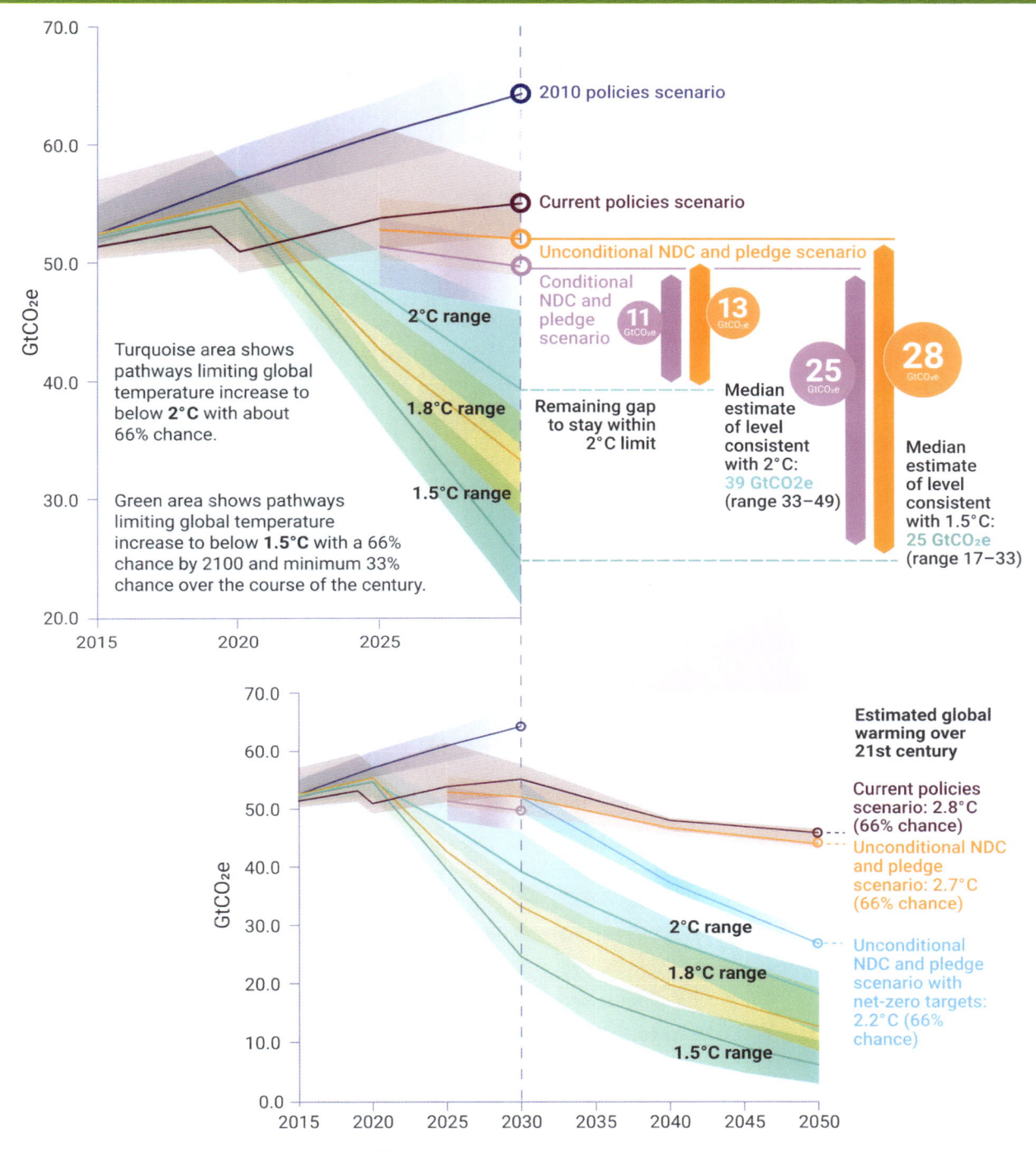

Exhibit 7: Global GHG emissions under Different Scenarios and the Emission Gap in 2030 (median and 10th and 90th percentile range)

Source: UNEP, "Emissions Gap Report 2021" (2021). www.unenvironment.org/emissions-gap-report-2021.

This brings us to the actions needed in response to warming that cannot be averted—in other words, to climate adaptation.

Climate Change Adaptation

Adapting to a changing climate involves adjusting to actual or expected future climate events, thereby increasing society's resilience to climate change and reducing vulnerabilities to its harmful effects. The faster the climate changes, the more challenging it is to adapt. The World Bank has aptly described adaptation and resilience as "two sides of the same coin."[47]

Most adaptation focuses on anticipating the adverse effects of climate change and taking appropriate action to prevent or minimize the damage they can cause, but there may also be opportunities (such as polar melting opening new maritime trade routes or the growth of viticulture in previously colder areas).

In light of humankind's ability to survive—and even thrive—in hostile climates, it is tempting to assume that adaptation is a less costly option than mitigation, but this is far from certain. Consider one of the most obvious examples of adaptation: air conditioning (AC), the use of which is becoming increasingly common as incomes and populations rise, particularly in the world's warmer regions. AC units are power intensive and use powerful GHGs as refrigerants. By 2050, it is anticipated that air conditioning alone may result in GHG emissions equivalent to that of India, the world's third-largest emitter today, which would create a vicious circle of more global overheating, which requires more AC, and so on.[48]

Alternatively, it is sometimes suggested that because CO_2 is a nutrient for plants, more CO_2 in the atmosphere will ultimately have a positive effect on agriculture around the world. However, other effects of climate change—in particular, increased droughts in some locations and stronger floods in others—are reducing yields and accelerating soil erosion, with the world already losing around 0.5% of its arable land every year.[49] Moreover, rising sea levels already flood some of the world's major rice-producing deltas with salt water. In light of these issues as well as signs of stagnating agricultural productivity, how the world will adapt to the food needs of a fast-rising global population is a crucial open question.

The more climate adaptation strategies are included in the investment plans of the finance sector and the industrial, agricultural, and even defense sector strategies of governments and the urban planning of municipalities, the higher their chances of success.

Examples of adaptation strategies include a variety of development plans on how to deal with

- protecting coastlines and adapting to sea-level rise,
- building flood defenses,
- managing land use and forestry practices,
- planning more efficiently for scarce water resources,
- developing drought-resilient crops,
- protecting energy and public infrastructure, and
- developing clean cooling systems.

---

47 World Bank, "Action Plan on Climate Change Adaptation and Resilience: Managing Risks for a More Resilient Future" (2019). http://documents1.worldbank.org/curated/en/519821547481031999/The-World-Bank-Groups-Action-Plan-on-Climate-Change-Adaptation-and-Resilience-Managing-Risks-for-a-More-Resilient-Future.pdf.
48 Ankit Kalanki and Sneha Sachar, "Revolutionizing the Air Conditioner Industry to Solve the Cooling Challenge," Rocky Mountain Institute (2018). https://rmi.org/revolutionizing-the-air-conditioner/.
49 See J. Grantham, "The Race of Our Lives Revisited," white paper, GMO (8 August 2018). www.gmo.com/europe/research-library/the-race-of-our-lives-revisited/.

Key Environmental Issues

As mentioned earlier, researchers have observed that some of the most effective climate policies (such as the protection of coastal and freshwater wetlands[50] and the promotion of sustainable agroforestry) contribute to both adaptation and mitigation simultaneously.[51]

Not just an issue of government policy, adaptation is also increasingly being factored into corporate business plans. For example, water risks are proving to be an issue of increased importance in the mining sector, which requires sufficient water to convey or help separate the desired ores. It is estimated that up to 50% of global production of copper, gold, iron ore, and zinc—metals with a key contribution to low-carbon energy technologies—is located in areas where water stress is already high.[52]

Too much water can also be a problem, because floods can shut down mines and cause significant local pollution. Close to half of the global production of iron ore and zinc is estimated to be in areas facing high flood risk.[53]

CASE STUDIES

Escondida Copper Mine

Located in one of the most arid places on earth, the Atacama Desert in Chile, Escondida is the world's largest copper mine by production. BHP, the mining company operating it, has been planning a transition away from using fresh groundwater.

In early 2020, BHP announced it was able to operate the mine using only desalinated water from the ocean. BHP already uses more than 50% of the water it needs from the ocean in an effort to reduce pressure on freshwater resources, which are often also used by local communities.[54]

States, provinces,[55] cities, and municipalities[56] are at the frontline of adaptation and resilience due to their high concentration of people, assets, and economic activities. Representing 80% of global gross domestic product (GDP), cities are heavily exposed to climate change risks in the forms of

- sea level rise,
- extreme weather events, such as flooding and drought, and
- increase in the spread of tropical diseases.

---

50 William R. Moomaw, G. L. Chmura, Gillian T. Davies, C. M. Finlayson, B. A. Middleton, Susan M. Natali, J. E. Perry, N. Roulet, and Ariana E. Sutton-Grier, "Wetlands in a Changing Climte: Science, Policy and Management," *Wetlands* 38 (2018): 183–205. https://link.springer.com/article/10.1007/s13157-018-1023-8.
51 I. Suarez, "5 Strategies that Achieve Climate Mitigation and Adaptation Simultaneously," World Resources Institute (10 February 2020). www.wri.org/blog/2020/02/climate-change-mitigation-adaptation-strategies.
52 Lindsay Delevingne, Will Glazener, Liesbet Grégoir, and Kimberly Henderson, "Climate Risk and Decarbonization: What Every Mining CEO Needs to Know," McKinsey (28 January 2020). www.mckinsey.com/business-functions/sustainability/our-insights/climate-risk-and-decarbonization-what-every-mining-ceo-needs-to-know#.
53 Delevingne, Glazener, Grégoir, and Henderson, "Climate Risk and Decarbonization."
54 C. Jamasmie, "BHP to Supply Water for Escondida Mine from Desalination Plant Only," Mining.com (4 February 2020). www.mining.com/bhp-to-supply-water-for-escondida-mine-from-desalination-plant-only/. See also BHP, "BHP Annual Report 2020" (2020). www.bhp.com/-/media/documents/investors/annual-reports/2020/200915_bhpannualreport2020.pdf.
55 Under2 Coalition: www.theclimategroup.org/under2-coalition.
56 Climate Mayors: https://climatemayors.org/.

All of these will have an economic and social cost to cities' inhabitants, infrastructure, and businesses and the built environment. At the same time, cities are a major contributor of GHG emissions, mainly from transport and buildings. Useful best practices of various cities' climate adaptation strategies include

- incorporating flood risk into building designs (in New York City) and planning for enhanced water absorption rates into city infrastructure ("sponge cities," such as Wuhan, China),[57]
- modeling the impact of natural disasters on energy supply (in Yokohama, Japan), and
- analyzing the resiliency to disruption of food supply systems (in Los Angeles and Paris).[58]

Estimates of the relative costs of adaptation to climate change vary. In the Adaptation Gap Report 2020, the UN Environmental Programme (UNEP) estimated that adaptation costs in developing countries alone were estimated to be in the range of US$70 billion (£50 billion), with the expectation of reaching US$140 billion to US$300 billion (£100 billion to £216 billion) in 2030 and US$280 billion to US$500 billion (£201 billion to £359 billion) in 2050.[59] And as with mitigation, expected costs must be set against the context of potential benefits: The Global Commission on Adaptation in 2019 estimated that approximately US$2 trillion (£1.4 trillion) of investment in adaptation measures would result in an over US$7 trillion (£5 trillion) return in avoided costs and other benefits.[60]

In late 2019, the Climate Bonds Initiative published the first Climate Resilience Principles, which provide a framework for developing location-specific climate resilience measures and financing them in the green bond market.[61] In addition, a group of multilateral development banks have put forward "A Framework and Principles for Climate Resilience Metrics in Financing Operations," which provides guidance on how to create effective climate resilience projects and how to measure direct outcomes and wider system impacts.[62]

It is important to recognize that there can be trade-offs between adaptation/resilience and mitigation. For example, the decision to invest in an a desalination plant that helps prevent a potential water shortage in a crisis may be warranted, despite its high associated emissions. Understanding and assessing such potential conflicts is critical to building resilience with limited impact on mitigation efforts.

---

[57] L. Jing, "Inside China's Leading 'Sponge City': Wuhan's War with Water," *Guardian* (23 January 2019). www.theguardian.com/cities/2019/jan/23/inside-chinas-leading-sponge-city-wuhans-war-with-water.
[58] C40 Cities and AXA, "Understanding Infrastructure Interdependencies in Cities" (2019). www.axa.com/en/press/publications/understanding-infrastructure-interdependencies-in-cities.
[59] UNEP, "Adaptation Gap Report 2020" (14 January 2021). www.unenvironment.org/resources/adaptation-gap-report-2020.
[60] Global Commission on Adaptation, "Adapt Now: A Global Call for Leadership on Climate Resilience" (2019). https://gca.org/wp-content/uploads/2019/09/GlobalCommission_Report_FINAL.pdf.
[61] Climate Bonds Initiative, "Climate Resilience Principles" (2019). www.climatebonds.net/climate-resilience-principles.
[62] African Development Bank, Asian Development Bank, Asian Infrastructure Investment Bank, European Bank for Reconstruction and Development, European Investment Bank, Inter American Development Bank, International Development Finance Club, and Islamic Development Bank, "A Framework and Principles for Climate Resilience Metrics in Financing Operations" (December 2019). https://publications.iadb.org/en/framework-and-principles-climate-resilience-metrics-financing-operations.

Pressures on Natural Resources

The relationship between businesses and natural resources is becoming increasingly important due to dramatically accelerating biodiversity loss and less secure access to natural resources. For the purposes of this section, natural resources cover

- fresh water,
- biodiversity loss,
- land use, and
- forestry and marine resources.

Natural resources also include non-renewable resources (such as fossil fuels, minerals, and metals), which cannot be replenished quickly enough to keep up with their consumption.

Governments and businesses are having to deal with increased pressure on natural resources, caused by

- population growth,
- health improvements leading to people living longer,
- economic growth, and
- the accompanying increased consumption in developed and emerging economies.

Simultaneously, these drivers are leading to the risk of resource scarcity. These developments are therefore compelling companies to become more efficient in the way that they use natural resources if they are to remain competitive and become more sustainable. This can help drive better financial management of resources but also spur technological innovations that can have a beneficial impact on the bottom line in support of a more sustainable and resilient economy and society.

Depletion of Natural Resources

According to the UN, the current world population of 7.6 billion is expected to reach

- 8.6 billion in 2030,
- 9.8 billion in 2050, and
- 11.2 billion in 2100.

The rising population will put increased strain on the world's natural resources, most notably in terms of access to food. This presents a number of related challenges:

1. "Modern agriculture is dependent on phosphorus derived from phosphate rock, which is a non-renewable resource, and current global reserves may be depleted in 50–100 years. While phosphorus demand is projected to increase, the expected global peak in phosphorus production is predicted to occur around 2030," with the quality of remaining reserves expected to fall while its costs—and the global population—continue to rise.[63]

---

[63] D. Cordell, J.-O. Drangerta, and S. White, "The Story of Phosphorus: Global Food Security and Food for Thought," *Global Environmental Change* 19 (May 2009): 292–305. https://doi.org/10.1016/j.gloenvcha.2008.10.009.

2. The world is already using half its vegetated land for agriculture. Avoiding worsening climate change, which itself would reduce agricultural productivity, requires feeding a rapidly growing population without further deforestation.[64]

3. The issue is compounded by changes in lifestyle: "While population growth was the leading cause of increasing consumption from 1970 to 2000, the emergence of a global affluent middle class has been the stronger driver since the turn of the century."[65] From the rare earths and other metals that go into smartphones and computers to the rising emissions associated with a higher standard of living (for example, bigger homes with higher heating and cooling needs, increased travel, and increased meat and dairy consumption), these dynamics are also set to increase the pressure on natural resources.

To a certain degree, technological innovation and moving from a linear to a circular economy has the potential to reduce the need for virgin resources. The decoupling of economic activities from resource usage has been observed; for example, in the past decade, the United Kingdom's GDP has risen by 18% while its carbon emissions have fallen by about 30%.[66]

However, a literature review of decoupling found a mixed picture: "Relative decoupling is frequent for material use as well as GHG and CO_2 emissions, [but] examples of absolute long-term decoupling are rare."[67]

One reason is that relative improvements in efficiency (using fewer resources per unit of production) may be offset by increased consumption of a given product—an effect known as the **Jevons paradox**.[68]

The issue of resource usage will remain crucial for investors and policymakers, who will have to navigate trade-offs and consider not just use efficiency but also how to facilitate changing the whole model (moving from linear to circular in products, processes, and ultimately, the economy) to reduce the strain on natural resources.

Another idea that is gaining ground is decoupling the definition of development and progress from GDP growth to a measurement of asset wealth and assigning economic value not just to produced capital and human capital but also to natural capital, as proposed in the Dasgupta Review.[69] Historically, growth in produced capital has been at the expense of natural capital, which has been ignored, and at the

---

64 Janet Ranganathan, Richard Waite, Tim Searchinger, and Craig Hanson, "How to Sustainably Feed 10 Billion People by 2050, in 21 Charts," World Resources Institute (5 December 2018). www.wri.org/blog/2018/12/how-sustainably-feed-10-billion-people-2050-21-charts.
65 B. Oberle, S. Bringezu, S. Hatfield-Dodds, S. Hellweg, "ETH Zurich UN Global Resources Outlook 2019: Natural Resources for the Future We Want" (March 2019). www.researchgate.net/publication/331683904_UN_Global_Resources_Outlook_2019_Natural_Resources_for_the_Future_We_Want. See also T. Wiedmann, M. Lenzen, L. T. Keyßer, and J. K. Steinberger, "Scientists' Warning on Affluence," *Nature Communications* 11 (19 June 2020). www.nature.com/articles/s41467-020-16941-y. As quoted in European Environment Agency, "Growth without Economic Growth" (2021). www.eea.europa.eu/publications/growth-without-economic-growth/growth-without-economic-growth.
66 S. Evans, "Analysis: UK's CO_2 Emissions Have Fallen 29% over the Past Decade," Carbon Brief (2 March 2020). www.carbonbrief.org/analysis-uks-co2-emissions-have-fallen-29-per-cent-over-the-past-decade.
67 H. Haberl, D. Wiedenhofer, D. Virag, G. Kalt, B. Plank, P. Brockway, T. Fishman, D. Hausknost, F. Krausmann, B. Leon-Gruchalski, A. Mayer, M. Pichler, A. Schaffartzik, T. Sousa, J. Streeck, and F. Creutzig, "A Systematic Review of the Evidence on Decoupling of GDP, Resource Use and GHG Emissions, Part II: Synthesizing the Insights," *Environmental Research Letters* 15 (June 2020). www.researchgate.net/publication/340243504_A_systematic_review_of_the_evidence_on_decoupling_of_GDP_resource_use_and_GHG_emissions_part_II_Synthesizing_the_insights.
68 "Jevons Paradox," Wikipedia (2021). https://en.wikipedia.org/wiki/Jevons_paradox.
69 HM Treasury, "Final Report—The Economics of Biodiversity: The Dasgupta Review" (2 February 2021). www.gov.uk/government/publications/final-report-the-economics-of-biodiversity-the-dasgupta-review.

Key Environmental Issues

expense of countries rich in natural resources, many of which have been left behind in the distribution of benefits in the form of human capital development and left with the impact of natural capital depletion and increasing social inequities. Valuing "ecosystem services" and their loss as the benefits and costs if they were supplied by the market is another alternative means of including natural inputs in the traditional GDP accounting.[70] There are also examples of individuals and governments paying someone for maintaining a beneficial ecosystem service.[71]

Water

Nearly 70% of the planet is covered by water, but only 2.5% of it is freshwater. Water is a vital natural resource, not only for human consumption but also for a range of agricultural, industrial, and household energy generation, as well as for recreational and environmental activities. It is critical to many industrial processes, including mineral extraction and cooling for industrial plants. Water demand is set to increase in all sectors.[72]

According to the World Economic Forum, water also connects these sectors to a broader economic system that must balance social development and environmental interests. As the world continues to face multiple water challenges, a decision to allocate more water to any one sector implies that less water will be available for other economic uses, for public water supply and other social services, or for environmental protection.[73]

Water scarcity is the lack of freshwater resources to meet water demand. Water scarcity is present on every continent and is one of the largest global risks in terms of potential impact over the next decade. UN-Water has reported that over 2 billion people experience high water stress in different countries, and about 4 billion people experience severe water scarcity at least one month of the year.[74]

The **UN's Sustainable Development Goal (SDG) 6** is the need "to ensure availability and sustainable management of water and sanitation to all" by 2030.[75] Water scarcity—caused either by economic factors, such as lack of investment, or by physical impacts related to climate change—continues to cause major concern, especially among the developing and emerging economies.

Biodiversity Loss

Biodiversity, land use, and associated ecosystems provide a range of invaluable services to society that underpin human health, well-being, and economic growth. Ecosystem services are the benefits that people and businesses derive from ecosystems. Biodiversity, as defined by the Convention on Biological Diversity, means the "variability

---

70 Robert Costanza, Rudolfde Groot, Paul Sutton, Sandervan der Ploeg, Sharolyn J. Anderson, Ida Kubiszewski, Stephen Farber, R. Kerry Turner, "Changes in the Value of Ecosystem Services," *Global Environmental Change* 26 (May 2014): 152–58. www.sciencedirect.com/science/article/pii/S0959378014000685.
71 B. Kelsey Jack, Carolyn Kousky, and Katharine R. E. Sims, "Designing Payments for Ecosystem Services: Lessons from Previous Experience with Incentive-Based Mechanisms," *Proceedings of the National Academy of Sciences* 105 (15 July 2008): 9465-70. www.pnas.org/doi/10.1073/pnas.0705503104.
72 UNESCO World Water Assessment Programme, "The United Nations World Water Development Report 2018: Nature-Based Solutions for Water" (2018). https://unesdoc.unesco.org/ark:/48223/pf0000261424.
73 World Economic Forum, "Shaping the Future of Global Public Goods" (2019). www.weforum.org/system-initiatives/shaping-the-future-of-environment-and-natural-resource-security.
74 United Nations, "The United Nations World Water Development Report 2019: Leaving No One Behind," (2019). www.unwater.org/publications/world-water-development-report-2019/.
75 United Nations Department of Economic and Social Affairs, "6: Ensure Availability and Sustainable Management of Water and Sanitation for All" (2021). https://sdgs.un.org/goals/goal6.

among living organisms from all sources including, among other things, terrestrial, marine and other aquatic ecosystems and the ecological complexes of which they are part; this includes diversity within species, between species and of ecosystems."[76]

The Summary for Policymakers for the 2022 IPCC report "Impact, Vulnerability and Adaptation," which was approved by all governments, made a strong connection between biodiversity, ecosystems, development, and climate change. The following are examples:

> *Safeguarding biodiversity and ecosystems is fundamental to climate resilient development, in light of the threats climate change poses to them and their roles in adaptation and mitigation (very high confidence). Recent analyses, drawing on a range of lines of evidence, suggest that maintaining the resilience of biodiversity and ecosystem services at a global scale depends on effective and equitable conservation of approximately 30% to 50% of earth's land, freshwater and ocean areas, including currently near-natural ecosystems (high confidence)....*
> *Building the resilience of biodiversity and supporting ecosystem integrity can maintain benefits for people, including livelihoods, human health and well-being and the provision of food, fibre and water, as well as contributing to disaster risk reduction and climate change adaptation and mitigation.*[77]

Unfortunately, global biodiversity is facing a dramatic decline. In 2019, the Intergovernmental Platform on Biodiversity and Ecosystem Services (IPBES) published a landmark report that showed that around 1 million animal and plant species are now threatened with extinction, many within decades, more than ever before in human history.[78] The report provides a stark and comprehensive set of scientifically proven findings that highlight the deterioration of biodiversity and its ecosystem functions and services. According to it, humans have impacted over 75% of the earth's land areas and 66% of the oceans. This deterioration is caused by a combined result of land and sea use change, direct exploitation, climate change, and pollution.

The World Wildlife Fund's (WWF's) "Living Planet Report" from 2020 noted that the world's wildlife populations have plummeted by 68% since 1970, with this trajectory likely to be further exacerbated by global warming. A major driver of this decline is loss of habitat linked to overexploitation.[79] In another report, WWF estimated that inaction on biodiversity may result in cumulative costs of approximately US$10 trillion (£7.2 trillion) up to 2050, through changes to crop yields and fish catches, economic damages from flooding and other disasters, and the loss of potential new sources of medicine.[80]

Already, biodiversity loss is presenting challenges to such industries as fishery and agriculture. Around 75% of global food crop types directly rely on animal pollination; given the decline in natural pollinators due to pollution and pesticides, US farmers paid approximately US$300 million (£215.6 million) for artificial (sometimes manual) pollination in 2017. Medicine and health is another area of concern, with an estimated 70% of cancer drugs being organic or derived from organic substances.[81]

---

76 United Nations, "Convention on Biological Diversity" (1992). www.cbd.int/doc/legal/cbd-en.pdf.
77 Sections D.4 and D.4.1 of IPCC, "Climate Change 2022: Impacts, Adaptation and Vulnerability: Summary for Policymakers" (2022).
78 IPBES, "The Global Assessment Report on Biodiversity and Ecosystem Services: Summary for Policymakers" (2019). https://ipbes.net/sites/default/files/inline/files/ipbes_global_assessment_report_summary_for_policymakers.pdf.
79 WWF, "The Living Planet Report 2020" (2020). www.wwf.org.uk/living-planet-report.
80 WWF, "Global Futures: Assessing the Global Economic Impacts of Environmental Change to Support Policy-Making" (2020). www.wwf.org.uk/sites/default/files/2020-02/GlobalFutures_SummaryReport.pdf.
81 A. Paun, "Biodiversity in the Balance," HSBC (17 June 2020). www.hsbc.com/insight/topics/biodiversity-in-the-balance.

Key Environmental Issues

Biodiversity underpins ecosystem services, provides natural resources and constitutes our "natural capital." Some of these ecosystem services are

- food,
- clean water,
- genetic resources,
- flood protection,
- nutrient cycling, and
- climate regulation.[82]

"The Economics of Biodiversity: The Dasgupta Review" from 2021 argued for assigning economic asset value to biodiversity to reverse its treatment as a free resource and attempt to halt depletion.[83] In the same vein, in 2020, PBL Netherlands Environmental Assessment Agency published an important report titled "Indebted to Nature," exploring the biodiversity risks for the Dutch financial sector, effectively identifying nature and biodiversity as a systemic risk.[84]

NATURAL CAPITAL

Natural capital is defined as:
"the world's stocks of natural assets which include geology, soil, air, water and all living things. It is from this natural capital that humans derive a wide range of services, often called ecosystem services, which make human life possible."[85]

The importance of taking a natural capital approach is explained in more detail in the section titled "Assessment of Materiality of Environmental Issues," which discusses investment opportunities.

It is estimated that the annual monetary value of ecosystem services is around US$125 trillion to US$140 trillion (£90 trillion to £100 trillion), more than 1.5 times the global GDP.[86] Biodiversity also has intrinsic value: The ideas that the beauty of nature is worth preserving and that mankind and other species should strive for a harmonious coexistence have been a mainstay of many cultures, religions, and belief systems.[87]

It is worth emphasising the potentially large *unrecognized value*. There are myriad interactions between different species, playing highly complex roles in cycling nutrients, regulating the numbers of (potentially invasive) plant and animal species, and even altering the formation of landscapes.

The Organisation for Economic Co-Operation and Development (OECD) has noted it is difficult to predict where biodiversity thresholds lie, "when they will be crossed, and what will be the scale of impact. Given this uncertainty and the potential impact of

---

[82] D. Juffe-Bignoli, "Biodiversity for Business: A Guide to Using Knowledge Products Delivered through IUCN" International Union for Conservation of Nature (2014). https://portals.iucn.org/library/node/43361.
[83] HM Treasury, "Final Report—The Economics of Biodiversity: The Dasgupta Review."
[84] PBL Netherlands Environmental Assessment Agency, "Indebted to Nature. Exploring Biodiversity Risks for the Dutch Financial Sector" (19 June 2020). www.pbl.nl/en/publications/indebted-to-nature.
[85] World Forum on Natural Capital, "What Is Natural Capital?" (2021). https://naturalcapitalforum.com/about/.
[86] OECD, "Biodiversity: Finance and the Economic and Business Case for Action" (2019). www.oecd.org/environment/resources/biodiversity/G7-report-Biodiversity-Finance-and-the-Economic-and-Business-Case-for-Action.pdf.
[87] See, for example, the Convention on Biological Diversity, signed by a majority of governments worldwide.

regime shifts, it is prudent to take a precautionary approach."[88] There is evidence that conservation can be effective: A study from 2009 found that conservation investments over more than a decade reduced extinction risk by almost a third for mammals and birds in 109 countries.[89] Without existing conservation efforts, the extinction risk of mammals, birds, and amphibians would have been at least 20% higher, according to the IPBES.[90] This is not just a conservation issue; the OECD noted the link between safeguarding biodiversity and human health: "Land-use change resulting from agricultural expansion, logging, infrastructure development and other human activities is the most common driver of infectious disease emergence."[91]

In summary, conserving nature and improving the sustainable use of natural resources is possible but can be achieved only through transformative changes across economic, social, political, and technological factors.

Land Use and Forestry

Land use management practices and forestry, also known as agriculture, forestry, and other land use (AFOLU), have a major impact on natural resources, including water, soil, nutrients, plants, and animals.

Covering approximately 30% of the world's land area, or just under 4 billion hectares, forests are a vital part of the carbon cycle.[92] They convert the CO_2 in the air to oxygen, through the process of photosynthesis, and are a natural regulator of CO_2, with the world's tropical forests playing a particularly important role in accumulating and storing carbon. The more mature and old growth trees in our forests, the less atmospheric CO_2 and the more oxygen there is in the atmosphere.[93]

Unfortunately, deforestation is accelerating: From 2001 to 2019, there was a total of 386 million hectares of tree cover loss globally, equivalent to a 9.7% decrease in tree cover since 2000 and 105 gigatonnes of CO_2 emissions, according to Global Forest Watch.[94]

The production of commodities (particularly relating to agriculture) is a key driver of deforestation—responsible for up to two-thirds of deforestation by some estimates.[95] As a result, there is increased investor focus on investee companies' contribution to deforestation. According to the CDP (previously the Carbon Disclosure Project), approximately US$1 trillion (£0.7 trillion) of turnover in publicly listed companies is dependent on commodities linked to deforestation, including soy, palm oil, cattle, and timber. The risks from these soft commodities can be transmitted across supply chains to affect companies' revenues, asset valuation, or costs, which can impact the creditworthiness or market value of the debt or equity of investee companies.[96]

---

88 OECD, "Biodiversity."
89 A. Waldron, D. C. Miller, D. Redding, A. Mooers, T. S. Kuhn, N. Nibbelink, J. T. Roberts, J. A. Tobias, J. L. Gittleman, "Reductions in Global Biodiversity Loss Predicted from Conservation Spending," *Nature* 551 (25 October 2017): 364–67. www.nature.com/articles/nature24295.
90 IPBES, "The Global Assessment Report on Biodiversity and Ecosystem Services."
91 OECD, "Biodiversity and the Economic Response to COVID-19: Ensuring a Green and Resilient Recovery" (2020). www.oecd.org/coronavirus/policy-responses/biodiversity-and-the-economic-response-to-covid-19-ensuring-a-green-and-resilient-recovery-d98b5a09/.
92 C. Nunez, "Deforestation Explained," National Geographic (2019). www.nationalgeographic.com/environment/global-warming/deforestation/.
93 Beverly E. Law, William R. Moomaw, Tara W. Hudiburg, William H. Schlesinger, John D. Sterman, and George M. Woodwell, "Creating Strategic Reserves to Protect Forest Carbon," *Land* 11 (May 2022). www.mdpi.com/2073-445X/11/5/721.
94 Global Forest Watch, "Global Deforestation Rates and Statistics by Country" (2020). www.globalforestwatch.org/dashboards/global/.
95 Global Canopy, "Time for Change: Delivering Deforestation-Free Supply Chains" (2021). https://forest500.org/publications/time-change-delivering-deforestation-free-supply-chains.
96 CDP and Global Canopy, "Financial Institution Guidance: Soft Commodity Company Strategy" (2017). www.cdp.net/en/reports/downloads/2913.

Key Environmental Issues

Companies with exposure to deforestation in their supply chains may face material financial risks, such as

- supply disruption,
- cost volatility, and
- reputational damage.

By contrast, shifting business practices to adopt more sustainable land management approaches contributes to

- agricultural and economic development, both locally and globally,
- the health and stability of forests and ecosystems and the continued provision of ecosystem services at an increasing scale, and
- the reduction of GHG emissions from deforestation and degradation.

Sustainable agriculture will remain an issue of growing focus for policymakers and companies. In 2019, the IPCC published its "Special Report on Climate Change and Land," which warned that the stability of the global food supply is projected to decrease as the magnitude and frequency of extreme weather events that disrupt food chains increases.[97]

In summary, the protection and management of land resources play a vital role in ensuring the balance of nature and the health of the ecosystem. Unsustainable management will negatively affect biodiversity, ecosystems, and all the natural resources that underpin economic growth and human flourishing.

Marine Resources

Storing 43 times more CO_2 than the atmosphere, the ocean is the planet's largest carbon reservoir. It is also the second largest sink in terms of removing CO_2 from the atmosphere.[98] Photosynthetic microorganisms on its surface layer also produce over half of the world's oxygen.[99] It is one of the earth's most valuable natural resources.

The OECD has estimated that ocean-based industries contribute roughly €1.3 trillion (£1.1 trillion) to global gross value added. Oceans provide seafood and are widely used for transportation (shipping). They are also mined for minerals (salt, sand, and gravel, as well as some manganese, copper, nickel, iron, and cobalt, which can be found in the deep sea) and drilled for crude oil. The oceans' resources are a source of economic growth and are also known as the **blue economy**. According to the World Bank, the blue economy is the "sustainable use of ocean resources for economic growth, improved livelihoods, and jobs while preserving the health of ocean ecosystem".[100] The blue economy as an investment opportunity is discussed in the section titled, "Applying Material Environmental Factors to Financial Modeling, Ratio Analysis, and Risk Assessment" of this chapter.

---

97 IPCC, "Climate Change and Land: Summary for Policymakers" (2019). www.ipcc.ch/srccl/chapter/summary-for-policymakers.
98 Global Carbon Project, "Global Carbon Budget 2021" (2022). www.globalcarbonproject.org/carbonbudget/21/publications.htm.
99 National Oceanic Service, "How Much Oxygen Comes from the Ocean?" (2021). https://oceanservice.noaa.gov/facts/ocean-oxygen.html.
100 World Bank, "What Is the Blue Economy?" (2017). www.worldbank.org/en/news/infographic/2017/06/06/blue-economy.

Communities in close connection with coastal environments, small islands (including Small Island Developing States), polar areas, and high mountains are particularly exposed to ocean change, such as sea level rise. Low-lying coastal zones are currently home to around 680 million people (nearly 10% of the 2010 global population), projected to reach more than 1 billion by 2050.[101]

Due to the increase in the human population, the oceans have been overfished, with a resulting decline of fish critical to the economy. In 2015,

- 33% of marine fish stocks were being harvested at unsustainable levels,
- 60% were fished to maximum capacity, and
- only 7% were harvested at levels lower than what can be sustainably fished.[102]

Although there are 66 international agreements governing regional fisheries management organizations, just 7 of them have a secretariat, a scientific body, and enforcement powers. In most cases, fishing quotas are politically agreed to and overrule the recommendation for maximum sustained yield recommended by the scientific body. This "legal overfishing" is in addition to the illegal, unreported, and unregulated catch. In addition, almost all fishing nations subsidize fishing fleets to be much larger than the fishery can sustain.[103] The control of the world's fisheries is a controversial subject, because production is unable to satisfy the demand, especially when there are not enough fish left to breed in healthy ecosystems. Environmental finance think-tank Planet Tracker estimated in 2020 that "if historic trends continue and coastal ecological health continues declining, total production forecasts for coastal farmed Atlantic salmon to 2025 may be 6% to 8% lower than predicted, equivalent to US$4.1 billion" (£3 billion). However, there are options to address this problem: By improvements in traceability and sustainability certifications, which have lower impacts on biodiversity, Planet Tracker estimated that "the typical seafood processor can double its EBIT [earnings before interest and tax] margin, which is currently at a low 3%, mainly due to lower recall, product waste and legal costs."[104]

Pollution, Waste, and a Circular economy

Air Pollution

Clean air is essential to health, the environment, and economic prosperity.
Increased air pollution

- adversely affects the environment,
- has a negative impact on human health,
- destroys ecosystems,
- impoverishes biodiversity, and
- reduces crop harvests as a result of soil acidification.

---

101 IPCC, "Special Report on the Ocean and Cryosphere in a Changing Climate" (2019). www.ipcc.ch/srocc/.
102 IPBES, "The Global Assessment Report on Biodiversity and Ecosystem Services."
103 William Moomaw and Sara Blankenship, "Charting a New Course for the Oceans" (April 2014). https://sites.tufts.edu/gdae/files/2019/10/MoomawFisheries_2014.pdf.
104 Planet Tracker, "Investors Face Financial Risk as Salmon Industry Approaches Ecological Brink, Says Planet Tracker" (27 May 2020). https://planet-tracker.org/investors-face-financial-risk-as-salmon-industry-approaches-ecological-brink-says-planet-tracker/.
See also Planet Tracker, "Traceability Could Double the EBIT Margin of Seafood Processors While Reducing Investor Risk, Says Planet Tracker" (13 October 2020). https://planet-tracker.org/traceability-could-double-the-ebit-margin-of-seafood-processors-while-reducing-investor-risk-says-planet-tracker/.

Indoor and outdoor air pollution are together responsible for over 7 million deaths globally each year, according to the World Health Organization (WHO). Research by the WHO further shows that in 2019, 99% of the world's population was living in places where the WHO air quality guideline levels were not met.[105] Urban air pollution is predicted to worsen, as migration and demographic trends drive the creation of more megacities.

Pollution is the largest environmental cause of disease and premature death in the world today. According to findings published in October 2017 by the Lancet Commission on Pollution and Health, diseases caused by pollution were responsible for an estimated 9 million premature deaths in 2015—16% of all deaths worldwide—which is three times more deaths than from AIDS, tuberculosis, and malaria combined and 15 times more than from all wars and other forms of violence.[106]

Research published in February 2021 in the journal *Environmental Research* focused on isolating the impact of fossil fuel combustion and concluded that "the burning of fossil fuels—especially coal, petrol, and diesel—is a major source of airborne fine particulate matter ($PM_{2.5}$), and a key contributor to the global burden of mortality and disease. . . . The greatest mortality impact is estimated over regions with substantial fossil fuel related $PM_{2.5}$."[107]

Using new modeling, the scientists estimated that parts of China, India, Europe, and the northeastern United States are among the hardest-hit areas, suffering a disproportionately high share of 8.7 million annual deaths attributed to fossil fuels, compared to a 2017 study, which had put the annual number of deaths from all outdoor airborne particulate matter—including dust and smoke from agricultural burns and wildfires—at 4.2 million.[108] These findings lend further support to the focus on reducing fossil fuel emissions.

Water Pollution

Water is essential to all living organisms. Yet water pollution is one of the most serious environmental threats faced. Water pollution occurs when contaminants (such as harmful chemicals or microorganisms) are introduced into the natural environment through the ocean, rivers, streams, lakes, or groundwater. Water pollution can be caused by spills and leaks from untreated sewage or sanitation systems and industrial waste discharge. Plastic waste also appears in waterways.

> **CASE STUDIES**
>
> ### Water-Related Fines
>
> Partially due to increased public interest litigation, fines for water pollution are increasing around the world. In 2014, Chinese media reported what was at the time the largest ever fine levied in the country—whereby six companies were fined a total of 160 million yuan (£18.1 million) for chemical discharges into rivers.[109]

---

105 "Air Pollution." World Health Organization. *World Health Organization* (2020). https://www.who.int/health-topics/air-pollution.
106 P. J. Landrigan et al., "The Lancet Commission on Pollution and Health," *Lancet Commissions* 391 (3 February 2018): 462–512. https://doi.org/10.1016/S0140-6736(17)32345-0.
107 Karn Vohra, Alina Vodonos, Joel Schwartz, Eloise A. Marais, Melissa P. Sulprizio, and Loretta J. Mickley, "Global Mortality from Outdoor Fine Particle Pollution Generated by Fossil Fuel Combustion: Results from GEOS-Chem," *Environmental Research* 195 (April 2021). www.sciencedirect.com/science/article/abs/pii/S0013935121000487.
108 M. Green, "Fossil Fuel Pollution Causes One in Five Premature Deaths Globally: Study," *Reuters* (9 February 2021). www.reuters.com/article/us-health-pollution-fossil/fossil-fuel-pollution-causes-one-in-five-premature-deaths-globally-study-idUSKBN2A90UB.
109 BBC, "Court in China Issues Record Pollution Fine" (31 December 2014). www.bbc.co.uk/news/world-asia-china-30640385.

> In 2020, the US Environmental Protection Agency announced its largest ever fine relating to the Clean Water Act. Almost US$3 million (£2.2 million) was charged to a horseracing facility for repeated discharge of animal waste into New Orleans waterways.[110]

Waste and Waste Management

In view of the concerns about growing pressures on natural resources—combined with opposition to all types of pollution—waste and waste management has, in recent decades, become a bigger priority for policymakers, businesses, and citizens. Increasing consumption and waste levels are putting more pressure on space for landfill waste, which, in turn, is causing landfill taxes to rise. Alongside tougher regulation on how waste is handled and managed, businesses are becoming increasingly incentivized to help economies, notably through recycling and by adopting a circular economy business model.

A recent striking example of the public's concern over excessive waste is the campaign against plastics, especially in relation to the serious damage that they are doing to the oceans. This has led to actions by national and local authorities on waste management and greater responsibility conferred on businesses to manage their waste responsibly.

In most developed countries, domestic waste disposal is funded from national or local taxes, which may be related to income or property values. Commercial and industrial waste disposal is typically charged for as a commercial service, often as an integrated charge that includes disposal costs. This practice may encourage disposal contractors to opt for the cheapest disposal option, such as using landfills or incineration—which generate GHG emissions and contribute to local pollution—rather than opting for such solutions as reuse and recycling.

Although many consumer products (such as metal cans and glass bottles) are recyclable, recycling practices are very uneven across (and sometimes even within) countries. However, there has been growing public concern with excessive waste, particularly for single-use plastics and the serious damage that they are doing to the oceans and marine wildlife. This has led to actions by national and local authorities on waste management and greater responsibility conferred on businesses to manage their waste responsibly. Coupled with a slowdown in the ability to export hazardous waste, including plastics, to a rising number of Asian countries (most notably China), this puts further pressure on those in Australia, Europe, and North America, in particular, to develop their own recycling and waste management solutions onshore.

In 2022 at the UN Environment Assembly, heads of state and government representatives from around the world committed to develop by 2024 an international legally binding agreement to end plastic pollution.[111]

A financial mechanism that is growing in popularity in the consumer space is the use of fees and taxes, including a charge on plastic bags, designed to discourage waste and promote recycled usage. The European Strategy for Plastics in a Circular Economy, agreed in January 2018, requires that all plastic packaging must be reusable or recyclable by 2030. This trend has material implications for investors. As the use of oil for transportation declines amid a shift to electric vehicles, numerous companies in the oil industry are looking toward petrochemicals—and plastics in particular—as an alternative source of growth. Yet, think-tank Carbon Tracker has estimated that

---

110 US Attorney's Office Eastern District of Louisiana, "United States Reaches Agreement to Protect New Orleans Waterways and Lake Pontchartrain" (29 September 2020). www.justice.gov/usao-edla/pr/united-states-reaches-agreement-protect-new-orleans-waterways-and-lake-pontchartrain.
111 UNEP, "Historic Day in the Campaign to Beat Plastic Pollution: Nations Commit to Develop a Legally Binding Agreement" (2 March 2022). www.unep.org/news-and-stories/press-release/historic-day-campaign-beat-plastic-pollution-nations-commit-develop.

Key Environmental Issues

if policymakers implement stricter recycling measures in response to ongoing public pressure, up to US$400 billion (£288 billion) of investments in new petrochemical facilities might become "stranded," unprofitable assets.[112]

Conversely, there are opportunities in better waste management, from the reuse or transformation of recovered waste (for example, using old tires to create road surfacing and expanded recycling programs under the TerraCycle initiative)[113] to finding new ways to break down waste into less harmful or useful materials (such as graphene).[114]

A global commitment by companies led by the Ellen MacArthur Foundation and UNEP has set a benchmark for "best practices" to address the plastic waste and pollution system.[115] In a sign of the times, the International Criminal Police Organization (INTERPOL) has also started tracking criminal trends in the global plastic waste market.[116]

Circular Economy

The **circular economy** is an economic model that aims to avoid waste and to preserve the value of resources (raw materials, energy, and water) for as long as possible. It is an effective model for companies to assess and manage their operations and resource management (see Exhibit 8); it is an alternative approach to the use-make-dispose economy. The circular economy is based on three principles:

1. design out waste and pollution,
2. keep products and materials in use, and
3. regenerate natural systems.[117]

The government of the Netherlands has developed a program for a circular economy, aimed at "preventing waste by making products and materials more efficiently and reusing them. If new raw materials are needed, they must be obtained sustainably so that the natural and human environment is not damaged."[118]

---

112 Carbon Tracker, "The Future's Not in Plastics: Why Plastics Demand Won't Rescue the Oil Sector" (4 September 2020). https://carbontracker.org/reports/the-futures-not-in-plastics/.
113 TerraCycle, "Recycle Everything with TerraCycle" (2021). www.terracycle.com
114 S. Snowden, "Ground-Breaking Method to Make Graphene from Garbage Is Modern-Day Alchemy," *Forbes* (24 July 2020). www.forbes.com/sites/scottsnowden/2020/07/24/ground-breaking-method-to-make-graphene-from-garbage-is-modern-day-alchemy/?sh=364742ed50d7#1d7e.
115 New Plastics Economy, "A Vision of a Circular Economy for Plastic" (2017). https://oceanfdn.org/wp-content/uploads/2010/08/npec-vision-of-a-circular-economy-for-plastic.pdf.
116 INTERPOL, "Emerging Criminal Trends in the Global Plastic Waste Market since January 2018" (2020). www.interpol.int/en/News-and-Events/News/2020/INTERPOL-report-alerts-to-sharp-rise-in-plastic-waste-crime.
117 Ellen MacArthur Foundation, "What Is a Circular Economy?" (2019). www.ellenmacarthurfoundation.org/circular-economy/concept.
118 Government of the Netherlands, "From a Linear to a Circular Economy" (2017). www.government.nl/topics/circular-economy/from-a-linear-to-a-circular-economy.

Exhibit 8: From a Linear to a Circular Economy

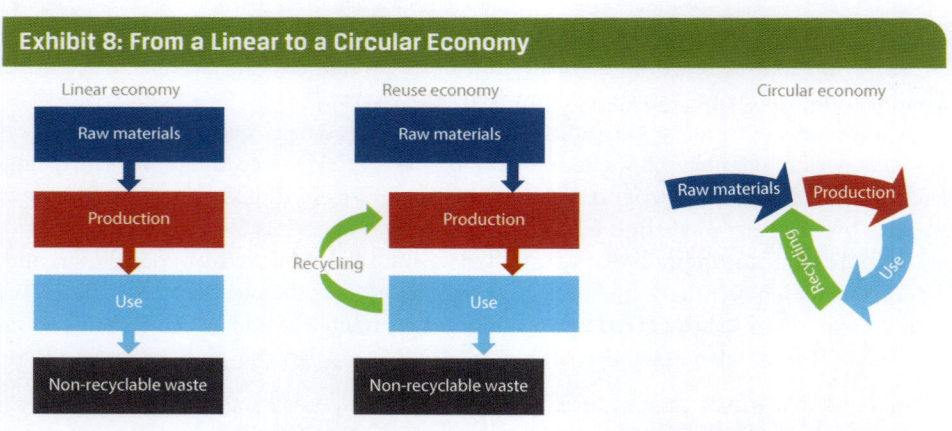

Source: Government of the Netherlands, "From a Linear to a Circular Economy" (2017). www.government.nl/topics/circular-economy/from-a-linear-to-a-circular-economy.

A report from the Ellen MacArthur Foundation stresses the importance of a circular economy as a fundamental step toward achieving climate targets.[119] To illustrate this potential, the paper argues that changes in the sources and use of energy could help halve the emissions associated with the production of goods; however, the other half of emissions comes from the use of materials, not energy. Applying circular economy strategies in just five key areas (cement, aluminium, steel, plastics, and food) can eliminate almost half of these remaining emissions. By 2050, the cumulative impact of these strategies would be equivalent to eliminating all current emissions from transport.[120]

The circular economy will also be covered in the section titled "Applying Material Environmental Factors to Financial Modeling, Ratio Analysis, and Risk Assessment."

3   SYSTEMIC RELATIONSHIPS BETWEEN BUSINESS ACTIVITIES AND ENVIRONMENTAL ISSUES

> **3.1.3** explain the systemic relationships between business activities and environmental issues, including systemic impact of climate risks on the financial system; climate-related physical and transition risks; the relationship between natural resources and business; supply, operational, and resource management issues; and supply chain transparency and traceability

Much of the understanding of key environmental factors with respect to business and investment centers on specific issues, such as climate change and unsustainable natural resource consumption and production, and on the negative impacts that businesses, consumption habits, and investment demand are having on the health of natural capital stocks. There is, however, less of an understanding of how businesses and financial activities depend on natural resources and properly functioning ecosystem services.

---

119 Ellen MacArthur Foundation, "Completing the Picture: How the Circular Economy Tackles Climate Change" (2019). www.ellenmacarthurfoundation.org/assets/downloads/Completing_The_Picture_How_The_Circular_Economy-_Tackles_Climate_Change_V3_26_September.pdf.
120 Ellen MacArthur Foundation, "Completing the Picture."

Systemic Relationships between Business Activities and Environmental Issues

Due to the difficulty in valuing and measuring natural resources, these detrimental impacts have not been fully priced into the costs of doing business (also known as pricing "negative externalities"). If such costs were to be fully internalized by businesses or their investors, there could be significant market disruptions.

Systemic Risks to the Financial System: Physical and Transitional Risks

Over the last 20 years, environmental themes have become an increasingly important consideration of the business agenda. Of note is the growing appreciation of the **physical risks** of climate change, stemming from more frequent or severe weather events, such as flooding, droughts, and storms. The associated costs are rising: Inflation-adjusted losses from extreme weather events have increased fivefold in recent decades.[121] In 2020, Munich RE estimated such losses to be over US$200 billion (£143.8 billion), with both overall losses and insured losses significantly higher than in previous years. Losses from the historic wildfires in the western United States alone were estimated to be around US$16 billion (£11.5 billion), with a similar loss figure due to floods in China.[122]

In 2022, a report by Swiss Re estimated that flood losses represented a third of the estimated US$270 billion global economic damages from natural catastrophes (see Exhibit 9), with 75% of flood risks remaining uninsured.[123]

Exhibit 9: Total Economic and Insured Losses from Natural Catastrophes (US$ billion, 2021 prices)

	2021	2020	Annual change
Total losses	270	217	33%
Insured losses	111	90	23%

Source: Lucia Bevere, "Natural Catastrophes in 2021: The Flood Gates Are Open," Swiss Re Institute (30 March 2022). www.swissre.com/institute/research/sigma-research/sigma-2022-01.html.

Insurers and reinsurers are particularly exposed to these effects, across both sides of their balance sheet. Their investment assets can be impacted if, for example, storms and floods affect real estate in their portfolio. Their liabilities can be affected if extreme weather leads to increases in property insurance claims or extreme-weather-induced diseases and mortality lead to increases in life insurance claims.

As the Bank of England has noted, physical risks can have significant macroeconomic effects: "For instance, if weather-related damage leads to a fall in house prices (and so reduces the wealth of homeowners) then there could be a knock-on effect on overall spending in the economy."[124]

There are also company- and sector-level implications, given the supply chains of a globalized economy.

---

121 S. Breeden, "Avoiding the Storm: Climate Change and the Financial System," speech, Bank of England (15 April 2019). www.bankofengland.co.uk/-/media/boe/files/speech/2019/avoiding-the-storm-climate-change-and-the-financial-system-speech-by-sarah-breeden.pdf.
122 Munich RE, "Record Hurricane Season and Major Wildfires—The Natural Disaster Figures for 2020" (2020). www.munichre.com/en/company/media-relations/media-information-and-corporate-news/media-information/2021/2020-natural-disasters-balance.html.
123 Lucia Bevere, "Natural Catastrophes in 2021: The Flood Gates Are Open," Swiss Re Institute (30 March 2022). www.swissre.com/institute/research/sigma-research/sigma-2022-01.html.
124 Bank of England, "Climate Change: What Are the Risks to Financial Stability?" (2021). www.bankofengland.co.uk/knowledgebank/climate-change-what-are-the-risks-to-financial-stability.

> **CASE STUDIES**
>
> ### Thai Floods
>
> In 2011, Thailand experienced its worst flooding in five decades, with US$45 billion (£32.4 billion) of economic damages, resulting in US$12 billion (£8.6 billion) in insurance claims. Although flooding is not uncommon in the region, the effects of the floods were felt across the globe: Over 10,000 factories of consumer goods, textiles, and automotive products had to close, disrupting the supply chain for such businesses as Sony, Nikon, and Honda, resulting in either reduced or delayed production. Many of these international businesses lodged contingent business interruption claims with their insurers and reinsurers, which cost Lloyd's of London US$2.2 billion (£1.6 billion).[125]

Occasionally, extreme weather events may lead not just to a hit to a company's finances but to full-scale bankruptcy.

> **CASE STUDIES**
>
> ### PG&E
>
> In what has been described as "the first climate-change bankruptcy, probably not the last,"[126] in January 2019, the US power supplier PG&E filed for voluntary Chapter 11 bankruptcy protection, as a result of liabilities stemming from wildfires in northern California in 2017 and 2018. It claimed that it faced an estimated US$30 billion (£21.6 billion) liability for damages from wildfires during those two years, a sum that would exceed its insurance and assets.

Whereas physical risks stem primarily from inaction on climate change, there are also climate risks and trade-offs associated with action—the so-called **transitional risks**—as the world shifts toward a low-carbon economy. As the Bank of England has explained:

> ▶ *such transitions could mean that some sectors of the economy face big shifts in asset values or higher costs of doing business. It's not that policies stemming from deals like the Paris Climate Agreement are bad for our economy—in fact, the risk of delaying action altogether would be far worse. Rather, it's about the speed of transition to a greener economy—and how this affects certain sectors and financial stability.*
>
> ▶ *One example is energy companies. If government policies were to change in line with the Paris Agreement, then two thirds of the world's known fossil fuel reserves could not be burned. This could lead to changes in the value of investments held by banks and insurance companies in sectors like coal, oil and gas. The move towards a greener economy could also impact companies that produce cars, ships and planes, or use a lot of energy to make raw materials like steel and cement."*[127]

---

125 Prudential Regulation Authority, "The Impact of Climate Change on the UK Insurance Sector" (September 2015). www.bankofengland.co.uk/-/media/boe/files/prudential-regulation/publication/impact-of-climate-change-on-the-uk-insurance-sector.pdf.
126 R. Gold, "PG&E: The First Climate-Change Bankruptcy, Probably Not the Last," *Wall Street Journal* (18 January 2019). www.wsj.com/articles/pg-e-wildfires-and-the-first-climate-change-bankruptcy-11547820006.
127 Bank of England, "Climate Change."

Transition risks are multiple in nature and include the following:

- policy risks, such as increased emission regulation and environmental standards,
- legal risks, such as lawsuits claiming damages from entities (corporations or sovereign states) believed to be liable for their contribution to climate change, and
- technology risks, such as low-carbon innovations disrupting established industries.

These risks are interlocking in nature and potentially have far-reaching impacts, which underscore their systemic relationship to business and financial activities. For example, a 2017 study from the Grantham Research Institute found that more than half of corporate bond purchases by the Bank of England and the European Central Bank (ECB) went to carbon-intensive sectors.[128] Such dependencies are increasingly being scrutinized by regulators, with the Bank for International Settlements—the "bank for central banks"—warning that climate change could "be the cause of the next systemic financial crisis."[129]

Exhibit 10 summarizes the main physical and transitional risks.

Exhibit 10: Risks to Financial Stability Due to Climate-Related Physical and Transition Risks

Physical and transition risks
The risks from climate change to the economy have two basic channels, but many potential impacts

Physical risks (Extreme weather events and gradual changes in climate)

Transition risks (Policy, technology, consumer preferences)

Economy:
- Business disruption
- Asset destruction
- Migration
- Reconstruction/replacement
- Lower value of stranded assets
- Increase in energy prices with dislocations

- Lower property and corporate asset value
- Lower household wealth
- Lower corporate profits, more litigation
- Lower growth and productivity affecting financial conditions

Negative feedback from tighter financial conditions

Financial system:
- Market losses (equities, bonds, commodities)
- Credit losses (residential and corporate loans)
- Underwriting losses
- Operational risk (including liability risk)

Source: International Monetary Fund, "Global Financial Stability Report: Lower for Longer," chapter 6 (October 2019). www.imf.org/en/Publications/GFSR/Issues/2019/10/01/global-financial-stability-report-october-2019.

The Relationship between Natural Resources and Business

In general, businesses and investment activities impact and depend on natural resources and ecosystem services in both direct and indirect ways.

---

[128] S. Matikainen, E. Campiglio, and D. Zenghelis, "The Climate Impact of Quantitative Easing," Grantham Research Institute (30 May 2017). www.lse.ac.uk/granthaminstitute/publication/the-climate-impact-of-quantitative-easing/.

[129] P. Bolton, M. Despres, L. A. Pereira Da Silva, F. Samama, and R. Svartzman, "The Green Swan: Central Banking and Financial Stability in the Age of Climate Change," Bank for International Settlements (January 2020). www.bis.org/publ/othp31.pdf.

The Global Reporting Initiative (GRI), which is a global sustainability reporting framework, explains the causes of direct and indirect impacts and dependencies of businesses on biodiversity resources.[130]

- A direct impact: An organization's activities directly affecting biodiversity—for example, when
  - degraded land is converted for the benefit of production activities,
  - surface water is used for irrigation purposes,
  - toxic materials are released, or
  - local species are disturbed through the noise and light produced at a processing site.
- An indirect impact: The impact is caused by parties in an organization's supply chain(s)—for example, when an organization imports fruits and vegetables, produces cotton shirts, sells construction materials, or publishes books, the production of the inputs for these goods will have indirect impacts on biodiversity.
- Indirect impacts can also include those from activities that have been triggered by the operations of the organization. For example, a road constructed to transport products from a forestry operation can have the indirect effect of stimulating the migration of workers to an unsettled region and encouraging new commercial development along the road.
- Indirect impacts may be relatively difficult to predict and manage, but they can be as significant as direct impacts and can easily affect an organization. Impacts on biodiversity can be either
  - negative (degrading the quality or quantity of biodiversity) or
  - positive (creating a net contribution to the quality or quantity of biodiversity).

Examples of sectors that rely significantly on natural resources and ecosystem services, with the potential to negatively affect biodiversity, include

- agriculture, aquaculture, fisheries, and food production,
- extractives, infrastructure, and activities or projects involving large-scale construction work,
- fast-moving consumer goods (FMCG) companies, primarily through the sourcing of raw materials in products,
- forestry (wood products, paper, fiber, and energy),
- pharmaceutical (in some cases),
- tourism and hospitality (in some cases), and
- utilities, including those involved in hydropower or open-cycle power plants generating significant thermal discharges.

Supply, Operational, and Resource Management Issues

Companies need to measure, manage, and disclose the environmental impact (both positive and negative) from their direct operations. Investors need to assess the extent to which companies understand the impact of their operations and manage resources that are material to their business.

---

130 Global Reporting Initiative, "Biodiversity: A GRI Reporting Resource" (2007).

Environmental impacts from direct operations can include

- toxic waste,
- water pollution,
- loss of biodiversity,
- deforestation,
- long-term damage to ecosystems,
- water scarcity,
- hazardous air emissions and high GHG emissions, and
- energy use.

Failure to address these challenges will expose businesses to additional risks, whereas working on solutions presents a business opportunity to develop climate-resilient business strategies. The previously described circular economy is a useful model for companies to assess and manage their operations and resource management.

The UK Government updated its Environmental Reporting Guidelines in March 2019, providing guidelines for businesses to measure and report their environmental impacts, including GHG emissions.[131] The guidelines emphasize the use of environmental key performance indicators (KPIs) to capture the link between environmental and financial performance.

In March 2019, the European Commission adopted the ambitious Circular Economy Action Plan to address the challenges of climate change and pressures on natural resources and ecosystems.[132] This was followed by European Commission guidelines under the Non-Financial Reporting Directive that introduced the concept of "double materiality"—in other words, asking companies to report both the impact of climate change on their activities and, conversely, the impact of a company's activities on climate change and the environment, stipulating that "companies should consider their whole value chain, both upstream in the supply chain and downstream."[133]

CASE STUDIES

Global Mining and Metals Sector

The global mining and metals sector has a considerable impact on the environment and the community in which it operates. In January 2019, Brazil's iron ore producer, Vale, experienced a deadly dam disaster, which resulted in the deaths of more than 250 people. The share price fell, wiping out BRL71.34 billion (£12.7 billion) in market value.[134]

---

131 Department for Environment, Food & Rural Affairs and Department for Business, Energy & Industrial Strategy, "Environmental Reporting Guidelines: Including Streamlined Energy and Carbon Reporting Requirements" (29 March 2019). www.gov.uk/government/publications/environmental-reporting-guidelines-including-mandatory-greenhouse-gas-emissions-reporting-guidance.

132 European Commission, "Report from the Commission to the European Parliament, the Council, the European Economic and Social Committee and the Committee of the Regions on the Implementation of the Circular Economy Action Plan" (2019). https://eur-lex.europa.eu/legal-content/EN/TXT/PDF/?uri=CELEX:52019DC0190&from=EN.

133 European Commission, "Guidelines on Reporting Climate-Related Information" (2019). https://ec.europa.eu/finance/docs/policy/190618-climate-related-information-reporting-guidelines_en.pdf.

134 P. Laier, "Vale Stock Plunges after Brazil Disaster; $19 Billion in Market Value Lost," Reuters (28 January 2019). www.reuters.com/article/us-vale-sa-disaster-stocks/vale-stock-plunges-after-brazil-disaster-19-billion-in-market-value-lost-idUSKCN1PM1JP.

> The disaster followed a similar incident in 2015, with the industry's use of a particular structure for the storage of waste—tailings dams—being thrown into the spotlight. Credit (and ESG) rating agencies downgraded Vale, with a number of funds selling out of the company, including from the world's largest sovereign wealth fund.[135]
>
> Recognizing the lack of transparency over the location and safety of such dams, a coalition of investors now representing over US$13 trillion (£9.3 trillion) in assets has written to over 700 extractive companies to call for investigations and reporting into this issue, with a view to the development of a global safety standard.
>
> Environmental (and social) scrutiny of the mining and metals sector has been increasing; many of the world's largest mining companies "have some of the worst scores on sustainability ratings compiled by fund managers . . . as well as external consultants."[136] This reinforces the role of adequate management of supply chain and operational impact.

Supply Chain Transparency and Traceability

Supply chain sustainability is the management of ESG impacts and practices beyond the factory gates, looking at the broader life cycle of goods and services, particularly with regard to the sourcing of raw materials and components.[137] Supply chains are complex to understand due to the fact that they are heavily interdependent. As such, the relationships between products and services and environmental risk factors are intertwined across sectors and throughout every level of the supply chain. Companies are increasingly expected to understand, manage, and disclose their exposure to supply chain ESG risks or be left exposed to reputational, operational, and financial risks. As such, it is becoming increasingly important for investors to factor into their due diligence and active stewardship a stronger understanding of the supply chain management of their portfolio companies.

Addressing emissions in industry and the food system presents a particularly complex challenge. In industry, a growing demand for materials, coupled with a slow adoption rate of renewable electricity and incremental process improvements, makes it especially difficult to bring emissions down to net zero by 2050. In the food system, significantly reducing emissions will also be challenging and will require changing the consumption habits of billions of people, changing the production habits of hundreds of millions of producers, and decarbonizing long and complex food supply chains.

Traceability is a useful practice to identify and trace the history, distribution, location and application of products, parts, and materials. This ensures the reliability of sustainability claims in the areas of human rights, labor (including health and safety), the environment, and anti-corruption.[138]

---

135 G. Freitas and V. Andrade, "Brazil Ore, Power Giants Excluded from Norway's Wealth Fund," Bloomberg (13 May 2020). www.bloomberg.com/news/articles/2020-05-13/brazil-iron-ore-power-giants-excluded-from-norway-s-wealth-fund.
136 N. Hume and H. Sanderson, "Global Miners Count the Cost of Their Failings," *Financial Times* (15 February 2019). www.ft.com/content/66965d68-2bc2-11e9-88a4-c32129756dd8.
137 UN Global Compact, "Supply Chain Sustainability: A Practical Guide for Continuous Improvement: Second Edition" (2015). www.unglobalcompact.org/docs/issues_doc/supply_chain/SupplyChainRep_spread.pdf.
138 UN Global Compact and BSR, "A Guide to Traceability: A Practical Approach to Advance Sustainability in the Global Supply Chains" (2014). www.unglobalcompact.org/library/791.

Systemic Relationships between Business Activities and Environmental Issues

In the context of environmental factors, GHG emissions in supply chains are estimated to be, on average, over five times as high as those from direct operations.[139]

Examples of sectors with particularly complex or high-risk supply chains include

- oil and gas,
- mining,
- beef,
- cocoa,
- cotton,
- fisheries,
- leather,
- palm oil,
- agriculture, and
- forestry.

It is therefore important for investors to understand key areas of environmental risks as a result of supply chain factors. Some of the main environmental risks in the supply chain are

- material toxicity and chemicals,
- raw material use,
- recyclability and end-of-life products,
- GHG emissions,
- energy use,
- water use and wastewater treatment,
- air pollution,
- biodiversity, and
- deforestation.

CASE STUDIES

Forest-Risk Commodities

Forests annually remove nearly one-third of emitted carbon dioxide[140] and are essential for meeting net-zero goals. Commodity production—mostly that of beef, palm oil, soy, and timber or pulp—is the leading cause of deforestation around the world, with significant amounts of financing devoted to these "forest-risk commodities." Trase Finance estimated that approximately US$1 trillion (£0.7 trillion) of investments are linked to deforestation, which are facing increased scrutiny from governments and civil society, bolstered by new data and tools (such as satellite monitoring). In 2020, the UK government announced that companies may face fines if they cannot demonstrate that their supply chains are free from illegal deforestation.

Investors have increased their engagement with relevant actors and begun to take action to address these risks. The Norwegian sovereign wealth fund has divested from over 30 palm oil companies, and a coalition of over 30 investors

---

139 CDP, "Global Supply Chain Report 2019" (2020). www.cdp.net/en/research/global-reports/global-supply-chain-report-2019.
140 Pierre Friedlingstein et al., "Global Carbon Budget 2021," *Earth System Science Data* 14 (26 April 2022): 1917–2005. https://essd.copernicus.org/articles/14/1917/2022/.

> with over US$4 trillion (£2.9 trillion) in assets under management has threatened divestment from commodity producers—and even government bonds—due to their impact in accelerating deforestation in the Amazon.[141]

Yet, much remains to be done. The results from Global Canopy's latest annual survey of the 500 most influential companies and financial institutions in forest supply chains shows that 43% do not have deforestation commitments for any of the forest-risk commodities they are exposed to (63% among financial institutions), and US$2.7 trillion (£1.9 trillion) of financing in the most influential high-risk companies comes from Forest 500 financial institutions with no deforestation policy.[142] The think-tank Planet Tracker has estimated that deforestation risks are rising in exchange-traded funds (ETFs), according to its 2020 report "Exchange Traded Deforestation."[143]

Measurement, frameworks, and investor expectations around supply chains keep evolving. For example, in terms of GHG emissions, the initial focus has been on direct emissions from core operations (Scope 1 emissions) and purchased energy (Scope 2 emissions). However, there is increasing focus on how to measure and incorporate indirect emissions from the whole value chain, including those produced by suppliers and customers (Scope 3 emissions).

CASE STUDIES

Scope 3 in the Spotlight

For companies in certain industries, the greatest contribution to their overall carbon footprint comes from outside "the factory gates." In the case of the fossil fuel industry, for example, most emissions come not from the extraction and processing of coal, oil, and gas but from the use of such products by consumers in vehicles, power plants, and steel mills around the world. Although to some degree, the emissions associated with suppliers or consumers (Scope 3) are not under a company's complete control, they nonetheless represent a source of potential business risk: A low-cost oil producer that captured all the emissions from its operations may nevertheless find the market for its main product shrinking or even vanishing as consumers shift to electric vehicles, for example. To address this issue, there has been growing investor pressure for companies to tackle emissions along the value chain that may lie outside "the factory gates."

A growing number of companies are now setting targets to also reduce Scope 3 emissions—associated with the burning of fossil fuels by customers (for miners, such as BHP, Glencore, and Vale), with the production of parts and raw materials by suppliers (in the case of Volkswagen), or with indirect emissions associated with food production, including land-use changes (in the case of Danone).

---

141 Multiple sources:
Fitch Ratings, "Financial Sector Confronts Deforestation as a Key ESG Risk" (2020). www.fitchratings.com/site/re/10134822.
Trase Finance, "Trase Finance Brings Transparency to More than $1 Trillion in Deforestation Financing" (7 October 2020). https://medium.com/trase/trase-finance-brings-transparency-to-more-than-1-trillion-in-deforestation-financing-a7123a5157e8.
M. McGrath, "Climate Change: New UK Law to Curb Deforestation in Supply Chains," BBC News (25 August 2020). www.bbc.com/news/science-environment-53891421.
Margaryta Kirakosian, "$4.6tn Investor Group Meets Brazilian Congress on Deforestation Concerns," CityWire Selector (2020). https://citywireselector.com/news/4-6tn-investor-group-meets-brazilian-congress-on-deforestation-concerns/a1380621.
142 Forest 500, "Time for Change: Delivering Deforestation-Free Supply Chains" (2021). https://forest500.org/publications/time-change-delivering-deforestation-free-supply-chains.
143 Planet Tracker, "Exchange Traded Deforestation" (2020).

For more information on classification of corporate emissions, see the section titled "Assessment of Materiality of Environmental Issues" on carbon footprinting.

Investors should assess whether a company in their portfolio has policies and systems in place that

1. clearly explain the environmental (and social) requirements that suppliers are expected to meet via a procurement policy (such as a supplier code of conduct) and
2. enable it to assess environmental (and social) risks throughout its supply chain and discuss whether it has a mechanism in place to improve poor practices.

Achieving full transparency and traceability across all stages in a supply chain in order to undertake a complete assessment of a company's environmental risks is often complex. This is a result of multiple actors involved with different systems and requirements in a supply chain that are required to produce an end product, often across international borders.

Despite these challenges, attempting to conduct this full value chain analysis is important for investors to obtain an accurate picture of investee companies and for companies to ensure that their own policies are not undermined by actions taken elsewhere in their supply chain. For example, CDP estimates that while 71% of its partner companies have zero deforestation targets, only 27% of their suppliers had policies to match this ambition. Conversely, corporate buyers polled by CDP stated that suppliers showing environmental leadership were more competitive over the long term.[144] As such, investors should continue to collaborate with and demand greater transparency from both companies and governments.

---

[144] CDP, "Changing the Chain: Global Supply Chain Report 2019/20" (2020). www.cdp.net/en/research/global-reports/changing-the-chain.

> **CASE STUDIES**
>
> ## Measurement Frameworks and Tools
>
> Not-for-profit organizations offer measurement frameworks and tools that can help trace critical sustainability issues in company supply chains. These include the following:
>
> - The Sustainability Consortium (TSC), which has built a set of performance indicators and a reporting system that highlights sustainability hotspots for more than 110 consumer product categories, covering 80%–90% of the impact of consumer products.
> - The WWF offers more than 50 performance indicators for measuring the supply chain risks associated with the production of a range of commodities, as well as the probability and severity of those risks.
> - CDP and the GRI have created standards and metrics for comparing different types of sustainability impact.
> - The Sustainability Accounting Standards Board (SASB) has developed standards that help public companies in 11 sectors, including consumer goods, to give investors material information about corporate sustainability performance along the value chain.
> - The EU Taxonomy and the Climate Bonds Sector Criteria provide sector-specific metrics and indicators to assess whether assets, projects, and activities in energy, transport, buildings, industry, agriculture and forestry, water and waste management, and so on, are compliant with the goals of the Paris Agreement.
> - Transparency for Sustainable Economies (Trase), a partnership between the Stockholm Environment Institute and Global Canopy
> - The Exploring Natural Capital Opportunities, Risks and Exposure (ENCORE) tool, an initiative of the UN Environment Programme World Conservation Monitoring Centre (WCMC), UN Environment Programme Finance Initiative, and Global Canopy
> - The Terra Carta (Earth Charter), an initiative under the patronage of the Prince of Wales, providing a roadmap for business action on climate change and biodiversity
>
> Companies and stakeholders in industries with complex supply chains, such as the agricultural and retail industries, have joined forces to build global multi-stakeholder initiatives in order to trace commodities collaboratively. Examples of global traceability schemes include the following:
>
> - the **Forest Stewardship Council (FSC)**,
> - the Marine Stewardship Council (MSC),
> - **Roundtable on Sustainable Palm Oil (RSPO)**, and
> - the Fairtrade Labelling Organizations International (FLO).

KEY "MEGATRENDS" AND DRIVERS INFLUENCING ENVIRONMENTAL CHANGE IN TERMS OF POTENTIAL IMPACT ON COMPANIES AND THEIR ENVIRONMENTAL PRACTICES

☐ 3.1.4 assess how megatrends influence environmental factors; environmental and climate policies; international climate and environmental agreements and conventions; international, regional, and country-level policy and initiatives; carbon pricing

Growth of Environmental and Climate Policies

There has been a considerable number of environmental and climate policies adopted in the last decade, with the majority coming from Europe. The Grantham Research Institute at the London School of Economics (LSE) undertook a global review and found that in 2017 there were approximately 1,400 climate change–relevant laws globally, a 20-fold increase over 20 years.[145] Since then, their number has only continued to increase: In January 2021, the Grantham Research Institute database counted a total of 2,092 climate laws and policies in countries across the globe.[146]

International Climate and Environmental Agreements and Conventions

International climate and environmental policy is particularly important in times of increasing globalization because many environmental problems, particularly climate change and loss of biodiversity, extend beyond national borders and can be solved only through international cooperation.

UN Framework Convention on Climate Change (1992)

The UN Framework Convention on Climate Change (UNFCCC) is the overarching international treaty relating to climate change. It set a general goal "to avoid dangerous anthropogenic interference with the climate system" and established the principle of "common but differentiated responsibilities" that distinguished responsibilities and obligations of developed and developing countries. All agreements including the legally binding Kyoto Protocol are protocols to this treaty. The UNFCCC secretariat is responsible for the annual Conference of the Parties established by the UNFCCC that are held each year so that national governments can evaluate progress and establish new goals, including the non-binding temperature limits established in 2015 in Paris at COP21.

---

[145] M. Nachmany, S. Fankhauser, J. Setzer, and A. Averchenkova, "Global Trends in Climate Change Legislation and Litigation: 2017 Update," Grantham Research Institute (2017). http://eprints.lse.ac.uk/80447/.
[146] Grantham Research Institute, "Climate Change Laws of the World" (2021). https://climate-laws.org/.

Kyoto Protocol (2005)

The Kyoto Protocol was adopted in 1997 and became effective in 2005 without US participation. It was the first international convention to set targets for emissions of the main GHGs:

1. CO_2,
2. methane (CH_4),
3. nitrous oxide (N_2O),
4. hydrofluorocarbons (HFCs),
5. perfluorocarbons (PFCs),
6. sulphur hexafluoride (SF_6), and
7. nitrogen trifluoride (NF_3).[147]

It established top-down, binding targets, but only for developed nations, recognizing the historical links between industrialization, economic development, and GHG emissions. The protocol's first commitment period began in 2008 and ended in 2012 but was subsequently extended to 2020. Negotiations on the measures to be taken after the second commitment period ends in 2020 resulted in the adoption of the Paris Agreement.

Paris Agreement (2015)

At the 21st Conference of the Parties to the UNFCCC in Paris in 2015 (COP21), a landmark agreement was reached to mobilize a global response to the threat of climate change in the form of the **Paris Agreement**.

The agreement's long-term goal is to keep the increase in global average temperature to well below 2°C (3.6°F) above pre-industrial levels and to limit the increase to 1.5°C (2.7°F), since this would substantially reduce the risks and effects of climate change.[148]

Although the Paris Agreement does not set any legally binding targets under international law, it serves as a significant landmark in tackling climate change on a global scale.

Nationally determined contributions (NDCs) are at the heart of the agreement.[149] Instead of top-down imposed contributions, they capture voluntary efforts by each country to reduce national emissions and adapt to the impacts of climate change, and they require every signatory (both developed and developing nations) to determine, plan, and report on its NDCs, with updates to commitments every five years. While commitments vary, they tend to fall in the 25%–30% range of GHG emissions (relative to 2005) by 2030. Unfortunately, many countries are not on track to achieving their targets, with existing NDCs estimated to be aligned with a dangerous trajectory of around 3°C (5.4°F) as of 2021.[150]

The deal has been formally endorsed by 191 nations, with only six parties to the UNFCCC that were not signatories to the agreement by February 2021.[151] However, the implementation of certain elements of the agreement—such as the development

---

147 United Nations Climate Change, "What Is the Kyoto Protocol?" (2021). https://unfccc.int/kyoto_protocol.
148 United Nations, "Paris Agreement."
149 United Nations Climate Change, "Nationally Determined Contributions (NDCs)" (2021). https://unfccc.int/process-and-meetings/the-paris-agreement/nationally-determined-contributions-ndcs/nationally-determined-contributions-ndcs.
150 Climate Action Tracker (2021). https://climateactiontracker.org/.
151 S. Apparicio and N. Sauer, "Which Countries Have Not Ratified the Paris Climate Agreement?" Climate Home News (13 August 2020). www.climatechangenews.com/2020/08/13/countries-yet-ratify-paris-agreement/.

of global carbon markets and the delivery of a proposed yearly US$100 billion (£71.9 billion) in climate finance—remains the subject of further negotiations under the UNFCCC.

Glasgow Climate Pact (2021)

The Glasgow Climate Pact[152] captures key outcomes of COP26 in Glasgow in 2021, marking the first time governments around the world were expected to announce their updated climate policies since the Paris Agreement.

As a diplomatic document, the Pact is notable for a commitment to phase down the use of unabated coal power and for the recognition of shorter-term emissions pathways (50% reduction in CO_2 emissions by 2030, net zero around mid-century) needed to reach the goal of limiting global warming to 1.5°C. The Glasgow Climate Pact has also seen progress made around carbon markets and other forms of international climate cooperation, including more stringent use around carbon offsetting and strengthened pledges from developed countries to increase the financing available for climate adaptation in emerging markets and to reduce the use of non-CO_2 GHGs—notably, methane.

In terms of aggregate impact, it is difficult to assess the outcomes of the Glasgow Climate Pact, because they involve a combination of individual NDCs submitted by countries via the formal UN process (pledges that only cover 5- or 10-year time frames, some of which are also conditional on access to development finance), as well as a swathe of longer-term unilateral and multilateral commitments (such as India's pledge to reach net zero by 2070 and the Global Methane Pledge made by over 100 countries).[153]

Analysis suggests that median projected levels of warming by 2100 would fall to around 2.4°C if all Glasgow NDCs were met, with the potential to reach 1.8°C if all other longer-term pledges were implemented on time.[154] Although compared to the policy trajectories before 2015, the Glasgow Climate Pact has potentially brought the Paris "well below 2°C" temperature goals within closer reach, the significant gaps and uncertainties surrounding the implementation and financing of policies still create the risk of missing the goals, potentially by a wide mark.

The following are other international agreements and frameworks that have impacted companies' environmental practices:

> The UN **Sustainable Development Goals (SDGs)** are a set of 17 global goals set in 2015 by the UN General Assembly seeking to address key global challenges, such as poverty, inequality, and climate change. Although primarily intended as a framework for government action, the SDGs are now regularly cited by corporate and investment actors as material to their business planning and operations. SDGs 7 (affordable and clean energy), 11 (sustainable cities and communities), 12 (responsible consumption and production), 13 (climate action), 14 (life below water), and 15 (life on land) are some of the most directly relevant to the environmental debate.

---

152 UNFCC, "Glasgow Climate Pact" (2021). https://unfccc.int/documents/310475.
153 P. Forster, C. Smith, and J. Rogelj, "Guest Post: The Global Methane Pledge Needs to Go Further to Help Limit Warming to 1.5C," Carbon Brief (2 November 2021). www.carbonbrief.org/guest-post-the-global-methane-pledge-needs-to-go-further-to-help-limit-warming-to-1-5c.
154 Z. Hausfather and P. Forster, "Analysis: Do COP26 Promises Keep Global Warming below 2C?" Carbon Brief (10 November 2021). www.carbonbrief.org/analysis-do-cop26-promises-keep-global-warming-below-2c.

The **Kigali Amendment to the Montreal Protocol of 2016** is a global agreement to phase out the manufacture of hydrofluorocarbons. These gases were used in an attempt to replace ozone-depleting chemicals but have the downside of causing a potent warming effect on the planet.[155]

The **International Maritime Organization (IMO) 2020 Regulation** caps the maximum sulphur content in the fuel oil used by ships. Limiting sulphur oxide emissions, which contribute to air pollution and acid rain, is estimated to have a very positive impact on human health and the environment.[156]

CORSIA (Carbon Offsetting and Reduction Scheme for International Aviation) is a UN mechanism designed by the UN International Civil Aviation Organization (ICAO) to help the aviation industry reach its aspirational goal to make all growth in international flights after 2020 carbon neutral, with airlines required to offset their emissions. The scheme is important because domestic aviation emissions are covered by the Paris Agreement, but international flights—which are responsible for around two-thirds of the CO_2 emissions from aviation—are under the remit of ICAO.[157]

International, Regional, and Country-Level Climate Policy and Initiatives

Over the last five years, there has been an acceleration in environmental and climate initiatives targeting the financial and business sector. The 2015 Paris Agreement has no doubt been the most instrumental driver in terms of bringing together all nations for a common cause to undertake ambitious efforts to combat climate change and adapt to its effects. It has also helped regulators and policymakers at national levels to take action.

Sustainable Finance in the EU

In December 2019, the European Union (EU) announced the **European Green Deal**, a plan to make the EU economy climate neutral by 2050 by boosting the efficient use of resources, restoring biodiversity, and cutting pollution. As part of this program, the EU has renewed its strategy focused on sustainable finance, whose main ambitions are as follows:

- **To reorient capital flows** by
  - establishing the following:
    - a classification system (taxonomy) for sustainable activities and
    - standards and labels for green bonds, benchmarks, and other financial products
  - increasing EU funding for sustainable projects

- **To mainstream sustainability into risk management** by efforts to incorporate sustainability into financial advice, credit ratings, and market research, as well as more technical proposals on the treatment of "green" assets in the capital requirements of banks and insurers (the so-called green supporting factor)

---

155 UNEP, "The Kigali Amendment to the Montreal Protocol: Another Global Commitment to Stop Climate Change" (8 December 2016). www.unenvironment.org/news-and-stories/news/kigali-amendment-montreal-protocol-another-global-commitment-stop-climate.
156 IMO, "IMO 2020—Cutting Sulphur Oxide Emissions" (2020). www.imo.org/en/MediaCentre/HotTopics/Pages/Sulphur-2020.aspx.
157 Note that, due to the impact of the pandemic, the emissions baseline was adjusted to 2019, not 2020. J. Timperley, "Corsia: The UN's Plan to 'Offset' Growth in Aviation Emissions," Carbon Brief (4 February 2019). www.carbonbrief.org/corsia-un-plan-to-offset-growth-in-aviation-emissions-after-2020.

▶ **To foster transparency and long-term thinking** by strengthening the disclosure requirements relating to sustainability (on both the financial industry and companies more broadly)[158]

These developments are intended to embed sustainability across the entire investment chain—from the owners of capital (such as pension funds and insurance companies) to the beneficiaries of capital (such as investee companies), as well as key intermediaries (banks, asset managers, financial advisers, consultants, and credit rating agencies).

EU Taxonomy

One of the most heavily debated topics in the investment community has been the EU taxonomy for sustainable activities. Approved by the EU Parliament in June 2020, the Taxonomy Regulation aims to significantly reduce the risk of green-washing financial products by providing a classification system to determine whether an economic activity is environmentally sustainable.[159] The taxonomy requires that economic activities make a substantial contribution to environmental objectives, do no significant harm to any other environmental objective, and comply with minimum social safeguards and the technical screening criteria (discussed below).

At a high level, inclusion in the taxonomy is restricted to activities that contribute to at least one of the six environmental objectives:

1. climate change mitigation,
2. climate change adaptation,
3. sustainable use and protection of water and marine resources,
4. transition to a circular economy, waste prevention, and recycling;
5. pollution prevention and control, and
6. protection of healthy ecosystems.

Further delegated acts in 2021 and 2022 have provided further clarifications, including screening criteria around each of the objectives—for example, the levels of GHG emissions associated with the manufacture of certain technologies and energy usage requirements for the construction of new buildings.[160] The inclusion of specific nuclear and gas energy activities, approved in principle by the EU Commission in February 2022, has been the subject of ongoing controversy among EU member states, industry groups, and civil society.[161]

Under the taxonomy regulation, institutional investors and asset managers offering investment products labeled as environmentally sustainable would need to explain whether and how they have used the taxonomy criteria. This forms a part of the growing disclosure requirements for investors relating to sustainability.

Sustainability Disclosures

Two further significant EU developments include the **Sustainable Finance Disclosure Regulation (SFDR)** and the **Corporate Sustainability Reporting Directive (CSRD)**.

---

158 European Commission, "Renewed Sustainable Finance Strategy and Implementation of the Action Plan on Financing Sustainable Growth" (2020). https://ec.europa.eu/info/publications/sustainable-finance-renewed-strategy_en.
159 European Commission, "Sustainable Finance Taxonomy—Regulation (EU) 2020/852." https://ec.europa.eu/info/law/sustainable-finance-taxonomy-regulation-eu-2020-852_en.
160 European Commission, "EU Taxonomy for Sustainable Activities" (2022). https://ec.europa.eu/info/business-economy-euro/banking-and-finance/sustainable-finance/eu-taxonomy-sustainable-activities_en. See also European Commission, "Commission Delegated Regulation (EU) 2021/2139" (4 June 2021). https://eur-lex.europa.eu/legal-content/EN/TXT/HTML/?uri=CELEX:32021R2139&from=EN.
161 BBC, "Climate Change: EU Moves to Label Nuclear and Gas as Sustainable Despite Internal Row" (2 February 2022). www.bbc.co.uk/news/world-europe-60229199.

Under SFDR, investors are required to provide more transparency around

- how the impacts of sustainability risks on their financial products are being systematically assessed (e.g., integrated into due diligence and research processes),
- how asset managers consider—and seek to address—the potentially negative implications of investment activities on sustainability factors, and
- products labeled with an explicit ESG focus.[162]

The SFDR introduces a categorization of the depth of ESG integration between so-called

- Article 6 products (which are not promoted as incorporating any ESG factors or objectives),
- Article 8 products (products claimed to promote environmental and social characteristics), and
- Article 9 products (products that have sustainable investment as an objective).

In October 2021, the final draft rules harmonizing disclosure requirements for financial products under SFDR and the Taxonomy Regulation were published by the European Supervisory Authorities, covering both pre-contractual and periodic disclosures.[163]

One challenge common to investors in meeting their obligations is the requirement for Article 8 and 9 funds, as of January 2022, to report the proportion of investments contributing to the first two objectives of the EU taxonomy. However, the companies (that in many cases represent a majority of the underlying holdings of these funds) are not required to report the alignment of their activities to the taxonomy until the following year.

The proposed Corporate Sustainability Reporting Directive (CSRD) would replace and strengthen the existing EU requirements around non-financial reporting, covering all large companies and all listed companies on EU-regulated markets (except for "micro-enterprises"). The companies in scope would have to report in line with upcoming EU sustainability reporting standards and have the resulting information audited and made available in a digital format to be incorporable into a "European Single Access Point" that aims to serve as a "one-stop-shop" for sustainability-related information regarding EU companies and investment products.[164]

One notable concept gaining prominence in EU non-financial reporting rules is that of "double materiality,"—that is, the two-way impacts between companies and climate change, the environment, and society (see Exhibit 11). This extends the historical focus on the micro, company level (for example, understanding a company's energy usage as a proxy for future production costs) to a broader discussion of a company's role in the macroeconomic environment. At the same time, it renders more explicit the challenge of navigating multiple dimensions of sustainability (e.g., selecting among energy producers for lower-cost sources of energy may inadvertently favor companies in countries with a problematic record on human rights).

---

162 European Commission, "Regulation (EU) 2019/2088 of the European Parliament and of the Council of 27 November 2019 on Sustainability-Related Disclosures in the Financial Services Sector" (2019). http://data.europa.eu/eli/reg/2019/2088/oj.

163 Joint Committee of the European Supervisory Authorities, "Final Report on Draft Regulatory Technical Standards with Regard to the Content and Presentation of Disclosures Pursuant to Article 8(4), 9(6) and 11(5) of Regulation (EU) 2019/2088" (2021).

164 European Commission, "Questions and Answers: Corporate Sustainability Reporting Directive Proposal" (2021). https://ec.europa.eu/commission/presscorner/detail/en/qanda_21_1806.

Exhibit 11: The Double Materiality Perspective in the Context of Reporting Climate-Related Information

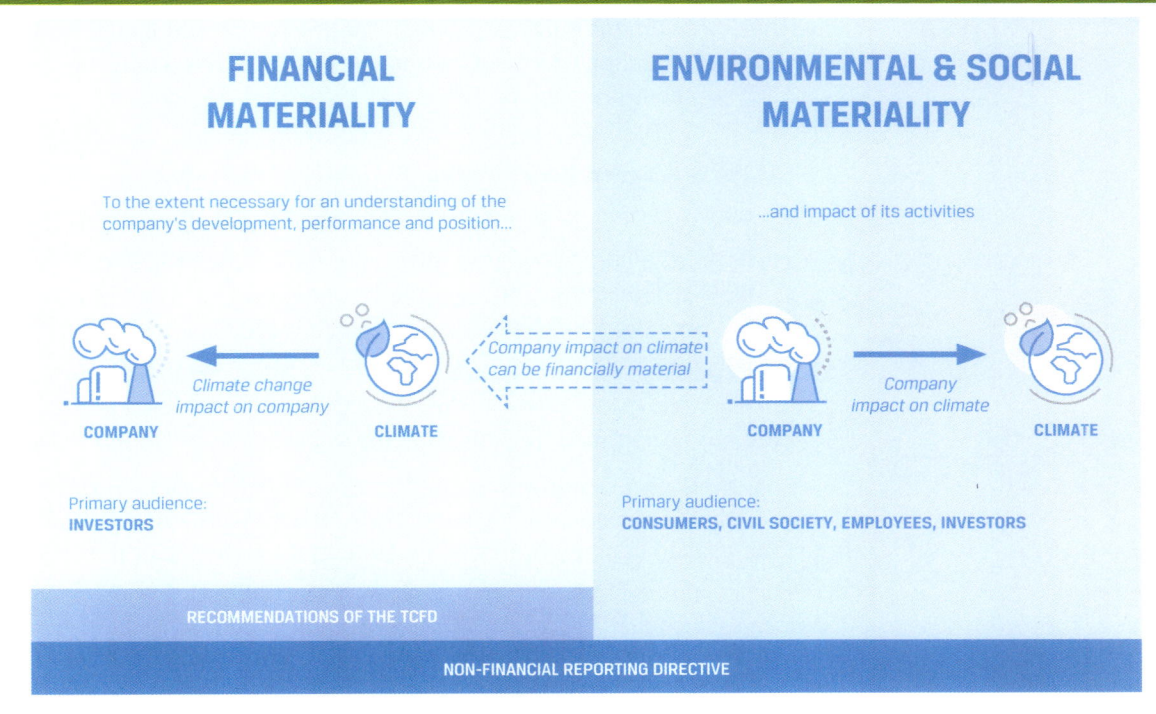

FINANCIAL MATERIALITY

To the extent necessary for an understanding of the company's development, performance and position...

Climate change impact on company

COMPANY ← CLIMATE

Primary audience: INVESTORS

Company impact on climate can be financially material

ENVIRONMENTAL & SOCIAL MATERIALITY

...and impact of its activities

Company impact on climate

COMPANY → CLIMATE

Primary audience: CONSUMERS, CIVIL SOCIETY, EMPLOYEES, INVESTORS

RECOMMENDATIONS OF THE TCFD

NON-FINANCIAL REPORTING DIRECTIVE

* Financial materiality is used here in the broad sense of affecting the value of the company, not just in the sense of affecting financial measures recognised in the financial statements.

Note: TCFD recommendations are explained in the following section.

Source: European Commission.[165]

Climate Benchmarks

Another area of EU activity is the creation of **climate benchmarks**. Benchmarks play an important role in investments, serving—as their name suggests—as a comparator to measure the performance of investments (in the case of actively managed funds) or as a target for the construction of investment solutions, which aim to replicate (or "track") the composition of certain widely used benchmarks (e.g., stock market indexes, such as the FTSE 100 Index and S&P 500 Index, in the case of so-called passive, tracker, or index funds).

However, the most widely used benchmarks are primarily based on company size (at least for equities) and thus do not directly reflect low-carbon considerations in their methodologies. This raises the possibility that a significant and, given the rising share of assets managed under index strategies, growing portion of the investment universe might be pursuing environmentally unsustainable investment strategies. In fact, research suggests that "current benchmarks are likely to be more aligned with a 'business-as-usual' scenario, where temperature rises range from 4°C to 6°C (7.2°F to 10.8°F), leading to catastrophic damage to the earth."[166]

---

[165] European Commission, "Guidelines on Reporting Climate-Related Information" (2019). https://ec.europa.eu/finance/docs/policy/190618-climate-related-information-reporting-guidelines_en.pdf.
[166] EU Technical Expert Group on Sustainable Finance, "TEG Interim Report on Climate Benchmarks and Benchmarks' ESG Disclosures" (June 2019). https://ec.europa.eu/info/sites/info/files/business_economy_euro/banking_and_finance/documents/190618-sustainable-finance-teg-report-climate-benchmarks-and-disclosures_en.pdf.

Therefore, the EU has developed two types of climate benchmarks for equities and corporate bonds that aim to start with lower associated carbon emission intensity relative to their investable universe and then continually cut emission thresholds each year by at least 7%, in line with IPCC estimates for annual reductions necessary for a 1.5°C (2.7°F) temperature scenario.

The following are the two main categories of benchmarks:

1. **EU Paris-Aligned Benchmarks (EU PABs)**, which must
   - reduce carbon emission intensity by at least 50% in their starting year,
   - have a four-to-one ratio of "green" to "brown" investments relative to the investable universe, and
   - not invest in fossil fuels

2. **EU Climate Transition Benchmarks (EU CTBs)**, which require a 30% intensity reduction in the starting year and at least an equal green-to-brown ratio but permit fossil fuel investments as part of a transition process[167]

One of the main innovations in the EU climate benchmarks is the attempt to compare company performance relative to the absolute emission pathways necessary for the global economy to reach climate targets, rather than the more relative approaches that exist in the market (whereby, for example, a company may receive a positive score as long as its emission performance was better than its sector average). However, concerns have also been raised as to whether the proposed approach sufficiently encourages the decarbonization of the *real economy*, across sectors, as opposed to the reduction of *portfolio-level emissions* by overly focusing on the exclusion of high-carbon sectors and stocks.[168]

Further progress on developments from the European Commission's Sustainable Action Plan will continue to play a pivotal role in the development of EU and global markets toward greater harmonization through the International Platform on Sustainable Finance (IPSF), thereby influencing policy.[169]

Country-Level Policy and Prudential Actions

Some countries and regions are leading the way in influencing the regulatory framework to promote the economic and financial mainstreaming of climate change and environmental factors.

France

France's Energy Transition for Green Growth Law took effect in January 2016. It requires mandatory disclosures from major institutional investors around their exposure to climate risks and efforts to mitigate climate change.[170] Because the law explicitly targets institutional investors but not banks, it provided a control group for

---

167 EU Technical Expert Group on Sustainable Finance, "TEG Final Report on Climate Benchmarks and Benchmarks' ESG Disclosures" (September 2019). https://ec.europa.eu/info/sites/default/files/business_economy_euro/banking_and_finance/documents/190930-sustainable-finance-teg-final-report-climate-benchmarks-and-disclosures_en.pdf.
168 N. Amenc, F. Goltz, and V. Liu, "Doing Good or Feeling Good? Detecting Greenwashing in Climate Investing," EDHEC Business School (August 2021). www.edhec.edu/sites/www.edhec-portail.pprod.net/files/210921-1_doing_good_or_feeling_good.pdf.
See also I. Daramus and R. Ram, "The Tracking Error Error: Why Climate Alignment Calls for Bolder Steps" (2022). www.fulcrumasset.com/inst/uk/en/white-papers/the-tracking-error-error-why-climate-alignment-calls-for-bolder-steps./.
169 European Commission, "International Platform on Sustainable Finance" (2021). https://ec.europa.eu/info/business-economy-euro/banking-and-finance/sustainable-finance/international-platform-sustainable-finance_en.
170 Gouvernement.fr, "Energy Transition" (2015).

a kind of natural experiment; a 2021 report by the Banque de France found "evidence of a sharp relative decrease in holdings of fossil energy securities in the portfolios" of the investors affected by the law.[171]

The United Kingdom

In 2020, the UK government announced a 10-point plan for a green industrial revolution that aims to

- scale up low-carbon technologies and infrastructure,
- increase protections for biodiversity, and
- further the green finance agenda.[172]

An important element of the plan is a roadmap toward mandatory climate-related disclosures for UK companies, starting with large financial institutions and premium listed companies and then gradually widening the scope to other UK-registered companies and financial actors.[173]

This plan follows a growing focus on sustainability from the main financial supervisors in the United Kingdom. Note that the United Kingdom is the first to introduce mandatory climate disclosures based on TCFD.

The Prudential Regulation Authority (PRA) and the Financial Conduct Authority published separate consultations on climate change in 2018, which resulted in increased requirements for UK banks and insurers—notably, the introduction of a climate change **stress test** for their liabilities and investments to investigate the resilience of the financial system by testing the implications of high-impact climate change scenarios.[174]

This has elements of a precautionary approach, which focuses not on forecasts of plausibility but on avoidance of worst-case outcomes.

CASE STUDIES

The Precautionary Principle

The precautionary principle states that "if an action or policy has a suspected risk of causing severe harm to the public domain (affecting general health or the environment globally), the action should not be taken in the absence of scientific near-certainty about its safety." It is intended to provide a safeguard "in cases where the absence of evidence and the incompleteness of scientific knowledge carry profound implications and in the presence of risks of 'black swans,' unforeseen and unforeseeable events of extreme consequence."[175]

---

171 J.-S. Méssonier and B. Nguyen, "Showing Off Cleaner Hands: Mandatory Climate-Related Disclosure by Financial Institutions and the Financing of Fossil Energy" (2021). www.banque-france.fr/sites/default/files/medias/documents/wp800.pdf.
172 HM Government, "Policy Paper: The Ten Point Plan for a Green Industrial Revolution" (2020). www.gov.uk/government/publications/the-ten-point-plan-for-a-green-industrial-revolution.
173 HM Treasury, "A Roadmap towards Mandatory Climate-Related Disclosures" (2020). https://assets.publishing.service.gov.uk/government/uploads/system/uploads/attachment_data/file/933783/FINAL_TCFD_ROADMAP.pdf.
174 Financial Conduct Authority, "FS19/6: Climate Change and Green Finance" (2018). www.fca.org.uk/publications/discussion-papers/dp18-8-climate-change-and-green-finance.
See also PRA, "Enhancing Banks' and Insurers' Approaches to Managing the Financial Risks from Climate Change" (2019). www.bankofengland.co.uk/prudential-regulation/publication/2018/enhancing-banks-and-insurers-approaches-to-managing-the-financial-risks-from-climate-change.
175 Nassim Nicholas Taleb, Rupert Read, Raphael Douady, Joseph Norman, and Yaneer Bar-Yam, "The Precautionary Principle (with Application to the Genetic Modification of Organisms)" (2014). https://arxiv.org/abs/1410.5787.
See also Joseph Norman, Rupert Read, Yaneer Bar-Yam, and Nassim Nicholas Taleb, "Climate Models and Precautionary Measures" (2015). https://fooledbyrandomness.com/climateletter.pdf.

> It is impossible to predict with full certainty the future evolution of the global climate system. But this does not mean it is impossible to state whether certain interventions are likely to increase, rather than decrease, climate risks. Moreover, by the time climate damages are confirmed, it may be too late—hence the importance of precaution.
>
> Environmental standards in certain jurisdictions, such as the EU, already embody elements of the precautionary principle. However, some have argued that financial authorities also "need to move towards precautionary approaches to maintaining the safety and soundness of the financial system. Precautionary policy prioritises preventative action and a qualitative approach to managing risk above quantitative measurement and information disclosure. It aims to steer away from tipping points and build system resilience as a superior means of managing radical uncertainty."[176]
>
> One notable area where precaution is a legal requirement concerns the duties of pension fund trustees.[177] Bound to act in the best interest of their beneficiaries, trustees in a number of jurisdictions are expected to act "as a prudent person acting in a like capacity would . . . in the conduct of an enterprise of like character and aims."[178] The implications of these duties with regard to, for example, the fossil fuel investments of pension funds have been the subject of significant debate in recent years.

Regulation is also increasing for pension funds, with successive clarifications from the United Kingdom's policymakers that ESG and climate considerations can have material financial impacts and therefore are not "to do with personal ethics, or optional extras,"[179] but fall within the remit of the risks that must be monitored and addressed by pension trustees as part of their investment duties.

The Pensions Regulator (TPR) in the United Kingdom has issued guidance to pension funds relating to ESG issues and climate change along similar lines. Since 1 October 2020, trustees of defined contribution (DC) pension schemes will be required to produce an implementation report setting out how they acted on the principles set out in the statement of investment principles. In February 2021, amendments to the **Pensions Schemes Act** required UK pension schemes, among increased climate requirements, to consider "the steps that might be taken for the purpose of achieving the Paris Agreement goal."[180]

In 2021, the UK government unveiled "Greening Finance: A Roadmap to Sustainable Investment,"[181] which detailed several policy areas, including the following:

► New disclosure requirements for corporates, asset managers, asset owners, and investment products, aligned with the recommendations of the TCFD and ISSB (discussed in the next section)

► The establishment of a "UK Green Taxonomy" of sustainable activities

---

176 K. Kedward, J. Ryan-Collins, and H. Chenet, "Managing Nature-Related Financial Risks: A Precautionary Policy Approach for Central Banks and Financial Supervisors," UCL Institute for Innovation and Public Purpose (18 August 2020). www.ucl.ac.uk/bartlett/public-purpose/wp2020-09.
177 I. S. Daramus, "Liability and Precaution," *Environment: Science and Policy for Sustainable Development* 59 (18 August 2017): 48–56. https://doi.org/10.1080/00139157.2017.1350012.
178 R. Galer, "'Prudent Person Rule' Standard for the Investment of Pension Fund Assets" (2021). www.oecd.org/finance/private-pensions/2763540.pdf.
179 Department of Work and Pension, "Consultation Outcome: Pension Trustees: Clarifying and Strengthening Investment Duties" (2018). www.gov.uk/government/consultations/pension-trustees-clarifying-and-strengthening-investment-duties.
180 UK Government, "Pension Schemes Act 2021" (2021). www.legislation.gov.uk/ukpga/2021/1/section/124/enacted.
181 HM Government, "Greening Finance: A Roadmap to Sustainable Investment" (2021). www.gov.uk/government/publications/greening-finance-a-roadmap-to-sustainable-investing.

The United States

The United States has historically had a more conservative stance on this issue compared to the United Kingdom and the EU. Notably, there has been ongoing debate (and successive policy shifts) as to whether trustees may, may not, or should consider ESG and climate factors in the management of their investments. Under the different administrations since 2015, the US Department of Labor's (DOL's) guidance on the issue has varied, and it is currently once more subject to review. Much of the discussion focuses on the extent to which the incorporation of ESG issues can be interpreted as prioritizing non-financial objectives (such as the pursuit of social and policy goals) over the long-term financial security of retirees. Recognizing the evolution of ESG investing, feedback from market participants in response to a DOL consultation in 2019 overwhelmingly stressed the financial materiality of ESG factors.[182]

In 2021, the Federal Reserve launched a Financial Stability Climate Committee and a Supervision Climate Committee to investigate the micro- and macro-prudential implications of climate change, respectively,[183] including the possibility of "climate stress testing" (see also the subsequent section on NGFS).

In 2022, the Securities and Exchange Commission (SEC) unveiled proposals[184] to require companies to report on

- the governance and impacts of climate-related risks,
- GHG emissions (Scope 1, Scope 2, and, where material, Scope 3 emissions) and other climate-related financial statement metrics, some of which would need to be subject to audit/assurance, and
- climate-related targets and goals and transition plans, if any.

China

Reckoning with the climate costs associated with decades of explosive economic growth, China's policymakers have begun combining its global leadership position on renewable energy with a greater desire for its financial system to address environmental issues. China is the world's largest manufacturer of solar cells, lithium-ion batteries, and electric vehicles, and these are areas of clear policy priority.[185] In 2020 alone, China doubled its construction of new wind and solar power plants compared to the previous year.[186] It remains the country with the highest levels of investment in the low-carbon energy transition and the highest absolute GHG emissions (see Exhibit 12).

---

182 T. Quinson, "Biden Administration Considers Reversing Trump's ESG Rule Change," Bloomberg (20 January 2021). www.bloomberg.com/news/articles/2021-01-20/biden-administration-considers-reversing-trump-s-esg-rule-change.
183 L. Brainard, "Financial Stability Implications of Climate Change" (2021). www.federalreserve.gov/newsevents/speech/brainard20210323a.htm.
184 Securities and Exchange Commission, "SEC Proposes Rules to Enhance and Standardize Climate-Related Disclosures for Investors" (2022). www.sec.gov/news/press-release/2022-46.
185 BloombergNEF, "China's Accelerated Decarbonization: Economic Benefits" (2020). https://assets.bbhub.io/professional/sites/24/BNEF-Chinas-Accelerated-Decarbonization-Pathways_12012020_FINAL.pdf.
186 J. Murtaugh, "China Blows Past Clean Energy Record with Wind Capacity Jump," Bloomberg (20 January 2021). www.bloomberg.com/news/articles/2021-01-20/china-blows-past-clean-energy-record-with-extra-wind-capacity.

Exhibit 12: Global Investment in Energy Transition by Country (2021, $ billions)

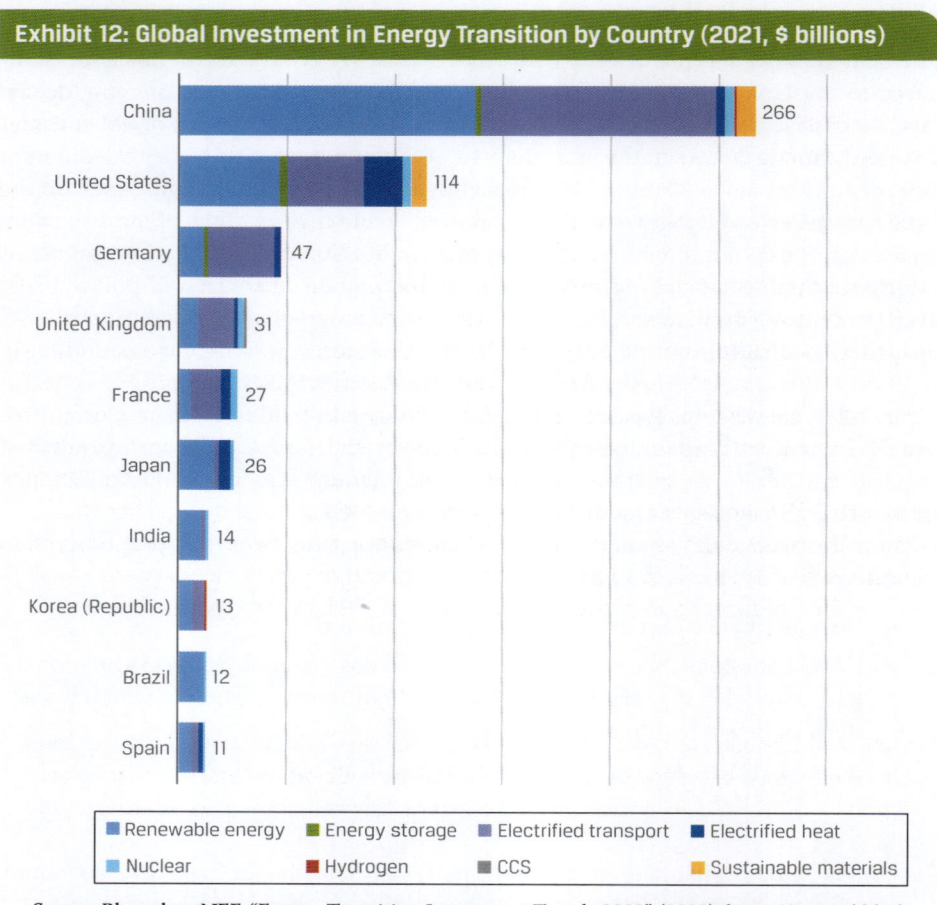

China	266
United States	114
Germany	47
United Kingdom	31
France	27
Japan	26
India	14
Korea (Republic)	13
Brazil	12
Spain	11

Legend: Renewable energy, Energy storage, Electrified transport, Electrified heat, Nuclear, Hydrogen, CCS, Sustainable materials

Source: BloombergNEF, "Energy Transition Investment Trends 2022" (2022). https://assets.bbhub.io/professional/sites/24/Energy-Transition-Investment-Trends-Exec-Summary-2022.pdf.

At the UN General Assembly in 2020, China's policymakers committed to have the country's CO_2 emissions peak before the year 2030, and in 2021 China published its roadmap to net-zero carbon by 2060. This was followed by an action plan for peak emissions, released a year later by the State Council.[187] More efforts to further embed environmental considerations into the economy are underway, with the rollout of a national carbon market and China's seven ministerial agencies, including the central bank, having previously indicated their support for institutional investors to perform environmental stress tests and for mandatory environmental disclosures for issuers of public debt and equity.[188]

The country's policymakers are increasingly engaging with international counterparts on issues pertaining to green finance and the green taxonomy. The country's green bond market is now the world's largest, but it has faced barriers regarding investor access and lack of international harmonization. Regulators announced they will exclude fossil fuel projects from their green bonds taxonomy, bringing the country closer to international practice.[189]

---

187 State Council of the People's Republic of China, "Full Text: Action Plan for Carbon Dioxide Peaking Before 2030" (2021). english.www.gov.cn/policies/latestreleases/202110/27/content_WS6178a47ec6d0df57f98e3dfb.html.
188 J. Ma, "Ma Jun on the Importance of Environmental Risk Analysis to Financial Institutions" (2017). www.climatebonds.net/files/files/Ma_Jun_Speech_17_07_17.pdf.
189 L. Fatin, "China's Top Regulators Announce They Will Exclude Fossil Fuels from Their Green Bonds Taxonomy. It's a Major Development!" Climate Bonds Initiative (10 June 2020). www.climatebonds.net/2020/06/chinas-top-regulators-announce-they-will-exclude-fossil-fuels-their-green-bonds-taxonomy-it.

India

The growing focus of financial regulators on environmental risks is reverberating in other Asian countries, too. In 2021, the Securities and Exchange Board of India strengthened and extended disclosure requirements, now covering the 1,000 largest listed companies, which are to report on certain social and sustainability aspects of their businesses.[190] India's central bank also published a study in 2020 arguing that climate change can exacerbate food price inflation, and the country also is host to one of the largest green bond markets among emerging markets.[191]

Japan

Japan has now committed to net-zero GHG emissions by 2050,[192] with multiple policy workstreams, including a new clean energy strategy expected in 2022, the development of a "Sustainability Standards Board of Japan" to systematize corporate disclosure in this area,[193] and the introduction of climate "stress testing" in the banking sector.[194]

Australia

The Australian Securities and Investments Commission is consulting on proposals to develop mandatory climate reporting rules and will investigate potential "greenwashing" with regard to ESG- or green-labeled financial products.[195]

As the science on climate change and its impact on the environment continues to improve and become more sophisticated, it would be reasonable to expect these issues to expand the agenda of financial regulators and policymakers. These are likely to have important implications for economic, financial, and business policies.

Task Force on Climate-Related Financial Disclosures

The most influential international framework for disclosure of climate change risks and opportunities affecting companies and financial institutions is the framework from the **Task Force on Climate-Related Financial Disclosures (TCFD)**.[196]

The TCFD was launched in 2015 following a request from the G20 countries' finance ministers and central bank governors for the Financial Stability Board—the organization that coordinates the work of national financial supervisors and international standard-setting bodies—to investigate the risks of climate change for the stability of the financial system and the appropriate response.

The TCFD set out to provide a set of recommendations and a framework for companies and financial institutions to provide better information to support investors, lenders, insurers, and other financial stakeholders to identify, build, and quantify climate-related risks and opportunities in their decisions. The TCFD also took the view that better information will help investors engage with companies on the resilience

---

190 Securities and Exchange Board of India, "SEBI Issues Circular on 'Business Responsibility and Sustainability Reporting by Listed Entities'" (2021). www.sebi.gov.in/media/press-releases/may-2021/sebi-issues-circular-on-business-responsibility-and-sustainability-reporting-by-listed-entities-_50097.html.
191 S. Tandon, "What Next for Sustainable Finance in India?" Grantham Research Institute (2020). www.lse.ac.uk/granthaminstitute/news/what-next-for-sustainable-finance-in-india/.
192 E. Lies, "Japan Aims for Zero Emissions, Carbon Neutral Society by 2050—PM," Reuters (26 October2020). www.reuters.com/article/uk-japan-politics-suga/japan-aims-for-zero-emissions-carbon-neutral-society-by-2050-pm-idUKKBN27B0C7?edition-redirect=ca.
193 Financial Accounting Standards Foundation, "Establishment of the Sustainability Standards Board of Japan (SSBJ) and Formation of the SSBJ Preparation Committee" (2021).
194 E. Milburn, "Japanese Regulator Gears Up for Climate Scenario Analysis Pilot for Banks," Responsible Investor (3 September 2020). www.responsible-investor.com/articles/japanese-regulator-gears-up-for-climate-scenario-analysis-pilot-for-banks.
195 Australian Securities and Investments Commission, "ASIC's Corporate Governance Priorities and the Year Ahead" (2022). https://asic.gov.au/about-asic/news-centre/speeches/asic-s-corporate-governance-priorities-and-the-year-ahead/.
196 TCFD, "Task Force on Climate-Related Financial Disclosures" (2020). www.fsb-tcfd.org.

of their strategies and capital spending, including more efficient allocation of capital, which should help promote a smooth transition to a more sustainable, low-carbon economy.

In July 2017, the TCFD published its final recommendations for how companies should report, structured around four thematic areas (see Exhibit 13):

1. governance,
2. strategy,
3. risk management, and
4. metrics and targets.

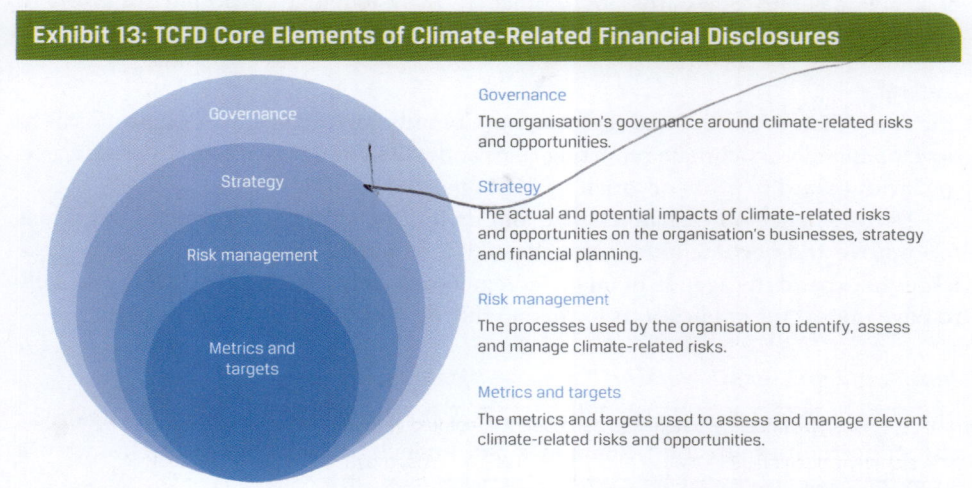

Exhibit 13: TCFD Core Elements of Climate-Related Financial Disclosures

Governance
The organisation's governance around climate-related risks and opportunities.

Strategy
The actual and potential impacts of climate-related risks and opportunities on the organisation's businesses, strategy and financial planning.

Risk management
The processes used by the organisation to identify, assess and manage climate-related risks.

Metrics and targets
The metrics and targets used to assess and manage relevant climate-related risks and opportunities.

Source: TCFD, "Final Report: Recommendations of the Task Force on Climate-Related Financial Disclosures" (2017). https://assets.bbhub.io/company/sites/60/2020/10/FINAL-2017-TCFD-Report-11052018.pdf.

The work of the TCFD introduced the influential classification of climate-related risks into physical and transition risks, recommending that companies report on both of these dimensions. One notable recommendation was the use of climate scenario analysis (which will be considered in more detail in the section titled "Assessment of Materiality of Environmental Issues."

A growing number of public and private sector organizations are showing their support for the TCFD recommendations, including over 1,300 companies with a total market capitalization of US$12.6 trillion (£9.1 trillion) and financial institutions responsible for assets of US$150 trillion (£107.8 trillion). Although initially intended as guidelines for voluntary reporting, some jurisdictions, including the United Kingdom, the EU, and New Zealand, have announced policies requiring TCFD-aligned disclosures.[197] Exhibit 14 illustrates climate-related risks, opportunities, and financial impact.

---

197 TCFD, "2020 Status Report" (2020). www.fsb.org/wp-content/uploads/P291020-1.pdf.

Exhibit 14: Climate-Related Risks, Opportunities, and Financial Impact According to TCFD

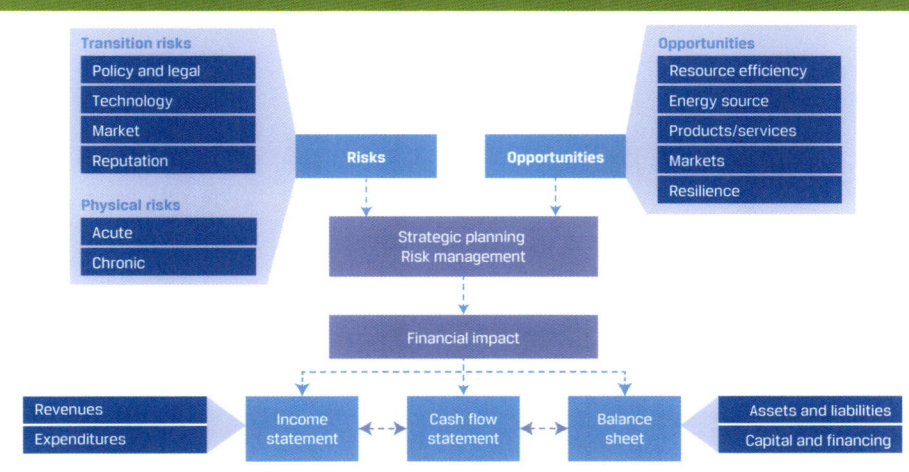

Source: TCFD, "Final Report: Recommendations of the Task Force on Climate-Related Financial Disclosures."

Network for Greening the Financial System

A notable related initiative is the **Network for Greening the Financial System (NGFS)**, comprising over 70 central banks and financial supervisors. It was set up to strengthen the global response required to meet the goals of the Paris Agreement and to enhance the role of the financial system to manage risks and to mobilize capital for green and low-carbon investments in the broader context of environmentally sustainable development. The NGFS has developed technical guidance—including publishing a set of climate scenarios—for the regulatory supervision of climate risks.[198] Elements of NGFS guidance for supervisors are increasingly being transposed into national or supranational regulation—most notably, the introduction of "climate stress tests" for banks and other financial institutions by the likes of the European Central Bank (ECB),[199] the Hong Kong Monetary Authority (HKMA), the Brazilian central bank, and other regulators.[200]

Carbon Pricing

There is a growing consensus among governments, the financial community, and businesses on the fundamental role of carbon pricing in the transition to a decarbonized economy. Putting a price on carbon emissions is viewed as one of the most effective methods of tackling climate change; it is often called the **polluter pays principle**.

There are many types of carbon pricing; the most common are the **emission trading system (ETS)** and **carbon taxes**, roughly corresponding to quotas and tariffs in international trade.

---

198 Network for Greening the Financial System, "NGFS Climate Scenarios for Central Banks and Supervisors" (2020). www.ngfs.net/sites/default/files/medias/documents/820184_ngfs_scenarios_final_version_v6.pdf.
199 European Central Bank, "ECB Economy-Wide Climate Stress Test: Methodology and Results" (2022). www.ecb.europa.eu/pub/pdf/scpops/ecb.op281~05a7735b1c.en.pdf.
200 NGFS, "Progress Report on the Guide for Supervisors" (2022). www.ngfs.net/sites/default/files/progress_report_on_the_guide_for_supervisors_0.pdf.

Emission Trading System

An ETS is a system based on the exchange of permits for emission units, where actors that exceed their emission limits are required to buy permits from those that have emitted less. The overall quantity of emissions is fixed, and market mechanisms are used to set their price.

In theory, this system creates an economic incentive for emission reductions to occur at the point of least cost; rather than mandating similar levels of reductions for all actors, price discovery helps reward those that can afford to reduce more.

The effectiveness in practice, however, depends crucially on the design of the ETS. If the scheme is too restrictive, it may encourage the offshoring of industries to jurisdictions with fewer constraints (a phenomenon known as "carbon leakage") and thus fail to reduce emissions. As a result, free allocation of allowances (to give industry an initial "buffer") has been a widely used feature of ETSs,[201] although in some cases, overallocation resulted in the price of an emission unit being too low to properly incentivize decarbonization.

Carbon Taxation

Carbon taxation takes a different approach by directly setting an explicit price for GHG emissions (e.g., per tonne of CO_2). This has the advantage of predictability, although the carbon tax rate, alongside the elasticity of demand for different products and the extent to which companies can pass on the carbon costs to their end consumers, will be key a determinant of effectiveness. It has been estimated that an explicit global carbon price of US$40 to US$80 (£29 to £58) per tCO_2 in the 2020s, more than doubling to US$50 to US$100 (£36 to £72) per tCO_2 by 2030, is required to meet the goals of the Paris Agreement.[202] This price is substantially higher than the current global average price, which the International Monetary Fund has estimated is US$2 (£1.4) per tCO_2.[203]

Carbon pricing and the trading of emission trading certificates began trial use in the United Kingdom in the early 2000s, a process that contributed substantially to the swift displacement of coal in the United Kingdom's electricity mix (which provided less than 1% of electricity in 2020,[204] compared to 40% as recently as 2012).[205] The EU subsequently adopted emission trading as one of its flagship climate policies with the establishment of the EU ETS in 2005. It covers the main energy and carbon-intensive industries, regulating about half the European economy with a carbon price. The EU carbon price has been rising in recent years, reaching an average of €53 (and a high of €89) per tCO_2 in 2021.[206] The EU ETS is undergoing significant developments—including plans to establish a "carbon border adjustment mechanism" that will seek to level the playing field with imported goods that do not face similar carbon costs in the country of origin.[207]

---

201 International Energy Agency, "Implementing Effective Emissions Trading Systems" (2020). www.iea.org/reports/implementing-effective-emissions-trading-systems.
202 Carbon Pricing Leadership Coalition, "Report of the High-Level Commission on Carbon Prices: Executive Summary" (2017). https://static1.squarespace.com/static/54ff9c5ce4b0a53decccfb4c/t/59b7f26b3c91f1bb0de2e41a/1505227373770/CarbonPricing_EnglishSummary.pdf.
203 World Bank, "State and Trends of Carbon Pricing 2021" (2021). https://openknowledge.worldbank.org/handle/10986/35620.
204 Department for Business, Energy & Industrial Strategy, "Energy Trends: December 2020" (2020). www.gov.uk/government/statistics/energy-trends-december-2020.
205 S. Evans, "Countdown to 2025: Tracking the UK Coal Phase Out," Carbon Brief (10 February 2016). www.carbonbrief.org/countdown-to-2025-tracking-the-uk-coal-phase-out.
206 Ember, "EU Carbon Price Tracker" (2022). https://ember-climate.org/data/carbon-price-viewer/.
207 European Council, "Council Agrees on the Carbon Border Adjustment Mechanism (CBAM)" (2022). www.consilium.europa.eu/en/press/press-releases/2022/03/15/carbon-border-adjustment-mechanism-cbam-council-agrees-its-negotiating-mandate/.

Key "Megatrends" and Drivers Influencing Environmental Change...

The growth of national and international carbon markets since then has been steady but sporadic, with growth in such regions as the East Coast and West Coast of the United States, New Zealand, South Korea, and some Canadian provinces. In early 2021, China launched its national ETS, becoming the world's largest carbon market, superseding the EU ETS.

Overall, as of 2021, there were 65 carbon pricing initiatives implemented or scheduled—split roughly equally between carbon taxation (35) and ETS mechanisms (30). They cover approximately 22% of global GHG emissions and are responsible for raising US$53 billion (£40 billion) in revenues.[208] Exhibit 15 provides an overview of carbon markets around the world.

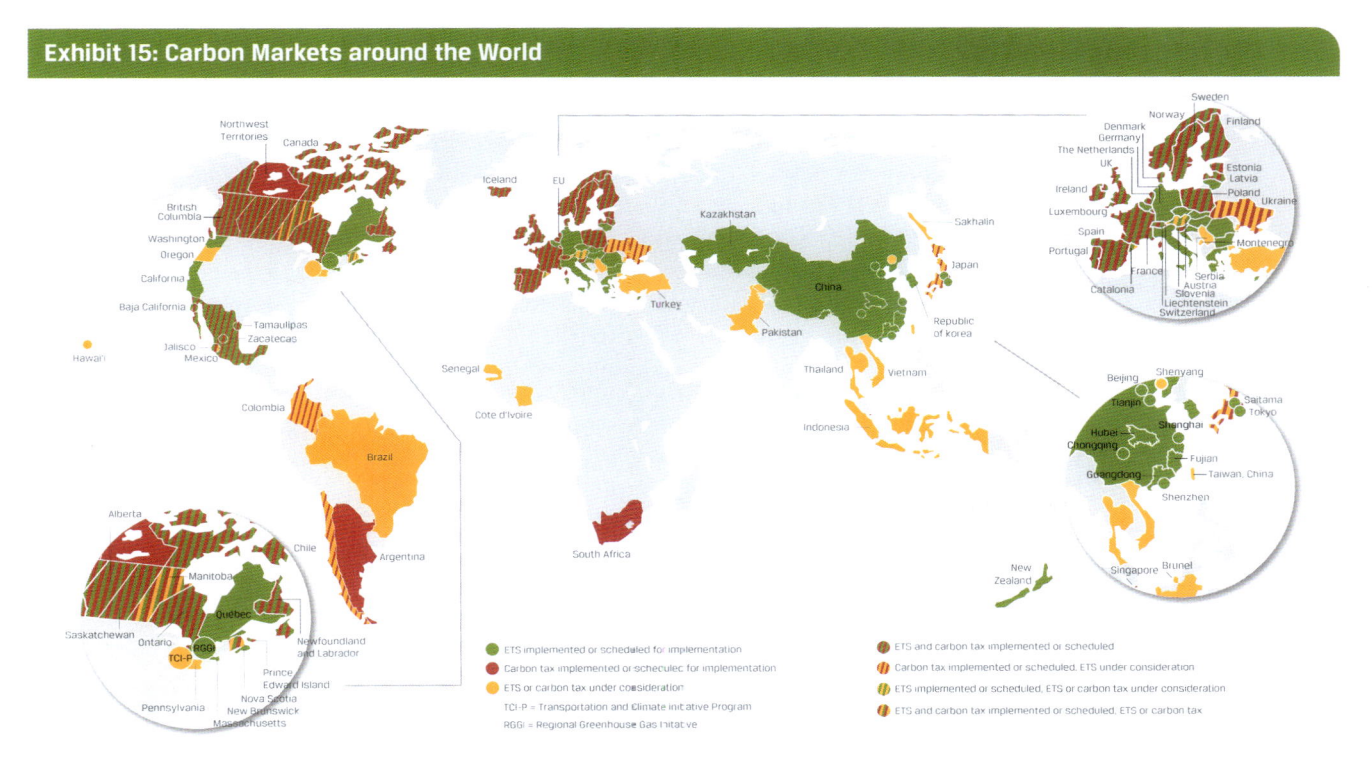

Exhibit 15: Carbon Markets around the World

Source: World Bank, "State and Trends of Carbon Pricing 2021."

Over the last 10 years, many companies—especially in energy-intensive sectors—have used the practice of shadow carbon pricing to guide their decision-making process. An internal or shadow price on carbon creates a theoretical or assumed cost per ton of carbon emissions. For example, the large oil company BP uses a price assumption of a US$100/te$CO_2$ by 2030[209] to better understand the potential impact of future climate regulation on the profitability of a project, a new business model, or an investment. Its use reveals hidden risks and enables businesses to build this factor into future valuations and estimates of capital expenditure. In addition, when emissions bear a cost in profit-and-loss statements, it helps uncover inefficiencies and incentivize low-carbon innovation within departments, cutting a company's energy use and carbon pollution.

---

208 World Bank, "State and Trends of Carbon Pricing 2021."
209 BP, "Progressing Strategy Development, BP Revises Long-Term Price Assumptions, Reviews Intangible Assets and, as a Result, Expects Non-Cash Impairments and Write-Offs," press release (15 June 2020). www.bp.com/en/global/corporate/news-and-insights/press-releases/bp-revises-long-term-price-assumptions.html.

Some governments are using internal carbon pricing as a tool in their procurement process, policy design, and project assessments in relation to climate change impacts. More recently, financial institutions have also begun using internal carbon pricing to assess their project portfolio. In 2019, approximately 1,600 companies—including more than 100 Fortune Global 500 companies, with a total annual revenue of about US$7 trillion (£5 trillion)—reported that they are currently using an internal price on carbon or plan to do so in the next two years.[210]

Carbon Offsetting

A concept that runs through different aspects of carbon markets is that of offsetting—the extent to which an activity providing an emission reduction in one part of the economy may be seen as compensating for the emission of greenhouse gases elsewhere.

The need for offsetting can be justified by the fact that, in a majority of scenarios compliant with the goals of the Paris Agreement, the world does not reach zero *absolute* GHG emissions in the next few decades—with some residual emissions being balanced out by natural or artificial "carbon sinks" (e.g., tree planting).[211] As such, companies or countries that are unable to reduce their emissions organically may require some accounting mechanism through which they can compensate those actors that are contributing *negative* emissions, in order for the global system to reach *net* zero.

However, there are substantial challenges around offsetting, because this market comprises both voluntary and regulated aspects, with uneven levels of transparency and scientific rigor. Part of the challenge stems from the *counterfactual* nature of offsetting and the risk of claiming credits for emission reductions that would have happened anyway, even if a given offset was not purchased (e.g., compensating a farmer to maintain a forest when the farmer had no intention of cutting it down in the first place), or that have not happened yet (e.g., netting present emissions against the *future* carbon sequestered by a newly planted tree over its lifetime). Additional complexities stem from how to account for carbon credits across jurisdictions and over time (i.e., should overachievement *in the past* allow actors to reduce their emission targets in the future?).

One of the positive outcomes of COP26 has been progress around carbon markets and international cooperation (Article 6 of the Paris Agreement), by introducing more stringent rules around the use of past credits, adjustments to avoid double counting of reductions, and restrictions around what projects are eligible to count as a genuine offset.[212]

5 ASSESSMENT OF MATERIALITY OF ENVIRONMENTAL ISSUES

3.1.5 assess material impacts of environmental issues on potential investment opportunities, corporate and project finance, public finance initiatives, and asset management

---

210 World Bank, "State and Trends of Carbon Pricing 2021."

211 Projected median GHG emissions across 1.5°C scenarios, both with and without "overshoot," range between 9 and 14 in scenarios from p. 63 of IPCC, "Climate Change 2022: Mitigation of Climate Change: Summary for Policymakers."

212 Simon Evans, Josh Gabbatiss, Robert McSweeney, Aruna Chandrasekhar, Ayesha Tandon, Giuliana Viglione, Zeke Hausfather, Xiaoying You, Joe Goodman, and Sylvia Hayes, "COP26: Key Outcomes Agreed at the UN Climate Talks in Glasgow," Carbon Brief (15 November 2021). www.carbonbrief.org/cop26-key-outcomes-agreed-at-the-un-climate-talks-in-glasgow.

Assessment of Materiality of Environmental Issues

Material environmental issues are factors that could have a significant impact—both positive and negative—on a company's business model and value drivers, such as operating and capital expenditure, revenue growth, margins, and risk. Materiality is not static, and it evolves in line with changes in the market, policies, and consumer attitudes. For example, the surge in public concern over plastic pollution seen in recent years—and the subsequent regulatory clampdowns on single-use plastics—has been quoted by the oil company BP as having the potential to have a "material impact" on the future oil demand.[213]

As such, efforts by investors to assess the material financial impacts caused by environmental risks have begun to increase in terms of their analytical scope and sophistication. This includes, for example, considering a wider range of environmental factors, such as those from policy and technology responses (transition risks), as well as the impacts of environmental events and physical risks.

Investors need to undertake relevant research and materiality analysis to determine the environmental impact—both positive and negative. The type of analysis and approach will mostly depend on the type of assets being assessed—company, sector, and geographic location and on a portfolio level. Based on both quantitative and qualitative data, environmental analysis will potentially determine adjustments to forecasted financials and ratios, valuation model variables, valuation multiples, credit assessments, and portfolio allocation weightings.

Without sufficient consideration of materiality, investors may be exposed to changes in policy, technology, and consumer sentiment or forgo investment opportunities. However, the challenge is that environmental issues unfold in complex ways over time and across regions and sectors, and there is significant variation in the definitions, classifications, and measurement of these risks and opportunities.

Corporate and Project Finance

At a company or project level, investors looking to identify and measure a company's environmental impact or materiality would need to analyze both quantitative and qualitative environmental factors in order to make an informed evaluation of the environmental risks embedded within. A judgment is then made on how material the risks are and whether those risks are priced in or not. A scoring system is also typically used to benchmark the company against its peers. Materiality is also highly influenced by the industry or sector of the company, as well as its country and jurisdictions where projects are located. This is also particularly relevant in the financing and investments of infrastructure projects.

A useful starting point is analyzing how a company or project uses energy, water, and waste:

- **Energy consumption** can be measured by the level of absolute emissions of GHGs from fossil fuel combustion and industrial processes and is measured by the amount of CO_2e. This could also include savings in energy and performance relative to a benchmark year and can be provided on an annualized or lifetime basis, based on estimates (particularly relevant for projects) or actual measurement (relevant to operational assets).

- **Water utilization** can be calculated as the costs generated by water usage efficiency in operations taken directly from the ground, taken from surface water, or purchased. Water and wastewater treatment can be assessed against indicators tracking reductions in pollutants and harmful substances in supply areas, as well as incident reports and sanctions.

---

213 E. Gosden, "Plastic May Do Less Harm Than Alternatives, Says BP," *The Times* (7 February 2019). www.thetimes.co.uk/article/plastic-may-do-less-harm-than-alternatives-says-bp-n7p0tt7w7.

▶ **Waste utilization** is measured as the costs generated from the disposal of waste in operations, such as through landfills, incinerated waste, or recycled or hazardous waste. Aspects that may need to be factored into the analysis include carbon capture and storage (e.g., for closed landfill and industrial operations), pollution control (soil, air, water), waste-to-energy facilities, and waste-to-biofuel facilities.

At a project finance level, when assessing project infrastructure initiatives, the International Finance Corporation's (IFC's) Equator Principles, which are based on IFC's Performance Standards, have become a globally recognized risk management framework and are adopted by financial institutions for determining, assessing, and managing environmental and social risk in project finance. They set out performance standards that address environmental factors (such as resource efficiency, biodiversity, and land resettlement), as well as other social-oriented standards. Examples of potential risks to be considered are presented in Exhibit 16.

Exhibit 16: Identification of Environmental Risks and Impacts at the Company or Project Level

Risks	Potential Impacts
Release of air pollutants (air emissions)	→ Pollution of air, land, and surface water
Release of liquid effluents or contaminated wastewater into local water bodies or improper wastewater treatment	→ Surface water pollution
Generation of large amounts of solid waste and improper waste management	→ Pollution of land and groundwater and surface water
Improper management of hazardous substances	→ Contamination of adjacent land and water
Excessive energy use	→ Depletion of local energy sources and release of combustion residuals leading to air pollution
Excessive water use	→ Depletion of water resources
High or excessive noise levels	→ Negative effects on human health and disruption of local wildlife
Improper or excessive land use	→ Soil degradation and biodiversity loss

Source: IFC, "Environmental and Social Management System Implementation Handbook" (2015). www.ifc.org/wps/wcm/connect/4c41260d-1ba8-4d10-a77d-f762d60a1380/ESMS+Handbook+General+v2.1.pdf?MOD=AJPERES&CVID=lllFYII.

While considering the potential negative impacts of investments can illuminate important sources of material risk, considering potential positive impacts (for example, whether a given investment contributes to nature conservation or emission reductions) can highlight opportunities.

Public Finance Initiatives

As governments continue to raise their climate targets in line with the Paris Agreement, resources are being allocated and investments from the public sector are being mobilized to implement these plans—including in partnership with private investors. For example, the **Helsinki Principles**, signed by a number of finance ministers around the world, encourage signatories to "take climate change into account in macroeconomic policy, fiscal planning, budgeting, public investment management, and procurement practices."[214]

Public finance is a key policy instrument to both incentivize and enable the transition to green growth. Domestically, governments are a significant economic actor—commissioning new buildings, roads, and other forms of infrastructure, for example—highlighting the importance of aligning public procurement and sustainability. Governments also contribute to international development, with public sector financing often blended with funding from multilateral development finance institutions in developing countries and disbursed through investment vehicles, such as

- green infrastructure funds (e.g., the Association of Southeast Asian Nations [ASEAN] Catalytic Green Finance Facility under the ASEAN Infrastructure Fund),
- specialized banks (e.g., Asian Infrastructure Investment Bank), and
- funding platforms (e.g., the Tropical Landscapes Finance Facility).[215]

A variety of financing initiatives leveraging public sector and development finance for sustainable agriculture, biodiversity conservation, and the blue economy are also emerging, particularly targeting more vulnerable and developing economies.[216]

The Climate Policy Initiative reported that the average annual public climate finance was around US$321 billion in 2019–2020,[217] out of a total of US$632 billion of climate finance, with the highest proportion dedicated to energy systems. Other areas of spending include adaptation and resilience, low-carbon transport, land use, and infrastructure projects with cross-sectoral impacts.[218] Direct finance flows (domestic and international) from governments accounting for 12% of public flows (US$38 billion) were driven by low-carbon transport and delivered primarily through grants.

---

214 J. Rydge, "Aligning Finance with the Paris Agreement: An Overview of Concepts, Approaches, Progress and Necessary Action" Grantham Research Institute (2020). www.lse.ac.uk/granthaminstitute/wp-content/uploads/2020/12/Aligning-finance-with-the-Paris-Agreement-3.pdf.
215 Climate Bonds Initiative, "ASEAN Green Financial Instruments Guide" (2019). www.climatebonds.net/resources/reports/asean-green-financial-instruments-guide.
216 Climate Bonds Initiative, "Latin America & Caribbean: Green Finance State of the Market 2019" (2019). www.climatebonds.net/resources/reports/latin-america-caribbean-green-finance-state-market-2019.
217 Barbara Buchner, Baysa Naran, Pedro de Aragão Fernandes, Rajashree Padmanabhi, Paul Rosane, Matthew Solomon, Sean Stout, Githungo Wakaba, Yaxin Zhu, Chavi Meattle, Sandra Guzmán, and Costanza Strinati, "Global Landscape of Climate Finance 2021," Climate Policy Initiative (14 December 2021). www.climatepolicyinitiative.org/publication/global-landscape-of-climate-finance-2021/.
218 Climate Policy Initiative, "Updated View on the Global Landscape of Climate Finance 2019" (2020). www.climatepolicyinitiative.org/wp-content/uploads/2020/12/Updated-View-on-the-2019-Global-Landscape-of-Climate-Finance-1.pdf.

Exhibit 17: The Landscape of Climate Finance, 2017–2018

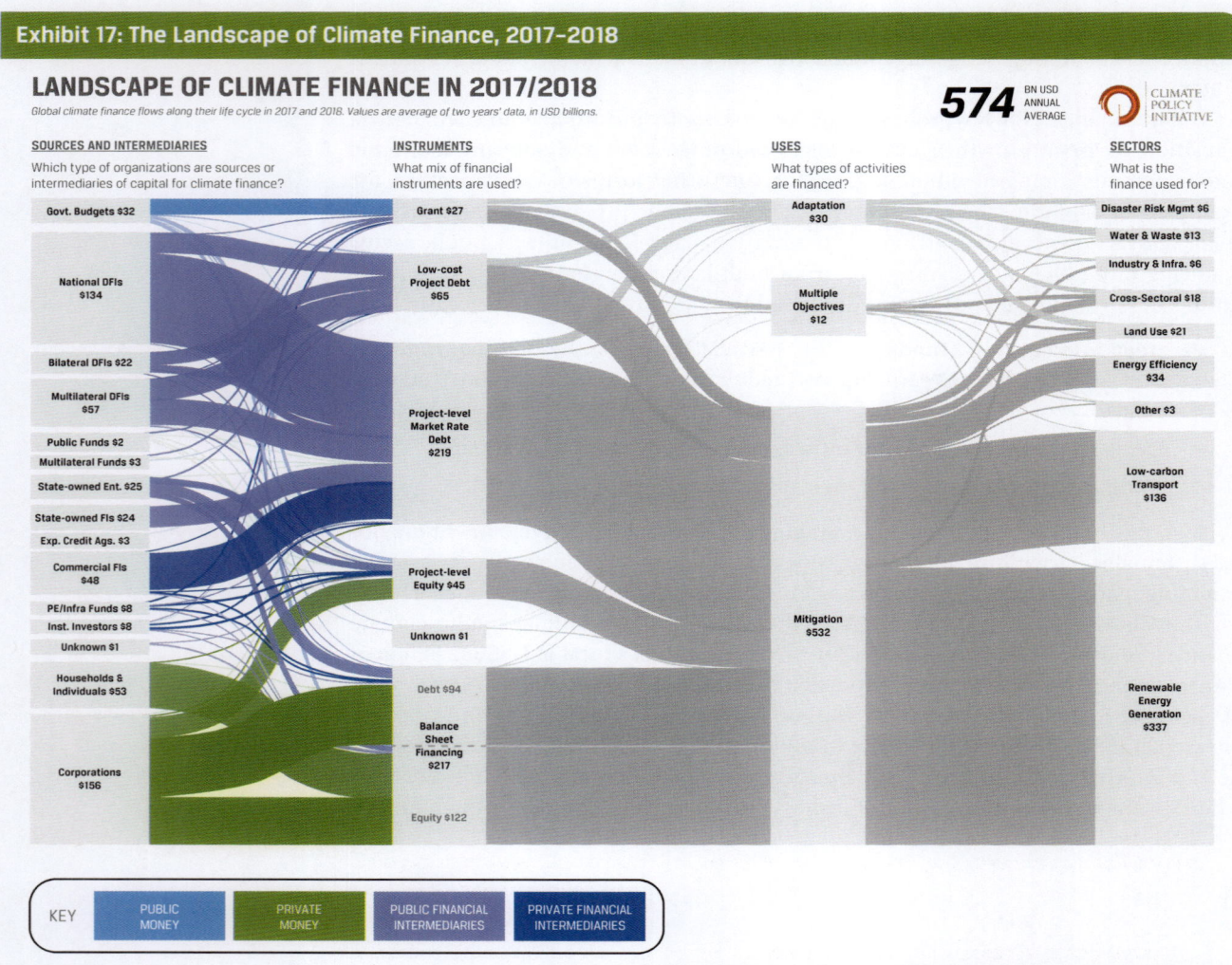

LANDSCAPE OF CLIMATE FINANCE IN 2017/2018

Global climate finance flows along their life cycle in 2017 and 2018. Values are average of two years' data, in USD billions.

574 BN USD ANNUAL AVERAGE — CLIMATE POLICY INITIATIVE

SOURCES AND INTERMEDIARIES — Which type of organizations are sources or intermediaries of capital for climate finance?
- Govt. Budgets $32
- National DFIs $134
- Bilateral DFIs $22
- Multilateral DFIs $57
- Public Funds $2
- Multilateral Funds $3
- State-owned Ent. $25
- State-owned FIs $24
- Exp. Credit Ags. $3
- Commercial FIs $48
- PE/Infra Funds $8
- Inst. Investors $8
- Unknown $1
- Households & Individuals $53
- Corporations $156

INSTRUMENTS — What mix of financial instruments are used?
- Grant $27
- Low-cost Project Debt $65
- Project-level Market Rate Debt $219
- Project-level Equity $45
- Unknown $1
- Debt $94
- Balance Sheet Financing $217
- Equity $122

USES — What types of activities are financed?
- Adaptation $30
- Multiple Objectives $12
- Mitigation $532

SECTORS — What is the finance used for?
- Disaster Risk Mgmt $6
- Water & Waste $13
- Industry & Infra. $6
- Cross-Sectoral $18
- Land Use $21
- Energy Efficiency $34
- Other $3
- Low-carbon Transport $136
- Renewable Energy Generation $337

KEY: PUBLIC MONEY | PRIVATE MONEY | PUBLIC FINANCIAL INTERMEDIARIES | PRIVATE FINANCIAL INTERMEDIARIES

Source: Climate Policy Initiative, "Updated View on the Global Landscape of Climate Finance 2019" (2020). www.climatepolicyinitiative.org/wp-content/uploads/2020/12/Updated-View-on-the-2019-Global-Landscape-of-Climate-Finance-1.pdf.

Examples of the types of **public finance** include

- export credit,
- development banks,
- concessionary lending to small and medium-sized enterprises (SMEs),
- guarantees,
- research and development (R&D), and
- investment in infrastructure.

Initiatives that typically require **public (and private) sector funding** with high environmental impacts are

- energy,
- water and waste,
- transport, and
- flood defenses.

Asset Management

As stewards of capital, asset managers play a key role in helping steer capital toward sustainability. Whether directly (e.g., by deciding to fund a particular green infrastructure project or to buy the debt of a high-carbon company) or indirectly (e.g., by using investor rights to appoint and reward company directors and through the related engagement with investee companies), the decisions made by asset managers can make positive or negative contributions to ESG factors, such as the global emission trajectory.

The environmental profiles of asset managers' portfolios have come under increased scrutiny from the media and civil society in recent years, often relating to campaigns for fossil fuel divestment. However, client mandates from asset owners may impose constraints on the options available to asset managers (particularly in the case of index-tracking funds). Exclusions are only one of a range of potential strategies that asset managers can deploy to manage environmental risks, alongside positive screening or impact investing funds.

Historically, however, the majority of the world's assets under management do not fall under either of these two categories but are invested in a variety of assets classes and strategies, which may not explicitly incorporate climate change or environmental objectives. This is changing, because both asset owners and asset managers are increasing their sustainability efforts. In December 2020, over 30 asset managers managing over US$9 trillion (£6.5 trillion) in assets joined the Net Zero Asset Managers initiative, pledging to support investing aligned with net-zero emissions by 2050 or sooner.[219] As of December 2021, 220 signatories representing US$57 trillion in AUM have joined the initiative over five waves of public announcements.[220] This initiative mirrors the growing number of asset owners who are setting net-zero emissions targets for their portfolios (e.g., the UN-convened Net-Zero Asset Owner Alliance, which gathers institutional investors with over US$5 trillion (£3.6 trillion) in assets).[221]

As a result of growing investor interest, asset managers are increasingly focused on the development of standardized frameworks and data points to be able to assess climate and environmental risks across multiple sectors, down to the level of individual companies or their securities. This recognizes that

1. companies in the same sector may face different levels of risk and
2. these risks are likely to be complex and interlocking and affect all sectors, not just those with high carbon emissions.

Such a framework, used by companies for reporting and disclosure and by investors in assessing the environmental, social, and governance risks of companies, comes from SASB, which was established in 2011 to develop and disseminate sustainability accounting standards. The standards identify financially material issues that are reasonably likely to impact the financial condition or operating performance of a company and therefore are most important to investors. SASB provides an interactive proprietary tool that identifies and compares disclosure topics across different industries and sectors, described as a "materiality map."[222] Environmental factors cover

- ▸ GHG emissions,

---

219 Net Zero Asset Managers Initiative, "The Net Zero Asset Managers Initiative" (2020). www.netzeroassetmanagers.org/.
220 Net Zero Asset Managers Initiative, "Net Zero Asset Managers initiative: Progress Report" (2021). www.netzeroassetmanagers.org/media/2021/12/NZAM-Progress-Report.pdf.
221 UNEP, "Institutional Investors Transitioning Their Portfolios to Net Zero GHG Emissions by 2050" (2020). www.unepfi.org/net-zero-alliance/.
222 Sustainability Accounting Standards Board, "SASB Materiality Map" (2018). https://materiality.sasb.org.

- air quality,
- energy management,
- water and wastewater management,
- waste and hazardous materials management, and
- ecological impacts.

SASB's analysis reflects the varied nature of different sectors. GHG emissions are assessed to be material for more than 50% of industries in such sectors as extractives and minerals processing and transportation but for less than 50% of industries in such sectors as health care and technology and communications—where the management of energy, waste, and hazardous materials features more prominently.

One initiative aims to identify "ESG upside" for large, listed companies if they were to bring ESG performance in line with that of top-rated peers. Controlling for industry, size, and sector, improving performance on carbon emissions is found to be the most material variable for over 2,000 large, listed companies. On average, companies could unlock up to a 3% share price increase across all sectors, with potential for double-digit increases in high-emitting sectors, such as energy (see Exhibit 18).[223]

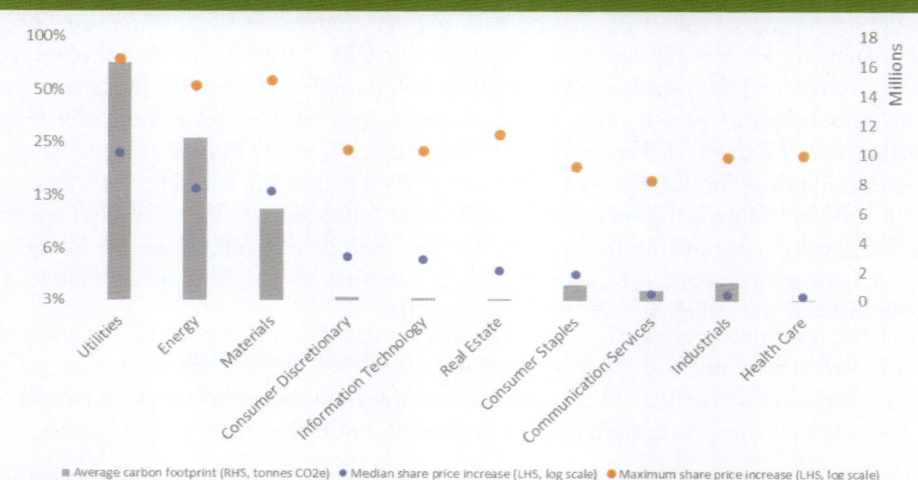

Exhibit 18: Potential Share Price Increase from Improving Emissions in Various Sectors

■ Average carbon footprint (RHS, tonnes CO2e) ● Median share price increase (LHS, log scale) ● Maximum share price increase (LHS, log scale)

Source: ESG for Investors, "Counting Down Carbon: Higher Share Prices through Lower Emissions" (24 January 2022). https://esgforinvestors.com/articles/detail/22/.

However, there are different definitions of materiality and related reporting metrics under the multiple standards and frameworks used for sustainability reporting, including the GRI, the Climate Disclosure Standards Board (CDSB), Integrated Reporting, and CDP. In 2021, the IFRS Foundation, which works on the development of accounting standards, announced the consolidation of CDSB, SASB, and Integrated Reporting into a single organization, the International Sustainability Standards Board (ISSB), which aims to develop a "comprehensive global baseline of high-quality sustainability disclosure standards to meet investors' information needs."[224]

---

223 ESG for Investors, "Counting Down Carbon: Higher Share Prices through Lower Emissions" (24 January 2022). https://esgforinvestors.com/articles/detail/22/.
224 IFRS Foundation, "IFRS Foundation Announces International Sustainability Standards Board, Consolidation with CDSB and VRF, and Publication of Prototype Disclosure Requirements" (2021). www.ifrs.org/news-and-events/news/2021/11/ifrs-foundation-announces-issb-consolidation-with-cdsb

At the same time, many investors are incorporating this increasingly available climate and environmental data into their own proprietary investment frameworks, which reflect their house views on the climate and energy transition.

While some environmental risks can be addressed quantitatively, others require a more qualitative approach—for example, through engagement with companies to align management incentives with sustainability goals. Asset managers have stepped up individual engagement efforts but are also collaborating to achieve this.

> **CASE STUDIES**
>
> ### Investor Collaboration on Climate
>
> Launched in 2017, Climate Action 100+ is an investor network with over 500 investors engaging the world's largest corporate emitters of GHGs.[225] Its members conduct joint company engagements and collaborate on shareholder proposals, and the initiative has been developing tools and benchmarks to be able to track company progress toward net-zero emissions.

APPROACHES TO ACCOUNT FOR MATERIAL ENVIRONMENTAL ANALYSIS AND RISK MANAGEMENT STRATEGIES

3.1.6 identify approaches to environmental analysis, including company-, project-, sector-, country-, and market-level analysis; environmental risks, including carbon footprinting and other carbon metrics; the natural capital approach; and climate scenario analysis

Environmental risks can be effectively integrated into company analysis and investment decision-making processes using various financial tools and models. According to a G20 green finance study, financial institutions need to combine two types of approaches to assess environmental risks:

1. understanding environmental factors that may pose risks to financial assets and liabilities (for example, the wrong pricing of a pollution liability or natural disaster insurance policy could be a risk to liability if the event probability is underestimated) and how such risks may evolve over time and

2. translating environmental risk factors into quantitative measures of financial risk that can, in turn, inform firms' risk management and investment decisions.[226]

The types of risk analysis tools and associated metrics primarily depend on the asset classes and risk types financial institutions are exposed to (for instance, a fixed-income analyst may be most interested in credit risk). Similarly, the choice of approach depends on the type of direct or indirect exposure to an environmental risk factor. For example, the probability of physical risks from flooding will have to

---

-vrf-publication-of-prototypes/.
225 Climate Action 100+, "About Climate Action 100+" (2021). www.climateaction100.org/about/.
226 UNEP, "Enhancing Environmental Risk Assessment in Financial Decision Making" (2017).

be incorporated differently than transition risks stemming from the transition to a low-carbon economy due to policy change. Depending on the investment strategy and objectives, different levels of analysis will likely be performed: at the individual asset level, portfolio level, and macroeconomic or systemic level.

It is important to analyze the extent to which environmental and climate-related impacts could affect a company's value chain—supply chain, operation and assets, logistics, and market—which would have an impact on financial performance.

Levels of Environmental Analysis

It is important to note that environmental risk assessments are conducted along with social and governance assessments at the

A. company or project level,
B. sector level,
C. country level, or
D. market level.

We will look at each of these in the following subsections.

Company or Project Level

At a company or project level, an assessment of material environmental risk factors will inform key financial metrics as monitored and disclosed in financial statements (such as profit and loss and balance sheet). For example, companies operating in water-scarce areas are exposed to higher risk than are those operating in areas where water availability is high. Therefore, it is important to undertake an analysis of how well the company is managing these risks (e.g., improvement in water efficiency over time).

Often, analysts and portfolio managers will have their own internal environmental (social and governance) scoring system that uses a combination of external third-party data providers and internal analysis. Qualitative and quantitative assessments are then made to determine the materiality of environmental risks for a particular company and how they will affect key efficiency or profitability ratios that might be used to value and compare across different companies. This could include a decision being made to adjust the target price-to-earnings ratio (P/E), which reflects a company's competitiveness in comparison to its peers with higher or lower environmental standards. Cost assumptions can also be adjusted according to future capital expenditure in environmental (mitigation or adaptation) spending.

> **THE "CARBON RISK PREMIUM"**
>
> A "carbon risk premium" is said to exist when investors require a higher compensation for the perceived risk from investing in high-carbon companies. Several studies have argued that companies with higher (absolute levels of or relative increases in) CO_2 emissions are associated with higher returns. However, studies have also found evidence for the converse—a positive link between reductions in carbon footprint and improvements returns.[227]

---

227 Multiple sources: P. Bolton and M. Kakperczyk, "Do Investors Care about Carbon Risk?" *Journal of Financial Economics* 142 (November 2021): 517–49. www.sciencedirect.com/science/article/abs/pii/S0304405X21001902?via%3Dihub.
Maximilian Görgen, Andrea Jacob, Martin Nerlinger, Ryan Riordan, Martin Rohleder, and Marco Wilkens, "Carbon Risk" (2020). https://ssrn.com/abstract=2930897.
Mats Andersson, Patrick Bolton, and Frédéric Samama, "Hedging Climate Risk," *Financial Analysts Journal* 72 (May/June 2016): 13–32. www.tandfonline.com/doi/abs/10.2469/faj.v72.n3.4.

Approaches to Account for Material Environmental Analysis and Risk Management Strategies

> These results illustrate the importance of defining investment beliefs, given that risk and return can be seen as two sides of the same coin. For some, remaining invested in sectors or stocks that may be shunned by a growing proportion of "climate-conscious" investors can create an opportunity for excess returns; others may see companies lagging on environmental metrics as being at risk of having permanently depressed future cash flows from changes in consumer preferences, technology, and regulation.
>
> Given the complex nature of the technologies, sectors, and commodities involved; the liquidity of underlying markets; and the availability of alternatives, conclusions around the existence of a carbon risk premium in one sector or industry may not be readily applicable in other sectors.
>
> For example, a study from the University of Oxford found an increase of 54% in loan spreads for coal mining (a perceived measure of the risk of corporate debt relative to government bonds) between 2017 and 2020 compared to the previous decade but that loan spreads for oil and gas had remained relatively stable, reflecting a more "ambivalent" attitude from lenders.[228]

Sector Level

Environmental and climate-related factors have varying degrees of impact on different sectors. Some sectors—whether through their higher carbon intensity or location of their assets—have higher exposure to

- environmental risks, such as
  - chemicals,
  - energy,
  - steel and cement,
  - extractives,
  - food or beverages, and
  - transportation, or
- physical risk from natural disasters—for example, to
  - buildings,
  - production facilities,
  - agricultural land, or
  - urban infrastructure.

Companies in these sectors tend to be influenced by an environmental risk premium, which may affect the discount rate used. Hence, alongside the previous company-level analysis, these sector-wide considerations need to be considered, and they should be overlaid on the company analysis. Adjustments are made to remove any regional or sector biases that align with the manager's investment strategy and process.

Gerald T. Garvey, Mohanaraman Iyer, and Joanna Nash, "Carbon Footprint and Productivity: Does the 'E' in ESG Capture Efficiency as Well as Environment?" *Journal of Investment Management* 16 (2018): 59–69. https://joim.com/downloads/carbon-footprint-and-productivity-does-the-e-in-esg-capture-efficiency-as-well-as-environment/.

228 X. Zhou, C. Wilson, and B. Caldecott, "The Energy Transition and Changing Financing Costs" (2021). www.smithschool.ox.ac.uk/research/sustainable-finance/publications/The-energy-transition-and-changing-financing-costs.pdf.

Country Level

A country's environmental regulations, emission targets, and enforcement may vary in emphasis across different jurisdictions. Often, investments may be multi-jurisdictional, and hence, several country-specific considerations and regulations will need to be factored into the valuation of a company based on the country in which it is located or where its operations lie. Disclosure and transparency of environmental data will also vary by region; for example, companies in emerging markets tend to have fewer comprehensive disclosures.

Country analysis is relevant not just to corporate securities but also to government bonds. Climate change, air quality, water stress, vulnerability to natural hazards, and food security can have an immediate and direct impact on a sovereign's ability or willingness to pay (credit risk) or its ESG profile. For example, the consistent deterioration in a country's rating scores on food security and high vulnerability to climate change could lead an asset manager to reduce its position despite the bond's scarcity and attractive relative value, but—conversely—it can also hold an overweight position based on a view that starting with a relatively low environmental score is acceptable when reforms and a green economy push from the government are expected to lead to ESG score improvements.[229]

Market Level

Recognizing the cross-cutting impacts of environmental risks, central banks and the Bank for International Settlements have warned of the potential systemic effects of both physical and transitional risks: "In the worst case scenario, central banks may have to confront a situation where they are called upon by their local constituencies to intervene as climate rescuers of last resort."[230]

Consideration of such market-wide impacts can influence investors' strategic asset allocation and long-term investment strategy, although research has sounded a note of caution with regard to the limits of some traditional risk mitigation strategies, such as diversification and hedging. In a report titled "Unhedgeable Risk," the Cambridge Institute for Sustainability Leadership warned that in a scenario where investor sentiment changes away from high-carbon sectors, there may not be sufficient available assets—including low-carbon assets—for investors to successfully reallocate capital. It found that around half of the potential decline in the modeled equity and fixed-income portfolios is "unhedgeable," meaning investors and asset owners would be exposed unless some system-wide action is taken to address the risks.[231]

This finding reaffirms the need for predictable policy measures, which prioritize real-world emission reductions and an orderly transition to the low-carbon economy. A growing number of investors (such as those under the Climate Action 100+ initiative) are advocating for this.

Analyzing Environmental Risks

It is not possible to outline all the available approaches for investors to assess environmental risks, because there is no one common standard. However, based on a combination of independent third-party research and data along with useful frameworks,

---

229 R. Agha and S. Singla, "ESG in LGIM's Active EMD Investment Process" (2020). www.lgim.com/uk/en/insights/our-thinking/esg-and-long-term-themes/esg-in-lgims-active-emd-investment-process.
230 P. Bolton, M. Despres, L. A. Pereira Da Silva, F. Samama, and R. Svartzman, "The Green Swan: Central Banking and Financial Stability in the Age of Climate Change," Bank for International Settlements (January 2020). www.bis.org/publ/othp31.pdf.
231 Cambridge Institute for Sustainability Leadership, "Unhedgeable Risk: How Climate Change Sentiment Impacts Investment" (2015). www.cisl.cam.ac.uk/resources/sustainable-finance-publications/unhedgeable-risk.

Approaches to Account for Material Environmental Analysis and Risk Management Strategies

practitioners are able to map out and analyze the environmental risks and costs for different types of asset classes by company and sector in order to make their own quantitative and qualitative risk assessments. The following outlines some of the approaches that are used by investors to assess material environmental risks (and opportunities):

A. carbon footprinting and other carbon metrics,

B. natural capital approach, and

C. climate scenario analysis.

We will look at each of these approaches in further detail in the following subsections.

Carbon Footprinting and Other Carbon Metrics

Carbon footprinting is one of the most common approaches used by companies and investors. A portfolio carbon footprint effectively measures carbon emissions and intensity associated with operations of the companies in a portfolio. Measuring the carbon footprint of a portfolio means that an investor can

- compare it to global benchmarks,
- identify priority areas and actions for reducing emissions, and
- track progress in making those reductions.

The use of carbon footprinting applies the international accounting tool of the GHG Protocol Standards. Scope 1 emissions are direct greenhouse emissions that occur from sources that are controlled or owned by an organization (e.g., emissions associated with fuel combustion in furnaces or company vehicles). Scope 2 emissions are indirect GHG emissions associated with the purchase of electricity, for example. Scope 3 emissions cover all indirect emissions arising from the activities of an organization. These include emissions from both suppliers and consumers, as shown in Exhibit 19.

Exhibit 19: GHG Protocol Standards: Examples of Direct and Indirect Emissions

Scope 1	Scope 2	Score 3
▶ Fuel combustion ▶ Company vehicles ▶ Fugitive emissions	▶ Purchased electricity, heat, and steam	▶ Purchased goods and services ▶ Business travel ▶ Employee commuting ▶ Waste disposal ▶ Use of sold products ▶ Transportation and distribution (upstream and downstream) ▶ Investments ▶ Leased assets and franchises

Source: Greenhouse Gas Protocol, "Standards" (2019). https://ghgprotocol.org/standards.

The benefits of carbon footprinting include the potential to aggregate emissions across industries and value chains (for countries and portfolios, enabling comparisons between companies or portfolios) and across sectors and geographies, as well as to focus the analysis on emission intensity. However, the analysis has its limitations and challenges as a risk measure and is increasingly seen as too backward looking or static.

Some of the main challenges of carbon footprinting are

- the lack of disclosure for unlisted or private assets,
- Scope 3 emissions rarely being included, thus failing to capture companies' full value chain,
- double counting' (e.g., a metallurgical coal miner's Scope 3 emissions can be a steel maker's Scope 1 emissions),
- the use of different estimation methodologies, and
- ignoring potential investment risks related to the physical impacts of climate change.

Depending on objectives, carbon footprinting can be an absolute or relative metric. It can be used to assess, for example, the **total carbon emissions** associated with a given investee company or portfolio. This recognizes that investments that are viewed as having a disproportionately high contribution to global emissions may have a higher exposure to future policy interventions on carbon emissions.

TOTAL CARBON EMISSIONS

Total carbon emissions

$$= \sum_n^i \frac{\text{Current value of investment}_i}{\text{Issuer's market capitalization}_i} \times \text{Issuer's Scope 1 and 2 emissions}_i. \qquad (1)$$

Source: TCFD, "Implementing the Recommendations of the Task Force on Climate-Related Financial Disclosures" (2017). www.fsb-tcfd.org/wp-content/uploads/2017/06/FINAL-TCFD-Annex-062817.pdf.

Alternatively, investors may wish to track carbon emissions **intensity** (e.g., emissions scaled in relation to a particular metric, such as a company's revenues). The TCFD recommends that asset owners and managers report the weighted average carbon intensity associated with their investments.[232]

WEIGHTED CARBON EMISSIONS

Weighted average carbon intensity

$$= \sum_n^i \frac{\text{Current value of investment}_i}{\text{Current portfolio value}} \times \frac{\text{Issuer's Scope 1 and 2 emissions}_i}{\text{Issuer's US\$m of revenue}_i}. \qquad (2)$$

Source: TCFD, "Implementing the Recommendations of the Task Force on Climate-Related Financial Disclosures."

This can provide a measure of how carbon efficient companies are, allowing for an element of comparability between companies of different sizes. The question of comparability (both between companies and different portfolios, which potentially harbor multiple asset classes) remains a complex one, and there is currently variation among different voluntary and mandatory frameworks in terms of the choice of denominator. Alternative methods of calculation include scaling emissions by companies' market capitalization or enterprise value (which takes into account companies' issuance of both equity and debt, as well as in some cases, the companies' cash reserves).

---

[232] TCFD, "Implementing the Recommendations of the Task Force on Climate-Related Financial Disclosures" (2017). www.fsb-tcfd.org/wp-content/uploads/2017/06/FINAL-TCFD-Annex-062817.pdf.

More broadly, high levels of carbon emissions are not a perfect proxy for high climate risks. A coal-burning power plant and a coal-burning steel plant may have very similar levels of emissions. But renewable energy can much more easily—and for two-thirds of the world's population, more cheaply[233]—replace the use of coal for generating electricity, whereas cleaner and economic alternatives to coal for steel production are not as widespread. As such, the policy focus and future profitability profile of the two plants may look radically different. A useful starting point is to consider companies' announced emission targets and related environmental ambitions, also in relation to carbon pricing in different climate scenarios.

Net-Zero/Science-Based Targets

As mentioned previously, companies are increasingly adopting **net-zero targets**. However, there is significant variation among these targets, because they can

- be absolute or relative targets,
- cover different scopes of emissions (just operational, or Scope 1 and 2) or include some or all of the value chain (Scope 3) and different types of emissions (just carbon dioxide or all GHGs),
- focus on differing or multiple time frames, or
- rely on offsets.

This can make it difficult for investors to accurately measure and benchmark their carbon emission reduction objectives.

One element of standardization comes from science-based targets (SBT): targets underpinned by the latest climate science and evaluated by the **Science-Based Target initiative (SBTi)**, a partnership between several environmental institutions that provides independent certifications of the strength of companies' targets. It has produced decarbonization guidance in different sectors, including power, apparel and footwear, and information and communication technology, and more recently for the financial sector. Over 1,000 companies have set targets through the SBTi.[234]

Public companies' and their commitments are only one—albeit an important—part of investors' portfolios. Methodologies to assess the environmental profile of private companies, sub- and supra-national debt, or other asset classes are still evolving. The UN Principles for Responsible Investment (PRI), UNEP Finance Initiative, and the Institutional Investor Group on Climate Change are developing frameworks to help benchmark investors' transition to net zero.[235] The Partnership for Carbon Accounting Financials (PCAF) has also developed guidance for financial institutions to assess the GHG emissions of their loans and investments.[236]

Emission Trajectories

Emission trajectories can be used to assess the required reductions to reach a stated goal (for example, net-zero carbon by 2050) and compare the pathways implied by corporate commitments, policies, or individual assets (for example, proposed refurbishments to a building to improve its energy efficiency). For instance, the Transition

---

233 BloombergNEF, "Scale-Up of Solar and Wind Puts Existing Coal, Gas at Risk" (2020). https://about.bnef.com/blog/scale-up-of-solar-and-wind-puts-existing-coal-gas-at-risk/.
234 SBTi, "Companies Taking Action" (2020). https://sciencebasedtargets.org/companies-taking-action.
235 See, for example, PRI and UNEP Finance Initiative, "Inaugural 2025 Target Setting Protocol" (2021). www.unepfi.org/wordpress/wp-content/uploads/2021/01/Alliance-Target-Setting-Protocol-2021.pdf. See also IIGCC, "Paris Aligned Investment Initiative" (2021). www.iigcc.org/our-work/paris-aligned-investment-initiative/.
236 For more information, go to https://carbonaccountingfinancials.com/.

Pathway Initiative is an asset owner–led collaboration that has developed a publicly available tool that aims to assess companies' preparedness for the low-carbon transition.[237]

Temperature Alignment

Another approach comes from measures of **temperature alignment**. It seeks to compare the climate profiles of companies, sectors, or portfolios against a benchmark of global temperature. Because global "carbon budgets" impose constraints on the amount of emissions that are compatible with maintaining a reasonable chance of global temperatures not exceeding certain levels, this allows a degree of quantification of the implied future temperature levels associated with a company or portfolio. For example, Japan's Government Pension Investment Fund (GPIF), the world's largest pension fund, estimates its portfolio of equities and bonds are aligned with a warming trajectory of around 3°C (5.4°F).[238]

As an illustration, Legal & General Investment Management analyzed the emission intensity trajectory of approximately 2,000 companies against various climate change scenarios and found that the majority were not aligned with the goals of the Paris Agreement. This raised "concerns that some institutional portfolios may be aligned with temperature outcomes of greater than three degrees (3°C)," leaving them exposed to tightening climate policies.[239]

While it is intuitively easy to understand the aim of these measures and seemingly easy to compare temperatures, there is significant variation in the market around such metrics. They

- include implied temperature rise, global warming potential, and temperature alignment,
- use different inputs for climate performance, including carbon footprint, share of investments in "green" technologies, and proportion of investee companies with (science-based) emissions targets, and
- result in a different quantification of output—a binary statement (aligned or not), a score, a percentage of misalignment, or a temperature number.

Lastly but importantly, different methodologies can offer significantly different alignment results.[240]

> **TEMPERATURE ALIGNMENT TOOLS**
>
> There are several analytical products, both commercial and freely available. In line with changes in investor demand, the major providers of environmental data (which had historically been backward looking) have expanded their toolkit to develop more forward-looking approaches, with temperature ratings emerging as a major area of focus.
>
> Free-to-use tools include the following:
>
> - The CDP temperature rating methodology [241]

---

237 TPI, "The TPI Tool" (2021). www.transitionpathwayinitiative.org.
238 GPIF, "Analysis of Climate Change-Related Risks and Opportunities in the GPIF Portfolio" (2020). www.gpif.go.jp/en/investment/GPIF_CLIMATE_REPORT_FY2019_2.pdf.
239 Legal & General, "LGIM Announces Climate Solutions Capability Powered by Risk and Alignment Framework Co-Developed with Baringa Partners" (2020). https://group.legalandgeneral.com/en/newsroom/press-releases/lgim-announces-climate-solutions-capability-powered-by-risk-and-alignment-framework-co-developed-with-baringa-partners.
240 Institut Louis Bachelier, "The Alignment Cookbook: A Technical Review of Methodologies Assessing a Portfolio's Alignment with Low Carbon Trajectories or Temperature Goal" (2020). www.louisbachelier.org/wp-content/uploads/2020/10/cookbook.pdf.
241 CDP, "CDP Temperature Ratings" (2020). www.cdp.net/en/investor/temperature-ratings.

Approaches to Account for Material Environmental Analysis and Risk Management Strategies

> - The Paris Agreement Capital Transition Assessment (PACTA), developed by the 2° Investing Initiative with backing from the UN PRI, which provides tools to model publicly listed securities (equity and fixed income) and an open-source data and modeling suite for private portfolios (such as bank loan books) [242]
> - The climate portfolio optimizer from ESG for Investors, which models temperature as part of a "3D" framework, covering risk, return, and climate impact [243]
>
> There is also a wide range of analytical products.

Green Capital Expenditures, Revenues, and Research and Development

A different approach looks in more detail at companies' level of **green capital expenditures**, **revenue streams**, and **R&D** to gauge the direction of travel for their business models.

For the oil and gas sector, the Carbon Tracker Initiative has created a framework to assess companies' potential **capital expenditures** on new oil and gas projects, compared against their cost of production, associated emissions, and demand levels in different climate scenarios.[244]

An alternative is to consider **existing revenues**. Data providers including FTSE Russell and HSBC have compiled proprietary databases to assess the sales companies generate from over 100 low-carbon products and services.[245]

Several data providers have constructed methodologies to analyze the **patents** for low-carbon technologies filed by companies. R&D is a potentially useful indicator; however, the mere accumulation of patents need not imply strategic commitment. For example, Kodak engineers invented and patented the digital camera that would eventually render its company's main business obsolete.[246]

Natural Capital Approach

A term often used to describe the relationship between nature and measuring and valuing nature's role in decision making is natural capital. **Natural capital** helps businesses identify, measure, value, and prioritize their impacts and dependencies on biodiversity and the ecosystem, which ultimately give businesses new insight into their risks and opportunities (see Exhibit 20).[247] Understanding the value of both natural capital impacts and dependencies helps business and financial decision makers assess the significance of these issues for their institution and therefore make more informed decisions.

---

242 2° Investing Initiative, "PACTA/Climate Scenario Analysis Program" (2020). https://2degrees-investing.org/resource/pacta/.
243 ESG for Investors, "3D Climate Optimiser" (2022). https://esgforinvestors.com/climate_optimiser/.
244 Carbon Tracker Initiative, "Breaking the Habit: Methodology" (2020). https://carbontransfer.wpengine.com/wp-content/uploads/2019/09/Breaking-the-Habit-Methodology-Final-1.pdf.
245 FTSE Russell, "Green Revenues 2.0 Data Model" (2020). www.ftserussell.com/data/sustainability-and-esg-data/green-revenues-data-model.
See also HSBC, "HSBC Climate Solutions Database" (2020). www.research.hsbc.com/C/1/1/315/KrqWFj9.
246 D. Gann, "Kodak Invented the Digital Camera—Then Killed It. Why Innovation Often Fails," World Economic Forum (23 June 2016). www.weforum.org/agenda/2016/06/leading-innovation-through-the-chicanes/.
247 Capitals Coalition, "Natural Capital Protocol" (2016). https://capitalscoalition.org/capitals-approach/natural-capital-protocol.

Exhibit 20: The Natural Capital Approach Explains the Complex Ways in Which Natural, Social, and Economic Systems Interact, Affect, and Depend on One Another

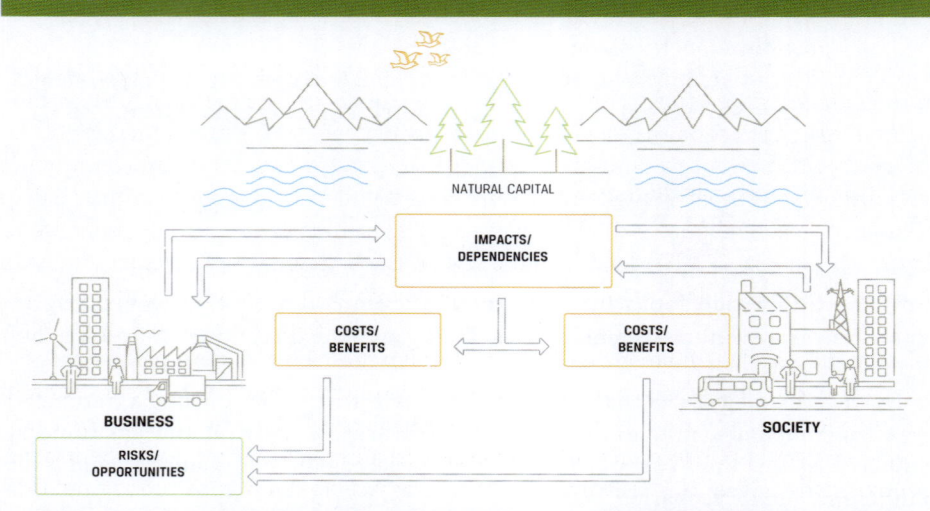

Source: Capitals Coalition, "Natural Capital Protocol" (2016). https://capitalscoalition.org/capitals-approach/natural-capital-protocol.

Assessing environmental factors using the Natural Capital Protocol (NCP), a decision-making framework, enables organizations to identify, measure, and value the direct and indirect impacts and dependencies of companies on natural capital. It currently provides guidance for the apparel sector, food and beverage sector, and forest products sector.

The protocol aims to allow companies to measure, value, and integrate natural capital impacts and dependencies into existing business processes, such as risk mitigation, sourcing, supply chain management, and product design.[248]

Recognizing the need for increased consideration of natural capital issues by financial decision makers, an initiative to establish the **Task Force on Nature-Related Financial Disclosures (TNFD)** was announced in mid-2020. It is a collaboration between Global Canopy and WWF, supported by financial institutions and governments.[249] In 2022, the TNFD released its first version of its nature-related risk management framework for market consultation.[250]

NATURAL RESOURCE RISK ASSESSMENT TOOLS FOR INVESTORS AND POLICYMAKERS

The Integrated Biodiversity Assessment Tool (IBAT), developed by the International Union for Conservation of Nature, is a central global biodiversity database that includes key biodiversity areas and legally protected areas. Through an interactive mapping tool, decision makers can easily access and use this up-to-date information to identify biodiversity risks and opportunities within a project boundary.[251]

---

248 Capitals Coalition, "Natural Capital Protocol."
249 TNFD, "Who We Are" (2020). https://tnfd.global/about/#who.
250 TNFD, "TNFD Releases First Beta Version of Nature-Related Risk Management Framework for Market Consultation" (2022). https://tnfd.global/news/tnfd-releases-first-beta-framework/.
251 IBAT, "Integrated Biodiversity Assessment Tool" (2022). www.ibat-alliance.org/.

Enabling a Natural Capital Approach (ENCA) is a policy tool and guidance developed by the UK Department for Environment, Food & Rural Affairs.[252]

CERES and WWF have developed water risk assessment tools, targeted at investors, lenders, and policymakers:

- ▸ The CERES Aqua Gauge, developed by CERES and CDP[253]
- ▸ The WWF Water Risk Filter[254]
- ▸ The World Resources Institute water tool, Aqueduct[255]

Climate Scenario Analysis

Scenario analysis is an approach for the forward-looking assessment of risks and opportunities. Scenario analysis is a process of evaluating how an organization, sector, country, or portfolio might perform in various future states, in order to understand its key drivers and possible outcomes.

Climate-related risk has been identified as one of the most complex macro-existential risks; it is not well understood and hard to quantify. The TCFD recommends that companies and financial institutions "describe the resilience of the organisation's strategy, taking into consideration different climate-related scenarios, including a 2°C (3.6°F) or lower scenario and, where relevant to the organisation, scenarios consistent with increased physical climate-related risks."[256]

In the current landscape, there is no common set of scenario analysis methodology used by investors. Instead, the types of approaches and models will depend largely on the objectives and scope of the work.

The **Institutional Investors Group on Climate Change (IIGCC)** published a practical investor guide, which provides a useful framework with which to approach climate-related scenario analysis.[257] The guide sets out two objectives of undertaking scenario analysis:

1. Financial impact: The use of scenario analysis enables the assessment and pricing of climate-related risks and opportunities.
2. Alignment: Aligning the portfolio(s) with a 2°C (3.6°F) or lower future, which is typically driven by a set of investment beliefs

At the overarching level, however, there is no one-size-fits-all methodology that investors can use to determine materiality, and they consequently use financial modeling and concepts, such as financial ratio analysis. The EU's Non-Financial Reporting Directive, which helps analysts and investors to evaluate the non-financial performance of large companies, sums up the most effective and recommended approach. It involves

- ▸ taking a set of transparent and credible data sources and assumptions, which can be quantitative or qualitative,

---

252 Department for Environment, Food & Rural Affairs, "Enabling a Natural Capital Approach (ENCA)" (2020). www.gov.uk/guidance/enabling-a-natural-capital-approach-enca.
253 Ceres, "Ceres Aqua Gauge: A Comprehensive Assessment Tool for Evaluating Corporate Management of Water Risk" (2021). www.ceres.org/resources/tools/ceres-aqua-gauge-comprehensive-assessment-tool-evaluating-corporate-management.
254 WWF, "WWF Water Risk Filter 6.0" (2022). https://waterriskfilter.org/.
255 World Resources Institute, "Aqueduct: Using Cutting-Edge Data to Identify and Evaluate Water Risks around the World" (2022). www.wri.org/aqueduct.
256 TCFD, "2019 Status Report: Task Force on Climate-Related Financial Disclosures: Status Report" (2019). www.fsb-tcfd.org/wp-content/uploads/2019/06/2019-TCFD-Status-Report-FINAL-053119.pdf.
257 IIGCC, "Navigating Climate Scenario Analysis—A Guide for Institutional Investors" (2019). www.iigcc.org/resource/navigating-climate-scenario-analysis-a-guide-for-institutional-investors/.

- applying recognizable, accepted methodologies, which will probably have the backing of an industry body, government department, or multilateral institution,
- focusing on materiality (looking in particular at business models, operations, and financial performance), and
- generating a set of outputs that can be measured in terms of key performance indicators.[258]

In order for the financial system to achieve a better appreciation of climate change risks (and opportunities), there is a need for more data, greater disclosure, better analytical toolkits, advanced scenario analysis, and new risk management techniques.[259]

7 APPLYING MATERIAL ENVIRONMENTAL FACTORS TO FINANCIAL MODELING, RATIO ANALYSIS, AND RISK ASSESSMENT

3.1.7 apply material environmental factors to financial modeling, ratio analysis, and risk assessment

The following case study is based on a 2018 WWF and Cadmus survey[260] of more than 20 infrastructure investors and related stakeholders and looks at how investors evaluate the sustainability of infrastructure assets. It can, however, be adapted for evaluating individual companies.

It demonstrates how and where to integrate the results of a comprehensive ESG assessment as input into the key financial ratios and variables of a financial model, such as the forecasting of revenues, operating costs, and capital expenditures, which form the basis of discounted cash flow (DCF) analysis.

Note that this example focuses only on the environmental impacts. In reality, the social and governance factors need to be considered in parallel for a full ESG materiality assessment.

> **CASE STUDIES**
>
> ### ESG Review—Environmental Factors and Materiality
>
> Over the lifetime of an infrastructure project—from development to construction, to operation, and all the way through to the decommissioning phase—infrastructure assets face all kinds of ESG issues. These vary depending on asset type, sector, size, geographic location, and stage in the life cycle.
>
> Some of the environmental issues may originate outside the asset but could impact its technical ability to operate or impact its profitability (for instance, temperature rise and increased water scarcity). Other issues may be caused by the asset itself and impact its surrounding environment and communities

---

258 European Commission, "Directive 2014/95/EU" (2014). https://ec.europa.eu/info/business-economy-euro/company-reporting-and-auditing/company-reporting/non-financial-reporting_en.
259 S. Breeden, "Avoiding the Storm."
260 WWF/Cadmus, "Valuing Sustainability in Infrastructure Investments: Market Status, Barriers and Opportunities — A Landscape Analysis," (2019). https://www.wwf.ch/de/unsere-ziele/sustainable-finance-nachhaltige-finanzfluesse-foerdern.

Applying Material Environmental Factors to Financial Modeling, Ratio Analysis, and Risk Assessment

(such as water effluence and the quality of life of the communities around it). In this latter case, these are called externalities, which can (and will) increasingly impact the asset's financial performance via various feedback loops (including protests of the surrounding community). It is thus important to realize that both directions of potential environmental impact (impact *on* the asset and impact *from* the asset) may have financial consequences for the investors.

For the purpose of arriving at a shortlist of environmental factors for which the potential impact of environmental risk on infrastructure financials can be demonstrated, a two-step process was followed:

1. A longlist of widely recognized environmental factors was derived. The longlist was reduced to a shortlist of environmental factors that are typically among those considered key to an environmental assessment in the context of infrastructure.
2. Whether and the extent to which any of the selected environmental factors have a material impact on the infrastructure asset will be revealed by the asset-specific ESG due diligence process.

Environmental Factors Material to Infrastructure Projects:

Typical Environmental Factors	Material Environment Factors for Infrastructure
Degradation and pollution →	**(A) Quantifiable**
▸ Air (climate)—GHG emissions	*Degradation and pollution*
▸ Air (health)—other pollution	1. Air (health) and water pollution
▸ Water	2. Air (climate)—GHG emissions
▸ Ground or contamination	*Resource efficiency—sourcing, use, or treatment*
▸ Noise and light	3. Energy (E)
▸ Biodiversity	4. Water (E)
Resource efficiency—sourcing, use, or treatment:	5. Solid waste (E)
▸ (Raw) materials including supply chain	6. (Raw) materials and supply chain (E/S)
▸ Energy	**(B) Difficult to quantify**
▸ Water	7. Biodiversity and habitat (E)
▸ Waste	8. Physical climate change impacts (E)
Physical risk—impact on asset, such as flooding	

Approach to Assess the Implications of Environmental Risk on Financial Ratios and Models

The approach used in this caSe study, which uses survey input across a range of infrastructure projects, simplifies the TCFD classification of risks introduced previously, while broadening it to ESG, not just climate, themes.

The following table helps show how the selected environmental factors may impact the financial performance of infrastructure organizations. It elaborates on the potential impact pathways from the selected environmental factors to specific financial ratios or inputs into financial models.

Environmental Factor	Risks Considered	Financial Ratio or Factor Impact	Impact of the Risk
Air pollution or water pollution	Tightening regulations	Asset write-off/capital expenditure (CapEx)	Write-offs, asset impairment, or early retirement of existing assets may result from the tightening of regulation.
		Provisions	Provisions may be needed to cover potential fines in case of non-compliance with new regulations. They may also need to be made for potential lawsuits or other legal proceedings.
	Costs for obtaining relevant permit increase	Operating expenditure (OpEx)	The overall production cost will increase due to an additional discharge cost.
	Imposition of new environmental tax	Tax	Taxes will increase.
	Enhanced disclosure requirements	OpEx	Monitoring, reporting, and auditing costs will increase.
	Reputational	Provisions	Reputational damage may lead to loss of revenues.
		Financing costs	Additional interest paid due to higher interest rate or lower credit rating.
GHG emissions	Client demand for lower-carbon products and services (e.g., cleaner electricity in the case of a utility company)	Revenues	Decrease in revenues from high-carbon activities.
	Introduction or increase of price for GHG emissions, implementation of a carbon tax, loss of subsidies for high-GHG-intensity energy sources	OpEx/tax/CapEx	Production cost increases (OpEx, tax). Preventive investment (CapEx) in measures of technology to reduce GHG emissions per unit of output or to reduce energy intensity of processes
Greenhouse gas emissions	In a utility example: Clients switch to electricity generated with lower GHG intensity than traditional electricity.	Revenues	Decrease in revenues due to lower demand for conventional fossil fuels
	Introduction or increase of price for greenhouse gas emissions, implementation of a carbon tax, loss of subsidies for high-GHG-intensity energy sources	OpEx/tax/Capex	Production cost increases (OpEx, tax). Preventive investment (CapEx) in measures of technology to reduce GHG emissions per unit of output or to reduce energy intensity of processes
Energy	Physical: rising temperatures	OpEx	Higher temperatures may influence the functioning of equipment and lead to an increase in fuel consumption or lower performance levels (OpEx).

Environmental Factor	Risks Considered	Financial Ratio or Factor Impact	Impact of the Risk
Water	Physical: increased water scarcity	Revenue/OpEx	Insufficient supply for water-reliant assets, such as hydro-power plants or district heating networks, leads to loss of revenues due to loss of energy production (hydro-power plant) or an increase in operating costs because of the rise in water prices.
	Reputational: conflicts with the surrounding community on water withdrawal	Revenues/provisions/OpEx	Conflicts with community may lead to project delays, which in turn may lead to loss of revenues or fines for late completion. Increase in operating expenses due to additional community engagement and marketing measures
	Regulatory: implementation of more stringent regulation regarding water withdrawal	CapEx/OpEx	Investments in water-saving measures may become necessary but may reduce water usage going forward. Implementation of new production processes, which substitute water with more expensive resources, leads to higher OpEx.
Solid waste	Regulatory: tightened regulation on waste disposal and land restoration	Provisions	Potentially stricter regulation for waste disposal, recycling, or land restoration during the decommissioning phase
(Raw) materials supply chain	Reputational: environmental, social, or governance issues may be found in the supply chain	Provisions	Dealing with reputational issues is time consuming and costly, and provisions may need to be made to cover for such cases.
Biodiversity and habitat	Regulatory/legal: tightening of regulations or other operating requirements regarding the protection of critical species or habitats	Revenues/CapEx/OpEx	Potential operating restrictions on certain days of the year or on certain times of the day leading to a reduction in sales (revenues) Investments into alterations to existing structures, such as implementation of sound curtains for offshore wind turbines, may be necessary. Adherence to stipulations may lead to increased monitoring and reporting cost.
Climate change impacts (E)	Physical: Extreme weather (storms and floods) can lead to disruptions.	Revenues	Periodic loss of energy production (windfarms) due to shutdown

Environmental Factor	Risks Considered	Financial Ratio or Factor Impact	Impact of the Risk
	Physical: Extreme weather may destroy the asset partially or fully.	Asset book value/revenues/CapEx/OpEx	A write-down or write-off of the assets and a loss of revenues may be the immediate result. Investments will be needed to repair or even rebuild the damaged asset. If the probability of extreme weather increases, the probability of damage or destruction increases; therefore, insurance policies are likely to increase.

Source: Adapted from WWF and B Capital Partners, "Guidance Note: Integrating ESG Factors into Financial Models for Infrastructure Investments" (2019). http://awsassets.panda.org/downloads/wwf_guidance_note_infra_.pdf.

8 OPPORTUNITIES RELATING TO CLIMATE CHANGE AND ENVIRONMENTAL ISSUES

> 3.1.8 explain how companies and the investment industry can benefit from opportunities relating to climate change and environmental issues: the circular economy, clean and technological innovation, green and ESG-related products, and the blue economy

Previous sections have covered the risks of neglecting the implications of key environmental factors for companies as a result of direct or indirect business activities. The increased awareness of climate change and environmental impact has resulted in an accelerating search for viable societal and economic solutions to enable a transition to a less carbon-intensive economy. Estimates for this transition reach trillions of dollars, and the magnitude of change required will be pervasive, across all aspects of life as we understand it today.

A 2016 study by the Global Commission on the Economy and Climate found that the world is expected to invest about US$90 trillion (£64.7 trillion) in infrastructure over the next 15 years, requiring an urgent shift to ensure that this capital is spent on low-carbon, energy-efficient projects. The report further described that "transformative change is needed now in how we build our cities, produce and use energy, transport people and goods, and manage our landscapes."[261] It is therefore no surprise that there is an increasing number of investment strategies that focus primarily on the opportunities of the low-carbon transition and green finance. Investing in such sectors as technology and resource efficiency, waste management, circular economy, and sustainable agriculture and forestry are just some of the available investment opportunities relating to climate change and environmental issues.

---

261 New Climate Economy, "The Sustainable Infrastructure Imperative" (2016). https://newclimateeconomy.report/2016/misc/downloads/.

Opportunities Relating to Climate Change and Environmental Issues

Already, the investment opportunities are becoming visible. FTSE Russell estimated that the green economy (the total market capitalization of the companies generating revenues from activities providing environmental benefits) in 2020 was "equivalent to 5% of the total listed equity market. It has grown faster than the overall equity market since 2009 and is estimated to have overtaken the size of the oil and gas sector."[262]

This section provides an overview of some of these opportunities as they relate to

- **A.** the circular economy,
- **B.** clean and technological innovation,
- **C.** green and ESG-related products, and
- **D.** the blue economy.

It also highlights how clean technology and innovation will play a critical role and be an investment opportunity in mitigating and adapting to the impacts of climate change and environmental degradation. This section also covers some of the financial products most prevalent in supporting environmental (green) considerations in investments.

Circular Economy

With only a fraction of material inputs being currently recycled (less than 12% in the EU in 2019, for example),[263] there are significant investment opportunities from innovations to encourage a shift toward a **circular economy**. This shift is already underway: In September 2020, assets managed through public equity funds with the circular economy as their sole or partial focus were estimated to have increased sixfold compared to the beginning of that year, from US$0.3 billion to US$2 billion (£0.2 billion to £1.4 billion), with the number of such funds almost doubling.[264]

Companies that factor in circularity in their business model are able to play a major role in safeguarding natural resources and transform the way we currently use natural resources and support a transition to a low-carbon economy.

In a circular economy, products and materials are repaired, reused, and recycled rather than thrown away, ensuring that waste from one industrial process becomes a valued input into another. The circular economy concept is now a core component of both the EU's 2050 Long-Term Strategy to achieve a climate-neutral Europe and China's five-year plans.

Due to the expanding market of investible opportunities, both in the private and public markets, companies are working to bring circularity closer to the heart of their business models.

> **CASE STUDIES**
>
> ### Jurong Island
>
> Singapore's Jurong Island is one of the world's top 10 chemical parks. The close proximity of industries on the island "provides an ecosystem where one company's product can become the feedstock of another. For example, waste from some companies is burned to generate steam for industrial use. Similarly,

---

262 FTSE Russell, "Investing in the Green Economy—Sizing the Opportunity" (2020). https://content.ftserussell.com/sites/default/files/investing_in_the_green_economy___sizing_the_opportunity_final.pdf.
263 European Environment Agency, "Growth without Economic Growth" (2021). www.eea.europa.eu/publications/growth-without-economic-growth/growth-without-economic-growth.
264 Ellen MacArthur Foundation, "Financing the Circular Economy: Capturing the Opportunity" (2020). www.ellenmacarthurfoundation.org/assets/downloads/Financing-the-circular-economy.pdf.

wastewater is recovered and recycled for industrial use."[265] Industrial developer JTC Corporation is partnering with local companies and regulators to explore further avenues for circularity, by mapping water, energy, and waste flows.

Heineken

As part of its Zero Waste Programme, 102 of Heineken's 165 production units sent zero waste to landfills in 2018. The waste from these sites was instead recycled into animal feed, material loops, or compost or used for energy recovery.[266]

Schneider Electric

This company specializes in energy management and automation. It uses recycled content and recyclable materials in its products, prolongs product lifespan through leasing and pay-per-use, and has introduced take-back schemes into its supply chain. Circular activities now account for 12% of its revenues and will save 100,000 metric tons of primary resources between 2018 and 2020.[267]

Stora Enso

This company provides renewable solutions in packaging, biomaterials, wooden construction, and paper. Reducing waste operates at the heart of the "bioeconomy and contributes to a circular economy."[268]

In 2019, the European Investment Bank launched an investment fund to support the circular bioeconomy.[269]

Close the Loop

This Australian company works to turn old printer cartridges and soft plastics into roads by mixing them with asphalt and recycled glass, resulting in a road surface that is estimated to be up to 65% more durable than traditional asphalt. For a kilometer of road, the equivalent of 530,000 plastic bags, 168,000 glass bottles, and the waste toner from 12,500 printer cartridges is used.[270]

Clean and Technological Innovation

Technological innovation and the development of new business ventures associated with the environment have been around for some time. However, the term cleantech as an umbrella term "encompassing the investment asset class, technology, and business sectors which include clean energy, environmental, and sustainable or green products and services" became increasingly popular approximately 20 years ago.[271]

As with many other technological innovations, such as the internet or GPS, state support and a favorable policy and regulatory environment have been instrumental in driving the early growth of technologies, such as wind and solar energy. However, as the technologies have matured, unsubsidized solar and wind have become the cheapest source of new electricity in most regions around the world. Moreover,

---

265 Singapore Ministry of the Environment and Water Resources, "Zero Waste Masterplan" (2019). www.towardszerowaste.gov.sg/zero-waste-masterplan/.
266 Heineken, "Drop the C: Reducing Our CO_2 Emissions" (2018). www.theheinekencompany.com/pt-pt/node/607.
267 Schneider Electric, "About Us" (2018). www.se.com/uk/en/about-us/.
268 Stora Enso, "About Stora Enso" (2018). www.storaenso.com/en/about-stora-enso.
269 European Investment Bank, "A European Fund to Support the Circular Bioeconomy" (2019). www.eib.org/en/press/all/2019-328-a-european-fund-to-support-the-circular-bioeconomy.
270 World Economic Forum, "These 11 Companies Are Leading the Way to a Circular Economy" (2019). www.weforum.org/agenda/2019/02/companies-leading-way-to-circular-economy/.
271 ISO, "Energy Management Systems—Requirements with Guidance for Use" (2018). www.iso.org/obp/ui/#iso:std:iso:50001:ed-2:v1:en.

Opportunities Relating to Climate Change and Environmental Issues

this dynamic is increasingly undercutting *operational* costs of some existing assets; research has shown that in 2020, on a levelized cost basis, it was cheaper to build new wind and solar capacity than to operate 60% of the existing coal power plants in the world.[272] See Exhibit 21 for data on the costs and adoption rates of several clean energy technologies.

Exhibit 21: Falling Costs (US$ 2020/MWh) and Growing Adoption (GW) of Selected Clean Energy Technologies, 2000–2020

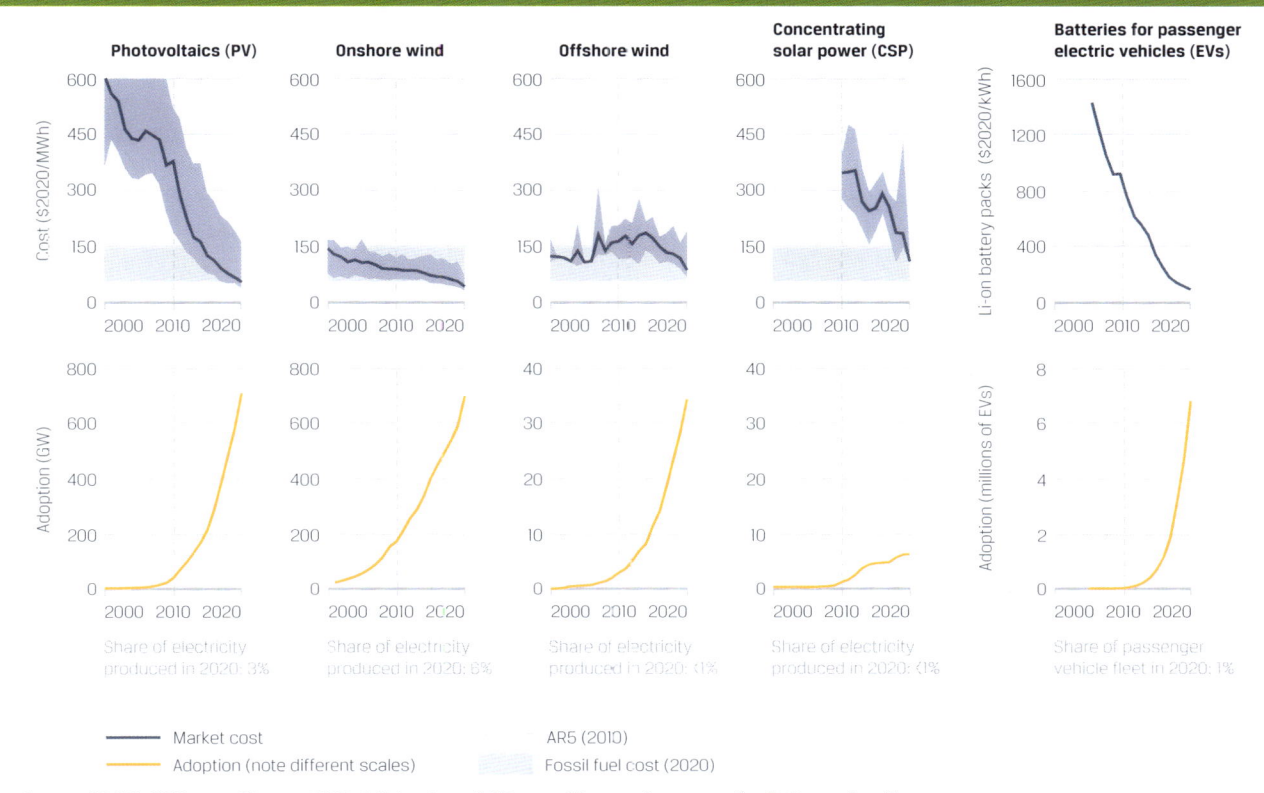

Source: IPCC, "Climate Change 2022: Mitigation of Climate Change: Summary for Policymakers" (2022). https://report.ipcc.ch/ar6wg3/pdf/IPCC_AR6_WGIII_SummaryForPolicymakers.pdf.

As a result, there is increased interest from private investors in this area. Over the past seven years—a period of intense digitalization and research into automation—it has been estimated that venture capital investment into cleantech grew three times faster than similar investments into artificial intelligence.[273]

Next, we discuss some of the technologies that can play a role in decarbonizing sectors, which contribute substantially to global emissions.

Energy is the "prime mover" of the economy, and reducing the emissions associated with energy production has knock-on effects across all sectors. The production of low-carbon **electricity** has been at the forefront of these developments, from such

---

[272] Lazard, "Levelized Cost of Energy, Levelized Cost of Storage, and Levelized Cost of Hydrogen 2020" (2020). www.lazard.com/perspective/levelized-cost-of-energy-and-levelized-cost-of-storage-2020/. See also Carbon Tracker Initiative, "Coal Developers Risk $600 Billion as Renewables Outcompete Worldwide" (2020). https://carbontracker.org/coal-developers-risk-600-billion-as-renewables-outcompete-worldwide/.

[273] PricewaterhouseCoopers, "The State of Climate Tech 2020: The Next Frontier for Venture Capital" (2020). www.pwc.com/gx/en/services/sustainability/publications/state-of-climate-tech-2020.html.

sources as solar photovoltaics, onshore and offshore wind, hydroelectricity, nuclear energy, tidal energy, and geothermal energy. Fuels derived from biomass (e.g., "biofuels," such as bioethanol) may also be considered as a renewable energy source, although this depends on the sustainability of the source, with significant debates around the environmental impacts of large-scale biofuel cultivation.[274]

A full, global accounting of the agricultural sector shows that it produces about 40% of global emissions when heat, electricity, and transportation are included, so biofuels are seldom the low-GHG source that some claim. Harvesting wood and burning it for electricity is slowly renewable but releases more carbon dioxide than burning coal or other fossil fuels and reduces the amount of CO_2 that can be removed by forests.[275] Wood burning also releases large amounts of fine particulates that damage human health, leave sunlight-absorbing black carbon on land, and darken ice and snow, hastening their melting.

Albeit very important, electricity is only one component of energy. The challenge is harder when it comes to decarbonizing **heat and cooling**. For residential and commercial properties, ground and air source heat pumps, combined heat and power, and district heating are some of the potential heating solutions. More difficult is the decarbonization of high-temperature processes. The use of renewable energy to produce hydrogen—which can burn at high temperatures—is increasingly the focus of governments' and investors' strategies, although the deployment of supportive green hydrogen infrastructure is currently lacking. Other speculative technologies include research into nuclear fusion (very long term) and next-generation battery storage.

The electrification of **industrial processes**—from clean sources—is an essential lever for the decarbonization of industry. In steel making, which has a substantial carbon footprint, the use of electric arc furnaces coupled with increased steel recycling and alternative reductants (e.g., hydrogen or gas instead of coal) are important avenues. The process CO_2 released from turning iron ore into iron can be captured and stored. In the chemicals industry, the use of green hydrogen, synthetic fuels, new catalysts, and alternative feedstocks (including the use of biogenic materials), as well as the development of lightweight materials and plastic alternatives, can contribute.

The **built environment** sector contributes up to 40% of total GHGs as a result of the whole life-cycle carbon of the building—the embodied carbon and the carbon associated with construction (building materials) and the operation (energy used to heat, cool, and light). Embodied carbon is associated with the construction materials, major refurbishments, and waste in their production, the building process, and the fixtures and fittings inside, as well as from deconstruction and disposal at the end of a building's lifetime.

In terms of technology drivers in this sector, CO_2 is an inevitable by-product of the chemical reaction used to create the most widely used form of cement. Developing alternatives to "clinkers" (one of cement's major components) will play a key role, as will capture and storage of the process CO_2 that is released. Several large cement producers have already begun to develop breakthrough technologies in producing cement with lower emissions and higher energy efficiency.

In the **transport** industry, many of the world's large automobile makers have begun to shift their business models toward battery electric vehicles (BEVs), with global sales of electric cars more than doubling in 2021 and capturing all the net growth in global

---

274 S. Evans, "CCC: UK Should 'Move Away' from Large-Scale Biomass Burning," Carbon Brief (15 November 2018). www.carbonbrief.org/ccc-uk-should-move-away-from-large-scale-biomass-burning.
275 John Sterman, William Moomaw, Juliette N. Rooney-Varga, and Lori Siegel, "Does Wood Bioenergy Help or Harm the Environment?" (10 May 2022). https://thebulletin.org/premium/2022-05/does-wood-bioenergy-help-or-harm-the-climate/.

Opportunities Relating to Climate Change and Environmental Issues

car demand.[276] Nearly half of the 6.5 million BEVs sold worldwide in 2021 were in China, and just 535,000 were sold in the United States.[277] In Norway, 65% of a much smaller but record number of car sales were BEVs; price and other incentives are rapidly transforming the market.[278] The extent to which batteries and electrification will play a substantial role in the decarbonization of heavy-duty transport or whether other fuel sources (such as ammonia, hydrogen fuel cells, or biofuels) may be used to power trucks, planes, and ships remains an open question and subject to intense research and investment.

Given the substantial emissions associated with food production, packaging, and consumption, innovation will be needed in the **food** industry. The development of protein alternatives (whether plant based, including algae,[279] or laboratory-grown meat, for example) is a fast-growing market. Further innovation in agricultural techniques (e.g., around precision and regenerative agriculture or the development of less toxic pest management and low–nitrous oxide emission nitrogen fertilizers) will also be needed.

Finally, in light of the interdependencies in the global economic system, it is often the case, as illustrated in Exhibit 22, that technologies have the potential to be used across multiple sectors.

Exhibit 22: Clean Energy Technologies' Level of Readiness and Applicability in Various Sectors

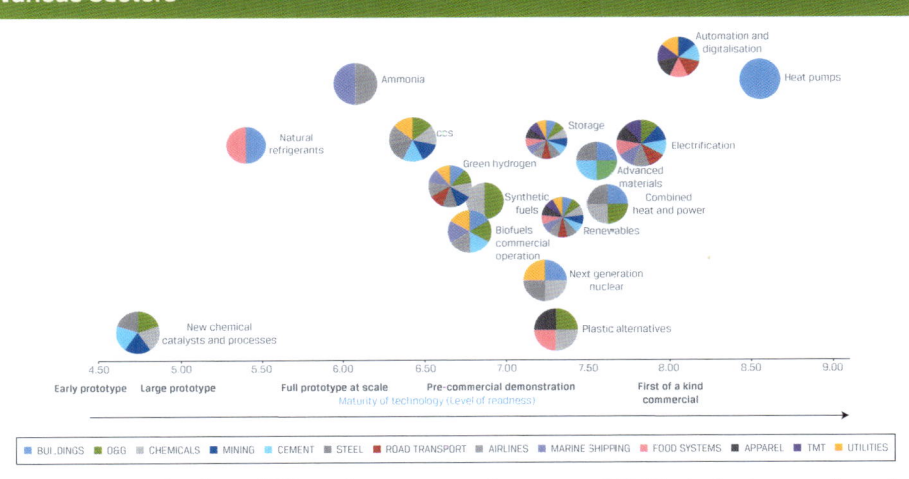

Note: O&G = oil and gas, CCS = carbon capture and storage, and TMT = technology, media, and telecommunications

Sources: LGIM; IEA, "ETP Clean Energy Technology Guide" (2020). www.iea.org/articles/etp-clean-energy-technology-guide.

---

276 Leonardo Paoli and Timur Gül, "Electric Cars Fend Off Supply Challenges to More Than Double Global Sales," IEA (2022). www.iea.org/commentaries/electric-cars-fend-off-supply-challenges-to-more-than-double-global-sales.

277 Canalys, "Global Electric Vehicle Sales up 109% in 2021, with Half in Mainland China" (14 February 2022). www.canalys.com/newsroom/global-electric-vehicle-market-2021

278 Victoria Klesty, "Electric Cars Hit 65% of Norway Sales as Tesla Grabs Overall Pole," Reuters (5 January 2022). www.reuters.com/business/autos-transportation/electric-cars-take-two-thirds-norway-car-market-led-by-tesla-2022-01-03/.

279 William Moomaw, Isaac Berzin, and Asaf Tzachor, "Cutting Out the Middle Fish: Marine Microalgae as the Next Sustainable Omega-3 Fatty Acids and Protein Source," *Industrial Biotechnology* 13 (October 2017). www.liebertpub.com/doi/10.1089/ind.2017.29102.wmo.

However, it is important to understand that the *technical potential* for a technology to contribute to decarbonization—the list of *possible use cases*—does not guarantee actual deployment, which will also be a function of economics, the availability of alternatives, social preferences, and other factors.

HYDROGEN: HOPE OR HYPE?

The clean-burning qualities of hydrogen, for example, make it a candidate for a variety of applications, including industrial (e.g., in certain high-temperature processes), transport (e.g., long-haul trucking), and domestic (such as replacing gas boilers). As a result, while some governments (notably Japan) have for decades been subsidizing hydrogen research, particularly around fuel cell vehicles, there is renewed policymaker interest in this area, with "hydrogen strategies" and funding commitments announced recently by such governments those in the United Kingdom, the EU, and China.

However, analysts have also highlighted barriers to adoption (e.g., the volumetric density and embrittling effect on steel pipes and the thermodynamic efficiency of transforming electricity into hydrogen and back via a fuel cell). Exhibit 23 shows one energy analyst's ranking of hydrogen use cases in various sectors. Inspired by the energy performance bands now common on electrical appliances, the "hydrogen ladder" aims to situate potential uses cases for clean hydrogen as a function of the availability (or lack thereof) of other, competing cleantech alternatives.

Exhibit 23: The Clean Hydrogen Ladder: An Analyst's Illustration of Clean Hydrogen Use Cases in Relation to Competing Technologies for Decarbonization

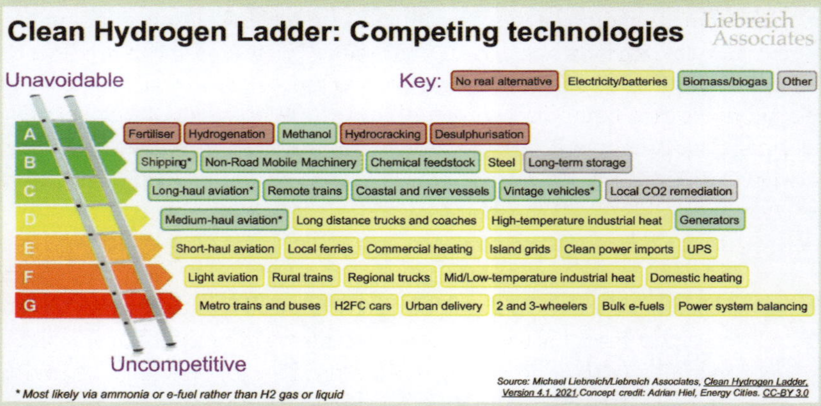

Source: Liebreich Associates, "The Clean Hydrogen Ladder" (2021) www.linkedin.com/pulse/clean-hydrogen-ladder-v40-michael-liebreich/.

The choice of technologies and scenario assumptions remains an area of intense debate in both academia and industry, and the technological realities on the ground are fast evolving. For example, according to Bloomberg New Energy Finance, the rise in gas prices in early 2022 has led to the costs of green hydrogen falling below those of "grey" hydrogen (produced from unabated fossil gas) in the Europe, Middle East, and Africa region and China—a point of price parity reached a decade earlier than in some previous estimates.[280]

---

[280] W. Mathis, R. Morison, and V. Dezem, "Russia's War Supercharges Push to Make New Green Fuel," Bloomberg (10 April 2022). www.bloomberg.com/news/articles/2022-04-10/russia-s-invasion-supercharges-push-to-make-a-new-green-fuel.

And as noted earlier, the development of cleantech often works in tandem with standard setting by governments and levels of policy support. One notable example of this is in the case of our built environment.

> **CASE STUDIES**
>
> ### Environmental Standards in Real Estate
>
> The real estate sector is currently undergoing significant change, with major property developers and managers stepping up their sustainability practices in their role to tackle climate change.
>
> In the United Kingdom, the Better Buildings Partnership (BBP), a coalition of some of the largest commercial property owners, has committed to achieving net-zero carbon by 2050. This is a bold ambition and one that will require significant changes in the current practices throughout the life cycle of a building. The BBP believes that the UK energy efficiency standard and regulations, which are intended to achieve better energy performance, are actually not "fit for purpose" and will certainly not support the BBP's net-zero carbon goal. These standards are focused on design intent rather than on how a building actually performs in use, hence creating a "performance gap."
>
> As such, the BBP has embarked on an initiative called Design for Performance (DfP), which is based on the National Australian Built Environmental Rating System (NABERS), which measures and rates the operational efficiency of commercial offices. NABERS has proven to be very successful as it focuses on target ratings, outcomes, and transparency, and so, it recently published the "NABERS UK Guide to Design for Performance," aimed at the UK market.
>
> In the near future, we can expect to see other governments that have made commitments to achieve carbon neutrality by 2050 start to strengthen their existing energy performance standards and regulations in the real estate sector and adopt best practice approaches such as this one.[281]

According to BloombergNEF, in 2021, total investment in the low-carbon energy transition worldwide was US$755 billion (£575 billion), with China as the largest investor, followed by the United States.[282] The largest area of funding in 2021 was renewable energy, followed by electrified transport and heat.

There has also been increasing activity in corporate venturing and investments by incumbent fossil fuel–based corporations into clean and renewable technologies. These private sector efforts have been complemented by greater supra-national and public sector support—for example, EIT **InnoEnergy**, which was established to invest in and accelerate sustainable energy innovations. Another initiative, still in the concept phase, is the World Economic Forum's **Sustainable Energy Innovation Fund (SEIF)**, which matches up private funding with public investment.

See also quote from BNEF in L. Collins, "Ukraine War | Green Hydrogen 'Now Cheaper than Grey in Europe, Middle East and China': BNEF," Recharge News (7 March 2022). www.rechargenews.com/energy-transition/ukraine-war-green-hydrogen-now-cheaper-than-grey-in-europe-middle-east-and-china-bnef/2-1-1180320.

281 Better Buildings Partnership, "BBP Climate Change Commitment" (2020). www.betterbuildingspartnership.co.uk/node/877.

282 BloombergNEF, "Energy Transition Investment Trends 2022" (2022). https://assets.bbhub.io/professional/sites/24/Energy-Transition-Investment-Trends-Exec-Summary-2022.pdf.

Green and ESG-Related Products

The risks and opportunities associated with environmental sustainability and mitigating climate change necessitate a realignment of financial products and services in order to facilitate the transition to a low-carbon economy. There are three attributes of energy and products: renewability, carbon (or GHG) intensity, and sustainability. For climate, low or zero carbon is the major criterion for determining whether it is "green." Sustainability is a second criterion: Is it "enduring"? Renewability means that the energy or material is replaced in a short time relative to its use. The overall assessment of these three factors determines what is green, but there is no universally agreed-on definition of "green." There have been several developments in this area, along with expectations for rapid expansion of the breadth and depth of these green products and services, over the next few years.

At the Glasgow Climate COP in 2021, the Glasgow Financial Alliance for Net Zero, a group of 450 financial institutions with assets of $130 trillion, announced a goal of net-zero carbon investments by 2050.[283] This goal is at odds with the large investments that have been made in heavy CO_2-releasing industries by many of these institutions.

Some specific financial products that have emerged are

- a range of green, sustainability, and ESG indexes,
- green bonds and loans, sustainability funds, and ETFs,
- retail and institutional deposit and savings products, and
- crowdfunding investments.[284]

Green Bonds, Loans, and Other Labeled ESG-Related Products

The first green bond issuance was announced in 2007 by the European Investment Bank to raise funding for climate-related projects. Green bonds were created to fund projects that have positive environmental or climate benefits. The majority are green "use-of-proceeds" or asset-linked bonds (see Exhibit 24).

Green bond issuances by banks and corporates have accelerated in recent years, with total cumulative issuance surpassing the US$1 trillion (£0.7 trillion) mark in late 2020, with annual issuance almost doubling in 2021 versus the previous year.[285]

---

283 J. Baker, "Mark Carney's Ambitious $130 Trillion Glasgow Financial Alliance for Net Zero," Forbes (8 November 2021). www.forbes.com/sites/jillbaker/2021/11/08/mark-carneys-ambitious-130-trillion-glasgow-financial-alliance-for-net-zero/?sh=5b6dd573a312.
284 Climate Bonds Initiative, "Green Bonds: The State of the Market 2018" (2019). www.climatebonds.net/resources/reports/green-bonds-state-market-2018.
285 L. Jones, "$1Trillion Mark Reached in Global Cumulative Green Issuance: Climate Bonds Data Intelligence Reports: Latest Figures," Climate Bonds Initiative (15 December 2020). www.climatebonds.net/2020/12/1trillion-mark-reached-global-cumulative-green-issuance-climate-bonds-data-intelligence. See also www.climatebonds.net/market/data/.

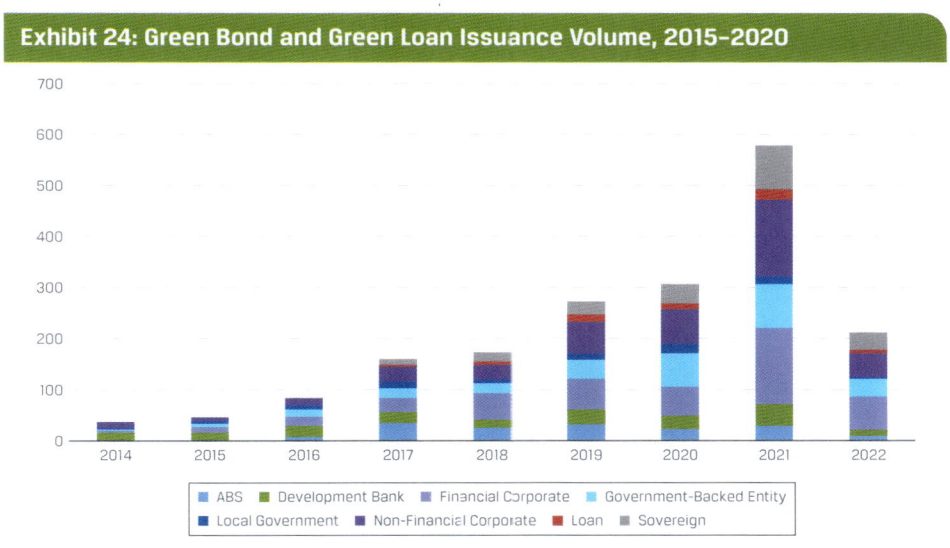

Opportunities Relating to Climate Change and Environmental Issues 209

Exhibit 24: Green Bond and Green Loan Issuance Volume, 2015–2020

[Stacked bar chart showing issuance volume from 2014 to 2022, with categories: ABS, Development Bank, Financial Corporate, Government-Backed Entity, Local Government, Non-Financial Corporate, Loan, Sovereign]

Notes: Data cover up to the end of 2021. All debt instruments have been screened in accordance with the Climate Bonds Initiative Green Bond Database Methodology[286] and Social & Sustainability Bond Database Methodology.[287] Definitions of *green* are derived from the Climate Bonds Taxonomy,[288] and issuer type classification follows Climate Bonds Initiative convention.

Source: Climate Bonds Initiative, "Climate Bonds Interactive Data Platform" (2022). www.climatebonds.net/market/data/.

While clean energy and low-carbon building investment continues to dominate allocations, funding for low-carbon transport has increased dramatically and issuers from the information and communications technology (ICT) and manufacturing sectors have entered the green bond market (see Exhibit 25).

---

286 Climate Bonds Initiative, "Green Bond Database Methodology" (2021). www.climatebonds.net/market/green-bond-database-methodolgy.
287 Climate Bonds Initiative, "Social & Sustainability Bond Database Methodology" (2021). www.climatebonds.net/market/social-sustainability-bond-database-methodology.
288 Climate Bonds Initiative, "Climate Bonds Taxonomy" (2020). www.climatebonds.net/standard/taxonomy.

Exhibit 25: Use of Green Bond and Loans Proceeds, 2021

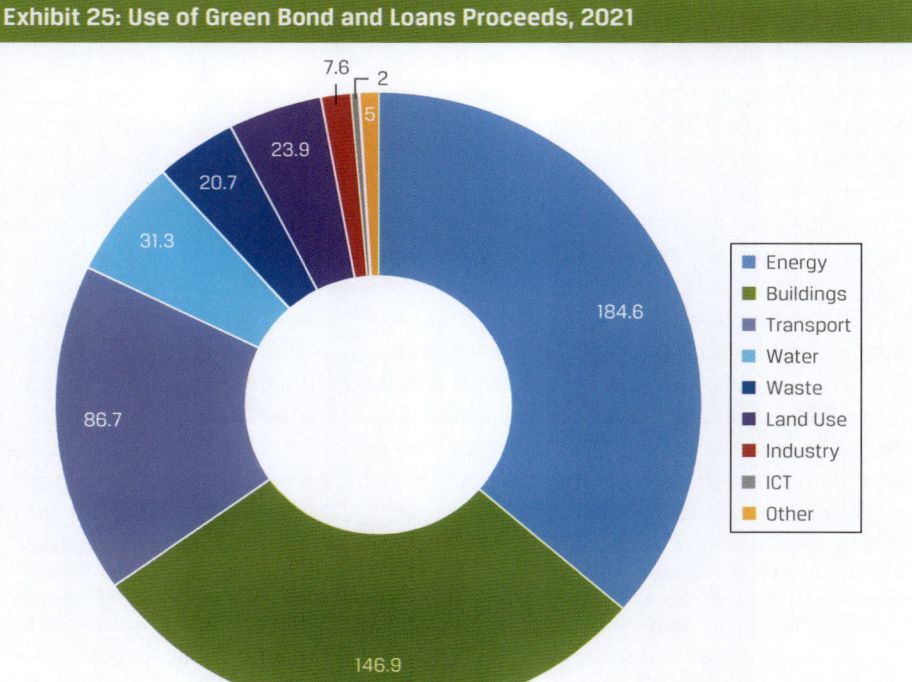

- Energy: 184.6
- Buildings: 146.9
- Transport: 86.7
- Water: 31.3
- Waste: 20.7
- Land Use: 23.9
- Industry: 7.6
- ICT: 2
- Other: 5

Note: Data cover up to the end of 2021. All debt instruments have been screened in accordance with the Climate Bonds Initiative Green Bond Database Methodology[289] and Social & Sustainability Bond Database Methodology.[290] Definitions of *green* are derived from the Climate Bonds Taxonomy,[291] and issuer type classification follows Climate Bonds Initiative convention.

Source: Climate Bonds Initiative, "Climate Bonds Interactive Data Platform" (2022). www.climatebonds.net/market/data/.

In addition to green bonds, which focus closely on climate change solutions, there has been increased issuance in other labeled debt (see Exhibit 26), primarily green and sustainability loans, where the financing terms are linked to climate or environmental performance indicators (for example, investors may receive an increase in the bond's coupon if the company fails to meet certain targets).

---

289 Climate Bonds Initiative, "Green Bond Database Methodology."
290 Climate Bonds Initiative, "Social & Sustainability Bond Database Methodology."
291 Climate Bonds Initiative, "Climate Bonds Taxonomy."

Opportunities Relating to Climate Change and Environmental Issues

Exhibit 26: Global Sustainable Debt Issuance, 2013–2021 (US$ billions)

[Stacked bar chart showing issuance by year:
- 2013: 28.7
- 2014: 68.2
- 2015: 88.2
- 2016: 144.7
- 2017: 241.6
- 2018: 314.8
- 2019: 577.0
- 2020: 762.7
- 2021: 1643.7

Categories: Sustainability-linked bond, Sustainability bond, Green loan, Sustainability-linked loan, Social bond, Green bond]

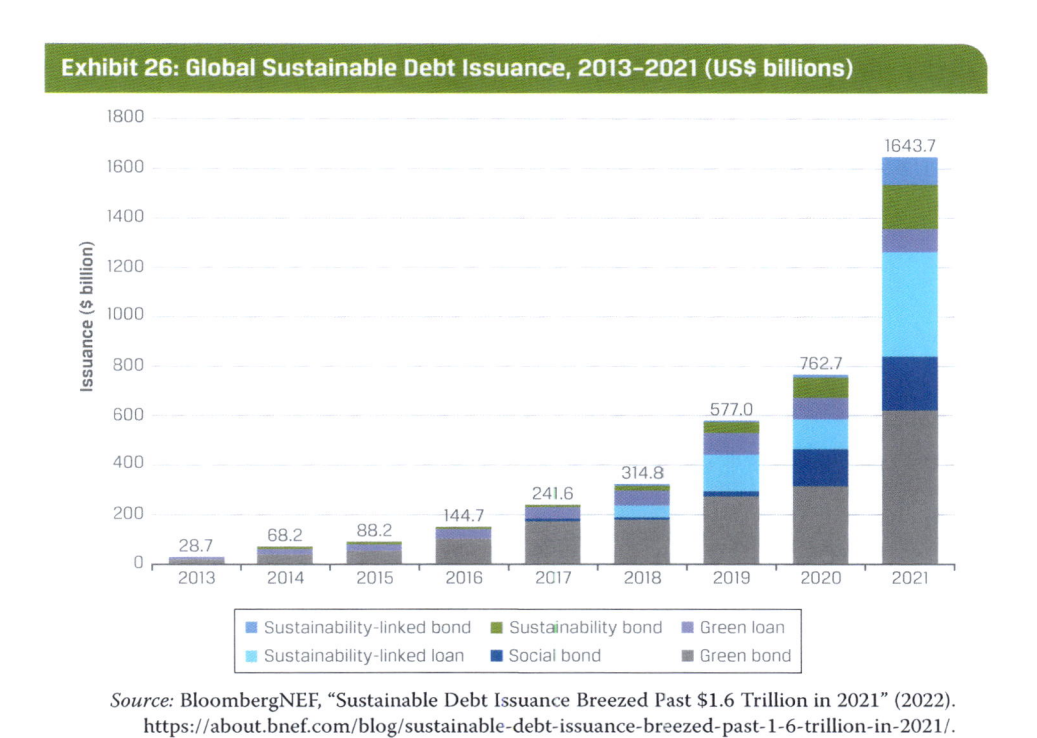

Source: BloombergNEF, "Sustainable Debt Issuance Breezed Past $1.6 Trillion in 2021" (2022). https://about.bnef.com/blog/sustainable-debt-issuance-breezed-past-1-6-trillion-in-2021/.

Exhibit 27 shows examples of such transactions, ranging from green bonds to sustainability or SDG-linked bonds and loans.

Exhibit 27: Examples of Sustainable Financing Transactions

Issuer and Type	Use of Proceeds
Green bond issued by Louisiana Local Government Environmental Facilities and Community Development Authority (2018)	Coastal flood defenses
Dutch sovereign green bond (2019)	Flood protection under its Delta Programme
First dedicated resilience bond under the Climate Resilience Principles by European Bank for Reconstruction and Development (2019)[292]	Climate-resilient infrastructure in Eastern Europe and North Africa
Chile's sovereign green bond (2019 and 2020)	The first issue in 2019 was focused on financing solar, low-carbon transport, low-carbon building upgrades, and water infrastructure. The 2020 issue was focused primarily on low-carbon transport.

---

[292] V. Bennett, "World's First Dedicated Climate Resilience Bond, for US$ 700m, Is Issued by EBRD," European Bank for Reconstruction and Development (20 September 2019). www.ebrd.com/news/2019/worlds-first-dedicated-climate-resilience-bond-for-us-700m-is-issued-by-ebrd-.html.

Issuer and Type	Use of Proceeds
Rizal Commercial Banking Corporation (RCBC), one of the Philippines' largest banks, issued the first ASEAN sustainability bond (2019)[293]	RCBC applied its Sustainability Finance Framework, which includes seven eligible green categories (energy, buildings, transport, urban and industrial energy efficiency, waste, water, and land use) and five eligible social categories (affordable basic infrastructure, access to essential services, employment generation, affordable housing, and socioeconomic advancement and empowerment).
First SDG-linked bond, launched by the Italian energy producer Enel (2019)	Proceeds were aimed at general corporate purposes. However, the new instrument requires Enel to measure its performance against several environmental and social KPIs, to which the coupon will be dependent.
First SDG-linked sovereign bond, launched by the government of Mexico[294]	Eligible categories need to meet two criteria: • geospatial (prioritizing location of vulnerable populations) and • governance (involvement of a UN organization).
Seychelles launched the world's first sovereign "blue bond"[295]	Proceeds were used to help finance the island's transition to sustainable fisheries and marine protection.
Starbucks issued a sustainability bond (2019), following its previous issues in 2016 and 2017.	Eligible categories fall under socioeconomic advancement and empowerment and access to essential services and under green (green buildings).
Thames Water became the United Kingdom's first corporation to issue a sustainability-linked revolving credit facility (£1.4 billion, 2018)[296]	Interest payments are linked to its Global Real Estate Sustainability Benchmark (GRESB) infrastructure score.
Solvay, a Belgium chemical company, issued a sustainability-linked loan.[297]	Linked to an ambitious GHG reduction target—in this case, 1 million tonnes of CO_2 by 2025
Luxembourg was the first European country to launch its own Sustainability Bond Framework, in line with the European taxonomy for green financing (2020)[298]	Combination of EU green projects and sustainability projects

From an investment perspective, as the supply of green or ESG-related products continues to grow, it is important to note that what may be considered green or sustainable for one investor may not be so for another. Therefore, investors need to have a clear framework by which to assess these assets. The following are some of the considerations:

▶ the eligibility of assets and criteria to meeting their green, ESG, or SDG-related objectives,

▶ the use of proceeds effectively allocated to eligible projects,

---

293 Rizal Commercial Banking Corporation, "RCBC to Issue First ASEAN Sustainability Bond in the Philippines," press release (2019). www.rcbc.com/Content/Web/img/about/pdf/disclosure/RCBC%20to%20issue%20First%20ASEAN%20Sustainability%20Bond%20in%20the%20Philippines.pdf.
294 International Institute for Sustainable Development, "Mexico Issues Sovereign SDG Bond for Most Vulnerable Municipalities" (2020). https://sdg.iisd.org/news/mexico-issues-sovereign-sdg-bond-for-most-vulnerable-municipalities/.
295 World Bank, "Seychelles Launches World's First Sovereign Blue Bond," press release (2018). www.worldbank.org/en/news/press-release/2018/10/29/seychelles-launches-worlds-first-sovereign-blue-bond.
296 Thames Water, "Press Release: Thames Water Ties Interest Rate on New £1.4 Billion Revolving Credit Facility to Sustainability Performance" (2019).
297 Solvay, "Solvay Links the Cost of €2 Bn Revolving Credit Facility to Its Ambitious Greenhouse Gas Reduction Commitments," press release (2019). www.solvay.com/en/press-release/solvay-links-cost-eu2-bn-revolving-credit-facility-its-ambitious-greenhouse-gas.
298 Gouvernement.lu, "Luxembourg—First European Country to Lunch a Sustainability Bond Framework," press release (2020). https://gouvernement.lu/en/actualites/toutes_actualites/communiques/2020/09-septembre/02-cadre-obligations-durables.html.

Opportunities Relating to Climate Change and Environmental Issues

- the transparency and reporting requirements and key measures of impacts, and
- the issuer or borrower has a clear sustainability and ESG strategy.

Exhibit 28 shows an example of the "shades of green" methodology developed by the Center for International Climate Research (CICERO) to provide second-party opinions that determine how a green or sustainability bond aligns with a low-carbon resilient future.

Exhibit 28: Example of the "Shades of Green"

Dark green	Solutions and projects that currently realize the long-term vision of a climate-resilient and low-carbon future. Typically, this equates to zero-emission solutions and government support that integrates environmental effects into all governance structures. Examples include renewable energy projects such as wind or solar.
Medium green	Solutions and projects that are making progress toward the long-term vision but that are not fully realized. Examples include sustainable buildings with good (but not excellent) energy efficiency ratings.
Light green	Solutions and projects that aren't a part of the long-term vision but are still environmentally friendly. Projects should be careful not to lock into fossil fuel systems permanently. Examples include short-term improvements in fossil fuel efficiency that result in reductions of greenhouse gas.
Brown	Solutions and projects that do not enable long-term vision of a climate-resilient and low carbon future. Examples include new infrastructure projects for coal.

Source: CICERO, "CICERO Shades of Green" (2015). https://cicero.green/.

At the intersection of "brown" and "green" in Exhibit 28, the term "transition bonds" has been coined for bonds issued by high-emission companies to finance their reduction in GHG emissions. Some of these products finance measures that may not be considered "green enough" but still aim to address climate change.

There will continue to be a proliferation of green financial products in the marketplace. The important consideration to note is that the quality and transparency of environmental and climate-related data and disclosure will need to improve in order to avoid "greenwashing." Efforts by the EU to harmonize and create a common language will be a significant development for green financial products.

CASE STUDIES

What Is "Green"?

The International Capital Markets Association (ICMA) sets out voluntary guidelines called the Green Bond Principles (GBP), which were established in 2014 by a consortium of investment banks to promote the integrity of the green bond market by recommending transparency, disclosure, and reporting.[299] As part of ensuring the integrity of the use of proceeds, external review is obtained through a second-party opinion provider that will track and report on whether proceeds are used as promised.

---

299 ICMA, "Green Bond Principles (GBP)" (2018). www.icmagroup.org/green-social-and-sustainability-bonds/green-bond-principles-gbp/.

The Climate Bonds Initiative has regular information about the state of the green bond market. The Climate Bonds Taxonomy and sector-specific criteria have been scientifically developed to meet the object of the Paris Agreement of keeping global warming under 2°C (3.6°F), and the range of sector criteria keeps expanding. The organization has started focusing on transition and published a framework for delineating green and transition finance.[300]

In 2018, the Green Loan Principles (GLP) were established by the Loan Market Association (LMA) and the Asia Pacific Loan Market Association (APLMA). The four pillars of the GLP are as follows:

1. There is clear green use of loan proceeds.
2. The project's sustainability objectives have been clearly evaluated and communicated to lenders.
3. Loan proceeds are strictly managed through project accounts.
4. Detailed and strict reporting is mandated.[301]

Further to the GLP, in 2019, the LMA, the APLMA, and the Loan Syndications and Trading Association launched the Sustainability-Linked Loan Principles.[302]

In addition to labeled debt, green and sustainable finance includes debt from companies that operate in such sectors. The Climate Bonds Initiative provides regular information on the scale of the unlabeled climate bond market relative to the green bond market.[303] Defined as entities that generate 75% or more of their revenues from green business lines, climate-aligned issuers had issued US$913 billion (£656 billion) in outstanding bonds as of 30 September 2020, up from US$811 billion (£583 billion) as of 30 June 2018.[304] LGX, the Luxembourg Green Exchange, launched a climate-aligned issuer segment to complement its existing green bond, sustainability, and social bond segment.[305]

Blue Economy

The World Bank defines blue economy as the "sustainable use of ocean resources for economic growth, improved livelihoods, and jobs while preserving the health of ocean ecosystems."[306] All other definitions of the term essentially relate to a broader perspective on sustainable economic and social activity associated with the world's oceans and coastal areas.

Examples of ocean-based industries representing the blue economy are shown in Exhibit 29.

---

300 Climate Bonds Initiative, "Financing Credible Transitions: How to Ensure the Transition Label Has Impact," white paper (2020). www.climatebonds.net/resources/reports/financing-credible-transitions-white-paper.
301 Loan Market Association, "Green Loan Principles: Supporting Environmentally Sustainable Economic Activity" (2018). www.lma.eu.com/application/files/9115/4452/5458/741_LM_Green_Loan_Principles_Booklet_V8.pdf.
302 Loan Market Association, "Sustainability Linked Loan Principles" (2019). www.icmagroup.org/assets/documents/Regulatory/Green-Bonds/LMASustainabilityLinkedLoanPrinciples-270919.pdf.
303 Climate Bonds Initiative, "Bonds and Climate Change: The State of the Market 2018" (2018). www.climatebonds.net/resources/reports/bonds-and-climate-change-state-market-2018.
304 2020 data provided by Climate Bonds Initiative in response to a data request by CFA UK.
305 Luxembourg Stock Exchange, "LGX Expands to Welcome Climate-Aligned Issuers" (2021). www.bourse.lu/pr-lgx-welcomes-climate-aligned-issuers. The segment is Luxembourg Stock Exchange, "Climate Bonds—LGX Climate-Aligned Issuers" (2021). www.bourse.lu/climate-bonds-lgx-climate-aligned-issuers.
306 World Bank, "The Potential of the Blue Economy: Increasing Long-Term Benefits of the Sustainable Use of Marine Resources for Small Island Developing States and Coastal Least Developed Countries" (2017). https://openknowledge.worldbank.org/bitstream/handle/10986/26843/115545.pdf.

Opportunities Relating to Climate Change and Environmental Issues

> **Exhibit 29: Examples of Ocean-Based Industries Representing the Blue Economy**
>
> - Aquaculture
> - Fisheries
> - Fish processing industry
> - Ports and warehousing
> - Ship building and repair
> - Coastal tourism
> - Marine extraction
> - Maritime transport
> - Desalination
> - Blue bioeconomy and biotechnology
> - Coastal and environmental protection
> - Offshore wind energy
> - Ocean energy
> - Deep water source cooling

The blue economy has more recently begun to gather more attention and has climbed the policy agenda. As covered in the previous section on oceans as a natural resource, it is clear that the ocean is already under stress from over-exploitation, pollution, declining biodiversity, and climate change.

Investors and policymakers are now beginning to recognize

- the growth prospects for the ocean economy,
- its capacity for future employment creation and innovation, and
- its role in addressing global challenges.[307]

There is growing scope for science and technology to manage the economic development of our seas and ocean responsibly. Marine ecosystems lie at the heart of many of the world's global challenges, providing food and medicines, new sources of clean energy and natural cooling systems, climate regulation, job creation, and inclusive growth. But safeguards are required to improve the health of these ecosystems to support an ever-growing use of marine resources. As we have seen in the section on biodiversity, the issue of accounting for natural capital remains a promising but underdeveloped area; this is also true in the case of the blue economy. The World Ocean Initiative has suggested the inclusion of **ocean accounting**—adding ocean-related services and assets—to national balance sheets.[308]

Based on a study by the OECD, three priority areas for action are presented:

1. approaches that produce win–win outcomes for ocean business and the ocean environment across a range of marine and maritime applications,
2. the creation of ocean-economy innovation networks, and
3. initiatives to improve the measurement of the ocean economy via satellite accounts of national accounting systems.

The OECD suggests that many ocean-based industries have the potential to outperform the growth of the global economy as a whole, both in terms of value added and employment. Projections suggest that the ocean economy could more than double its contribution to global value added, to over US$3 trillion (£2.2 trillion), in addition to huge potential in employment growth by 2030.

---

307 OECD, "The Ocean Economy in 2030" (2016). https://doi.org/10.1787/9789264251724-en.
308 World Ocean Initiative, "The Wealth of Oceans: New Research Shines a Light on Ocean Accounting" (2020). https://ocean.economist.com/blue-finance/articles/the-wealth-of-oceans-new-research-highlights-importance-of-ocean-accounting.

> **CASE STUDIES**
>
> **Blue Economy Development Framework**
>
> The World Bank and the European Commission have launched the Blue Economy Development Framework (BEDF), which is a new step in the area of international ocean governance.[309] It helps (developing) coastal states transition to diverse and sustainable blue economies while building resilience to climate change.
>
> The BEDF aims to create a roadmap that assists governments in
>
> - preparing policy, fiscal, and administrative reforms,
> - identifying value creation opportunities from blue economy sectors, and
> - identifying strategic financial investments.
>
> The BEDF intends to help coastal countries and regions develop evidence-based investment and policy reform plans for its coastal and ocean resources.

---

[309] World Bank and European Commission, "World Bank and European Commission Promote Blue Economy through New Tool" (2019). https://oceans-and-fisheries.ec.europa.eu/news/world-bank-and-european-commission-promote-blue-economy-through-new-tool-2019-02-14_en.

KEY FACTS

1. The range of environmental factors that have a material impact on investments are broad and far reaching. They include but are not limited to:
   a. a rapidly changing climate,
   b. natural resources (including water, biodiversity, land use and forestry, and marine resources), and
   c. pollution, waste, and the circular economy.

2. Driven by the emissions of greenhouse gases (GHGs) into the atmosphere, accelerating climate change carries significant risks to human health, economies, and ecosystems. Effective responses will involve a combination of climate mitigation and adaptation measures.

3. The Paris Agreement of 2015 was reached to mobilize a global response to the threat of climate change, amid growing concern reported by scientific experts. The agreement's long-term goal is to keep the increase in global average temperature well below 2°C (3.6°F) above pre-industrial levels and to limit the increase to 1.5°C (2.7°F).

4. Since the Paris Agreement was signed, a global consensus has begun to emerge that reaching net-zero carbon dioxide emissions around 2050 is required to turn its goals into reality. Governments, companies, and investors are increasingly adopting net-zero targets as a result. It is essential to understand that this goal is not an end point but a midpoint in a century-long effort to stabilize atmospheric concentrations in the atmosphere. It should be seen as a floor under aspirations and not a ceiling over accomplishments.

5. Putting a price on carbon emissions is seen by many economists as one of the most effective methods of tackling climate change. Carbon markets have steadily grown around the world, but current levels of carbon pricing remain low.

6. Policymakers and investors must navigate both
   - the physical risks of climate change (associated with climate inaction) and
   - the transition risks of climate change (associated with climate action).

   Rising carbon costs carry financial risks of their own, because they can affect the value of high-carbon assets, with potential knock-on effects across sectors. This reinforces the need for an orderly and just transition to the low-carbon economy.

7. Environmental degradation, the depletion of natural resources, and the associated losses in biodiversity are presenting multiple, interrelated challenges for governments, the public, and businesses. Such issues as water scarcity, deforestation, degradation of land and oceans, unsustainable agricultural practices, waste, and pollution are increasingly impacting business and investment activities. To help alleviate some of these pressures, the model of the circular economy promotes a more efficient use of raw materials, coupled with increased reuse, recycling, and waste management.

8. Material environmental issues are factors that could have a significant impact—both positive and negative—on a company's business model and value drivers, such as operating and capital expenditure, revenue growth, margins, and risk. The material factors differ from one sector to another.

9. Environmental risks can be effectively integrated into company analysis and investment decision-making processes, using various financial tools and models. The types of risk analysis tools and associated metrics primarily depend on the asset classes and risk types financial institutions are exposed to. Similarly, the choice of approach depends on the type of direct and indirect exposure to an environmental risk factor. Investors have developed a combination of metrics, from carbon footprinting to forward-looking climate scenario analysis. Many solutions for reducing risk bring economic benefits; for example, increasing energy and material productivity (efficiency of use) and such renewables as wind and solar reduce production costs and often have a higher rate of economic return than continuing the use of inefficient technologies and fossil fuels.

10. There is an increasing number of policy initiatives at both the country and regional levels to promote the economic and financial mainstreaming of climate change and environmental factors in jurisdictions around the world. Requirements for climate-related disclosures (both mandatory and voluntary) are increasing in different parts of the entire investment chain, from the owners of capital (pension funds and insurance companies) to the beneficiaries (investee companies).

11. Coupled with regulatory tailwinds, technological innovation is giving rise to increasing investment opportunities from the provision of climate and environmental solutions, in areas including clean energy and mobility, sustainable buildings, and advanced materials. For a majority of the world's population, unsubsidized clean energy represents the cheapest source of new electricity.

12. There is a growing number of specialized investment products, including low-carbon (active and index) funds and sustainability-linked debt, that aim to capture this opportunity set.

FURTHER READING

Temperature Alignment Tools

Raynaud, Julie, Stephane Voisin, Peter Tankov, Anuschka Hilke, Alice Pauthie. 2020. "The Alignment Cookbook: A Technical Review of Methodologies Assessing a Portfolio's Alignment with Low-Carbon Trajectories or Temperature Goal." https://gsf.institutlouisbachelier.org/publication/the-alignment-cookbook-a-technical-review-of-methodologies-assessing-a-portfolios-alignment-with-low-carbon-trajectories-or-temperature-goal/.

Climate Scenario Analysis

Zürich, E. T. H. 2020. "Taming the Green Swan: How to Improve Climate-Related Financial Risk Assessments." www.research-collection.ethz.ch/handle/20.500.11850/428321.

Principles for Responsible Investment 2020. "Pathways to Net Zero: Scenario Architecture for Strategic Resilience Testing and Planning." www.unpri.org/climate-change/pathways-to-net-zero-scenario-architecture-for-strategic-resilience-testing-and-planning/6006.article.

Task Force on Climate-Related Financial Disclosures 2020. "Guidance on Scenario Analysis for Non-Financial Companies." www.fsb.org/wp-content/uploads/P291020-3.pdf.

Green and ESG-Related Products

Climate Bonds Initiative 2018. "Bonds and Climate Change: The State of the Market 2018." www.climatebonds.net/resources/reports/bonds-and-climate-change-state-market-2018.

SELF PRACTICE AND SELF ASSESSMENT

1. The Paris Agreement:
   a. is legally binding under the local law of each signatory country.
   b. requires every signatory to provide an annual update on its national emission commitments.
   c. aims to limit the increase in global average temperature to 2°C above pre-industrial levels by the end of the century.

2. The first international convention to set targets for emissions of the main greenhouse gases was the:
   a. Kyoto Protocol.
   b. Paris Agreement.
   c. United Nations Sustainable Development Goals.

3. In relation to the European Green Deal, the "green supporting factor" refers to:
   a. standards and labels for green bonds.
   b. a classification system for sustainable activities.
   c. the treatment of "green" assets in the capital requirements of banks and insurers.

4. Sustainability integration is *most* effective when sustainability is embedded in the practices of:
   a. asset owners and investee companies.
   b. asset owners and financial intermediaries.
   c. asset owners, investee companies, and financial intermediaries.

5. Which of the following countries has the highest level of investments in the low-carbon energy transition?
   a. Japan
   b. China
   c. United States

6. A sustainability bond funding a climate-friendly project that may be exposed to physical and transitional climate risks yet has no strategies in place to mitigate their impact would be graded by CICERO as:
   a. brown.
   b. light green.
   c. medium green.

7. Which of the following initiatives recommends that signatories incorporate climate change effects into macroeconomic policy and fiscal planning?
   a. Helsinki Principles
   b. Equator Principles
   c. Climate Resilience Principles

8. The Network for Greening the Financial System (NGFS) comprises:
   a. multilateral institutions and agencies.
   b. asset managers and investment banks.

Self Practice and Self Assessment

    c. central banks and financial supervisors.

9. Which of the following carbon pricing methods is used by companies to determine the impact of climate change on the profitability of a new project?

    a. Carbon taxation
    b. Shadow carbon pricing
    c. Emission trading system (ETS)

10. In relation to ESG analysis, investors should make adjustments to the credit assessment of a company based on:

    a. solely quantitative environmental factors.
    b. the sector and geographic location of the company's assets.
    c. all environmental effects on the company, irrespective of their materiality.

The following information relates to questions 11-25
Self Assessment Questions

These questions are provided only to enable you to test your understanding of the chapter content. They are not indicative of the types and standard of questions you may see in the examination. The Self-Assessment questions do not include an explanation of the correct answer.

11. Which of the following would be considered a climate change adaptation strategy?

    a. Releasing sunlight-reflecting aerosols into the atmosphere to reduce temperatures
    b. Retrofitting buildings to become more energy efficient
    c. Developing clean cooling systems
    d. Protecting coastlines from erosion

12. What is "natural capital"?

    a. Natural resources (such as oil, gas, or timber) that can be sold for a profit in a capitalist economy
    b. The stock of natural assets, which include geology, soil, air, water, and all living things
    c. An international collaboration to increase the proportion of natural spaces in capital cities
    d. The sum total of monetary benefits that are directly dependent on nature

13. Which of the following has the highest potential to contribute to global decarbonization?

    a. The electrification of industrial processes, powered by clean energy sources
    b. Coal gasification combined with carbon capture and storage
    c. A global shift to a flexitarian diet
    d. Shifting all passenger cars to hydrogen fuel cells

14. What is the most common method of waste management globally?

    a. Recycling
    b. Incineration
    c. Landfills

d. Treatment

15. Which of the following best describes the principles of a circular economy?

    a. Extracting natural resources for products that are then used and eventually discarded
    b. Designing out waste and pollution, keeping materials in use, and regenerating natural systems
    c. Ensuring that all products are returned to the manufacturers to reuse component parts
    d. Producing goods only for consumption by customers in the manufacturer's domestic market

16. For a reasonable chance of limiting the global average temperature rise to 1.5°C (2.7°F), the Intergovernmental Panel on Climate Change (IPCC) recommends that global emissions of CO_2 must reach "net zero" around:

    a. 2050.
    b. 2030.
    c. 2100.
    d. 2075.

17. What is the blue economy?

    a. Industrial activities that generate pollution of oceans and inland waterways
    b. The global network of shipping that transports people and manufactured goods
    c. Products and processes used to clean up water-based environmental pollution
    d. Sustainable economic and social activity related to oceans and coastal areas

18. Which of the following represents a transition risk?

    a. Policy change to encourage low-carbon technologies
    b. Occurrence of extreme weather events
    c. Breakdowns in business supply chains
    d. Long-term rises in global temperatures

19. In relation to shadow carbon pricing, which of the following is incorrect?

    a. Shadow carbon pricing is used to understand the potential impact of external prices on the profitability of a project.
    b. Shadow carbon pricing is used to reduce a business's carbon footprint.
    c. Shadow carbon pricing is used to reveal hidden risks and to factor these into future valuations and estimates of capital expenditure.
    d. Shadow carbon pricing is used to create a theoretical cost per tonne of carbon emissions by establishing a business's internal price on carbon.

20. Which of the following is not a Task Force on Climate-Related Financial Disclosures (TCFD) core element of climate-related disclosures?

    a. Governance
    b. Impact
    c. Risk management
    d. Strategy

Self Practice and Self Assessment

21. Which of the following is not an explicit UN Sustainable Development Goal (SDG)?
    a. Ending poverty in all its forms everywhere
    b. Access to affordable, clean nuclear energy
    c. Ensuring healthy lives and promoting well-being for all ages
    d. Taking urgent action to combat climate change and its impacts

22. What is the primary objective of the EU Taxonomy?
    a. Clear labeling of the use of proceeds for green bonds
    b. An EU-wide classification system of sustainable activities.
    c. A classification of what "green" activities states can finance domestically without breaching competition rules
    d. A classification system of the Scope 1, 2, and 3 emissions associated with the activities of EU companies

23. Scope 3 of the GHG Protocol Standards covers which of the following emission sources?
    a. Company vehicles
    b. Company facilities
    c. Purchased electricity
    d. Purchased goods and services

24. Which of the following is *not* a requirement for a bond or a loan to be considered "green" under such frameworks as the Green Bond Principles (GBP) or Green Loan Principles (GLP)?
    a. A description of the environmental benefits associated with the use of proceeds
    b. A minimum of 10 tonnes of certified emissions reductions per every US$1 (£0.7) of debt
    c. A clear process for the evaluation and selection of eligible projects
    d. Detailed and regular reporting

25. The long-term goal of the Paris Agreement, adopted in 2015, is to keep the increase in the global average temperature above pre-industrial levels to well below what level?
    a. 1.0°C (1.8°F)
    b. 1.5°C (2.7°F)
    c. 2.0°C (3.6°F)
    d. 2.5°C (4.5°F)

SOLUTIONS

1. C is correct. The aim of the international Paris Agreement on climate change is to pursue efforts to limit the temperature increase to 2°C (3.6°F) above pre-industrial levels by the end of the century. The Paris Agreement does not set any legally binding targets under international law. Signatories to the Paris Agreement are required to determine, plan, and report on its NDCs, with updates to commitments every five years.

2. A is correct. The Kyoto Protocol was adopted in 1997 and became effective in 2005. It was the first international convention to set targets for emissions of the main GHGs.

3. C is correct. The treatment of "green" assets in the capital requirements of banks and insurers is referred to the "green supporting factor."

4. C is correct. Effective ESG integration is intended to embed sustainability across the entire investment chain—from the owners of capital (asset owners) to the beneficiaries of capital (such as investee companies), as well as key intermediaries.

5. B is correct. China remains the country with the highest levels of investment in the low-carbon energy transition.

6. B is correct. In the light green grade, projects may be exposed to physical and transitional climate risks without appropriate strategies in place to protect them.

7. A is correct. Helsinki Principles encourage signatories to "take climate change into account in macroeconomic policy, fiscal planning, budgeting, public investment management, and procurement practices."

8. C is correct. The NGFS comprises over 70 central banks and financial supervisors.

9. B is correct. An internal or shadow price on carbon creates a theoretical or assumed cost per tonne of carbon emissions. This is used to better understand the potential impact of future climate regulation on the profitability of a project, a new business model, or an investment.

10. B is correct. Investors should consider quantitative and qualitative environmental factors, the company, the sector, and the geographic location. Investors should assess the material financial impacts caused by environmental risks.

11. D is correct.

12. B is correct.

13. B is correct.

14. C is correct.

15. B is correct.

16. A is correct.

17. D is correct.

18. A is correct.

Solutions

19. B is correct.
20. B is correct.
21. B is correct.
22. B is correct.
23. D is correct.
24. B is correct.
25. C is correct.

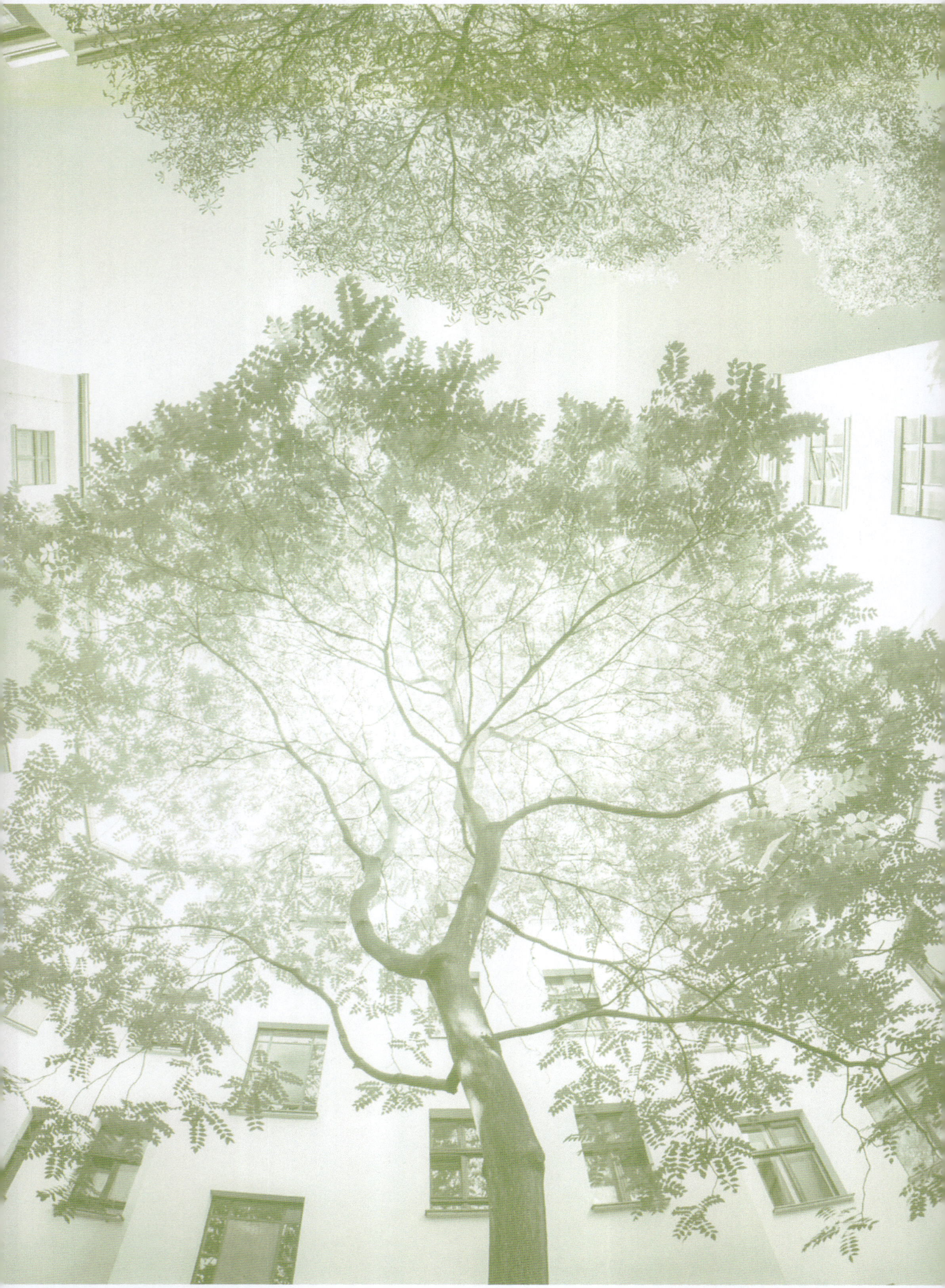

CHAPTER 4

Social Factors

LEARNING OUTCOMES

Mastery	The candidate should be able to:
☐	4.1.1 explain the systemic relationships and activities between business activities and social issues, including: globalization; automation and artificial intelligence (AI); inequality and wealth creation; digital disruption, social media, and access to electronic devices; changes to work, leisure time, and education; changes to individual rights and responsibilities and family structures; changing demographics; urbanization; and religion
☐	4.1.2 assess key megatrends influencing social change in terms of potential impact on companies and their social practices: climate change; transition risk; water scarcity; pollution; mass migration; and loss and/or degradation of natural resources and ecosystem services
☐	4.1.3 explain key social concepts, including: human capital: development, employment standards, and health and safety; product liability/consumer protection: safety, quality, health and demographic risks, and data privacy and security; stakeholder opposition/controversial sourcing; social opportunities: access to communications, finance, and health and nutrition; social and news media; animal welfare and microbial resistance
☐	4.1.4 assess material impacts of social issues on potential investment opportunities and the dangers of overlooking them, including: changing demographics; digitization; individual rights and responsibilities; family structures and roles; education and work; faith-based ESG investing and exercise of religion; inequality; and globalization
☐	4.1.5 identify approaches to social analysis at country, sector, and company levels
☐	4.1.6 apply material social factors to: risk assessment; quality of management; ratio analysis; and financial modeling

1. INTRODUCTION TO SOCIAL FACTORS

Social factors are relevant from both a business and an investment perspective and are increasingly being factored into investment analysis and investment decisions. In many cases, investors expect companies to manage these issues by using a best-in-class approach, whereby a company is better than its peers on a number of material issues relevant to its sector (e.g., occupational health and safety or managing its impact on local communities). In other cases, a social issue can become the focus of an investable opportunity (e.g., gender equality funds). Companies are increasingly expected to engage with their stakeholders openly, transparently, and responsively.

This chapter first gives an overview of various social factors and their material impact on potential investment opportunities. It then outlines the most relevant social megatrends, highlighting their relationship with business activities and investment opportunities. Descriptions are then provided of how to identify and apply material social factors, focusing on social analysis at country, sector, and company levels in both developed and emerging economies. Finally, all the above-mentioned topics are practically applied in case studies.

2. SOCIAL AND ENVIRONMENTAL MEGATRENDS

☐ **4.1.1** explain the systemic relationships and activities between business activities and social issues, including: globalization; automation and artificial intelligence (AI); inequality and wealth creation; digital disruption, social media, and access to electronic devices; changes to work, leisure time, and education; changes to individual rights and responsibilities and family structures; changing demographics; urbanization; and religion

☐ **4.1.2** assess key megatrends influencing social change in terms of potential impact on companies and their social practices: climate change; transition risk; water scarcity; pollution; mass migration; and loss and/or degradation of natural resources and ecosystem services

Investors need to note the different **social megatrends** that could have an effect on the businesses of the investee companies. This section looks at the systemic relationships between these social megatrends and business activities of the investee companies, and it elaborates on the material impacts of these trends on potential investment opportunities.

What Are Social Megatrends?

Social megatrends are long-term social changes that affect governments, societies, and economies permanently over a long period of time.

The following megatrends will be described in this section:

A. Globalization

B. Automation and artificial intelligence (AI)

C. Inequality and wealth creation

D. Digital disruption, social media, and access to electronic devices
E. Changes to work, leisure time, and education
F. Changes to individual rights and responsibilities and family structures
G. Changing demographics, including health and longevity
H. Urbanization
I. Religion

Some **environmental megatrends** have a severe social impact as well. These include the following:

- Climate change and transition risks
- Water scarcity
- Mass migration

All of these could, in an extreme case, result in mass migration. These social megatrends will change the way we live, work, consume, and perceive the world and, as such, will pose new risks or opportunities for investors. Next, we will look at each of these megatrends in further detail.

Globalization

One of the biggest megatrends is the integration of local and national economies into a global (and less regulated) market economy. The growth in global interactions has increased international trade and the exchange of ideas and culture. This process is also called **globalization**.

Globalization is caused by a rapid increase in cross-border movement of goods, services, technology, people, and capital. Depending on the viewpoint, it can be viewed as either a positive or a negative phenomenon. On the one hand, it is stated to have led to increased efficiency in the markets, resulting in wider availability of products at lower costs. On the other hand, it is claimed to be detrimental to social well-being due to social structural inequality.

Examples of its implications include the following:

- **Offshoring**. Due to the lower wages of workers in the garment industry in developing countries, clothes are now mainly produced in such countries as Vietnam, Bangladesh, and China. This has led to the disappearance of the textile industry in Western countries. Offshoring also takes place in other sectors.
- **Dependency**. As US-based and Asian companies dominate the industry for mobile telephones, computers, and other IT products, European countries are more dependent on these suppliers.

Automation and Artificial Intelligence (AI)

Linked to the increased economic globalization is the trend of **automation**, which is the technology by which a process or procedure is performed with minimal human assistance. Some of the biggest advantages of automation in industry are that it is:

a. associated with faster production and lower labor costs; and it
b. replaces hard, physical, or monotonous work.

The largest (social) disadvantage, however, is that it displaces workers due to job replacement, as technology renders their skills or experience unnecessary. It is expected that this trend will increase due to the rise of AI.

AI is expected to have a significant effect on such sectors as:

a. healthcare;
b. automotive;
c. financial services and auditing;
d. security (including military); and
e. creative (in particular, advertising and video games).

> **EXAMPLE 1**
>
> ### Implications for Investors
>
> The transportation industry is currently on the brink of becoming more automated, and it is expected that some jobs for drivers (of taxis, buses, and trucks, for example) will disappear due to self-driving vehicles. This will be beneficial for companies that develop the best self-driving cars, but less so for traditional heavy goods vehicle (HGV) companies that do not innovate. One of the largest expected implications of this is that by automating the transport industry, major job losses will occur. One possible solution is to invest in upskilling staff to enable their transition to a more AI-enabled world. Investors should take this into account when assessing the risks of an investee company.

Inequality and Wealth Creation

The Organisation for Economic Co-operation and Development (OECD) analyzes trends in inequality and poverty for advanced and emerging economies. It examines the drivers of growing inequalities, such as globalization, skill-biased technological change, and changes in countries' policy approaches. It also assesses the effectiveness and efficiency of a wide range of policies, including education, labor market, and social policies, in tackling poverty and promoting more inclusive growth. According to the OECD Centre for Opportunity and Equality (COPE) 2015 report, the average income of the richest 10% of the population is about nine times that of the poorest 10% across the OECD.[1] This is also called **economic** or **income inequality.**

There is increasing evidence that growing inequality affects economies and societies. Educational opportunities and social mobility may be reduced, resulting in a less skilled and less healthy society with lower purchasing power among the lower and middle classes. This limits total economic growth.

An issue related to the topic of inequality is corporate tax strategies and whether companies are too aggressive in their tax optimization strategies. As regulators put more focus on this issue, some companies (for instance, in the technology sector) have had to pay huge fines. Others will need to adopt more conservative tax strategies in the future that will impact their bottom line.

---

1 The Organisation for Economic Co-operation and Development (OECD). 2015. *OECD Insights: Income Inequality – The Gap between Rich and Poor*. Available at: www.oecd.org/publications/income-inequality-9789264246010-en.htm

Digital Disruption, Social Media, and Access to Electronic Devices

Another important social trend is the rise of **digital disruption**, which is the change that occurs when new digital technologies and business models affect the value proposition of existing goods and services. This trend is closely related to the increased automation and rise of AI discussed in sub-section B above.

Some exemplary cases of disrupting companies include Amazon, Uber, and Airbnb. They have managed to enter an existing market but with different and more digital business approaches than their competitors, effectively challenging existing business models. There are opportunities for investors who are about to invest, preferably at an early stage, in such companies, although such investments can carry a high-risk profile.

A related consequence of digital technologies is the huge amount of data that can be collected, stored, and processed (**big data**) as well as the ownership or use of the data (including data privacy, monetization of data, etc.).

Big data has many opportunities, including more personalized services, products, and (health) treatments. However, controversies have arisen because some data are being used and sold in more extreme or socially unacceptable ways. Examples include social media companies—such as Facebook, Twitter, and LinkedIn—selling data for political or marketing campaigns (e.g., the case of Cambridge Analytica allegedly using Facebook data to try to manipulate elections).

Due to these types of scandals, there is a debate around the growing need for regulating the industry. This can affect the profitability of these companies and should be considered by investors.

Finally, electronic devices are now found everywhere. Almost everyone, both in developed and emerging economies, owns a mobile phone (in many cases a smartphone) and a tablet. The **Internet of Things (IoT)** is the next frontier, where semi-intelligent appliances (called 'embedded systems') communicate directly with each other and with the internet and make autonomous decisions.

For investors, disruption represents both risks and opportunities. Analysts need to take a forward-looking approach to determine which sectors and companies will thrive and which will struggle in a digital society.

Changes to Work, Leisure Time, and Education

The way we spend our lives has changed dramatically over the last few decades. Various measures have emerged that aim to provide a broad sense of the state of our societies and of how people's lives are evolving. The OECD examines issues of well-being in its *Better Life Index*, which rates a wide range of developed and emerging economies in a number of areas, including life satisfaction.

Most countries in the developed world have seen average hours worked decrease significantly. In the UK, the average annual hours actually worked per person in employment decreased from 1,775 hours in 1970 to 1,538 in 2019.[2] This is partially caused by increases in automation and part-time employment.

New technologies increasingly enable workers to be connected to their work from remote locations. This creates an opportunity for employers and employees to adopt more flexible working patterns. However, the constant connection also makes the notion of work–life balance more elusive and can cause stress-related illnesses.

---

2 OECD. 2020. *Average Annual Hours Actually Worked per Worker*. Available at: https://stats.oecd.org/index.aspx?Datasetcode=ANHRS#

While the number of average working hours has decreased, the average level of education has increased. The percentage of employees with a higher education degree has grown over the last few decades. Yet, some sectors suffer from a lack of qualified employees and are facing an intense 'war on talent' to attract the most skilled workers.

Investors who are assessing companies that rely heavily on employees as a key asset need to pay attention to those companies' human capital management strategies. They should evaluate how the companies are coping with these structural changes in the labor market.

Changes to Individual Rights and Responsibilities and Family Structures

In recent decades, not only has the way we divide work and leisure time changed but also the role and importance of family (especially in developed countries). Individuals are also less reliant on the structure of the family for (economic and physical) security.

The workforce has become more diverse: More women are now entering the labor market, which has provided women with more financial independence. However, in comparison to men, women are still more likely to become and remain unemployed, have fewer chances to participate in the labor force, and often have to accept lower quality jobs when they do secure employment. Women also face wage gaps in comparison to men. To improve gender equality, a number of different initiatives have been created, and there is growing evidence that a more diverse workforce leads to better (financial) results for the company. Some best-in-class funds and impact investors take diversity (gender and other types of diversity) into account in their risk analysis and stock selection.

Changing Demographics, Including Health and Longevity

Due to improvements made in healthcare and changes in lifestyle, life expectancy is increasing. For example, female and male life expectancy (from birth) in the United Kingdom increased by two years between 2002 and 2010 (to 78.4 years for men and 82.5 for women).[3] As of 2019, this stood at 79.4 for men and 83 for women.

This increased life expectancy, combined with a falling birth rate, have caused many developed countries' populations to age. The overall median age rose from 28 in 1950 to 41 in 2015, and it is forecast to rise to 45 by 2050.[4]

An aging population has substantial effects on society:

1. The ratio between the active and the inactive part of the workforce drops, impacting national tax revenues and challenging pension systems, including an impact on pension pots that need to last longer.
2. Older people have higher accumulated savings per person than younger people but spend less on consumer goods, which is a business risk for some industries. In some categories, such as healthcare, expenditure rises sharply when populations age.

---

[3] Office for National Statistics. 2018. *National Life Tables: UK*. Available at: www.ons.gov.uk/peoplepopulationandcommunity/birthsdeathsandmarriages/lifeexpectancies/datasets/nationallifetablesunitedkingdomreferencetables

[4] United Nations. 2015. *World Population Ageing 2015*. Available at: www.un.org/development/desa/pd/sites/www.un.org.development.desa.pd/files/files/documents/2020/May/un_2015_worldpopulationageing_report.pdf

Social and Environmental Megatrends

> **CASE STUDIES**
>
> ### The Impact of the Global COVID-19 Pandemic
>
> The COVID-19 pandemic is one of the largest global health, economic, and social crises in recent history. Although it affects every population segment, it is particularly detrimental to those in the most vulnerable situations, including people living in poverty, older people, people with disabilities, adolescents, and the indigenous peoples. Health and economic impacts are being felt disproportionately by poor people, particularly among the homeless as they are unable to safely shelter and are therefore highly exposed to the dangers of the virus. People without access to running water, refugees, migrants, or displaced people also stand to suffer disproportionately both from the pandemic and its aftermath. This could include limited movement, fewer employment opportunities, and increased xenophobia.[5]
>
> Other impacts include the following:
>
> - Educational: Potential learning loss may occur due to the widespread closures of schools and universities.
> - Increased inequality: It has been found that low-income individuals are more likely to contract COVID-19 and die from it. This is likely because poorer families are more likely to live in crowded housing and work in low-skilled jobs, such as supermarkets and elderly care, which are deemed essential during the crisis. In the United States, millions of low-income people may lack access to healthcare due to being un- or underinsured.
> - Psychological: There is a concern for a potential spike in suicides, exacerbated by social isolation due to quarantining and social distancing guidelines, fear, unemployment, and financial factors.
> - Reshoring: Companies and countries may decide to reduce supply chain risk by relocating production of strategic importance back to high-wage countries.[6]
> - Work environment: There has been a changing demand for office buildings with increased working from home.[7]

Investor Initiatives: Equitable Circulation of COVID-19 Vaccines

To ensure a more equitable global circulation of the COVID-19 vaccine, different investor initiatives have been launched. The pharma group Moderna faced a shareholder proposal demanding to open up its COVID-19 vaccine technology to poorer countries and requesting an explanation regarding the high prices given the amount of government assistance it had received. Another initiative concerns vaccine manufacturers being asked to increase the availability and deployment of vaccinations around the world. A group of 65 institutional investors have demanded that the global

---

[5] United Nations. 2020. *Everyone Included: Social Impact of COVID-19.* Available at: www.un.org/development/desa/dspd/everyone-included-covid-19.html
[6] UNCTAD. 2020. *How COVID-19 Is Changing Global Value Chains.* Available at: https://unctad.org/news/how-covid-19-changing-global-value-chains
[7] Pew Research Center. 2020. *How the Coronavirus Outbreak Has – and Hasn't – Changed the Way Americans Work.* Available at: www.pewresearch.org/social-trends/2020/12/09/how-the-coronavirus-outbreak-has-and-hasnt-changed-the-way-americans-work/

availability of vaccines would become part of the remuneration policy of managers and directors. In this way, investors have aimed to hold them accountable for their contribution to solving this problem.

Urbanization

The places where people live also change. Globally, the population has been increasingly shifting from rural to urban areas. In the 1950s, approximately 30% of the world population lived in an urban environment. This is expected to increase to 68% by 2050.

This shift can have different kinds of implications for societies, including the following:

- **Economic**: Dramatic increases and changes in costs can often price the local working class out of the market
- **Environmental**: 'Urban heat islands,' where urban areas produce and retain heat, have become a growing concern.
- **Social**: There has been increased mortality from non-communicable diseases associated with lifestyle, including cancer and heart disease. Residents in poor urban areas (such as slums) also suffer "disproportionately from disease, injury, premature death, and the combination of ill-health and poverty entrenches disadvantage over time."[8]

These societal implications provide business opportunities because of the growing need for infrastructure development, but they also require companies to address social and environmental issues related to urban living (for instance, pollution and waste management systems).

Religion

As a social factor, the changing religious landscape around the world has consequences for consumer preferences. Religion-based politics and conflicts can also have a profound impact on specific local economies.

All investors (faith-based or not) should therefore judge if investee companies take these changes into account from a financial perspective. A distinction should be made between exercise of religion as a social factor and faith-based investing.

Faith-based investors aim to invest their money in line with a specific named faith. The two most common types are:

- **Christian investors**, who aim to align their investment principles to the Bible. This means that they may refrain from investing in certain companies whose activities or processes are considered to not be aligned with Christian values.
- **Islamic investors**, who look to invest in line with Shariah principles. They would not invest in companies that profit from alcohol, pornography, or gambling or companies involved in pork. They will not own investments that pay interest or invest in firms that earn a substantial part of their revenue from interest.

Norms-based exclusion has been one of the first environmental, social, and governance (ESG) investing instruments; many of these first movers were faith-based investors. The Church of England, the Church Investors Group, the Interfaith Center

---

[8] International Institute for Environment and Development/United Nations Population Fund. 2012. *Urbanization and Emerging Population Issues – Working Paper 7.* Available at: https://www.unfpa.org/sites/default/files/resource-pdf/UEPI%207%20Tacoli%20Mar%202012.pdf

Social and Environmental Megatrends

on Corporate Responsibility, and other faith-based investors continue to play an important role in ESG advocacy and company engagement and in submitting shareholder resolutions.

Environmental Megatrends with Social Impact

Climate change and transition risk

Climate change and the neighboring effect of **transition risk** have social implications. A widespread call is that the transition should be a 'just' transition. In the process of adjusting to an economy that does not adversely affect the climate, sectors that employ millions of workers (such as energy, coal, manufacturing, agriculture, and forestry) must restructure. It is feared that the period of economic structural change will result in ordinary workers bearing the costs of the transition, leading to unemployment, poverty, and exclusion for the working class.

Water scarcity

Climate change has a negative impact on the availability of fresh water. Some corporations with high water usage pose a significant threat to clean and affordable water for communities. The construction of wastewater treatment plants and reduction of groundwater over-drafting appear to be obvious solutions to the worldwide problem. However, this is not as simple as it seems for the following reasons:

- ▶ Wastewater treatment is highly capital intensive, so there is restricted access to this technology in some regions.
- ▶ The rapid increase in the population of many countries makes this a race that is difficult to win.
- ▶ There are enormous costs and skillsets involved in maintaining wastewater treatment plants, even if they are successfully developed.

Mass migration

The scarcity of fresh water and desertification due to climate change in several emerging countries is believed to be one of the reasons for **mass migration** streams from developing countries to developed countries where these issues are less present. Climate change might result in an increase of 'environmental migrants,' with the most common projection being that the world will have 150 to 200 million climate change migrants by 2050.

Pollution and loss and/or degradation of natural resources and ecosystem services

Factors like pollution and land degradation can also result in stakeholder opposition, social unrest, and/or migration.

Conclusion

As discussed in this section, different social megatrends provide both opportunities and risks for investors and analysts. It is therefore important to be aware of these trends and take them into account when making investment decisions.

More specific information on how to apply these trends to investing can be found in Section 7. The next section, Section 3, considers key social issues and business activities.

3 KEY SOCIAL ISSUES AND BUSINESS ACTIVITIES

> 4.1.3 explain key social concepts, including: human capital: development, employment standards, and health and safety; product liability/consumer protection: safety, quality, health and demographic risks, and data privacy and security; stakeholder opposition/controversial sourcing; social opportunities: access to communications, finance, and health and nutrition; social and news media; animal welfare and microbial resistance

Where should investors start when implementing social factors in their investment decision?

1. A good starting point is to determine which social factors are most controversial or financially material in each industry.
2. As a next step, investors can assess how exposed certain companies are to these sector-specific social factors and if and how the company manages these risks. This might depend on their business models or on the nature and geographical location of their business operations.
3. Finally, where relevant, investors should assess critical social factors in the supply chain.

It should be noted that the social elements that are considered to have the largest financial materiality depend on specific aspects mostly related to their field of industry. The Sustainability Accounting Standards Board (SASB) framework gives guidance on the financially material topics within industries.

Social factors can also be categorized between those impacting external stakeholders (such as customers, local communities, and governments) and groups of internal stakeholders (such as the company's employees). See Exhibit 1 for examples of social factors that may affect these stakeholders.

Exhibit 1: Examples of Social Factors That Impact Internal and External Stakeholders

Social factors that impact internal stakeholders:	Social factors that impact external stakeholders:
Human capital development.	Stakeholder opposition and controversial sourcing.
Working conditions, health, and safety.	Product liability and consumer protection.
Human rights.	Social opportunities.

Social factors that impact internal stakeholders:	Social factors that impact external stakeholders:
Employment standards and labor rights.	Animal welfare and antimicrobial resistance.

INTERNAL SOCIAL FACTORS

> 4.1.3 explain key social concepts, including: human capital: development, employment standards, and health and safety; product liability/consumer protection: safety, quality, health and demographic risks, and data privacy and security; stakeholder opposition/controversial sourcing; social opportunities: access to communications, finance, and health and nutrition; social and news media; animal welfare and microbial resistance

This section will provide an overview of the key internal social factors that can be of interest for investors.

Human Capital Development

A company's long-term strategy should take into account the development of its workforce.

This ensures that the workforce:

1. is well equipped for performing its tasks and responsibilities;
2. operates under the latest standards and regulations; and
3. remains motivated.

Good human capital management generates a culture and behaviors where the workforce is positively disposed and productive, rather than taking excessive risks or harming customer relationships. It enhances social inclusion, active citizenship, and personal development while increasing competitiveness and employability.

For an investor, the following business requirements could be assessed when analyzing a company on human capital development. Questions should include:

Does the business...

- identify required skills or competencies to deliver on its strategy as well as identify gaps within the company and areas of skill shortage in the industry ('war on talent')?
- develop an attractive value proposition to attract talent as well as ways to develop competencies of internal employees to retain talent?
- develop measures to monitor its investment in human capital development (e.g., training hours, coaching) and its return on investment (key performance indicators, or KPIs, such as employee engagement, turnover, and ability to fill vacancies with internal candidates)?

Working Conditions, Health, and Safety

One of the most widely felt social factors that has been incorporated by institutional investors is health and safety. Its focus is on protecting the workforce from accidents and fatalities. A specific subtopic is occupational health, which is about limiting workforce exposures to minimize the risk of occupational diseases (such as silicosis) or injury (for example, vibration white finger).

An example of a health and safety factor can be seen in the Rana Plaza disaster, examined in the following case study.

> **CASE STUDIES**
>
> #### Rana Plaza Disaster
>
> On 24 April 2013, a structural failure resulted in the collapse of the Rana Plaza, an eight-story commercial building in Dhaka, Bangladesh. This resulted in a death toll of 1,134 people. Approximately 2,500 injured people were rescued from the building alive. It is considered the deadliest structural failure accident in modern human history. The building's owners ignored warnings to avoid using the building after cracks had appeared the day before. Garment workers were ordered to return the following day, and the building collapsed during the morning rush hour.
>
> The high death toll of this disaster is at least partially caused by the managers' decision to send workers back into the factories despite knowing the risks. Managers claimed they ignored the warnings due to the pressure to complete orders for buyers on time. Some have argued that the demand for fast fashion and low-cost clothing motivated minimal oversight by clothing brands and that collectively organized trade unions could have responded to the pressure of management.
>
> This massive tragedy drew attention to pervasive human rights abuses in the garment sector, as well as the failure of the Bangladesh government and corporations sourcing there to create workplaces that respect and protect the lives of workers and mitigate the risk to companies and their investors. As a result of the Rana Plaza disaster, over 175 brands, such as Adidas, Marks and Spencer, and H&M, have signed the Bangladesh Accord,[9] where they pledge to commit to higher fire and health and safety standards in Bangladesh.
>
> Led by the Interfaith Center on Corporate Responsibility, the Bangladesh Investor initiative, an investor coalition comprising 250 institutional investors and representing over US$4.5 trillion (£3.2 trillion) in assets under management, was formed in May 2013 to urge a strong corporate response to Rana Plaza, including participation in the Accord.[10]

Health and safety performance indicators should be assessed for both permanent employees and contractors. For example, several oil and gas companies report only fatalities of their permanent employees but not of their contractors. Given the volume of contracted workers in this sector, it is critical for investors to understand if the company is providing a safe place to work. This is particularly pertinent in emerging market extractive companies.

---

[9] Bangladesh Accord. 2019. *The Accord on Fire and Building Safety in Bangladesh.* Available at: http://bangladeshaccord.org/
[10] Interfaith Center on Corporate Responsibility. 2019. *Protecting Worker Rights: Garment Workers.* Available at: www.iccr.org/our-issues/human-rights/protecting-worker-rights-garment-workers

Besides minimizing accidents and fatalities, health and safety has evolved a broader concept of working conditions that promotes employee well-being, as seen for instance through ergonomic workplaces and flexible working hours. The focus is also increasingly on mental health (such as burn out risks in the finance industry) and other employee benefits to promote their well-being outside of the workplace (including medical checks, gym membership sponsorship, and training programs on nutrition-related risks). Another example is "financial wellness," which is a fairly well-established term among US employers and HR departments. Assistance with personal financial issues like personal budgeting and retirement planning/saving leads to less distracted and less stressed workers.

Human Rights

Another important social factor for investment professionals is **human rights**. These are rights inherent to all human beings, regardless of:

1. race;
2. sex;
3. nationality;
4. ethnicity;
5. language;
6. religion; or
7. any other status (e.g., age, ability, socioeconomic level, or gender identity).

Human rights include the following:

1. the right to life and liberty;
2. freedom from slavery and torture;
3. freedom of opinion and expression; and
4. the right to work and education.

Everyone is entitled to these rights, without discrimination.

The most important foundation for international human rights is the **Universal Declaration of Human Rights (UDHR).** This declaration was proclaimed by the United Nations General Assembly on 10 December 1948 by General Assembly resolution 217A and is a common standard of achievement for all peoples and all nations.[11]

Human rights violations usually occur deep within supply chains. Companies to which major investors most often have direct exposure, and even their first and second tier suppliers, are less likely to be directly implicated in such practices. For example, in the garment industry, it is more likely that human rights violations will take place in emerging countries where clothing is produced, rather than at the stores where the clothing is being sold. However, both clients and governments expect companies to take responsibility for activities within their supply chain.

UN Guiding Principles and OECD Guidelines for Multinational Enterprises

There are many different guidelines with respect to human rights. However, two have a direct effect on companies and investors:

- The **United Nations Guiding Principles on Business and Human Rights (UNGPs)**
- The **OECD Guidelines for Multinational Enterprises (MNEs)**

---

11 United Nations. 1948. *Universal Declaration of Human Rights*. Available at: www.un.org/en/universal-declaration-human-rights/index.html

United Nations Guiding Principles on Business and Human Rights

The UNGPs[12] are a set of guidelines implementing the United Nations' "Protect, Respect and Remedy" framework for the responsibilities of transnational corporations and other business enterprises with regard to human rights. Developed by the Special Representative of the Secretary-General (SRSG) John Ruggie, these guiding principles provided the first global standard for preventing and addressing the risk of adverse impacts on human rights linked to business activity. They also continue to provide the internationally accepted framework for enhancing standards and practice regarding business and human rights.

The UNGPs encompass three pillars outlining how states and businesses should implement the framework:

1. The state duty to protect human rights
2. The corporate responsibility to respect human rights
3. Access to remedy for victims of business-related abuses

OECD Guidelines for Multinational Enterprises

The OECD Guidelines for MNEs are a comprehensive set of government-backed recommendations on responsible business conduct. The governments adhering to the Guidelines aim to encourage and maximize the positive impact MNEs can make to sustainable development and enduring social progress. The Guidelines are important recommendations addressed by governments to multinational enterprises operating in or from adhering countries. They provide voluntary principles and standards for responsible business conduct in such areas as:

1. employment and industrial relations;
2. human rights;
3. environment;
4. information disclosure;
5. combating bribery;
6. consumer interests;
7. science and technology;
8. competition; and
9. taxation.

The study, *Responsible Business Conduct for Institutional Investors*,[13] helps institutional investors implement the due diligence recommendations of the OECD Guidelines for MNEs in order to prevent or address adverse impacts related to human and labor rights, the **environment**, and corruption in their investment portfolios.

It is important to note that these guidelines do not focus on the impact social factors can have on investments (financial materiality) but rather on the responsibility investors have for the adverse impacts their investments/ companies can cause to society. Nowadays, many investors are convinced that they should take ESG factors into account, but these guidelines require governments and investors to adopt a so-called double (or dual) materiality approach and take the (positive and negative) "social return on investments" into account.

---

12 Business & Human Rights Resource Centre. 2019. *UN Guiding Principles*. Available at: www.business-humanrights.org/en/un-guiding-principles

13 OECD. 2017. *Responsible Business Conduct for Institutional Investors: Key Considerations for Due Diligence under the OECD Guidelines for Multinational Enterprises*. Available at: https://mneguidelines.oecd.org/RBC-for-Institutional-Investors.pdf

Internal Social Factors

The OECD guidelines and UNGPs are further backed by the European Union (EU) corporate social responsibility (CSR) strategy, its regulation on sustainability-related disclosures in the financial services sector, and its taxonomy for minimum social safeguards for sustainable activities.

In the Netherlands, the government, non-governmental organizations (NGOs), and institutional investors have signed a Responsible Investment Agreement in which investors agree to adopt this double materiality approach, follow the OECD guidelines, and take responsibility to try to mitigate the negative impact of their investments.[14]

Corporate Human Rights Benchmark

The **Corporate Human Rights Benchmark (CHRB)**[15] is a collaboration led by investors and civil society organizations dedicated to creating the first open and public benchmark of corporate human rights performance.

The CHRB provides a comparative snapshot year-on-year of the largest companies on the planet, looking at the policies, processes, and practices they have in place to systematize their human rights approach and how they respond to serious allegations. Initially, only companies from three industries — agricultural products, apparel, and extractives — were chosen on the basis of their size and revenues. The measurement themes and indicators within the CHRB provide a truly rigorous and credible proxy measure of corporate human rights performance, which can be used by analysts and investors. The themes consist of multiple questions that are listed in the report. These questions address:

1. governance and policy commitments;
2. embedding respect and human rights due diligence;
3. remedies and grievance mechanisms;
4. performance — company human rights practices;
5. performance — responses to serious allegations; and
6. transparency.

Human Rights 100+

Following in the footsteps of Climate Action 100+, Principles for Responsible Investment (PRI) has recently launched a new collaborative initiative for investors to address human rights and social issues through their stewardship activities: Human Rights 100+. The initiative acts as a platform that can encompass a broad range of social issues, allowing investors to prioritize the most severe human rights risks and outcomes within their stewardship activities. It includes investor collaborative engagement with companies, along with potential further escalation where needed, and also supports investor engagement with policymakers and other stakeholders to make progress on the overall goal.

Labor Rights

Assessing how companies uphold labor rights is important for investors to gain insights into the corporate culture and the level of employee satisfaction. The most important labor rights have been summarized in **International Labour Standards.** These are

---

14 International RBC/SER. 2021. *Agreements on International Responsible Business Conduct.* Available at: www.imvoconvenanten.nl/en
15 Corporate Human Rights Benchmark (CHRB). 2020. *Corporate Human Rights Benchmark.* Available at: www.corporatebenchmark.org

aimed at promoting opportunities for women and men to obtain decent and productive work with freedom, equity, security, and dignity. These standards are included in the eight fundamental conventions of the International Labour Organization (ILO):

1. Freedom of Association and Protection of the Right to Organise
2. Right to Organise and Collective Bargaining
3. Forced Labour
4. Abolition of Forced Labour
5. Minimum Age
6. Worst Forms of Child Labour
7. Equal Remuneration
8. Discrimination (Employment and Occupation)

We will now explore some of these conventions in further detail.

Freedom of Association and Employee Relations

A company operates most effectively and efficiently when the workforce is positive and productive. This ensures that the costs of turnover, absenteeism, or strike actions are reduced. In order to ensure that the rights of the employees are well served, employees should have the freedom to form or join an association or a trade union that advocates for the interests of the employees.

In some countries or industries this right is limited. For example, several companies within the retail industry are renowned for their anti-union stance. Walmart has been targeted by several international institutional investors to adopt a more pro-union stance. When freedom of association is established, often other labor rights violations — such as forced labor, child labor, and discrimination — are better safeguarded.

The lack of freedom of association can occur directly at the level of the investee companies, but it is more likely to be an issue in companies' supply chains. By engaging with their investee companies on this topic, investors can press for better industrial relations within a specific sector or country.

Modern Slavery and Forced Labor

Two topics that are less frequently mentioned in responsible investment policies are modern slavery and forced labor.

Modern slavery refers to situations of exploitation that a person cannot refuse or leave because of threats, violence, coercion, deception, and/or abuse of power. This is considered to be an umbrella term encompassing such practices as forced labor, debt bondage, forced marriage, and human trafficking.[16]

Forced labor is defined by the ILO as:

> *"All work or service which is exacted from any person under the menace of any penalty and for which the said person has not offered himself voluntarily."*[17]

Modern slavery and forced labor can take place in every kind of work or service, either in the private, public, informal, or formal marketplace, but it typically occurs in industries that are poorly regulated and where the production process requires many workers. In total, no fewer than 25 million people are estimated to be in forced labor.

---

16 United Nations. 2021. *Slavery Is Not Merely a Historical Relic*. Available at: www.un.org/en/observances/slavery-abolition-day
17 International Labour Organization. 2019. *Forced Labour, Modern Slavery and Human Trafficking*. Available at: www.ilo.org/global/topics/forced-labour/lang--en/index.htm

Internal Social Factors

It is often hidden away in supply chains in the second tier and beyond. Most companies that address modern slavery and forced labor, however, both start and end their due diligence by focusing on their first-tier contractors and suppliers. Beside modern slavery, forced labor can take subtle forms, which makes detecting it very difficult.

The use or threat of physical violence is not essential to characterize a labor relationship as forced labor. Debt bondage, threatening to denounce a worker to immigration authorities, or the retention of identity papers can 'force' workers as well. The increasing complexity and international character of supply chains makes more transparency essential.[18]

In 2015, the Parliament of the United Kingdom adopted the **Modern Slavery Act,** which was designed to combat modern slavery.

Further information on the UK Modern Slavery Act is provided in Section 6 of this chapter.

Living Wage

In sectors that employ and rely on masses of manual labor (such as the garment and footwear, food and beverage, consumer electronics, or retail sectors), wages are often insufficient to cover workers' basic living expenses (food, clothing, housing, healthcare, and education).

The benefits of paying a **living wage** are clear. Workers who earn a living wage can meet their own basic needs and those of their families and put savings aside, thus being more likely to find their way out of poverty. They work regular working hours instead of excessive overtime to make 'ends meet' and are more likely to send their children to school instead of work.

In short, the focus on a living wage also advances the respect for a number of other fundamental human rights in global supply chains.

EXAMPLE 2

Platform Living Wage Financials

The Platform Living Wage Financials (PLWF)[19] was established at the end of 2018. This is a coalition of (mainly Dutch) financial institutions that encourage and monitor investee companies to address the non-payment of a living wage in their global supply chains. The investor coalition has over €2.6 trillion (£1.9 trillion) of assets under management and uses its influence and leverage to engage with its investee companies. They:

1. measure their performance on living wage;
2. discuss the assessment results; and
3. support innovative pilots.

Finally, they make sustainable investment decisions based on (the lack of) progress subject to individual choices and policy preferences of each member of the platform.

---

18 Holtland, H., and A. Höften. 2018. *Dutch Pension Funds and Forced Labour – Speak up*. Available at: www.vbdo.nl/wp-content/uploads/2018/12/SPEAK-UP7.pdf
19 Platform Living Wage Financials (PLWF). 2020. *Platform Living Wage Financials*. Available at: www.livingwage.nl/platform-living-wage-financials/

5 EXTERNAL SOCIAL FACTORS

☐ 4.1.3 explain key social concepts, including: human capital: development, employment standards, and health and safety; product liability/consumer protection: safety, quality, health and demographic risks, and data privacy and security; stakeholder opposition/controversial sourcing; social opportunities: access to communications, finance, and health and nutrition; social and news media; animal welfare and microbial resistance

This section will provide an overview of the key external social factors that can be of interest for investors.

Stakeholder Opposition and Controversial Sourcing

When a company operates in a certain area, it should strive for good relationships with stakeholders, including its local communities. This ensures that the company can continue operating without political interference or informal protest and disruption. Companies should focus on local communities (located near companies' operations) and recognize how they can be involved in stakeholder engagement processes to understand their needs and concerns and how these can be addressed. A way to establish bottom-up participation is to use **Free Prior Informed Consent (FPIC)**.

EXAMPLE 3

Free Prior Informed Consent

A company that plans to develop on ancestral land or use resources of a territory owned by indigenous people should establish FPIC:

- **Free** simply means that there is no manipulation or coercion of the indigenous people and that the process is self-directed by those affected by the project.
- **Prior** implies that consent is sought sufficiently in advance of any activities being either commenced or authorized, and time for the consultation process to occur must be guaranteed by the relative agents.
- **Informed** suggests that the relevant indigenous people receive satisfactory information on the key points of the project, such as:
  - its nature;
  - its size;
  - its pace;
  - its reversibility;
  - the scope of the project;
  - the reason for it; and
  - its duration.

"Informed" is the more difficult term of the four, as different groups may find certain information more relevant. The indigenous people should also have access to the primary reports on the economic, environmental, and cultural impact that the project will have. The language used must be able to be understood by the indigenous people.

- Finally, **consent** means a process in which participation and consultation are the central pillars.[20]

Controversial sourcing is also an issue for companies, with suppliers operating in emerging economies. Companies enjoy the cheap products of their suppliers, but when the cost-driven practices of many of them in these chains come to light, there is often considerable debate over the ethics of these practices.

A rather well-known example is the case of conflict minerals and blood diamonds, which are natural resources extracted in a conflict zone and sold to perpetuate the fighting. The most prominent contemporary example has been in the eastern provinces of the Democratic Republic of Congo (DRC), where various armies, rebel groups, and outside organizations have profited from mining while contributing to violence and exploitation during wars in the region.

Investors should be aware of issues around controversial sourcing and stakeholder opposition because they can become a business and reputational risk for the investee company.

Product Liability and Consumer Protection

Consumer protection refers to laws and other forms of government regulation designed to protect the rights of consumers. It is based on consumer rights, or the idea that consumers have an inherent right to basic health and safety. These are safeguarded by:

a. enforcing product safety;
b. distributing consumer-related information; and
c. preventing deceptive marketing.

Product liability is the legal responsibility imposed on a business for the manufacturing or selling of defective goods. The laws are built on the principle that manufacturers and vendors have more knowledge about the products than the consumers do. Therefore, these businesses bear the responsibility when things go wrong (even when consumers are somewhat at fault).

Product liability cases can result in civil lawsuits and lucrative monetary judgments for the plaintiffs. They can have consequences for the share price of a company if it has regular product recalls or lawsuits. Investors should take this into account in their investment analysis. There are three main types of product liability:

1. businesses being found liable to consumers when a court finds design flaws;
2. manufacturing defects; or
3. a failure to warn consumers of a possible danger.[21]

---

20 Food and Agriculture Organization of the United Nations. 2016. *Free Prior and Informed Consent – Manual for Project Practitioners*. Available at: www.fao.org/3/a-i6190e.pdf
21 Dugger, A. 2019. "What Is Consumer Protection? – Product Liability, Laws & Rights." *CLEP Introductory Business Law*. Available at: https://study.com/academy/lesson/what-is-consumer-protection-product-liability-laws-rights.html

Product liability is likely to lead to reputational risks since consumers can easily express their opinions via social media or boycott the product or service when it is found to be liable. Especially around consumer products, analysts should be aware of such risks.

Social Opportunities

Lack of social opportunities, especially in developing countries, is an important social issue. Many of the **Sustainable Development Goals (SDGs)** focus around this area. The most closely linked are access to basic needs and services in different areas related to health (including water), education, energy, housing, and financial inclusion.

Originally, only such specific investors as development finance institutions, NGOs, and foundations focused on these topics. For example, they invested in microfinance institutions and other impact funds to ensure that people have access to products and services related to communications, finance, and health and nutrition. However, enabling broad and affordable access to basic products and services has proved to be a good business model as well and is increasingly seen as an opportunity for both businesses and investors. This is especially true when aligning the investments with the SDG framework or trying to achieve both a financial and social return on investments.

A similar tool that can be used by investors is the **Access to Medicine Index.** The tool analyzes how 20 of the world's largest pharmaceutical companies are addressing access to medicine in 106 low- to middle-income countries for 82 diseases, conditions, and pathogens. It evaluates these companies in areas where they have the biggest potential and responsibility to make change, such as research and development (R&D) and pricing.[22]

Animal Welfare and Antimicrobial Resistance

Concerns around animal welfare have become more prevalent among consumers and investors as they increasingly recognize that it is not only ethical to minimize harm caused to animals, but it is also important to understand the negative impacts on human health resulting from intensive farming practices. As a result of antimicrobial resistance (i.e., bacteria, viruses, and some parasites becoming more resistant to antibiotics, antivirals, and antimalarials), standard treatments become increasingly ineffective and infections persist, which can result in deaths and increased spread to others.

A growing investor initiative that is focused and engaged on the risks and opportunities linked to intensive livestock production is **Farm Animal Investment Risk and Return (FAIRR).** FAIRR focuses particularly on the increased prevalence of antimicrobial resistance due to intensive farming practices and poor antibiotic stewardship. Companies operating in these ways are more likely to face lawsuits and pressures to change their practices.

---

22 Access to Medicine Foundation. 2021. *2021 Access to Medicine Index.* Available at: https://accesstomedicinefoundation.org/publications/2021-access-to-medicine-index

IDENTIFYING MATERIAL SOCIAL FACTORS FOR INVESTORS

- ☐ **4.1.4** assess material impacts of social issues on potential investment opportunities and the dangers of overlooking them, including: changing demographics; digitization; individual rights and responsibilities; family structures and roles; education and work; faith-based ESG investing and exercise of religion; inequality; and globalization
- ☐ **4.1.5** identify approaches to social analysis at country, sector, and company levels

Given the wide range of social trends and factors that could have an effect on the risks and opportunities in a portfolio, these should be considered by investors.

Until now, these factors and trends have been discussed in a general sense, as if these factors would have an impact on each country, sector, or company equally; however, this is not the case.

Analyzing which social topics are material from an investment point of view should start with an understanding of materiality at both the geographical and industry level. Once this is established, the company-level exposure can be determined by looking at the sector it operates in and which countries/regions it mostly operates in as well as by considering locations of key suppliers, plants, customers, and main tax jurisdictions.

Country

The importance or relevance of a specific social issue depends on the regional or country context, including the level of economic development, regulatory framework (e.g., when local labor laws do not fully comply with ILO principles), and cultural or historical factors. For example, population aging is an important problem in the developed world, but it is less so in emerging markets. Furthermore, the difference between rural and urban areas is greater in emerging markets than in developed ones.

Government legislation also plays an increasing role, as the legal responsibility for companies to take responsibility and check the conditions in their supply chains is becoming mandatory in certain jurisdictions. Examples include the UK Modern Slavery Act, the French Corporate Duty of Vigilance Law, the EU Conflict Minerals Regulation, and the Dutch Child Labour Due Diligence Law. Investors should look closely at how social factors and trends impact investee companies in the different countries where they operate.

CASE STUDIES

Two examples of local regulatory frameworks are the EU taxonomy for sustainable activities and the UK Modern Slavery Act.

EU Taxonomy for Sustainable Activities

The EU taxonomy sets performance thresholds for economic activities that make a substantive contribution to one of six environmental objectives:

1. climate change mitigation;
2. climate change adaptation;
3. sustainable and protection of water and marine resources;
4. transition to a circular economy;

5. pollution prevention and control; and
6. protection and restoration of biodiversity and ecosystems.

The activity should substantially contribute to one of the objectives to become taxonomy-aligned (while doing no significant harm to the other five, where relevant) and should comply with minimum safeguards (e.g., OECD Guidelines on MNEs and the UN Guiding Principles on Business and Human Rights), as shown in the following figure.

The European Parliament and the Council established that for an economic activity to be taxonomy-aligned, the activity should be carried out "in alignment with the OECD Guidelines for Multinational Enterprises and UN Guiding Principles on Business and Human Rights, including the International Labour Organization's ('ILO') declaration on Fundamental Rights and Principles at Work, the eight ILO core conventions and the International Bill of Human Rights." Where applicable, more stringent requirements in EU law still apply.

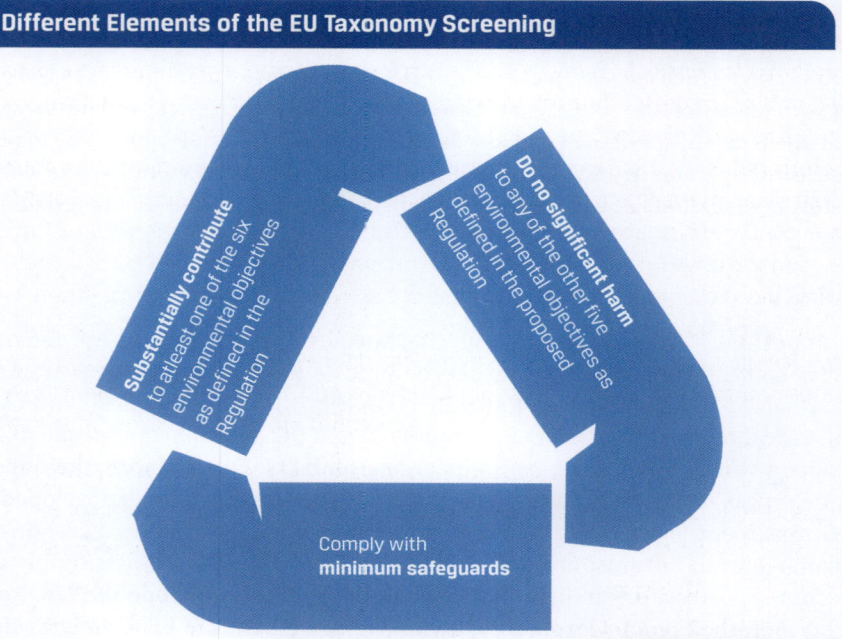

Different Elements of the EU Taxonomy Screening

- **Substantially contribute** to atleast one of the six environmental objectives as defined in the Regulation
- **Do no significant harm** to any of the other five environmental objectives as defined in the proposed Regulation
- Comply with **minimum safeguards**

Source: EU Technical Expert Group on Sustainable Finance. [23]

UK Modern Slavery Act

The Modern Slavery Act requires both medium- and large-sized companies to provide a slavery and human trafficking statement each year, which sets out the steps taken to ensure modern slavery is not taking place in their business or supply chains. Many of these statements provide not only general information but also specific numerical data, such as the number of audits initiated for suppliers at high risk or the number of suppliers that have established corrective action plans, which can help investors assess materiality.

The regulatory pressure on companies to provide useful social data is likely to increase further. For example, in the United States, the Human Capital Management Coalition, which includes such influential investors as leading

---

23 EU Technical Expert Group on Sustainable Finance. 2020. *Taxonomy: Final Report of the Technical Expert Group on Sustainable Finance* . Available at: https://ec.europa.eu/info/sites/info/files/business_economy_euro/banking_and_finance/documents/200309-sustainable-finance-teg-final-report-taxonomy_en.pdf

Application of Social Factors in Investments 249

> US pension funds, has petitioned the Securities and Exchange Commission to require issuers to disclose information about their human capital management policies, practices, and performance. International collaboration is also key. The International Organization of Securities Commissions (IOSCO) connects regulators over the world and provides global frameworks to support worldwide standardization, which regulators in each country can use as a basis for their own regulations.

Sector

It is important to determine what the most material social factors and trends are per sector.

Certain sectors have deeper inherent social risks, for example, due to child labor in the supply chain (clothing/cotton) or the nature of the business (mining).

Social trends also impact sectors differently. For example, automation and artificial intelligence (AI) will have a very different impact on transport (self-driving cars) compared to maintenance (very hard to automate). Demographic change, however, will have a specific impact on the healthcare sector.

Technological developments can also help in tackling injustices in certain sectors, such as satellite imagery that can help to identify illegal deforestation.

Company Level

Companies within a sector may not all be exposed to social trends and factors in the same way.

Much will depend on a company's culture, systems, operations, and governance. For example, older, more established companies might have better systems in place to manage social risks in their supply chain, but at the same time they may find it harder to respond when a company with a disruptive business model enters their market.

Most social issues mentioned above could:

1. impact a company's bottom line;
2. increase workforce issues (including supply chain); and
3. decrease the corporate responsibility (human rights) and its consumer expectations (e.g., animal welfare).[24]

APPLICATION OF SOCIAL FACTORS IN INVESTMENTS 7

☐ | 4.1.6 apply material social factors to: risk assessment; quality of management; ratio analysis; and financial modeling

This section provides information on how to apply social factors in investments.

---

24 EU Technical Expert Group on Sustainable Finance. 2020. *Taxonomy: Final Report of the Technical Expert Group on Sustainable Finance.* Available at: https://ec.europa.eu/info/sites/info/files/business_economy_euro/banking_and_finance/documents/200309-sustainable-finance-teg-final-report-taxonomy_en.pdf

Materiality or Risk Assessment

The first step of a financial materiality or risk assessment could be to determine what the impact of social factors and trends could be on the investee companies in the different sectors, operating in the different countries (which is also briefly described in Section 3). For example, some sectors, such as the mining and oil and gas industry, are more susceptible to human rights violations or health and safety issues.

This financial materiality assessment should be part of a company's traditional risk assessment. Non-financial risks, such as social risks, could have a material impact on the performance of the investments and should therefore be taken into account. Besides risks, certain companies or sectors could also provide investment opportunities because they identify social trends early on and adapt their company strategy to benefit from these trends instead of being caught at a disadvantage.

Recent EU and UK regulation is asking for double materiality reporting. The concept of double materiality acknowledges that a company should report both on sustainability matters that are: 1) financially material in influencing business value and 2) 'impact material,' which is the impact of the company on the environment and people. For assessment of material negative impact, the OECD Due Diligence Guidance for Responsible Business Conduct and the UN Guiding Principles on Business and Human Rights can be used. For a focus on positive impact and adding value for 'the organization, society, and the environment' rather than just 'financial materiality' enhancements, reference to the United Nations Sustainable Development Goals are often made.

CASE STUDIES

Amazon, Apple, and Thai Union

In this case study, we will look in detail at the social aspects of Apple and Amazon.

Amazon

Amazon is a multinational technology company based in Seattle, USA, that focuses on e-commerce, cloud computing, digital streaming, and AI. Amazon is known for its disruption of well-established industries through technological innovation and mass scale. Former employees, current employees, the media, and politicians have criticized Amazon for poor working conditions at the company. Some examples include the following:

a. In 2011, workers had to carry out tasks in 38°C heat (100°F) at a warehouse in Breinigsville, Pennsylvania. As a result of these inhumane conditions, employees became extremely uncomfortable and suffered from dehydration; some employees collapsed. Although loading bay doors could have been opened to bring in fresh air, this was not allowed due to concerns over theft.[25]

b. Some workers, known as 'pickers,' who travel the buildings with a trolley and a handheld scanner 'picking' customer orders, can walk up to 15 miles during their workday. If they fall behind on their targets, they can be reprimanded. The handheld scanners give real-time information to the employee on how quickly or slowly they are working; the scanners

---

[25] Yarow, J., and C. Kovach. 2011. "10 Crazy Rules That Could Get You Fired from Amazon Warehouses." *Business Insider* (20 September). Available at: www.businessinsider.com/amazon-warehouse-rules-2011-9?international=true&r=US&IR=T

Application of Social Factors in Investments

also serve to allow team leaders and area managers to track the specific locations of employees and how much 'idle time' they use when not working.[26]

c. In March 2019, it was reported that emergency services responded to 189 calls from 46 Amazon warehouses in 17 US states between 2013 and 2018, all relating to suicidal employees. The workers attributed their mental breakdowns to employer-imposed social isolation, aggressive surveillance, and the hurried and dangerous working conditions at these fulfilment centers.[27]

d. In response to criticism that Amazon does not pay its workers a livable wage, the CEO, Jeff Bezos, announced that from 1 November 2018, all US and UK Amazon employees will earn a minimum of US$15 or £10.78 per hour. Amazon also announced that it would begin lobbying the US Congress to increase the federal minimum wage.

e. Although it might seem that by paying lower wages or applying other strict labor conditions has a positive effect on profitability from an investor perspective, analysts should, from a financial materiality perspective, consider the possibility that legislation, social unrest, or higher than expected employee turnover/low morale will likely at some point result in disruptions and increased costs. From a double materiality perspective, the impact on employees as a stakeholder group also should be considered.

Apple/Foxconn/Inventec

Apple is an American multinational technology company based in Cupertino, California, that designs, develops, and sells consumer electronics, computer software, and online services. Apple has been criticized on the labor practices at their suppliers Foxconn and Inventec:

a. In 2006, it was reported that the working conditions in the factories where contract manufacturers Foxconn and Inventec produced the iPod were poor. One complex of factories that assembled the iPod, among other items, had over 200,000 workers living and working within it. Employees regularly worked more than 60 hours per week and made around US$100 (£71) per month. A little over half of the workers' earnings was required to pay for rent and food from the company. Apple immediately launched an investigation and worked with their manufacturers to ensure acceptable working conditions. In 2007, Apple started yearly audits of all its suppliers regarding workers' rights, slowly raising standards and removing suppliers that did not comply.[28]

---

26 O'Connor, S. 2013. "Amazon Unpacked." *FT Magazine* (8 February). Available at: www.ft.com/content/ed6a985c-70bd-11e2-85d0-00144feab49a

27 Zahn, M., and S. Paget. 2019. "'Colony of Hell': 911 Calls from Inside Amazon Warehouses.." *The Daily Beast* (8 May). Available at: www.thedailybeast.com/amazon-the-shocking-911-calls-from-inside-its-warehouses

28 Dean, J. 2007. "The Forbidden City of Terry Gou." *The Wall Street Journal* (11 August). Available at: www.wsj.com/articles/SB118677584137994489

b. In 2010, Apple led an investigation into the employment practices at Foxconn, the world's largest contract electronics manufacturer at the time, after the Foxconn suicides. These took place between January and November 2010, when 18 Foxconn employees attempted suicide, resulting in 14 deaths, and drew much media attention.[29]

c. A 2014 BBC investigation found excessive hours and other problems persisted, despite Apple's promise to reform factory practice after the 2010 Foxconn suicides. Reporters gained access to the working conditions inside a factory through recruitment as employees. While the BBC maintained that the experiences of its reporters showed that labor violations were continuing since 2010, Apple publicly disagreed with the BBC and stated: "We are aware of no other company doing as much as Apple to ensure fair and safe working conditions."[30]

d. Controversies like these can impact customer loyalty, resulting in fines or employee/supplier strikes. The stock price of Apple, for example, took a 5% hit on 24 April 2012, believed to be linked to the Foxconn riots that day, which is a consequence from the high financial materiality of the topic. From a double materiality perspective, the effects or impact on the employees within the supply chain should be considered.[31]

Thai Union

Thai Union is a Thailand-based producer of seafood-based food products with a global workforce of over 49,000 people. The company's global brand portfolio includes such international brands as Chicken of the Sea, John West, Sealect, and Petit Navire. In 2015, Greenpeace accused Thai Union of being "seriously implicated in horrendous human rights and environmental abuses" and warned shareholders and investors "of the financial risks associated with these destructive and harmful practices":

a. Such controversies led to a loss of revenue[32] as consumers and supermarkets boycotted the products. This led to a required termination of sub-contractors and, in turn, increased transition and future costs.

b. In 2015, Thai Union released new codes of conduct and stated that it had terminated the relationships with 17 suppliers as a result of forced labor or human trafficking violations since the start of 2015. It also ended the use of employment brokers to source for workers for its seafood processing plants to stop debt bondage.

c. In a statement issued on 10 December 2015, Thai Union declared that it would cease working with all shrimp processing sub-contractors by the end of 2015 and bring all shrimp processing operations in-house to enable full oversight. All processing work would be directly controlled by Thai Union Group to ensure that all workers, whether migrants or Thai, would have safe, legal employment and be treated fairly and with dignity.

---

29 Pomfret, J., H. Yan, and K. Soh. 2010. "Foxconn Worker Plunges to Death at China Plant: Report." *Reuters* (5 November). Available at: www.reuters.com/article/us-china-foxconn-death/foxconn-worker-plunges-to-death-at-china-plant-report-idUSTRE6A41M920101105

30 Agence France-Presse. 2014. "Apple under Fire Again for Working Conditions at Chinese Factories." *The Guardian* (19 December). Available at: www.theguardian.com/technology/2014/dec/19/apple-under-fire-again-for-working-conditions-at-chinese-factories

31 Seeking Alpha. 2012. *Did Foxconn Bring Down Apple Stock?* Available at: https://seekingalpha.com/article/926801-did-foxconn-bring-down-apple-stock

32 Seafood Source. 2016. *Are US Buyers Boycotting Thailand Shrimp?* Available at: www.seafoodsource.com/news/supply-trade/are-u-s-buyers-boycotting-thailand-shrimp

Application of Social Factors in Investments

   d. In December 2016, Thai Union and the World Tuna Purse Seine Organization (WTPO) signed a memorandum of understanding (MOU) to establish a framework to ensure fair labor practices.
   e. In May 2018, Thai Union announced it had made an agreement with Greenpeace in which both parties stated that it had made substantial, positive progress on its commitment to implement measures that tackle illegal fishing and overfishing and had also improved the livelihoods of hundreds of thousands of workers throughout its supply chains. According to Greenpeace: "There is much work still to do, but it's clear the company takes its commitments seriously and is making progress to deliver them."
   f. After the agreement was reached, Thai Union released a Vessel Code of Conduct, developed in collaboration with Greenpeace and the International Transport Workers' Federation.

When evaluating the financial materiality of such issues for a company investment, both social risks and the level of mitigation and management of these risks should be considered. When such issues persist, a consumer boycott or divestment by investors is possible, which could affect the share price of the company. However, improving performance can lead to the strengthening of the brand and possibly increasing or future-proofing revenues. In considering double materiality, investors should manage and take responsibility for both the actual and the potential adverse impacts of their investment decisions on people, society, and the market.

Quality of Management

Having identified which social factors are relevant for a particular company, analysts will assess the way the company manages the risks and opportunities associated with these social factors compared to its peers. This includes looking at the corporate strategy, policies in place, the processes and measures implemented, performance indicators, and public disclosure. They will look at current performance and progress over time and investigate how they compare to industry averages and key competitors. It should be noted that poor management of social factors could be an indicator of poor (stakeholder) management in general, and it could, therefore, be an effective warning for investors.

Ratio Analysis and Financial Modeling

It is very useful to quantify the potential impact of social factor scenarios and include these in the ratio analysis and financial modeling of the investment.
   Some scenarios that can be included in the ratio analysis are:

1. occupational health and safety issues (accident and fatalities), which can result in huge fines and liabilities;
2. human capital management issues, which can lead to greater operating costs if new employees need to be trained due to high employee turnover;
3. supply chain issues, which can impact brand reputation and revenues if consumers choose to boycott certain products;
4. local protests that lead to business disruptions at plants or factories; and
5. poor working conditions, which can result in issues with product safety.

Besides specific impacts on estimates regarding future revenues, costs, and potential liabilities in a company's financial analysis, analysts might decide to raise the discount rate to reflect a higher risk profile if a company does not manage social factors appropriately.

> **CASE STUDIES**
>
> ### Tesco Equal Pay Claim
>
> Tesco plc is a British multinational groceries and general merchandise retailer. It is the 16th largest retailer measured by gross revenues.[33] The company reported in financial reporting period 2017/2018 total group sales of £51 billion and £1,837 million in operating profits.
>
> However, since July 2018, the company is facing a demand for up to £4 billion in back pay from thousands of mainly female shopworkers in what could become the UK's largest ever equal pay claim. The retailer is claimed to have breached its duty under Section 66 of the **Equality Act 2010** by paying staff in its distribution centers more than those on the shop floor, despite the roles being of 'comparable value.' Shop floor staff — the majority of whom are female — are paid up to £3 less per hour than the predominantly male warehouse and distribution center workforce.
>
> Section 66 is a 'sex equality clause' that states:
>
> > *"If the terms of A's work do not (by whatever means) include a sex equality clause, they are to be treated as including one."*
>
> A sex equality clause has the following effect:
>
> - If a term of A's is less favorable to A than a corresponding term of B's is to B, A's term is modified so as not to be less favorable.
> - If A does not have a term that corresponds to a term of B's that benefits B, A's terms are modified so as to include such a term.
>
> The employees have formed a Tesco Action Group, which is made up of around 8,000 current and former Tesco staff, to take the claim forward. The claim was formed in addition to a separate legal challenge by Leigh Day, which is representing around 1,000 current and former Tesco staff in a similar equal pay dispute.
>
> A spokesman of the company responded:
>
> > *"Tesco works hard to make sure all our colleagues are paid fairly and equally for the jobs they do and are recognised for the great job they do every day serving our shoppers. There are only a very small number of claims being made, and there are strong factual and legal arguments to defend against those claims."*
>
> This case is groundbreaking, financially material, and goes to the heart of social factors in labor rights. Its outcome could have significant financial consequences for the company and others in the sector.

---

33 National Retail Federation. 2020. *Top 50 Global Retailers 2020.* Available at: https://nrf.com/resources/top-retailers/top-50-global-retailers/top-50-global-retailers-2020

KEY FACTS

In this chapter, an overview was given of the main social megatrends that now influence societies.

Megatrends

The social megatrends have a rather broad range and include:

a. globalization;
b. automation and AI in manufacturing and service sectors;
c. inequality and wealth creation;
d. digital disruption and social media;
e. changes to work, leisure time, and education;
f. changes to individual rights and responsibilities and family structures;
g. changing demographics, including health and longevity;
h. urbanization; and
i. religion.

Environmental megatrends with social impact include:

a. climate change and transition risk;
b. water scarcity; and
c. mass migration.

The most important internal and external factors were described earlier in the chapter. These factors are:

Internal Social Factors

a. human capital development;
b. health and safety;
c. human rights;
d. labor rights;
e. freedom of association and employee relations;
f. forced labor; and
g. living wage.

External Social Factors

a. stakeholder opposition/controversial sourcing;
b. product liability/consumer protection;
c. social opportunities; and
d. animal welfare and antimicrobial resistance.

Countries, sectors, and companies are not affected equally by the different social megatrends and social factors. The analysis of which social factors are material from an investment point of view should start with an understanding of materiality at the geographical and industry levels. Once this is established, the company-level exposure can be determined by looking at the sector it operates in and which countries or regions it mostly operates in (looking at locations of key suppliers, plants, customers, and main tax jurisdictions).

Having identified which social factors are relevant for a particular company, analysts will assess the way the company manages the risks and opportunities associated with these social factors compared to its peers. This includes looking at:

1. corporate strategy;
2. policies in place;
3. processes and measures implemented;
4. performance indicators; and
5. public disclosure.

This process involves looking at:

1. current performance;
2. progress over time; and
3. how that progress compares to industry averages and key competitors.

Increasingly, investors are integrating social factors into the ratio analysis or financial models of investee companies to gain a better understanding of the potential impacts of social factors on a company's financial performance.

FURTHER READING

Methodology of the Corporate Human Rights Benchmark 2019, which provides clear guidance on main human rights questions that can be included in ESG integration or engagement activities:

> Corporate Human Rights Benchmark Ltd. 2019. *Corporate Human Rights Benchmark Methodology 2019*. Available at: www.corporatebenchmark.org/chrb-methodology

Exclusion list of the Norges Bank Investment Management, which is used by many asset owners as guidance for their own exclusions:

> Norges Bank Investment Management. 2019. *Observation and Exclusion of Companies*. Available at: www.nbim.no/en/responsibility/exclusion-of-companies/

The 2018 sector takeaways and the 2018 engagement outcomes of the Platform Living Wage Financials (PLWF):

> New York University's Stern Center for Business and Human Rights' publication on the 'S' of ESG

> O'Connor, C., and S. Labowitz. 2017. *Putting the 'S' in ESG: Measuring Human Rights Performance for Investors*. Available at: www.stern.nyu.edu/experience-stern/global/putting-s-esg-measuring-human-rights-performance-investors

> PLWF. (2019. *2018 Engagement Outcomes*. Available at: www.livingwage.nl/garment-and-footwear/2018-engagement-outcomes

> PLWF. 2019. *2018 Sector Takeaways*. Available at: www.livingwage.nl/garment-and-footwear/2018-sector-takeaways/

The Principles for Responsible Investment (PRI) supports investors' efforts to address social issues, such as human rights, working conditions, and modern slavery, with companies in their portfolio. The different human rights and labor standards publications are also recommended reading material:

> PRI. 2019. *Human Rights and Labor Standards*. Available at: www.unpri.org/esg-issues/social-issues/human-rights-and-labor-standards

> PRI. 2019. *Social Issues*. Available at: www.unpri.org/esg-issues/social-issues

> PRI. 2020. *Why and How Investors Should Act on Human Rights*. Available at: www.unpri.org/human-rights-and-labor-standards/why-and-how-investors-should-act-on-human-rights/6636.article

The World Economic Forum's Global Risk Report is an authoritative publication concerning more than just social issues:

> World Economic Forum. 2019. *The Global Risks Report 2019*. Available at: www.weforum.org/reports/the-global-risks-report-2019.

SELF PRACTICE AND SELF ASSESSMENT

1. Which of the following social trends is *most* closely associated with environmental trends?

    a. Mass migration

    b. Digital disruption

    c. Increasing inequality

2. Over the last few decades, developed countries have *most likely* experienced declining:

    a. average annual working hours.

    b. levels of part-time employment.

    c. proportions of employees with higher education.

3. A developed country with an aging population is *most likely* to:

    a. achieve higher per capita savings levels.

    b. spend more per person on consumer goods.

    c. have a proportionately larger active workforce.

4. Which of the following scenarios *best* illustrates the concept of a 'just' transition?

    a. A region transitioning to renewable power prioritizes equipment installations in historically underserved areas.

    b. A government pledges a multibillion-dollar fund to employ displaced oil industry workers in safely decommissioning abandoned drill sites.

    c. A logistics company builds a new warehouse on the ancestral land of indigenous people and commits to employing a minimum number of indigenous workers.

5. Which of the following is *most likely* to be assessed in an institutional investor's evaluation of employee health performance indicators? Programs that:

    a. assist employees with personal financial issues, like budgeting.

    b. limit employee exposure to conditions that lead to occupational diseases.

    c. support employee mental health by providing free, confidential counseling.

6. In which area of a food processing company's business is forced labor *most likely* to be found?

    a. Producers of the raw agricultural ingredients processed by the company

    b. Casual laborers who work for the company only during busy seasons

    c. Purchasing agents that source the raw agricultural ingredients

7. Which of the following social issues is likely to be *most* relevant to low-to-middle income countries?

    a. An aging population

    b. Access to medicines

    c. Anti-microbial resistance

8. An investment fund scores its potential investments on a scale of one to ten based on the contributions they make to the environmental objectives under the EU taxonomy for sustainable activities. The following table shows how each

Self Practice and Self Assessment

company's score has changed over the past year.

	Transition to a Circular Economy	Climate Change Adaptation	Pollution Prevention and Control	Total
Company 1	+4	−2	+1	+3
Company 2	0	+3	0	+3
Company 3	+1	+1	+1	+3

Which company *most likely* complies with the EU taxonomy for sustainable activities?

a. Company 1
b. Company 2
c. Company 3

9. Within the transportation sector, advances in artificial intelligence are *most likely* to result in fewer employment opportunities for:

a. mechanics.
b. taxi drivers.
c. bulldozer operators.

10. An investment fund requires that its analysts consider an extensive list of potential social factors and trends that could affect the performance of individual investments. Which of the following steps should its analysts take first when evaluating the social suitability of a potential acquisition?

a. Carry out a materiality assessment
b. Model potential impacts of the social factors on key ratios
c. Consider the impact of the UN Sustainable Development Goals

11. An appliance retailer is facing a consumer boycott due to reports of forced labor in its supply chain. The ratio *most likely* to be affected by the consumer action is:

a. leverage.
b. asset turnover.
c. the current ratio.

12. A portfolio analyst is modeling the potential impact of a safety incident with multiple fatalities on its mining sector holdings. Which of the following ratios is *most likely* to be affected as a result?

a. Asset turnover
b. Days of receivables
c. Liabilities-to-assets ratio

The following information relates to questions 13-22

Self Assessment Questions

These questions are provided only to enable you to test your understanding of the chapter content. They are not indicative of the types and standard of questions you may see in the examination. The Self-Assessment questions do not include an explanation of the correct answer.

13. What does 'offshoring' mean?
    a. Protecting coastal areas by building offshore dykes to protect cities against climate change
    b. Climate migrants moving from shore areas to more inland cities
    c. Moving company production to low-income countries
    d. Tax avoidance by companies

14. Of the following, what is the increase in automation and AI not associated with?
    a. Data privacy concerns in social media companies
    b. Employment losses in the garment sector
    c. Employment gains in the IT sector
    d. Future employment losses in the transportation sector

15. What is an example of an internal and an external social factor?
    a. Internal: biodiversity; external: product liability
    b. Internal: health and safety; external: social opportunities
    c. Internal: animal welfare; external: employee relations
    d. Internal: ESG analysis; external: engagement service providers

16. What is meant by the concept of a just transition?
    a. A transition that is aligned with the Paris Agreement
    b. A transition that shares the financial and social burden in a fair way
    c. A transition that is just in time to prevent stranded assets
    d. A transition that respects labor and human rights

17. What is the FAIRR initiative?
    a. It is a collaboration that aims to reach a just transition.
    b. It is an initiative to stimulate fair trade.
    c. It is an investor network to engage on equal pay.
    d. It is an initiative that focuses on the increased prevalence of antimicrobial resistance.

18. What kinds of cases require Free Prior Informed Consent (FPIC)?
    a. Developments on ancestral land or the use of resources of a territory owned by indigenous people
    b. Consumer acceptance of limitation of product liability
    c. Workplace relationships
    d. Investments in alcohol, gambling, or tobacco

19. What does the Access to Medicine Index analzye?
    a. How pharmaceutical companies are addressing access to medicine in low- to middle-income countries
    b. How affordable medicines are in the major developed markets
    c. The percentage of employees covered under a health insurance scheme
    d. How much time it takes to access medical assistance in developing countries

Self Practice and Self Assessment

20. The OECD Guidelines for Multinational Enterprises:
    a. state that companies should adhere to the UN Guiding Principles for Business and Human Rights.
    b. is a voluntary agreement of multinational enterprises to improve their social performance.
    c. is a comprehensive set of government-backed recommendations on responsible business conduct.
    d. prescribe that multinational enterprises should perform a financial due diligence on their suppliers to prevent bribery and corruption.

21. Which social megatrends are important to consider within the investment analysis?
    a. Human rights, health and safety, and employee relations
    b. The Millennium and Sustainable Development Goals
    c. Automation, globalization, and longevity
    d. Natural capital, biodiversity, and climate change adaptation

22. Why is a (social) materiality assessment important?
    a. It is standard procedure in investment analysis, which makes it an important tick-box exercise.
    b. It is always recommendable to conduct assessments because these provide you with invaluable insights.
    c. Not all countries, sectors, and companies are affected equally by the different social megatrends and social factors.
    d. A social materiality assessment is required by law in many jurisdictions.

SOLUTIONS

1. A is correct. Environmental changes, including water scarcity, rising sea levels, and increased flooding, will result in mass migration wherein people relocate to more hospitable regions in large numbers. Social strains are likely to develop in both the migrant communities and the receiving communities.

2. A is correct. OECD studies indicate that most developed countries have experienced declining average working hours over the past few decades. Over the same period, part-time employment has increased as has the proportion of employees with higher education.

3. A is correct. Older populations in developed countries have higher accumulated savings per capita than younger populations. Older people are more likely to be retired, leading to proportionately smaller active workforces. Finally, older populations spend less on consumer goods compared to younger populations.

4. B is correct. A 'just' transition is one that avoids burdening ordinary workers with unemployment, poverty, and exclusion as part of the transition to a low carbon economy. The government's pledge to employ displaced oil industry workers provides transitional employment to workers in a vulnerable sector (oil industry) and thus best illustrates a 'just' transition.

5. B is correct. Occupational health practices, such as limiting workforce exposures to harmful conditions, are well established and widely accepted as fundamental health and safety measures. The broadening of the health and safety concept to incorporate the mental health and "financial wellness" of employees is still gaining acceptance.

6. A is correct. Egregious labor rights violations, such as the use of forced labor, are often hidden deep within supply chains in the second tier and beyond. Of the options, producers of raw agricultural ingredients are deepest within the food processor's supply chain and thus the most likely to employ forced labor.

7. B is correct. Lack of social opportunities, including lack of access to medicines, is identified under the UN's Sustainable Development Goals as an issue in developing or low-to-middle income countries. Aging populations are more closely associated with developed countries, and anti-microbial resistance is not specifically linked to either developed or developing countries.

8. B is correct. Company 2 best fulfills the requirements to substantially contribute to one objective (climate change adaptation at +3 points) while doing no significant harm to the others.

9. B is correct. Artificial intelligence is suited to structured tasks that can be carried out with minimal human assistance. The development of self-driving cars suggests that taxi drivers are most at risk of being displaced because of advances in artificial intelligence. Less routine work, such as troubleshooting mechanical problems and operating bulldozers in varied physical environments, is subject to lower displacement risk.

10. A is correct. Carrying out a materiality assessment, or determining which of the social factors and trends is likely to have a significant impact on the performance of the investments, is the next logical step. Once the materiality assessment is complete, the potential impacts can be modeled and the impact of the UN Sustainable Development Goals can be considered.

Solutions

11. B is correct. Consumer boycotts are most likely to result in lower revenues. The ratio that will be most directly affected by lower revenues is the asset turnover ratio, defined as revenues/assets.

12. C is correct. A safety incident is most likely to result in increased costs and liabilities for fines, lawsuits, and equipment with better safety features. The liabilities-to-assets ratio will be most directly affected by the increased liabilities. Asset turnover and days of receivables are not directly affected by either expenses or liabilities.

13. C is correct.

14. B is correct.

15. B is correct.

16. B is correct.

17. D is correct.

18. A is correct.

19. A is correct.

20. C is correct.

21. C is correct.

22. C is correct.

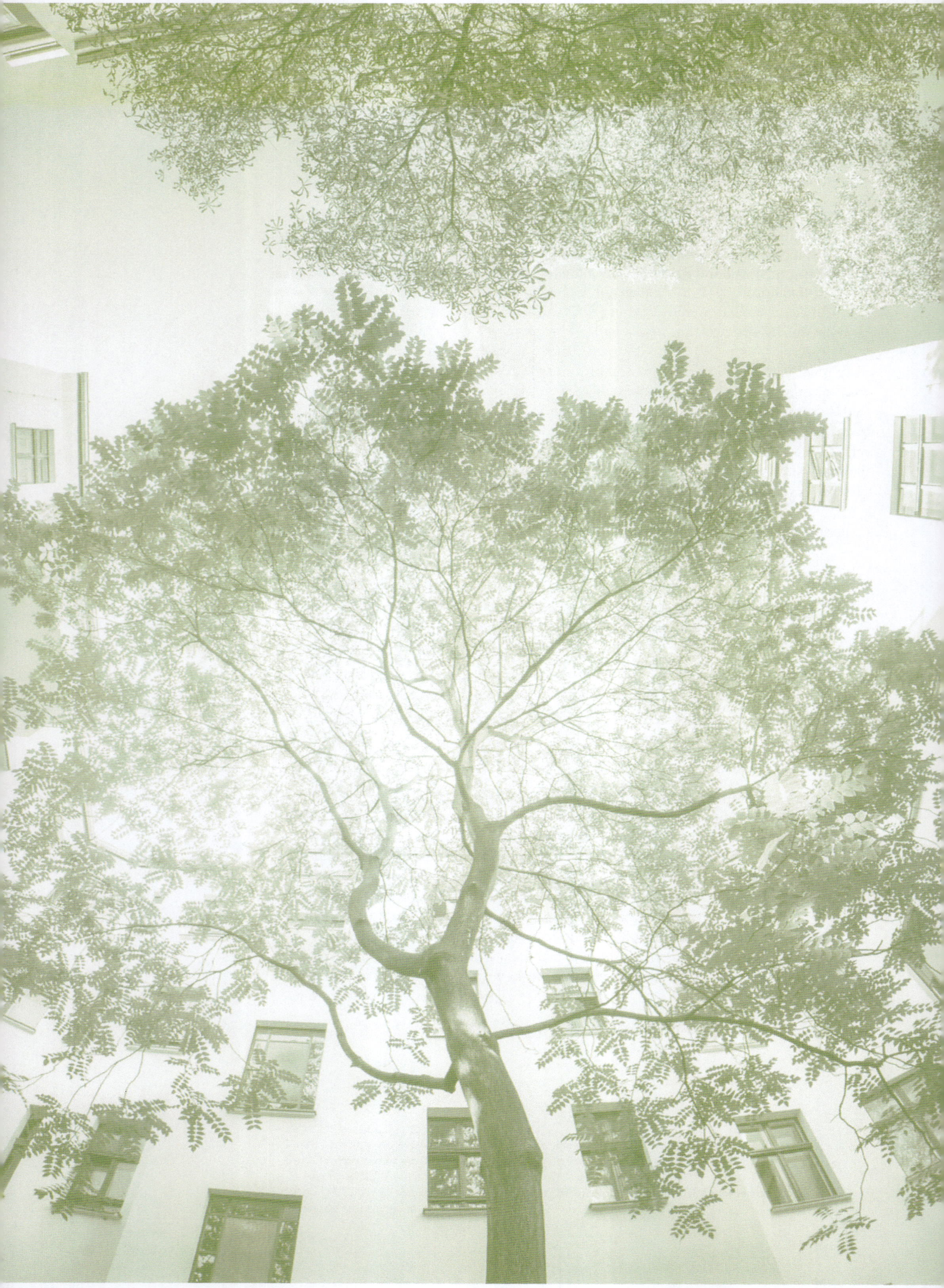

CHAPTER 5

Governance Factors

LEARNING OUTCOMES		
Mastery	\multicolumn{2}{l	}{*The candidate should be able to:*}
☐	5.1.1	explain the evolution of corporate governance frameworks: development of corporate governance; roles and responsibilities; systems and processes; shareholder engagement; minority shareholder alignment
☐	5.1.2	assess key characteristics of effective corporate governance, and the main reasons why they may not be implemented or upheld: board structure, diversity, effectiveness, and independence; executive remuneration, performance metrics, and key performance indicators (KPIs); reporting and transparency; financial integrity and capital allocation; business ethics
☐	5.1.3	assess and contrast the main models of corporate governance in major markets and the main variables influencing best practice: extent of variation of best practice; differences in legislation, culture, and interpretation
☐	5.1.4	explain the role of auditors in relation to corporate governance and the challenges in effective delivery of the audit: independence of audit firms and conflicts of interest; auditor rotation; sampling of audit work and technological disruption; auditor reports; auditor liability; internal audit
☐	5.1.5	assess material impacts of governance issues on potential investment opportunities, including the dangers of overlooking them: public finance initiatives; companies; infrastructure/private finance vehicles; societal impact
☐	5.1.6	apply material corporate governance factors to: financial modeling; risk assessment; quality of management

1 CORPORATE GOVERNANCE: ACCOUNTABILITY AND ALIGNMENT

☐ 5.1.1 explain the evolution of corporate governance frameworks: development of corporate governance; roles and responsibilities; systems and processes; shareholder engagement; minority shareholder alignment

Corporate governance is the process and structure for overseeing the business and management of a company. From the Latin word for the steering of a boat, *gubernare*, governance incorporates that sense of guiding and controlling. Corporate governance has become more complex as the scale and complexity of companies have grown and as ownership has become more dispersed.

As a result, the role of the board of directors has become more important. The board is responsible for representing the owners of the company and for holding management teams accountable for running the business in the interest of its owners. The effectiveness of the board depends on whether good corporate governance practices are applied. The principles that shape these practices have been developed over the years and codified into corporate governance codes. Increasingly, investors are expecting companies to disclose their corporate governance structures and processes so that external investors and other stakeholders can understand where the company stands on the spectrum of good governance.

The types of issues that investors will address when considering a company's governance include, but are not limited to:

- shareholder rights;
- the likely success of the intended company strategy, and the effectiveness of the leadership in place to deliver it;
- executive pay;
- audit practices;
- board independence and expertise;
- transparency or accountability;
- related-party transactions; and
- dual-class share structures.

This chapter considers the *G* of environmental, social, and governance (ESG) factors, corporate governance, and gives readers insight into the core fundamentals of what the concept means, its history and development, global practices, and how governance analysis is used by investment professionals to deliver value to their clients and beneficiaries and minimize the risk of value destruction.

What is Governance? Why Does It Matter?

Corporate governance is the process by which a company is managed and overseen. There are different rules worldwide—governance grows out of the legal system of the country in which the company is incorporated—but at its heart, governance is about people and processes. Good governance also involves developing an appropriate culture that will underpin the delivery of strong business performance without excessive risk-taking through appropriate conduct of business operations. Good corporate governance should lead to strong business performance and long-term prosperity

Corporate Governance: Accountability and Alignment

to the benefit of shareholders and the company's other stakeholders. The corporate culture needs to be supportive of that long-term business success in the interests of all stakeholders.

While at its heart corporate governance is about people (the individuals in the boardroom and how they interact with the individuals outside the boardroom), in order to exercise their responsibilities effectively, board members are supported by processes. These processes bear an increased burden in large and complex companies; at smaller companies there is greater scope for individuals at the top to have direct knowledge across a business, but at larger companies this is impossible. Companies will typically have policies and codes of conduct in place, but they will rely on processes to be confident that those policies are indeed delivered in practice. Investors will judge a company's governance based on the quality of its policies and processes and on the diligence and care with which the board oversees their implementation. Most fundamentally, they will judge governance by the quality and thoughtfulness of the people on the board.

Assessing the effectiveness of corporate governance systems within a firm gives investors insight into the accountability mechanisms and decision-making processes that support all critical decisions affecting the allocation of investors' capital and the likely delivery of long-term value. A company with sound governance is better able to address the key risks that the business faces, including environmental and social issues. Conversely, a company that is failing to manage a key long-term risk (again including environmental and social issues) may have an underlying governance failure that is blocking its ability to address the issue.

In practice, corporate governance comes down to two A's: **accountability** and **alignment**.

These concepts are reflected in many of the core elements of corporate governance standards and investor expectations.

Accountability

People need to be:

- given authority and responsibility for decision-making; and
- held accountable for the consequences of their decisions and the effectiveness of the work they deliver.

Accountability and the Board

Just as people are most effective when they are conscious of being accountable to someone—typically their manager—in the same way, senior executives need to feel accountable to the non-executive directors on their board. In turn, that board will be most effective when its non-executive members feel accountable to shareholders for effective delivery. Therefore, corporate governance has a strong focus on board structure and the independence of directors.

The mixed skill sets of directors are also important, so that discussions and debate are appropriately informed by a range of perspectives and the risk of "groupthink" is avoided. Increasing diversity and the range of perspectives in the boardroom—through gender diversity, but also diversity in terms of professional backgrounds and experiences—has been demonstrated to deliver a more challenging culture and thus the greater accountability that is more likely to enhance long-term value.

The role of the chair of the board is vital in facilitating a balanced debate in the boardroom. Consequently, many investors prefer that the chair be an independent non-executive director. If the chair is not independent, and especially if that individual combines the role of chair with the role of CEO, this situation can lead to an excessive concentration of powers and hamper the board's ability to:

- exercise their oversight responsibilities;
- challenge and debate performance and strategic plans;
- set the agenda, both for board meetings and for the company as a whole;
- influence succession planning; and
- debate executive remuneration.

Exhibit 1 illustrates the flow of accountability through company structures and the investment chain.

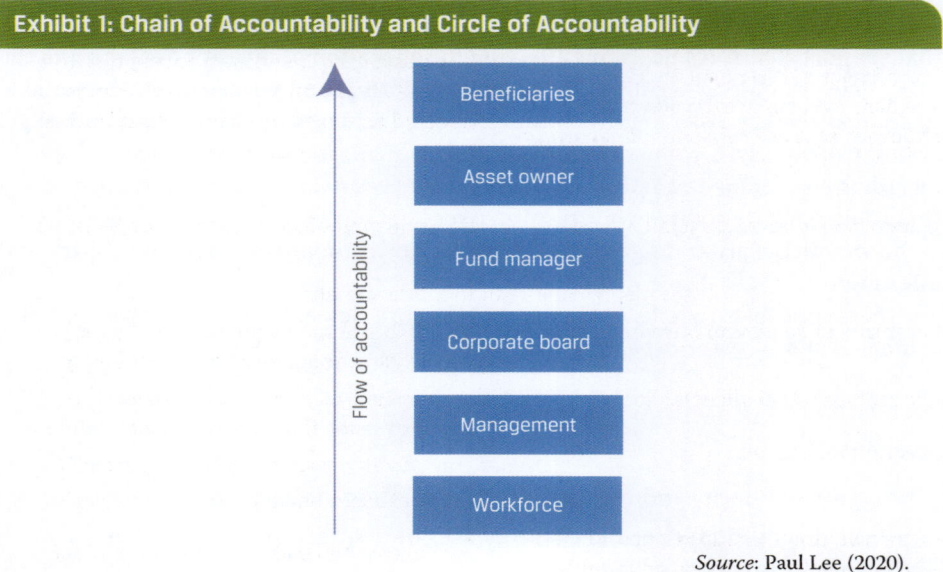

Exhibit 1: Chain of Accountability and Circle of Accountability

Flow of accountability (bottom to top):
- Beneficiaries
- Asset owner
- Fund manager
- Corporate board
- Management
- Workforce

Source: Paul Lee (2020).

Accountability and Accounts

Accurate accounts are needed for accountability. The annual accounts of the company represent the formal process of the directors making themselves properly accountable to the shareholders for financial and broader business performance, which is why the first item at many annual general meetings (**AGM**s) is acceptance of the report and accounts, often through a formal vote. Hence, the central importance of transparent and honest accounting by companies, and of the independence of the audit of those accounts by the auditor. Again, it is not by chance that the auditor reports formally to shareholders each year and is reappointed annually in most countries at the AGM. The integrity of the numbers that investors look at when assessing business performance is central to their ability to hold management and boards to account. The votes to "discharge" board directors in some countries (such as Germany) effectively absolve them of liability for any actions over the year and are usually dependent on the annual report providing a full, true disclosure of activity in the year and the position at year-end.

Alignment and the Agency Problem

Alignment comes down to the challenge of the agency problem. Since the seminal publication of *The Modern Corporation and Private Property* by Adolf Berle and Gardiner Means in 1932 (seen by many as the starting point for the modern understanding of corporate governance), the **agency problem** has been identified as an inevitable consequence of the separation of ownership and control. The agency problem arises in that the interests of the professional managers—the agents—may not always be wholly aligned with the interests of the owners of the business, and so the company may not be run in the way the owners wish. This challenge is magnified at larger corporations, not least public companies, where ownership is fragmented among many investors owning a small fraction of the company.

Any discussion of the agency problem needs to acknowledge that the issues it raises are not so simple that they can be solved by management and the board simply doing what they are instructed to do by the shareholders. First, it will usually be difficult to discern a single message from the shareholder base of most companies, which will include multiple investors. Even where there is a single shareholder or a clear single message from the shareholders, the duty of directors under the company law of most countries is to care for the success of the company and not of the shareholders directly. There is also a risk that directors will fail in their duty if they simply abdicate their responsibilities and respond thoughtlessly to the input received from shareholders. Promoting short-term share price increases is not the same thing as promoting the long-term success of the business.

Furthermore, there can be agency problems within the investment chain itself, as a disconnect can develop between the interests of fund management firms and individual portfolio managers and those of their clients and/or ultimate beneficiaries. This agency problem is discussed in more detail in Chapter 9.

Nonetheless, the challenge of the agency problem is a risk of some divergence between the interests of shareholders, on the one hand, and the interests of company directors and management, on the other. Corporate governance attempts to ensure that there is greater alignment of the interests of the agents with the interests of the owners, through both incentives and appropriate chains of accountability, to mitigate the potential negative consequences of the agency problem.

Alignment and Executive Pay

With regard to alignment, the major focus in terms of executive pay is always on addressing the agency problem and helping to ensure that executives are not subject to incentives to perform in their own interests and contrary to the interests of the owners. Thus, executive pay structures aim to align the interests of management with those of the owners, usually by creating a balanced compensation package that includes performance-related remuneration based on long-term goals and that vests over a long term. The goals ideally include a mix of key performance indicators (KPIs) related to business and share price performance. Many of the incentives often come with some form of equity linkage—which can, on occasion, make risk management more focused on share price than on the performance of the business itself.

Accountability: Board Committees

The three key committees of the board, usually required by corporate governance codes, are established to respond to each of the key challenges discussed above (accountability and the board, accountability and accounts, and alignment and executive pay). These committees are:

- The **Nominations Committee** (in some markets, this is called the Corporate Governance Committee or some combination of these terms) aims to ensure that the board overall is balanced and effective, ensuring that management is accountable.

- The **Audit Committee** oversees financial reporting and the audit, delivering accountability in the accounts. The Audit Committee also oversees internal audits (where they exist) and is responsible for risk oversight unless there is a separate risk committee.
- The **Remuneration Committee** (in some markets, this is called the Compensation Committee) seeks to deliver a proper alignment of interests through executive pay.

The roles of these committees are considered more thoroughly in the next section.

2. FORMALIZED CORPORATE GOVERNANCE FRAMEWORKS

5.1.1 explain the evolution of corporate governance frameworks: development of corporate governance; roles and responsibilities; systems and processes; shareholder engagement; minority shareholder alignment

Corporate failures and scandals have been a powerful driver for the formalization of corporate governance and the development of codes. When companies fail and investors lose money, there is often pressure for an improved approach. Examples include the Walker Review,[1] following the 2008 financial crisis, and the recent Kingman[2] and Brydon[3] reviews in the wake of Carillion's failure.

See Scandals in Brief (below) for further (and international) discussion.

Corporate Governance Codes

The world's first formal corporate governance code emerged in the United Kingdom in 1992. The Cadbury Committee had been brought together in May 1991 by the Financial Reporting Council, the London Stock Exchange, and the accounting profession to consider what were called "the financial aspects of corporate governance." Its creation followed the Caparo and Polly Peck scandals.

Caparo had mounted a successful takeover bid for Fidelity, only to subsequently discover that Fidelity's profits were significantly overstated. The market had pumped up the share price of Polly Peck for years on the basis of financial reporting that later turned out to be misleading. The Cadbury Committee was created because of the perceived problems in accounting and governance. Once the committee began its work (but before the planned publication of its report), the Maxwell/Mirror Group scandal was beginning to emerge, and the Bank of Credit and Commerce International (BCCI) collapsed spectacularly in the wake of money laundering and other regulatory breaches. It was clear that much needed to change.

---

1 D. Walker, *A Review of Corporate Governance in UK Banks and Other Financial Industry Entities: Final Recommendations* (2009). Available at: https://webarchive.nationalarchives.gov.uk/+/www.hm-treasury.gov.uk/d/walker_review_261109.pdf.

2 Financial Reporting Council, *Financial Reporting Council: Review 2018* (2018). Available at: www.gov.uk/government/publications/financial-reporting-council-review-2018.

3 D. Brydon, *Assess, Assure and Inform: Improving Audit Quality and Effectiveness; Report of the Independent Review into the Quality and Effectiveness of Audit* (2019). Available at: https://assets.publishing.service.gov.uk/government/uploads/system/uploads/attachment_data/file/852960/brydon-review-final-report.pdf.

Much of what the Cadbury Committee recommended is still considered best practice today and has been incorporated into codes and guidelines globally. For example, the committee proposed that every public company should have an audit committee that meets at least twice a year. Notably, when the report was released, only two-thirds of the largest 250 companies in the UK had such committees at all (although nowadays they are commonplace). The report's core theme is that no individual should have "unfettered powers of decision"; so, for example, the roles of chair and CEO should not be combined, as they frequently were at the time.

A codified set of guidelines for good governance has grown from the basic concepts of accountability and alignment. Governance differs from country to country based on cultures and historical developments as well as local corporate law. At the most basic level, some countries, including Germany and the Netherlands, have **two-tier boards**, with wholly non-executive supervisory boards overseeing management boards; others have **single-tier boards**, with some dominated by executive directors (as in Japan), some having a combined CEO and chair (most commonly seen in the United States and France), and some lying in between these models (as in the UK).

The Cadbury Code model of recommendations with which companies should comply or explain any non-compliance has also been followed throughout much of the world. It is now highly unusual for any market to be without an official corporate governance code.

Since Japan adopted one in 2015, the USA is now the only major world market that does not have such a code, which is largely a consequence of corporate law being set at the individual state, rather than the federal, level. Most markets adopt the language of "comply or explain," although the Netherlands favors "apply or explain," and the Australians use the blunt "if not, why not?" The thought process, however, is the same: the code expects adherence to the relevant standard or the publication of a thoughtful and intelligent discussion of how the board delivers on the underlying principle. These discussions are gaining increased attention, not least because they offer the board an opportunity to explain how it operates to deliver value to the business on behalf of both shareholders and other stakeholders.

Companies' willingness to provide thoughtful discussions of their divergences from guidance varies. Some companies may look negatively on corporate governance, as they consider it inflexible. Indeed, there can be a risk that investors will approach corporate governance codes with inflexibility, expecting much more compliance than explanation—which is not the code's intent. Sometimes, this apparent inflexibility can arise from a failure of communication, particularly due to the reliance on proxy advisory firms (a highly concentrated group led by ISS and Glass Lewis) to mediate some of the discussions on governance and voting matters. These advisory firms tend to adhere to the details of corporate governance codes in giving recommendations on how their clients might vote. Some argue that it is the role of the proxy adviser to interpret the standards strictly, and it is for the actual shareholder to apply the flexibility that arises from a closer understanding of the specific circumstances of the individual company. Under this analysis, the problem of inflexibility may arise more from the investor client's tendency to follow the proxy adviser's recommendations, with too little independent judgment about whether those recommendations are the right ones, than from the strictness of the recommendations themselves.

These issues are discussed in more detail in Chapter 6.

Just as the Caparo and Polly Peck scandals sparked the establishment of the Cadbury Committee, and the Mirror Group and BCCI scandals provided a firm context for the publication and acceptance of its report, later scandals have continued to fuel the development of governance standards around the world:

- In the UK, shocks around pay levels at newly privatized utilities led to the **Greenbury Report**, which revised the UK's corporate governance code in 1995. It increased the visibility of remuneration structures and pressed toward transparency over the KPIs that drive performance pay and the time horizons over which pay is released (for long-term schemes, the time horizon is a minimum of three years).

- The Enron, Tyco, and WorldCom scandals in the USA led to the **Sarbanes-Oxley Act** in 2002. This law lifted expectations for greater integrity in financial reporting and created the Public Company Accounting Oversight Board (PCAOB) as the country's audit standard setter and inspector, establishing a standard for auditor independence and challenge.

- The 2003 failures at Ahold and Parmalat in the Netherlands and Italy, respectively, led to pressure for heightened standards of corporate governance and for both board and auditor independence across Europe. No longer could Europe pretend that Enron represented a problem isolated to the USA.

- The financial crisis of 2008 led to various changes around the world and to a renewed focus on corporate culture and executive pay as well as questions around audit. It also led to the creation of stewardship codes, in the UK initially and then around the world. Most notable of the legislative changes was the **2010 Dodd-Frank Act** in the USA (formally, the Dodd-Frank Wall Street Reform and Consumer Protection Act), which, among its multiple clauses, tightened standards for, and oversight of, banks.

- In Japan, the Olympus scandal of 2011–12 revealed long-running market deceit, whereby more than US$1.5bn (£1.07bn) in losses were hidden, apparently not for personal gain but to maintain the apparent health of the company and jobs for its workforce. When the much larger Toshiba revealed its own scandal of overstated profits in 2015, some felt that there might be something culturally wrong in Japanese companies that sought to hide the truth and failures of governance. The combination of these shocks has helped fuel the rapid advance of Japanese governance standards and also expectations for ESG disclosures across the market.

SCANDALS IN BRIEF

Enron (USA, 2001): An electric utility turned energy-trading business, Enron used a range of off-balance-sheet vehicles and other aggressive accounting techniques to appear hugely profitable, even on projects that had barely begun. Its collapse led to the dismantling of its auditor, Arthur Andersen, which split apart rapidly after some of its staff in Houston were discovered to have shredded documents linked to Enron and the US Securities and Exchange Commission's (SEC) investigation.

Governance failings included weak oversight of the executives (reinforced by the founder, Ken Lay, remaining as executive chair) by the non-executive directors. There were also failures of commission, most clearly the decision to waive the board's own code of conduct to enable the CFO to participate personally in some of the off-balance-sheet structures whose purpose was to facilitate the removal of losses from Enron's accounts.

HIH (Australia, 2001): This insurer collapsed before ever revealing the scale of its multi-million-dollar losses for the last six months of 2000. Having grown rapidly, insured aggressively, and under-reserved, the business had insufficient assets to cover its liabilities by a huge margin: the deficit was estimated to be up to AU$5.3bn (£2.7bn).

The Royal Commission that looked into the HIH scandal concluded that while the board was unusually well qualified (including insurance specialists and accounting experts), the way it operated was subservient to the CEO and failed to offer independent oversight and challenge. Management controlled the board agenda and the information provided to directors—who, in turn, failed to question assumptions and gain an independent view. The board also handled conflicts of interest poorly, or simply ignored them, and had only limited debate on major strategic decisions, including acquisitions.

Tyco International (USA/Bermuda, 2002): When losses mounted from unsuccessful deals by this aggressive Bermuda-incorporated acquisition vehicle, questions were raised about the behavior of CEO Dennis Kozlowski. Allegations centered on inflated profits, but also on ill-gotten earnings by senior management. In the end, the trial of Kozlowski and of CFO Mark Swartz centered on payments of US$150mn (£107mn), which they claimed the board had authorized as their remuneration. They were convicted, but the suggested level of actual theft is believed to have exceeded US$500mn (£359mn).

The culture at Tyco had long been one of lavish lifestyles for corporate leadership using corporate money and perks. Kozlowski had already grown accustomed to this culture prior to becoming CEO and extended it further. Deal-making (some 750 acquisitions in the four-year period up to 2001) became a basis for personal aggrandizement and even personal entertainment. Tyco apparently financed Kozlowski's wife's $2 million birthday party, for example. The board at best turned a blind eye to these behaviors, enabling this wasteful and unhealthy culture to persist.

WorldCom (USA, 2002): The internal audit function of this telecom business uncovered its use of one of the simplest accounting deceits—booking current expenses as capital investment, boosting profits by some US$3.8bn (£2.7bn). A subsequent investigation concluded that, in total, assets were exaggerated by US$11bn (£7.9bn). The fraud was undertaken to hide falling growth in a more challenging market.

At WorldCom, the board's checks and balances worked, although belatedly. An internal audit team uncovered suspicious transactions (or, rather, suspicious accounting treatments of transactions) and raised them with the chair of the audit committee. Though the chair did not immediately call a meeting of the committee, he did invite the internal audit team to discuss the issues directly with KPMG, the external auditor; in the meantime, the internal audit team persisted with its work and uncovered the full scale of the misleading accounting. When the committee was finally called, it confronted the executives leading the finance function with full evidence from the internal audit and with the support of KPMG. Executive departures and public announcements—and an SEC investigation—followed. So did bankruptcy.

Ahold (the Netherlands, 2002–03): Ahold was a Dutch grocery chain that went international through acquisitions, principally in the USA, in part because management had a 15% earnings growth target. Deteriorating performance was hidden through fraud—dubious joint venture accounting, hidden costs, and vendor rebates.

While making decisions to grow internationally, the board failed to ensure that its skills and its processes also developed so that it could oversee the new broader spread of the business. Instead, the US operations faced more limited oversight and challenge than they might have, allowing frauds to develop without being uncovered until they were very substantial.

Parmalat (Italy, 2003): False accounting spiraled from an initial 1990 decision by this Italian milk business to hide losses in its South American operations, mainly through inflating apparent revenues by double billing. In the end, in 2003, more than €4bn (£3.4bn) in cash and equivalents on the company's reported balance sheet turned out to be imaginary.

Parmalat's fraud began the way many frauds begin—accounting sleight of hand to cover up local losses. The fraud got so big because the losses persisted and the fraud was not uncovered for more than a decade, while the scale of the hole in the profits, and the efforts needed to conceal it, snowballed. Again, it appears that board oversight of international operations was less effective than it might have been. Further, audit checks and balances seem to have failed. At the time, Italy had a rule requiring a change in audit firm every nine years. Parmalat sidestepped this rule by changing the parent company's auditor, Grant Thornton, but retaining them internationally. The market missed signals that appear obvious in retrospect, not least Parmalat's reported profit margins being far in excess of peers'.

Satyam (India, 2009): The founder and chair admitted to falsifying the accounts of this IT services company. For around five years, the company had inflated revenues using thousands of false invoices; the auditor had apparently failed to check the bank statements that might have uncovered the fraud. The entire board was removed by regulators, the chair was jailed, and following a lengthy regulatory procedure, the company's auditor, PwC, was banned in 2018 from auditing any Indian public company for two years.

The founder's confession followed a proposed related-party transaction whereby Satyam would buy a real estate company from him. Though announced, the plan was retracted within a few hours after a highly negative response from shareholders—and the news that the World Bank would no longer do business with the company, barring it for eight years. The World Bank alleged that Satyam had provided improper benefits to its staff and had failed to provide proper accounts for its charges. Once problems emerged, as is so often the case, the fraud rapidly unraveled and the founder's losses in real estate ventures were revealed. The board had provided limited oversight and had perhaps believed the myth of the company's success and rapid growth. The extensive fraud was also missed by the audit process.

Olympus (Japan, 2011–12): Following his appointment, new CEO Michael Woodford soon became concerned about the profitability of Olympus. He was ousted but acted as a whistle-blower. Slowly it emerged that the Japanese camera maker had hidden losses for many years, principally through over-priced acquisitions whereby some of the excess fees paid were returned to the company to cover losses and shore up its finances.

Like many Japanese companies, Olympus was run by long-standing executives who had sought to protect the company at all costs, with remarkably few independent checks and balances. They had clearly concluded that hiding losses through convoluted schemes was preferable to honesty about the company's issues and the potential negative consequences for its workforce. Also, the supposedly independent oversight from the statutory auditors failed because they too appear to have lacked independence from the company (or at least enough of them did).

> **Volkswagen (Germany, 2015):** Volkswagen was revealed to have cheated on US emissions tests on its diesel engines through software, so-called defeat devices. Although, on the face of it, this was not a governance scandal, many investors had long been concerned about the lack of accountability at the German company, where the voting shares were predominantly held by the founding families, the local government, and the government of Qatar.
>
> The differential voting rights served to entrench these groups, enabling them to dominate the board. Management was thus able to operate in an insular and unaccountable way. Furthermore, the company's culture was driven by the view that engineers always knew best and that their actions were largely above criticism. The company needed an engineering response to the new diesel regulations, but when it failed to find one that worked on the road, it chose to seek one that at least worked during testing. The board, accustomed to not having to listen to external voices, never felt the need to ask enough questions to uncover the issue.
>
> **Wirecard (Germany, 2020):** Wirecard, a hard-driving fintech and global payments processor, collapsed in June 2020 when long-running allegations of fraud and questionable accounting were largely confirmed by a special audit. The audit revealed that some €1.9bn (£1.6bn) were missing from its accounts. It became apparent that substantial elements of its business in the Middle East and Asia were no more than an elaborate sham and that the core payments-processing operations in Europe were barely profitable.
>
> One of the most remarkable aspects of the scandal was the way that the press investigation—persistently pursued by the *Financial Times*—was fought at each step by the German regulator, BaFin, which was supposed to be overseeing the business. Apparently, both the regulator and the board were so taken by the opportunity for Europe to build its own fintech star that they failed to spot the red flags about the business and failed to ask enough questions as it expanded overseas. The auditor also failed to identify warning signs, especially around the overseas operations.

SHAREHOLDER ENGAGEMENT AND ALIGNMENT

5.1.1 explain the evolution of corporate governance frameworks: development of corporate governance; roles and responsibilities; systems and processes; shareholder engagement; minority shareholder alignment

Shareholder engagement is the active dialogue between companies and their investors, with the latter expressing clear views about areas of concern (which often include ESG matters). Engagement helps ensure that the board directors are accountable for their actions, which hopefully in time helps to improve the quality of their decision-making.

Engagement is discussed in depth in Chapter 6.

For minority shareholders—which institutional investors will almost always be—a crucial issue is that they not be exploited by the dominant or controlling shareholders. In many cases, protections for minorities are built into company law, and they often exist in listing rules and other formal protections. These protections are usually bolstered by corporate governance codes, but the issues are so fundamental (because they relate to avoiding exploitation of minorities and protection of their ownership rights) that in most countries, minority shareholders benefit from underlying legal protections.

Exploitation of minorities could involve money being siphoned out of the business in ways that benefit the controlling shareholders but not the wider shareholder base, which explains why there are typically higher disclosure requirements around related-party transactions and rights for non-conflicted shareholders to approve them. Minority shareholders will also be unwilling to see the company they invested in change dramatically without their having the chance to vote on the issue. For example, in the UK listing regime, class tests are applied as follows:

- If a transaction affects more than 5% of any of a company's assets, profits, value, or capital, there must be additional disclosures (Class 2 transactions).
- If a transaction affects more than 25% of any of a company's assets, profits, value, or capital, there must be a shareholder vote to approve the deal based on detailed justifications (Class 1 transactions).

Another key area for shareholder protection is pre-emption rights. These rights ensure that an investor has the ability to maintain its position in the company. Fundamental to many markets' company laws (though not, for example, in the USA) is the idea that a company should not issue shares without giving existing shareholders the right to buy an amount sufficient to maintain their existing shareholding. Because these rights come before the prerogative of potential external investors, they are called pre-emptive, and the existence of these rights is why a large equity fundraising by companies is often called a "rights issue."

As rights issues are cumbersome, particularly if a company is issuing a relatively small number of shares, companies typically seek authority at AGMs to issue a relatively small proportion of shares (up to 5% or 10%) non-pre-emptively—that is, without having to offer them fairly to existing shareholders. Investors are usually prepared to grant such authority but with certain protections in place. Even where issues are not on a fully pre-emptive basis, there is usually an expectation that the larger institutional shareholders will be offered a so-called soft pre-emption, meaning an allocation equivalent to their existing shareholding but in a less formal, less legalistic way (which may enable the issuance to be made more swiftly). Larger issuances are more controversial, as are issues at a price possibly less than the prevailing share price. An example of a particularly unpopular model with defenders of minority shareholder rights is the "general mandate" resolutions in Hong Kong SAR, which seek to enable issuance of up to 20% of the share capital, potentially at a discount. There is a clear detriment from such transactions to the existing shareholders.

A final area in which minority shareholders can feel exploited is the mechanism of dual-class shares. Typically, one of the classes is restricted to the founders of a company (or a limited group chosen early in a company's life), who receive multiple votes compared to the class of shares that subsequent shareholders can invest in—the shares that are usually more freely traded on the stock market (and those issued freely as compensation to staff, particularly in the case of US technology businesses). Moreover, management, which typically benefits directly from multiple voting rights and often voting control, will feel less accountable to the broader shareholder base, with whose interests management is less aligned.

Dual-class shares are often frowned upon by many investors and are rare outside the USA (though Volkswagen, as discussed in the Scandals in Brief section, is a European example). They are, however, becoming more visible and more common because of the current success of technology businesses, the founders of which have been keen to retain voting control. The Council for Institutional Investors, the main organization for US institutions, has taken a nuanced stance on dual-class stock,[4] recognizing that it can provide some stability in the early life of a company, but urging that it be subject to sunset clauses so the two classes are unified after, at most, seven years (the time horizon after which academic evidence suggests that dual-class stock will usually have a negative performance impact). Controversially, Snap Inc. (the parent company of Snapchat) took the dual-class stock route further and issued shares without any voting rights at all; indeed, given that the company indicated there was little likelihood of a dividend, the instruments sold were actually more like warrants than shares.

CHARACTERISTICS OF EFFECTIVE CORPORATE GOVERNANCE: BOARD STRUCTURE AND EXECUTIVE REMUNERATION

5.1.2 assess key characteristics of effective corporate governance, and the main reasons why they may not be implemented or upheld: board structure, diversity, effectiveness, and independence; executive remuneration, performance metrics, and key performance indicators (KPIs); reporting and transparency; financial integrity and capital allocation; business ethics

The current iteration of the Corporate Governance Code in the UK was published in 2018. It includes 18 principles under five themes:

- board leadership and company purpose;
- division of responsibilities;
- composition, succession, and evaluation;
- audit, risk, and internal control; and
- remuneration.

These themes are consistent across most of the world's corporate governance codes, as are (largely) the expectations and duties of the three principal board committees that almost all major companies have in place:

- the audit committee (sometimes the audit and risk committee);
- the nominations committee (sometimes the corporate governance committee or some combination of the two); and
- the remuneration committee (or the compensation committee in the USA; some companies also now incorporate into the name some reflection of a responsibility to the broader employee base).

The expectation is that the audit and remuneration committees will be populated solely by independent non-executive directors, and such directors should form a majority of the nominations committee (the chair should not lead this committee while it is seeking to appoint a successor). Some companies will establish other board committees to address issues ad hoc or on an ongoing basis, but they should use appropriate judgment in how those committees should best be populated. For example, most financial services businesses now have a separate risk committee, which is

---

4 Council of Institutional Investors, *Dual-Class Stock* (2021). Available at: www.cii.org/dualclass_stock.

usually made up of independent non-executive directors. Other companies may have sustainability committees, or committees considering their key operational risks—such as a people committee at companies highly dependent on their workforce or a health and safety committee. Such committees assist the board in overseeing major exposures and in dealing with the workload of oversight. They are not compulsory, and certainly at smaller businesses, this workload is likely to be handled by the audit committee or by the board itself. The Code also determines appropriate disclosures to make the workings of the board transparent and to demonstrate their effectiveness to shareholders.

Published alongside the 2018 Code was a *Guide to Board Effectiveness*, which applies the same structure as the Code under the same five themes. It provides not only guidance but also questions to assist board members in considering whether they are being fully effective in their roles. The guide also provides questions that board members might choose to ask management to gain additional clarity on corporate culture. Almost half of the main body of the guide is taken up with the first theme, board leadership and company purpose—essentially, this theme focuses on culture, strategy, and maintaining appropriate relationships with key stakeholders. While this guide is a UK document that is explicitly aimed at assisting boards, the themes are useful to investors in considering the effectiveness of governance globally.

Board Structure, Diversity, Effectiveness, and Independence

As governance at its core is about people, the key to exercising effective governance is having the right people with relevant skills and experience around the boardroom table, as well as having the right board culture to enable each of them to contribute effectively to boardroom debate.

This goal is easily summarized but difficult to achieve. As can be seen from the case study sample of BHP's annual report disclosures on its board skills and diversity, there are multiple skills that boards seek to have available within the boardroom, often many more than the number of individual directors. If an issue is of high importance to the business, the usual expectation is that more than one person should have knowledge of that issue, because a board will rarely feel comfortable relying on a single perspective, particularly as that person may not always be available. Compromises need to be made, and plans need to be considered for the future to prepare for expected departures from the board—and to respond to unexpected changes (such as death or conflicts of interest). Of course, a board can have access to specialist skills through advice from experts invited to present at board meetings or to provide input in other ways. A question to consider is what skills and experience are regularly needed around the boardroom table and what skills and experience would be better accessed on an occasional, independent advisory basis.

One skill set, or at least depth of understanding, increasingly expected for every board concerns climate change—as highlighted by the specific attention to this issue in the BHP disclosures. Not every board can have a climate scientist, and indeed few boards may actually want one. But all boards need to be competent in dealing with the business complexities of the issues around climate change, so that they can appropriately consider how to adjust their business models and investment approach to reflect the coming scrutiny on greenhouse gas emissions. A company that fails to consider this issue is likely to misspend capital expenditures either currently or in the near future, as it invests in assets that will not have the same value in a carbon-constrained world—having a board with climate change competency could help avoid this waste. To achieve this goal, it is likely that education and training will be needed, for at least some directors. A growing number of appropriate courses are available. Boards may also increasingly have to consider skills and training in other areas, such as environmental and social risk.

As well as training for directors, boards must consider the need for refreshment of skills, which have a half-life and will decrease over time. The needs of the board will also change over time as its strategy evolves, and it is important to keep the skills matrix updated. The issue of director tenure and independence is discussed below.

There are many types of diversity needed for a board to be successful, though the most important is diversity of thought. The other types include diversity of gender, race, age, culture, nationality, economic background, and experience, each of which can also often help to deliver diversity of thought. The aim is to avoid groupthink in the boardroom, which may lead to a lack of questioning and challenge.

While this broad concept of diversity—diversity of thought—is well understood, most diversity initiatives focus on the most visible issues: gender and race. A number of markets now have quotas for female directors (notably Norway, which pioneered the approach, and France), and most are moving toward an expectation that at least 30% of public company directors should be women. The issue of racial diversity has been actively debated in the USA for some years, and the UK's 2017 Parker Review called for at least one non-white director on every FTSE-100 company board by 2021 and on every FTSE-250 board by 2024.[5] A 2022 update of the review (https://assets.ey.com/content/dam/ey-sites/ey-com/en_uk/topics/diversity/ey-what-the-parker-review-tells-us-about-boardroom-diversity.pdf) noted that 89 of the FTSE-100 companies had met the goal by the end of 2021 and that some 55% of the FTSE-250 had also already reached the goal. These initiatives gained fresh impetus from the momentum of the Black Lives Matter campaign in 2020, which could mean that more change is likely.

An effective chair brings out the contributions of each board member, which is less visible to outsiders but is a vital part of delivering board effectiveness. Investors can gain some insight into how the chair operates in the boardroom from direct dialogue with the chair and with other board members, but often the clearest indicator is the quality of the individuals on the board overall. Good directors tend not to join boards that do not allow them to contribute effectively, or if they do, they are quick to leave them. The unfortunate consequence of all this for those who invest broadly is that weak boards tend to remain weak and it is difficult to improve them without substantive changes.

Board appraisals (sometimes known as board assessments or self-assessments) are required under many corporate governance codes and can help boards to become more effective by bringing problems to the surface. Some investors are often cynical about these appraisals, as weak boards and weak chairs can relatively easily limit their impact without its being apparent to investors. It is hard to determine whether a board appraisal has been effective—though it has a better chance of succeeding if it is an external process with an independent facilitator rather than simply an internal review. In some markets, both the delivery and the findings of board appraisals are expected to be disclosed, which can help investors gain insight into a company.

---

5 UK Government, *Ethnic Diversity of UK Boards: The Parker Review* (2017). Available at: www.gov.uk/government/publications/ethnic-diversity-of-uk-boards-the-parker-review.

CASE STUDIES

BHP Annual Report 2021, pp. 82–83: Disclosures on Board Skills, including Specifically on Climate Change Matters and Diversity

Board Skills and Experience

Total Directors	**12**

Mining — 4
Senior executive who has:

- deep operating or technical mining experience with a large company operating in multiple countries;
- successfully optimized and led a suite of large, global, complex operating assets that have delivered consistent and sustaining levels of high performance (related to cost, returns and throughputs);
- successfully led exploration projects with proven results and performance;
- delivered large capital projects that have been successful in terms of performance and returns; and
- a proven record in terms of health, safety and environmental performance and results.

Oil and gas — 2
Senior executive who has:

- deep technical and operational oil and gas experience with a large company operating in multiple countries;
- successfully led production operations that have delivered consistent and sustaining levels of high performance (related to cost, returns and throughputs);
- successfully led exploration projects with proven results and performance;
- delivered large capital projects that have been successful in terms of performance and returns; and
- a proven record in terms of health, safety and environmental performance and results.

Global experience — 10
Global experience working in multiple geographies over an extended period of time, including a deep understanding of and experience with global markets, and the macro-political and economic environment.

Strategy — 11
Experience in enterprise-wide strategy development and implementation in industries with long cycles, and developing and leading business transformation strategies.

Risk — 12
Experience and deep understanding of systemic risk and monitoring risk management frameworks and controls, and the ability to identify key emerging and existing risks to the organisation.

Commodity value chain expertise — 8
End-to-end value or commodity chain experience – understanding of consumers, marking demand drivers (including specific geographic markets) and other aspects of commodity chain development.

Characteristics of Effective Corporate Governance: Board Structure and Executive Remuneration

Total Directors	12
Financial expertise Extensive relevant experience in financial regulation and the capability to evaluate financial statements and understand key financial drivers of the business, bringing a deep understanding of corporate finance, internal financial controls and experience probing the adequacy of financial and risk controls.	12
Relevant public policy expertise Extensive experience specifically and explicitly focused on public policy or regulatory matters, including ESG (in particular climate change) and community issues, social responsibility and transformation, and economic issues.	5
Health, safety, environment and community Extensive experience with complex workplace health, safety, environmental, and community risks and frameworks.	10
Technology Recent experience and expertise with the development, selection, and implementation of leading and business transforming technology and innovation, and responding to digital disruption.	5
Capital allocation and cost efficiency Extensive direct experience gained through a senior executive role in capital allocation discipline, cost efficiency	11

Twelve Directors meet the criteria of financial expertise outlined above. The Risk and Audit Committee Report contains details of how its members meet the relevant legal and regulatory requirements in relation to financial experience.

Board Skills and Experience: Climate Change

"Board members bring experience from a range of sectors, including resources, energy, finance, technology and public policy. The Board also seeks the input of management and other independent advisers. This equips them to consider potential implications of climate change on BHP and its operational capacity, as well as understand the nature of the debate and the international policy response as it develops. In addition, there is a deep understanding of systemic risk and the potential impacts on our portfolio.

The Board has taken measures designed to ensure its decisions are informed by climate change science and expert advisers. The Board seeks the input of management (including Dr Fiona Wild, our Vice President Sustainability and Climate Change) and other independent advisers. In addition, our Forum on Corporate Responsibility (which includes Don Henry, former CEO of the Australian Conservation Foundation and Changhua Wu, former Greater China Director, the Climate Group) advises operational management teams and engages with the Sustainability Committee and the Board as appropriate."

Board Tenure and Diversity (as at 30 June 2021)

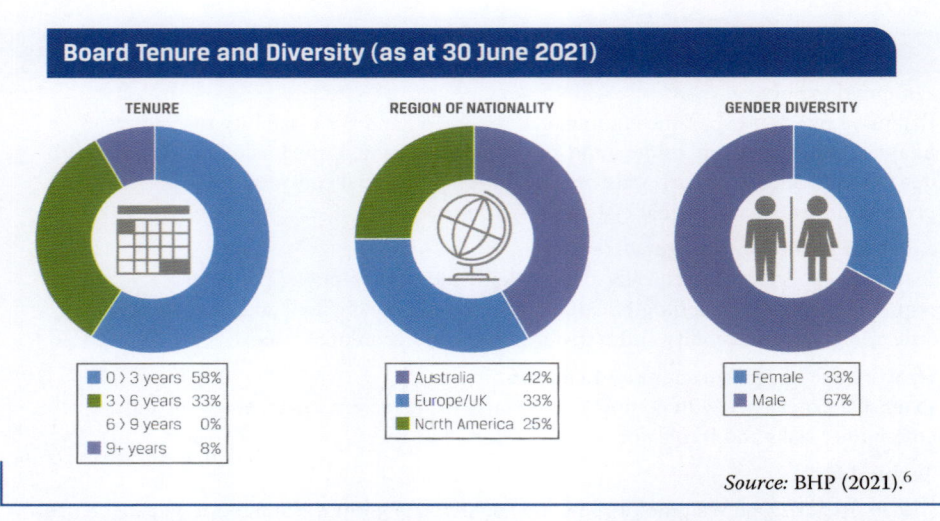

TENURE
- 0 › 3 years 58%
- 3 › 6 years 33%
- 6 › 9 years 0%
- 9+ years 8%

REGION OF NATIONALITY
- Australia 42%
- Europe/UK 33%
- North America 25%

GENDER DIVERSITY
- Female 33%
- Male 67%

Source: BHP (2021).[6]

Board independence is also a key concern. The aim must be to have a board that is independent of the management team and operates with independence of thought so that it can challenge both management and previous decision-making at the company (including prior board decisions).

The ICGN's Global Governance Principles set out an unusually complete investor perspective on independence criteria; these extend and elucidate some of the criteria embedded in standards in various Codes around the world. These criteria suggest that there will be questions about the independence of an individual who:

▶ had been an executive at the company or a subsidiary, or an adviser to the company, and there was not an appropriate gap between their employment and joining the board;

▶ receives, or has received, incentive pay from the company, or receives fees additional to directors' fees;

▶ has close family ties with any of the company's advisers, directors, or senior management;

▶ holds cross-directorships or has significant links with other directors through involvement in other companies or bodies;

▶ is a significant shareholder in the company, or is an officer of, or otherwise associated with, a significant shareholder, or is a nominee or formal representative of a shareholder or the state; and

▶ has been a director of the company for a long enough period that their independence may have become compromised.

The intent is not to suggest that boards should never include directors whose independence is questioned. Indeed, such individuals may provide useful skills and perspectives. However, every board needs a sufficient weight of clearly independent individuals so that it is able to operate independently and is not subject to bias or inappropriate influence. Investors recognize that independence is a state of mind, and that some individuals can be fully independent notwithstanding some of the issues raised, while others, whatever their appearance of independence, will support only a CEO or a dominant shareholder. One of the challenges for investors is being able to identify both sorts of individuals.

---

[6] BHP, *Annual Report 2021* (2021). Available at: https://www.bhp.com/investors/annual-reporting/annual-report-2021.

Characteristics of Effective Corporate Governance: Board Structure and Executive Remuneration

Most investors would prefer that a company acknowledge that an individual will not be perceived as independent (for one of the various reasons) but will nevertheless bring real value to the business, rather than assert that the individual remains fully independent notwithstanding some obvious challenge(s). As ever, the way a board approaches an issue in its disclosures will determine how shareholders consider it.

The issue of length of tenure on the board and independence is generally recognized around the world (though it is not acknowledged as an issue in some major markets, most notably the USA), though different standards are applied. As can be seen in Exhibit 2 (from the OECD Corporate Governance Factbook 2019), different markets have different expectations as to how long it takes for independence to erode. Investors may often seek to apply a single global standard, while companies may expect that their local standard will be respected.

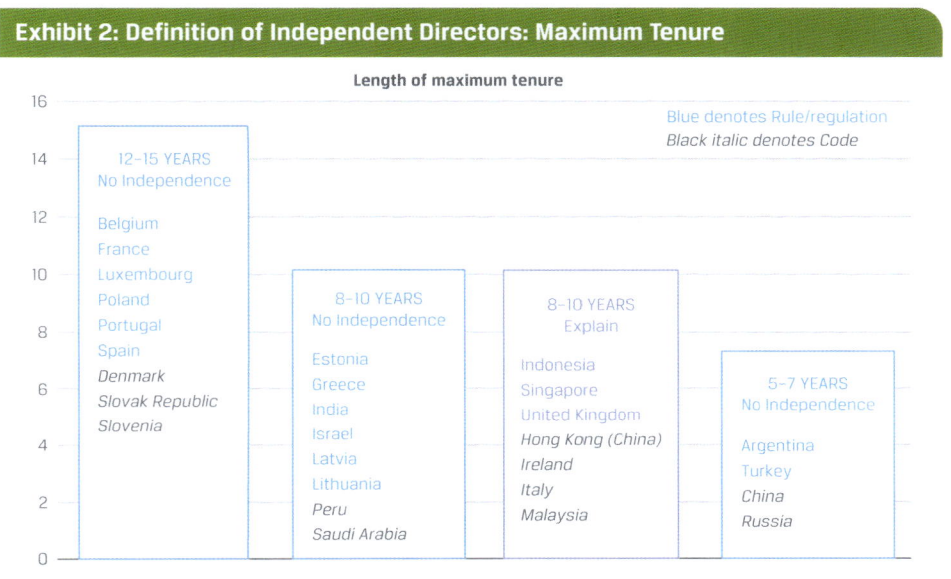

Exhibit 2: Definition of Independent Directors: Maximum Tenure

Length of maximum tenure

Blue denotes Rule/regulation
Black italic denotes Code

12–15 YEARS — No Independence
Belgium
France
Luxembourg
Poland
Portugal
Spain
Denmark
Slovak Republic
Slovenia

8–10 YEARS — No Independence
Estonia
Greece
India
Israel
Latvia
Lithuania
Peru
Saudi Arabia

8–10 YEARS — Explain
Indonesia
Singapore
United Kingdom
Hong Kong (China)
Ireland
Italy
Malaysia

5–7 YEARS — No Independence
Argentina
Turkey
China
Russia

Blue denotes Rule or Regulation. *Black italic denotes Code.*

The countries that apply an "Explain" standard are essentially asserting a rebuttable presumption that the relevant individual is not independent; if a company wishes to argue that the individual remains independent notwithstanding their tenure, an explanation is needed, which shareholders may or may not accept.

Source: OECD (2019).[7]

Executive Remuneration

Pay is where the clearest conflict of interest between management and shareholders occurs. As (in public companies at least) it is not possible for investors to negotiate pay directly with management, shareholders need to rely on remuneration committees to do so effectively on their behalf, and they need to have confidence that the non-executive directors on those committees will negotiate well and with shareholder interests in mind.

---

[7] OECD, *OECD Corporate Governance Factbook 2019* (2019). Available at: www.oecd.org/corporate/corporate-governance-factbook.htm.

There is a broader challenge, however: the directors' obligation is to the success of the individual company, while shareholders, in most cases, have an eye to the broader market. Therefore, while shareholders may be more concerned about a ratcheting effect of increased pay across the market as a whole (often driven by companies seeking to respond to pay benchmarks and remain competitive in terms of remuneration), directors will want to ensure the best possible candidate is appointed to their company, which may tempt them to pay up for the given individual. Often, many of the arguments about executive pay arise directly from this difference between the mindsets of the board and the shareholders.

While pay levels differ in different markets, the pay structures for top executives are broadly similar. In brief, executive pay structures in much of the world come in four categories:

- fixed salary, usually increased annually;
- benefits, including pension (typically calculated as a percentage of the salary, often at a more generous rate than is enjoyed by the wider employee base);
- annual bonus; and
- share-linked incentive (usually in the form of a long-term incentive plan, or LTIP).

While the scale of fixed salaries, and the way in which they increase (often ahead of inflation in general wages), can be controversial, most attention is focused on the variable incentives: the bonus and equity-linked portions. Bonuses are typically calculated on the basis of annual performance against metrics (often called key performance indicators, or KPIs) set at the start of a year; they are paid in cash at the end of the year—though increasingly some of the bonus is deferred for a further two or three years, often into shares that are released only at the end of the deferral period. The KPIs for bonuses will predominantly be financial metrics (usually profit-related), but often around 20% of the KPIs concern personal performance or non-financial measures, including ESG factors. Investor expectations on this matter have shifted notably in the last few years, and it is now a predominant view that at least a portion of the bonus should be driven by such ESG metrics—typically, factors that are closely aligned with the strategic aims of the business.

The longer-term equity rewards usually measure performance over at least three years and are typically paid out in shares that must be held for a further period (currently the expected minimum overall period, including the performance period and lock-up thereafter, is five or more years). Performance for these schemes is usually measured by broad-brush financial metrics, typically a combination of total shareholder return (TSR) and earnings per share (EPS).

While this brief discussion may sound complex, it is a significant simplification, as can be seen by looking at the multiple pages devoted to remuneration in an annual report.

Trust, or a lack of it, has driven much of the problem with executive reward. This issue has developed because of failures of understanding between investors who see ongoing payments for poor performance and corporations that find shareholders voting against schemes they have supported for years or have previously indicated they will support. Companies are faced with various views from investors, many of which are incompatible and so strongly held that they allow little flexibility. The fear of significant votes against a board's remuneration proposals leads many companies to produce a compromised structure, rather than something the directors fully believe will drive value in the business. This action can lead to a further escalation of quantum (the amount paid to executives, aggregated across all forms of remuneration), as a compromised structure means that executives lack confidence they can deliver what is needed to unlock the company's full potential. The higher quantum also leads to media and investor attention, and tension between the company and its shareholders is likely to escalate.

Disputes also arise from other differences in mindset. Investors tend to look for pay outcomes that match the corporate performance they enjoy as shareholders, and they are unlikely to oppose even the most generous packages when share price performance is strong (though there is increasing evidence that US companies in particular are testing the boundaries of this shareholder indifference to quantum—for instance, the 34% shareholder opposition in the say-on-pay vote at Apple's 2022 AGM, where the company's generous executive rewards raised concerns for shareholders, even given its stellar business and share price performance). Companies tend to consider performance within the business itself (seeing the share price as a function of market sentiment as much as business performance), and directors believe they need to honor contractual obligations, paying out according to the terms of the agreed incentives. This situation can sometimes lead to a disconnect in expectations: the reward that is due under the contractual incentives may seem excessive to shareholders because it does not reflect the market performance of the shares.

Overcoming these differing perspectives is necessary, but as yet no proposed alternative structure has gained sufficient traction among both investors and companies to become the universal solution to the problem.

Discussions about executive pay are also complicated by concerns about fairness and the extent to which executive pay outcomes far exceed the experience of ordinary people, as exemplified by the pay ratio disclosures now mandated by some markets (notably the UK and the USA). These disclosures compare the remuneration of the CEO with that of the firm's average-paid worker and reveal very sizable differences, often hundreds to one. While investors will often have sympathy for companies that are keen to have the best leadership, the growing tensions about income and wealth disparity make the question of fairness, as exemplified by pay ratios, an issue that is increasingly hard to ignore. These considerations are part of what is now driving the debate about the overall quantum of executive pay.

CHARACTERISTICS OF EFFECTIVE CORPORATE GOVERNANCE: TRANSPARENCY, CAPITAL ALLOCATION, AND BUSINESS ETHICS

5.1.2 assess key characteristics of effective corporate governance, and the main reasons why they may not be implemented or upheld: board structure, diversity, effectiveness, and independence; executive remuneration, performance metrics, and key performance indicators (KPIs); reporting and transparency; financial integrity and capital allocation; business ethics

Reporting and Transparency

Principle N of the 2018 Corporate Governance Code states:

"The board should present a fair, balanced and understandable assessment of the company's position and prospects."[8]

The starting responsibility for the oversight of company reporting sits with the audit committee, but as Principle N indicates, this responsibility is shared by the whole board. The phrase "fair, balanced and understandable" was arrived at after considerable debate and has led many companies to undertake a rigorous restructuring of their processes and reporting. Reporting and transparency are led first by the management team and then overseen by the audit committee and the board as a whole. Independent challenge then comes from the auditor.

Investors often learn much about the management team from their reporting. That is especially true where a company appears to be masking a weakening performance. One way in which this masking is sometimes done is through alternative performance metrics (APMs). These measures are adjusted forms of the accounting standard–approved measures of performance, often referred to as "adjusted" or "underlying." Their use sometimes indicates a management that is keen to flatter performance rather than admit a failure to generate better performance, as the omission of elements through these adjustments may be difficult to justify objectively. Investors are particularly wary when the APM calculations vary from one reporting period to another. A further indicator of an attempt to obscure an issue is where numbers in the narrative disclosures of the annual report do not entirely tally with the numbers revealed in the financial accounts in the back half of the report.

One area where there is a particular danger of inconsistency between the narrative and the financial reporting, and currently a major concern to many institutional investors, is climate change. Too often, the fine words in the narrative reporting in response to the Task Force on Climate-related Financial Disclosures (TCFD) and other reporting standards are not reflected in changes to the associated financial reporting. The International Accounting Standards Board (IASB), which sets the International Financial Reporting Standards (IFRS) for most of the world, has recently commented that material climate issues should be reflected in financial reporting, and the Principles for Responsible Investment (PRI) and other institutions have called on companies and their auditors to ensure that this reporting is delivered in practice.[9]

The area of reporting on environmental and social factors is rapidly developing. New Zealand and the UK were the first countries to mandate that all large public companies must report according to TCFD standards, but they will not be the last.

In collaboration with the International Organization of Securities Commissions (IOSCO), the IFRS Foundation announced at COP26 the formation of a new International Sustainability Standards Board (ISSB). (IOSCO, the international body that brings together the world's securities regulators, is recognized as the global standard setter for the securities sector; COP26, held in 2021, was the 26th UN global summit to address climate change.)

The ISSB will develop a comprehensive global baseline of high-quality sustainability disclosure standards to meet investors' information needs and will consolidate the Climate Disclosure Standards Board (CDSB, an initiative of CDP) and the Value Reporting Foundation (VRF, which houses the Integrated Reporting Framework and the SASB Standards) into the IFRS Foundation.

---

[8] Financial Reporting Council, *The UK Corporate Governance Code*. Available at: www.frc.org.uk/getattachment/88bd8c45-50ea-4841-95b0-d2f4f48069a2/2018-UK-Corporate-Governance-Code-FINAL.pdf.

[9] Principles for Responsible Investment (PRI), *Accounting for Climate Change* (2020). Available at: www.unpri.org/sustainability-issues/accounting-for-climate-change; See also Flying Blind: The Glaring Absence of Climate Risks in Financia Reporting. Available at https://carbontracker.org/flying-blind-pr/.

This new body will have a multi-location structure, drawing together many of the disparate groups independently seeking to set sustainability reporting standards. It aims to ensure that the different needs of the various regions are reflected as the standards are developed.

The advent of ISSB provides the potential for unprecedented uniformity based on a consistent common standard of high-quality sustainability reporting, assessment, and analysis.

A strong audit committee should strictly oversee the reporting process to ensure fair and balanced reporting, preventing these sorts of discrepancies from occurring. A strong and challenging auditor, assisted by regulations, should also intervene to prevent any misleading of investors. Auditors also have a specific duty to highlight any apparent inconsistencies between the financial statements and other reporting by the company.

The European Securities and Markets Authority (ESMA) published a set of guidelines on the use of APMs in 2015.[10] These guidelines require consistency, with the APMs not to be disclosed more prominently than the official measures and with a full reconciliation between the two. Unfortunately, enforcement of these standards is variable.

In a similar way, in December 2019 the IASB published an *Exposure Draft on Primary Financial Statements*, which would allow the disclosure of a management-preferred measure of performance on the face of the income statement—but only alongside the permitted standard measures and with a full reconciliation between them.[11] The IASB continues to consider how best to respond to the feedback it has received. It remains to be seen how effectively companies will respond to any new standard.

See the section titled "Corporate Governance and the Independent Audit Function" for a detailed discussion of audit and the challenges that arise in that area.

Financial Integrity and Capital Allocation

The key concern active shareholders usually have about a company's strategy is capital allocation (the way a company applies its financial resources to generate the most value over the long term). Key questions to be asked include how much of its cash flow does it distribute to shareholders and how much does it reinvest in existing or new business activities. It is rare for a company to have large enough resources to pursue every opportunity it identifies, and so capital allocation is as much about what a company will *not* do as about what it will. These investment decisions are crucial—whether a company can successfully deliver on them will determine the returns the company receives over future years.

Often, in part, capital allocation is a function of history: a company retains a legacy business operation, even a sizable operating business, when the opportunity for the company as a whole has in fact moved on. Shareholders can be more clear-minded than management about disposing of older businesses or operations—often, perhaps, because they may not understand the full complexities that would be involved in fully moving on from the legacy activity nor be fully aware of the consequences for stakeholders. Even where the issue is not a legacy activity, most companies have to make decisions that will see their business operations diverge over time. Conglomerates are now firmly out of favor, and most investors prefer to invest in focused businesses—with

---

10 European Securities and Markets Authority (ESMA), *ESMA Guidelines on Alternative Performance Measures* (2015). Available at: www.esma.europa.eu/press-news/esma-news/esma-publishes-final-guidelines-alternative-performance-measures.
11 IFRS Foundation, *Exposure Draft and Comment Letters: General Presentation and Disclosures (Primary Financial Statements)* (2019). Available at: www.ifrs.org/projects/work-plan/primary-financial-statements/comment-letters-projects/ed-primary-financial-statements/.

investors themselves providing diversification across their portfolio holdings. The crucial decision for the boards of such companies is how to allocate capital among the various businesses and make the most of the opportunities they have identified. Even where there is no active investor pressing for a different approach to capital allocation, the board may need to have an active dialogue with the shareholder base because different decisions about which business opportunities to pursue will appeal to different investors. In particular, some of the capital allocation options may require a change in the dividend payout to ensure that more resources can be retained for reinvestment in the business.

In a similar way, the capital structure of a company is a crucial area of debate within the boardroom and between the board and shareholders. Companies without debt on their balance sheets are often thought to be inefficient and failing to deliver the full extent of possible returns—failing to maximize return on equity. However, the 2008 financial crisis—and the more recent challenges to business resilience arising from the COVID-19 pandemic—reminded all investors that there is a danger in seeking to load companies with excess debt in order to generate greater returns on the remaining equity capital. That danger is the risk of insolvency if interest rates rise and/or if there is a downturn in the business. Having a sustainable capital structure means there must be some compromise between the extremes of maximizing returns on equity in the short term and making the company entirely robust to a downturn. Unless the company is operating in a highly volatile business (where the gearing is operational rather than financial), the board should seek to optimize the capital structure by taking on some debt.

A key financial resilience question that boards will need to answer is how they strike a balance between full resilience and maximizing short-term returns. Many shareholders will be willing to sacrifice some short-term returns so the business will be strong enough to survive a downturn. The experience of the COVID-19 pandemic has reminded investors and company boards that having such a buffer is good stewardship of a business in the long term. But the prudent balance is delicate: most shareholders would not wish businesses to be so financially secure that they could cope with any financial crisis. The multiple fundraisings by companies during the pandemic demonstrated this point in practice: good businesses with long-term futures were refinanced.

Decisions regarding share buybacks and the issuance of shares are key elements of these overall capital structure decisions and should be considered as such by both boards and shareholders. Similarly, considerations with regard to the payment of dividends to shareholders need to encompass decisions about what is a sustainable level of capital to support ongoing business success. Paying dividends beyond the cash flow from the business is clearly not sustainable and is likely to raise significant questions among shareholders, even though they may welcome the immediate cash payments. But the opposite circumstance—a low dividend payout ratio—is also likely to cause concerns, especially if the company already has significant cash on its balance sheet. This latter circumstance has proved central to disagreements between several Japanese companies and their shareholders over recent years

Business Ethics

A company needs to abide by the laws of its home country (formally known as its country of incorporation), and a multinational group must act within the laws of any country in which it operates. In some respects, such as bribery and corruption, many jurisdictions impose extraterritorial laws, meaning that a company can be guilty of an offense anywhere in the world it is involved in corruption. For example, both the USA's Foreign Corrupt Practices Act and the UK's Bribery Act have extraterritorial effect; the latter also explicitly requires every company to maintain procedures to ensure that no bribery is carried out by agents or others on its behalf.

Many companies, particularly those based in legalistic environments, tend to believe that obedience to the law is sufficient. However, many investors expect more than that, and companies aspiring to be responsible world citizens and to enjoy ownership on the public markets will need to go further. Companies need to operate while being conscious of business ethics and broader responsibilities to stakeholders and communities. By doing so, they are more likely to prosper in the long term, not least because a failure to deliver on these ethical aims may lead to a breakdown in relations with one or more key stakeholders. At its extreme, an ethical failure might lead to a loss of license to operate in a market or even as a business. An ethical approach to business will encompass such issues as:

- corporate culture and having a set of expected behavioral standards for all staff, not tolerating inappropriate behaviors;
- treating employees fairly by upholding high standards in health and safety, human rights, and avoiding modern slavery;
- offering value to customers and avoiding discriminatory or other exploitative behavior, including avoiding collusion with rivals or other anti-competitive activity;
- avoiding bribery and corruption, and fraudulent behavior;
- paying suppliers appropriately and promptly, and not seeking unfair benefit from any dominant negotiating position;
- developing appropriate relationships with local communities close to relevant business operations, and being ready to enter into dialogue on any key concerns they may have;
- approaching any regulatory or political lobbying activity honestly (including ensuring that the lobbying is not inconsistent with the company's publicly stated approach to particular issues) and without seeking unfair advantage;
- seeking to pay a fair and appropriate level of tax by approaching tax compliantly and recognizing that tax avoidance, not just tax evasion, can be inappropriate; and
- acknowledging that a company's reputation is a valuable asset that can be harmed by unethical or inappropriate behavior by the business or its staff.

Usually, the audit committee is asked to oversee business ethics as part of its broader risk remit, but different companies address these issues through different structures. A company with a robust ethical approach and culture will have robust whistle-blowing procedures in place that are well publicized to staff and to which all employees (and perhaps others, such as contractors and suppliers) have access. These procedures will allow any concerned party to raise issues with people of appropriate seniority and independence, so that any apparent failure to live up to the asserted ethical standards can be identified and addressed promptly. Typically, these whistle-blowing processes will be overseen by the audit committee (and sometimes by the risk committee or other appropriate board-level group), so non-executive directors can assure themselves of the independence of the process and have confidence that the company is living up to the standards that the board expects.

In practice, the approach to business ethics within a company is, like corporate culture, generally difficult for outsiders to discern, as it will always be a challenge for both non-executive directors and shareholders to have real insight into the matter.

6 STRUCTURAL CORPORATE GOVERNANCE DIFFERENCES IN MAJOR WORLD MARKETS

☐ 5.1.3 assess and contrast the main models of corporate governance in major markets and the main variables influencing best practice: extent of variation of best practice; differences in legislation, culture, and interpretation

The division between the supervisory board and the management board marks one of the fundamental structural differences in governance globally. The so-called two-tier boards are seen, for example, in Germany, the Netherlands, Scandinavia, and China; the single-tier (also called unitary) boards are more typical of the UK, the USA, Japan, France, and most of the rest of the world. But this structural difference covers other differences; for example, there are multiple forms of the single-tier board:

- In the USA and France, a single executive sits on the board and often bears the responsibility of both chair and CEO (though this long-held tradition of combining the two very different roles is declining in the USA, with around half of S&P 500 companies now having an independent chair). In Australia, the CEO is usually the board's single executive director (and does not usually chair the board), but is typically not subject to election by shareholders.
- In Japan, there is usually a single-tier board dominated by executive directors, with only a small handful of non-executive directors (not necessarily independent).
- In most other countries, single-tier boards have a few executive directors and a majority of non-executives (most of whom are independent), one of whom acts as chair.

By contrast, supervisory boards are all largely constituted in the same way, with all members being non-executives. In some cases, however, they are not perceived as independent, as some members may be direct representatives of major shareholders or representatives of employees, and in some cases the chair of the supervisory board is the former CEO of the company (though this tradition is slowly being abandoned).

No one model of corporate governance is better than the others. They are creatures of the legal histories and cultures of the countries in question. Best practices have been identified and incorporated into global initiatives such as the **ICGN Principles** and the **Organisation for Economic Co-operation and Development (OECD) Principles**. In the same vein, investors will often expect companies to adopt international best practices and go beyond local standards in country-specific codes. The **OECD's Corporate Governance Factbook** is a good source for details on the governance structures and approaches in 49 jurisdictions. Inevitably, the following brief survey covers a much smaller set of geographies and highlights the unusual features in the governance of a handful of leading markets.

Corporate Governance in Australia

Australia has a single-tier board structure, with just a single executive director (often called the managing director instead of, or as well as, CEO). This individual is typically not subject to election by shareholders, who vote on the appointment of the non-executive directors annually. Boards are also relatively small in comparison to public companies in most other major markets, with six or seven directors being typical. While some companies have moved to annual elections for all directors (other than the CEO), many still face re-election only every third year.

The Australian bluntness of their version of comply or explain—"if not, why not?"—can be reflected in a sometimes-combative relationship between companies and their shareholders. Australia was one of the first countries to make superannuation (pension) saving compulsory in order to increase that form of saving to meaningful levels, so the "super funds" are now significant. They increasingly seek to wield their influence forcefully, and a number of organizations—in particular, the Australian Council of Superannuation Investors (ACSI)—help them present shared views to companies.

Investors have a strong influence on Australian companies, as can be seen in the case of the mining company Rio Tinto in 2020. The CEO and two other senior executives were ousted following a public outcry after the company destroyed the Juukan Gorge site (caves that showed evidence of continuous human habitation for 46,000 years and were considered sacred by the local Puutu Kunti Kurrama and Pinikura peoples) to develop it for iron ore mining. Despite the company's having a license to take these actions, the public outcry and the concerns expressed by both politicians and investors made it impossible for the company not to take action against top executives.

Shareholder resolutions are relatively common in Australia, with only US companies facing more such proposals. The reason is partly because Australian law has been interpreted in a relaxed way, and partly because of the strength and organization of the shareholders. The approach can be seen in the appointment of directors, where law and regulations are deemed to mean that only a minimal shareholding is needed to make a proposal, provided the notice period for proposing a candidate has been followed. Though the thresholds for other shareholder resolutions are higher—5% of the issued capital or 100 shareholders—campaigners using social media find it relatively easy to reach the required number of shareholders.

Corporate Governance in France

While there is scope for two-tier boards in France, the vast majority of French boards are single-tier and led by a combined chair/CEO, sometimes still referred to as the Président-Directeur Général (PDG). Standards require that 40% of the directors be female and that around a third of the board be employee representatives, ensuring that the stakeholder voice is clearly heard in the boardroom. French law takes conflicts of interest particularly seriously, and shareholders are invited to vote on related-party transactions (often multiple resolutions in a single year), even those of relatively small value.

Two aspects of French governance are particularly unusual and worthy of discussion: the requirement for joint auditors and the existence of double voting rights for some shareholders. With regard to the audit, France is the only major market to require two audit firms to look at financial statements rather than the usual one firm; these firms are generally one of the Big Four (Deloitte, EY, KPMG, and PricewaterhouseCoopers, or PwC) and one from the next tier of firms. Some consider this requirement controversial, as it is seen as possible for issues to fall between the cracks between the two firms; however, the proponents of this approach suggest that there are likely to be fewer issues missed because there are more pairs of eyes considering the key concerns. The duplication of work effort (and cost) is minimized, as the only entity audited by both joint auditors is the top company and the consolidated accounts—the firms split the audit of the rest of the business units between them (with the smaller firm typically covering less than half). The staggered rotation of the audit firms provides continuity despite the requirement for regular changes of audit firm.

Under 2014's so-called Florange Act (named after a steelworks in northern France that closed and became a symbol of the risk of further industrial decline), unless there is a two-thirds shareholder vote to the contrary, French companies can award double voting rights to long-standing shareholders, defined as those who have held shares in a particular way for at least two years. The structure of this requirement means that few institutional investors qualify (certainly those outside France do not). Even a long-standing pension fund or insurance investor may find its continuity of ownership perceived as having been affected by such normal practices as a change of custodian or fund manager or by a stock-lending program. Thus, in practice, these double voting rights are perceived as a mechanism to establish management control, or control by majority shareholders, and to limit the influence of minority shareholders.

The controversial nature of the Florange Act and the potential long-term consequences of its double voting rights are illustrated in two cases.

First, at Renault: the French government was a 15% shareholder and failed to persuade the company's management and its business partner, Nissan, not to propose an opt-out from the Florange Act at its 2015 AGM. Instead, shortly before the AGM, the French government bought an additional near-5% stake in the company—enough to defeat the opt-out from the law, having given the French state double voting rights for its shareholding, which it soon reverted to the 15% level. In retrospect, this maneuver (agreed to by Emmanuel Macron, the economy minister at the time) is seen as one of the moments when the partnership between Renault and Nissan began to break down.

The second example is Vivendi, the French media conglomerate. Businessman Vincent Bolloré effectively secured his control of the company in 2015, when he was able to defeat a resolution to opt out of the Florange Act. At the time, his shareholding in Vivendi was just under 15%, and while a majority of shareholders supported the opt-out, it failed to gain the necessary two-thirds majority. As a result, Bolloré's shareholding soon gave him 20% of the votes (and more since then), which proved sufficient for him to gain full control of the company and to radically reshape its strategy.

Corporate Governance in Germany

The two-tier board structure in Germany distances shareholders from the operations and from holding management accountable. Shareholders appoint half the members of the supervisory board, and the other half are appointed from among the workforce. All supervisory board members are charged with acting in the best interests of the corporation. This inclusion of workers in the boardroom is called co-determination; in theory, it enables boards to make longer-term decisions and to gain staff support even for difficult decisions. Certainly, German business has been highly successful over the last 70 years, and many world-leading German companies have been built. Anecdotal reports, however, tend to suggest that there are usually meetings of the supervisory board without the workforce members in attendance (where many of the crucial discussions happen) and that the full board meetings are more formalized.

As shareholders vote on the appointment of half the supervisory board—which, in turn, is responsible for the appointment of the management board—the supervisory board, but not the management board, is accountable to shareholders. This sense of distance between the management board and shareholders is increased by the co-determination structure, which allows management to feel at least as accountable to other stakeholders as it does to shareholders. A symbol of the distancing of shareholders from decision-making is the position on remuneration: the German code on corporate governance, the Kodex, insists that shareholders vote on management remuneration structures through advisory votes only, with the actual decision-making resting with the supervisory board.

The independence of thought on the supervisory board has been improved by a move away from the former tradition of an outgoing executive becoming the chair of the supervisory board. Helpfully, from an independence perspective, German law (s. 100(2) of the Aktiengesetz, or German Stock Corporation Act) now requires a two-year gap between departure from the management board and joining the supervisory board, unless the individual is elected after having been nominated for the role by 25% of shareholders. The Kodex confirms that any such individual should not be regarded as independent and that no more than two former members of the management board should be on the supervisory board.

It is intended that strategies be developed by the supervisory board and the management board working together, though the management board is usually expected to initiate the thought process. Principally, the role of the supervisory board is to hold the management board to account, and all major transactions (according to the Kodex, these "include decisions or measures that fundamentally change the company's net assets, financial status or results of operations") need the supervisory board's approval. The supervisory board structure thus keeps shareholders one step further away from holding management to account.

The most controversial item in the Kodex is in Principle 7:

> "The Supervisory Board Chair should be available—within reasonable limits—to discuss Supervisory Board–related issues with investors."[12]

This sentence was opposed by a number of leading supervisory board chairs. In contrast to many countries, in Germany it can, in practice, be difficult for shareholders to meet with the chair (and all but impossible to meet with any other members of the supervisory board). This challenge of access is slowly improving, but investors do rely on the goodwill of the individual chair.

Corporate Governance in Italy

Italy has a single-tier board structure, with typically a single executive director and an independent chair. An unusual feature of Italy's governance framework arises from its history: most company shareholder bases have been dominated by a single shareholder or group of shareholders (often led by the state, local or national, or the founding family or, in some cases, by the country's major financial institutions). The dominance of these shareholder groups could mean that the nomination and election of the boards of such companies would be entirely in their hands, leaving minority shareholders feeling unrepresented and facing wholly non-independent boards. To reassure minority shareholders that their interests would be represented, the *voto di lista* approach was developed: a designated portion of the board (typically around 30%) is reserved for minority shareholders only. Shareholders with a minimum level of shareholding (usually 1%) have the ability to propose a slate (i.e., a group) of directors, and typically there is more than one slate. The slate with the most votes is the dominant one, and the chair is appointed from it; the slate with the next most votes is considered the successful minority slate and fills the board roles designated for minority investors. The Italian investor association Assogestioni organizes minority slates for board elections each year.

At companies with a broad institutional investor base and only a limited shareholding by the "major" shareholder, there is a chance that the *voto di lista* approach could lead to the slate intended as the minority slate gaining more votes than the one intended to be dominant. In such unusual situations, the proxy agencies will recommend that their clients support the slate intended as the dominant one, so that

---

[12] Regierungskommission, *Deutscher Corporate Governance Kodex* (2020). Available at: https://dcgk.de/en/home.html.

it provides the chair and the bulk of board seats as intended. In most circumstances, the proxy agency recommendation is that clients support the Assogestioni minority slate to ensure some board participation by independent directors.

Another unusual feature of the Italian governance structure is that there are elections for statutory auditors. These auditors are not the independent auditors, who are charged with assessing the accuracy of the financial statements. Rather, the statutory auditors have a legal role to affirm the legality of certain actions by the board. Usually, one of the three to five proposed candidates is a lawyer and another is a former (financial statements) auditor. Statutory auditors are also appointed through a *voto di lista* slate process and form an additional protection for minority shareholders.

Both the boards and the statutory auditors are elected for multi-year periods, usually five years, and are not eligible for re-election in the following period. Though this approach provides a clear planning horizon, it can lead to challenges in the last year of a mandate, as there may be a sense of a weaker board that does not wish to bind its successor inappropriately. There is of course no reason why the same board should not be reappointed for a second mandate, but this happens less frequently than might be assumed.

Corporate Governance in Japan

Many companies in Japan (and also in markets such as Taiwan and South Korea) enjoy the structure of having statutory auditors (*kansayaku*), who are in addition to the independent audit firm that ensures the accuracy of the accounts. There is typically a small odd number of statutory auditors (usually three or five), each of whom is appointed individually by shareholders, typically on a four-year rotation. In theory, these auditors are independent individuals, but in many cases, this independence may be questionable as many come from family companies or the lending banks, which can have a close relationship with large companies. While in some ways these statutory auditors serve an independent challenge role somewhat equivalent to independent non-executive directors, their scope to do so is limited by their narrowly defined role and also by the questionable independence of some.

Since the changes to governance introduced by the third "arrow" of Abenomics (the moves toward economic liberalization and renewal under former Prime Minister Shinzo Abe), some companies in Japan have started moving away from the statutory auditor approach and have instead adopted the alternative structure of a "board with committees," similar to board structures seen elsewhere in the world, with non-executive directors. This move has created some challenges, as there has not been a tradition of non-executive directors in Japan, and the culture of loyal and lifetime service to single companies and of strong rivalries within industries has halted the development of a body of non-executives ready to offer advice and challenge a range of businesses. The focus in the Japanese Corporate Governance Code, introduced in 2015 and revised in mid-2018, is on the independence of non-executive directors rather than on the value they can bring to companies through their insights. This focus purely on independence has led to the appointment of some individuals whose value in a business boardroom might be doubted, but this focus is changing over time and a greater understanding of the role of the non-executive director is developing.

Although the *zaibatsu*[13] conglomerates that dominated the Japanese economy for decades were officially dismantled after 1945, the culture of family groups of companies held together by cross-shareholdings persisted. There was a perception that these cross-shareholdings acted as deadweights on fresh strategic thinking and innovation.

---

13 *Zaibatsu* is a Japanese term meaning "financial clique" and refers to industrial and financial business conglomerates in Japan, usually family controlled, whose influence and size allowed control over significant parts of the Japanese economy up until the end of World War II.

For this reason, the Japanese Corporate Governance Code includes provisions that discourage the maintenance of cross-shareholdings (a specific principle, 1.4, discusses cross-shareholdings and, in effect, requires the disclosure of a policy to reduce them over time). Another main focus in the code is on increasing independence on Japanese boards by requiring at least two independent non-executive directors to be in place on every board, even where the statutory auditor model is still in use.

Corporate Governance in the Netherlands

The 2017 contested takeover bid for Dutch chemicals firm AkzoNobel by US rival PPG put corporate governance in the Netherlands firmly in the spotlight. While in most countries, the bid—certainly the revised terms offered by PPG after its initial and second approaches were rebuffed—and the strong support for discussions from significant shareholders would have led to active negotiations, AkzoNobel never even came to the negotiating table. Instead, the Dutch firm successfully argued that the board owed as strong a duty to other stakeholders, particularly employees, as it did to shareholders, and further argued that the value offered to shareholders was unattractive (though the shareholders themselves largely and often publicly disagreed) and that the protections for staff were insufficient.

AkzoNobel declined to hold an extraordinary general meeting (**EGM**) proposed by several shareholders that would have considered ousting the supervisory board chair, Antony Burgmans. A May 2017 court decision by the Enterprise Chamber backed the board's understanding of Dutch corporate governance, including both its basis for not entering into discussions on a deal despite investor support and its decision not to hold the proposed EGM. Burgmans finally departed the board ahead of the 2018 AGM. In effect, the court decision backed the board's stance on the bids, and the company also benefited from significant political support—further takeover protections for all Dutch companies have since been proposed. In some ways, however, shareholders got the bulk of what they wanted in the end. Subsequently, the company sold off its specialty chemicals business, focusing instead on paints and coatings, and returned the bulk of the proceeds to shareholders.

As with other countries with supervisory board structures, shareholders in the Netherlands appoint the supervisory board and are kept at a distance from holding management accountable for performance and strategy. The AkzoNobel case demonstrates that shareholders do not necessarily come first in the Dutch corporate governance model and that other stakeholder interests must be taken into account. That is particularly true in the case of takeovers, which have long been a sensitive issue in the Netherlands and remain so—long after the dismantling of most of the Stichting structures,[14] which were able to keep shareholders at arm's length if there was a hostile bid, securing the role of management and the supervisory board. But the AkzoNobel example also shows that, other than in the case of takeovers, the influence of shareholders is strong: the longer-term outcome of the dispute was board change and a significant streamlining of the company and return of value to shareholders.

Corporate Governance in Sweden

Governance in Sweden has been shaped by the dominance of major shareholders in the registers of many leading companies. Most prominent of these is the Wallenberg family vehicle, Investor AB. Investor AB is itself a public company but is controlled

---

14 *Stichting* is a legal structure that can be used for any purpose. In the context of corporate governance and control, it usually refers to an organization that itself owns the shares in the underlying company and issues depositary receipts to the market. Investors would buy these instead of shares, meaning that they would not enjoy all the rights of legal shareholders.

by the Wallenbergs through the mechanism of two classes of shares with differential voting rights—a feature of Swedish governance that persists at many businesses despite its controversial nature. Investor AB's ownership of other Swedish companies includes, among others:

- Atlas Copco (16.9% of the shares and 22.3% of the votes);
- ABB (12.2% of the shares and votes);
- AstraZeneca (3.9% of the shares and votes);
- SEB (20.8% of the shares and votes);
- Ericsson (7.7% of the shares and 23.6% of the votes); and
- Electrolux (16.4% of the shares and 28.4% of the votes).

Investor AB argues that its investments, and its voting influence, enable it to avoid short-term pressures and to build these businesses for the long term.

This dominance of the share capital, and particularly of the votes, could lead to Investor AB being able to appoint the bulk of corporate boards in Sweden and having even more disproportionate influence than it already does. To mitigate this dominance, Sweden has developed an unusual structure whereby a company's nominations committee is not a board committee but is instead appointed from among the shareholders—with the largest shareholders invited to participate in descending order of their shareholdings until the committee is fully populated. At the AGM, this nominations committee proposes a board (which may include no more than a single executive, with independent non-executive directors in the majority) and a chair for shareholder approval. The outcome of this procedure is reasonably positive: skilled and generally well-balanced boards. The Wallenberg family still appear in many Swedish boardrooms, frequently providing the chair. In contrast to most countries, in Sweden the proposed board is usually put forward as a single slate, meaning that shareholders have a vote on the board as a whole rather than votes on each proposed director.

Similar structures and approaches can be found in other Scandinavian markets.

Corporate Governance in the UK

The UK issued the world's first Corporate Governance Code, and the current, 2018 version—overseen by the regulator Financial Reporting Council—goes further than most others. In particular, it focuses more attention on board behaviors and corporate culture than do other Codes. Of course, it does set expectations for:

- board skills and structure;
  - the UK discourages combined chair/CEO roles and expects chairs to be independent at appointment;
  - independent non-executive directors should compose the majority of the board, though there should be at least two and preferably three or more executive directors;
- audit and risk (the board is charged with considering the company's emerging and principal risks, including ESG risks, and making a statement regarding the viability of the business over at least a three-year period from the date of the accounts);
- remuneration;
  - the UK has detailed expectations around pay, in theory linking executive pay to performance and limiting the scope of payments for failure (long-term schemes need to be genuinely long term);

- these expectations are layered with extensive corporate law disclosure standards that apply to large UK-incorporated companies, which means that generally UK annual reports are the most coherent and informative in the world.

The UK Code's focus on board behaviors and corporate culture is much more in-depth than that of other Codes around the world and really makes the UK stand out. The second Principle of the current Code is particularly striking in this regard: "The board should establish the company's purpose, values and strategy, and satisfy itself that these and its culture are aligned. All directors must act with integrity, lead by example and promote the desired culture." The second provision reinforces this message: "The board should assess and monitor culture. Where it is not satisfied that policy, practices or behaviour throughout the business are aligned with the company's purpose, values and strategy, it should seek assurance that management has taken corrective action."

This focus on culture means that the Code places particular emphasis on a company's *workforce*, a deliberately chosen term intended to include not only those directly employed by the company but also workers more generally. Boards are expected to explain their approach to investing in and rewarding their workforce. They are also expected to stay informed about the views and attitudes of the workforce through one of three mechanisms: a director appointed from the workforce, a formal workforce advisory panel, or a non-executive director who serves as a liaison to the workforce. The last mechanism is by far the most popular; workforce directors remain highly unusual in the UK and are part of only some already fairly idiosyncratic boards (such as those at Frasers Group and JD Wetherspoon). The link to the interests of the workforce is also seen in the Code's standards on pay: the remuneration committee is expected to take account of workforce pay and culture in its consideration of executive pay, and there is a specific expectation that executive pension rates be aligned with those of the general workforce.

UK governance standards are also, in effect, set by best practice groupings, with some degree of regulatory and political backing. Most notable among these are the Hampton-Alexander Review and the Parker Review, which are pressing, respectively, for greater female representation on boards and for each board to include at least one director from a minority ethnicity. The initial goal of the former has nearly been reached (broadly, 30% female board membership); more remains to be done to reach the initial goal set by the latter.

Corporate Governance in the USA

The USA stands out in terms of governance. Now that Japan has introduced its own Corporate Governance Code, the USA is the only major market—and almost the sole country—without a Code of its own. The reason is a fundamental issue in US politics: the relationship between the federal government and the individual states. Corporate law is a matter for the states, and so there is no scope for a federal set of rules to govern corporations. Indeed, the fact that each state has its own corporate laws led to a race to the bottom for company standards among the states, competing with one another for the tax revenue from incorporating businesses. This race was comprehensively won by the small state of Delaware, which is now home to more than half of all publicly traded US corporations. The decisions of the Delaware courts are therefore of disproportionate importance to US corporate life.

In the absence of countrywide US governance standards, there have been various attempts to establish market-led best practices, of which these are the leading ones:

1. The Commonsense Corporate Governance Principles, first published in July 2016 and revised in October 2018. These principles were created by a coalition of company representatives, including the leadership of Berkshire Hathaway, BlackRock, General Electric, General Motors, JPMorgan Chase, and Verizon Communications, along with representatives of the largest US investors. These principles focus mostly on the inner workings of corporate governance, board effectiveness and accountability, and alignment through pay.
2. The Investor Stewardship Group's (ISG) Corporate Governance Principles for US Listed Companies, which came into effect at the start of 2018. As the name suggests, these principles were created by a coalition of investors (a number of whom were involved in creating the Commonsense Corporate Governance Principles). These principles are also more about the relationship between US companies and their shareholders than about their internal governance. The ISG has also produced a set of Stewardship Principles—in effect, the reciprocal responsibilities of investors in response to these corporate responsibilities.
3. The Corporate Governance Policies of the Council of Institutional Investors (CII). These policies set out in detail the approach of the CII—the pre-eminent representative of long-term investors in the USA—to the full range of corporate governance issues. These policies are less a set of principles and more an indication of the likely positions of CII members on issues that might go to a shareholder vote or be the subject of a public policy debate.

In combination, the first two initiatives represent a corporate governance code as it would be understood elsewhere in the world.

With reference to governance, what *is* regulated on a federal level in the USA is securities law: hence, the importance of the US Securities and Exchange Commission (SEC) and the rules it sets. For example, the SEC sets requirements for the independence and skills of members of the audit committees of companies listed in the USA. These standards were set by the Sarbanes-Oxley Act. Typically, the SEC creates rules based on statutes that reflect pre-existing expectations set down as principles in other markets. Here are two examples under the Dodd-Frank legislation:

1. There is a resolution to consider executive remuneration, usually referred to as a say-on-pay vote. Under Dodd-Frank, such a resolution must be put to a shareholder vote at least every third year, though shareholders must also be offered a vote on whether they wish to have a "say on pay" more frequently; most institutional investors favor holding such votes annually.
2. The "access to the proxy" standard permits shareholders that fulfill certain criteria to add a candidate to the company's formal proxy statement, avoiding the cost and administrative complexity of mounting a full proxy fight over board membership.

In practice, the access-to-the-proxy right has rarely been used. However, the combination of these two rights has led to a positive dynamic in company–shareholder relations. More companies are now making non-executive directors—particularly an independent chair where there is a lead independent director—available for shareholder meetings. Such a dialogue would have been highly unusual just a few years ago.

CORPORATE GOVERNANCE AND THE INDEPENDENT AUDIT FUNCTION

☐ 5.1.4 explain the role of auditors in relation to corporate governance and the challenges in effective delivery of the audit: independence of audit firms and conflicts of interest; auditor rotation; sampling of audit work and technological disruption; auditor reports; auditor liability; internal audit

The modern concept of the auditor evolved from the financial scandals of another era.

The earliest trading businesses of the 17th century (perhaps most famously, the Dutch East India Company, or VOC) were established for a specific trade journey or a set period, after which they needed to account for their performance and share the proceeds before being allowed to renew their mandate for a further period. This procedure sometimes included an expected independent oversight of the accounts. The Industrial Revolution (circa 1760–1840) saw for the first time the creation of many more large-scale corporations that sought to raise capital from outside parties. As many of these companies were expected to have an ongoing life beyond a set period or a particular endeavor, finance providers started to insist that management account for their use of this capital at least annually, leading to requirements for both annual reports and accounts and an AGM.

The failures and downright frauds of the UK's 1840s railway boom (an early investment bubble) saw minority shareholders suffer significant losses. The law was changed in response to the inevitable outcry, requiring an audit of the annual accounts by an independent party, thus providing shareholders with assurance that the numbers presented to them were true and fair.

The concept of the audit has not changed: the auditor is there to provide an independent pair of eyes assessing the financial reports prepared by management, and to provide some assurance that those reports fairly represent the performance and position of the business. There is no absolute assurance that the numbers are correct, nor certainty that there is no fraud within the business. Auditing is a sampling process that tries to identify anomalies that can then be followed up. According to the 1896 UK Court of Appeal judgment re Kingston Cotton Mill (No. 2)—following yet another corporate failure, this time when the auditor had taken a management assertion on inventory at face value—auditors should be watchdogs, not bloodhounds. There has been an ongoing debate following every corporate failure since, as to both whether the watchdogs were asleep on the job and whether we ought to expect a little more bloodhound-like—or perhaps, to use a more modern simile, sniffer dog–like—behavior from auditors.

Reviewing Financial Statements, Annual Reports, and Wider Reporting (Including Sustainability Reports)

Despite the lack of global uniformity in ESG reporting standards, companies increasingly seek to burnish their sustainability credentials by publishing detailed reports that have been independently assured by auditors.

The auditor independently examines and provides third-party assurance of the financial statements, affirming that the detailed information is free from material misstatement and inconsistencies. As a result of an audit, stakeholders may evaluate and improve the effectiveness of governance, risk management, and control over the subject matter.

This assurance work may be conducted by leading audit firms or by smaller groups of alternative assurance providers that specialize in ESG matters. Investors need to read the assurer's report carefully to understand what ESG standards have been achieved in practice and then consider what additional weight they can place on the sustainability reporting. The intention in sustainability reporting is to encourage organizations to go beyond the fundamental duty of legal compliance.

The key elements of an ESG audit that investors should consider include the scope—business strategy, policies, and operations; the timeline covering when the assessment is being carried out, and which periods are being reviewed; and how the audit is conducted, including information on checks and balances to ensure as much accuracy as possible. Although the auditor's work is often procedural, providing limited substantive assurance, a well-conducted ESG audit fosters an increase in the confidence that both current and future investors can place in reported ESG data and analysis.

Audit methods include:

- third-party certification of data and information included in the ESG report;
- provision of an independent guarantee that both data and analysis are credible and accurate; and
- attestation that published communication from management details how activities are transparently reported for ESG issues.

Examples of issues that can be evaluated in an ESG audit include:

- environmental standards, and management systems;
- energy-saving initiatives;
- facilities, water, and waste management, including recycling activities;
- product development and manufacturing processes, and efforts to reduce waste in all stages of production;
- plans for monitoring carbon emissions and mitigating or even eliminating production of toxic waste (the way the company's supply chain moves goods to customers, emissions from transportation vehicles, and fuel use can be assessed);
- use of hazardous materials in products;
- compensation for community impacts and environmental damage due to location of facilities;
- corporate transparency;
- performance on social issues related to human rights, diversity, labor standards, and working conditions; and
- remuneration policies for employees.

Assurance of ESG reporting is currently entirely voluntary and (in contrast to the financial audit) is not based on a single set of universally accepted regulatory standards. E, S, and G data are largely drawn from several organizations that expend considerable resources in developing and setting comprehensive global standards. These standards are focused on identifying and evaluating ESG risk factors that are financially important to companies.

Disclosures and frameworks can be quite detailed, yet not uniform. It is important to differentiate between management system standards and those that simply offer guidance on reporting about sustainable activities. In the case of the latter, these standards are not designed for certification purposes or for regulatory or contractual use; thus, any offer to certify, or claims of certification, would be a misrepresentation of the intent and purpose—and a misuse—of audit.

The Independence of Audit Firms and Conflicts of Interest

The independence of the audit firm is critical. Large audit firms, including the Big Four, typically offer non-audit services (consultancy work and tax advice, principally) to the companies they audit, despite the obvious risks arising from conflicts of interest. As they spend so much time within a business and interact with the finance department, auditors can build closer relationships with the management of the companies they audit than with the non-executive directors on the audit committee to whom they report, or the shareholders for whom they formally perform their work. Audit firm staff also sometimes will later work at companies they have audited. Investors often assess potential conflicts of interest by looking at how much an audit firm is being paid for its audit work versus its consultancy work and whether a company has a policy to limit this risk, though this issue is not the only sign of conflicts.

Regulators have intervened to remove the most obvious conflicts of interest, which has led to a significant decline in recent years of the scope for auditors to provide non-audit services to their clients. This trend can be seen within the EU. For example, EU law now not only provides a list of non-audit services that are the only ones an audit firm may provide to clients, but also places a monetary limit (calculated in relation to the audit fee) on their overall value. The UK's Competition and Markets Authority has proposed much more separation between the audit and non-audit arms of accountancy firms, so that audit is much less likely to be influenced by other concerns.[15]

Another important question surrounds behavioral independence. There is a natural tendency for individuals to seek consensus and for people to want to avoid disagreement or even confrontation with those they spend time with. These natural human behaviors run counter to the very role of the auditor, which must be to question and challenge the information that the audited entity provides. Every member of the audit team must work to avoid succumbing to such tendencies, and the audit partner overseeing the whole process needs to ensure that skepticism has been maintained throughout. In particular, there must be enough time allowed for questions to be pursued fully, and enough scope for additional staffing if necessary. These ideas both run contrary to the frequent mindset that the audit firm should be efficient in its work, adhere to a timetable dictated by the company, and keep within a budget that allows the firm to generate a profit. In practice, it is not always easy for investors to be confident that the audit has been done as thoroughly as they might wish.

Auditor Rotation

The concentration of the audit market makes it more difficult to address the issues of auditor independence and effectiveness. In the EU, public companies are obliged to change auditors after 20 years at most (and to tender the audit after 10 years). With the incumbent barred from competing after 20 years and the other audit firms sometimes unwilling to give up valuable non-audit services contracts, there is a sub-optimal level of competition. Prior to the rule changes, it was frequently argued that auditor rotation might lead to issues being missed, either in the last year of a departing auditor or in the first year of a new auditor, but the reported impact has been positive: companies that have changed auditors have found the refreshed perspectives valuable yet challenging.

---

15 Competition and Markets Authority, *Statutory Audit Services Market Study: Final Report* (2019). Available at: www.gov.uk/cma-cases/statutory-audit-market-study.

Sampling and Audit Work

The sampling process that underlies audit work has been mentioned previously; however, technological and AI developments may see this process change. Significant effort should go into assessing what is an appropriate level of sampling to gain a good insight into the accuracy of the underlying numbers, and also into assessing the output of that sampling. On occasion, though, it seems that the budget for the audit does more to determine the work undertaken than the need for clarity of assurance. The depth of sampling is highly dependent on the auditor's assessment of the quality of the company's own systems and financial controls (see below for a discussion of disclosures of performance **materiality**). In this matter, the external auditor leans on the work of the company's internal audit (the company's own process for assessing risks and the quality of reporting, also discussed below), and well-run audit committees sensibly coordinate the internal and external audits so they can get an appropriate level of assurance across the company.

Sir Donald Brydon's recent independent review of the quality and effectiveness of audit proposes that every audit committee produce an annual audit and assurance plan that discloses the committee's expectations for overall assurance of company reporting, including both internal and external audits, which should make this coordination more apparent and perhaps more effective. Under Sir Donald's proposals, shareholders would be invited to provide input into the development of this plan.[16]

In theory at least, the world of big data is changing the sampling approach, and the leading audit firms are exploring methods of using technology to consider every single transaction rather than merely sampling a proportion of them. A number of independent software firms have developed packages that deliver this capability, though these firms currently seem to be more focused on the small and mid-sized end of the corporate market than on larger businesses. The challenge with any approach to assessing every transaction is spotting anomalies in this barrage of data, not just checking that the numbers add up. The technology potentially removes the need to sample—but not the need to consider intelligently the information that is delivered. This area remains a work in progress.

Enhanced Auditor Reports

Shareholders today have more insight than ever before into the work of auditors because of the new enhanced auditor reports. Originated in the UK, enhanced auditor reports have now been adopted globally. These reports include three crucial elements:

- **Scope of the audit:** This element concerns how many parts of the company the audit has covered and in what depth. Typically, an auditor will apply a full audit to the largest segments (usually geographies, but sometimes business segments) and will apply tailored audit procedures to others, but some segments may be ignored altogether.
- **Materiality:** While materiality is a qualitative concept and should vary depending on the significance of the issue and its circumstances, in practice the disclosure tends to focus on a quantitative measure of materiality: the level of transaction or valuation below which the auditor spends little time. For the biggest companies, this number can be surprisingly large (US$500m, or £359m, is not unusual). Of more interest to investors are the levels of materiality applied to the different segments and—where it is disclosed—the

---

16 D. Brydon, *Assess, Assure and Inform: Improving Audit Quality and Effectiveness; Report of the Independent Review into the Quality and Effectiveness of Audit* (2019). Available at: https://assets.publishing.service.gov.uk/government/uploads/system/uploads/attachment_data/file/852960/brydon-review-final-report.pdf.

performance materiality number (the level below the materiality threshold that the auditor uses in its audit procedures to prevent problems from arising when the numbers analyzed are aggregated). The performance materiality number indicates the extent to which the auditor trusts the company's financial systems: 75% of the overall materiality threshold is typical, whereas anything around 50% to 60% suggests a low level of confidence in the company's financial controls. Such lower levels of performance materiality might indicate a highly devolved organization or one whose controls should perhaps be enhanced, which can be a useful insight for investors.

▶ **Key audit matters:** The third element concerns a handful of key areas of judgment in the accounts. While the areas covered will rarely come as a surprise to investors, the way in which these issues are discussed and what auditors choose to highlight in their open discussion can reveal interesting and important insights. The best auditor reports not only highlight the key areas of judgment but also indicate whether the company's reporting on them is conservative, neutral, or aggressive. This so-called graduated audit adds real value to investors' understanding of the company's reported performance.

These enhanced auditor reports upgrade prior practice, where the sole piece of insight was the auditor's opinion on whether the financial statements represented a true and fair view of the company's performance and position at the end of the financial year. When an annual report was published, it would be quick work to find out whether an auditor had given a negative opinion. Auditors' past unwillingness to provide much insight was driven by their fear of litigation in the case of a corporate failure. Investors learned that auditor reports were not worth reading—a lesson that now needs to be unlearned. Investors have much to learn from these enhanced auditor reports if they can begin to navigate the tone and specialist language used in them (or if auditors could begin to make them more accessible to the general user). These reports may be further enhanced if some of the proposals in the independent Brydon Review are adopted—indeed, Sir Donald's review proposes that auditors do a lot more to inform investors and the market as a whole. He emphasizes the importance of this role for auditors by using *inform* as one of the three key words in the title of his final report: "assess, assure and inform."[16]

Auditor Liability

One reason that auditors give for not providing more than they are strictly required to, in terms of the audit or auditor reporting, is liability. In most markets, the auditor has unlimited liability. Indeed, the US SEC has established a rule that any company subject to its jurisdiction (which includes many foreign companies that have US listings of either their equity or their debt) may not in any way limit the liability of the auditor. Even where audit firms enjoy the benefit of a limited liability partnership (meaning that all the partners are no longer exposed to risk because of a potential failure by one of the partners), the individuals who are directly responsible for any failure, especially the partner involved, can face losing everything. This risk is seen as significant, in part, because auditors are often among the few deep-pocketed players when there is a corporate failure, and so they are regularly included in lawsuits. The extent to which the courts would attribute liability to the individuals and their firms, however, is less clear, because most of these cases are settled before they get anywhere near a judgment. Most of the settlements are private, and so it is unclear whether, in practice, the liability risk is as large as the profession tends to indicate.

Internal Audit

Internal audit should not be confused with external audit. The latter can be outsourced, but most of the time, internal audit is part of the company itself, with a formal reporting line to the executive team (though usually with a dotted line to the audit committee). It functions largely as a risk management tool, used to ensure that the company's procedures and expected behaviors are delivered in practice and to uncover misbehavior or problematic management.

Internal audit has a highly variable status in different businesses—indeed, it does not exist at all in some organizations. Where it is deployed most effectively, internal audit is a tool for both the executive team and the non-executive directors to gain confidence and comfort about the company's delivery on the ground, helping the company operate more effectively and efficiently. It can help the board feel closer to the real operations—a significant challenge for modern, large multinational businesses. There is a sea change taking place in internal audit, involving directing the work toward helping the board and senior managers protect their organization's assets, reputation, and sustainability. The Internal Audit Code of Practice,[17] issued by the Chartered Institute of Internal Auditors in January 2020, is, in effect, a pathfinder for the profession to help it deliver fully on this promised change.

8. CORPORATE GOVERNANCE AND THE INVESTMENT DECISION-MAKING PROCESS

☐ **5.1.5** assess material impacts of governance issues on potential investment opportunities, including the dangers of overlooking them: public finance initiatives; companies; infrastructure/private finance vehicles; societal impact

☐ **5.1.6** apply material corporate governance factors to: financial modeling; risk assessment; quality of management

Of the three ESG factors, governance is the one most often considered by traditional investment analysts. A 2017 CFA Institute ESG survey showed that 67% of global respondents took governance into consideration in their analysis and investment decision-making (up from 64% in 2014), ahead of environmental and social factors (both at 54%).[18] In the EMEA region, the number of analysts indicating that they took governance into account was 74%.

The primacy of governance is logical. Academic research indicates that of the three ESG factors, governance has the clearest link to financial performance. Friede, Busch, and Bassen's 2015 meta-study on ESG and financial performance notes that:

▶ 62% of the studies they reviewed showed a positive correlation between governance and corporate financial performance; and

---

17 Chartered Institute of Internal Auditors, *Internal Audit Code of Practice: Guidance on Effective Internal Audit in the Private and Third Sectors* (2020). Available at: www.iia.org.uk/media/1691066/internal-audit-code-of-practice-report.pdf.

18 CFA Institute, *Environmental, Social and Governance (ESG) Survey* (2017). Available at: https://www.cfainstitute.org/-/media/documents/survey/esg-survey-report-2017.ashx.

- 58% of environmental studies and 55% of social studies showed the same correlation.[19]

Similarly, in mid-2016, one UK investment manager estimated that companies with good or improving governance tended to outperform companies with poor or worsening governance by 30 basis points per month, on average, in the prior seven years.[20] Environmental and social factors also demonstrated their ability to guide investors toward better-performing companies and away from poorly performing ones, but the dispersion in performance was about half as large.

Good governance is fundamental to a company's performance, in terms of both long-term shareholder value creation and the creation of broader prosperity for society and all stakeholders. If a company delivers good governance, it is more likely to approach environmental and social issues with the right long-term mindset and thus avoid, or effectively manage, significant risks and seize relevant opportunities. Failures can be devastating to shareholders and other capital providers. The description of the board's failings in the Enron case (where the company's market value fell from US$60bn, or £43bn, in December 2000 to zero in October 2001) is bracing, as seen in this excerpt from the special investigation committee's report:

> *Oversight of the related-party transactions by Enron's Board of Directors and Management failed for many reasons. As a threshold matter, in our opinion the very concept of related-party transactions of this magnitude with the CFO was flawed. The Board put many controls in place, but the controls were not adequate, and they were not adequately implemented. Some senior members of Management did not exercise sufficient oversight and did not respond adequately when issues arose that required a vigorous response. The Board assigned the Audit and Compliance Committee an expanded duty to review the transactions, but the Committee carried out the reviews only in a cursory way. The Board of Directors was denied important information that might have led it to take action, but the Board also did not fully appreciate the significance of some of the specific information that came before it. Enron's outside auditors supposedly examined Enron's internal controls but did not identify or bring to the Audit Committee's attention the inadequacies in their implementation.*[21]

Governance matters because the wrong people—or just not enough of the right people—around the boardroom table are less likely to make the best decisions, resulting in the likelihood of significant value erosion and a failure to address key risks, including environmental and social issues. And if the interests of management and shareholders are not aligned, there is also a risk of value erosion for stakeholders generally.

Thus, companies with poor governance risk destroying value—or at least adding less value than they might have done. These issues are as true of private companies as they are of public companies: governance, good or bad, is not the exclusive preserve of the public company or the exclusive concern of the public equity investor. Governance is just as much an issue in private equity investments and infrastructure vehicles (including public finance initiatives), where value can be lost as easily. The building blocks for understanding good governance—accountability and alignment,

---

19 G. Friede, T. Busch, and A. Bassen, "ESG and Financial Performance: Aggregated Evidence from More Than 2000 Empirical Studies," *Journal of Sustainable Finance & Investment* 5, no. 4 (2015): 210–33. Available at: www.tandfonline.com/doi/full/10.1080/20430795.2015.1118917.
20 Hermes Investment Management, *ESG Investing: It Still Makes You Feel Good, It Still Makes You Money* (2016). Available at: www.hermes-investment.com/wp-content/uploads/2018/10/hermes-esg-investing.pdf.
21 W. C. Powers, R. S. Troubh, and H. S. Winokur, *Report of Investigation by the Special Investigative Committee of the Board of Directors of Enron Corporation* (2002). Available at: http://i.cnn.net/cnn/2002/LAW/02/02/enron.report/powers.report.pdf.

with governance being, at its heart, about people (allowing boards to get the right mix of skills and experience and an array of perspectives in the boardroom)—can be applied to any situation.

Some will say that governance is less of an issue in private equity because investors are directly represented on the board, and the same is often true in many infrastructure vehicles. Although this factor reduces the risk of misinformation and a lack of responsiveness, it does not, in itself, remove all governance risks. Indeed, given the highly indebted nature of many such investments, the margin for error is not always large, and so failure can be swift if it does occur, often overwhelming even more responsive governance structures. Certainly, as the following brief case studies (on Theranos, Uber, and WeWork) indicate, there are significant risks to consider from failures of governance within private businesses.

CASE STUDIES

Theranos Board

In 2014, around the time Theranos was raising money from private market investors at a valuation that confirmed it was—at least temporarily—a so-called unicorn (a private company valued at more than US$1bn, or £718m), the company, which claimed to be reinventing blood testing with exclusive technology, had the following board of directors:

- Elizabeth Holmes, 30 — founder, CEO, and chair
- Sunny Balwani, 48 — president and COO (former software engineer)
- Riley Bechtel, 62 — chair of the board of the construction company Bechtel Group
- William Frist, 62 — former heart and lung transplant surgeon before becoming a US senator
- Henry Kissinger, 90 — former US secretary of state
- Richard Kovacevich, 70 — former CEO of Wells Fargo
- James Mattis, 63 — retired US Marine Corps general
- Sam Nunn, 75 — former US senator and chair of the Senate Armed Services Committee
- William Perry, 86 — former US secretary of defense
- Gary Roughead, 61 — retired US Navy admiral
- George Shultz, 93 — former US secretary of state

Thus, overseeing an innovative blood-testing technology company was a board where the non-executive directors were exclusively male, mostly with military or foreign service backgrounds rather than medical or scientific experience, and with an average age of 73 (excluding the two executives). There were more former secretaries of state in their 90s on the board than people with medical training. None had any expertise, or even basic experience, in blood testing.

The degree of oversight offered by this board of the management and operations was always likely to be limited, and its influence was further hindered by the company's dual-class share structure that saw the founder hold 99% of the voting rights. In addition, it appears that the board met infrequently, and several directors had poor attendance rates. All this suggests that the board was not operating as effectively as it might have been. Perhaps that should not be surprising. The *Wall Street Journal* investigative reporter John Carreyrou, in his striking account of the Theranos story, *Bad Blood*, notes that Elizabeth Holmes told someone interviewing for a job at the company in 2011: "The board is just a placeholder. I make all the decisions here."

In the end, all of the US$700m (£503m) invested in the business was lost (together with its largely theoretical estimated valuation of US$10bn, or £7.1bn) when the company was revealed to have falsified test results and misled investors about the nature and effectiveness of its technology.

In retrospect, the Theranos board's many red flags indicated that something was amiss—at the very least, the board could have been better designed to deliver effective oversight of an early-stage, high-risk technology business with unproven leadership. The red flags at other boards may be less obvious, but the two key questions that investors will always need to ask are:

1. Is there the right mix of skills and experience, and *enough* of the right skills and experience, to properly oversee the next stage of development of this business? If there are obvious gaps, investors need to consider how those gaps might best be filled.

2. Is there the right dynamic around the boardroom table to enable the views of the appropriately skilled board members to be heard? This question is about behaviors, which are inevitably harder to identify from outside; nonetheless, there are often indications that the board dynamic is not as effective as it might be.

Theranos is not the only unicorn to experience governance challenges that affected its estimated value.

Uber, the transportation network company, felt obliged to change its governance practices in the wake of a series of damaging scandals that were affecting its growth. The founder CEO's responsibilities were reallocated, preferential voting rights were adjusted, and the board's independence was strengthened.

In 2019, WeWork was obliged to abandon its planned initial public offering (IPO)—and its valuation plummeted from the intended capitalization at listing—when investors balked at the company's approach to several governance issues, including the dominant decision-making position of the founding CEO (which would persist even after his death, when his wife was to be handed the choice of his successor) and related-party deals with the CEO. While these governance issues were addressed in the latter stages of the planned IPO process, they were enough to raise broader questions in investors' minds, including the crucial ones about business model and the absence of a clear path to profitability. In a *Financial Times* article about the company's downfall, a financial adviser who is particularly insightful on the company's governance and the CEO's management style is reported as saying, "How do you go from succeeding by not listening to succeeding by listening?"[22]

Few governance failures are as extreme in their destruction of value as Theranos and WeWork, and few boards are as lacking in diversity and the relevant skill set as the Theranos board was. There is good evidence in the academic literature of the beneficial effect of diversity. Carter, Simkins, and Simpson's 2003 study of the *Fortune* 1000 firms found statistically significant positive relationships between the presence of women or minorities on the board and firm value, as measured by Tobin's q (a valuation measure based on the ratio between a company's market value and the replacement cost of its assets).[23] Bernile, Bhagwat, and Yonker's 2017 study concluded

---

22 E. Platt and A. Edgecliffe-Johnson, "WeWork: How the Ultimate Unicorn Lost Its Billions," *Financial Times*, 20 February 2020. Available at: www.ft.com/content/7938752a-52a7-11ea-90ad-25e377c0ee1f.
23 D. A. Carter, B. J. Simkins, and W. G. Simpson, "Corporate Governance, Board Diversity, and Firm Value," *Financial Review* 38, no. 1 (2003): 33–53. Available at: https://doi.org/10.1111/1540-6288.00034.

that diversity in the board of directors reduces stock return volatility (consistent with diverse backgrounds working as a governance mechanism) and that firms with diverse boards tend to adopt policies that are more stable and persistent (consistent with the board decisions being less subject to idiosyncrasies).[24] In addition, while diverse boards take less financial risk, "this behavior does not carry over onto real risk-taking activities," with diverse boards investing more in research and development (R&D). Overall, their study found that greater heterogeneity among directors leads to higher profitability and firm valuations, on average.

Governance failures lead to fines and additional liabilities, as well as litigation and other costs. Revenues fall as trust is eroded and customers boycott the company or buy from competitors, and profits fall as additional cost burdens are placed to mitigate future risks. All these effects harm security values. Governance analysis should be a core component of valuation practice.

Integrating Governance into Investment and Stewardship Processes

Different fund managers integrate governance factors into their investment decision-making in different ways. For many, it is a threshold assessment—a formal minimum criterion to consider *before* they will consider making an investment at any price. Often, it is talked about as quality of management, which, despite the name, is never simply an assessment of the CEO and CFO but, rather, of the overall team and the governance structure by which they oversee the company and (hopefully) drive the success of the business.

For others, it is a risk assessment tool, which may represent the level of confidence about future earnings or the multiple on which those earnings are placed in a valuation—or it may be reflected less in full financial models and more in a simple level of confidence in the valuation range or investment thesis.

If the analysis of corporate governance is specifically built into valuation models, this analysis is most typically done by recognizing negative governance characteristics by way of adding a risk premium to the cost of capital or raising the discount rate applied. Others regard weak governance as an engagement and investment opportunity—the logic being that governance can be improved through active dialogue with management and proxy voting, so that past underperformance, on which the company is currently valued in the market, is reversed and the valuation can be enhanced by stronger performance and an expectation of more positive performance in the future.

Many governance issues lend themselves to stewardship dialogue with companies, not least because many of these issues will be directly addressed in the AGM agenda. Investors will be obliged to take a stance on them (for many investors, that is why governance has a longer heritage than environmental and social issues—particularly because in many markets, the obligation to consider voting decisions actively is well established). In almost every market, investors will be faced annually with voting decisions on at least the following:

- accepting the report and accounts;
- board appointments;
- the appointment of the auditor, and perhaps their fees; and
- executive remuneration.

---

[24] G. Bernile, V. Bhagwat, and S. Yonker, "Board Diversity, Firm Risk, and Corporate Policies," *Journal of Financial Economics* 127, no. 3 (2018): 588–612. Available at: https://doi.org/10.1016/j.jfineco.2017.12.009.

Corporate Governance and the Investment Decision-Making Process

Thus, there is a natural driver, at least annually, for engagement on these issues—though investors are increasingly keen to avoid the critical points of all such discussions during the AGM season (largely April to June in the Northern Hemisphere, July in Japan, and September to November in the Southern Hemisphere). To avoid this problem, dialogue is held throughout the year, with the conclusions reached in the dialogue reflected in the voting.

Engagement is covered in depth in the next chapter.

Thus far, this chapter has considered the G in ESG as meaning corporate governance. While many may see corporate governance as an issue particularly for public equity investments, in fact many investments across the asset classes are in company structures in one form or another. Therefore, corporate governance concerns will have relevance for many investments, including, for example, fixed income, private equity, property, and infrastructure. The intent of this chapter is to discuss corporate governance at a level whereby its relevance across this broad range of asset classes is apparent, and the analysis can be applied and tailored as appropriate.

However, there is one asset class where the G of ESG will always have a very different meaning. In the sovereign debt arena, G means the effectiveness of the governance and robustness of the state and its institutions, the approach to the rule of law, and the general business environment (including such issues as competition and anti-corruption). In effect, the concern is about gaining assurance that the economy can prosper through good governance, so that sovereign debt obligations can continue to be covered. ESG-minded investors are increasingly integrating the analysis of these issues into their broader financial analysis of sovereign credits.

KEY FACTS

1. Corporate governance is the process by which a company is managed and overseen. It is framed by local law and culture, and almost all countries now have a formal but non-binding corporate governance code to set standards and expectations.

2. However, within these formal frames, governance comes down to people and how they interact; they need information and they need to be able to make the relevant people accountable for their decisions.

3. Accountability is reflected in sufficient oversight of management so that management is encouraged, pressed, and challenged to efficiently deliver for the long-term good of the business.

4. Alongside accountability sits alignment as the other core tenet of good governance. This tenet is seen most clearly in the area of pay, where the aim is an alignment of the interests of management with those of the long-term shareholder. It means that long-term value creation in the business is reflected as a reward to individual managers.

5. To deliver these two main aims of accountability and alignment, each board is expected to establish three independent and effective committees to cover the crucial areas of nominations, audit, and remuneration.

6. Corporate governance codes and guidelines, and the laws that underpin them, typically get changed in reaction to scandals in individual companies. In the UK, the Cadbury Code was the world's first governance code and was used as a model for many others.

7. The scandals frequently feature excessive, acquisitive growth and ambition, combined with overconfident management and boards that practice little challenge.

8. Effective boards need a mix of skills and experience across their membership, and a boardroom culture that enables those different perspectives to be brought to bear on the key issues facing the company. Independence matters—independence of thought, most of all—but knowledge and expertise also matter.

9. Good boards ensure that the company operates in an ethical and appropriate way and has a corporate culture that is conducive to long-term value creation in the interests of all stakeholders.

10. Two-tier boards are typical in Germany, the Netherlands, Scandinavia, and China; single-tier boards are typical in the USA, the UK, Japan, France, and most of the rest of the world. In the USA and France, boards generally have a single executive member, often acting as both chair and CEO. Japanese single-tier boards are dominated by executive directors, with only a handful of non-executives; most unitary boards lie somewhere in between these models.

11. Audits focus on close attention to, and assurance of, the financial statements. However, they entail only a limited requirement to read other material published alongside the financial statements and disclose inconsistencies.

12. The new enhanced auditor reports offer more valuable insights into the work of the auditor and also, potentially, into the quality of the controls and reporting at the audited company.

FURTHER READING

Armour, T., M. Barra, E. Breen. 2019. *Commonsense Principles 2.0.* Available at: www.governanceprinciples.org.

Brydon, D. 2019. *Assess, Assure and Inform: Improving Audit Quality and Effectiveness; Report of the Independent Review into the Quality and Effectiveness of Audit.* Available at: https://assets.publishing.service.gov.uk/government/uploads/system/uploads/attachment_data/file/852960/brydon-review-final-report.pdf.

Chartered Institute of Internal Auditors 2020. *Internal Audit Code of Practice.* Available at: www.iia.org.uk/media/1690932/iia-internal-audit-code-report-final.pdf.

Council of Institutional Investors 2018. Corporate Governance Policies. Available at: www.cii.org/files/10_24_18_corp_gov_policies.pdf.

Financial Reporting Council 2018. *Guidance on Board Effectiveness.* Available at: www.frc.org.uk/getattachment/61232f60-a338-471b-ba5a-bfed25219147/2018-Guidance-on-Board-Effectiveness-FINAL.PDF.

International Corporate Governance Network (ICGN) 2017. *ICGN Global Governance Principles.* Available at: www.icgn.org/policy/global-governance-principles.

Investor Stewardship Group 2019. *Corporate Governance Principles for US Listed Companies.* Available at: https://isgframework.org/corporate-governance-principles.

Organisation for Economic Co-operation and Development (OECD) 2019. *OECD Corporate Governance Factbook* 2019. Available at: www.oecd.org/corporate/corporate-governance-factbook.htm.

Recommended Books on Individual Scandals

Carreyrou, J. 2019. Bad Blood: Secrets and Lies in a Silicon Valley Startup. London: Pan Macmillan.

Woodford, M. 2012. Inside the Olympus Scandal: How I Went from CEO to Whistleblower. New York: Portfolio/Penguin.

SELF PRACTICE AND SELF ASSESSMENT

1. Which element of governance *most likely* has heightened importance in larger companies as opposed to smaller ones?
   a. The effective operation of governance processes
   b. The quality and thoughtfulness of board members
   c. A culture of strong performance without excessive risk taking

2. In the evolution of corporate governance frameworks, which practice developed *most* recently?
   a. Establishment of auditor oversight regulatory bodies
   b. Decreasing prominence of combined CEO/chair roles
   c. Establishment of, and regularly scheduled meetings of, audit committees

3. The interests of institutional investors are *most likely* protected through:
   a. pre-emptive rights.
   b. related-party transactions.
   c. dual-class share structures.

4. Which of the following is considered a principal committee, in place on the boards of most major companies?
   a. Risk committee
   b. Nominations committee
   c. Social and ethics committee

5. The effectiveness of a board chair is *best* evaluated by:
   a. engaging in direct dialogue with directors.
   b. referring to a board self-assessment report.
   c. assessing the quality of the directors on the board.

6. Which executive remuneration concern is *most likely* expressed by board members?
   a. Across the market as a whole, executive pay rates continue to ratchet up.
   b. Executive pay does not reflect the market performance of the shares.
   c. The executive pay structure does not incentivize executives to deliver maximum value.

7. French and American corporate governance practices are *most likely* similar with respect to:
   a. audit requirements.
   b. institutional investor power.
   c. board structure and type of chair.

8. Which element of enhanced auditor reports *most likely* provides insight into the auditor's assessment of the company's financial controls?
   a. Key audit matters
   b. Scope of the audit
   c. Performance materiality

Self Practice and Self Assessment 313

9. Compared to companies financed by public equity, those financed by private equity are *most likely* to face governance challenges arising from:
   a. a small margin for error.
   b. a lack of board responsiveness.
   c. investor susceptibility to misinformation.

10. The governance analysis of a public equity investment will differ *most* significantly from that of an investment in:
    a. fixed income.
    b. sovereign debt.
    c. property and infrastructure.

The following information relates to questions 11-25
Self Assessment Questions

These questions are provided only to enable you to test your understanding of the chapter content. They are not indicative of the types and standard of questions you may see in the examination. The Self-Assessment questions do not include an explanation of the correct answer.

11. What are the "two As" that lie at the heart of corporate governance?
    a. Advocacy and alignment
    b. Advocacy and argument
    c. Accountability and advocacy
    d. Accountability and alignment

12. Which of the following is NOT a reason why the role of the chair of a company board is so important?
    a. The chair sets the agenda for board discussions.
    b. The chair helps ensure that all directors make their full contribution.
    c. The chair will usually also be the CEO.
    d. The chair leads the process of selecting and appointing new directors.

13. Which of the following scandals did NOT help set the context for the creation of the first corporate governance code?
    a. Polly Peck
    b. Enron
    c. Mirror Group Newspapers
    d. Caparo

14. What was the model created by the Cadbury Code for adherence to its principles, still followed in the UK code?
    a. If not, why not?
    b. Comply or else.
    c. Apply and explain.
    d. Comply or explain.

15. What US legislation led to the creation of the Public Company Accounting Over-

sight Board (PCAOB)?

- a. Glass-Steagall Act
- b. Sarbanes-Oxley Act
- c. Dodd-Frank Act
- d. Accountable Capitalism Act

16. What were the two major scandals in Europe in 2003 that led to a reassessment of the continent's approach to governance?

- a. Ahold and Parmalat
- b. WorldCom and Tyco
- c. HIH and Satyam
- d. BCCI and Caparo

17. Which is the only major country that does NOT, as of 2022, have a corporate governance code?

- a. Japan
- b. France
- c. UK
- d. USA

18. Which of the following is NOT a board committee expected to be established at all companies?

- a. Audit
- b. Risk
- c. Nominations
- d. Remuneration

19. Which element of executive pay is most likely to include some metric based on ESG performance?

- a. Salary
- b. Benefits
- c. Annual bonus
- d. Long-term incentive or share scheme

20. Which of the following is NOT typically seen as a driver of concern regarding an individual director's independence?

- a. A family tie to an executive
- b. Recent senior role in a firm that provides advisory services
- c. Receiving share options in the company
- d. Not having been on the board long enough to fully understand the business

21. Which area of ethical corporate behavior is most likely to be subject to extraterritorial legislation?

- a. Anti-corruption
- b. Employee health and safety
- c. Supplier payments
- d. Lobbying activities

22. Which statement outlines the auditor's role in relation to both the financial state-

ments and the rest of the annual report and accounts?

a. Assurance on the financial statements and a report on inconsistencies in narrative reporting

b. Guarantee of accuracy of the financial statements and a report on inconsistencies in narrative reporting

c. Assurance on the financial statements and on narrative reporting

d. Assurance on the financial statements and on numbers within narrative reporting

23. How long can an audit firm remain in that role at an EU public company?

a. 5 years
b. 7 years
c. 10 years
d. 20 years

24. Which of the following is NOT one of the three key elements of disclosure in the new enhanced auditor reports?

a. Scope
b. Materiality
c. Skepticism
d. Key audit matters

25. Which of the following is NOT likely to be considered a *G* factor by a sovereign debt investor?

a. Corruption
b. Rule of law
c. Regulatory effectiveness
d. Proportion of investors that are PRI signatories

SOLUTIONS

1. A is correct. Board members of larger, more complex companies rely more heavily on governance processes to carry out their responsibilities. It is not possible for an individual board member to maintain sufficient direct knowledge across a complex organization, but it may be possible across smaller companies.

2. A is correct. Auditor oversight bodies are a relatively recent development, first established in the USA under the 2002 Sarbanes-Oxley Act. The emphasis on audit committees and the separation of the chair and CEO roles started in 1991 through the work of the Cadbury Committee in the UK.

3. A is correct. Pre-emptive rights ensure that investors, including institutional investors, can avoid dilution of their interest in a company by a dominant shareholder seeking to gain more control. Both related-party transactions and dual-class share structures are disadvantageous to minority shareholders such as institutional investors, as they can enable dominant shareholders to siphon resources from the company or maintain disproportionate control of voting rights, respectively.

4. B is correct. The nominations committee, the audit committee, and the remuneration committee are the principal committees on most public company boards.

5. C is correct. The quality of the directors on the board provides an indirect but otherwise clear signal of the chair's effectiveness, as strong board members are unlikely to stay on a board led by a weak chair. The other evaluation approaches can be used, but they are considered less likely to provide accurate assessments of the chair's effectiveness.

6. C is correct. Misunderstandings between board members and investors over executive pay have led to a lack of trust between the two parties, with board members concerned that their remuneration proposals could be voted down by investors. This situation may lead to the negotiation of a compromised executive pay structure that does not necessarily enable the executives to unlock the full potential of the company but is likely to receive voting support from investors. Broader concerns about market rates for executive pay and potential disconnects between executive pay and market performance are more often expressed by investors who are not on the board.

7. C is correct. Single-tier boards with combined chair and CEO roles are more common in the USA and France than in other countries. Institutional investor power is more constrained in France than in the USA because of the Florange Act of 2014. Audit requirements also differ between the two countries, as France is the only major market with a joint audit requirement.

8. C is correct. The auditor's assessment of the company's financial controls is implied by the magnitude of the discount from materiality used in the auditor's calculation of performance materiality. Larger discounts can signal that the company's financial controls have room for improvement.

9. A is correct. Companies financed by private equity are more likely to be highly indebted, leading to little margin for error even in an otherwise well-functioning governance system. Because private equity investors are often directly represented on the board, private equity boards are often more responsive and less subject to investor misinformation than their public board counterparts.

Solutions

10. B is correct. The assessment of governance for a sovereign debt investment includes elements not typically evaluated in assessing fixed-income or property and infrastructure issuers. Examples of sovereign-specific governance issues include corruption, competition in the economy, and adherence to the rule of law in the country's legal systems.

11. D is correct.

12. C is correct.

13. B is correct.

14. D is correct.

15. B is correct.

16. A is correct.

17. D is correct.

18. B is correct.

19. C is correct.

20. D is correct.

21. A is correct.

22. A is correct.

23. D is correct.

24. C is correct.

25. D is correct.

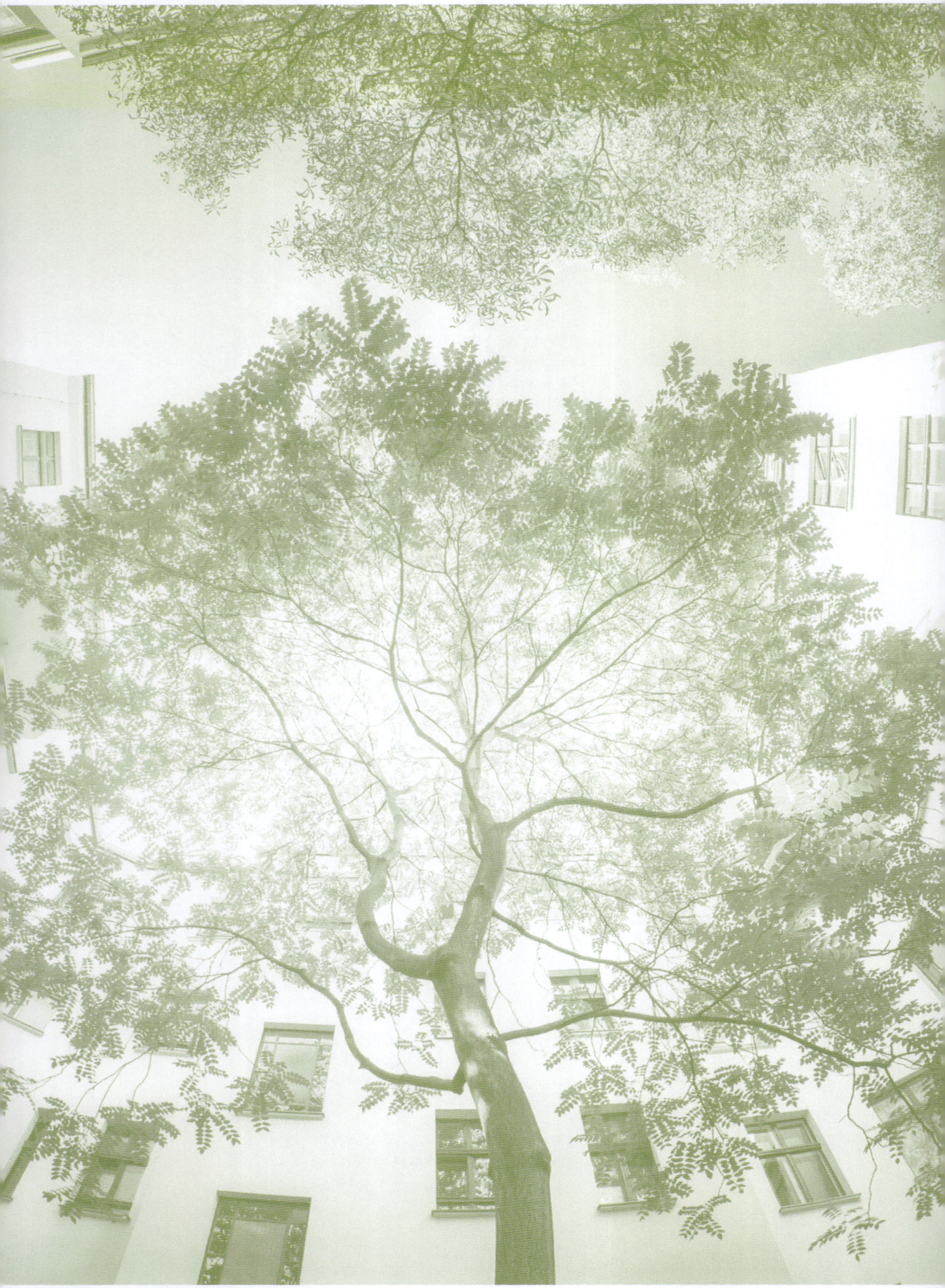

CHAPTER 6

Engagement and Stewardship

LEARNING OUTCOMES

Mastery	The candidate should be able to:
☐	**6.1.1** explain the purpose of investor engagement and stewardship
☐	**6.1.2** explain why engagement is considered beneficial and some of the key criticisms of engagement
☐	**6.1.3** explain the main principles and requirements of stewardship codes as they apply to institutional asset management firms: UK Walker Review (2009) and Stewardship Code (2020); US Employee Retirement Income Security Act (ERISA) guidelines; EU European Fund and Asset Management Association (EFAMA) Stewardship Code
☐	**6.1.4** explain how engagement is achieved in practice, including key differences in objectives, style, and tone
☐	**6.1.5** apply appropriate methods to establish an engagement approach: strategy and tactics-goal-setting; identifying who to talk with; formalities-hosting/agenda/managing expectations; communication-approach/tone/managing tensions; working towards agreement; escalation techniques, including collective engagement; ESG investment forums; proxy voting
☐	**6.1.6** describe approaches of engagement across a range of asset classes

1. STEWARDSHIP & ENGAGEMENT: WHAT'S INVOLVED AND WHY IT'S IMPORTANT

☐	**6.1.1**	explain the purpose of investor engagement and stewardship
☐	**6.1.2**	explain why engagement is considered beneficial and some of the key criticisms of engagement

Stewardship is typically used as an overarching term encompassing the approach that investors take as active and involved owners of the companies and other entities in which they invest through voting and engagement. Voting is one aspect of stewardship activity and tends to focus on corporate governance matters raised at shareholders' meetings.

Engagement is the way in which investors put into effect their stewardship responsibilities in line with the Principles for Responsible Investment (PRI) principle 2 ("We will be active owners and incorporate environmental, social and governance (ESG) issues into our ownership policies and practices"). It is often described as purposeful dialogue with a specific objective in mind; that purpose will vary from engagement to engagement but often relates to improving companies' business practices, especially in relation to the management of ESG issues.

Stewardship ought to be a consequence of investment. By contrast, activism is typically a specialist form of such engagement and stewardship, where an investment institution initiates an investment with the intent of generating investment outperformance through driving change with respect to a company's governance, capital allocation, or business practices. Most frequently now associated with activist hedge funds, the activism mindset appears increasingly short-term and involves extraction of value rather than the longer-term value creation that is the driver for most engagement.

This chapter considers what we mean by stewardship and engagement and covers the emergence of different styles of engagement. We consider the framework of guidelines and rules that direct the approach to stewardship and discuss how engagement can be delivered most effectively.

What Is Stewardship? What Is Engagement?

Stewardship is an odd word that does not translate easily, yet it is regularly used globally to describe the responsibilities of institutional investors. It is a term that has a long history. The word "steward" is derived from two Old English words ("stig" and "weard") describing a guardian of a home—to protect the owner's assets. What in the Middle Ages was the home and its estate, in the 21st century is assets bought on financial markets. The steward is the representative of the owner, charged with acting in the owner's interests and delivering returns and long-term value from their assets.

As the first stewards emerged, the concept of fiduciary duty was developed. Fiduciary duty is an obligation by the person (fiduciary) to look after another person's assets; a person with a fiduciary duty must seek to protect and enhance the value of the assets with which they have been charged so that they are able to return them in good order to their owner. As the representative of the owner, caring for assets on the owner's behalf, the steward should always feel the burden of fiduciary duty.

Stewardship is the process of intervention to make sure that the value of the assets is enhanced over time, or at least does not deteriorate through neglect or mismanagement. The process can encompass the buying and selling of assets to maintain value within the fund as a whole, as well as acting as a good owner of assets. Engagement is one aspect of good stewardship; it is the individual interventions in specific assets to preserve and/or enhance value. In modern investment terms, this is the dialogue with the management and boards of investee companies and other assets. Voting is a particular form of engagement. It is the most visible form because public company annual general meetings (AGMs) are public events and many institutions now make their voting actions public (some even ahead of the relevant meetings). However, by its nature it is formulaic because the nature of the resolutions on which shareholders vote is restricted by law. Engagement is much broader than just voting.

Given its focus on preserving and enhancing long-term value on behalf of the asset owner, engagement can encompass the full range of issues that affect the long-term value of a business, including

- strategy;
- capital structure;
- operational performance and delivery;
- risk management;
- pay; and
- corporate governance.

ESG factors are clearly integral to these. Opportunities and challenges offered by ESG developments need to be reflected in the business's strategic thinking. Equally, a full assessment of operational performance must encompass not only financials but also vital areas relevant to the company's stakeholders:

- highlighting the long-term health of the business, such as relations with the workforce;
- establishing a culture that favors long-term value creation;
- dealing openly and fairly with suppliers and customers; and
- having proper and effective environmental controls in place.

An understanding of the complete range of key risks facing a business will always include ESG factors; and clearly remuneration and governance are integral to the **G** in ESG.

Stewardship and engagement are beneficial because they enhance shareholder value and support investors in the execution of their fiduciary duty—indeed for many, stewardship is simply putting fiduciary duty into effect. When done well, stewardship and engagement encourage enhanced information flows between investors and investees as the parties discuss and debate issues. These exchanges allow them to learn from each other and to build relationships and, most importantly, encourage change as shareholders communicate their perspectives on key issues that the company is facing.

As stewardship is a reflection of fiduciary duty, it needs to be actively considered by any party charged with fiduciary duties. This will include most parties in the modern investment chain from underlying beneficiary through to asset owner (pension fund, insurer, or other fund) to fund manager and those directing the investment asset. Any of these parties could carry out stewardship functions, but in practice, the role typically rests with those with the greatest aggregated scale—usually, the fund manager. Only the very largest asset owners seek to carry out stewardship activities themselves. The expectations for stewardship are typically set out in the investment mandate, the contract between asset owner and fund manager (which is discussed in detail in Chapter 9).

In a 2018 report, the Principles for Responsible Investment highlighted three ESG engagement dynamics that it believes create value:

- communicative dynamics (the exchange of information);
- learning dynamics (enhancing knowledge); and
- political dynamics (building relationships).[1]

---

1 PRI, *How ESG Engagement Creates Value for Investors and Companies – Executive Summary* (2018). Available at: www.unpri.org/academic-research/how-esg-engagement-creates-value-for-investors-and-companies/3054.article

Developing these dynamics requires investors to go beyond a superficial understanding of the company and its activities. Unless the steward strives to build communication and relationships and has a desire to learn, engagement is unlikely to be successful. In order to be successful in engagement, investors need to respect the individual circumstances of the company, seeking understanding and rapport, and not simply declare that things need to change. This means that good engagement is time consuming and tailored to the individual company.

Different investors may have varying definitions of what successful engagement is. The usual definition of engagement—a purposeful dialogue with a specific objective in mind—presupposes something vital: that the engager sets objectives for their engagement at the start of the process, and the dialogue's purpose is to deliver those objectives over time. While various investors both set objectives and measure their delivery differently, engagement is successful only to the extent that it delivers the pre-agreed objectives. Financial success in terms of business performance or share price performance may consequently occur but will always be subsidiary to the first measurement of success. This is because much engagement is about safeguarding value rather than increasing it, and it is not possible to know what might have been in the absence of engagement.

This mindset of success being measured against the delivery of pre-agreed objectives fits well with the new thought process revealed in the UK's Stewardship Code (2020) (discussed in further detail later in this chapter). The Financial Reporting Council, in the Code, repeatedly discusses the need for signatories to disclose the outcomes of their engagement work as well as the concrete benefits from stewardship activity for clients and beneficiaries. The Code also repeatedly uses the word "outcome" to describe "delivery of objectives that benefit clients."

Just as with ESG and investment performance, there is a growing body of evidence that engagement adds value to portfolios. One of the earliest articles to provide a detailed academic analysis of engagement impact was "Returns to Shareholder Activism: Evidence from a Clinical Study of the Hermes UK Focus Fund".[2] This looked at the early years of the Hermes Focus Fund business (which was launched in late 1998) and considered the first 41 investments by the fund. It studied the internal records of Focus Fund team activities and considered their impact both in terms of delivering change at the companies in question and in delivering returns for the investors. To assess this, the study sought to identify engagement success by analyzing the objectives that were set for each engagement at the start. It found that the majority of these stated objectives were achieved, with a 65% success rate overall, with greatest success in restructuring and financial policies and slightly less success with regard to board change. Ironically perhaps, the lowest success rate was found in areas where shareholder engagement occurs more frequently, with only 25% of the remuneration policy changes sought achieved and only 44% of the sought improvements to investor relations. While analyzing this success, the study also found that the fund achieved positive financial returns. At the time, the overall performance of the fund was 4.9% net of fees a year in excess of the FTSE All-Share Performance; 90% of this excess return is attributed to activist outcomes.

In *Active Ownership* a different (anonymous) fund manager's engagement record was studied in depth, looking at the years 1999–2009.[3] This study considered less activist investing and more what would now be considered standard ESG engagement and stewardship. One benefit of studying this style of engagement is that the number

---

[2] M. Becht, J.R. Franks, C. Mayer, and S. Rossi, "Returns to Shareholder Activism: Evidence from a Clinical Study of the Hermes UK Focus Fund," *ECGI – Finance Working Paper No 138* (2006). Available at: https://ssrn.com/abstract=934712

[3] E. Dimson, O. Karakaş, and X. Li, "Active Ownership," *Review of Financial Studies (RFS)* 28, no. 12 (2015): 3225–68. Available at: https://ssrn.com/abstract=2154724

of cases covered in the study is substantial. Even though it considered only US activity by the fund manager, it covered more than 2,000 engagements, involving over 600 investee companies, and had an overall success rate of 18%.

The core finding of this study was clear: Successful engagement activity was followed by positive abnormal financial returns. For example, for successes in climate change engagements over the study period, the excess return in the year following engagement was more than 10% and was nearly 9% for successful corporate governance engagements. Typically, the time between initial engagement and success was 1.5 years, with two or three engagements being required. On average, ESG engagement generated an abnormal return of 2.3% in the year after the initial engagement, rising to 7.1% for successful engagements and with no adverse response to unsuccessful engagement.

A more recent study finds that ESG engagement leads to a reduction in downside risk and that the effect is stronger the more successful the engagement is.[4] In this case, the effects were strongest in relation to governance (which also counts for the majority of engagement cases) and then for social issues (so long as these are also associated with work on governance).

These studies show that engagement—if carried out well, so that it is focused on material and relevant issues and pursued with persistence—can work. Engaged companies change their behaviors against ESG factors, and this leads to increased value.

Engagement also works, often, to further inform investment analysis and fill out an investor's understanding of the potential for a business model to adapt to a changing business environment and evolving expectations and of the willingness of a particular management team and board to strategically address these challenges. Thus, engagement for many is a crucial part of active investment decision making.

Why Engagement?

Engagement helps investee companies to understand their investors' (and potential investors') expectations, allowing them to shape their long-term strategies accordingly to suit them. Engagement also enables companies to explain how their approach to sustainability relates to their broader business strategy and can provide an opportunity for companies to comment on ratings or scores driven by templates that they feel do not reflect the complexity of an issue.

Engagement also clearly allows investors to work closely with an investee over time on specific governance, social, or environmental issues that the investor regards as posing a downside risk to the business. By working with companies' management—either individually or collectively—investment firms are able to influence companies to adopt better ESG practices, or at least to relinquish poor practices.

The Investor Forum, a UK group set up to facilitate collective dialogue between investors and investees, describes engagement as "active dialogue with a specific and targeted objective … the underlying aim … should always be to preserve and enhance the value of assets."

In a 2019 white paper, *Defining Stewardship and Engagement*, the Investor Forum provides a framework for understanding the nature and key elements of stewardship.[5] Not least by defining stewardship in terms of assets with which an organization has been entrusted, this framework deliberately frames stewardship within the context of fiduciary duty. Trustees (of pension funds or other assets) and directors fully understand that they are fiduciaries because they are charged with caring for assets on behalf of

---

[4] A.G.F. Hoepner, I. Oikonomou, Z. Sautner, Z. et al, "ESG Shareholder Engagement and Downside Risk," *AFA 2018 Paper* (2018). Available at: https://ssrn.com/abstract=2874252
[5] The Investor Forum, *Defining Stewardship and Engagement* (2019). Available at: www.investorforum.org.uk/wp-content/uploads/securepdfs/2019/04/Defining-Stewardship-Engagement-April-2019.pdf

others. Because they are also entrusted with assets, similar fiduciary duties apply to investment institutions as well. The Forum argues that stewardship is one aspect of delivering on those duties.

Exhibit 1: The Components of Stewardship

Stewardship
Preserving and enhancing the value of assets with which one has been entrusted

... delivered through ...

Investment approach and decision
Allocation of capital in accordance with investment purpose, mandate, and client interests, at portfolio and individual asset levels

Dialogue
Active discussions between companies and investors, of which there are two principal forms:

Monitoring	**Engagement**
Dialogue for investment purposes: to understand the company, its stakeholders and performance. Informs incremental buy/sell/hold decisions.	Purposeful dialogue with a specific and targeted objective to achieve change. Individual or collective basis, as appropriate.

... typified by ...

Detailed and specific questioning; investors seeking insights	Two-way dialogue; investors expressing opinions

... characteristics of high-quality delivery ...

- Framed by close understanding of the nature of a company and drivers of its business model and long-term opportunity to prosper.
- Appropriately resourced, so dialogue can be delivered professionally in the context of full understanding of individual company.
- Dialogue must be consistent, direct, and honest.
- Dialogue is respectful and seeks to build mutual trust.

▸ Set in a context of mutual understanding of fund manager's investment style and approach.	▸ Set in a context of long-term ownership and focus on long-term value preservation and creation, so that engagement is aligned with investment thesis.
▸ Recognizes that change within companies is a process and sometimes takes time to be reflected in external indicators of performance.	▸ Recognizes that change is a process; while haste may at times be needed, change cannot be inappropriately rushed.
▸ Resources are used efficiently so that neither party's time is wasted.	▸ Overall resources used efficiently, so engagement coverage is as broad as possible, while also proving effective.
▸ Fuller insight leads to better informed decisions.	▸ Clear and specific objective leads to effective change.
▸ Includes feedback so that mutual understanding can be reinforced over time.	▸ Involves reflection, so lessons are learned and taken fully into account in future.

... resulting in ...

▸ Changed investor decision making.	▸ Changed company behaviors.
▸ Efficient capital allocation by investors.	▸ Efficient capital allocation by companies.
▸ Appropriate risk-adjusted returns for clients.	▸ Appropriate risk management by companies.
▸ Preserved/enhanced value.	▸ Preserved/enhanced value.
▸ Delivery of client objectives and investment purpose.	▸ Delivery of corporate purpose and culture, through effective oversight.

Source: The Investor Forum.[5]

Particularly key in this analysis is the contrast that it draws between monitoring and engagement dialogues. As the paper articulates, monitoring dialogues are the conversations between investors and management to more fully understand performance and opportunity, which are typified by detailed questions from the investor and which are likely to inform buy, sell, or hold investment decisions. In contrast, engagement dialogues are conversations between investors and any level of the investee entity (including non-executive directors) featuring a two-way sharing of perspectives, such that the investors express their position on key issues and, in particular, highlight any concerns that they may have. This two-way dialogue and expression of clear positions is necessary for engagement to deliver on its intended outcomes, of changed company behaviors, and so on. If engagement is to be effective in generating change outcomes, it requires that a clear objective has been set from the start.

This distinction between monitoring dialogues and genuine engagement shows the ways in which stewardship can sometimes be ineffective or inappropriate. There can be occasions where engagement activity is directed at companies that are unlikely to change and have no intent to enter into a productive dialogue with their investors. Engagement with these companies has limited benefit, yet some clients may suspect that it is an excuse to continue to hold onto a company that is otherwise unsuitable for a portfolio but the portfolio manager wishes to keep exposure to for performance reasons. This is not considered real engagement, but more like a cover for investment decision making.

The opposite can also occur: engagement as a response to poor investment decision making. Very often, a desire to engage arises from a share price fall. Active fund managers may then become concerned about issues that may have been apparent for a time but which may have been ignored as the performance was positive. Experience tends to show that such knee-jerk engagement is less likely to be effective than long-standing consistent messaging (where intensity may increase at moments of difficulty, but messaging does not just begin at those moments). Key identifiers of successful genuine engagement include clarity and consistency about objectives and ensuring that it is clear when the investor is communicating messages to the company and not just seeking information from it.

The delivery of concrete outcomes is core to the "why" of engagement. Effective engagement generates change, and if the intended engagement outcomes have been chosen well, that change will preserve and enhance long-term value at the company subject to the engagement itself. Thus, engagement delivers on the promise of fiduciary duty: preserving and enhancing the value of assets that the investor is overseeing on behalf of clients and beneficiaries.

As well as this need for clear objectives, focused on effecting change, the paper also identifies a series of other characteristics of effective engagement. These are a gathering of the "characteristics of high-quality delivery" set out in Exhibit 1 and require that high-quality delivery

- is set in an appropriate context of long-term ownership and has a focus on long-term value preservation and creation, so that the engagement is aligned with the investment thesis;
- is framed by a close understanding of the nature of the company and the drivers of its business model and long-term opportunity to prosper;
- recognizes that change is a process and that, while haste may at times be necessary, change should not be inappropriately rushed;
- employs consistent, direct, and honest messages and dialogue;
- is appropriately resourced so that it can be delivered professionally in the context of a full understanding of the individual company;
- uses resources efficiently so that engagement coverage is as broad as possible while using all the tools available, including collective engagement; and
- involves reflection so that lessons are learned in order to improve future engagement activity.

These characteristics are explored through the case studies and wider discussion in the following.

Engagement in Practice

Some examples of how this form of process can influence companies to adopt improved ESG practices are described in this section.

EXAMPLE 1

Examples of Engagement in Practice

A PRI case study[6] describes Boston Common Asset Management's long-term engagement with VF Corporation (VF Corp) around the water risks in its cotton and leather supply chains. This multi-year engagement—during which Boston Common submitted and then withdrew a shareholder resolution (withdrawing it in response to the company's commitment to address the issue)—saw VF Corp improve relevant reporting, undertake material risk assessment and sign up to good practice standards in the Better Cotton Initiative.

Hermes EOS's (Equity Ownership Services')[7] engagement with Siam Cement has seen that company improve from a level one company (the lowest score) to level three as rated by the Transition Pathway Initiative (an asset-owner-led initiative that assesses companies' preparation for the transition to a low carbon economy).[1] In early 2018, the investment firm met senior management to discuss its 2020 emissions targets. It then held a TCFD (Task Force on Climate-Related Financial Disclosures) workshop with senior executives at Siam Cement to share industry best practice and to encourage the company to improve assessment of physical risks of its assets, take part in industry collaboration, and establish a

---

[6] C. Bichta, *Growing Water Risk Resilience: An Investor Guide on Agricultural Supply ChainsCase Study: Engagement* (2018). Available at: www.unpri.org/environmental-issues/long-term-engagement-on-water-risk-management-in-the-supplychain/2811.article

[7] C. Chow, *Siam Cement* (2018). Available at: www.hermes-investment.com/uki/eos-insight/eos/siam-cement/

group-wide climate governance mechanism. The company has now committed to the Paris Agreement's global temperature limitation goal, extended its scenario planning, and improved its governance and business management around climate.

In 2018, the Investor Forum worked with its members to address concerns around Imperial Brands' strategic direction, operational execution, and disclosures. The chair engaged "rapidly and constructively ... announcing a disposal programme, enhancing its communications on its approach to Next Generation Products and implementing changes to segmental reporting at the full year results".[8]

There are also situations where engagement (or at least some form of stewardship) is *required* and when an investor must take a view. These could be corporate actions, such as share issuances in which the investor can choose to participate or not, or proposed takeovers where the investor must decide whether to sell up or, if it is permitted, to hold on to their shares. For most investors, some dialogue with the company will be needed before reaching the relevant conclusion.

Most investors now regard the vote as a client asset like any other, and thus as something to be considered carefully and exercised with due thought. Voting comes around annually, at the AGM, and occasionally in between at special meetings, in most countries called extraordinary general meetings (EGMs). In addition to voting to receive the report and accounts, the issues considered at each AGM depend on local law but are often fundamental issues about the structure of the board, audit and oversight, executive pay, and the capital structure of the company. Not considering such issues with due care can clearly be seen to be a failure of fiduciary duty, and due care will often require active dialogue with the company in order to understand the issues and express any concerns and perspectives.

Another driver for investors to act as good stewards is the growing expectations enshrined in codes, standards, and regulations.

CODES/STANDARDS & ENGAGEMENT STYLES

6.1.3 explain the main principles and requirements of stewardship codes as they apply to institutional asset management firms: UK Walker Review (2009) and Stewardship Code (2020); US Employee Retirement Income Security Act (ERISA) guidelines; EU European Fund and Asset Management Association (EFAMA) Stewardship Code

6.1.4 explain how engagement is achieved in practice, including key differences in objectives, style, and tone

Regulators are convinced that engagement adds value, not just within investment portfolios but for markets as a whole. In his powerful 2008 report on the financial crisis, Sir David Walker stated:

> *Before the recent crisis phase there appears to have been a widespread acquiescence by institutional investors and the market in the gearing up of the balance sheets of banks ... as a means of boosting returns on equity.*

---

8 The Investor Forum, *Review 2018* (2018). Available at: www.investorforum.org.uk/wp-content/uploads/2019/01/Annual_Review_2018.pdf

The limited institutional efforts at engagement with several UK banks appear to have had little impact in restraining management before the recent crisis phase.[9]

Regulatory interest in stewardship has grown from the disappointment of that financial crisis. As an adjunct to the institutional investor soul-searching that followed the crisis, the Walker report ushered in a new era of shareholder engagement. The report formally called for the Financial Reporting Council (FRC) to issue a stewardship code to provide a framework for shareholder engagement and for this code to be reinforced by a Financial Services Authority (FSA, now the Financial Conduct Authority or FCA) requirement that any registered fund manager must make a statement as to whether and how it approached its principles.

Following consultation, in 2010 the FRC issued the world's first stewardship code —largely unchanged from the existing *Statement of Principles on the Responsibilities of Institutional Shareholders and Agents* issued by the Institutional Shareholders Committee in 2005 (itself built upon a 1991 document, *The Responsibilities of Institutional Shareholders in the UK*). Industry best practice had not delivered in the run-up to the financial crisis, but a code with regulatory backing was thought likely to have greater force. Industry acceptance of the code was relatively rapid, particularly among fund managers.

The 2010 Stewardship Code had seven principles: Institutional investors should

1. publicly disclose their policy on how they will discharge their stewardship responsibilities;
2. have a robust policy on managing conflicts of interest in relation to stewardship and this policy should be publicly disclosed;
3. monitor their investee companies;
4. establish clear guidelines on when and how they will escalate their activities as a method of protecting and enhancing shareholder value;
5. be willing to act collectively with other investors where appropriate;
6. have a clear policy on voting and disclosure of voting activity; and
7. report periodically on their stewardship and voting activities.

This UK Code went through a further iteration in 2012, clarifying the distinction between the roles of asset owners (pension funds and the like) and their fund managers and other agents but leaving the principles themselves almost entirely unchanged. While some of the largest pension funds may seek to carry out stewardship activities themselves, most delegate this role, either by a specific contract or as part of their fund management services. Thus, the role of most asset owners is overseeing, challenging, and assessing the stewardship activities of their service providers.

The UK Stewardship Code model has been followed around the world, and at the time of writing, there are now such codes in 20 markets, either developed by stock exchanges or regulators or by investor bodies themselves keen to advance best practice. Among these are the following:

▶ Global—*ICGN Global Stewardship Principles* (2016).[10]

---

[9] HM Treasury, *A Review of Corporate Governance in UK Banks and Other Financial Industry Entities: Final Recommendations* (2009). Available at: https://webarchive.nationalarchives.gov.uk/+/www.hm-treasury.gov.uk/d/walker_review_261109.pdf

[10] ICGN, *ICGN Global Stewardship Principles* (2016). Available at: https://www.icgn.org/icgn-global-stewardship-principles

Codes/Standards & Engagement Styles

- Europe—*EFAMA Stewardship Code* (2018).[11]
- Australia—*Australian Asset Owner Stewardship Code* (2018).[12]
- Brazil—*AMEC Stewardship Code* (2016).[13]
- Japan—*Principles for Responsible Institutional Investors* (2020).[14]
- Singapore—*Singapore Stewardship Principles (SSP) for Responsible Investors* (2016).[15]
- United States—*The Principles* (2016).[16]

It is notable that while there is great consistency between the principles in each of these codes, as they are modeled closely on the seven principles of the 2010 UK Code, conflicts of interest are dealt with very differently. It has been stated that those codes drafted by the fund management industry are more likely to downplay the issue of conflicts, while those codes with greater regulatory backing place greater emphasis on the issue. Perhaps most striking is the European Fund and Asset Management Association (EFAMA) Code, which is almost a direct copy of the 2012 UK Code except that it does not include a separate principle on conflicts and avoids the issue almost entirely.

Code Revisions 2020

The UK Stewardship Code went through a more fundamental redrafting to produce the 2020 version of the code, published in late 2019.[17] The new code, which came into effect on 1 January 2020, includes 12 principles (plus an alternate 6 for service providers), where formerly there were 7, and three times the number of pages as the 2012 code. But the biggest change is not the growth of the document, but the increased ambition for practical delivery by signatories. The former focus on statements of intent no longer exists. Instead, investors are now expected to report annually on activity and, most importantly, on outcomes from that activity. The first such annual reports were expected to be delivered by the end of March, setting out policy, activity, and outcomes during 2020.

Merely reporting on activity is not enough; each of the new principles has associated outcomes that must be reported on and requires concrete examples of what has been delivered practically for clients and beneficiaries. Signatories will no longer fulfil the demands of the Code by publishing policy statements filled with ambitious assertions, instead they must deliver practical effects from their actions.

The 12 new principles fall into four categories but cover two distinct functions:

- Principles 1 through 8 address the foundations for stewardship.

---

11 European Fund and Asset Management Association, *EFAMA Stewardship Code* (2018). Available at: www.efama.org/newsroom/news/efama-stewardship-code-principles-asset-managers-monitoring-voting-engagement
12 Australian Council of Superannuation Investors, *Australian Asset Owner Stewardship Code* (2018). Available at: https://acsi.org.au/members/australian-asset-owner-stewardship-code/
13 Associação de Investidores no Mercado de Capitais, *Codigo AMEC de Principios e Deveres dos Investidores Institucionais Stewardship* (2016). Available at: https://en.amecbrasil.org.br/stewardship/amec-stewardship-code/
14 The Council of Experts on the Stewardship Code, *Principles for Responsible Institutional Investors* (2020). Available at: www.fsa.go.jp/en/refer/councils/stewardship/20200324/01.pdf
15 Stewardship Asia, *Singapore Stewardship Principles (SSP) for Responsible Investors* (2016). Available at: www.stewardshipasia.com.sg/enable/investors
16 Investor Stewardship Group, *The Principles* (2019). Available at: https://isgframework.org/stewardship-principles/
17 Financial Reporting Council, *UK Stewardship Code* (2020). Available at: www.frc.org.uk/investors/uk-stewardship-code

- Principles 9 through 12 focus on the practical discharge of engagement responsibilities.

The need to report on concrete outcomes applies even to the foundational principles 1, 2, 3, 5, and 6 of the new code. These cover such structural issues within the investment institution as governance, culture, and conflicts of interest management. The outcomes that need to be disclosed in relation to these issues are evidence that those structures concretely work in practice in the clients' best interests.

Principles 7 and 8 require the integration of ESG factors into the investment process and include an effective oversight of service providers. The disclosures of related outcomes need to be explanations of how these processes have delivered effectively on behalf of clients and beneficiaries.

Principles 9 through 12 cover engagement (and voting) activities. The intended outcome of these principles (that must be part of the annual reporting) is to show substantive change at companies (or other investee assets) as a result of the engagement activity. The disclosure of at least some voting outcomes, not just the investor's voting activity, is also expected.

Perhaps the most challenging of the 12 is principle 4, which charges signatories with identifying and responding to marketwide and systemic risks. Some investment institutions already recognize their obligation on behalf of beneficiaries and clients to maintain and promote well-functioning markets and social and environmental systems, but for many this may feel like a significant additional burden. The requirement to "disclose an assessment of their effectiveness in identifying and responding to" such risks imposes a new and significant burden even for those who already recognize this as being a stewardship responsibility. Only the Australian Asset Owner Stewardship Code, developed by the industry body Australian Council of Superannuation Investors (ACSI), had a similar expectation in place, in its principle 5:

> *Asset owners should encourage better alignment of the operation of the financial system and regulatory policy with the interests of long-term investors. (ACSI 2018)*

While this new UK Code may prove as much of a model for global stewardship codes as its predecessors, the latest country to propose changes is Japan, which has not followed the UK's example closely. There is a move to require reporting on the outcomes of engagement activity, but this is downplayed and given little prominence so may have only a limited impact (the contrast to how central this is to the new UK Code is significant). Beyond this, the latest changes made to the Japanese Code were as follows:

- to extend coverage to all asset classes, not only equity;
- to incorporate sustainability and ESG;
- to add encouragement for asset owners to become involved in stewardship and provide a little more clarity on their role in the stewardship hierarchy; and
- to clarify the position of service providers in the hierarchy and add higher expectations of proxy advisers.

Code Provisions

Other than the new UK Stewardship Code, the principles of all the codes around the world are remarkably similar. Typically, there are six or seven principles, with the first often requiring investors to have a public policy regarding stewardship, and the last noting the need for honest and open reporting of stewardship activities. The main body of the principles between these two usually call for

- regular monitoring of investee companies;
- active engagement where relevant (sometimes termed "escalation," or sometimes escalation is deemed worthy of a separate principle of its own); and
- thoughtfully intelligent voting.

The two principles that are sometimes but not always present (though they appear in the UK Code in both its former and current iterations) require the following:

- investors are required to manage their conflicts of interest regarding stewardship matters; and
- the escalation of stewardship activity to include a willingness to act collectively with other institutional investors.

The collective engagement issue is controversial because there are concerns about the creation of concert parties (groups of shareholders so influential that they in effect take control of companies without mounting a formal takeover). This is not the intention of collective engagement, as is shown by the related discussion in this section.

Stewardship codes are usually now expressed to apply to all asset classes, but their language tends to reveal an initial focus in practice on public equity investment. The stewardship thought process, both by regulators and by investors, and the practical delivery of stewardship actions by those investors, is most developed in public equities. There is a discussion about the application of stewardship to other asset classes later in this chapter; it is more straightforward than some practitioners may indicate.

In 2016, the FRC went through a process of assessing the quality of the UK Code signatories (against the then-extant Code, the 2012 version). This was not based on the substance of the stewardship activity delivered but simply on the basis of the stewardship statements published by each signatory in response to principle 1. The regulator gave signatories an indication of which tier (1, 2, or 3) the quality of these disclosures placed them in, which led to a rapid improvement in the quality of disclosures.

The final results of this process showed that out of the 300 signatories in total, 120 were deemed to be tier 1 and best practice ("Signatories provide a good quality and transparent description of their approach to stewardship and explanations of an alternative approach where necessary"), compared with the 40 deemed by the FRC to be in that category in their initial assessment of Code disclosures at the start of the process. It is not yet clear whether or how the FRC will conduct a tiering process in relation to the new Code. If it does do so, the tougher expectations (and particularly the focus on outcomes) in the new 2020 Code seem likely to lead to a greater differentiation being drawn between signatories.

The number of stewardship codes in Europe is likely to increase significantly following the Shareholder Rights Directive II that came into force in June 2019. Among other things, SRD II, as it is known, will raise expectations in each country about the level of stewardship carried out by local investors. This is likely to supersede such initiatives as the voluntary EFAMA Code (updated in 2018 from the original 2011 version) and may move European markets towards expanding expectations that have regulatory backing. While by name, it is about shareholder rights, the directive in reality is more about shareholder responsibilities.

Expectations with regard to stewardship are set by legislation as well as codes. Foremost among these is the US ERISA legislation, the **Employee Retirement Income Security Act of 1974.** Among the Act's requirements, a number are relevant to stewardship, in particular, that advisers should act as fiduciaries in relation to the beneficiaries (under the US regime, fund management firms are deemed to be advisers and so subject to this standard). Among the obligations expected under fiduciary duty (as narrowly defined in the Act; it is worth noting that elsewhere in this chapter "fiduciary duty" refers to the general common law understanding of that duty and not this US-legislated definition) is that the fund will vote at investee company general meetings and engage with companies.

In the past, the legal interpretation of the Act was thought to discourage ESG stewardship because of a bulletin statement indicating that engagement and proxy use on environmental and social issues would be rare. But fresh interpretative statements from 2018 are more supportive of stewardship. The regulator's views, set out in the US Department of Labor's *Field Assistance Bulletin No. 2018-01*, confirm that fiduciaries can vote and use proxies if there is a reasonable expectation that such activities are likely to enhance the economic value of the investment after taking costs into account.[18] The *Bulletin* added that engagement might be prudent for indexed portfolios where ESG issues represent significant operational risks and costs. There continues to be a clear view that engagement, and indeed ESG investing, needs a firm basis in value for beneficiaries—so engaging would not be permissible to achieve purely social policy goals without making a clear link to value.

Engagement Styles

Some asset owners will choose to engage with companies directly, through team members who act as stewards of the investment portfolios. Others expect their external fund managers to deliver this work, either through the portfolio managers who also take stewardship responsibility, or through stewardship specialists (or some combination of the two). Engagement activities can also be entirely outsourced to specialist stewardship service providers.

Almost all institutional investors lean at least in part on one group of these service providers, the proxy voting advisory firms. These proxy advisers offer analysis and (in most cases) voting recommendations across many public companies, and almost all institutions hire them to provide the framework that ensures their voting decisions are delivered. Most also pay for their advice on those voting decisions.

Other stewardship service providers offer various degrees of engagement services, by effectively stepping into the shoes of the investor to engage on their behalf. By aggregating the interests of clients, the scale that is necessary to be present and visible enough in dialogue and engagement with company management and boards can be built. Boards can offer a form of collective engagement, enabling investors to have a greater reach and influence by working alongside others and sharing precious resources. Collaborative engagement can also take place through industry initiatives and collaboration platforms, such as one offered by the PRI or by the Investor Forum in the UK.

---

18 United States Department of Labor, *Field Assistance Bulletin No. 2018-01* (2018) Available at: www.dol.gov/agencies/ebsa/employers-and-advisers/guidance/field-assistance-bulletins/2018-01

Styles: Top-Down and Bottom-Up

To an extent, engagement styles vary depending on the heritage of stewardship teams. There is a distinction in mindset and approach between those teams with a history of governance-led engagement and those that have worked more on the environmental and social side.

The most obvious distinction is as material **E** and **S** issues arise from the nature of a company's business activities, teams with this heritage tend to be organized by sector, whereas as **G** is determined more by national law and codes, and such teams are usually split according to geography. Engagement style also follows this structure to some extent. Teams tend to focus on individual environmental and social issues and to pursue those vigorously across sectors or markets as a whole. This can encompass trying to establish better practice standards and highlighting leading practice as well as targeting those perceived as laggards. The dialogue would tend to start with investor relations or sustainability teams and then be escalated upwards, both to senior management and to the board level. Firms with a governance heritage tend to focus on individual companies, starting with the chair (often with the assistance of the company secretary) and working through the board and down to management from there.

These are generalizations, but they illustrate the distinction between top-down and bottom-up activity. Most investment houses mix the two, though company-focused, bottom-up engagement fits most naturally with active investment approaches, particularly those with concentrated portfolios; whereas issues-based, top-down engagement tends to align more closely with passive or otherwise broadly diversified investment portfolios.

Styles: Issue-Based and Company-Focused

Passive investors, and others with broadly diversified portfolios, typically start with an issue, whether identified by the team from news or broader analysis or through a screening or other research provider, and seek to engage with all the companies impacted by that issue (which may be a sector as a whole, or even broader). Usually, the starting point is a letter written to all those impacted, which is then followed up by dialogue. Active investors, particularly those with focused portfolios, start with the company itself and its business issues and develop a tailored engagement approach cutting across a range of issues, often with the investment teams taking a leading role. Companies selected for this approach are often identified from investment underperformers or ones that trigger other financial or ESG metrics. The starting point is typically to seek a direct discussion with senior management and then the board.

Larry Fink's annual letter to CEOs setting out BlackRock's engagement plans is an example of the issue-based approach taken by passive investors. In the 2019 letter, Fink wrote that their priorities for the year were,

> *Governance, including your company's approach to board diversity; corporate strategy and capital allocation; compensation that promotes long-termism; environmental risks and opportunities; and human capital management. These priorities reflect our commitment to engaging around issues that influence a company's prospects not over the next quarter, but over the long horizons that our clients are planning for.*[19]

Issue-based approaches to engagement are often accompanied by examples of what best practice in a particular area looks like. These may be developed in advance of the first engagement dialogues but usually come out of the engagement process with

---

[19] BlackRock, *Larry Fink's 2019 Letter to CEOs* (2019). Available at: https://www.blackrock.com/corporate/investor-relations/2019-larry-fink-ceo-letter

those companies that are deemed to have leading practices. By expecting all companies in a given sector to adopt these best practices, investors may over time move sector or industry practice forward overall. Company-focused engagement seeks to improve practice across a number of relevant ESG issues at an individual company; the aim is to enhance performance of the portfolio overall, in terms of both ESG and investment performance.

3 EFFECTIVE ENGAGEMENT: FORMS, GOAL SETTING

6.1.5 apply appropriate methods to establish an engagement approach: strategy and tactics-goal-setting; identifying who to talk with; formalities-hosting/agenda/managing expectations; communication-approach/tone/managing tensions; working towards agreement; escalation techniques, including collective engagement; ESG investment forums; proxy voting

Forms of Engagement

An Investor Forum white paper published in November 2019, "Collective Engagement: An Essential Stewardship Capability," identifies 12 different forms of engagement (The Investor Forum 2019b). Of these, 5 are types of individual engagement (engagement by a single investment institution):

1. *generic letter*: these are broad communications across a swathe of investment holdings;
2. *tailored letter*: these are more targeted and can cover a range of topics at varied levels of detail;
3. *"housekeeping" engagement*: this is annual dialogue to help maintain and enhance a relationship with a company, but with only limited objectives;
4. *active private engagement*: targeted and specific engagement; and
5. *active public engagement*: engagement deliberately made public by the institution.

The others are forms of collaborative engagement (where an institution works with one or more others):

1. *informal discussions*: institutions discuss views of particular corporate situations;
2. *collaborative campaigns*: collaborative letter-writing or market/sector-wide campaigns;
3. *follow-on dialogue*: company engagement dialogue led by one or more investors in follow-up to a broader group letter or expression of views;
4. *soliciting support*: solicitation of broader support for formal publicly stated targets (e.g., "vote no" campaigns or support for a shareholder resolution);
5. *group meeting(s)*: one-off group meeting (or a series of meetings) with a company, followed up either with individual investor reflections on the discussion or with a co-signed letter;

6. *collective engagement*: a formal coalition of investors with a clear objective, typically working over time and with a coordinating body; and
7. *concert party*: formal agreement, in any form, with concrete objectives and agreed steps (e.g., collectively proposing a shareholder resolution or agreeing how to vote on a particular matter).

The Investor Forum paper argues that as you go through the lists, there is a greater need for formality in approach and potentially greater regulatory attention. That greater formality requires increased clarity of the engagement objective(s) and can perhaps provide greater scope for influencing the change that is sought.

Gaining greater clarity of the engagement objective is particularly important as it forms one of the key success factors for effective engagement that the Investor Forum paper identifies (based on its own practical experience and a study of the academic literature).[20] In full, these six success factors are as follows:

Success Factor Characteristics of Engagement Approach

SF1. Objective(s) should be specific and targeted to enable clarity around delivery.

SF2. Objectives should be strategic or governance-led, or linked to material strategic and/or governance issues.

SF3. The engagement approach should be bespoke (tailored) to the target company.

Success Factor Characteristics of Investor Collaboration

SF4. The participants should have clear leadership with appropriate relationships, skills and knowledge.

SF5. The scale of coalition gathered (both scale of shareholding and overall assets under management of the group) should be meaningful.

SF6. The coalition should have a prior relationship and/or cultural awareness of the target company.

The Investor Forum paper continues by adding these success factors to a matrix alongside the 12 forms of engagement (listed earlier), indicating how likely each engagement is to fulfil the six stated success factors (the darker color shows a greater likelihood). Exhibit 2 shows the conclusions that are reached (which include a number of assumptions and generalizations yet are informative).

---

20 The Investor Forum, *Collective Engagement: An Essential Stewardship Capability* (2019). Available at: www.investorforum.org.uk/wp-content/uploads/securepdfs/2019/11/The-case-for-collective-engagement-211119.pdf

Exhibit 2: Success Factors and Styles of Institutional Investor Engagement

Success factor	CHARACTERISTICS OF ENGAGEMENT FOCUS			CHARACTERISTICS OF INVESTOR GROUPING AND APPROACH		
	SF1: Clear objective	SF2: Material and strategic	SF3: Bespoke	SF4: Effective leadership	SF5: Scale of coalition	SF6: Depth of relationship
Potential impact on effectiveness (low to high)	Express concern ↔ Specify change	Narrow ESG focus ↔ Include strategy and finance	Generic approach ↔ Close cultural awareness	Informal grouping ↔ Formal coalition	Limited ownership ↔ Broad and material share ownership	Limited relationship ↔ Top-level access
Individual institutional engagement						
Generic letter-writing				n/a	n/a	
Tailored letter-writing				n/a	n/a	
Housekeeping engagement				n/a	n/a	
Active private engagement				n/a	n/a	
Active public engagement				n/a	n/a	
Collaborative engagement						
Informal discussions						
Collaborative campaigns						
Follow-on dialogue						
Soliciting support						
Group meeting(s)						
Collective engagement						
Concert party						

Source: The Investor Forum.[20]

Strategy and Tactics: Goal-Setting

There are several challenges in engagement, the most significant being the question of resources. Does the investment firm have the time, the expertise, and sufficient leverage with its investees to engage successfully?

Given the scale of most fund management firms, the number of companies in which they invest client money is large, meaning that just the monitoring element of stewardship is a significant obligation on its own. Even where individual portfolios are concentrated, the aggregate is a rather broader exposure, with many moderate-sized investment firms owning a few thousand companies and the largest fund management houses holding tens of thousands. Having enough resources to engage effectively across all the companies in a firmwide portfolio is a significant challenge. In practice, every investor is resource-constrained.

Given these resource constraints, engagement strategies must be designed to deliver meaningful results in the most cost- and time-effective manner. In practice, this translates into a few operational challenges that need to be addressed in the following order.

1. Investors need to define the scope of the engagement and prioritize their engagement activities carefully in order to ensure it is value-adding for their clients/beneficiaries and impactful in terms of delivering improved corporate practices.

2. Investors need to frame the engagement topic (be it climate risk or supply chain risk) into the broader discussion around strategy and long-term financial performance with the management team and the board.

3. Investors must develop a clear process that articulates realistic goals and milestones so that both investment institutions and their clients have a clear indicator to measure their expectations and the effectiveness of the engagement strategy.

4. The engagement process needs to be adapted to the local context, language, and cultural approaches to doing business. Beyond dialogue, investors also need to have clear escalation measures in case engagement fails.

In many ways, this represents two different forms of necessary prioritization:

- identifying which company in a portfolio is most in need of engagement; and
- determining which engagement issues should be prioritized in the dialogue between the investor and company (if change is to be delivered effectively, it is impossible for an investor to raise every possible concern with the company—not least because they risk creating confusion as to what issues the investor believes are most in need of attention).

The approach to engagement must always sit within the framework of the fund manager's investment approach, and an active manager may well find it easier to prioritize both the company and the issue as those where most value is at risk within portfolios. The existence of risk suggests that if the manager is an active manager, selling a holding in a company (or other investment asset) will always be a possible appropriate action for a responsible fiduciary to take.

For passive investors, the same value-at-risk dynamic should be the driver, but it may come less naturally to the decision-making teams, because they are less used to identifying where the most value is at risk in the portfolio. This approach will tend to mean a focus on the largest companies and on the most material issues, although there may be issues that certain clients put particular emphasis on. These issues and companies are then deemed to deserve greater attention and so move up the prioritization list.

Many fund managers are building their stewardship resources by adding to their specialist stewardship teams. Passive fund managers (who invest in the broadest range of companies) perhaps have no option but to do so, while many active investment houses are working to ensure that their active portfolio managers can deliver stewardship alongside their regular monitoring of investee companies. Even where portfolio managers take the lead, they will typically need the support and partnership of a specialist stewardship team.

Potentially, another key additional resource is external collective vehicles—commercial stewardship operations or investor groups. Many of these have staff with a different and complementary range of skills that fund managers can use. For example, engagement on a particular theme, such as palm oil or water, is likely to require particular knowledge and experience that may be difficult to resource internally. Collaboration with an investor with particular skill in an area or with a collective vehicle that can bring alternative skills to bear can enable an investor to make progress that might not be possible alone. In addition, working collectively can help those investors whose individual holdings might be relatively small to gain traction in their discussion with management and boards.

The behavioral challenges involved in working as part of investor coalitions are significant. These include the challenges of reaching consensus, conflicts of interest, and competition.

Investors will often agree that there is a problem at a company or at least that they share concerns about a company. But discussions about collective action often fail because the investors are unable to reach any consensus about what might need to change at the company to address the problem. Having said that, agreement is not always possible between investors even on the nature of the problem. Companies sometimes rightly feel that they receive such a range of views from investors that responding to them all is impossible (although some investors often feel this is an excuse rather than a reason for inaction).

The PRI's 2018 report on how engagement adds value for investors and companies found that individual engagement can be more strategically valuable (and might allow an investor to resolve an ambiguous or anomalous position that they might prefer to deal with alone), but that individual approaches can be time-consuming and costly (PRI 2018d). The report suggests that "engagement practices should be adapted to balance the trade-offs of individual and collective forms of engagement."

In the same report, the PRI identified common enablers and barriers to successful engagement from both corporate and investor perspectives.

Exhibit 3: Contrasting Perceptions of the Enablers and Barriers to Engagement Success

	Corporate Perspectives		Investor Perspectives	
	Enablers	**Barriers**	**Enablers**	**Barriers**
Relational Factors	▶ Existence of an actual two-way dialogue. ▶ Being honest and transparent in the dialogue, and having an 'open and objective discussion'.	▶ Language barriers and communication issues. ▶ Lack of continuity in interactions.	▶ Good level of commitment on both sides to meet objectives. ▶ Reciprocal understanding of the engagement process and issues on both sides. ▶ Good communication and listening capacities on both sides.	▶ Language barriers and cultural differences can hamper dialogue.
Corporate Factors	▶ Responsiveness and willingness to act upon investor requests. ▶ Selecting appropriate internal experts. ▶ Knowing your investors, access to prior discussions to tailor conversations. ▶ Systematic tracking of interactions with investors.	▶ Company bureaucracy preventing changes in internal practices and/or external reporting on (new) practices. ▶ Lack of resources, insufficient knowledge to meet investor demands. ▶ Lack of actual ESG policies, practices and/or results that can be reported externally.	▶ Corporate reactivity to requests. ▶ Board-level access in targeted companies. ▶ Access to appropriate corporate experts. ▶ Long-standing relationships with key corporate actors. ▶ Corporate proactivity to inform investors when engagement objectives/targets have been met.	▶ Refusal by top executives to be engaged on ESG issues. ▶ Functional/sustainability manager struggles to advance ESG related issues. ▶ Too small a shareholding to attract sufficient attention. ▶ Corporate inability to meet (on-going) objectives and targets.

Effective Engagement: Forms, Goal Setting

| | Corporate Perspectives || Investor Perspectives ||
	Enablers	Barriers	Enablers	Barriers
Investor Factors	▸ Listening capacities of investors. ▸ Communicating in different languages. ▸ Providing questions in advance. ▸ Prior knowledge of corporate ESG practice and performance. ▸ Genuine interest in (improving) the management of ESG issues at the company. ▸ Patience and understanding regarding corporate ability to address ESG challenges.	▸ Lack of investor preparation, overly generic questions/requests. ▸ Lack of knowledge about the company (e.g., ESG policy, track record). ▸ Lack of sufficient investor tracking process to determine whether engagement requests have been met. ▸ Changing engagement objectives and targets.	▸ Client or beneficiary requests for the consideration of ESG issues. ▸ Top-management support for ESG-related investment activities. ▸ Well-resourced and experienced ESG team. ▸ Clear engagement objectives and targets. ▸ In-house tracking tools to monitor and evaluate engagement progress. ▸ Pooling of resources through collective engagement.	▸ Lack of buy-in from clients and/or top management for ESG-related investment activities. ▸ Small, under-resourced ESG team. ▸ Lack of clear engagement policies, objectives and monitoring systems. ▸ Underdeveloped relationships with key corporate actors. ▸ Difficulty demonstrating materiality of engagement. ▸ For (interested) asset owners: Insufficient mechanisms to guarantee asset managers conduct successful engagements.

Source: PRI (2018).[21]

Conflicts of interest can also be a behavioral barrier to engagement. The fact that many stewardship codes call for transparency around conflicts that might impinge on stewardship activities, explicitly acknowledges this issue. The PRI notes,

> *Conflicts can arise when investment managers have business relations with the same companies they engage with or whose AGMs they have to cast their votes at. A company that is selected for engagement or voting might also be related to a parent company or subsidiary of the investor. Conflicts can occur when the interests of clients or beneficiaries also diverge from each other. Finally, employees might be linked personally or professionally to a company whose securities are submitted to vote or included in the investor's engagement programme. The disclosure of actual, potential or perceived conflicts is best practice.*[22]

A final barrier is the emergence of competition. Historically, few people worked in this once considerably under-resourced area, and stewardship professionals had been content to work together, both informally and in more formal collaborations, recognizing that working together on thematic and specific issues might be the best way to deliver change on behalf of clients. As stewardship is becoming more important to clients and an increased focus for investment consultants and fund managers, there are signs that this collaborative approach may be waning. There are exceptions however, such as the Climate Action 100+ (CA 100+) collaborative engagement to which most major institutional investors now adhere. Even there, however, various institutions are seeking to differentiate themselves by adopting different approaches (individual

---
21 PRI, *How ESG Engagement Creates Value for Investors and Companies – Executive Summary* (2018). Available at: www.unpri.org/academic-research/how-esg-engagement-creates-value-for-investors-and-companies/3054.article
22 PRI, *A Practical Guide to Active Ownership in Listed Equity: Developing an Active Ownership Policy* (2018). Available at: www.unpri.org/listed-equity/developing-an-active-ownership-policy-/2724.article

CA 100+ engagements are very distinct), and although each company engagement is seemingly led by a single investor, in a number of cases, other institutions are taking forward their own initiatives under the CA 100+ banner.

As engagement practices evolve, a degree of competition between service providers in terms of the quality of their resources and reporting is helpful because that enables innovative and effective services to be developed at a greater scale, lowering costs for individual fund managers. It is important that the benefits of collective activity are not forgotten and that the investor sector should continue to explore synergies in engagement priorities and amplify their collective impact.

4 EFFECTIVE ENGAGEMENT: OBJECTIVES, PRACTICALITIES, ESCALATION, COLLECTIVE STRATEGIES

6.1.5 apply appropriate methods to establish an engagement approach: strategy and tactics-goal-setting; identifying who to talk with; formalities-hosting/agenda/managing expectations; communication-approach/tone/managing tensions; working towards agreement; escalation techniques, including collective engagement; ESG investment forums; proxy voting

Setting Engagement Objectives

The first key step in engagement is to set clear objectives. Given that engagement is dialogue with a clear purpose—not just dialogue for the sake of dialogue—knowing what the purpose is matters. This is why the stewardship service providers all apply some milestone measure or set of key performance indicators (KPIs) to their engagements so that their clients can hold them to account for delivery. This also explains why the PRI sets itself a key KPI that its members should set objectives for the majority of their engagements. The PRI's 2020 annual report confirms that 71% of members implement this, although this is short of its 80% target.[23]

Outcomes matter more than activity, and given the impossibility of attributing share price movements to any individual engagement success (indeed, even attributing changes in corporate practices to any individual engagement success can be a challenge), having some mechanism to test whether the objectives have been achieved is the best way for clients to have confidence about the success of engagement. Some investors also have objectives that provide a practical roadmap of concrete measures that the engagee company can adopt to move toward the broader objective of the engagement dialogue.

Having clear objectives helps set a clear agenda. Though successful engagement is always a conversation and so may cover much ground, the engager needs to know those handful of issues (at most) that really need to be probed hard and brought into real focus in the discussion. In many cases, the investor will share at least a version of this agenda with the company so that there are few surprises and a framework of honesty and openness is set from the start.

---

23 PRI, *Annual Report* (2020). Available at: https://www.unpri.org/annual-report-2020

Clarity around objectives will also help to identify the right company representative to work with. For ESG operational matters, this will typically be the sustainability and/or investor relations teams, with escalation to the senior management and then to the board. For business strategy or operational matters, the starting point will typically be the CEO or CFO, with escalation if need be to the non-executive directors. For governance matters, the usual starting point will be the chair, often with the company secretary (or equivalent role) as a part of the conversation, with the ability to seek further discussions with the senior independent director or lead independent director—or with other non-executives.

Practicalities of Engagement

If the matter is purely a voting issue, the first contact is normally with the company secretary (at least in those markets where such a role has prominence; in the United States and some of continental Europe, the contact is more likely to start with the investor relations team), and then further dialogue may be with the chair of the relevant board committee (remuneration or audit) and/or the chair of the board. There are no fixed rules, and these models are often not what happens in practice. Investors need to respond accordingly to what is appropriate at the individual company. Occasionally, it can take some effort to persuade a company that the dialogue an investor is seeking is worthy of the relevant corporate representative's, particularly non-executive director's, time.

Meetings can be held at the corporate head office or at the investment firm. Typically, the choice between the two is only a matter of mutual convenience, although visiting the company's office can help to demonstrate the investor's interest. On rare occasions, engagement may happen on an operational or supplier site visit. An investor fully educating themselves through dedicated time on operational site visits, or through visits to one or more supplier(s), can provide further standing to their engagement dialogue and serve to reinforce the points that they are seeking to make.

The engager typically has an hour with a single individual to explore a set of issues, perhaps only one of which will be the main focus for the meeting. Listening is as important—often more important—than speaking. Good engagement seeks understanding and constructive dialogue as the engager explains how a proposed course of action is in the company's best interests, not purely those of the single investor. It is helpful to demonstrate knowledge of the company and the sector to build relations because it shows an earnest approach and helps the investor be most convincing in engagement actions (hence, the additional status in engagement gained from site visits).

There is also a need to identify possible reasons why the company may not want to adopt a measure that is commonly understood as beneficial. Frequently, a company's culture, history, or individuals might stand in the way of change—one reason why successful engagement is often a multi-stage, multi-year activity. Investors can find that their role has been to add weight to one side of a discussion that is already ongoing at the company, helping those who are already seeking change to win that debate in the boardroom.

In order to be constructive, the dialogue should initially take place privately without media attention, not least because media interest often entrenches positions rather than allowing the fluidity that may be necessary for change to occur.

Nevertheless, over time it may become clear that greater force is required for the investor's message to be heard properly in a dialogue. This is where escalation tools may be needed.

Escalation of Engagement

While escalation is dealt with in the new Stewardship Code under Principle 11, the former UK Code set out a helpful list of escalation measures that can be considered to advance engagements. While the first three might be seen by many engagement professionals as part of a standard set of tools in normal dialogue with companies, the subsequent four will certainly be recognized as forms of escalation:

- holding additional meetings with management specifically to discuss concerns;
- expressing concerns through the company's advisers;
- meeting with the chair or other board members;
- intervening jointly with other institutions on particular issues;
- making a public statement in advance of general meetings;
- submitting resolutions and speaking at general meetings; and
- requesting a general meeting, in some cases proposing to change board membership.

Additional methods used by some as part of their escalation models might include the following:

- writing a formal letter setting out concerns, usually following one of the previously mentioned meetings, and typically to the chair; such letters are usually private, but may occasionally be leaked publicly if frustrations worsen (sometimes those leaks come from within the company, if there are internal individuals who are frustrated by a lack of progress);
- seeking dialogue with other stakeholders, including regulators, banks, creditors, customers, suppliers, the workforce and non-governmental organizations (NGOs) (stakeholder dialogue is most typically a tool in European markets and is specifically referenced as important in the Shareholder Rights Directive II, but is increasingly being used elsewhere as well);
- formally requesting a special audit of the company (a right for shareholders in certain countries, most notably Germany, to consider particular areas of concern);
- taking concerns public in the media or in some other form, not only as the code said in relation to AGMs or other general meetings;
- seeking governance improvements and/or damages through litigation, other legal remedies, or arbitration; and
- formally adding the company to an exclusion list or otherwise exiting or threatening to exit from the investment.

The idea of escalation is that it is a ladder of additional steps to raise the stakes in an engagement. Many engagement objectives can be managed without any escalation, and indeed investors may choose to move slower in an engagement rather than escalate so as to maintain positive relations with a company they wish to remain invested in for many years. But where escalation is seen as necessary, the investor must consider what additional steps might be needed to generate the change that is sought, and this consideration may go through a number of stages so that the escalation goes step by step up the ladder, or occasionally by jumping up several steps at once if change is felt to be particularly urgent. There is no particular ordering of the steps, although some steps are clearly more significant than others.

Given resource constraints, an investor must always be prepared to take the view that little further progress can be made at any given time and so an engagement should be paused. The investor will also need to consider whether the steps are warranted by the objective; on occasion, the right thing may be to withdraw and step away from the objective for some time. Typically, this is done by a formal letter setting out the investor's concerns, which can be referred to in future years when the board may be different or in different circumstances and so may be more responsive to engagement.

Many escalation tools need to be used wisely and not overexploited. For example, litigation must be used rarely, not least because of the expense and the staff time taken up with any legal case; the step of making concerns public through the media or social media needs to be applied with care because the investor who rarely raises issues in public will be listened to more on the occasions when it does than an investor who is always expressing views publicly. But often, moving an engagement from the private sphere into the public is seen as one of the most important ways to bolster influence.

One form of public engagement is putting forward a shareholder resolution—a shareholder right in most jurisdictions, although local law often restricts the nature of the resolution that can be proposed, as well as the size and period of shareholding that the proponents of the resolution must represent in order to hold the right. In many jurisdictions, the proposal of a resolution must be made public by the company; but in the United States, where they are most common, they do not typically enter the public domain until the papers for the relevant AGM are published. Typically, this will be after the company has tried to exclude the resolution from the AGM agenda and sought a ruling from the US Securities and Exchange Commission (SEC) as to whether this exclusion is permitted. Proposing a shareholder resolution in the United States can therefore be the trigger for private engagement, which may reach enough of a satisfactory conclusion for the investor to withdraw the resolution, thus never coming to public attention.

Collective engagement is sometimes seen as an alternative model of engagement, but we will treat it in this chapter as another form—often the most powerful form—of escalation. This is looked at in further detail in the following discussion.

Perhaps counterintuitively, one form of escalation that is considered by many institutions is disinvestment. This can only really escalate influence when it is done through a formal process so that the company is aware that it is approaching the point where the investor may feel obliged to sell its shares. An example of a public and influential divestment process is that followed by the Norwegian Government Pension Fund Global. There, an independent ethics council considers whether companies should be excluded from the fund because of business activities (such as the production of indiscriminate weaponry or thermal coal) or because of breaches of behavioral norms (the UN Global Compact standards).

For example, in recent years the ethics council has recommended divestments based on a criterion adopted in 2016: behavior that leads to unacceptable carbon emission levels, including an assessment of companies' willingness and ability to change such behavior in the future. The manager running the fund (Norges Bank Investment Management, usually referred to as NBIM) considers these recommendations and can exclude companies on these grounds. It has, for example, excluded four companies involved in oil sands production as a result.

NBIM makes the full list of its exclusions public and publicizes its decisions to exclude individual companies (and on occasions remove the exclusion).[24] This publicity forms part of an escalation process with the companies in question and also has a potential influence on other companies. The NBIM exclusion list is observed by a number of other investors with some of its exclusions being adopted by others.

---

24 Norges Bank Investment Management, *Observation and Exclusion of Companies* (2021). Available at: www.nbim.no/en/the-fund/responsible-investment/exclusion-of-companies/

Collective Engagement

Another way in which investors can share resources is through collective engagement. This may be done informally, through quiet and nonspecific dialogue between individual fund managers' stewardship teams, while taking care to avoid reaching agreements or even sharing concrete plans, because of the constraints of acting in concert and other regulations. In addition to these informal dialogues, there are also active collective engagement vehicles of various sorts.

Collective engagement is often the most resource-efficient method for engagement; every investor is inevitably resource-constrained and pooling those limited resources should enable greater efficiency. Such efficiency has a benefit for the corporate recipient too because it reduces the weight of messages received, which in some cases can feel like a broad spectrum of conflicting opinions of which it is difficult to make much sense. The pooling of resources by investors can aid their own education about an issue, and also add weight and emphasis to their concerns, which may mean they are more likely to be heard.

The challenges around collective engagement are perhaps the obvious ones of coordinating a potentially disparate group of separate investors and trying to maintain a consistent perspective, or at least enough consistency of perspective, that the company receives a clear message from its investors in the key areas. A number of investors are also concerned by the rules in particular markets around anti-competitive behavior or activities that abuse or exploit the market (such as those dealing with acting in concert, where a number of separate investors work together to use their holdings as a single bloc). Some market regulators have made clear that there is a safe harbor for institutional engagement, but such safe harbors do not exist everywhere and none have been tested robustly. Thus, unless they are careful, such investors may be seen to be acting in concert and so may potentially face serious regulatory consequences, the most significant of which being a possible need to launch a takeover bid for the company. Hence, the care with which collective engagement is approached is essential.

A number of asset owner organizations globally support their members in their stewardship work, such as the following:

- the Asian Corporate Governance Association (ACGA);
- Associação de Investidores no Mercado de Capitais (AMEC) in Brazil;
- Assogestioni in Italy;
- the Australian Council of Superannuation Investors (ACSI);
- the Council of Institutional Investors (CII) in the United States;
- Eumedion in the Netherlands; and
- the Pensions and Lifetime Savings Association (PLSA—formerly the National Association of Pension Funds or NAPF) in the United Kingdom.

Most of these organizations have a much broader remit, with stewardship being just one element of their offering.

In addition, investor coalitions covering ESG have been created recently, with environmental issues in particular rallying investors together. Among these is Climate Action 100+ (CA 100+). Climate change groups—such as the Asia Investor Group on Climate Change (AIGCC), Australia's Investor Group on Climate Change (IGCC), Europe's Institutional Investor Group on Climate Change (IIGCC), and Ceres (which coordinates US investor efforts in this regard), each of which has a regional remit but all of which now seek to coordinate their actions—have largely focused on lobbying and playing an effective role in the political debates on climate. These are increasingly developing company engagement, however, not least by performing a coordinating role on CA 100+.

CA 100+ targets the most polluting companies, appointing one institution as lead engager and a number of small groups of institutions to work alongside it. In theory, there is a common approach and agenda, but the coordination is flexible and the lead engager is invited to respond to the specific circumstances of each company so there can be a good deal of inconsistency between the engagements. CA 100+ has had some notable successes, not least in relation to strategic changes by the European oil majors, such as Spain's Repsol, France's Total, Italy's ENI, UK's BP, and Royal Dutch Shell of the UK/Netherlands, each of which has in recent years dramatically shifted its planned scope of future investments.

The PRI also has its own collective engagement service: the Collaboration Platform. Its main focus is on company engagements, occasionally targeting just a single company but more frequently identifying an issue that a number of companies face and proposing a collective approach to engaging with the relevant companies. Usually, a single investor raises something on the platform and invites other PRI members to participate in the proposed engagement; typically, the engagement is then led by a small working group of investors. According to the PRI's statistics, there have been more than 2,500 groups and more than 600 engagements run through the Collaboration Platform, targeting 24,667 companies with the involvement of over 2,000 signatories.

CASE STUDIES

Slave Labor and Rainforest Charcoal in the Brazilian Pig Iron Supply Chain

An early example of the PRI's Collaboration Platform in action was its collective engagement regarding the use of slave labor and rainforest wood charcoal in the Brazilian pig iron supply chain, which is an important source of raw materials for many iron and steel producers and consumers, particularly in North America. This collaboration formed in 2006/2007 following a *Bloomberg Markets* cover story, "The Secret World of Modern Slavery."[25]

The collaboration identified several companies whose supply chains were impacted by this issue, among them was US steel producer Nucor. US ethical investment house, Domini Social Investments performed the leadership role in the investor coalition in relation to Nucor and wrote to the company in April 2007 in a letter co-signed by 10 investors from around the world. Nucor's response was inadequate in the view of the investors, and Domini and another group of (this time, predominantly US) investors co-filed shareholder resolutions at the company on the issue, at the end of 2008, 2009, and 2010.

The company continued to make a weak response, leading to a 2009 shareholder resolution winning support from some 27% of shareholders voting on the issue. This set the scene for more constructive discussions in relation to the 2010 shareholder resolution. In the end, Nucor and Domini announced an agreement that led Domini to withdraw the shareholder resolution for that year. Nucor had agreed to work with two key NGO initiatives in Brazil: the National Pact for the Eradication of Slave Labor and the Citizens Charcoal Institute (ICC). Specifically, it would require all its top-tier Brazilian pig iron suppliers either to join the ICC or to endorse and commit to the National Pact. Nucor also agreed to provide funding to ICC to give it the resources needed to be truly effective, and to report annually on its delivery around commitments to appropriate behavior in its supply chain.

---

25 M. Smith, "The Secret World of Modern Slavery," *Bloomberg*, 14 March 2007.

> Domini later published this story, "Fighting Slavery in Brazil: Strengthening Local Solutions".[26]

Formal collective stewardship vehicles take different forms. There are the commercial approaches, predominantly offered by fund managers that offer stewardship overlay services, taking forward engagement work on behalf of clients whether they invest money on their behalf or not. Some of the main players in the overlay market are Columbia Threadneedle Investments "Responsible Engagement Overlay" (REO) Service, Federated Hermes EOS, Robeco, and Sustainalytics (which bought the former GES International in 2019 and is part of Morningstar).

These operations cover both voting advice and direct engagement activities. There are also noncommercial operations, offering collaborative vehicles to members. Prominent among these is the UK's The Investor Forum, created in 2014 as a response to the Kay Review call for such a vehicle.[27] The forum is being watched closely in other markets as a potential model to follow.

The Investor Forum has a detailed collective engagement framework (available in full only to its members), through which its engagements avoid falling foul of the rules around acting in concert and market abuse. Many investors see such market abuse rules as limiting their ability to carry out collective engagement effectively. The Investor Forum publishes 10 key features of this private collective engagement framework.

1. **Trusted facilitator, not an adviser.** Members retain full voting and other investment rights in respect of their shareholdings. No control is ceded to the forum or other members.

2. **Opt in/opt out.** A member actively chooses to participate in an engagement involving a company in which it is a shareholder. It can also choose to opt out of an engagement at any time.

3. **Complementary to members' direct engagement**. Members are actively encouraged to continue their direct interaction with companies outside the forum's auspices.

4. **Confidentiality**. Members must agree to comply with confidentiality obligations during an engagement. Disclosure of identities and public statements must be agreed upon by participants during an engagement.

5. **Nominated key engagement contact**. Members retain full control as to whether or not they receive information and who receives that information.

6. **Hub and spoke model**. A bilateral model is the usual method of communication between the executive and members involved in engagements.

7. **No inside information**. The forum is not intended to be a means of facilitating the exchange of inside information between companies and members or among members themselves. Participation in an engagement will not exempt any person from any law or regulation governing the use and dissemination of inside information.

8. **No-concert party and no-group**. Members agree that while participating in a forum engagement they will not form a concert party in respect of the relevant company, including by requisitioning a board control-seeking resolution or seeking to obtain control of the company.

---

26 A. Kanzer, Domini Social Investments, "Fighting Slavery in Brazil: Strengthening Local Solutions" in ICCR's *Social Sustainability Resource Guide: Building Sustainable Communities through Multi-Party Collaboration* (2011). Available at: www.iccr.org/sites/default/files/ICCRsBuildingSustainableCommunities.pdf
27 The Investor Forum, *The Investor Forum* (2020). Available at: www.investorforum.org.uk

9. **Heightened procedures**. At various points in an engagement, heightened procedures may be deemed necessary, including seeking specialist advice. Particular attention will be paid to the case of engagements involving companies with dual US or other foreign listings and companies or members that are subject to the Bank Holding Company Act.
10. **Conflict of interest avoidance**. The forum maintains control procedures to avoid conflicts of interest that could impact either its own governance or individual engagements. Members are reminded of their own obligations to manage conflicts of interest and should note that participation in an engagement is not a substitute for, and does not release them from, those obligations.

It is this formal structure that the forum has developed—and its apparent effectiveness in engagement (such as in relation to Unilever's retreat from its plan to shift its headquarters)[28]—that has led to international interest in the forum as a model for other markets (for example, in a November 2019 report, France's Club des Juristes proposed that France ought to seek to create a similar organization).[29]

In particular, the collective engagement framework is seen as a key mechanism to mitigate the risks that sometimes impedes collective engagement, that is, the regulatory rules against seeking control of public companies except through formal takeover bids or market abuse and insider trading constraints.

SPECIAL CONSIDERATIONS: PROXY VOTING, ASSET CLASSES

☐ 6.1.5 apply appropriate methods to establish an engagement approach: strategy and tactics-goal-setting; identifying who to talk with; formalities-hosting/agenda/managing expectations; communication-approach/tone/managing tensions; working towards agreement; escalation techniques, including collective engagement; ESG investment forums; proxy voting

☐ 6.1.6 describe approaches of engagement across a range of asset classes

Voting

As mentioned earlier, shareholders have the right to vote at AGMs and EGMs, and in some markets, occasionally at other investor gatherings. In almost all cases, voting is proportionate to the percentage shareholding in the company and resolutions are usually passed when more than half of those voting support a vote. In a few cases, special resolutions require support by 75% of those voting, and there are unusual circumstances where the number of votes cast must exceed a threshold in terms of the overall share capital (and rarer still when the number of shareholders is important). Institutions typically vote for or against, although in many markets, there is also scope

---

28 A. Mooney, "Unilever U-turn Shows How Angry Shareholders Are Securing Change," *Financial Times*, 14 Oct 2018. Available at: www.ft.com/content/d7211dba-ce21-11e8-9fe5-24ad351828ab
29 Le Club des Juristes, *Activisme Actionnarial* (2019). Available at: www.leclubdesjuristes.com/les-commissions/activisme-actionnarial/

for a conscious abstention (for example, in the UK these votes are collated despite not legally being considered votes as such). This is considered an active decision rather than just an absence of a vote. Abstention can sometimes be a useful tool in an engagement process where the investor does not have a fixed view on an issue but certainly does not want to be in the potential position later of being hampered in its criticism of an action that it has in effect endorsed through its voting.

Given the public nature of company general meetings, where the results are announced publicly by the company and the events themselves are often open to the media, voting decisions are often the most visible element of stewardship and engagement. It thus gains disproportionate media attention, and major votes against earn significant media coverage. Fund managers are therefore often held to account, both in the public arena and by their clients, for individual voting decisions.

Voting is often referred to as "proxy voting" because the investor rarely physically attends the meeting where the voting occurs, but instead appoints an individual as proxy to cast the votes on their behalf (in most cases, this will be the chair of the company, although anyone physically at the meeting can be appointed). Votes vest in the legal owner of the shares, which may be the custodian or a unit trust vehicle or some other intermediary, meaning that even an institutional investor will usually need various formal paperwork in order to attend the meeting and to vote, not least that clearly identifying the individual who is physically representing the investor at the meeting.

With sizable portfolios of companies and AGMs usually occurring over compressed time periods (a few months in some markets, with the extreme being Japan where thousands of AGMs are held over just a few days), resourcing is a particular issue in the area of voting. Institutional investors typically lean on proxy firms to assist in processing votes and in providing advice on them. There are two dominant firms in this market:

- ISS, with around 80% of the market; and
- Glass Lewis, with the bulk of the remaining 20%; along with
- a few much smaller rivals, which have some market share, especially in a few localized markets.

The proxy advisers are often criticized by companies for taking what may appear to be narrow, inflexible approaches to voting and not facilitating the "explain" aspect of "comply/apply or explain." But most investors would argue that the advisers' role is to lack flexibility and to focus on the general guidance and that it must be up to investors to display their closer understanding of individual companies and respond appropriately to explanations. The extent to which investors do indeed use their own judgment and avoid relying on their proxy advisers—particularly in often long tails of smaller holdings outside of their home market—is variable.

The vote is a key tool for the active investor, and any voting decision should be aligned with the investment thesis for the holding and any stewardship agenda that the institution has in relation to the company. Thus, for example,

- If there are concerns about the **capital structure and financial viability of the business**, investors need to pay close attention to votes in relation to dividends, share buybacks, share issuance, or scope for further debt burden.
- If there are concerns about the **effectiveness or diversity of the board**, that needs to be reflected in voting decisions on director reelections (and particularly in relation to the members of the nominations committee).
- Worries about the **independence or effectiveness of the audit process** should be taken into account when voting on the reappointment of the auditor, its pay, and the reappointment of members of the audit committee.

Special Considerations: Proxy Voting, Asset Classes

Given the level of attention on executive pay, it is perhaps not surprising that investors take a close interest in resolutions on remuneration. In many markets there are both nonbinding annual resolutions to approve pay in the year and binding votes on forward-looking policies and any new pay schemes. These are in addition to votes on the appointment of the members of the remuneration committee.

Investors will also often reflect concerns about financial or sustainability reporting in their votes to approve the report and accounts. In most markets, this is a symbolic resolution, but the message sent by voting against it can still be significant. It is important to remember that even though most resolutions are seen as being purely G issues (e.g., the approval of the accounts and the dividend, the election of directors, related party transactions, appointment of the auditor, and capital structure decisions— share issuance and buyback authorities), there is no reason why investor decisions on such resolutions should be driven solely by G considerations.

This can be seen for example with the recent debate about the incorporation of climate change issues into the financial accounts (the financial statements in the back of the annual report, rather than the narrative reporting in the front half). In September 2020, investor groups representing more than US$100 trillion (£71 trillion) in assets published an open letter calling for companies to follow International Accounting Standards Board (IASB) guidance and incorporate material climate change issues in their financials, fully disclosing their relevant assumptions.[30] The investor groups also asked that auditors play their part in ensuring the delivery of this and indicated their preference that the assumptions used should be compatible with the goals of the Paris Agreement. A number of investors are considering how their voting might respond to any failures to live up to this call from investors. In particular, some are likely to vote against reports and accounts where it is not clear that climate change has been incorporated or that the assumptions are not disclosed. Some are considering voting against auditors of heavily climate-exposed companies that do not include climate issues among the key audit matters in their auditor reports. And others expect to vote against key board directors of companies that do not show sufficient signs of climate awareness where they have key risk exposures.

Any vote will rarely be meaningful in itself because there may be a range of reasons that an investor might have for voting in any particular way. Institutions therefore usually have active programs to communicate to companies why they have voted in particular ways, either in writing or in dialogue. Many seek to have active discussions with companies as they work towards their voting decisions (helping them to tailor decisions to companies' particular circumstances) and use that as an opportunity to explain the thought process that lies behind any decision making. This dialogue is a form of low-level engagement, but it will only ever have limited impacts.

Even though institutional investors mostly do not physically attend shareholder meetings, perhaps stewards should give this opportunity more active consideration. Particularly at mid-sized and smaller companies, the attendance at AGMs can be small or negligible, and so an investor can gain unusually direct access to many directors at one time, with much scope for informal dialogue. Furthermore, because the full board typically attends most AGMs, these meetings can offer investors an unusual insight into board dynamics and the ease of relationships within the boardroom. Shareholder meetings usually offer opportunities for formal questioning of many board members (typically any committee chair will respond directly to questions, as well as the chair and executive directors; in some circumstances, the audit partner is in attendance too and may answer relevant questions—something that ought to increase if the recommendations of the Brydon Review are reflected in this respect), and this

---

30 PRI, *Accounting for Climate Change* (2020). Available at: www.unpri.org/sustainability-issues/accounting-for-climate-change

formal questioning can provide scope for both insight and influence. But many will find that the informal insights from actually participating in general meetings are of as much value.

Asset Classes

Although most stewardship codes assert that they are intended to apply to all asset classes, their language and approach seems very much based in the world of public equity investment. This chapter has reflected that tendency of thinking first of public equity investment, but its application is much broader. That is because the codes (and this chapter) are written in terms of principles, which can be applied with good sense and intelligence across the full range of asset classes.

Many investment structures involve businesses investing in assets that in some ways look like public companies, with the immediate responsibility for managing direct property or infrastructure assets within their own boards and where directors and investors can engage. Private equity and other fund investment structures (including indirect property or infrastructure investments) will usually see the interface for investors being with the fund management organization rather than the underlying assets. However, the sense of accountability and the need for alignment arises just as much in these relationships as it does in any corporate governance structure.

The concepts of engagement need to be applied in a different way to respond to the circumstances and the levers of influence that are available. Because engagement is usually about influence rather than control, investors should have some scope for engagement success whichever formal structure they invest through.

Usually in these latter, more indirect, investment structures, the engagement issues are related to policies and approaches to ESG issues rather than specific individual asset concerns, but if a concern about an individual asset demonstrates that policy approaches may not be what the investor expects, then the engagement can be very specific indeed. An interesting case study of this has been the exclusion from private equity holdings of gun manufacturers and retailers by a number of asset owners, most notably CalSTRS (the Californian teachers' pension scheme, which was responding in particular to the number of shootings on US school premises). For example, Cerberus enabled its investors, including CalSTRS, to exit underlying holdings in retailer Remington Outdoor in 2015.

Although, in these cases, investors will not generally have a vote and do not have formal sanction on the parties, the sanction of selling a position or being unwilling to invest in future opportunities remains. That is clearly a powerful sanction in most circumstances (especially if the asset owner is a large one) and is certainly enough for the investor's counterparty to pay attention to concerns that are raised.

Corporate Fixed Income

Fixed income investors may ultimately be concerned with the likelihood of default, but ESG factors can impact credit ratings and affect spreads, leading to short-term changes in value. Companies that regularly raise capital in fixed income markets are becoming more conscious of investors' interest in ESG as a material factor in their pricing of debt.

ESG engagement is also important to private debt, private equity, and property and infrastructure investments. These investments are often illiquid, relatively long term, and involve close partnership between the investor and investee. As a consequence, there is both motive and opportunity for ESG engagement.

Special Considerations: Proxy Voting, Asset Classes

In relation to fixed income, the PRI's guide *ESG Engagement for Fixed Income Investors: Managing Risks, Enhancing Returns* recommends that investors should prioritize engagement based on the following:

- the size of a holding in the portfolio;
- lower credit quality issuers (with less balance sheet flexibility to absorb negative ESG impacts);
- key themes that are material to sectors; and
- issuers with low ESG scores.[31]

The greatest opportunity to push for conditions and disclosures around ESG is likely to be preissuance. This can be difficult to implement in fast-moving public markets but is easier to effect in private debt issuance.

The investor's interaction with corporate debt issuers is most commonly with corporate treasury rather than more senior officials. In most cases, the parties are used to dialogue in relation to strategy, risk, financial structure (especially where the proposed debt sits in the debt hierarchy), and also, the covenants and protections for debt investors. Increasingly, however, dialogue about risk encompasses ESG matters, and debt investors are finding they can have some influence on the approach of fixed income issuers.

This scope for influence is particularly clear where debt investors engage alongside equity investors (or where single investment firms bring together their engagement approaches in relation to investments in a single issuer regardless of the asset class exposure and the portfolio in which it is held). There are instances where equity and debt investors are direct rivals over issues; for example, in the case of some transactions or capital structurings or in the case of the company nearing insolvency. In almost all cases relating to ESG matters at companies that are going concerns, however, the interests of long-term investors (whether they are exposed to equity or debt) very much align, and it will benefit all if the corporation effectively deals with an ESG concern.

Sovereign Debt

The stewardship interaction with sovereign debt issuers is likely to be much more limited. Here, only the largest investors are likely to have any scope to influence the stance of nation states, and even then, the influence may be minimal. Therefore, the ESG approach usually applied in this asset class is screening or an ESG tilt in the investment process rather than engagement.

Having said that, there are early signs of steps to advance investor activity in this area, and the PRI has produced a guide for those seeking to engage with sovereign issuers.[32] This guide makes clear the fledgling nature of engagement in this area and is focused on learning how engagement might happen rather than on highlighting successful case studies. There is a particular focus on educating sovereign issuers about the value of green bonds and the strong market appetite for such instruments.

The leading case study for sovereign debt engagement is the work by a group of 29 investors with assets of around US$3.7 trillion (£2.6 trillion) to encourage the Brazilian government to do more to limit the destruction of the Amazon rainforest. Having also had contact through the Brazilian embassies in their home nations, the group wrote to the government in June 2020 noting among other things that "Brazilian

---

31 PRI, *ESG Engagement for Fixed Income Investors: Managing Risks, Enhancing Returns* (2018). Available at: www.unpri.org/download?ac=4449
32 PRI, *ESG Engagement for Sovereign Debt Investors* (2020). Available at: www.unpri.org/download?ac=12018

sovereign bonds are also likely to be deemed high risk if deforestation continues".[33] At least some of the group are reported to be considering divesting existing holdings and excluding Brazilian debt from their sovereign portfolios to reflect these concerns. Sadly, it is unclear if this effort has had any positive influence, as other reports suggest that Amazon destruction accelerated through 2020, reaching a 12-year high.

Private Equity

Within private equity investments, direct ESG engagement will be undertaken by the general partner (GP, the private equity house) rather than the limited partner (LP, the asset owner), although individual LPs may wish to engage with their GPs on the ways in which they are monitoring and acting on ESG issues across their portfolios. As the PRI report *ESG Monitoring, Reporting and Dialogue in Private Equity* points out:

> *The process of portfolio monitoring has value protection and enhancement potential in itself, as a systematic approach for identifying material ESG issues, setting objectives and regularly tracking progress. It enables GPs: to identify anomalies and achievements; support regular engagement with the portfolio company on these issues; and strengthen company reporting practices that could have implications at exit.*[34]

Given that private equity provides a form of share ownership, the logic of extending the principles of the Stewardship Code to such investments may come more naturally. That's especially true when the companies are early stage and the investor has a more substantial influence. The poor quality of the governance of a number of companies coming through the private equity system—for example, the very public failure of WeWork's initial public offering (discussed briefly in Chapter 5) was in significant part caused by poor corporate governance—suggests that often, less effective ESG is instilled in private equity companies than ought to be the case given the levers that private equity investors hold.

Infrastructure

Infrastructure investors are exposed to ESG across the economic lifetime of their assets. These exposures extend beyond issues related directly to a specific asset, such as health and safety, supply chains, and environment, to such factors as climate change, bribery and corruption, and the social license to operate. The PRI (2018a) recommends that investors consider eight potential mechanisms to act as engaged owners in infrastructure:

1. Use ESG assessments undertaken during due diligence to prioritize attention to ESG considerations and potential for improving profitability, efficiency, and risk management.
2. Include material ESG risks and opportunities identified during due diligence into the post-acquisition plan of each asset or project company and integrate this into asset management activities.
3. Engage with, and encourage, the management of the business to act on the identified ESG risks and opportunities using the mechanisms available.
4. Define and communicate the expectations of ESG operations and maintenance performance to the infrastructure business managers.

---

33 B. Harris, "Investors Warn Brazil to Stop Amazon Destruction," *Financial Times*, 23 June 2020. Available at: www.ft.com/content/ad1d7176-ce6c-4a9b-9bbc-cbdb6691084f
34 PRI, *ESG Monitoring, Reporting and Dialogue in Private Equity* (2018). Available at: www.unpri.org/download?ac=4839

5. Ensure ESG factors identified as material during due diligence are explicitly woven into asset-level policies.
6. Advocate a governance framework that clearly articulates who has responsibility for ESG and sustainability.
7. Set performance targets for preserving or improving environmental and social impact, including regular reports to the board and investors.
8. Where possible, make ESG information and expertise available to the asset or project company to help it develop capacity.[35]

Like private equity and property, many investors in infrastructure will work through specialist managers. In these situations, the investor's responsibility is to monitor and engage with the manager. AustralianSuper, one of Australia's largest pension schemes, has been investing in infrastructure since 1994. In a 2012 case study for the PRI, AustralianSuper reported that one of their infrastructure managers had used detailed questionnaires based on the Global Reporting Initiative to analyze the impact of ESG issues for each of its 28 existing assets.[36] This analysis and benchmarking across the assets enabled the fund manager to

- improve the governance at each of the boards on which it sits;
- arrange for four Australian airports to work together to develop market best practice health and safety processes based on practices from each of the airports; and
- measure the electricity and water usage and carbon emissions of each its assets on a regular basis, enabling the identification of energy savings for many assets.

Property

As with fixed income, there is good evidence of the positive effect of ESG on returns to real estate investments. Friede, Busch and Bassen's 2015 study determined that 57% of equity studies showed a positive effect, although the positive share for bond studies was 64%, rising to 71% for real estate.[37]

A 2014 INREV study[38] indicated that there was a 2.8% difference in return spread between the top 10% and the bottom 10% of Global Real Estate Sustainability Benchmark (GRESB) rated properties.[39] Regulatory changes are also driving a need for greater engagement in relation to ESG in real estate.

Investors should engage indirectly by requiring their managers to report on the frameworks and metrics that they use to monitor holdings. In addition, UNEP Financial Initiative et al. recommend that real estate investment stakeholders:

- engage, directly or indirectly, on public policy to manage risks;
- support research on ESG and climate risks; and

---

35 PRI, *Applying Principle 2* (2018). Available at: www.unpri.org/infrastructure/applying-principle-2-to-infrastructure-investing/2706.article
36 PRI, *ESG and the Long-Term Ownership of Infrastructure Assets* (2012). Available at: www.unpri.org/infrastructure/esg-and-the-long-term-ownership-of-infrastructure-assets/129.article
37 A. Bassen, T. Busch, and G. Friede, "ESG and Financial Performance: Aggregated Evidence from More than 2,000 Empirical Studies," *Journal of Sustainable Finance & Investment* 5, no. 4 (2015): 210–33. Available at: https://papers.ssrn.com/sol3/papers.cfm?abstract_id=2699610
38 INREV, *Transparency and Performance of the European Non-Listed Real Estate Market* (2014). Available at: www.inrev.org/library/transparency-and-performance-european-non-listed-real-estate-fund-market
39 GRESB, *How GRESB Works* (2020). Available at: www.gresb.com

- support sector initiatives to develop resources to understand risks and integrate ESG.[40]

Fund Investments

For funds of funds as an asset class, engagement with fund vehicles, covering any underlying asset class, sometimes becomes a little more complex. However, there is typically a fund board, which should be there to represent investor interests and that can be subject to engagement. Investors are often distanced from the underlying assets, but the role is then to hold to account the managers of the fund for their own investment and stewardship efforts. Closing the agency gap in these sorts of vehicles can be harder and take more effort, but as long as the investor has this in mind, there is certainly a role for engagement to play.

---

[40] UNEP Finance Initiative et al, *Sustainable Real Investment & Framework for Action* (2016). Available at: www.unepfi.org/fileadmin/property/SustainableREI_DirectInvestment.pdf

KEY FACTS

1. Stewardship is active, responsible ownership of companies or other assets on behalf of a long-term owner, a reflection of the investor's fiduciary duty to its clients and beneficiaries.
2. Engagement is active dialogue with companies with a particular purpose. Typically, it covers one or more ESG matter(s).
3. Voting at shareholder meetings is one element of stewardship. Often it is the most public, so it gains external attention, but it is nevertheless a limited element with limited influence on its own. Few investors attend company general meetings but could benefit from the insights and influence that come from doing so.
4. There is strong evidence that engagement, if carried out well, can positively influence corporate behavior and that the changes made can deliver long-term value.
5. Many markets have stewardship codes in place, and growing numbers are developing such codes; increasingly, these are codes with regulatory backing.
6. Generally, engagement is most successful if carried out positively and consensually, recognizing that the changes sought are in the company's interests not in an investor's self-interest.
7. Yet sometimes engagement must be escalated in order to have effect. This can be through a range of mechanisms, including making concerns publicly known, proposing shareholder resolutions, or working collectively with other shareholders.
8. One of the most significant constraints on investors delivering effective stewardship and engagement is resources—particularly where the investor has broad investment portfolios. Finding responses to these resource constraints is currently one of the major challenges, and among the answers being found are
    - hiring new resource;
    - prioritizing with care;
    - expecting more ESG delivery from mainstream fund management teams; and
    - using collective and collaborative engagement resources.
9. Some forms of engagement start bottom-up, by focusing on the specific issues faced by an individual company, while others operate top-down by applying a perspective on particular issues (e.g., climate change) across all companies in a sector or market as a whole. Typically, the approach is linked to the investor's investment approach.
10. The most effective engagement starts with clarity over the engagement objective and how delivery against that objective will be measured over time. Greater clarity in these respects will be required by the focus on outcomes in the new UK Stewardship Code and, increasingly, by clients. Engagement success often takes years to deliver in full.
11. Collective engagement is a key route to maximizing effectiveness from limited resources, but investors must beware of regulatory constraints, such as rules against acting in concert.

12. Engagement can be carried out across the full range of investment asset classes. The principles and mindset of engagement and stewardship need to be applied with good sense and judgment to the different circumstances and the levers that the investor controls.

FURTHER READING

Australian Council of Superannuation Investors (ACSI) 2018. Australian Asset Owner Stewardship Code. Available at: https://acsi.org.au/members/australian-asset-owner-stewardship-code

Financial Reporting Council 2020. *UK Stewardship Code.* Available at: www.frc.org.uk/investors/uk-stewardship-code

Forum, Investor. 2019. "Defining Stewardship and Engagement." Available at: www.investorforum.org.uk/wp-content/uploads/securepdfs/2019/04/Defining-Stewardship-Engagement-April-2019.pdf

International Corporate Governance Network (ICGN) 2016. *ICGN Global Stewardship Principles.* Available at: https://www.icgn.org/icgn-global-stewardship-principles

Principles for Responsible Investment (PRI) 2018. *ESG Engagement for Fixed Income Investors: Managing Risks, Enhancing Returns.* Available at: www.unpri.org/download?ac=4449

Principles for Responsible Investment (PRI) 2014. *Integrating ESG in Private Equity: A Guide for General Partners.* Available at: www.unpri.org/download?ac=252

US Department of Labor 2018. *Field Assistance Bulletin No. 2018-01 – Superseded by 85 FR 72846 and 85 FR 81658.* Available at: www.dol.gov/agencies/ebsa/employers-and-advisers/guidance/field-assistance-bulletins/2018-01

SELF PRACTICE AND SELF ASSESSMENT

1. An investor embarks on engagement with a mindset that respects the investee's individual circumstances and seeks understanding. The PRI would suggest that her approach is *most closely* related to which ESG engagement dynamic?

    a. Political
    b. Learning
    c. Communicative

2. Successful investor engagement tends to have *most* positive impact:

    a. on changes to remuneration policies.
    b. on abnormal financial returns.
    c. within six months of the initial engagement contact.

3. Which of the following is *most likely* an engagement dialogue according to the Investor Forum Framework?

    a. An analyst asks the CFO to explain the impact of a bottom-of-the-pyramid initiative on a division's cost structure
    b. An investor asks the CEO to identify the current stage of the consultation process for a development on a native reserve and the likely completion date
    c. A board member asks the purchasing executive about the labor audits underway and shares information about child labor detected in other firms' supply chains

4. In the United Kingdom, institutional engagement activities aimed at fulfilling stewardship responsibilities are *most likely* carried out by:

    a. regulators.
    b. asset owners.
    c. fund managers.

5. The most significant change in the 2020 version of the UK Stewardship Code is *most likely* the:

    a. increased emphasis on clear, robust policy statements.
    b. addition of a principle requiring conflict of interest management.
    c. requirement to report on the practical effects of engagement actions.

6. Collective engagement activities are *most likely* to be controversial when they:

    a. result in the creation of concert parties.
    b. are outsourced to specialist stewardship providers.
    c. are carried out through platforms such as the UK Investor Forum.

7. Engagement teams organized by geography rather than by markets or sectors are *most likely* focused on:

    a. social issues.
    b. governance issues.
    c. environmental issues.

8. Which form of collaborative engagement is *most likely* to require greater formal-

ity in approach?

- a. Group meetings with the company
- b. Collaborative letter-writing campaigns
- c. Soliciting broader support for a shareholder resolution

9. Which of the following activities is *most likely* associated with the early stages of a successful engagement action?

    - a. Ensuring that there is media interest
    - b. Registering to speak at an annual general meeting
    - c. Engaging in site visits to understand the company culture

10. A fund management entity that advances clients' engagement activities even if not investing the client's funds is *best* described as:

    - a. a proxy firm.
    - b. an overlay service provider.
    - c. an ESG investment consultant.

11. A portfolio has equal holdings of the following investments:

	Credit rating	ESG score (1 is low, 10 is high)
Bond 1	BBB+	2
Bond 2	AA-	8
Bond 3	AAA-	2

    According to PRI's guide to *ESG Engagement for Fixed Income Investors*, which investment is *most likely* to be highest priority for engagement?

    - a. Bond 1
    - b. Bond 2
    - c. Bond 3

12. The opportunity for fixed income investors to engage on ESG issues is greatest with:

    - a. public debt.
    - b. private debt.
    - c. sovereign debt.

The following information relates to questions 13-27
Self Assessment Questions

These questions are provided only to enable you to test your understanding of the chapter content. They are not indicative of the types and standard of questions you may see in the examination. The Self-Assessment questions do not include an explanation of the correct answer.

13. Which principle in the Principles of Responsible Investment (PRI) is the "engagement principle"?

    - a. Principle 1
    - b. Principle 2
    - c. Principle 3

d. Principle 4

14. What are the origins of the term "stewardship"?
    a. A butler, or steward, delivering food to the lord's table
    b. The steward responsible for mixing appropriate ingredients for a feast
    c. The steward left in charge of an absentee landlord's estate
    d. A steward steering a ship

15. What is the most significant difference between monitoring dialogues and engagement?
    a. Monitoring will influence trading decisions, engagement voting decisions
    b. Monitoring is only done by portfolio managers, engagement only by stewardship staff
    c. Monitoring occurs with investor relations staff, engagement with board directors
    d. Monitoring is one-way information seeking, engagement is two-way dialogue

16. What post-financial crisis report led to the creation of the first stewardship code?
    a. The Walker Report.
    b. The Oban Report.
    c. The Kay Report.
    d. The Arthur Report.

17. Which of the following is NOT among the seven areas typically covered by the top-level principles of a stewardship code?
    a. Engagement and escalation
    b. Voting
    c. Reporting and transparency
    d. Stock lending (or securities lending) policies

18. Which principle, more typical in regulatory codes, is frequently neglected in codes developed by investor groups?
    a. Conflicts of interest
    b. Reporting and transparency
    c. Stock lending (or securities lending) policies
    d. Voting

19. Which of the following is a new area of focus in the UK Stewardship Code 2020?
    a. Voting
    b. Outcomes
    c. Collaboration
    d. Conflicts

20. Which of the following is *not* one of the prioritization decisions that an investor must make in relation to stewardship?
    a. Which company to focus engagement attention on
    b. Which annual general meeting (AGM) resolutions to vote on
    c. Which sectors face the greatest ESG risks

Self Practice and Self Assessment

d. Which are the key engagement issues for the individual company in question

21. Which of the following is NOT among the main barriers to effective engagement?
    a. Limited resources
    b. Difficulty of reaching consensus
    c. Unwillingness to act without specific client instruction
    d. Conflicts of interest

22. Which of the following is *not* among the identified key mechanisms for the escalation of engagement?
    a. Holding additional meetings
    b. Operating collectively with other shareholders
    c. Withdrawing a shareholder resolution
    d. Proposing new board members

23. When might escalation *not* be the right step in an engagement that has made no progress?
    a. When collective engagement is prevented by regulatory standards
    b. When no progress has been made and the objective does not warrant excess activity
    c. When divestment is the likely step should no change be made
    d. Pending a forthcoming shareholder resolution

24. Which of the following is *not* a typical form of collective engagement?
    a. Informal collaboration between investors
    b. Specialist stewardship service providers
    c. Investor associations aggregating member views
    d. Internet campaigns aggregating consumer perspectives

25. What is the major constraint on collective engagement approaches?
    a. Acting in concert rules
    b. Client best interests
    c. Maintaining discretion over institutional shareholding
    d. Investors are never in contact with each other

26. Which of these is *not* a way for investors to make their voting activity more effective and influential?
    a. Hold an active dialogue with the company ahead of the decision
    b. Attend the AGM, perhaps to make a spoken intervention
    c. Writing afterwards to highlight the reasons for the voting decision
    d. Only vote on resolutions where they have a clear opinion

27. An active investor concerned about the financial viability of the business is most likely to reflect that concern in their voting on:

   a. board director re-appointment.
   b. auditor pay.
   c. dividends issue.
   d. Audit Committee member re-appointment.

SOLUTIONS

1. A is correct. Respecting the individual investee's circumstances and seeking understanding are features of relationship building, which is most closely associated with the political dynamic.

2. B is correct. Academic studies have consistently shown that, on average, successful engagement activity has been followed by positive abnormal financial returns. The same studies showed that of the engagement objectives investigated, those related to changes in remuneration policies were least likely to be successful. Finally, the studies showed that successful engagement is time consuming, as the average timeframe for success was 1.5 years.

3. C is correct. The board member's dialogue with the purchasing executive features the two-way communication typical of engagement dialogues. The analyst and investor dialogues are aimed at more fully understanding performance and opportunity, which is typical of monitoring dialogues.

4. C is correct. Fund managers typically take responsibility for stewardship activities as part of their service agreements with institutional investors (asset owners). Only a few large pension funds carry out the activities directly.

5. C is correct. The most significant change is the requirement to report on the practical effects of engagement activities. Conflict of interest regulations and robust policy statements were in place within earlier versions of the Code.

6. A is correct. Concert parties are groups of investors acting in concert as part of a takeover bid and are subject to regulatory oversight. Even though a takeover is not the intention of collective ESG engagement activities, formalized agreements between investors to act in concert to achieve ESG objectives can raise concerns with regulators and other market participants.

7. B is correct. Governance issues are organized geographically because they are typically regulated nationally. This is demonstrated by the range of governance traditions found between different countries. In contrast, social and environmental issues cut across markets and sectors as do social and environmental engagement teams.

8. A is correct. An Investor Forum white paper rated 12 forms of engagement in terms of the need for formality in approach. Of the three options listed, direct engagement between groups of investors and the company was considered most likely to require an organized, formal approach and clear engagement objectives.

9. C is correct. Engagement activities are most likely to be successful when an open, earnest approach is combined with a strong understanding of the company's culture and history. Site visits are particularly helpful in demonstrating investors' willingness to educate themselves and engage in constructive dialogue. Involving media or speaking at general meetings are escalation strategies that are unlikely to be helpful in the early stages of engagement.

10. B is correct. Overlay service providers (such as Columbia Threadneedle Investments [REO] and Sustainalytics) provide stewardship overlay services, such as voting advice and direct engagement activities, for clients regardless of whether they invest funds on the client's behalf. Proxy advisers (such as ISS and Glass Lewis) provide voting advice and assist with processing votes, but don't directly advance engagement on their clients' behalf. ESG investment consultants (such

as Mercer) typically rate the ESG expertise of fund managers.

11. A is correct. The guide recommends prioritizing engagement with issuers that have weak ESG scores and lower credit quality. Bond 1 has the lowest credit score and along with Bond 3, the lowest ESG score. Issuers with low ESG scores are prioritized because there is greater scope for improvement; those with lower credit quality are prioritized because they are less able to absorb negative ESG impacts.

12. B is correct. Private debt is typically less liquid than public or sovereign debt, resulting in closer, longer-term relationships between investors and issuers of private debt. Opportunities to engage on ESG issues are enhanced because of these relationships.

13. B is correct.

14. C is correct.

15. D is correct.

16. A is correct.

17. D is correct.

18. A is correct.

19. B is correct.

20. B is correct.

21. C is correct.

22. C is correct.

23. B is correct.

24. D is correct.

25. A is correct.

26. D is correct.

27. C is correct.

CHAPTER 7

ESG Analysis, Valuation, and Integration

LEARNING OUTCOMES

Mastery	The candidate should be able to:
☐	7.1.1 explain the aims and objectives of integrating ESG into the investment process
☐	7.1.2 describe different approaches of integrating ESG analysis into the investment process
☐	7.1.3 describe qualitative approaches to ESG analysis across a range of asset classes
☐	7.1.4 describe quantitative approaches to ESG analysis across a range of asset classes
☐	7.1.5 identify tangible and intangible material ESG-related factors through both qualitative and quantitative approaches
☐	7.1.6 describe how scorecards may be developed and constructed to assess ESG factors
☐	7.1.7 assess ESG issues using risk mapping methodologies
☐	7.1.8 explain how ESG complements traditional financial analysis
☐	7.1.9 analyze how ESG factors may affect industry and company performance
☐	7.1.10 analyze how ESG factors may affect security valuation across a range of asset classes
☐	7.1.11 interpret a company's disclosure on selected ESG topics
☐	7.1.12 apply the range of approaches to ESG analysis and integration across a range of asset classes
☐	7.1.13 describe the challenges of undertaking ESG analysis across different geographic regions and cultures
☐	7.1.14 describe the challenges of identifying and assessing material ESG issues
☐	7.1.15 describe the challenges of integrating ESG analysis into a firm's investment process
☐	7.1.16 explain the approaches taken across a range of ESG integration databases and software available, and the nature of the information provided

LEARNING OUTCOMES

Mastery	The candidate should be able to:
☐	**7.1.17** identify the main providers of screening services or tools, similarities and differences in their methodologies, and the aims, benefits and limitations of using them
☐	**7.1.18** describe the limitations and constraints of information provided by ESG integration databases
☐	**7.1.19** describe primary and secondary sources of ESG data and information
☐	**7.1.20** describe other uses of ESG and sustainability systems data
☐	**7.1.21** explain how Credit Rating Agencies (CRAs) approach ESG Credit Scoring

1 WHY INVESTORS INTEGRATE ESG

☐   **7.1.1** explain the aims and objectives of integrating ESG into the investment process

Many approaches to ESG analysis are used, and a multitude of ESG integration tools and techniques are available. These methods include company analysis, asset valuation, portfolio decision making, and stewardship.

ESG analysis methods use various data sources, ranging from commercially available databases to primary analytical research.

This chapter gives an overview of common and major techniques, a summary of major ESG research providers, and case studies of ESG integration in practice across a range of investment strategies.

Why Investors Integrate ESG

An investment firm might have several different aims and objectives for integrating ESG into an investment process. These can include

- meeting requirements under fiduciary duty or regulations,
- meeting client and beneficiary demands,
- lowering investment risk,
- increasing investment returns,
- giving investment professionals more tools and techniques to use in analysis,
- improving the quality of engagement and stewardship activities, and
- lowering reputational risk at a firm level and investment level.

We will look at each of these objectives in the following sections.

The aims can differ depending on the nature of the firm. Some firms are pure asset managers, some are asset owners (e.g., pension plans), and some have mixed characteristics of both an asset manager and an asset owner (e.g., some insurance entities or large endowments that use both in-house asset managers and third-party firms).

Meeting Requirements under Fiduciary Duty or Regulations, or Meeting Client and Beneficiary Demands

A significant number of investment professionals still do not integrate ESG. According to a 2017 CFA Institute global ESG survey, 24% of equity investors, 55% of fixed income investors, and between 79% and 92% of alternative asset investors (across private equity, real estate, infrastructure, and hedge funds) do not integrate ESG into their processes. More recent studies continue to suggest ESG integration is not universally accepted. The Royal Bank of Canada *2020 Responsible Investment Survey* noted that 25% of respondents and, on a regional basis, 36% of US respondents did not integrate ESG.[1]

However, these investors, or their asset owner clients, might fall under certain country regulations, such as the **EU Shareholder Rights Directive**, the UK Department for Work and Pensions' regulations, or the UK **Stewardship Code**. In these cases, the regulations or clients could demand a certain level of ESG integration, even though the investor might not believe that ESG integration enhances return or lowers risk. The aim is to meet minimum regulatory obligations or client demands.

The debate has evolved over the past two decades. Historically, legal questions arose as to whether some aspects of exclusionary strategies (e.g., excluding tobacco companies) were consistent with fiduciary duties (modeled on what a prudent person might do). Today, some legal and regulatory standards suggest that failing to integrate aspects of ESG might be inconsistent with fiduciary duties. The United Nations Environment Programme Finance Initiative (UNEP FI), along with legal firm Freshfields and the **United Nations Principles for Responsible Investment (PRI)**, examined these questions over the past decade. Their analysis (across jurisdictions) argued that the fiduciary duties of investors require them to do the following:

- Incorporate ESG issues into investment analysis and decision-making processes, consistent with their investment time horizons
- Encourage high standards of ESG performance in the companies or other entities in which they invest
- Understand and incorporate beneficiaries' and savers' sustainability-related preferences, regardless of whether these preferences are financially material[2]

As of 2021, regulatory updates include the EU Shareholder Rights Directive II, the UK Stewardship Code, and guidance from the US Department of Labor (DoL).

Of note, over the past decade, the tone of the US DoL guidance has fluctuated but regardless, the point has been that investors have to take note of regulatory requirements with respect to integrating ESG.

See Chapter 6 on the main principles of stewardship codes and standards.

Lowering Investment Risk and Increasing Investment Returns

Many investors seek to integrate ESG into investment processes to better understand and lower investment risk. Some also wish to enhance returns via ESG by seeking higher alpha. Recent surveys suggest that more firms do so to lower risk rather than enhance returns, but some firms do so for both reasons.[3,4]

---

1 RBC Global Asset Management, *2020 Responsible Investment Survey Key Findings* (2020). www.rbcgam.com/documents/en/other/esg-key-findings.pdf.
2 United Nations Global Compact, United Nations Environment Programme (UNEP) Finance Initiative, PRI, and UNEP Inquiry (2019), *Fiduciary Duty in the 21st Century*. www.unepfi.org/fileadmin/documents/fiduciary_duty_21st_century.pdf.
3 CFA Institute (2017). *Global Perceptions of Environmental, Social, and Governance Issues in Investing* (2017). www.cfainstitute.org/en/research/survey-reports/esg-survey-2017.
4 A. Amel-Zadeh and G. Serafeim, "Why and How Investors Use ESG Information: Evidence from a Global Survey," *Financial Analysts Journal* 74(3) (2017): 87–103. http://dx.doi.org/10.2139/ssrn.2925310.

Exhibit 1: Why and How Investors Use ESG information: Evidence from a Global Survey

Survey responses to the following question: Do you consider ESG information when making investment decisions?	All (1)	Significant difference in proportion vs. rows (2)	AUM size Large (3)	AUM size Small (4)	Diff. (3)–(4) (5)	ESG Allocation High (6)	ESG Allocation Low (7)	Diff. (6)–(7) (8)	Region US (9)	Region Europe (10)	Diff. (11)
N^i=419	82.1%		85.9%	80.3%		93.2%	75.0%	***	75.2%	84.4%	*
Yes, because …											
1 … ESG information is material to investment performance.	63.1%	2–8	60.3%	64.5%		69.3%	58.3%	**	55.7%	64.4%	
2 … of growing client/stakeholder demand.	33.1%	1, 7–8	54.3%	22.4%	***	35.3%	31.8%		33.0%	39.3%	
3 … we believe such policy to be effective in bringing about change at firms.	32.6%	1, 7–8	31.9%	32.9%		46.0%	22.4%	***	25.8%	40.7%	**
4 … it is part of our investment product strategy.	32.6%	1, 7–8	43.1%	27.2%	***	38.7%	28.1%	**	47.4%	30.4%	***
5 … we see it as an ethical responsibility.	32.6%	1, 7–8	25.0%	36.4%	**	41.3%	26.0%	***	18.6%	40.7%	***
6 … we anticipate it to become material in the near future.	31.7%	1, 7–8	31.9%	31.6%		34.0%	30.2%		29.9%	37.0%	
7 … of formal client mandates.	25.0%	1–3, 5–6, 8	37.1%	18.9%	***	33.3%	18.8%	***	23.7%	30.4%	
No, because …	17.9%		14.1%	19.7%		6.8%	25.0%	***	24.8%	15.6%	*
1 … there is no stakeholder demand for such policy.	26.7%	3–5, 6–8	15.8%	30.4%		9.1%	29.7%	*	21.9%	24.0%	
2 … we lack access to reliable nonfinancial data.	21.3%	6–7	21.1%	21.4%		9.1%	23.4%		18.8%	32.0%	
3 … ESG information is not material to investment performance.	13.3%	1, 7	5.3%	16.1%		18.2%	12.5%		21.9%	4.0%	**

Why Investors Integrate ESG

Survey responses to the following question: Do you consider ESG information when making investment decisions?	All (1)	Significant difference in proportion vs. rows (2)	AUM size Large (3)	AUM size Small (4)	Diff. (3)–(4) (5)	ESG Allocation High (6)	ESG Allocation Low (7)	Diff. (6)–(7) (8)	Region US (9)	Region Europe (10)	Diff. (11)
4 … we believe such policy to be ineffective in inducing change at firms.	12.0%	1, 7	15.8%	10.7%		18.2%	10.9%		12.5%	16.0%	
5 … it would violate our fiduciary duty to our stakeholders.	12.0%	1, 7	5.3%	14.3%		9.1%	12.5%		21.9%	8.0%	
6 … such information is not material to a diversified investment portfolio.	10.7%	1–2	5.3%	12.5%		9.1%	10.9%		6.3%	16.0%	
7 … including such information is detrimental to investment performance.	4.0%	1–5, 8	5.3%	3.6%		0.0%	4.7%	*	6.3%	4.0%	
p-value of difference (yes vs. no) <0.001	<0.001	<0.001		<0.001	<0.001		<0.001	<0.001		p-value of difference (yes vs. no) <0.001	<0.001

^{Ni} = *the number of respondents*
Source: Amel-Zadeh and Serafeim (2017).[4]

More Tools and Techniques to Use in Analysis and Improving the Quality of Engagement and Stewardship Activities

Judging by ESG surveys undertaken by both academics and investment practitioners, not all firms believe that ESG integration leads to better risk-adjusted returns. However, many ESG integration tools, such as scorecards, can be used to engage with company management teams and aid stewardship activities. These same tools can also enhance the clarity of a company's business model.

Further details on this can be found in Chapter 6.

Reputational Risk at a Firm Level

Firms might view ESG integration as necessary to ensure a strong reputation and limit reputational risk with stakeholders. Evidence of varying views in the corporate world can be found in Business Roundtable's "Statement on the Purpose of a Corporation"

(August 2019) signed by 181 CEOs (including those of major investment banks and asset managers) who committed to lead their companies for the benefit of all stakeholders—customers, employees, suppliers, communities, and shareholders.[5]

These CEOs wrote:

> *While each of our individual companies serves its own corporate purpose, we share a fundamental commitment to all of our stakeholders. We commit to:*
>
> ▶ *Delivering value to our customers. We will further the tradition of American companies leading the way in meeting or exceeding customer expectations.*
>
> ▶ *Investing in our employees. This starts with compensating them fairly and providing important benefits. It also includes supporting them through training and education that help develop new skills for a rapidly changing world. We foster diversity and inclusion, dignity and respect.*
>
> ▶ *Dealing fairly and ethically with our suppliers. We are dedicated to serving as good partners to the other companies, large and small, that help us meet our missions.*
>
> ▶ *Supporting the communities in which we work. We respect the people in our communities and protect the environment by embracing sustainable practices across our businesses.*
>
> ▶ *Generating long-term value for shareholders, who provide the capital that allows companies to invest, grow and innovate. We are committed to transparency and effective engagement with shareholders.*
>
> *Each of our stakeholders is essential. We commit to deliver value to all of them, for the future success of our companies, our communities and our country.*

A core component of consumer brand surveys are attitudes toward sustainability and climates, as well as perceptions of diversity and inclusion. Managing ESG risks and opportunities therefore becomes an important part of managing brand and reputational value.

2. THE DIFFERENT APPROACHES TO INTEGRATING ESG

☐	7.1.2	describe different approaches of integrating ESG analysis into the investment process
☐	7.1.3	describe qualitative approaches to ESG analysis across a range of asset classes
☐	7.1.4	describe quantitative approaches to ESG analysis across a range of asset classes

---

5 Business Roundtable, *Business Roundtable Redefines the Purpose of a Corporation to Promote "An Economy That Serves All Americans"* (2019). www.businessroundtable.org/business-roundtable-redefines-the-purpose-of-a-corporation-to-promote-an-economy-that-serves-all-americans.

The Different Approaches to Integrating ESG

A firm can use a multitude of approaches to integrate ESG analysis into its investment process. This section provides a summary of these approaches.

What is important to note is that ESG analysis can be either **qualitative** or **quantitative** (sometimes contracted to "quant"). Similarly, the way the analysis is integrated can also be **purely qualitative** (e.g., opinion on quality of management added to the investment thesis) or **quantified** (e.g., impact on financial models or valuation). Some techniques could be considered a hybrid of both techniques, such as scorecards, where a qualitative judgment is turned into a quantitative score.

These tools and techniques cover different types of strategy (passive, systematic, fundamental, active or activist) and different asset classes. Certain tools tend to be asset class or strategy specific.

Qualitative ESG Analysis

Qualitative ESG analysis is likely to be used in investment processes that are based on company-specific research, fundamental analysis, and stock picking.

- ▶ Investment teams analyze ESG data to form an opinion on a firm's ability to manage certain ESG issues.
- ▶ They combine this opinion with their financial analysis by linking specific aspects of the company's ESG risk-management strategy to different value drivers (e.g., costs, revenues, profits, and capital expenditure requirements).
- ▶ Analysts and portfolio managers then seek to integrate their opinion in a quantified way into their financial models by adjusting assumptions used in the model (e.g., growth, margins, or costs of capital).

Certain qualitative techniques might be more suitable (or weighted differently) for different asset classes. For instance, a judgment on management incentives (a part of G analysis) could have more weight in public equity and private equity, have less weight for fixed-income investors, and be deemed irrelevant for sovereign bond investors.

Quantitative ESG Analysis

Quantitative ESG (QESG) analysis is likely to be used in investment processes that use quant models to identify attractive investment opportunities. In such cases, the ESG data are typically aggregated into an ESG factor (an ESG score), which is added to the quant models. This could be a screen that creates the investment universe or a quant model used to adjust valuations based on several factors (including ESG).

Quantitative, Systematic, and Thematic Approaches to Integrated ESG Analysis

Quantitative practitioners might assess ESG factors at the research stage typically using a third-party database or a mix of third-party data and internal proprietary data. This assessment is typically done with large datasets of stocks or bonds, rather than individual company assessment, though some firms will create their own proprietary scores from individual company assessment. The data gathering can be similar to that done by fundamental investors but tends to be over larger datasets. For instance, a global dataset might contain 2,000 to 4,000 companies with 100 data points per company.

Quantitative factor investors typically integrate ESG factors alongside other factors, such as value, size, momentum, growth, and volatility. Some of these factors might be from third-party models.

ESG data are included in their investment processes and could result in upward or downward adjustments to the weights of securities, including to zero. For instance, a strong score on an environmental factor might be sought. Systematic approaches can attempt to derive correlations to understand how ESG factors might affect financial performance over time and then weight those ESG factors appropriately. Investors can try to assess relationships in existing ESG third-party scores as well as proprietary scores. Algorithmic approaches use ESG data (e.g., scraped from internet news articles to adjust company or sector weights after parsing the ESG data through rules-based formulas).

See further sections within this chapter for more information on data sources.

Passive and index approaches might tilt toward ESG factors chosen by investors. For instance, the Japanese Government Pension Investment Fund has created, with index providers, gender-tilted, rules-based indexes to invest in. These could be considered rules-based strategies. This shows that asset owners can set certain mandate rules accordingly to integrate ESG across differing strategies and in line with their own ESG polices and philosophies.

This is explored in further detail in Chapter 9.

Thematic funds might assess alignment with priority themes, which could have an ESG nature (e.g., climate, gender). This alignment can be done with a material opportunity mapping process or using ESG data to adjust weights accordingly.

Application Programming Interfaces

Investors use application programming interfaces (APIs) to compile and assess data. APIs are used to more easily access and interface with underlying databases and other datasets.

Companies are more forthcoming with their sustainability practices, and financial practitioners are increasingly using APIs to compile and integrate this rapidly growing dataset into their processes. The number of total unique ESG data points captured is on the rise.[6]

Artificial Intelligence and Algorithms

Much of the ESG data available on companies is unstructured. Artificial intelligence (AI) and machine learning algorithms attempt to bring structure and numerical value to part of that unstructured dataset. Some practitioners

- focus on using AI techniques to measure ESG performance tied to measures developed by the **Sustainability Accounting Standards Board (SASB)**,
- attempt to provide immediate access to scores based on material ESG events as they occur, or
- focus on intangible ESG factors, such as corporate culture, that could drive company value.

Natural language processing (NLP) and other quantitative techniques are likely to continue to develop over time. NLP is broadly defined as the automatic manipulation of natural language, such as speech and text, by software. In particular, investors are interested in how to program computers to process and analyze large amounts of natural language data related to ESG. The aim is to obtain a computer capable of "understanding" the ESG contents of documents, including the contextual nuances of the language within them. The technology can then accurately extract information and insights contained in the documents as well as categorize and organize the documents themselves.

---

6 ProgrammableWeb, *Growth in Financial Related (Financial, Banking, Payments, Monetization) APIs since 2005* (2020). www.programmableweb.com/news/financial-apis-have-seen-two-growth-spikes/research/2017/08/09.

Highlights between the Quantitative Approaches and Qualitative Approaches and Terminology Confusion

Combining this information can be confusing because of the different meanings investors give to the term *quantitative*. As a description of an analytical technique, it tends to be used when a numeric score is assigned. But it can also be used to describe a whole class of investment strategy that tends to use stock, bond, derivative, or other security factor properties as the main basis for investment.

In terms of investment strategies, quantitative investing can be known as "systematic investing." It can include the following strategies:

- high-frequency trading
- use of algorithms based on news or factors and statistical arbitrage
- trend following
- risk parity
- use of beta strategies

The approach tends to use heavy mathematical modeling, computing power, and data analysis, potentially including machine and natural language learning processes. Some firms use these approaches exclusively, and some use them to supplement human decision making.

Typically, computer and mathematical models are built and then backtested. Where these models use ESG data or information (e.g., through raw data or ratings agencies), this is considered a form of ESG integration. This produces many challenges because the length of time series for ESG data (usually 7–15 years, depending on the series) is much shorter than for financial data. This typically might be viewed as a quantitative investment form of integrating ESG technique.

See Chapter 8 and further sections within this chapter for more on the types of challenges that can arise from ESG integration.

Qualitative forms of analysis typically use human judgment of non-numerical forms of analysis. However, advances in techniques are blurring these traditional boundaries. For instance, machine learning's use of natural language processing and scanning of management commentary from meeting transcripts are using those qualitative words in a quantitative fashion.

See Chapter 8 for more on ESG and quantitative investment factors.

Fundamental active strategies, where human judgment is used, tend to use ESG techniques that have both qualitative and quantitative elements to them but are typically not considered quantitative investment. And similarly, with quantitative investment strategies that use ESG ratings data, those ESG ratings data might be based on qualitative human judgment.

Overall, ESG techniques can be considered quantitative or qualitative or have elements of both. Investment strategies are typically classified as

- quantitative (systematic, algorithmic),
- fundamental,
- active,
- passive, or
- beta.

Investors interchange the term *quantitative* but provide different meanings when applying it to overall investment strategies and processes rather than specific ESG integration techniques.

Tools and Elements of ESG Analysis

Regardless of whether the ESG analysis is classified as qualitative or quantitative, investors use many types of tools. These tools and elements of ESG analysis can include the following:

- Red flag indicators – Securities with high ESG risk are flagged and investigated further or excluded. For instance, a company that has a board that lacks majority independence might be flagged for deep scrutiny on management incentives or simply be excluded from an investable universe.

- Company questionnaires and management interviews – For example, if the detail on management aspects or other material ESG information is insufficient, the investor might ask the company for specific data. Or the investor might have a prepared list of standard ESG data they ask for. These questionnaires are also used in parallel with regular company meetings, where investors and companies meet to discuss the most material ESG issues.

- Checks with outside experts – For instance, an investor might interview key industry thought leaders or other stakeholders of the company, including customers, suppliers, or regulators. These checks might be complemented via interviews, surveys, or third-party sourcing, such as the use of expert networks.

- Watch lists – These lists might include securities with high ESG risk added to a watchlist for monitoring, or securities with high ESG opportunities that are put on a watchlist for possible investment. For instance, once an investor has assessed ESG risks or opportunities, a news or stock price watchlist is created and monitored for stock price entry levels or for change in ESG events. For example, a highly carbon-intense company identified with high E risk might be monitored against changing policies on carbon taxes.

- Internal ESG research – This research could be based on a variety of techniques and data sources. Proprietary ESG research and analysis is performed, and the output can be provided in scores, rankings, or reports. The research can be based on a variety of data sources, and proprietary ESG research or scores could be created. Furthermore, research could consist of the following:
  - materiality frameworks;
  - ESG-integrated research notes;
  - research dashboards;
  - strengths, weaknesses, opportunities, and threats (SWOT) analysis with ESG factors;
  - scenario analysis; and
  - relative rankings.

- External ESG research – For this research, sell-side, ESG specialists, or third-party databases can all be used, and a materiality framework is created.

- ESG agenda items at investment committee– or chief information officer– level meetings – One technique to ensure consistent integration is to ensure an ESG section as a standing item at committee meetings. This approach might guarantee scrutiny from senior level investors and signal importance to the investment firm.

Elements of ESG Integration

The elements of ESG integration include the following:

- adjusting forecast financials (e.g., revenue, operating cost, asset book value, capital expenditure)
- adjusting valuation models or multiples (e.g., discount rates, terminal values, ratios)
- adjusting credit risk and duration
- managing risk, including exposure limits, scenario analysis, and value-at-risk models
- ESG factor tilts
- ESG momentum tilts
- strategic asset allocation, including thematic and ESG objective tilts
- tactical asset allocation
- ESG controversies and positive ESG events

This can be summed up by the ESG integration framework shown in Exhibit 2.

Exhibit 2: ESG Integration Framework

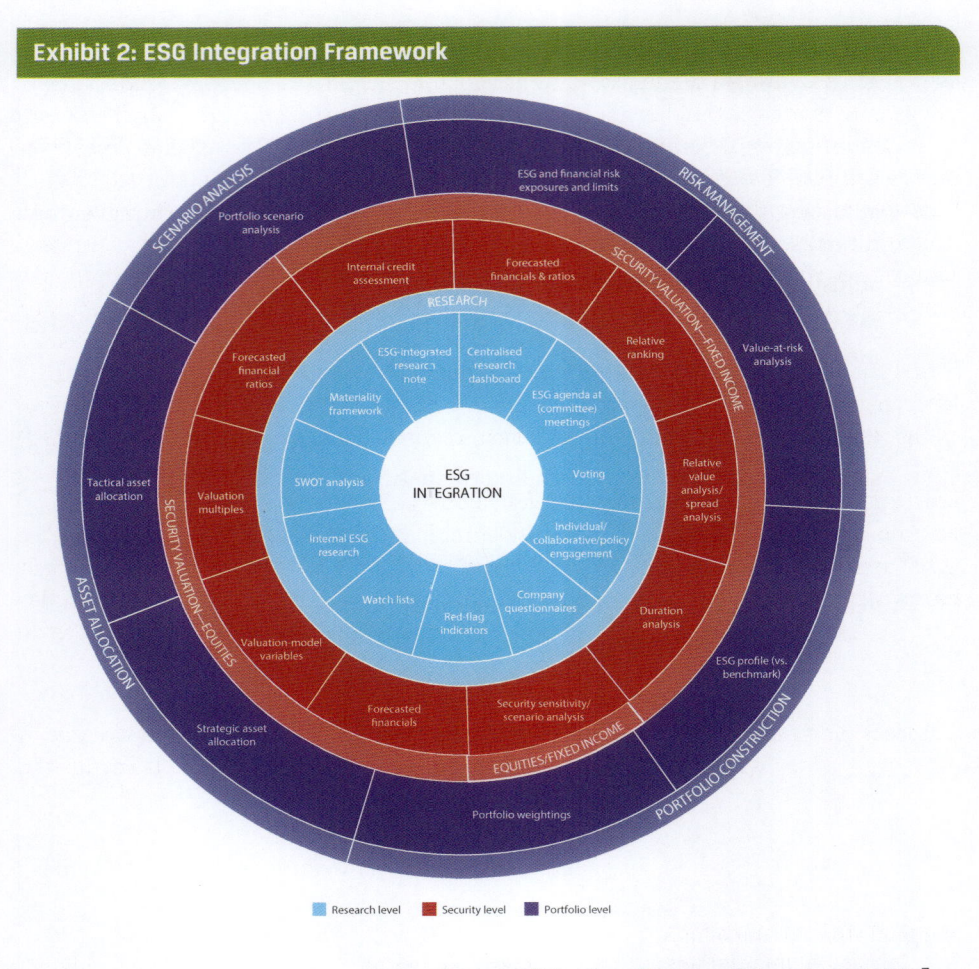

Source: CFA Institute 2018, in collaboration with PRI.[7]

The ESG integration framework, shown in Exhibit 2, is not meant to illustrate the perfect ESG-integrated investment process. Because every firm is unique, the ESG integration techniques of one firm are not necessarily the right techniques for all firms. However, many firms will use a selection of the techniques referenced in the figure.

Firms typically use various tools and techniques to identify material factors. These tools can be qualitative or quantitative, or a mix of both.

Differences between Company or Business Analysis and Security Analysis

Many investment practitioners make two distinctions in fundamental investment analysis:

1. the difference between a company or business assessment, and
2. a security, stock, bond, or convertible (or other tradeable construct, including derivatives) assessment.

---

7 CFA Institute and PRI, *Guidance and Case Studies for ESG Integration: Equities and Fixed Income* (2018). www.unpri.org/investor-tools/guidance-and-case-studies-for-esg-integration-equities-and-fixed-income/3622.article.

While the differences are often interchanged in ordinary language, many investors give them different meanings. Stocks and bonds can have properties that companies do not, such as stock beta or volatility, which are potentially expressed in different ways.

A company or business assessment typically examines fundamental properties of a business, such as its competitive advantages (or lack of), sometimes described as a business moat (after the popular Warren Buffett Annual Letters). These properties could appear in the company's products or services, suppliers, employees, management, organizational structure, incentives, corporate culture, or resources (natural, intellectual, or innovation). Many of these properties could be considered as under an ESG category. For instance, natural capital could be under E, corporate culture or supplier analysis under S, and management structure or incentives under G.

A business might have strong aspects of ESG, which lead to an assessment of a strong or competitive advantage, that can then lead to a positive judgment on that business or company.

The statistical properties of a company stock or bond might differ from its fundamental business properties. For instance, beta or stock volatility are properties of a stock, not of a company or business per se. This distinction is important because of the debate among investors who use security factors to invest. The debate here is whether these properties are ESG components that are robust QESG stock or bond factors.

See Chapter 8 for more detail on this debate.

This debate is important because of how an assessment of the strength or weakness of a company or business can then lead to a valuation of its securities.

TYPICAL STAGES OF INTEGRATED ESG ASSESSMENT (RESEARCH AND IDEA GENERATION STAGE)

7.1.5 identify tangible and intangible material ESG-related factors through both qualitative and quantitative approaches

Firms and investment teams might not have ESG factors embedded in their philosophy but still use ESG techniques within investment processes. These techniques can run alongside a financial analysis or have integrated aspects to the analysis. The stages typically are research, valuation, and portfolio construction, which leads to investment decisions.

Each of these stages is considered in further detail in the following subsections.

Research and Idea Generation Stage

Gathering Information

Practitioners gather financial and ESG information from multiple sources, typically a mix of company reports, third-party research, and primary research, and the data might be qualitative or quantitative, or both.

For example, qualitative data might include company questionnaires and management interviews, whereas quantitative data might include environmental emissions data.

Materiality Assessments

The research stage typically includes a materiality assessment to identify the ESG issues that are likely to have an impact on the company's financial performance. Materiality is typically measured in terms of both the likelihood and magnitude of impact.

The materiality assessment is considered important because evidence shows that nonmaterial factors do not affect financials, valuations, or company **business models**.[8] It is distinguished from some exclusionary socially responsible investing strategies, which might also consider nonmaterial factors (e.g., exclusion of pork-based product companies for certain religious stakeholders) that a typical investor would not deem a material ESG factor.

Investors who primarily see ESG analysis and ESG integration as a way to enhance investment processes are likely to focus on ESG issues they consider financially material (i.e., a factor that they consider likely to have a financial impact in the future, either positive or negative).

As of 2021, debates are ongoing about the taxonomy and definitions to be used surrounding ESG and sustainability. For instance, the EU is proposing a taxonomy on sustainability investments.[9] Also, some investors label their strategies as either "ethical" or "impact." Such ethical strategies might consider issues that an ESG-integrated investor does not deem as being material.

Tangible versus Intangible Factors; Different Forms of Capital

A tangible asset (or a hard asset) is a physical asset, whereas an intangible asset is a non-physical one that is difficult or impossible to touch physically.

Exhibit 3: Examples of Tangible and Intangible Assets

Tangible Assets	Intangible Assets	Applicable to Both Tangible and Intangible Assets
▶ Land	▶ Goodwill	▶ ESG analysis techniques
▶ Manufacturing plants	▶ Patents	▶ Materiality
▶ Inventories	▶ Copyrights	
▶ Furniture	▶ Intellectual property and know-how	
▶ Machinery	▶ Software and innovation assets	
	▶ Corporate culture	
	▶ Incentives	
	▶ Employee productivity	
	▶ Other forms of social and relationship assets	

Evaluating Different Forms of Tangible or Intangible Factors

One framework for evaluating different forms of "capital" or tangible or intangible factors was developed by the International Integrated Reporting Council (IIRC).

---

8 M. Khan, G. Serafeim, and A. Yoon, "Corporate Sustainability: First Evidence on Materiality," *The Accounting Review* 91(6) (2016): 1697–724. https://ssrn.com/abstract=2575912.
9 European Commission, *EU Taxonomy for Sustainable Activities* (2021). https://ec.europa.eu/info/business-economy-euro/banking-and-finance/sustainable-finance/eu-taxonomy-sustainable-activities_en.

The IIRC Framework (to which certain companies report) describes capitals (both intangible and tangible) as follows:

- Financial capital — the pool of funds that is available to an organization for use in the production of goods or the provision of services and that is obtained through financing, such as debt, equity, or grants or generated through operations or investments.
- Manufactured capital — manufactured physical objects (distinct from natural physical objects) that are available to an organization for use in the production of goods or the provision of services, including buildings, equipment, and infrastructure (e.g., roads, ports, bridges, and waste and water treatment plants).
  - Manufactured capital is often created by other organizations but includes assets manufactured by the reporting organization for sale purposes or when they are retained for their own use.
- Intellectual capital – organizational, knowledge-based intangibles, including intellectual property (e.g., patents, copyrights, software, rights, and licenses) and "organizational capital" (e.g., tacit knowledge, systems, procedures, and protocols).
- Human capital – people's competencies, capabilities, and experiences and their motivations to innovate, including the following:
  - their alignment with and support for an organization's governance framework, risk management approach, and ethical values
  - the ability to understand, develop, and implement an organization's strategy
  - their loyalties and motivations for improving processes, goods, and services, including their ability to lead, manage, and collaborate
- Social and relationship capital – the institutions and relationships between communities, groups of stakeholders, and other networks and the ability to share information to enhance individual and collective well-being. These include the following:
  - shared norms and common values and behaviors
  - intangibles associated with the brand and reputation that an organization has developed
  - an organization's social license to operate
- Natural capital – all renewable and non-renewable environmental resources and processes that provide goods or services that support the past, present, or future prosperity of an organization (see Chapter 3 in particular), including air, water, land, minerals, and forests, as well as biodiversity and ecosystem health.

Clearly, not all forms of capital (intangible or tangible) would be material or relevant to all companies; however, determining this might require a materiality judgment (see the later section on materiality assessments and risk mapping).

Many of the nonfinancial capitals would be considered under ESG, with a large number also intangible. A qualitative identification and judgment would be considered a form of qualitative approach to ESG.

We will now briefly examine how some of these forms of capital can be assessed with some examples across company constituents, such as regulators, customers, employees, and suppliers.

A positive relationship with regulators could lead to less friction and litigation. Examples include

- social media and advertising companies,
- pharmaceutical companies,
- airlines,
- financial services, and
- any company that has a significant regulator, which could be found in many industries.

The relationship between a regulator and a company would be considered an intangible asset (or a liability if the relationship is negative). A negative relationship might be more likely to lead to litigation, which adds to costs and could lead to penalties, both of which affect cash flows.

The amount of capital that banks and insurers are required to hold might depend on an analyst's view of their relationships and on their reputation with regulators and the public. This in turn could affect return on capital metrics, cash flows, and valuation estimates.

Pharmaceutical companies with a positive reputation and products that meet previously unmet medical needs might have quicker or more certain regulatory approval pathways. This can be assessed by differing estimates of probability of success for future products. For example, the probability of success might be lowered from an industry average of 70% to 60% for a company with a poor reputation, or it could be raised to 80% for a company with a positive reputation. This adjustment would affect risk-adjusted **discounted cash flow (DCF)** calculations: Faster approval positively affects cash flows, so reputation and brand are intangible assets.

Customer service, perceived brand value, and overall customer satisfaction can be inputs to determine future sales growth rates and therefore cash flows. Differing growth rates might be affected by an investor's view of reputation and brand value for both positive opportunity and negative risk. A company with high customer satisfaction or strong brand reputation might be expected to grow revenue faster than the industry average in investor estimates.

High employee satisfaction might also affect forward estimates by investors. For instance, a hotel group with high employee satisfaction might find recruiting new talent easier and might be assessed to provide a better customer experience, which could lead to higher repeat revenue modeled by investors, or by investors prepared to assign higher valuation ratios (e.g., prepared to buy stocks with higher P/E ratios or bonds at lower credit spreads).

A poor supply chain or a weak relationship with suppliers might lead to a lower forecast by investors or lower valuation ratios, for instance, in food supply chains for supermarkets when a poor supply chain has led to instances of horse meat in lasagna food products. Alternatively, this could be seen in the questioning of the sustainable sourcing of supply chains. On the other hand, strong supply chain management in agile, fast inventory management from short robust supply chains might lead to a more positive view from investors.

These factors can be intersectional. For instance, a poor supply chain and labor practices might be negatively affected by modern slavery laws or regulation, which might incorporate both a regulator assessment and a supply chain assessment from investors.

Generating Ideas

Investment ideas can be generated from the data. Some practitioners begin this stage using a valuation screen, or fundamental screen, which might incorporate ESG factors—perhaps a mix of positive (seek high G), negative (avoid low G), or momentum (seek rising G or avoid declining G)—to create an attractive investment universe. This is commonly referred to as "positive" or "best-in-class" screening.

Investment ideas can also be generated by themes associated with specific ESG megatrends. For instance, an ESG opportunity theme might be to seek improving access to clean water or to energy services. This approach is commonly referred to as "thematic" investing.

At this stage, checklists—internal or externally sourced—might "red flag" companies and be used to narrow the investable universe. For instance, an acceptable low governance score or an unacceptable number of ESG controversies (real-world ESG events that are contested by different stakeholders or that affect society, such as a dam failing). Red flag techniques can also be used in later stages.

These risks might be ESG risks judged on an absolute hurdle basis or judged against what can be "priced into the asset."

A materially negative assessment of a particular ESG factor or collection of factors could lead to a decision that an investment fails to meet a specified hurdle. For example, an incentive structure deemed to be poorly aligned under a G assessment might disqualify a possible investment and, the assessment triggers a "sell" or "do not invest" signal.

This assessment could be either **quantitative** (e.g., the carbon intensity of company A is too far above an index benchmark to meet a practitioner's investment criteria) or **qualitative** (e.g., the experience of the management team in managing environmental risk and the lack of disclosed policies might indicate risks too great for an investor on a qualitative basis).

TYPICAL STAGES OF INTEGRATED ESG ASSESSMENT (SCORECARDS CAN BE USED TO ASSESS ESG RISK AND OPPORTUNITY, AND MATERIALITY ASSESSMENTS AND RISK MAPPING)

4

- ☐ 7.1.6 describe how scorecards may be developed and constructed to assess ESG factors
- ☐ 7.1.7 assess ESG issues using risk mapping methodologies

As an example, a credit analyst identifies a company that has no third-party ESG rating available but that is issuing investment-grade bonds that might be investable. In this case, the analyst creates their own ESG assessment. A custom ESG self-assessment tool that reflects the sector-specific risk issues relevant to the issuer is created, and the company management or investor relations team is asked to fill this out. An ESG scorecard based on the self-assessment response is created with ESG factor scores ranging from 0 to 5, and high or low scores are then used in valuation or further assessment work.

Ethical marketing might, for example, be identified as a key ESG social risk (perhaps via a risk-mapping process, which is covered in the next subsection) for pharmaceutical companies X, Y, and Z:

- Company X has no policy and a history of violations, so it scores a 0.
- Company Y has a brief policy and no violations, so it scores a 3.
- Company Z has a detailed policy and one minor violation, so it scores a 4.

Scores of 0 could make a company unattractive, and scores of 5 could lead to further investment work. Alternatively, total scores of all factors in the scorecard are used in further assessment or valuation work.

The scorecard can take a qualitative judgment of a factor and put a form of quantitative score on it.

ESG rating agencies can provide scores, and a form of scoring is typically used in commercially available ESG rating services. These can be used raw or adjusted by practitioners to reflect their own views. These scores can then be compiled for use in assessment or idea generation.

The scorecard technique could be used on private companies as well as public companies. Challenges to creating private company scorecards is that a rating agency score is less likely to be available for a private company, and less information about it is available in the public domain. This scorecard technique can be adapted to scoring countries for sovereign bond analysis or to infrastructure and real estate. For example, environmental policies could be scored for infrastructure and commitments to a carbon net zero plan, or corruption levels could be scored for countries.

See more on ESG ratings agencies later in this chapter.

In summary, developing a scorecard involves the following steps:

1. Identify sector- or company-specific ESG items.
2. Break down issues into a number of indicators (e.g., policy, measures, disclosure).
3. Determine a scoring system based on what good/best practice looks like for each indicator/issue.
4. Assess a company and give it a score.
5. Calculate aggregated scores at issue level, dimension level (ESG level), or total score level (depending on the relative weight of each issue).
6. Benchmark the company's performance against industry averages or peer group (optional).

Materiality Assessments and Risk Mapping

Some ESG issues might be material for companies in a specific industry (e.g., water stress can disrupt the operations of mining or beverages companies, which rely heavily on clean water in their production processes) but not for those in other sectors (e.g., water stress has little affect on media or financial companies).

One should note that not all risks can be managed. Material ESG risk that has not been managed by a company takes two types: (1) unmanageable risk, which cannot be addressed by company initiatives, and (2) the management gap, which represents risks that could be managed by a company through suitable initiatives but which might not yet be managed.

As explained, some risks are manageable, such as the risk of on-the-job injuries, which can be managed, for example, through establishing stringent safety procedures, having emergency response plans and safety drills, and promoting a safe culture.

Some risks are not (fully) manageable, such as the carbon emissions of airplanes in flight. An airline can manage some of the issues (e.g., by modernizing aircraft, installing winglets, and working on information and communication technology systems to minimize the time that airplanes spend idling on the runway), but it cannot easily manage all of an airplane's flight emissions. As a result, the airline has some unmanageable risk on carbon emissions, which should contribute to its unmanaged risk score on that issue.

Unmanageable risk is only one of the two components of unmanaged risk. The second component is the management gap, which relates to the manageable part of a company's material ESG risks and reflects the failure of the company in managing these risks sufficiently, as reflected in the company's management score.

EXAMPLE 1

Human Capital

Human capital is difficult to manage. A company can employ hundreds of thousands of people, and imagining a management program that could eliminate all risk of sexual harassment, low morale, or high turnover is very hard. But companies are expected to have full control over these policies. Moreover, Sustainalytics has confidence that strong policies can effectively promote a working culture that limits material risk from sexual harassment or a workplace with destructive low morale and turnover. However, companies have challenges in mitigating risks in the labor supply chain. Therefore, a manageable risk factor is applied to distinguish that some risk within the issue cannot be managed.

In terms of a company's risk management capabilities, a review of controversy cases can be helpful.

A controversy case is defined as an instance, or ongoing situation, in which a company's operations or products allegedly have a negative ESG impact.

Determining which ESG issues are most material is not an exact science, and there might be important differences between what each investor considers most material, even when analyzing the same company.

Determining which ESG issues are most material is not an exact science, and there might be important differences between what each investor considers most material, even when analyzing the same company. This is because forecasting how much one ESG or risk factor will affect a financial metric such as future cash flow is typically a matter of judgement.

Frameworks such as the materiality maps provided by the SASB are helpful in providing some guidance, but investment professionals often develop their own view on what is most material. This spectrum of opinions concerning materiality is exemplified through the different examples of materiality maps provided in Exhibit 4, Exhibit 5, and Exhibit 6, which highlight the differing views investors might take.

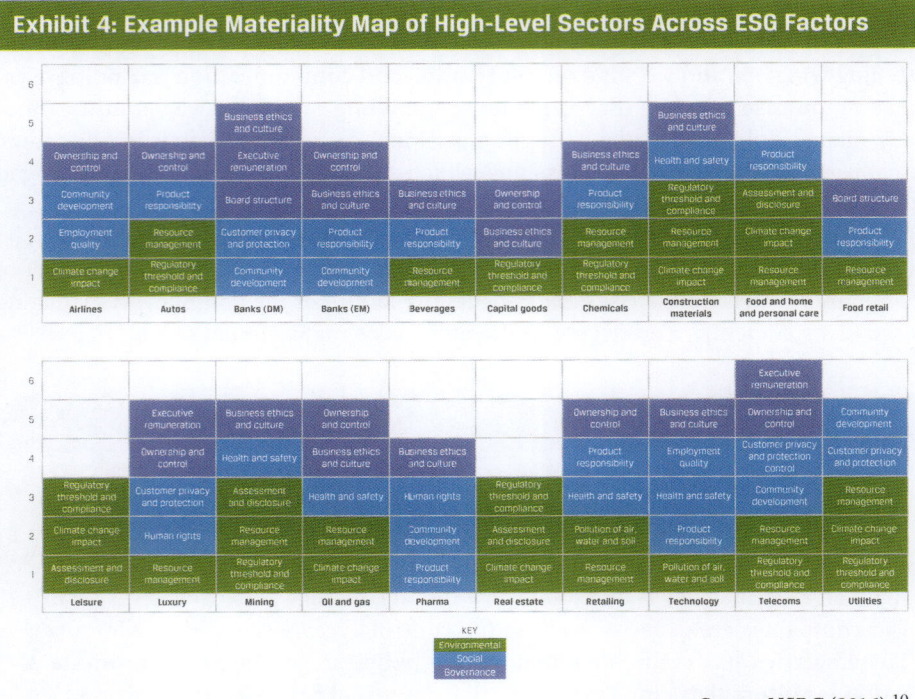

Exhibit 4: Example Materiality Map of High-Level Sectors Across ESG Factors

Source: HSBC (2016).[10]

Exhibit 4 highlights the numerous and shifting nature of many ESG factors.

One publicly available sector materiality assessment is provided by the SASB (see Exhibit 5). This shows that different industries can have different exposures (compare with Exhibit 6 on health care).

One can deduce that individual companies in the same market-defined sector might be judged to have different material ESG factors affecting their business. For instance, within insurance, a US health care insurer will have different factors affecting it than a car insurance firm would.

Investors can find more direct comparisons useful in analysis. In the health care industry example (Exhibit 6), using the SASB materiality map, a pharmaceutical company is judged to have a material exposure to fair marketing practices.

- Pharmaceutical company A is judged to have a low risk exposure to this factor because it has up-to-date policies and training programs and has never had a regulatory warning letter.

- Pharmaceutical company B is judged to have a high risk to this factor because it lacks a strong policy, training is minimal, and the company has received several fines and warnings from regulators.

- Pharmaceutical company C is judged to have no risk to this factor because it engages only in pharmaceutical research and does not have any commercially marketed products. Here we can see that even though the factor is material to the sector, it is of limited risk or arguably no risk to the company because the company is not exposed.

These pharmaceutical companies can be more directly assessed on this same factor compared to each other.

---

10 HSBC and Equity Strategy, *Global ESG Sector Playbook* (2016).

Exhibit 5: Example

Issues	Health Care	Financials	Technology and Communications	Non-renewable Resources	Transportation	Services	Resource Transformation	Consumption	Renewable Resources and Alternative Energy	Infrastructure
Environment										
Greenhouse gas (GHG) emissions			x	x	x	x	x	x	x	x
Air quality				x	x	x	x		x	x
Energy management	x		x	x	x	x	x	x	x	x
Fuel management	x			x	x	x		x		x
Water and wastewater management	x		x	x		x	x	x	x	x
Waste and hazardous materials management	x		x	x	x	x	x	x		x
Biodiversity impacts				x	x	x		x	x	x
Social capital										
Human rights and community relations	x			x					x	x
Access and affordability	x	x				x			x	x
Customer welfare	x	x			x	x	x	x		x
Data security and customer privacy	x	x	x			x	x	x		
Fair disclosure and labelling	x					x		x		
Fair marketing and advertising	x	x				x		x		
Human capital										

Issues	Health Care	Financials	Technology and Communications	Non-renewable Resources	Transportation	Services	Resource Transformation	Consumption	Renewable Resources and Alternative Energy	Infrastructure
Labor relations			x	x	x			x		x
Fair labor practices			x		x	x		x		
Employee health, safety and well-being	x		x	x	x	x	x	x	x	x
Diversity and inclusion		x	x			x		x		
Compensation and benefits		x				x		x		
Recruitment, development, and retention	x		x		x	x		x		
Business model and innovation										
Lifecycle impacts of products and services	x	x	x	x	x	x	x	x	x	x
Environmental, social impacts on assets and operations	x	x		x		x		x		
Product packaging	x					x	x	x		
Product quality and safety	x				x	x	x	x		
Leadership and governance										
Systemic risk management		x	x			x	x			x
Accident and safety management				x	x	x	x		x	x

Issues	Health Care	Financials	Technology and Communications	Non-renewable Resources	Transportation	Services	Resource Transformation	Consumption	Renewable Resources and Alternative Energy	Infrastructure
Business ethics and transparency payments	x	x		x	x	x	x			x
Competitive behavior		x	x	x	x	x	x			x
Regulatory risk				x		x	x	x	x	x
Materials sourcing			x	x	x		x	x	x	
Supply chain management	x		x	x	x	x	x	x	x	

Source: SASB, *SASB Materiality Map* (2018). https://materiality.sasb.org/.

As seen earlier, the same technique can be applied to whole sectors or sub-sectors, as well as companies. For instance, biodiversity as an E factor is not seen to affect the whole pharmaceutical sector but might have an impact on the agriculture sector.

Using the SASB as a Baseline Framework in a Materiality Assessment

One example of where you might want to use the SASB as a baseline framework in a fundamental active investment process might be for a bio-pharmaceutical company that has a cannabis plant as its raw active ingredient. (This applies to the company GW Pharmaceuticals.)

As is shown in Exhibit 6, "materials sourcing" is not considered a material ESG risk for biotechnology and pharmaceutical companies.

However, an analyst might judge that a cannabis-derived medication would be a material risk on two accounts:

1. Growing the plants is potentially a complex operation with enhanced risks compared to standard manufacturing.

2. The regulatory oversight is more complex because both the drug regulator and the pharmaceutical regulator (in the United States, the Drug Enforcement Agency and the Food and Drug Administration, respectively) would be involved. For a standard pharmaceutical, only the pharmaceutical regulator would be involved.

The analyst might further judge that an ESG opportunity exists here as well because of the technology needed to harvest the plants, the knowledge protection around that technology, and the barriers involved in having to satisfy two regulators.

This might lead to longer intellectual property protection (and longer cash flows) as well as higher barriers to entry (and lower likelihood of competition). In this example, the social impacts might be more complex to judge as well, whereas all other aspects of the company's analysis might correspond to where the SASB has judged most risk to be (e.g., energy, water, and waste under E; see Exhibit 6).

As of 2019–2020, a trend has developed in company reporting to include more material ESG factors. However, various stakeholders do not agree on materiality and how to report, so developing proprietary materiality assessments could continue to be an important technique for investors to potentially develop their own analytical framework alongside standardized frameworks, such as those of the SASB or the Global Reporting Initiative (GRI). As the SASB becomes more established as a leading materiality framework, it might be worth further investigation because calls are increasing from stakeholders for such standardization.

ESG Risk-Mapping Methodologies

ESG risk mapping can also be done at the research stage. Here, an individual company (equity or credit) or sector has its risk mapped to a specific theme or factor, usually one that has been judged "material."

Risk mapping could also mean mapping a portfolio or investable universe against a specific ESG risk (e.g., climate risk, water-related risks) to identify which sectors or companies contribute the most to this particular risk profile (e.g., carbon- or water-intensive companies). Examples of risk-mapping methodologies include carbon footprinting or testing portfolios against different climate scenarios.

Exhibit 6: Example Materiality Map of Health Care Subsectors from the SASB

			Health Care		
Issues	Biotechnology	Pharmaceuticals	Medical Equipment and Supplies	Health care Delivery	Health care Distribution	Managed Care
Environment						
GHG emissions						
Air quality						
Energy management	x	x	x	x		
Fuel management	x	x	x		x	
Water and wastewater management	x	x	x			
Waste and hazardous materials management	x	x	x	x		
Biodiversity impacts						
Social capital						
Human rights and community relations	x	x				
Access and affordability	x	x	x	x		x
Customer welfare	x	x	x	x		x
Data security and customer privacy				x		x
Fair disclosure and labelling				x		x
Fair marketing and advertising	x	x	x			
Human capital						
Labor relations						
Fair labor practices						
Employee health, safety, and well-being	x	x				
Diversity and inclusion						
Compensation and benefits						
Recruitment, development, and retention	x	x		x		
Business model and innovation						
Lifecycle impacts of products and services	x	x	x		x	
Environmental, social impacts on assets and operations		x		x		x
Product packaging					x	
Product quality and safety	x	x	x		x	
Leadership and governance						

Systemic risk management			
Accident and safety management			
Business ethics and transparency payments	x	x	x
Competitive behavior		x	
Regulatory capture and political influence	x		
Materials sourcing	x		
Supply chain management	x	x	x

Source: SASB, *SASB Materiality Map* (2018). https://materiality.sasb.org/.

Mapping can also be done for material opportunities (e.g., opportunity from recycling or the transition to renewable energy) as well as risks. It can be scored, for instance, on a 10-point scale or given a qualitative label, such as low or high risk. This shows how the scorecard technique (described earlier) can be combined with a mapping technique.

VALUATION AND COMPANY INTEGRATED ASSESSMENT STAGE AND THE CHALLENGE OF COMPANY DISCLOSURE ON ESG TOPICS

☐	7.1.8	explain how ESG complements traditional financial analysis
☐	7.1.9	analyze how ESG factors may affect industry and company performance
☐	7.1.10	analyze how ESG factors may affect security valuation across a range of asset classes
☐	7.1.11	interpret a company's disclosure on selected ESG topics

After the research stage and any relevant risk and materiality mapping, practitioners assess the impact of material financial and ESG factors on the corporate and investment performance of a company.

This can lead to adjustments to the following:

- forecasted financials
- valuation-model variables, such as cost of capital or terminal growth rates in discounted cash flow analysis;
- valuation multiples
- forecasted financial ratios
- internal credit assessments
- assumptions in qualitative or quantitative models

Regardless of whether a hurdle process is used, adjustments in models can be made—positively or negatively—on assessment.

Model Adjustments Based on ESG Assessment

Discounted cash flow input adjustments

A company's environmental management processes and policies are judged strong or weak. After this judgment, the cost of capital used to discount cash flows in a DCF analysis is adjusted down or up by 1% to account for this. This can also be on a country or sector basis, where a country or sector ESG risk factor can contribute to a change in a cost of capital or terminal value growth assumption. For example, the coal sector might be judged to have a negative environmental impact.

> Note how the judgment on the E factor leads to a change in the financial model assumption. This is a complement. A higher cost of capital would lead—all other factors being equal—to a lower intrinsic value estimate from the model. This is an example of how the E factor then affects a valuation model.

> Also note that the sizing of the adjustment is typically at the discretion of the analyst, though the analyst might use certain guidelines.

Explicit Profit and Loss Sales, Balance Sheet and Margin Adjustments from ESG Assessment

Rather than changing model discount assumptions, explicit sales or margin assumptions can be adjusted. For example, an analysis of a company's strong management of its employees (as assessed by employee engagement or satisfaction metrics) leads to an assessment of strong future customer satisfaction, which in turn leads to sales forecasts five years out being raised to above the industry average to account for this strong social factor score.

See the Further Reading section on academic work on employee satisfaction found in Professor Alex Edmans's work.

An adjustment can be a direct impact (e.g., an assessment of an environmental litigation fine being USD400m, or GBP288m) or the risk-adjusted impact of a carbon tax might be forecast to be an absolute dollar amount per year in a model.

Adjustments can be made directly to the balance sheet or capital expense lines. A practitioner might believe that ESG factors will lead a company to decrease or increase its future capital expenditure. A forecast ESG impairment event (e.g., a substandard factory) could result in an impairment charge being made to bring the company's book value down.

Valuation Ratio Adjustments with ESG Integration

Adjustments can also be made to valuation ratios.

- An investor might decide that a company is worth a certain P/E ratio premium or discount versus its peers because of ESG factors.
- Alternatively, an investor might be prepared to invest in a company with, for example, a 50% discount on a P/E ratio versus an index benchmark simply because the company is judged to have a high ESG risk.
- Conversely, an investor might be willing to invest in a company at a 50% premium on a P/E ratio because of strong ESG characteristics.

The adjustment might also be absolute. For instance, the investor might assign a "fair value P/E" of 16x to a strong ESG company versus 14x for an average ESG company and 12x for a weak ESG company.

How ESG Analysis Can Complement Traditional Financial Analysis

A few theoretical examples can now be examined. (These examples might be useful for thinking about how ESG factors affect industry and company performance. They show how integrated many ESG techniques and thinking are.)

One theoretical concept in fundamental analysis might be weak or strong ESG factor:

- weak or strong business driver or moat
- up or down sales or margins
- up or down long-term cash flow
- up or down intrinsic value
- up or down share price

This might be expressed as high employee engagement or satisfaction (proved by being number one versus the competition on surveys or having an X% higher score against a threshold):

- high customer satisfaction (judged by high net promoter score)
- higher sales growth than competition
- higher valuation than competition

The judgment of an intangible ESG factor, such as employee relations, complements an analysis of customer satisfaction and the assumptions that lead into a model of sales growth (a traditional financial factor).

Alternatively, high carbon intensity (proved by scope 1 and 2 carbon intensity being both absolute and relative to sector):

- increased risk from carbon taxes
- increased cost of debt for new project financing
- higher taxes
- increased balance sheet risk of default on debt
- change in debt rating
- lower value of corporate debt

Here, the judgment of an E factor, such as exposure to carbon, leads to analysis on the risk to debt pricing. It complements a traditional take on default risk.

Alternatively, weak governance identified in a private company (proved by a board with poor skills, not independent, non-diversified thinking):

- increased risk of negative capital allocation decisions
- lower future cash flows or difficulty in IPO to capital markets
- lower valuation or increased bankruptcy risk

Here, a judgment on a G factor in a private company affects both a valuation and possible exit for a private equity investor.

Active Ownership as an ESG Technique

What is worth noting here is how integration with a stewardship function—whether outsourced or part of the same investment team—might work in an integrated ESG approach. For instance, a stewardship-led investment team might gain a commitment or an action to improve (e.g., weak governance by gaining a commitment to recruit independent board members and an independent chair, thereby influencing future cash flows and valuations). Such strategies could come under an active ownership or ESG activist approach. Information gained from an active engagement might also inform the ESG and traditional analysis; for instance, a management team's unwillingness to disclose carbon emissions and not commit to future disclosure could affect an investment team's ESG analysis.

The Challenge of Company Disclosure on ESG Topics

Companies have variable disclosure policies and reporting. While for listed companies, minimum accounting reporting standards are adhered to, these standards vary from one region to the next. Disclosure of ESG data is often not compulsory under typical reporting standards. Although "material factors affecting financials" is a standard reporting idea, management has large flexibility in what is chosen to be reported. Conversely, over-disclosure can be a problem, particularly of non-material ESG information.

Simply because a company does not disclose relevant ESG data does not necessarily mean it is managing its ESG risks or opportunities poorly. Smaller companies with fewer resources typically put less effort into reporting disclosure. There are geographical differences in reporting, so cultural differences can lead companies to assume different judgments on the materiality of certain ESG factors. Management might also assume that certain information is of limited importance to investors or is commercially sensitive. ESG information might be available to other stakeholders (e.g., supply chain information to suppliers, supply chain audit to business customers) but not publicly available to investors.

Disclosure varies by geography and is influenced by company size (because of company resources) and industry practice. Certain ESG data might be easier to collect and disclose but might not be considered material by investors. However, in terms of ESG reporting, data might be important to other stakeholders (even if it is not material to investors), so a company might choose to disclose this non-financially material information.

That said, a lack of disclosure could be an indicator of poor management, and many investors prefer to see relevant disclosure so judgments can be made. One common technique is to ask company management, often investor relations, to disclose, where possible, missing ESG data or explain why the data might be missing.

Other issues are that an ESG disclosure, when revealed, might be unaudited, incomplete, or incomparable to other companies.

While poor disclosure is a challenge to market efficiency, this relative inefficiency could arguably be a source of superior risk-adjusted return for the skilled investor. This argument would suggest this type of investment analysis is about superior judgments concerning qualitative, non-computable factors and how things are likely to unfold in the future.

EXAMPLE 2

Assessing What an E Disclosure Might Imply

A cement company discloses its carbon mitigation strategy but discloses only its carbon scope 1 emissions, omitting scopes 2 and 3 (see Chapter 3).

Some of its competitors do not disclose any carbon data, and some disclose data on all three scopes. The carbon data the company discloses would have been assured by an independent third party.

An analyst might want to ask the following questions:

- *What is the size of the company?* A company that is smaller with respect to employees, resources, or market capitalization might not be expected to report to the same standard as a larger company, though over a material item, this might be a weakness.

- *Does the presence of a narrative and strategy (and its strength or weakness) improve an analyst's view on disclosure?* Is this narrative reporting aligned with best practice guidance (for instance, the International Accounting Standards Board's *IFRS Practice Statement on Management Commentary*)?[11]

- *How well does the company compare to its competitors?*

- *Are there any signs from reading the strategy or the size of the scope 1 data?*

---

11 IFRS, *IFRS Practice Statement 1: Management Commentary* (2010). www.ifrs.org/issued-standards/list-of-standards/management-commentary-practice-statement/.

- *Would the business model suggest scope 2 would be a material matter?* The fact that the scope 1 data has third-party assurance should, with all other matters being equal, give more weight to the disclosure.
- *How long has the company been disclosing, and has management made other commitments to future disclosure?* Answers and judgments to these types of questions will sway how an analyst rates a company (e.g., on a scorecard approach) or the discount rate they might use in a DCF or valuation.

As a follow-up, the analyst could call the company and ask for an explanation of the data's absence and the company view on its materiality, then judge its willingness to engage or commit to publishing the data. Or the analyst could estimate the data and find a third-party data source.

- A quantitative approach would have to consider how to deal with missing data.
- The analyst also has to judge the materiality of the missing information and might view cement as a carbon-intense industry.
- A disclosure on carbon intensity would be viewed as more material for a cement company than a software service business.
- A software service business would not be expected to be carbon intense.

On occasion, a lack of disclosure can be enough to red flag an investment completely. For example, a company hires a new CEO but will not disclose in sufficient detail what the long-term incentive plans for management are based on. This might be too strong a red flag for the analyst to recommend any investment.

Another factor to consider is the strength of environmental accounting. Consensus is currently lacking on how best to account for natural capital. Also, how selective disclosure affects firm value is unclear; academic and practitioner work is currently exploring this issue.[12]

The example also shows both qualitative ESG and QESG tools and demonstrates the intertwined nature with traditional assessments.

INVESTMENT DECISION AND PORTFOLIO CONSTRUCTION AND ESG INTEGRATION TECHNIQUES IN PRACTICE (SEVEN CASES)

☐ 7.1.12 apply the range of approaches to ESG analysis and integration across a range of asset classes

---

12 Please refer to the following three articles: D. Crilly, M. Hansen, and M. Zollo, "The Grammar of Decoupling: A Cognitive-Linguistic Perspective on Firms' Sustainability Claims and Stakeholders' Interpretation," *Academy of Management Journal* 59(2) (April 2016). https://journals.aom.org/doi/10.5465/amj.2015.0171. A. Saad and D. Strauss, "The New 'Reasonable Investor' and Changing Frontiers of Materiality: Increasing Investor Reliance on ESG Disclosures and Implications for Securities Litigation," *Berkeley Business Law Journal* 17.2 (May 2020). https://papers.ssrn.com/sol3/papers.cfm?abstract_id=3590809. F. Zhang, X. Qin, and L. Liu, "The Interaction Effect between ESG and Green Innovation and Its Impact on Firm Value from the Perspective of Information Disclosure," *Sustainability* 12(5) (March 2020). www.mdpi.com/2071-1050/12/5/1866.

Several adapted case studies across equities and fixed income will be highlighted in this section. Although this section does not provide detailed case studies in private equity, infrastructure, or other alternative investments, many similar techniques can be used in those asset classes. The end of this section allows for some discussion.

Unless mentioned otherwise, the case studies are adaptations from CFA Institute case studies (see the Further Reading section).

We will look at the following case studies:

- Case Study 1 – Quantitative Systematic Approach to an Environmental Tilted Mandate in Global Equities
- Case Study 2 – Fundamental ESG Integration
- Case Study 3 – ESG Analysis Supporting a Premium Valuation Ratio
- Case Study 4 – ESG DCF Scenario Analysis
- Case Study 5 – Credit Analysis Integrating ESG
- Case Study 6 – Credit ESG Integration Practice
- Case Study 7 – Sovereign Debt Analysis

A detailed look at how quantitative investment approaches work at a portfolio level is provided in Chapter 8.

CASE STUDY 1 – QUANTITATIVE SYSTEMATIC APPROACH TO AN ENVIRONMENTAL TILTED MANDATE IN GLOBAL EQUITIES

(This is a theoretical case study based on the author's knowledge and experience.)

A foundation endowment with an underlying mission to fund climate science wishes to invest part of its endowment funds in a systematic global equities strategy tilted to companies that have positive environmental characteristics.

The endowment discusses a mandate with a quantitative systematic investment manager. The endowment decides that the following rules and factors are important:

- the use of at least two third-party ESG scoring systems
- a proprietary scoring system
- all invested companies have a publicly available environmental management policy
- the average blend of the rating systems meet a minimum criterion on an E score
- rebalance quarterly

In practice, for specific mandates, many further detailed rules and conditions can be set on other aspects of ESG or other established quantitative and fundamental factors (e.g., quality or geography).

The fund manager converts the third-party E scores through its own formula. They use the database to flag companies with no environmental management policy. The manager has an in-house team that uses a scorecard approach to score companies on material, relevant environmental risks and opportunities. This score is combined with the third-party scores and a minimum threshold set, where the bottom 20% of companies are deemed ineligible for the fund.

See earlier parts of this chapter for more on the scorecard approach.

The remaining companies are weighted to approximately match a specified global benchmark with respect to momentum, quality, and volatility factors, as well as other ESG factors, and within the bounds of other construction criteria, such as tracking error and market beta.

These calculations are performed once a quarter, and the portfolio is adjusted accordingly. The rules are examined once a year in consultation with the end client. Performance and ESG measurements are recorded and assessed. An engagement or stewardship program could be implemented for companies not meeting, or in danger of not meeting, the specified environmental criteria.

CASE STUDY 2 – FUNDAMENTAL ESG INTEGRATION

This fund manager adjusts the most relevant financial forecasts (revenue, profits or returns on capital, capital and operational expenditures, and cash flows) based on material ESG factors. They also consider the potential ESG impact on the overall security valuation by adjusting the target multiples (discount or premium and discount rate) on ratio analysis.

The chemical sector is analyzed. The following trends are assessed:

- aging populations that will require more health and well-being products
- regulations that influence a move toward biodegradable or bio-derived plastics
- evolving consumer sensitivity to "green" issues

A company is sought after if it reflects positively on those trends.

Company A is one of the world's leading suppliers of specialty chemicals based on renewable raw materials that are used in personal care, life sciences, and industrial chemicals. It enjoys an industry-leading position in sustainability, having differentiated itself from its petrochemical-based specialty chemical peers.

Two-thirds of Company A's raw materials come from natural sources, and it is well positioned to participate in the trends described earlier.

Company A has opened a new chemicals plant with a renewable-source, plant-based feed stock. The fund manager judges that the new plant will allow the company to capture more of the value chain in surfactants and to charge a premium because consumers are willing to pay more for sustainable products. This will improve revenue growth through increased share and pricing.

The company is forecast to grow sales two whole percentage points above the industry average for the next 10 years for this. This is embedded in a DCF forecast and a value calculated.

This value is then cross-checked with a P/E ratio. The fund manager is prepared to pay a 50% premium on a P/E basis because of the company's strong sales and earnings growth.

Company A currently trades at only a 10% P/E premium to the chemicals sector, and the DCF is forecast to have 35% target price upside. The company is selected to go into the fund manager's portfolio.

Thanks to Hyewon Kong for the case study example upon which this case study is based.

CASE STUDY 3 – ESG ANALYSIS SUPPORTING A PREMIUM VALUATION RATIO

An investor is reviewing their portfolio.

Company Z has been performing well and now has a 50% premium to the sector on a P/E basis.

To achieve long-term value creation, in accordance with its investment philosophy, the investor needs to have a strong conviction regarding the company's ability to maintain its industry-leading products and profitability.

Key operational risks to the company include the following:

- the maintenance of the company's technical leadership through investment in human and physical capital
- the potential for manufacturing delays or product defects that could affect its reputation and market share

E and S data were assessed using third-party databases. The company ranked as a top 10% performer over the relevant criteria. The following three major areas were considered strong enough that an even higher P/E premium was recommended, and the company was kept in the portfolio:

1. Asset quality and efficiency: The company had industry-leading resource (water and energy) intensity per unit of revenue, higher performance regarding water and waste recycling, and lower carbon emission intensity than its peers.

2. Attracting and retaining talent: The investor evaluated employee engagement and compensation to help gauge the risks associated with attracting and retaining talent. The company's average employee wage was significantly higher than that of its peers, and it had low employee turnover. In a highly complex research and development–intensive industry, this suggested that the company is well positioned to attract and retain top talent. This in turn should enhance the company's innovation potential.

3. Sustainable business model: These elements were considered superior to those of the company's competitors:

   - its positioning as enabling smaller, faster, and more energy-efficient electronics
   - its customer-centric approach of providing aftermarket enhancements and refurbishments to improve customers' capital efficiency
   - its culture of innovation and collaboration with internal and external stakeholders that have the potential to generate both new business opportunities and broader social benefits

Thanks to GS Sustain for their case study example upon which this study is based.

CASE STUDY 4 – ESG DCF SCENARIO ANALYSIS

This investment team uses an integrated approach. Rather than having separate ESG analysts, the team's portfolio managers perform and integrate ESG analysis. They believe this is a better way to value and assess stocks. The team uses multiple sources of ESG information as it represents an abundance of ESG-related opinions that require interpreting, and portfolio managers are best placed to filter this advice and ascertain how it relates to a company's business model and valuation.

The team starts with a fundamental analysis to identify any material positive or negative ESG factors. The team embed that assessment into an analysis of the competitive position and the sustainability of the business, which they put into valuation models. They aim to invest only in companies that perform strongly in four areas:

1. business model;
2. market share opportunity;
3. end-market growth; and
4. management and ESG.

The Global Equities team identified several ESG risks (contingent liabilities) and ESG opportunities (contingent assets) for a leading health care insurer and a health care cost management and IT provider managing 5% of US health care spending.

ESG Risks

As custodians of the personal and medical details of millions of people, the company needs to keep the data secure: False savings here can have long-term consequences, including regulatory and political risks and the potential impairment of the company's social contract with customers and the wider society.

The team challenged management on the risk of privacy data breaches, asking how that risk is being managed and what policies are in place to mitigate that risk. Management acknowledged that information about their data security was not available on the company's website, but several management members reassured the team about the quality of the policies, training, and general operation management of data handling and security that are in place. Nevertheless, the team modeled a DCF valuation scenario looking at the possible impact of privacy data breaches.

ESG Opportunities

The data analytics business was viewed as an ESG potential. The analytics business allows to create cheaper, better health care options for businesses, governments, and patients, creating strong competitive advantage and an ESG contingent asset. For instance, it identified 150 diabetic patients not taking their medication properly, 123 of whom were in Texas, which enabled its client to implement location-specific measures using preventive health care techniques.

In another instance, using the company's data analytics, a US state department discovered clusters of patients with asthma on certain streets and in certain buildings, and found that those areas correlated with cockroach infestations, allowing the state department to successfully prosecute inefficient landlords and ultimately raise living standards for tenants.

The team assessed the materiality of all this information and assigned a rating for the four components of the company's strengths:

- business model;
- market share opportunity;
- end-market growth; and
- management and ESG.

The team then performed a DCF scenario analysis embedding the material ESG risks and opportunities. The team prefers DCF and explicit model scenarios for sales, margins, and asset turns because they are judged to be a more accurate method of modeling than an adjustment to a discount rate or terminal value for a company-specific assessment. Sum-of-the-parts and standard financial ratio assessments are also performed.

The analysis was peer-reviewed within the team, and the assumptions were stress-tested, challenged, and refined before the rating and valuation were confirmed. In the peer review, assumptions are flexed in real time to see how further valuation scenarios change. These include:

- for the upside scenario: increasing EBIT margins and sales growth
- for the downside scenario: normalizing sales to a lower growth rate (3%) and looking at the sales impact over more than one year

The core findings supported significant valuation upside and limited probability of mild downside. The stock was then added to the portfolio after a portfolio construction process.

Adapted from RBC (Royal Bank of Canada) Global Asset Management example case study.[13]

CASE STUDY 5 – CREDIT ANALYSIS INTEGRATING ESG

This credit investor, when analyzing a corporate bond for investment, evaluates an issuer's business profile, market position, and competitive profile, as well as fundamental credit measures (such as margins, leverage, and cash flow). The analysis then turns to an evaluation of management and sector-specific material ESG indicators, such as carbon emissions, workplace injury rates, and the composition of the board of directors.

The ESG analysis consists of a quantitative score and qualitative-based research.

The quantitative score is derived from a proprietary framework that aggregates metrics from ESG research providers as well as from other third-party sources.

The corporate credit analysts also perform a qualitative assessment by reviewing a company's ESG policies and targets, which might be outlined in its corporate sustainability report or on its website, and consider information learned from the engagement call.

The analyst evaluates both the score and qualitative research when assigning a sustainability rating for the company. This measure of an issuer's ESG risk profile could affect the analyst's overall internal rating. Specifically, the analyst might upgrade the internal rating to reflect a corporation's low ESG risks or downgrade the rating if the ESG risks are considered high or poorly managed.

A beverages company is examined. The research identifies several strengths and challenges, some of which might be material from a financial perspective. For example, because water is a key input for the ingredients used in the company's beverage products, efforts to ensure a steady supply of water would be considered both an ESG strength and a credit strength. Furthermore, water management is a material issue for the sector because a lack of water can affect crop yields and prices, increasing the cost of goods sold.

---

13 CFA Institute and PRI, *Guidance and Case Studies for ESG Integration: Equities and Fixed Income* (2018). www.unpri.org/investor-tools/guidance-and-case-studies-for-esg-integration-equities-and-fixed-income/3622.article.

The analyst weighs the strengths and challenges, and compares the performance of (hypothetical) beverage brands to its industry peers.

Strengths and Challenges of Considered Brands

	Strengths	Challenges
E	▶ Collaboration with suppliers to improve water efficiency by 15% in high-risk areas ▶ Its GHG goal is aligned with a science-based target initiative.	▶ There is weak disclosure on progress being made to reduce packaging waste.
S	▶ It has a comprehensive human rights strategy and strong supplier code-of-conduct protocols.	▶ Certain talent retention and recruitment strategies trail best practices. ▶ Products are primarily sugary drinks, despite introduction of healthier brands.
G	▶ Robust antibribery policies govern interactions with suppliers. ▶ Board of directors formally oversees sustainability initiatives. ▶ Rigorous, year-round stakeholder engagement includes consumer groups.	▶ No significant challenges seen.

The totality of material ESG information depicts a company judged to have a strong ESG profile, and a high sustainability rating is assigned, which is also incorporated into the company's final internal credit rating. This credit rating was analyzed to be wrongly priced, so an investment was made.

Thanks to Robert Fernandez for the original case study upon which this example is based.

CASE STUDY 6 – CREDIT ESG INTEGRATION PRACTICE

The credit team uses several inputs. It relies on a central ESG/responsibility team for firm policies, approaches, and investment tools.

At a company-specific level, the credit team reviews the proprietary measures of ESG risk, that is, its **quantitative ESG (QESG)** score that the firm has developed. This QESG score represents a snapshot of the company's overall ESG performance.

The QESG score is supported by the **company information** provided by a separate steward and engagement team (whom some practitioners consider an active ownership team) to give a sense of the potential forward trajectory.

A state-owned oil producer was examined. ESG factors emerged as recurring themes in the credit discussion: The company's labor safety track record was below the industry average, and the company had experienced frequent oil spills and leaks in the past. Spills and leaks could result in fines and production downtime, damaging the company's cash flow profile.

After the initial credit committee analysis, an ESG score of 4 was assigned (below average on a scale of 1 to 5, with 1 being the best). Bonds acquired through the new issue process were kept, but because of the low ESG score, there was no further exposure to credit.

Later that year, the ESG score was upgraded to 3 (from 4) to reflect the company's improvement in the following ESG factors:

1. improvement in worker safety (injury frequency per million man-hours worked declined 35% year-over-year)
2. progress in reducing environmental waste and emissions (water reuse increased 66% year-over-year, while sulfur oxide emissions declined 45% year-over-year)

After the score upgrade, the investors added to the bond position. The company's ability to manage ESG risks was assessed to be improved and adequate.

Thanks to Mitch Reznick and Audra Stundziaite for the original case study upon which this example is based.

CASE STUDY 7 - SOVEREIGN DEBT ANALYSIS

An investor uses ESG as an enhanced analysis of sovereigns to better assess their ESG-related risks and opportunities.

The investor assigns a **financial stability score (FSS)** to a country based on the overall balance sheet strength and ESG factors. The FSS ranges from +4 to −4 for those countries and currencies deemed to make it into the opportunity set and will lead to exclusion for those rankings below −4. However, the FSS is determined after a review of the ESG factors, and a strong sovereign balance sheet might be heavily penalized because of weak ESG factors. In this example, a country with a strong balance sheet can be significantly negatively affected by ESG factors.

At the time of analysis, the investor believed that the Russian 10-year government bonds offered an attractive real yield of 3% with a Russian ruble undervaluation of over 10% versus the US dollar in purchasing power parity. But the investor thought that the valuation needed to be considered in conjunction with a thorough balance sheet analysis and ESG factors to ascertain the underlying investment risk.

The strength of the balance sheet was judged by looking at the following:

- gross domestic product (GDP)
- inflation
- government revenue
- fiscal balance
- gross debt
- current account
- currency reserves
- external debt

It was given a strong score on this measure.

Although Russia's balance sheet is strong in this assessment, its governance factors rank very low according to the World Bank's worldwide governance indicators. The investor believes the governance factor strongly influences the social and environmental factors because the government sets the policies for environmental and social matters and, in turn, influences the country's long-term sustainable economic growth.

These **G** factors were considered:

- political stability;
- absence of violence or terrorism;
- government effectiveness;
- regulatory quality;
- rule of law;
- control of corruption, and
- voice of accountability

Third-party rating scores were used. The investor determined a low and deteriorating score on the government indicator. The rankings for rule of law and control of corruption were judged to be relatively low and unchanged over time. The investor believed that did not bode well for foreign direct investment inflows because of the absence of clearly defined property rights, international sanctions, and therefore long-term economic growth. These factors weighed on the FSS score.

The investor then used the following indexes to judge social capital strength:

- a life expectancy index;
- an education index; and
- the human development index.

The investor judged that Russia's low levels of health spending, coupled with an unfavorable demographics profile, might affect life expectancy negatively. This, in turn, would reduce the overall future workforce, leading to lower productivity and future economic growth, and would likely negatively impact sovereign creditworthiness in the long term. Again, although the social aspect does not have an imminent economic impact, it was judged to be unfavorable in the long term with regard to the FSS.

Combining all factors, Russia was given a −4 score on FSS, the lowest possible score.

When completing portfolio construction between two countries with equal real yields, the one with the higher FSS will be favored. This happens because a country with higher standards on all or some factors is believed to have a better return outcome over the investment horizon.

Thanks to Claudia Gollmeier for the original case study upon which this example is based.

See the following section for a discussion on the challenges of sovereign analysis and ESG.

7. DISCUSSION OF PRIVATE MARKETS, REAL ESTATE, AND INFRASTRUCTURE; DISCUSSION OF ESG IN FIXED INCOME AND DIFFERENCES TO EQUITY; AND CHALLENGES TO ESG INTEGRATION

☐ 7.1.12 apply the range of approaches to ESG analysis and integration across a range of asset classes

☐ 7.1.13 describe the challenges of undertaking ESG analysis across different geographic regions and cultures

☐ 7.1.14 describe the challenges of identifying and assessing material ESG issues

☐ 7.1.15 describe the challenges of integrating ESG analysis into a firm's investment process

Real assets (including vacant land, farmland, timber, infrastructure, intellectual property, commodities, and private real estate)[14] carry certain advantages and challenges compared to the equities and corporate fixed income investment universe. In many cases, investors are majority owners or own the asset outright. Majority or full ownership stakes offer investors much greater control over the definition, application, and reporting of ESG data alongside or outside of existing reporting standards like those of the GRI or like the 2009 **Global Real Estate Sustainability Benchmark (GRESB)**. The materiality frameworks used might have philosophical similarities—as in material ESG factors—but the identification of those factors can differ.

GRESB's full benchmark report (see Chapter 8) provides the following:

- a composite of peer group information,
- overall portfolio key performance indicator (KPI) performance,
- aggregate environmental data in terms of usage and efficiency gains,
- a GRESB score that weights management, policy, and disclosure; risks and opportunities; and monitoring and Environmental Management Systems (EMS),
- environmental impact reduction targets, and
- data validation and assurance

This type of report depends heavily on companies participating in the GRESB reporting assessment process.

Looking at commercial and residential real estate historically, the sectors arguably had little regard for ESG factors (especially pre-2009, before GRESB). Often the tenants and operators might think differently from the owners and constructors (sometimes called a "split incentive problem") because tenants must pay ongoing energy bills, whereas constructors do not.

Buildings also have a carbon footprint. An integrated ESG view might look at reducing a building's carbon footprint by using more efficient materials and standards and thereby lowering the risk of impact from carbon prices or deriving gains from energy efficiencies.

---

14 D.R. Chambers, K. Black, and N.J. Lacey, *Alternative Investments: A Primer for Investment Professionals* (CFA Institute Research Foundation, Research Foundation Books, 2018). www.cfainstitute.org/en/research/foundation/2018/alternative-investments-a-primer-for-investment-professionals.

Like unlisted credit and real asset private markets, ESG integration in private equity faces a number of challenges, foremost being the lack of public transparency, established reporting standards, regulatory oversight, and public market expectations around ESG. Current initiatives aim to address these challenges, such as the PRI's reporting framework for infrastructure.[15]

In addition, smaller, private companies are often capacity challenged by ESG reporting requirements. Private equity investors might have to negotiate with a strong founder or founder team.

But early investors and significant shareholders can be strategic and long-term oriented, creating a powerful incentive to establish a strong set of ESG KPIs early in the company's life cycle or by setting important cultural values. Some investors will perform a materiality analysis much like public equity investors might do; the same SASB framework might be used or developed via the private equity industry, e.g. the British Venture Capital Association (BVCA) *Responsible Investment Framework*.[16]

Another way of looking at this is shown in the GRESB Benchmark Portfolio Report in Chapter 8.

Two case study examples from recent years show the role governance analysis played in the IPO and valuation of Uber[17] and the failed IPO of WeWork.[18]

These examples show how ESG can add or detract value.

Asset owners might also assess private equity managers on ESG criteria, especially when they might be co-investors on an asset. A typical assessment might include policy, people, process, transparency, and collaboration assessments.

Discussion of ESG in Fixed Income and Differences to Equity

Historically, corporate bond practitioners adapted the materiality and sustainability frameworks, as well as the ESG techniques equity investors use, to meet their needs. More recently, newer techniques focused specifically on bonds have been used because bonds differ in the following ways:

- credit quality
- duration
- payment schedules
- embedded options
- seniority
- currencies
- collateral
- time horizon

Equity securities tend to not have these qualities, so different integration techniques are needed.

Fixed-income investors in corporate bonds might use principles in materiality and ESG frameworks that are similar to those used by equity investors but adapt them to where materiality is different between equity and bonds. Bond investors might

---

15 PRI, *PRI Reporting Framework 2019:Direct – Infrastructure* (2019). www.unpri.org/Uploads/l/h/o/09.inf2019_843342.pdf.
16 British Private Equity & Venture Capital Association, *Responsible Investment* (2021). www.bvca.co.uk/Our-Industry/Responsible-Investment.
17 D.F. Larcker and B. Tayan, "Governance Gone Wild: Misbehavior at Uber Technologies," *Harvard Law School Forum on Corporate Governance* (20 Jan. 2018). https://corpgov.law.harvard.edu/2018/01/20/governance-gone-wild-misbehavior-at-uber-technologies/.
18 D.C. Langevoort and H.A. Sale, "Corporate Adolescence: Why Did 'We' Not Work?" (8 Jan. 2021). https://papers.ssrn.com/sol3/papers.cfm?abstract_id=3762718.

find ESG factors that affect balance sheet strength (and therefore, the risks of debt defaults) more material than equity investors, who might be more concerned about future growth opportunities.

The opportunity side of ESG might be less relevant for bond investors because what is typically foremost in a bond investor's analysis is the impact of ESG factors on a company's ability to pay its debt obligations. For instance, an equity investor might view a green technology acquisition more favorably than a bond investor would because the equity investor is positive about future value from the technology, whereas the bond investor might be worried about the amount of debt required to fund the acquisition. ESG scores (whether third party or internal) go alongside or are integrated into internal credit analysis and investment decisions.

Sovereign debt investors have started to analyze ESG, but borrowing the same materiality frameworks as equity or corporate debt investors has not been easy because some country-level factors (e.g., peace, corruption, ease of doing business, freedom of expression, education levels, and regulatory and legal robustness) might not be material to equity or corporate bond investors. Furthermore, a material factor (e.g., climate or carbon policy) will interact with analysis and valuations differently. Turning ESG analysis into meaningful judgments on the credit ratings or spreads for sovereign nations is therefore difficult. That said, investors have typically integrated certain ESG factors (e.g., political risk and governance factors) into sovereign debt, even if not explicitly labelled ESG.

Municipal credit ESG analysis can differ as well. In the municipal space (region, state, or city) the issuer's governance and management practices can both be assessed, as well as their

- overall transparency,
- reporting,
- corruption levels,
- budgetary practices,
- pension liabilities, and
- contracts.

Some investors will view municipals investing for inclusive communities as lower-risk investment because of the social benefits. Alternatively, co-primary outcomes are possible, where market rate returns are expected alongside social impact. This differs from social impact, which is not always expected to make market rate (risk-adjusted) returns. Environmental factors (e.g., a region's air quality and the associated health risks for its constituents) and the quality of public infrastructure (e.g., wastewater treatment plants) can all pose risks that could affect an issuer's ability to repay its debt.

Overall, while there are philosophical similarities in identifying material ESG factors and then applying those to the analysis, the type of factors used can differ across asset classes, as can the type of integration techniques.

Challenges to ESG Integration

There are many hurdles and challenges for ESG integration. These include:

- Disclosure and data-related challenges, such as: data consistency, data scarcity, data incompleteness, and a lack of audited data.
- Comparability difficulties include a lack of comparability between ESG ratings agencies, comparisons across different accounting and other standards, comparisons across geographies and cultures, and inconsistent use of jargon terminology.

- Materiality and judgment challenges, such as: judgments that are difficult and uncertain, and judgments that are inconsistent.

The challenges in ESG integration across asset classes arise because different types of assets and different strategies integrate ESG using different techniques.

Challenges from Incomplete Datasets and Identifying and Assessing ESG Data

As can be seen from the case studies and ESG techniques, many of the processes start with data gathering and original research gathering. However, a few challenges exist:

- ESG data are not consistently reported across companies, geographies, and sectors.
- Most ESG data are not audited.
- Some ESG data are not easily available in public databases and are difficult to obtain.

ESG factors can be judged material and useful, but the data might be incomplete. For instance, carbon pollution is often judged material, but it can be measured in at least three scopes: **scope 1, 2, and 3 emissions**. Currently, in the top 2,000 companies in the world, few data are available on scope 3 (as of 2018, 10% of companies reported scope 3, and by 2020, this had increased to 18%),[19] yet evidence indicates that scope 3 makes up more than 50% of the world's carbon (and GHG equivalent) pollution impact.

ESG data can be incomplete, unaudited, unavailable, or incomparable between companies because of the different reporting methodologies used. These issues make the assessment of ESG factors impossible in certain situations. A lack of data or a company unwilling to disclose information can make identification of relevant ESG factors difficult.

Data Disclosure Challenge

A debate is ongoing over ESG data disclosures at a company level. These disclosures vary between companies and regionally. Also ongoing are efforts via organizations such as the SASB and the GRI, and continuous evolution from the IASB on "broader corporate reporting."[20]

Surveys suggest that a range of investors view ESG disclosure at companies as inadequate. This might be partly because investors and management teams view materiality differently and might also have conflicting aims. Investors could claim that assessing a material piece of ESG information is difficult without data disclosure. Companies can argue that the vast range of possible ESG data and the differing demands of investors, stakeholders, and rating agencies make the resource demands unreasonable.

A further challenge is that there is no consensus agreement on the details of what good ESG disclosure might look like (although again, see the SASB's evolving work here) and that this might differ by strategy and asset class. Historically, public markets disclosure has been higher than private markets disclosure. The needs of fixed-income and sovereign bond investors can (and do) differ from those of equity investors.

See earlier parts of this section for more information on company disclosure.

---

19 B. Baker, "Scope 3 Carbon Emissions: Seeing the Full Picture," *MSCI Blog* (17 Sep. 2020). www.msci.com/www/blog-posts/scope-3-carbon-emissions-seeing/02092372761.
20 IFRS, *Management Commentary* (2021). www.ifrs.org/projects/work-plan/management-commentary/.

Comparability and Materiality Judgment Challenges

ESG ratings agencies use different techniques and assessments so that their ratings are not easily comparable. ESG ratings do not correlate like bond credit ratings, nor do agencies use the same methods of scoring.

Judgments on ESG materiality might differ between analysts. Many ESG terms are used inconsistently and are difficult for non-specialists to interpret.

These differences can be magnified by cultural or regional differences. For instance, different countries have different governance best practices or differing views on risk and materiality. Japanese companies have a much lower number of independent directors on their boards than European and US companies do on average, which is reflected in the Corporate Governance Code of Japan. Different countries might also put different weights on social factors (e.g., US companies are less concerned about having a policy on work or labor unions than German companies are).

Where materiality can be judged, assessing the level of impact can be difficult, and how ESG factors interact with financial performance over time is uncertain.

The field has many jargon terms (e.g., responsible, impact, sustainable, socially responsible, and ethical and green investment). Many of these terms are not used consistently by specialists and are confusing to non-specialists.

Integration Challenges

Because of the different third-party databases, many QESG factors are not agreed upon, and the data are relatively short run. Also, to what degree the ESG factors might correlate with other established quantitative factors, such as "quality," "value," or "momentum," is uncertain. Index-tilting strategies might therefore fail to reflect desired factors appropriately.

Many investment firms have separate ESG analyst teams. This separation can move ESG expertise away from investment decision makers and thereby create a challenge to integration. Perhaps ESG analysts are more junior (perhaps because the focus on this area at, for example, the business school level is still recent), so lower weight is given to their views and providing a challenge.

In fundamental active strategies, many ESG factors are difficult to judge and quantify. Impacts to cash flows, growth rates, or DCF assumptions are also hard to express. As noted earlier, in quantitative strategies, limited consensus remains, and historical data provide an integration challenge.

See Chapter 8 for a detailed discussion on this topic.

Investment Firm Culture Challenge

A significant number of investment professionals still do not integrate ESG or believe that ESG has limited financial impact; this can be challenging for teams and within firms. Firms might not have significant resources to buy third-party ESG data, or a firm's global nature might make culturally different attitudes to ESG factors difficult to integrate globally across the firm.

ESG integration is often different across asset classes, which can make being consistent or explaining across a firm difficult. Investors are likely to make differing judgments on materiality or weight factors, which causes a lack of comparability or a difference of opinion, even within firms.

Additional resources are typically needed for ESG integration, finances, and personnel, which raises both financial and operational challenges within firms.

ESG integration techniques have only recently started to become part of the curriculum at business schools and within universities. Typically, this means that investment professionals would not have had as much detailed training on how to deal with the challenge of integration.

Despite advances in techniques and understanding, significant challenges to ESG integration remain.

Criticism for ESG Integration

One of the most common criticisms of ESG investing is the difficulty for investors to correctly identify, and appropriately weigh, ESG factors in investment selection. Critics tend to express four primary concerns about the precision, validity, and reliability of ESG investment strategies:

1. Too inclusive of poor companies – ESG mutual funds and exchange-traded funds (ETFs) often hold investments in companies that might be seen as "bad actors" in one or more of the ESG spaces.

2. Dubious assessment criteria – The criteria used for selecting ESG factors are too subjective and can reflect narrow or conflicting ideological or political viewpoints. Non-material or sociopolitical factors might be overemphasized. Materiality assessments might be considered flawed.

3. Quality of data – The information used for selecting ESG factors often comes (unaudited, or assured) from the companies themselves. This complicates the ability to verify, compare, and standardize this information.

4. Potential lack of emphasis on long-term improvements – Some financial advisers screen investments first for performance and only after that for ESG factors. This initial emphasis on performance can exclude companies with high ESG practices that focus on longer-term performance.

Finally, some critics would argue that evidence for the benefits of ESG are mixed or not proven.[21] These critics suggest that the time horizon for assessing ESG is too short to prove benefits. Critics also point out time periods during which certain sectors that are often excluded (e.g., tobacco) perform well as evidence that ESG detracts value. Note that as discussed earlier, exclusionary strategies are only one type of strategy, which some investors do not consider part of ESG integration but rather a separate type of investment process.

RANGE OF ESG INTEGRATION DATABASES AND SOFTWARE AVAILABLE   8

- [ ] 7.1.16 explain the approaches taken across a range of ESG integration databases and software available, and the nature of the information provided
- [ ] 7.1.17 identify the main providers of screening services or tools, similarities and differences in their methodologies, and the aims, benefits and limitations of using them
- [ ] 7.1.18 describe the limitations and constraints of information provided by ESG integration databases

---

21 D. Vogel, *The Market for Virtue: The Potential and Limits of Corporate Social Responsibility* (Washington, DC: Brookings Institution Press, 2005).

Typical mainstream investment research often includes an ESG or sustainability offering, and most major investment research departments (the "sell-side") will have analysts producing research in this area.

One way of classifying providers is by business type:

- *For-profit large providers* that offer multiple ESG-related products and services, as well as non-ESG-related products and services (e.g., MSCI, S&P, Sustainalytics, Fitch, and Moody's)
- *For-profit boutique providers* that offer speciality ESG products and services (e.g., RepRisk, Urgentum, Truvalue Labs [prior to its October 2020 acquisition by FactSet], and ISS [prior to its November 2020 acquisition by Deutsche Börse AG])
- *Nonprofit providers* that offer ESG-related products and services (e.g., Carbon Disclosure Project [CDP], IMF economic data, and World Bank, with the World Bank's ESG data portal; these services are free to the general public and in the public domain)

Another way of thinking about the services is by type of product or service; this is a non-exhaustive list:

- **ESG data** – quantitative or qualitative information on the environmental, social, economic and corporate governance practices of companies.
- **ESG ratings** – quantitative or qualitative evaluations of a company, country, financial product, or fund, based on a comparative assessment of their approach, disclosure, strategy, or performance on ESG issues. Different methodologies are discussed later.
- **ESG screening** – tools that evaluate companies, countries, and bonds based on their exposure or involvement-specific factors, sectors, products, or services
- **Voting and governance advice** – typically, proxy vote advisory services. These include voting guidelines on governance and other proxy voting items, including compensation and board directorships.
- **ESG benchmarks and indexes** – a set of securities (e.g., stocks, bonds) designed to represent some aspect of the total market by including some ESG criteria in the selection
- **ESG news and controversy alerts** – a company or a country conducts assessments that highlight events, behaviors, and practices that might lead to reputational and business risks and opportunities
- **Integrated research** – typically sell-side (investment bank or broker reports) research of contextualized, data-informed, analytical opinion designed to support investment decision making
- **Advisory services** – ESG strategy, integration, investment process, reporting, and corporate advice. Within this are also many specific ESG-related services, such as the following:
  - class action litigation
  - Sustainable Development Goals (SDGs) reporting and alignment
  - carbon and water analysis
  - norms and sanctions
  - policy development
  - real estate assessment
  - factor databases

Range of ESG Integration Databases and Software Available

- supply chain assessment
- assurance services

Exhibit 7 provides a non-exhaustive list of ESG ratings and database providers. New entrants, as of 2020, are continuing to appear.

MSCI ESG ratings and Sustainalytics ESG ratings are examined in greater detail later, and SASB materiality maps were examined earlier in this chapter. See also the exhibit titled "Examples of ESG Indexes, Benchmarks, and Their Methodologies" in Chapter 8.

Many ESG tools look at a broad range of ESG factors, although some, such as CDP, which has an environmental focus, are more specific. One challenge is that the agreement or correlation between the various ratings agencies is low.

▶ A study by Chatterji, Levine, and Toffel (2009) finds an approximate 0.3 correlation.[22] (Or more technically, this analysis found pairwise tetrachoric correlations for three years among the six raters, with a mean correlation of 0.30 [about two standard deviations].) However, this also included some negative ones' correlations, meaning that what one rater found responsible another found "irresponsible.") A 2019 study by Gibson, Krueger, and Schmidt shows a range of correlations (see Exhibit 8).

▶ Yet another study by Berg, Koelbel, and Rigobon (2019) shows a range of correlations as well; Berg et al. look at a dataset of ESG ratings from six different raters: KLD (MSCI Stats), Sustainalytics, Vigeo Eiris (Moody's), RobecoSAM (S&P Global), Asset4 (Refinitiv), and MSCI. The correlations between the ratings are on average 0.54 and range from 0.38 to 0.71.

Berg et al. note, "This means that the information that decision-makers receive from ESG rating agencies is relatively noisy."[23]

Berg et al. further suggest:

Three major consequences follow:

> ▶ *First, ESG performance is less likely to be reflected in corporate stock and bond prices, as investors face a challenge when trying to identify outperformers and laggards. Investor tastes can influence asset prices, but only when a large enough fraction of the market holds and implements a uniform nonfinancial preference. Therefore, even if a large fraction of investors have a preference for ESG performance, the divergence of the ratings disperses the effect of these preferences on asset prices.*
>
> ▶ *Second, the divergence hampers the ambition of companies to improve their ESG performance, because they receive mixed signals from rating agencies about which actions are expected and will be valued by the market.*
>
> ▶ *Third, the divergence of ratings poses a challenge for empirical research, as using one rater versus another may alter a study's results and conclusions. Taken together, the ambiguity around ESG ratings represents a challenge for decision-makers.*[23]

---

22 A. Chatterji, D.I. Levine, and M.W. Toffel, "How Well Do Social Ratings Actually Measure Corporate Social Responsibility?" *Journal of Economics & Management Strategy* 18(1) (2009): 125–69. https://ssrn.com/abstract=1394704.

23 F. Berg, J.F. Koelbel, and R. Rigobon, "Aggregate Confusion: The Divergence of ESG Ratings" (2019). https://papers.ssrn.com/sol3/papers.cfm?abstract_id=3438533.

Exhibit 7: Summary of Major ESG Service Providers

Product	Bloomberg	Morningstar / Sustainalytics	Deutsche Börse (ISS)	RepRisk	FactSet (TruValue Labs)	MSCI	LSE (FTSE Russell)	Reuters (Refinitiv)	Moody's (Vigeo Eiris)	CDP	Real Impact Tracker	Mercer / Other Investment Consultants	World Bank
Data	✓	✓	✓	✓	✓	✓	✓	✓	✓	✓			✓
Ratings	✓	✓	✓	✓	✓	✓	✓	✓	✓	✓	✓	✓	
Screening		✓	✓			✓					✓		
Voting advisory			✓										
Benchmarks	✓		✓			✓	✓		✓				
Controversies	✓	✓	✓	✓	✓	✓		✓					

Source: Benjamin Yeoh (2020); also see Publications Office of the European Union, *Study on Sustainability-Related Ratings, Data and Research* (2021). https://op.europa.eu/en/publication-detail/-/publication/d7d85036-509c-11eb-b59f-01aa75ed71a1/language-en/format-PDF/source-183474104%E2%80%9D.

Range of ESG Integration Databases and Software Available

Most of the tools are available only commercially. However, the completeness of coverage varies substantially across ESG tools. The correlations might well change with time, as providers evolve the way ratings are produced. For example, Sustainalytics experienced a major change in its ESG ratings system in 2019, and all main providers are currently evolving their processes, annually at least. This is expected for some time to come.

This evolving process also makes historic comparisons difficult. The different methodologies might also mean like-for-like comparisons are not being made in the correlations between rating agencies.

Many factors are still debated by investors:

- what the correlations are
- the timeframe over which they are studied
- the relevance of any potential correlations (could be spurious data-mined)

Practitioners debate how important strong correlations are.

- On one hand, high correlations could lead to groupthink and a lack of rigorous thinking. Some think this was one of the problems with credit rating agencies' (CRAs') (highly correlated) assessment of mortgage-backed bonds in the financial crisis (2007–2009). To some, a low correlation is a healthy and useful outcome from ESG rating providers noting the distinction between ratings and raw data.
- On the other hand, simplicity and correlation could bring credibility to ESG ratings as a discipline and give more consistent messages to companies. As described in the quantitative investment sections, quantitative investors use these data differently than they do fundamental active investor judgments.

This area is expected to be discussed for some time to come.

Exhibit 8: ESG Rating Correlation Among Six Third-Party Data Providers

	N	Mean	Median	StdDev	Pearson Correlations			
	(1)	(2)	(3)	(4)	(5)	(6)	(7)	(8)	(9)
					Asset 4	Sust.	Inrate	Bloom.	KLD
Panel A: Total Rating									
Asset 4	31424	0.501	0.501	0.289					
Sustainalytics	32703	0.501	0.499	0.289	0.762				
Inrate	25945	0.501	0.534	0.284	0.233	0.303			
Bloomberg	32410	0.501	0.501	0.289	0.749	0.708	0.122		
KLD	32485	0.501	0.507	0.288	0.584	0.619	0.290	0.538	
MSCI IVA	32450	0.501	0.502	0.289	0.418	0.460	0.319	0.308	0.452
Average correlation							0.458		
Panel B: Environmental Pillar									
Asset 4	31261	0.501	0.501	0.289					
Sustainalytics	32532	0.501	0.501	0.289	0.710				
Inrate	25880	0.501	0.518	0.286	0.305	0.488			
Bloomberg	28258	0.501	0.501	0.289	0.651	0.566	0.206		
KLD	32403	0.501	0.498	0.281	0.629	0.654	0.422	0.472	

	N	Mean	Median	StdDev	Pearson Correlations				
	(1)	(2)	(3)	(4)	(5)	(6)	(7)	(8)	(9)
					Asset 4	Sust.	Inrate	Bloom.	KLD
MSCI IVA	32361	0.501	0.502	0.289	0.174	0.325	0.403	0.140	0.284
Average correlation							**0.429**		
Panel C: Social Pillar									
Asset 4	31424	0.501	0.501	0.289					
Sustainalytics	32703	0.501	0.504	0.289	0.617				
Inrate	25945	0.501	0.522	0.288	0.133	0.143			
Bloomberg	32322	0.501	0.507	0.288	0.682	0.530	0.061		
KLD	32485	0.501	0.505	0.288	0.397	0.423	0.128	0.302	
MSCI IVA	32450	0.501	0.500	0.289	0.282	0.323	0.236	0.207	
Average correlation							**0.321**		
Panel D: Governance Pillar									
Asset 4	31424	0.501	0.501	0.289					
Sustainalytics	32703	0.501	0.504	0.289	0.312				
Inrate	25945	0.501	0.502	0.283	0.297	0.401			
Bloomberg	32410	0.501	0.487	0.283	0.421	0.340	0.343		
KLD	32485	0.501	0.489	0.237	0.059	0.034	0.083	0.095	
MSCI IVA	32450	0.501	0.501	0.288	0.141	0.129	0.144	0.045	0.152
Average correlation							**0.200**		

Source: © Rajna Gibson Brandon, Philipp Krueger and Peter S. Schmidt 2021.[24]

The sources of information used to assess ESG investments also vary across the ESG tools. Information can be collected directly (via surveys, company communication, company reports, presentations, and public documents) or indirectly (via news articles, third-party reports, and analysis).

The assessments can be given in raw form or used to determine index weights or processed to determine specific ratings and scores.

The Berg et al. study[23] also argues that low correlations pose these challenges:

▶ Sustainability performance is less likely to be reflected in company stock and bond prices. Investors are not able to easily identify sustainability outperformers and laggards. Low correlation could have consequences for investors who rely on one single ESG rating in their investment strategies and fail to account for sustainability-related rating disagreement among rating and data providers.

▶ Divergence restricts companies from being able to improve their ESG performance because they receive mixed signals from ESG rating providers about which actions are expected and will be valued by the market.

▶ Low correlation poses a challenge for academic and empirical research. Using one rating provider versus another might alter a study's conclusions.

---

24 R. Gibson, P. Krueger, and P. S. Schmidt, "ESG Rating Disagreement and Stock Returns," Swiss Finance Institute Research Paper No. 19-67 (2019). https://papers.ssrn.com/sol3/papers.cfm?abstract_id=3433728.

However, some investors argue that variability in methodology and output can be beneficial for investors and a source of insight, as long as there is transparency about how they have been derived.

Another consideration when thinking of providers is where they have come from and which stakeholders are served. Here are some examples:

- "Traditional" ESG data and research providers: founded from the SRI industry to provide investors with sustainability data and ratings about primarily large, publicly traded companies. More recent consolidation activity has turned these providers into conglomerates with different offerings and research focuses. The level of automation is low or medium because human judgment is still used.
- "Nontraditional" ESG data and research providers: More recently, nontraditional providers, such as credit-rating agencies (e.g., Fitch, Moody's, and S&P), entered the space by acquiring Trucost (2016) and Vigeo Eiris (2019), respectively. As with traditional ESG data and research providers, the level of automation is low or medium because human judgment is still used.
- AI or algorithm-driven ESG research: Launched more recently, in the past five years, these providers use new technologies, such as Natural Language Processing, to identify ESG risks and opportunities from web-based sources. The level of automation is high.

Some of these providers might serve corporate issuers and bank and insurance companies as well as asset owners and asset managers. One way to think about these ratings and data providers is through their broad styles and techniques:

- raw or partially transformed data (e.g., absolute carbon emissions, or carbon intensity, which is emissions or sales)
- ratings based on backward-looking reported data
- ratings or information based on internet, third-party, and web-reported data, aiming to be current
- aggregators of data or ratings

The considerations that investors could take into account when choosing providers include:

- the number of companies covered
- the length of history of datasets
- the languages used
- the stability of methodology
- the regularity of updates
- asset class coverage
- the quality of methodology
- the range of datasets
- the range of tools and services offered

Consensus on ESG ratings is currently limited among investors. In that sense, it is similar to current discussions on sell-side equity research, which is investment research typically generated by investment banks. These sell-side ratings (e.g., buy/sell/hold, overweight/underweight versus index, or target prices and credit spreads) are not expected to agree. The rating divergence in opinions can be helpful for investors in decision making because it allows both positive and negative arguments to come to light and to be assessed. However, this is somewhat different from CRAs, which typically have highly correlated credit ratings.

One gap is the forward-looking forecasts for ESG data or ratings. Such forecasts are still typically performed by sell-side (at investment banks) and buy-side (at asset management firms) analysts, although not necessarily in a systematic fashion.

Areas of Focus for Investors Compared to Rating Agencies

Investors often focus on these types of issues over and above what rating agencies do:

- ▶ subsector and company-specific material issues
- ▶ a focus on product impacts and actual financial (sales) or extra-financial performance (e.g., customer retention)
- ▶ more focus on interpreting raw data
- ▶ drawing deeper insights into associated financial risks for companies

Investors might focus less on company policies and common disclosures, and might also focus less on history and put a stronger emphasis on forward-looking factors.

9. MUTUAL FUND AND FUND MANAGER ESG ASSESSMENT, COMPANY ESG ASSESSMENT AND RATING, PRIMARY AND SECONDARY ESG DATA SOURCES, AND OTHER USES OF ESG AND SUSTAINABILITY SYSTEMS DATA

7.1.19 describe primary and secondary sources of ESG data and information

7.1.20 describe other uses of ESG and sustainability systems data

Morningstar's sustainability ratings and Real Impact Tracker (RIT) are examples of ESG fund and fund manager assessments.

EXAMPLE 3

Morningstar's Sustainability Ratings

As of 2021, Morningstar covered more than 20,000 mutual funds and more than 2,000 ETFs with a 1 to 5 score (the system was started in 2018). It uses company-level ratings from Sustainalytics (now part of Morningstar) to develop its fund ratings, and the headline rating is freely available. Morningstar takes a "holdings-based approach"—a weighted average of portfolio companies' ESG scores. No credit or assessment is given to managers' efforts on shareholder engagement and public advocacy or on their sophistication, culture, or investment strategy. One key critique of this approach is that holdings-based approaches ignore intentional ESG strategy and that the approach is necessarily backward looking.

Given that the correlation of the two major rating systems (Sustainalytics and MSCI) is low and variable and that Morningstar uses only the Sustainalytics data for its calculations, there is limited comparability between the ratings and others.

> **EXAMPLE 4**
>
> ### Real Impact Tracker
>
> The RIT takes a more holistic approach, doing deep-dive due diligence on its manager assessments. Its "certified community" is publicly available, with details of the assessment undertaken.
>
> Rather than using a "holdings-based approach," the RIT assesses
>
> - culture,
> - philosophy,
> - process impact, and
> - public policy efforts.

> **EXAMPLE 5**
>
> ### Mercer's Point System
>
> Investment consultants, such as Mercer, will also rate the ESG capabilities of fund managers, which is often done at a fund strategy level. Mercer has a 4-point score, where its highest rating of ESG = 1 is given to less than 5% of investment teams.
>
> Mercer's investment consultants might look for the following features:
>
> - A demonstration that ESG factors are featured in investment teams' decision-making process and corporate culture.
> - An effort has been made to build ESG factors into valuation metrics, using the investment team's own judgment about materiality and time frames.
> - There is a long-term investment horizon and low portfolio turnover.
> - Ownership policies and practices include sufficient oversight, integration with investment decision making, and transparency.
> - For alternative assets, there is evidence of pursuing best practices in transparency and evaluation, with monitoring and improvement of ESG performance as relevant for portfolio companies and sectors.
> - There is a demonstrated willingness to collaborate with other institutional investors to improve company, sector, or market performance.
> - Commitment to ESG integration can be seen across the organization.
>
> *Source:* Adapted from Mercer (2018).[25]

The aim of these types of ESG assessors is to form a view on the ESG integration practices and processes of different fund managers and strategies so that end users, both retail and institutional, can match ESG and investment needs with funds that provide the best fit services. These limitations include:

- different methodologies (some focus on investment processes, others on portfolio holdings)
- different data sources or rating providers
- the unaudited limited data sources

---

[25] The example was adapted from "Mercer ESG Ratings" (2018). www.mercer.com/our-thinking/mercer-esg-ratings.html.

- the time resource to make the comparisons
- the relatively nontransparent and noncomparable way these assessments are performed

Company ESG Assessment and Rating

In 2018, MSCI and Sustainalytics had the largest market shares in company-focused ESG ratings. Both rating agencies have grown by acquiring other ESG rating providers over the past decade. However, new entrants are still entering.

The different types of assessment include the following:

- fundamental, including risk, business model, policies, and preparedness
- operational, including carbon impact, water stress, and human capital management
- disclosure-based assessment
- algorithm and news based, including controversies (Truvalue Labs and RepRisk predominantly use this assessment, though most ratings companies use fundamental, operational, and disclosure based.)

A few ESG ratings companies have attempted to look at the opportunities side of ESG factors as well.

As noted earlier, each provider has different methodologies and differing benefits and limitations. Consensus between the databases is limited.

Typically, a rating provider will establish a methodology to inform the rating by identifying a set of relevant ESG issues, assigning indicators to evaluate performance on those issues, and then developing a weighting and scoring process to evaluate a company.

See the appendix for further details on the Sustainalytics and MSCI Methodologies.

Most establish systems whereby a certain level of performance on an issue is assigned a certain number of points or a grade. Points or grade assignments can be attached to a quantitative metric (e.g., the number of female directors or emissions reduced) or to qualitative assessments (e.g., a "high," "medium," or "low" assessment based on policies, procedures, or performance). Topics are also often assigned a given weight, establishing different levels of influence for different topics or sets of topics on the final rating.

ESG ratings are primarily based on historical company data and alternative data sources (e.g., media sources). Rating agencies try to synthesize these data to provide investors with information to inform investment decisions. Some ESG rating providers are also developing measures of "climate risk" that attempt to assess forward-looking risk informed by the Paris Agreement and by such initiatives as the Task Force on Climate-Related Financial Disclosures.

To produce a rating, a provider will typically perform the following tasks.

- Identify indicators that determine which ESG indicators are most material to the sector in question (see materiality mapping elsewhere in this chapter).
- Gather a set of data points for the identified indicators on the company in question from company public disclosures, survey responses, unstructured company data, or third-party data. Assess the data gathered for consistency and, on occasion, estimate any missing data points (not all rating providers estimate data points).
- Quantify qualitative data points through scoring or ranking methodologies; score or evaluate quantitative data points through scoring or ranking methodologies. Combine these data points with regard to the predetermined

weighting system applied to the indicators to create either a sector-relative score for a company that assesses its performance relative to its peer group or an absolute score—or both.

ESG factor identification is up to the rating provider; therefore, dispersal of opinions starts at this step, even before consideration of different weighting and scoring methodologies.

Several rating providers exist, though historically, MSCI and Sustainalytics have had some of the largest market shares in the equity rating space. Country-specific, or more bond-specific, services are also available at, for instance, the World Bank.

We are not elevating one method over another, and the methodologies have great detail and differences.

This is looked at in the appendix, where we consider the approaches of two ESG risk-rating systems: Sustainalytics' and MSCI risk ratings.

Further detail is also available from the EU's *Study on Sustainability-Related Ratings, Data and Research* (2020).[26]

ESG Index Providers

The likes of FTSE Russell and MSCI provide ESG index benchmarks. These indexes can be custom built to an investor's preferences (typically at the institutional level) and are generally commercially available in more standard versions.

The index typically relies on rules-based criteria assessed on underlying ESG scores or metrics. These criteria then go into a formula to tilt company weightings or exclude entire companies based on ESG scores and hurdles. These scores can be sourced by other ESG service providers. For instance, Sustainalytics started providing FTSE Russell with underlying data from 2019 (and had provided Morningstar with data before this).

These indexes can be used as benchmarks for fund managers to be measured against or as model funds for investors to directly invest into in a form of beta or passive management.

These types of indexes have been developed into different ranges of "ESG ETFs." ETFs are made up of a basket of securities (stocks, bonds, and other assets).

These ETFs follow the underlying index or basket construction in a rules-based fashion. These can be thematic, namely investing only in certain sectors, or tilt weightings based on ESG scores, as described earlier. These scores can be data based (e.g., carbon emissions) or ratings based (e.g., on a provider's ratings) or a mix of the two. Debates continue as to how well these ETFs capture potential ESG factors.

Primary and Secondary ESG Data Sources

Many ESG databases provide secondary ESG data or ratings. These are assessments transformed by a process of scoring or by a formula from a primary data source. Some providers (e.g., Bloomberg) will provide primary data sourced from company reports in an easier or consistent form to digest, along with a secondary rating (e.g., Bloomberg Disclosure score).

Primary data can be sourced from companies directly via surveys, direct company communication, and company reports, presentations, and public documents.

---

[26] Publications Office of the European Union, *Study on Sustainability-Related Ratings, Data and Research* (2021). https://op.europa.eu/en/publication-detail/-/publication/d7d85036-509c-11eb-b59f-01aa75ed71a1/language-en/format-PDF/source-183474104%E2%80%9D.

These public documents can be sourced from nonprofit organizations, such as the *UN Global Compact* or the GRI, as well as the companies' own websites. A primary source might be audited or not audited, but as of 2020, many ESG performance indicators are not audited (though the number has increased since 2018 and is expected to continue to increase, verification and auditing of carbon emissions being one important data point that is increasingly audited).

Alternatively, the source may be indirect, via news articles, third-party reports and analysis, or investment and consulting research.

Indirect assessment can be via a third-party source (e.g., Glassdoor for employee satisfaction data and scores, which are directly sourced from employee surveys). They could also come from government, regulatory bodies or non-governmental organization (NGO) reports into different segments of ESG.

Some of these data or assessments might be used widely between organizations. For instance, CDP carbon data are used as an input by many of the major ESG rating providers, such as FTSE Russell, MSCI, and Sustainalytics.

Secondary data sources typically involve transforming the primary ESG data in some way and creating new scores, assessments, or ratings based on these transformations. These are available from commercial organizations, both financial and nonfinancial, as well as from regulators, NGOs, and other nonprofit or charitable bodies.

Other Uses of ESG and Sustainability Systems Data

Looking at all aspects, ESG data clearly have wide and varied uses within investment. This section presents some other techniques that can go beyond a company assessment but are useful for companies and analysts to consider.

"Big Data" Analysis of Multiple ESG Factors

As can be seen earlier in this chapter, regarding quantitative analysis, algorithms and natural language processes are using ESG datasets to determine company quality, reputational risk, and many forward-looking aspects of business strength and valuation. These trends can also be analyzed at the industry or country level. Companies are starting to use big data analysis of various ESG factors in their strategic and operational analysis.

More detailed information on this can be found in Chapter 8.

Resource, Supply, and Operational Risk Mitigation

Assessment here is not only at a company level but can also be carried out at a systems or sector level. This would include assessments of supply chain risk (e.g., from forced labor or supply constraints) or policy changes (e.g., on carbon pricing or water usage).

These risks could include climate adaptation and transition risk to physical infrastructure or the location of human resources in risk areas—environmentally or politically.

This then ties into resource-, supply-, and operations-related decision making in terms of investments and capital allocation, where investors and companies might decide to invest further money (e.g., low-carbon technology) or withdraw further funding (e.g., thermal coal mines).

Modeling Future Sustainability Scenarios, Including Climate Change, Wage Growth, and Social Effects

Future scenarios can be useful at the country, industry, and company level, as well as for investors. One example is climate change scenarios. One set of scenarios examines different policy interventions (e.g., levels of carbon tax). These different policy assumptions can then lead to contrasting impacts on fires and storms from varying levels of warming. These natural disasters could then affect companies (e.g., with insurers and their infrastructure) as well as countries via human migration. This type of data can be used to guide sustainability strategy and manage risk.

The World Economic Forum (WEF) shows two examples of risk mapping at this level (see Exhibit 9 and Exhibit 10). Furthermore, some would consider the analysis in Exhibit 10 a form of risk mapping.

Exhibit 9: The Global Risk Landscape 2019

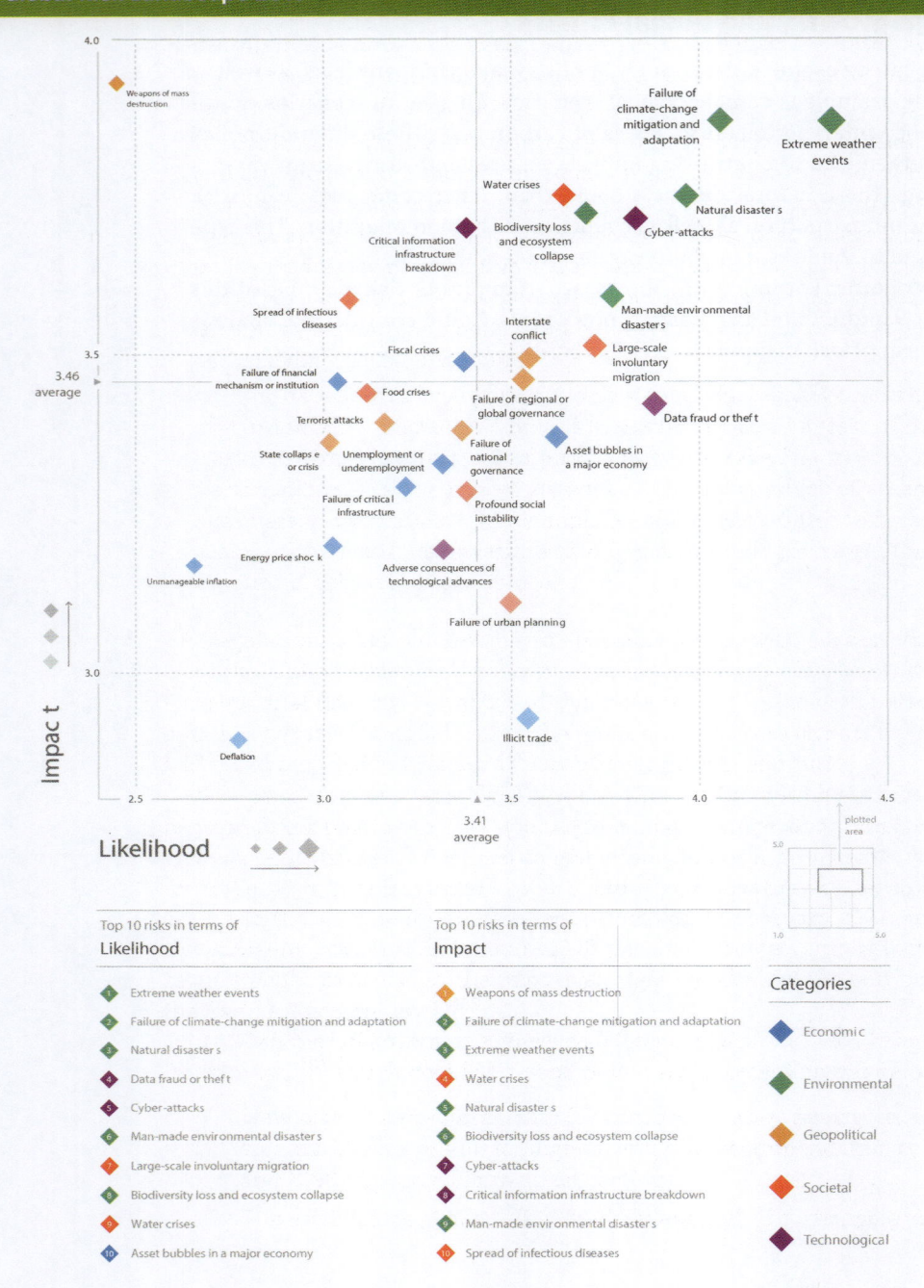

Source: World Economic Forum (2019).[27]

---

[27] World Economic Forum, *WEF Global Risk Report 2019* (2019). www.weforum.org/global-risks/reports.

Mutual Fund and Fund Manager ESG Assessment, Company ESG Assessment and Rating... 423

Exhibit 10: The Global Risk Interconnections Map 2019

Source: World Economic Forum (2019).[28]

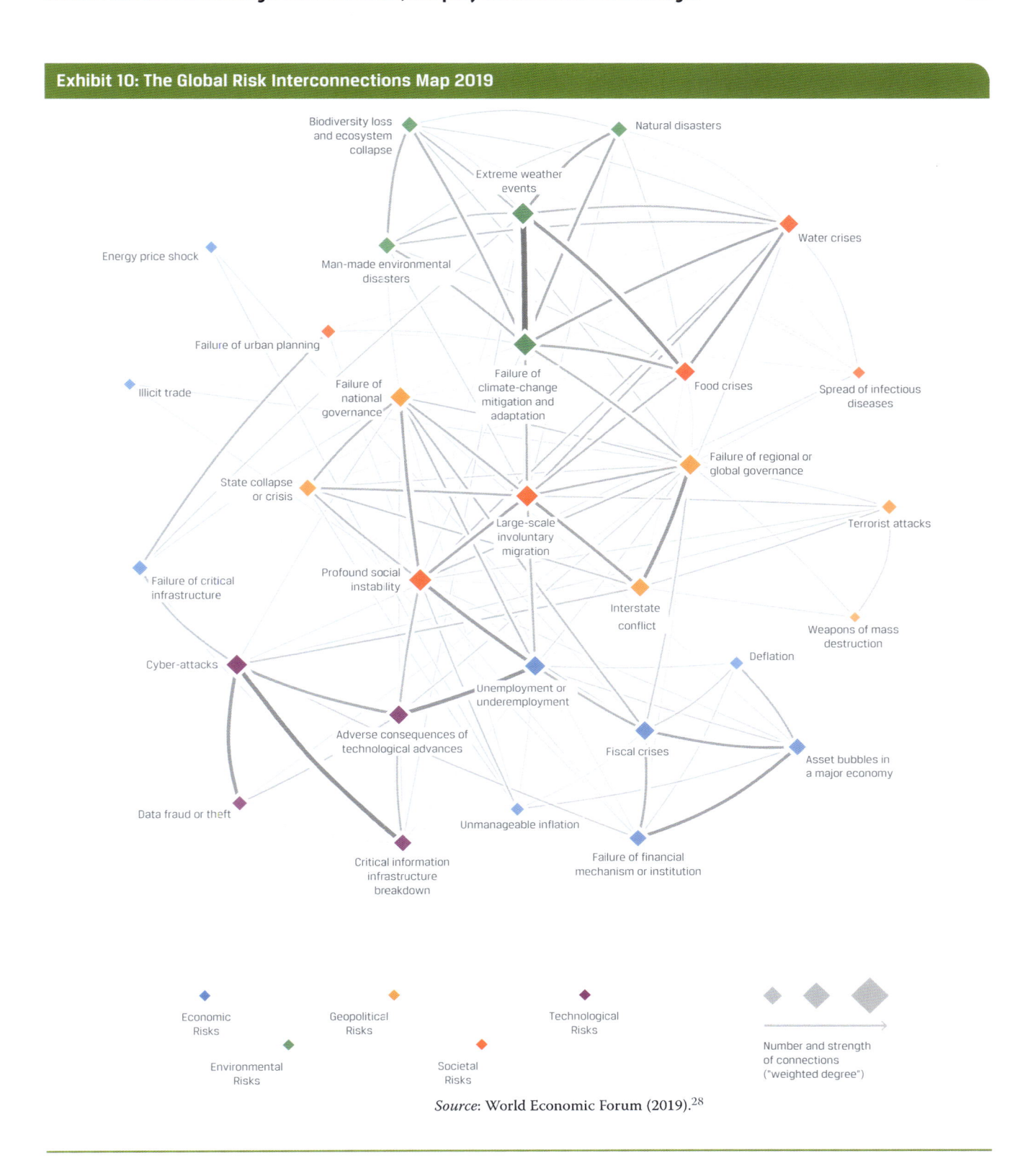

See the subsection titled "Materiality Assessments and Risk Mapping" for more information on risk mapping.

---

28 World Economic Forum, *The Global Risks Interconnections Map 2019* (2019).

Real-Time Dynamic Analysis

The analysis at the frontiers of data science is being extended to real-time analysis. For instance, geospatial data are used to track deforestation, mining, construction, shipping, and traffic, and natural language processes are used to track social sentiment on the internet.

Overall, ESG investment analysis does not occur in a vacuum. The techniques and analysis are intersectional with the real world, as well as with the impact and risk on companies and countries.

10 FIXED INCOME, CREDIT RATING AGENCIES, AND ESG CREDIT SCORING

> 7.1.21 explain how Credit Rating Agencies (CRAs) approach ESG Credit Scoring

The direct physical infrastructure impact of climate change, corporate scandals and the importance of human capital are ESG risks that impact bonds. These are influenced by oversight, transparency and accountability.

ESG integration techniques can extend across asset classes. This section concentrates on the fixed-income asset class.

Different Levels at Which ESG Factors Can Affect Bond Price Performance and Credit Risk

Broadly speaking, ESG factors can affect the price performance of a bond and its credit risk at different levels.

- Issuer and company level: These are risks that affect a specific bond issue and not the whole market. They are related to factors such as the governance of an issuer, its regulatory compliance, the strength of its balance sheet, and company-specific items, such as brand reputation. For example, the yield on the corporate debt of the car manufacturer Volkswagen rose and stayed high for a prolonged period of time in the aftermath of the fraudulent emission scandal (see Chapter 1 for more information on this).
- Industry and geographic level: These risks stem from wider-ranging issues affecting the entire industry or region. They can be related to regulatory and legal factors, technological changes associated with the business activity the company is involved in, and the markets it sources or sells to (e.g., the idea that utilities are relatively more exposed to climate change risks than media companies).

Some investors assume that some ESG factors might affect a bond's price performance but not actually influence an issuer's creditworthiness. This is because an ESG factor might not be considered to affect bankruptcy risk, even if it might have an impact on price performance. This would highlight a difference between a rating analysis and an asset valuation.

Good ESG risk management not only affects asset prices but can also fundamentally protect people's lives. For instance, no one was injured in the 2013 landslide at a Rio Tinto mine in Utah. Rio Tinto's laser scanning system sent early warning signals, enabling a prompt evacuation of the site. However, the 2019 Vale dam failure in Brazil cost many lives.

Continuing Evolution for Credit and ESG Since PRI Releases

Practice in the area of credit and ESG has evolved in the past few years. By 2020, CRAs were in a different place than when the first observations were made by the PRI in 2016–2017, which was when the PRI's Statement on ESG in Credit Risk and Ratings[29] and its report on CRAs were both released.

The PRI statement was designed to commit CRAs and fixed-income investors to incorporate ESG into credit ratings and analysis in a systematic and transparent way. As of May 2022, the statement remains open for investors and CRAs to sign.

Global and Regional Credit Rating Agencies

There are global and regional CRAs. Historically, ESG analysis was not typically considered by CRAs. But this has changed in recent years. A major evolutionary step was taken by S&P (a global CRA) when it rolled out ESG as part of its credit assessments in 2019. The World Bank also launched its Sovereign ESG database in late 2019. In addition, the IMF launched its Climate Change Indicators Dashboard in April 2021.

Surveys from investors suggest that the G factor remains more important to credit investors than E and S. Credit investors argue that this is because downside risk (as in bankruptcy risk and therefore the chance of losing a credit investor's entire capital) is more important than any upside or opportunity risk. Arguably, opportunity is more important to equity investors. Upside is limited for most credit investors, but downside risk from bankruptcy will hurt returns. Credit investors view fraud prevention and governance as important factors in protecting from downside risk (negative credit events). As **G** is directly related to preventing downside risk, its direct relevance is easier to trace for credit investors.

Many of the challenges are similar to equity ESG ratings. These challenges include:

- the lack of transparency
- inconsistent or changing methodologies
- the use of estimated data
- the lack of comparability through time and between providers and companies

The following also give some specific fixed income challenges (see also case studies and discussion of sovereign and fixed income expressions of ESG elsewhere in this chapter):

- time horizon (e.g., three-month paper or 50-year bonds),
- lack of proxy vote,
- different levels of management engagement, and
- unique qualities of sovereign credit.

---

29 PRI, *Statement on ESG in Credit Risk and Ratings* (2020). www.unpri.org/credit-ratings/statement-on-esg-in-credit-risk-and-ratings-available-in-different-languages/77.article.

Corporate Credit Risk Assessments

When assessing credit risk, pre-2016 CRAs typically did not attempt to capture the environmental, ethical, or social impact of a bond issue.[30] For example, CRAs may have somewhat ignored environmental damage measurements (e.g., CO_2 emissions of a company) or environmental opportunities.

Before 2016, when analyzing a carbon-intense company, CRAs might have typically focused on other material impacts, including financial, regulatory, and legal factors, that could affect the company's credit profile. As of 2020, though, many CRAs look at a range of ESG factors (and judge materiality). They judge the company's response to ESG risks and "ESG events" and link that response to potential financial and balance sheet or cash flow considerations, such as the ability to meet debt obligations.

In addition, during 2018–2019, Moody's and S&P developed further ESG evaluation systems, which continue to evolve today.

Typically, CRAs assess the predictability and certainty of an issuer's ability to generate future cash flow to meet its debt obligations. To this end, they look at whether companies can sell their assets to cover obligations (and certain assets might be impaired through ESG concerns, such as coal assets).

The levels of litigation risk are often analyzed as well, including environmental litigation, employment litigation, and human rights violations (e.g., modern slavery laws).

To that degree, ESG risk, which comes to litigation, has always been incorporated into CRA analysis.

On the quantitative side, CRA analysis focuses on the issuer's overall bankruptcy risk, the strength of its balance sheet, and how it compares to other issuers.

Using standard credit ratio analysis, CRAs might test the following:

- how ESG factors affect an issuer's ability to convert assets into cash (profitability and cash flow analysis)
- the impact that changing yields—due to an ESG event—could have on the cost of capital, depending on the share of debt used in the issuer's capital structure (interest coverage ratio and capital structure analysis)
- the extent to which ESG-related costs affect an issuer's ability to generate profits and add to refinancing risks
- how well an issuer's management uses the assets under its control to generate sales and profit (efficiency ratios)

In summary, a CRA rating is typically

- based on analytical judgment (both quantitative and qualitative), using all the information deemed material by the analysts;
- forward looking, with a varying time horizon;
- composed of dynamic and relative measures; and
- a statement of the relative likelihood of default.

An interested fixed-income investor may conduct different materiality assessments or judgments to a CRA (see case studies). This is considered true of equity ESG ratings by many investors as well.

Indeed, credit investors typically use the information provided by credit ratings to help them price, trade, and assess the credit risk of fixed-income securities and to determine whether these are suitable investments, but ratings are not the only input.

---

30 PRI, *Shifting Perceptions: ESG, Credit Risk and Ratings* (2017). www.unpri.org/credit-ratings.

A combination of investor research, analysis and judgment determines the suitability of a bond investment based on a range of factors, of which credit ratings may be one. Other factors may include proprietary indicators and recommendations by security analysts. It is notable that not all credit will have a rating.

With that said, credit ratings have an important role in the credit risk assessment of a bond issue and are typically used to define and limit investment mandates set by a wide range of institutional investors. Many investors in investment grade credit have limited or no ability to invest in high-yield speculative-grade credit, for example.

Certain Fixed-Income Investors Use QESGs

Certain fixed-income investors use quantitative ESG scores (QESGs) – not to be confused with what investors often mean by quantitative investing (see the section titled "The Different Approaches to Integrating ESG") – in their fixed income assessments. These QESGs might be based on quantitative data (such as carbon intensity) or be judgments based on data and/or policy (e.g. policy or commitment to align business model to science-based targets). Not all investors use the term and different investors may be referring to different proprietary systems when referring to QESGs.

Green Bonds Considered a Different Class of Credit

Green bonds (bonds financing green projects) or bonds assessed to meet B-corp criteria are sometimes considered a different class of credit. Once certain ESG or sustainability criteria are met, a green bond's credit risk is often assessed in the same manner as a standard credit.

Typically, a green bond is a fixed-income instrument tied to projects that create an environmental benefit. Issuers use proceeds for a variety of activities aimed at contributing to climate change mitigation, adaptation, or some other environmental benefit, such as conservation or pollution control. Examples include projects associated with renewable energy, public transportation, energy-efficient buildings and manufacturing processes, agricultural land management, waste management, and water management.

Often a green bond has some form of verification or assurance from a third-party organization. This organization ensures that the financing meets the criteria set out in the bond, though the covenants related to this will vary by different bonds. Debate continues as to what makes a bond "green" because no global consensus exists on the types of capital projects that fit within the scope of green bonds. There are, however, several frameworks, which may start to standardize with the publication of the *EU Green Taxonomy* and with the EU Green Bond Standard potentially evolving in 2021.[31]

Note that B-corporation certification is a private certification issued to for-profit companies by B Lab, a global nonprofit organization that verifies social and environmental performance, public transparency, and legal accountability to balance profit and purpose.

---

31 European Commission, *European Green Bond Standard* (2021). https://ec.europa.eu/info/business-economy-euro/banking-and-finance/sustainable-finance/eu-green-bond-standard_en.

Sovereign Credit Risk Assessment

A country's competitiveness, growth and potential growth, governance, and political stability are all important ingredients of prosperity. There are many ESG factors to possibly take into account, including the availability and management of:

- resources (including population trends, human capital, education and health),
- emerging technologies, and
- government regulations and policies.

Beyond this though, a CRA is typically most interested in a government's ability to generate enough revenues to repay its financial debt obligations.

Each CRA uses a different framework when assessing sovereign debt, but typically looks at some form of:

1. economic growth; and
2. governance.

The ways that E and S factors transmit to economic growth and potential can also be indirect, and the way CRAs assess this is still evolving. The G factor is a more obvious and direct assessment, which has been analyzed historically. On G, each major CRA has a different framework to assess it, so in that sense, this replicates some of the difficulties around equity stock ESG ratings.

Also see discussion in the case studies.

ESG and Credit Ratings: Discussion over Relationship

The link between ESG ratings and credit ratings is still hotly debated among investors. Proponents might point to a Barclays' study (see Chapter 8) looking at a high ESG portfolio versus a low ESG portfolio using two different ESG datasets (MSCI and Sustainalytics).

Fixed Income, Credit Rating Agencies, and ESG Credit Scoring

Exhibit 11: Investment-Grade Bond Portfolio Performance (High ESG over Low ESG)

Cumulate performance % of a high-ESG portfolio over a low-ESG portfolio using MSCI ESG data[33]

Cumulate performance % of a high-ESG portfolio over a low-ESG portfolio using Sustainalytics ESG data[34]

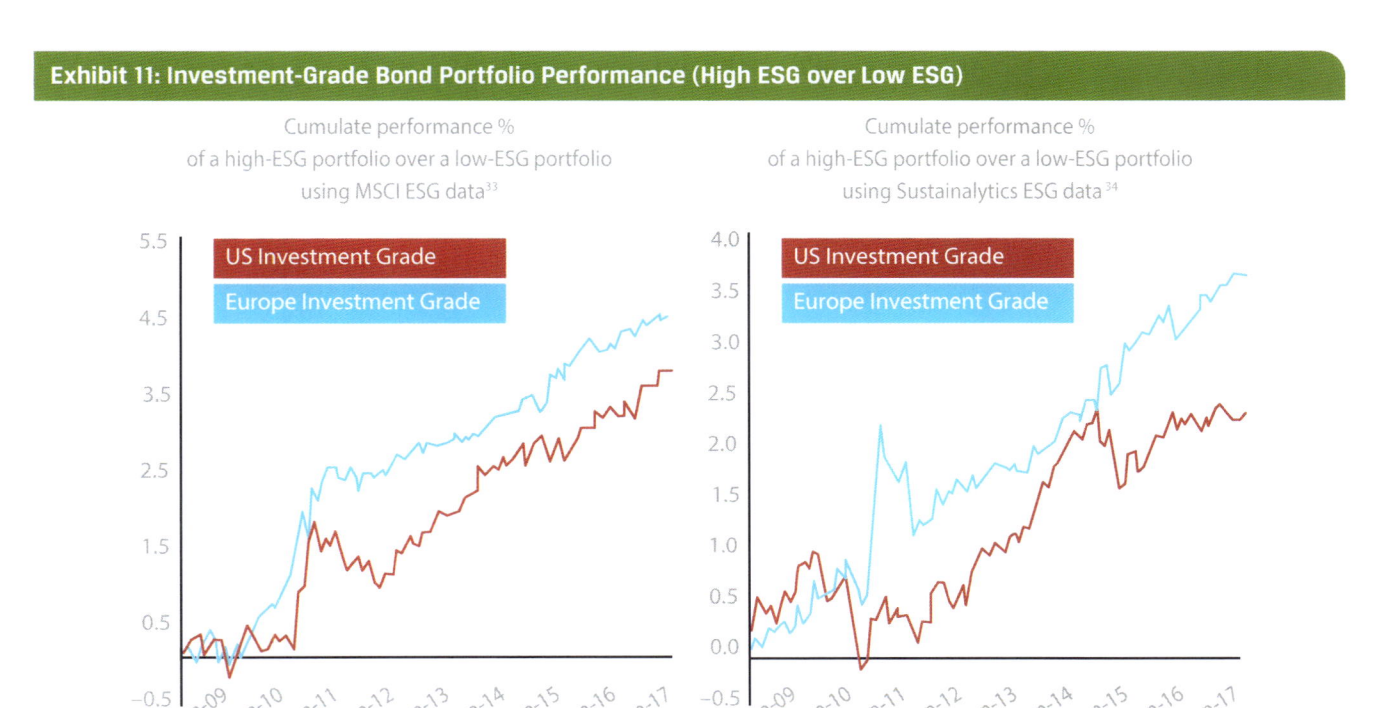

Source: Barclays (2018).[32]

The case for sustainable bond investing strengthens, but critics would point out the flaws of correlational studies as well as the short 2009–18 time period. Critics further point out that the factor attributions post-2008/2009 (the financial crisis), and some ESG ratings correlate with quality factors (though not all).

Portfolio managers are developing more sophisticated approaches beyond simple ESG tilts. Chapter 8 illustrates some of the ratings distribution features developed by a fixed-income specialist asset manager within its portfolio ESG evaluation framework. The framework uses third-party ESG data but combines the data to produce proprietary ESG metrics for that firm, including a fundamental, absolute-oriented ESG rating and a relative investment ESG score. The internal investment teams can see an ESG risk from the single-issuer level to the portfolio level, which is a value added part of the process.

The impact can be seen in the credit default swap (CDS) market as well as on a single-issuer basis, such as with Volkswagen and emissions testing.[33] This would be an argument for the impact an ESG event can have on CDS.

However, the timing of subsequent CDSs does not perfectly correspond to when all the information was first released. The lag in timing might suggest inefficient markets or the lagged delays that market participants have in assessing material ESG information into CDS prices.

The research on ESG and credit is historically less well developed than in equity, but interest continues to grow and techniques are developing, with CRAs recently embedding ESG into their processes. There is some evidence that ESG ratings and

---

32 Barclays, *The Case for Sustainable Bond Investing Strengthens* (2018), Sustainalytics data based on the firm's legacy ESG ratings. www.investmentbank.barclays.com/content/dam/barclaysmicrosites/ibpublic/documents/our-insights/ESG2/BarclaysIB-ImpactSeries4-ESG-in-credit-5MB.pdf.
33 Multiple sources (including Volkswagen AG), as detailed in P.A. Griffin and D.H. Lont, "Game Changer? The Impact of the VW Emission Cheating Scandal on the Co-Integration of Large Automakers' Securities" (2016). http://ssrn.com/abstract=2838949.

CDSs may have a relationship. Still, the overall principles of gathering ESG data or ratings, assessing material ESG factors, and then embedding them into asset assessment and valuation hold.

Potential Bias in Ratings

ESG ratings in the credit area could suffer bias as is seen in other asset classes. Three key types of bias are typically encountered:

1. Company size bias, where larger companies might obtain higher ratings because of the ability to dedicate more resources to nonfinancial disclosures.
2. Geographical bias, where a geographical bias exists toward companies in regions with high reporting requirements or some other cultural factor (e.g., higher unionization in Europe).
3. Industry and sector bias, where rating providers oversimplify industry weighting and company alignment.

Bias can potentially also be seen in how certain industries (e.g., technology) are assessed in comparison to other industries, or through the lens of other factor labels, such as "growth" or "value."

KEY FACTS

1. Investors integrate ESG techniques to improve investment returns, lower investment risk, meet client needs, and comply with regulatory requirements.
2. A multitude of approaches can be used to integrate ESG analysis into a firm's investment process. Many approaches can be combined, and some are more suitable to specific asset classes and risks.
3. Quantitative and qualitative approaches can be used at all stages of the investment process, from idea and research generation to asset valuation and portfolio construction.
4. Materiality assessment is an important ESG technique because investors typically distinguish between important, material ESG factors and less important, nonmaterial ESG factors. Nonmaterial factors are considered to not affect investment considerations.
5. Primary ESG data come from direct sources. Secondary ESG information has been transformed or assessed. Investors can use both types of ESG sources in their analysis. ESG data, like all data, need to be interpreted in the correct contexts.
6. ESG rating agencies use a mix of ESG information and proprietary assessments to give ESG ratings to stocks and credits. Current ESG rating agencies have variable correlation between their ESG ratings because of methodological differences.
7. CRAs are increasingly using ESG factors, particularly G, in their credit assessments. This has developed and is expected to continue to develop quickly.
8. Investment consultants and asset owners will use ESG assessment to judge investment managers and as part of their decision criteria.
9. Index providers use ESG factors in establishing ESG indexes. These can be thematic or general.
10. Investors use a range of ESG ratings and techniques, both internally generated and sourced from third parties, to enhance their investment valuation and decision processes.
11. ESG tools and integration techniques continue to develop at a fast pace because of investor and end-customer demand.

Conclusion

There are many techniques for ESG integration across asset classes, though most investors are aligned in seeking to maximize risk-adjusted returns in using these ESG tools. While certain tools are asset-class specific, the overall framework of identifying material ESG factors and then embedding them in valuation and assessment remains similar.

As of 2021, the field remains dynamic, as it has been over recent years, and expert techniques and tools for analysis continue to evolve.

FURTHER READING

Reports and standards concerning ESG practice

CFA Institute 2017. *Global Perceptions of Environmental, Social, and Governance Issues in Investing*.www.cfainstitute.org/en/research/survey-reports/esg-survey-2017.

CFA Institute and PRI 2018. *Guidance and Case Studies for ESG Integration: Equities and Fixed Income*.www.cfainstitute.org/-/media/documents/survey/guidance-case-studies-esg-integration.ashx.

CFA Institute and the Principles for Responsible Investment 2018. *ESG Integration in the Americas: Markets, Practices, and Data*. www.cfainstitute.org/en/research/survey-reports/esg-integration-americas-survey-report.

Financial Reporting Council 2020. *UK Stewardship Code*.www.frc.org.uk/investors/uk-stewardship-code.

Financial Services Agency 2017. *Principles for Responsible Institutional Investors "Japan's Stewardship Code."* www.fsa.go.jp/en/laws_regulations/pc_stewardship.html.

Generation Investment Management 2019. *Generation Philosophy*.www.generationim.com/generation-philosophy/.

Global Asset Management R. B. C. 2019. *RBC Global Equity*.http://global.rbcgam.com/global-equities/default.fs.

PRI 2016. *Credit Risk and Ratings Initiative*.www.unpri.org/credit-ratings.

Tuan, M. T. 2008. *Measuring and/or Estimating Social Value Creation: Insights into Eight Integrated Cost Approaches*. https://docs.gatesfoundation.org/Documents/wwl-report-measuring-estimating-social-value-creation.pdf.

United Nations Global Compact, United Nations Environment Programme (UNEP) Finance Initiative, PRI, and UNEP Inquiry 2019. *Fiduciary Duty in the 21st Century*. www.unepfi.org/fileadmin/documents/fiduciary_duty_21st_century.pdf.

Books and Articles

Chatterji, A., D. I. Levine, M. W. Toffel. 2009. "How Well Do Social Ratings Actually Measure Corporate Social Responsibility?" Journal of Economics & Management Strategy18 (1): 125–69. https://ssrn.com/abstract=139470410.1111/j.1530-9134.2009.00210.x

Edmans, A. 2011. "Does the Stock Market Fully Value Intangibles? Employee Satisfaction and Equity Prices." Journal of Financial Economics101 (3): 621–40. https://ssrn.com/abstract=98573510.1016/j.jfineco.2011.03.021

Flammer, C. 2013. "Does Corporate Social Responsibility Lead to Superior Financial Performance? A Regression Discontinuity Approach." Journal of Economic Literature27. https://ssrn.com/abstract=2146282

Haskel, J., S. Westlake. 2017. Capitalism Without Capital: The Rise of the Intangible Economy. Princeton University Press. 10.2307/j.ctvc77hhj

Khan, M., G. Serafeim, A. Yoon. 2016. "Corporate Sustainability: First Evidence on Materiality." Accounting Review91 (6): 1697–724. https://ssrn.com/abstract=257591210.2308/accr-51383

Krosinsky, C. 2018. "The Failure of Fund Sustainability Ratings." Medium.com. https://medium.com/@cary_krosinsky/the-failure-of-fund-sustainability-ratings-bea95c0b370f.

OECD 2017. *Responsible Business Conduct for Institutional Investors: Key Considerations for Due Diligence Under the OECD Guidelines for Multinational Enterprises*.https://mneguidelines.oecd.org/RBC-for-Institutional-Investors.pdf.

PRI 2014. *A GP's Guide to Integrating ESG Factors in Private Equity*.www.unpri.org/private-equity/a-gps-guide-to-integrating-esg-factors-in-private-equity/91.article.

APPENDIX

This appendix provides further information on Sustainalytics and its ESG products as well as MSCI Research.

This content will not be assessed. It is provided to give more insight into two major rating providers' methodology but does not suggest that these are the only ways in which ESG ratings can be performed.

Sustainalytics and Its ESG Products

- Sustainalytics is an ESG and corporate governance research and rating provider. As of 2018, it was considered a top-three provider of ESG ratings, and in 2020, it was acquired by Morningstar. It has strategic partnerships with:
- Morningstar;
- Glass Lewis (proxy adviser);
- STOXX (index provider); and
- since 2018, FTSE Russell (index provider).

It has several products ranging from compliance and screening, index research, portfolio analysis, carbon and country risk research to ESG integration research.

The Sustainalytics' ESG Risk Rating

The Sustainalytics' ESG Risk Rating measures the degree to which a company's economic value is at risk driven by ESG factors or, more technically speaking, the magnitude of a company's unmanaged ESG risks.

The rating system gives points for specific risk factors. Each point of risk is equivalent, no matter which company or issue it applies to. Points will add up across issues to create overall scores, which are then rated.

The rating sorts companies into five risk categories:

1. Negligible
2. Low
3. Medium
4. High
5. Severe

These risk categories are absolute, meaning that a "high" risk assessment reflects a comparable degree of unmanaged ESG risk across the research universe, whether it refers to an agriculture company, a utility, or any other type of company.

According to Sustainalytics, an issue is considered "material" within the ESG Risk Rating if its presence or absence in financial reporting is likely to influence the decisions made by a reasonable investor.

To be considered "relevant" in the risk rating, the issue must have a potentially substantial impact on the economic value of a company and, hence, the financial risk and return profile of an investor investing in the company.

Distinguishing the ESG Risk Rating's use of materiality as a concept from narrower legal or accounting-focused definitions is important Not every issue Sustainalytics considers "material" in the rating is legally required to be disclosed in company reporting. Some issues are "material" from an ESG perspective, even if the financial consequences are not fully measurable today.

The ESG Risk Rating's emphasis on materiality incorporates an additional dimension—the exposure dimension. It reflects the extent to which a company is exposed to material ESG risks identified at the industry level and affects the overall rating score for a company as well as its rating score for each material ESG issue. ESG issue risk exposure is estimated at the sub-industry level and further adjusted at the individual company level.

The ESG Risk Rating's second dimension is management. ESG management can be considered a set of company commitments and actions that demonstrate how a company approaches and handles an ESG issue through policies, programs, quantitative performance. and involvement in controversies, as well as its management of corporate governance. Sustainalytics considers management in the ESG Risk Rating because company commitments and actions provide signals about whether companies are managing ESG risks.

Unmanaged Risk: How Sustainalytics Arrives at the Scores

The ESG Risk Rating scoring system for a company is best thought of as occurring in three stages on the issue level:

1. the starting point is exposure,
2. the next stage is management, and
3. the final stage is calculating unmanaged risk, using the concept of risk decomposition.

The final ESG Risk Rating score is a measure of unmanaged risk. This is defined as material ESG risk that has not been managed by a company. As noted in the subsection titled "Materiality Assessments and Risk Mapping", it includes two types of risk:

1. Unmanageable risk, which cannot be addressed by company initiatives
2. The management gap, which represents risks that could be managed by a company through suitable initiatives but which may not yet be managed

The share of risk that is manageable versus the share of risk that is unmanageable on a material ESG issue is predefined at a sub-industry level by a manageable risk factor. Every material ESG issue has an issue manageable risk factor (MRF), ranging from 30% (indicating that a high level of the issue risk is unmanageable) to 100% (indicating that the issue risk is considered fully manageable).

Calculating the Final Unmanaged Risk Score

The assessment of unmanaged risk (the final ESG Risk Rating score) requires three steps:

1. Assess the share of the overall exposure of companies and compare to a material ESG issue in a given sub-industry that can be managed by a company (manageable risk assessment).
2. At the company level, the degree to which a company has managed the manageable risk portion of its overall exposure, with regard to an issue being calculated based on the management assessment (overall management score assessment).
3. Finally, the unmanaged risk score is calculated by subtracting managed risks from a company's overall exposure score in relation to a material ESG issue (final unmanaged risk score calculation).

Appendix

Exhibit 12 shows how the companies Sustainalytics has used for testing and validation are allocated across the five ESG risk categories that were defined for the ESG Risk Rating.

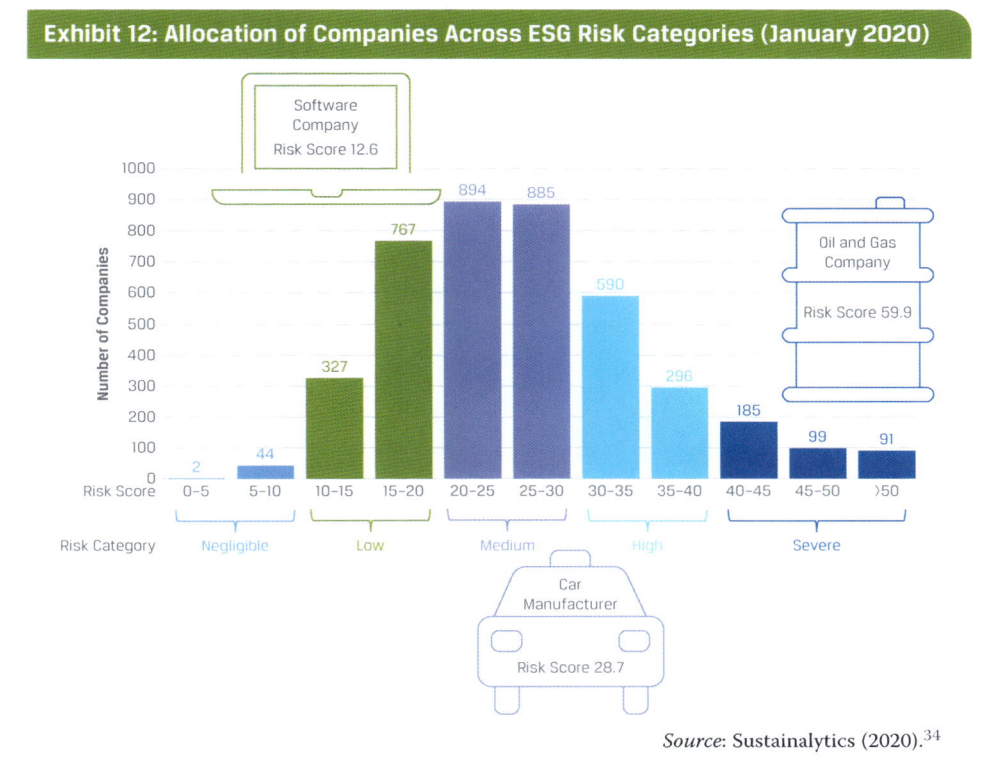

Exhibit 12: Allocation of Companies Across ESG Risk Categories (January 2020)

Risk Score	Number of Companies	Risk Category
0–5	2	Negligible
5–10	44	Negligible
10–15	327	Low
15–20	767	Low
20–25	894	Medium
25–30	885	Medium
30–35	590	High
35–40	296	High
40–45	185	Severe
45–50	99	Severe
>50	91	Severe

Software Company Risk Score 12.6
Car Manufacturer Risk Score 28.7
Oil and Gas Company Risk Score 59.9

Source: Sustainalytics (2020).[34]

Further details on how research looks at materiality, governance, and idiosyncratic issues can be found in Further Reading.

MSCI ESG Research

According to the MSCI ESG Rating, ESG risks and opportunities are posed by large-scale trends (e.g., climate change, resource scarcity, or demographic shifts) and the nature of the company's operations.

The MSCI considers a risk or an opportunity to be material to industry as follows:

- ▶ A risk is material to an industry when companies in a given industry are likely to incur substantial costs in connection with it (e.g., a regulatory ban on a key chemical input).
- ▶ An opportunity is material to an industry when companies in a given industry could likely capitalize on it for profit (e.g., opportunities in clean technology for the LED lighting industry).

Note that this definition of "materiality" is different from that of Sustainalytics but is still a judgment (and might differ from other investors' judgments).

MSCI assesses material risks and opportunities for each industry through a quantitative model that compares ranges and average values in each industry for externalized impacts (e.g., carbon intensity, water intensity, and injury rates). Exceptions are

---
34 Sustainalytics, *Our Solutions* (2019). www.sustainalytics.com/our-solutions.

allowed for companies with diversified business models or that are facing controversies, or based on industry rules. Once identified, these "key issues" are assigned to each industry and company.

Exhibit 13 summarizes the MSCI ESG hierarchy (note the overlaps with, but also differences from, the SASB mapping seen in Exhibit 6.

Exhibit 13: MSCI ESG Hierarchy

3 Pillars	10 Themes	37 ESG Key Issues
Environment		
	Climate change	Emissions
		Financing environmental impact
		Product carbon footprint
		Climate change vulnerability
	Natural resources	Water stress
		Biodiversity and land use
		Raw material sourcing
	Pollution and waste	Toxic emissions and waste
		Packaging material and waste
		Electronic waste
	Opportunities	Opportunities in clean tech
		Opportunities in green building
		Opportunities in renewable energy
Social		
	Human capital	Labor management
		Health and safety
		Human capital development
		Supply chain labor standards
	Product liability	Product safety and quality
		Chemical safety
		Financial product safety
		Privacy and data security
		Responsible investment
		Health and demographic risk
	Stakeholder opposition	Controversial sourcing
		Access to communications
	Social opportunities	Access to finance
		Access to health care
		Opportunities in nutrition and health

Appendix

3 Pillars	10 Themes	37 ESG Key Issues
Governance		Board
	Corporate governance	Pay
		Ownership
		Accounting
		Business ethics
		Anti-competitive practices
	Corporate behavior	Tax transparency
		Corruption and instability
		Financial system instability

Source: MSCI (2019).[35]

Final MSCI ESG Ratings are derived by the weighted averages of the key issue scores. These scores are aggregated, and companies' scores are normalized by their industries. After any overrides are factored in, each company's final industry-adjusted score corresponds to a rating between the best (AAA) and the worst (CCC). These assessments of company performance are not absolute but are explicitly intended to be relative to the standards and performance of a company's industry peers.

MSCI ESG Risk Score

MSCI argues that to understand whether a company is adequately managing a key ESG risk, it is essential to understand both:

- what management strategies it has employed (i.e. risk management); and
- how exposed it is to the risk (i.e. risk exposure).

The MSCI ESG Ratings model attempts to measure both of these. For MSCI to score a company highly on a key issue, the management needs to be judged commensurate with the level of exposure:

- a company with high exposure must also have very strong management, but
- a company with limited exposure can have a more modest approach.

The risk exposure and management scores are combined so that a higher level of exposure requires a higher level of demonstrated management capability in order to achieve the same overall key issue score. Key issue scores are also on a 0 to 10 scale, where 0 is very poor and 10 is very good.

MSCI ESG Opportunity Score

The assessment of MSCI ESG opportunities works similarly to risks, but the model for combining exposure and management differs:

- exposure indicates the relevance of the opportunity to a given company based on its current business and geographic segments, and
- management indicates the company's capacity to take advantage of the opportunity.

---

35 MSCI, *MSCI ESG Ratings Methodology: Executive Summary, September 2019* (2019). www.msci.com/documents/1296102/14524248/MSCI+ESG+Ratings+Methodology+-+Exec+Summary+2019.pdf.

Where exposure is limited, the key issue score is constrained toward the middle of the 0 to 10 range, while high exposure allows for both higher and lower scores.

MSCI Controversy Assessment

MSCI ESG Ratings also reviews controversies, which may indicate structural problems with a company's risk-management capabilities.

As noted earlier in this chapter, a controversy case is defined as an instance, or ongoing situation, in which company operations or products allegedly have a negative environmental, social or governance impact.

> **EXAMPLE 6**
>
> ### Controversy Cases
>
> The ESG rating model is applied to two controversy cases:
>
> 1. A case that is deemed by an analyst to indicate structural problems
> 2. A case that is deemed to be an indicator of recent performance, but that does not offer clear signals of future material risk
>
> The rating system finds that Case 1 poses future material risks for the company and therefore triggers a larger deduction from the key issue score than Case 2.

MSCI Data Sources

These data sources that MSCI ESG Ratings use are similar to what Sustainalytics and other in-house teams might use, including the following:

- macro data at the segment or geographic level from academic, government, and NGO datasets
- company disclosure (e.g., annual report filings, sustainability report, proxy report, or annual general meeting results)

MSCI Final Letter Rating Summary

To arrive at a final letter rating, the weighted average key issue score is normalized by industry. The range of scores for each industry is established annually by taking a rolling three-year average of the top and bottom scores among the MSCI ACWI Index constituents; the values are set at the 97.5th and 2.5th percentile.

Using these ranges, the weighted average key issue score is converted to an industry-adjusted score from 0 to 10, where 0 is worst and 10 is best. The industry-adjusted score corresponds to a rating between best (AAA) and worst (CCC).

MSCI ESG Research

MSCI is historically most well-known for its market index products, but it also provides ESG and corporate governance research and ratings, a index and fund research.

As of 2018, it was considered a top-three provider of ESG ratings. Like Sustainalytics, it has several products ranging from compliance and screening, index research, portfolio analysis, and carbon risk research to ESG integration research.

MSCI has the intellectual property from legacy companies KLD, Innovest, IRRC, and GMI (Governance Metrics International) Ratings.

SELF PRACTICE AND SELF ASSESSMENT

1. Which of the following is an objective for integrating ESG into an investment process? Lowering:
   a. reputational risk.
   b. quality of engagement activities.
   c. risk-adjusted investment returns.

2. Tools of ESG analysis include:
   a. ESG factor tilts.
   b. red flag indicators.
   c. ESG momentum tilts.

3. Elements of ESG integration include:
   a. watch lists.
   b. scenario analysis.
   c. ESG momentum tilts.

4. The typical stages of an integrated ESG assessment are:
   a. research, valuation, and portfolio construction.
   b. materiality assessment, risk mapping, and valuation.
   c. materiality assessment, risk mapping, and portfolio construction.

5. ESG risk mapping refers to:
   a. positive or best-in-class screening.
   b. testing a portfolio against different climate scenarios.
   c. identifying the ESG issues that are likely to have an impact on the company's financial performance

6. Weak governance identified in a private company mostly likely leads to higher:
   a. valuation.
   b. future cash flows.
   c. risk of negative capital allocation decisions.

7. High carbon intensity of a project most likely leads to lower:
   a. valuation.
   b. cost of debt.
   c. risk of default on debt.

8. Which of the following is an example of an ESG-integrated valuation adjustment? Upward adjustment in:
   a. sales growth due to high employee engagement.
   b. valuation due to weak governance of a company.
   c. cost of debt for new project financing with low carbon intensity.

9. Which of the following is a criticism of ESG integration?
   a. Rapid advances in ESG integration techniques
   b. ESG screening emphasizes longer-term performance

c. ESG investment strategy being too inclusive of poor companies

10. Which of the following best describes the relationship between ESG and credit ratings?

    a. ESG and credit ratings are positively correlated.
    b. The link between ESG ratings and credit ratings is still hotly debated among credit investors.
    c. Surveys from credit investors suggest that S factor remains more important than E and G factors.

The following information relates to questions 11-25
Self Assessment Questions

These questions are provided only to enable you to test your understanding of the chapter content. They are not indicative of the types and standard of questions you may see in the examination. The Self-Assessment questions do not include an explanation of the correct answer.

11. Qualitative ESG analysis is likely to be used in investment processes that are based on:

    a. company-specific research.
    b. fundamental analysis.
    c. stock picking.
    d. all of the above.

12. Qualitative analysts and portfolio managers seek to integrate their qualitative investment opinion by incorporating:

    a. negative screening.
    b. quantitative adjustments to financial models and valuations.
    c. qualitative measures only.
    d. none of the above.

13. Elements of ESG integration include:

    a. ESG factor tilts.
    b. red flag indicators.
    c. company questionnaires and management interviews.
    d. watch lists.

14. Which of these statements is *not* true?

    a. The ESG integration framework is not meant to illustrate the perfect ESG-integrated investment process.
    b. The ESG integration techniques of one firm are not necessarily the right techniques for all firms.
    c. There is a consensus amongst firms on which techniques to use to identify and assess ESG factors
    d. Every firm is unique and will use a selection of the techniques referenced in the ESG Integration Framework.

15. In relation to materiality assessment, which of the following is correct?

    a. The materiality assessment is typically contained in the valuation stage.

Self Practice and Self Assessment

b. Materiality is measured in terms of likelihood and magnitude of impact on a company's financial performance.

c. Evidence that non-material factors impact financials, valuations, and company business models.

d. Ethical or impact investors judge material factors affecting social, environmental, and maximum financial returns.

16. Which of the following best represents the chronological order for ESG scorecard development?

   a. Approach a)

Step 1	Determine a scoring system based on what good or best practice looks like for each indicator or issue.
Step 2	Assess a company and give it a score.
Step 3	Identify sector- or company-specific ESG items.
Step 4	Benchmark the company's performance against industry averages or peer group.
Step 5	Calculate aggregated scores at issue level, dimension level, or total score level.
Step 6	Break down issues into a number of indicators.

   b. Approach b)

Step 1	Determine a scoring system based on what good or best practice looks like for each indicator or issue.
Step 2	Break down issues into a number of indicators.
Step 3	Assess a company and give it a score.
Step 4	Identify sector- or company-specific ESG items.
Step 5	Calculate aggregated scores at issue level, dimension level, or total score level.
Step 6	Benchmark the company's performance against industry averages or peer group.

   c. Approach c)

Step 1	Identify sector- or company-specific ESG items.
Step 2	Break down issues into a number of indicators.
Step 3	Determine a scoring system based on what good or best practice looks like for each indicator or issue.
Step 4	Assess a company and give it a score.
Step 5	Calculate aggregated scores at issue level, dimension level, or total score level.
Step 6	Benchmark the company's performance against industry averages or peer group.

   d. Approach d)

Step 1	Identify sector- or company-specific ESG items.
Step 2	Assess a company and give it a score.
Step 3	Break down issues into a number of indicators.
Step 4	Determine a scoring system based on what good or best practice looks like for each indicator or issue.

Step 5   Calculate aggregated scores at issue level, dimension level, or total score level.

Step 6   Benchmark the company's performance against industry averages or peer group.

17. Which of these is *not* an ESG-integrated valuation technique?
    a. Adjusting sales growth assumptions due to weak employee engagement scores
    b. Adjusting cost of capital due to poor governance ratings
    c. Adjusting cash flows due to cash tax adjustments
    d. Changing fair value price/earnings (PE) ratio due to strong sustainability scores

18. An analyst assesses a company as below average on ESG metrics. All other matters being equal, she is most likely to:
    a. give a PE premium to the stock.
    b. increase the company's cost of capital.
    c. increase the terminal growth rate assumption in a DCF model.
    d. reduce the risk of default in her forecast models.

19. This question relates to the case study focusing on the beverages company. Which of the following are examples of material environmental factors that should be considered?
    a. Talent retention, recruitment strategy.
    b. Water efficiency, greenhouse gas emissions (GHG).
    c. Supplier code-of-conduct protocols, product mix.
    d. Human rights strategy, anti-bribery policy.

20. The aims and objectives for integrating ESG into an investment process may include:
    a. Meeting requirements under Principles for Responsible Investment (PRI) regulations.
    b. Increasing reputational risk at a firm and investment level.
    c. Meeting internal audit demands.
    d. Improving the quality of engagement and stewardship activities, and increasing investment returns.

21. Disclosure and data-related challenges for ESG integration include:
    a. data consistency.
    b. data scarcity.
    c. data incompleteness and lack of audited data.
    d. all of the above.

22. Which of the following is NOT used by a fixed-income practitioner when evaluating ESG aspects?
    a. Bankruptcy risk
    b. Proxy voting
    c. Negative credit events
    d. Time horizons

Self Practice and Self Assessment

23. Which of the following best represents factors least considered by CRAs?
    a. Bankruptcy risk, standard credit ratio analysis, litigation risk
    b. Bankruptcy risk, litigation risk, human capital risk
    c. Environmental risk, religious or ethical risk
    d. Environmental risk, standard credit ratio analysis, governance risk

24. Which of the following factors is generally considered the most important when evaluating ESG considerations around sovereign debt?
    a. Environmental factors
    b. Social factors
    c. Governance factors
    d. Human capital factors

25. Which of the following statements best describes a green bond?
    a. Bonds that finance green projects
    b. Bonds that meet certain ratings criteria
    c. Bonds that get the green light based on governance guidelines
    d. Bonds that are evergreen and roll on for a specified duration

SOLUTIONS

1. A is correct. An investment firm might have several different aims and objectives for integrating ESG into an investment process. These can include the following:

    - meeting requirements under fiduciary duty or regulations
    - meeting client and beneficiary demands
    - lowering investment risk
    - increasing investment returns
    - giving investment professionals more tools and techniques to use in analysis
    - improving the quality of engagement and stewardship activities
    - lowering reputational risk at a firm level and investment level

2. B is correct. Regardless of the ESG analysis classification as qualitative or quantitative, there are many types of tools used by investors. These tools of ESG analysis may include:

    - red flag indicators
    - company questionnaires and management interviews
    - checks with outside experts
    - watch lists
    - internal ESG research
    - external ESG research

3. C is correct. The elements of ESG integration include the following:

    - adjusting forecast financials
    - adjusting valuation models or multiples
    - adjusting credit risk and duration
    - managing risk
    - ESG factor tilts
    - ESG momentum tilts
    - strategic asset allocation
    - tactical asset allocation
    - ESG controversies and positive ESG events

4. A is correct. Firms and investment teams might not have ESG factors embedded in their philosophy but still use ESG techniques within investment processes. These can run alongside a financial analysis or have integrated aspects to the analysis. The typical stages of an integrated ESG investment are

    - a research stage,
    - a valuation stage, and
    - a portfolio construction stage, which leads to investment decisions.

5. B is correct. Risk mapping means mapping a portfolio or investable universe against a specific ESG risk (e.g., climate risk or water-related risks). Examples of risk-mapping methodologies include carbon footprinting or testing portfolios against different climate scenarios.

Solutions

6. C is correct. Weak governance identified in a private company (proved by board with poor skills, not independent, non-diversified thinking):

    ▸ increased risk of negative capital allocation decisions
    ▸ lower future cash flows or difficulty in initial public offering (IPO) to capital markets
    ▸ lower valuation or increased bankruptcy risk

7. A is correct. The judgment of an E factor, such as exposure to carbon, leads to analysis on the risk to debt pricing. It complements a traditional take on default risk. High carbon intensity:

    ▸ increased risk from carbon taxes
    ▸ increased cost of debt for new project financing
    ▸ higher taxes
    ▸ increased balance sheet risk of default on debt
    ▸ change in debt rating
    ▸ lower value of corporate debt

8. A is correct. Practitioners assess the impact of material financial and ESG factors on the corporate and investment performance of a company and make adjustments to:

    ▸ forecasted financials
    ▸ valuation-model variables (e.g., cost of capital or terminal growth rates in DCF analysis)
    ▸ valuation multiples
    ▸ forecasted financial ratios
    ▸ internal credit assessments
    ▸ assumptions in qualitative or quantitative models

    Rather than changing model discount assumptions, explicit sales or margin assumptions may also be adjusted. For example, an analysis of a company's strong management of its employees (as assessed by employee engagement or satisfaction metrics) leads to an assessment of strong future customer satisfaction, which in turn leads to sales forecasts five years out being raised to above the industry average to account for this strong social factor score.

9. C is correct. One of the most common criticisms of ESG investing is the difficulty for investors to correctly identify, and appropriately weigh, ESG factors in investment selection. Critics express concerns about the precision, validity, and reliability of ESG investment strategies. One concern is of ESG mutual funds and exchange-traded holding investments in companies that may be acknowledged as "bad actors" in one or more of the ESG spaces.

10. B is correct. The ways that E and S factors transmit to economic growth and potential can also be indirect, and the way CRAs assess this is still evolving. The G factor is a more obvious and direct assessment, which has been analyzed historically. *The link between ESG ratings and credit ratings is still hotly debated among investors.* Proponents might point to a Barclays' study looking at a high ESG portfolio versus a low ESG portfolio using two different ESG datasets (MSCI and Sustainalytics). The case for sustainable bond investing strengthens, but critics would point out the flaws of correlational studies as well as the short 2009–18 time period. Critics further point out that the factor attributions post-2008/2009

(the financial crisis) and some ESG ratings correlate with quality factors (though not all).

11. D is correct.
12. B is correct.
13. A is correct.
14. C is correct.
15. B is correct.
16. C is correct.
17. C is correct.
18. B is correct.
19. B is correct.
20. D is correct.
21. D is correct.
22. B is correct.
23. C is correct.
24. C is correct.
25. A is correct.

CHAPTER 8

Integrated Portfolio Construction and Management

LEARNING OUTCOMES

Mastery — The candidate should be able to:

- ☐ 8.1.1 explain the impact of ESG factors on strategic asset allocation
- ☐ 8.1.2 describe approaches for integrating ESG into the portfolio management process
- ☐ 8.1.3 explain approaches for how internal and external ESG research and analysis is used by portfolio managers to make investment decisions
- ☐ 8.1.4 explain the different approaches to screening and the benefits and limitations of the main approaches
- ☐ 8.1.5 explain the main indexes and benchmarking approaches applicable to sustainable and ESG investing, noting potential limitations
- ☐ 8.1.6 apply ESG screens to the main asset classes and their sub-sectors: fixed income; equities; and alternative investments
- ☐ 8.1.7 distinguish between ESG screening of individual companies and collective investment funds: on an absolute basis; relative to sector/peer group data
- ☐ 8.1.8 explain how ESG integration impacts the risk–return dynamic of portfolio optimization
- ☐ 8.1.9 evaluate the different types of ESG analysis/SRI investment in terms of key objectives, investment considerations, and risks: full ESG integration; exclusionary screening; positive alignment/best-in-class; active ownership; thematic investing; impact investing; other
- ☐ 8.1.10 describe approaches to managing passive ESG portfolios

1 INTRODUCTION TO INTEGRATED PORTFOLIO CONSTRUCTION AND MANAGEMENT

Environmental, social, and governance (ESG) integration occurs at different levels of the investment process, each necessitating its own framework for analysis and implementation. Where previous chapters have described ESG integration at the underlying security level, this chapter examines different approaches, research, and methodologies for integrating ESG assessment at higher levels of the investment decision-making process, starting at strategic asset allocation (SAA) and moving on to portfolio construction and management.

Much of the existing evidence supporting ESG integration draws upon single security and issuer case studies. The fact that ESG integration is comparatively less developed as investors elevate the decision-making process to higher levels — asset allocation, fund manager selection, and portfolio investment — makes it an exciting area for innovation. This is particularly true as investors build more robust ESG capabilities outside of the traditional equities focus of ESG. These areas include:

- mixed assets;
- real assets; and
- sovereign debt.

Nonetheless, investors should recognize the trade-offs — both explicit and implicit — to risk-adjusted returns when integrating ESG screening approaches.

Accordingly, this chapter draws upon portfolio management theory complemented with examples of investment best practices to:

- discuss research, approaches, and challenges to embedding ESG investing risk into global asset allocation models;
- examine how ESG investing can be applied to approaches across asset classes and different strategy types;
- consider how ESG can leverage quantitative research methods to understand risk exposure and performance return dynamics in portfolios; and
- differentiate between actively and passively managed ESG strategies.

2 INTEGRATING ESG: STRATEGIC ASSET ALLOCATION MODELS

☐ **8.1.1** explain the impact of ESG factors on strategic asset allocation

One of the most exciting, yet least developed, areas in ESG integration is the degree and means to which it can inform and shape the strategic asset allocation decision-making process. For asset owners and multi-asset managers, asset allocation represents the most important, top-down decision that will carry wide-ranging implications depending on exposure to asset classes and investment strategy types. Indeed, the strategic asset allocation policy may account for as much as 90% of the variability in investment returns of a typical fund over time.[1]

---

[1] Ibbotson, R.G., and P.D. Kaplan. 2000. "Does Asset Allocation Policy Explain 40, 90, or 100 Percent of Performance?" *Financial Analysts Journal* 56 (1): 26–33. Available at: www.jstor.org/stable/4480220

Traditionally, institutional investors have managed systemic, macro-economic factors by coupling asset allocation strategies alongside asset/liability management (ALM). Where strategic asset allocation establishes return targets across asset classes (equities, fixed income, real assets, etc.) and investment strategy types (i.e., alternatives), ALM provides investors the tools with which to match the cash flows of assets to payment of liabilities. For example, both of these elements are vital for the sustainability of a pension fund's risk-adjusted returns and its ability to pay out pension benefits for its beneficiaries.[2]

A considerable misalignment exists between investors' traditional efforts, which emphasize integrating ESG in individual securities, assets, and companies, and the much broader, systemic exercise of strategic asset allocation. As discussed in both Chapter 7 of this book and later on in this chapter, ESG is most commonly integrated at the security level, complemented by more recent, increasingly sophisticated efforts to express ESG risk at a composite portfolio level. As a consequence, asset allocators often cede responsibility for active ESG integration to these underlying levels. Said another way, if an allocator believes that ESG risk resides at the underlying, security selection level, then integrating ESG at the asset allocation level may prove a redundant exercise. If, on the other hand, the allocator believes that ESG risk (e.g., climate risk) represents a top-down risk factor, then integrating ESG within the asset allocation process makes sense in light of more specific climate implications (e.g., coastal retreat to coastal property exposure).

Different asset allocation approaches carry important implications for the degree of ESG integration. A strategic asset allocation approach is constructed over a multi-decade period representing several economic cycles, an investment timeframe that clearly warrants the long-term consideration of financial and non-financial ESG effects like climate risk. Dynamic (or tactical) asset allocation, on the other hand, establishes an initial asset allocation mix with the aim to continually review and recalibrate this allocation mix under much shorter intervals using traditional factors to maintain the original target mix. However, there is a risk that continual rebalancing in shorter time intervals may ultimately diminish the value of ESG integration in **dynamic asset allocation**.

It could be argued that one result of the emphasis of ESG integration on equities exposure (versus other asset classes) is the relative underdevelopment of other asset classes and investment strategies. Challenges clearly exist in many alternative areas, but greater coverage beyond equities and corporate fixed income has now made ESG integration at the strategic asset allocation level more relevant. In addition, ESG research on top-down strategic asset allocation has tended to focus on environmental criteria, essentially exposure and sensitivity to assumptions around climate risk rather than through a broader ESG lens.

---

2 Bohne, A., and M. Elkenbracht-Huizing. 2018. *The Handbook of ALM in Banking: Managing New Challenges for Interest Rates, Liquidity and the Balance Sheet*. London: Risk Books.

Exhibit 1: Strategic Asset Allocation Models and Their Suitability to ESG

Model	Features	Potential link to ESG issues	Outputs to reflect ESG issues
Mean–variance optimization (MVO)[3]	MVO results in the construction of an efficient frontier that represents a mix of assets that produces the minimum standard deviation (as a proxy for risk) for the maximum level of expected return. It is based on defined asset class buckets and long-term expected returns, risks, and correlations. The Black-Litterman Global Asset Allocation is an MVO model, using the Markowitz portfolio optimization model or modern portfolio theory (MPT).	MVO is highly sensitive to baseline assumptions, making it imperative to fully understand any revised assumptions due to ESG considerations. MVO is highly dependent on historical data as the baseline, with adjustments made to reflect future expectations. Volatility as a proxy for risk does not work well in cases of fat tail risk and large market swings.	ESG issues could have an impact on assumptions regarding expected return, volatility, and correlation at the asset and sub-asset class level. ESG issues also have the potential to expand the regional and asset class mix and to add new sub-asset classes to align with the pursuit of positive real-world impact.
Factor risk allocation[4]	Factor risk frameworks seek to build a diversified portfolio based on sources of risk. They typically include such factors as fundamental risks (gross domestic product [GDP], interest rates, and inflation) as well as market risks (equity risk premium, illiquidity, and volatility).	The macroeconomic links to ESG issues are more difficult to quantify with precision from a purely top-down perspective. Market risk factors can be built from the bottom-up using asset and sector level analysis.	ESG issues could require a change to baseline factor risk assumptions. Factor risk allocation offers the potential to build in new ESG-related risk factors (such as climate change) to improve diversification (particularly across market risk factors).
Total portfolio analysis (TPA)[5]	Similar to factor risk allocation, TPA allows for closer review and interplay between the strategy setting process and alignment of investment goals. Based on an agreed risk budget, asset allocations are made on expected risk exposures and are less constrained by asset class 'buckets' than are traditional MVO approaches.	TPA is relevant to consider ESG issues that require the interplay between judgment about the future and quantitative analysis. TPA requires specialist knowledge to make informed judgments about future risk.	TPA's emphasis on risk budgeting and allocation of capital to opportunities within that budget (bringing alignment between top-down and bottom-up) would provide greater flexibility to capture the potential winners and losers in scenario analysis that also incorporate ESG-related issues.

---

3 Markowitz, H. 1952. "Portfolio Selection." *Journal of Finance* 7 (1): 77–91. Available at: https://doi.org/10.1111/j.1540-6261.1952.tb01525.x Widely-used models to generate the inputs for portfolio optimization (including estimates of asset returns) include Black Litterman (1991) (www.blacklitterman.org), with a range of asset return estimation techniques subsequently being developed.

4 For example, see: Idzorek, T. M., and M. Kowara. 2013. "Factor-Based Asset Allocation vs. Asset-Class-Based Asset Allocation." *Financial Analysts Journal* 69 (3). Available at: www.cfainstitute.org/research/financial-analysts-journal/2013/factor-based-asset-allocation-vs-asset-class-based-asset-allocation

5 Bass, R., S. Gladstone, and A. Ang. 2017. "Total Portfolio Factor, Not Just Asset, Allocation." *Journal of Portfolio Management Special QES Issue* 43 (5): 38–53. Available at: https://media.top1000funds.com/wp-content/uploads/2017/10/25154404/Total-portfolio-factor-not-just-asset-allocation-2.pdf

Model	Features	Potential link to ESG issues	Outputs to reflect ESG issues
Dynamic asset allocation (DAA)[6]	DAA is driven by changes in risk tolerance, typically induced by cumulative performance relative to investment goals or an approaching investment horizon.	DAA could introduce an additional source of estimation errors due to the need for dynamic rebalancing.	DAA has the potential to reflect changes in baseline assumptions over different time horizons.
Liability driven asset allocation[7]	Liability driven investment (LDI) seeks to find the most efficient asset class mix driven by a fund's liabilities. It is simultaneously concerned with the return of the assets, the change in value of the liabilities, and how assets and liabilities interact to determine the overall portfolio value.	LDI encounters the same limitations as MVO, with high sensitivity to baseline assumptions.	Some ESG issues could potentially impact on inflation and alter liability assumptions.
Regime switching models[8]	Regime switching approaches model abrupt and persistent changes in financial variables due to shifts in regulations, policies, and other secular changes. They capture fat tails, skewness, and time-varying correlations.	Regime switching approaches are relevant for considering ESG issues where an abrupt shift is expected over time. They are also typically based more on forward looking rather than historical data.	These approaches have the potential to capture dramatic shifts in the investment environment. These models are not yet widely used by investment practitioners.

Source: Adapted from Principles for Responsible Investment (PRI).[9]

Within the asset allocation framework shown in Exhibit 1, one of the most promising approaches may well be the **Black–Litterman asset allocation model (BLM)**.

While the Markowitz-derived MVO approach has garnered significant academic support, mean–variance theory poses a number of limitations. For it to function, MVO requires estimates for asset returns across each asset class, which makes the model incredibly sensitive and input-dependent. Any adjustments (even minor ones) to these return estimates will produce a dramatic change in allocation output, so investors may find the model hard to practically implement.

By comparison, BLM represents a more intuitive approach. Anchored by the global equilibrium market and not requiring return estimates for each asset class, it can arguably better accommodate areas like pricing climate risk.[10]

Notwithstanding ESG integration, diversification is a key consideration within any asset allocation framework. Because ESG research has traditionally been equities focused, its relevance has tended to be muted or at best underrepresented within multi- and mixed-asset allocation. As ESG research improves — from a better quantitative understanding of ESG risk implications to the extension into other asset classes beyond equities and fixed income — its relevance within a multi-asset allocation context should increase.

---

[6] For an overview of various dynamic asset allocation techniques, see: Jarvis, S., A. Lawrence, and S. Miao. 2012. "Dynamic Asset Allocation Techniques." *British Actuarial Journal* 15 (3): 573–655.

[7] For example, see: Hoevenaars, P. M. M., R. D. J. Molenaar, P. C. Schotman, and T. B. M. Steenkamp. 2008. "Strategic Asset Allocation with Liabilities: Beyond Stocks and Bonds." *Journal of Economic Dynamics and Control* 32 (9): 2939–2970.

[8] Ang, A., and Timmerman. 2011. "Regime Changes and Financial Markets." NBER Working Paper No. 17182. Available at: www.nber.org/papers/w17182

[9] PRI. 2019. "Embedding ESG Issues into Strategic Asset Allocation Frameworks." Discussion paper. Available at: www.unpri.org/embedding-esg-issues-into-strategic-asset-allocation-frameworks-discussion-paper/4815.article

[10] For more information, see: Daniel, K. D., R. B., Litterman, and G. Wagner. 2018. "Applying Asset Pricing Theory to Calibrate the Price of Climate Change." NBER Working Paper No. 22795. Available at: www.nber.org/papers/w22795

Despite an increasing amount of academic work (see such meta-analyses as those by Friede, Busch, and Bussen)[11] supporting ESG's effect on risk-adjusted returns, introducing ESG into the asset allocation process will undoubtedly carry exposure and weighting implications that must be considered relative to a standard, non-ESG asset mix strategy. In other words, integrating a given ESG methodology (e.g., positive screening that tilts the overall asset mix to a higher-than-mean ESG rating) will introduce some diversification effect or skewness.

To be sure, this effect may well be intended. In theory, managing a mixed-asset portfolio according to a carbon constraint or desired exposure level should reduce the risk to a carbon pricing shock through lower commensurate exposure to carbon-intensive, coal-reliant utilities and potential stranded assets. There are trade-offs that investors must consider when allocating to ESG or 'sustainability' more broadly. Portfolio risk can be divided into two portions:

1. the isolated risk of the individual asset or individual investment strategy; and
2. the correlation risk that emerges from the combination of all the assets and strategies.

Climate change — and thus climate risk — has emerged as the most material ESG factor for institutional investors to address within asset allocation strategies. Climate risk is both systemic and local. It threatens the financial system and the global means of production as much as it poses risk on a more localized level for specific regions, sectors, and companies. Its potential physical risks will manifest in both acute, event-driven forms (such as extreme weather) and longer-term, chronic shifts driven by the effects of elevated temperatures and rising sea levels.

Exhibit 2: Macro-Economic Climate Considerations by Asset Class

Asset Classes	Subtypes	SAA/ALM Implications	Climate Change Considerations
Equities	▸ Industries or sectors; ▸ growth vs. value; ▸ large, mid, or small cap; and ▸ long vs. short positions.	▸ Hedge against inflation, which can result from supply shocks and high government spending; and ▸ sensitive to growth, macro-economic performance.	▸ Sensitive to climate impacts on macro-economic performance.

---

11 Friede, G., T. Busch, and A. Bussen. 2015. "ESG and Financial Performance: Aggregated Evidence from More than 2,000 Empirical Studies." *Journal of Sustainable Finance & Investment* 5 (4): 210–233. Available at: https://doi.org/10.1080/20430795.2015.1118917

Asset Classes	Subtypes	SAA/ALM Implications	Climate Change Considerations
Fixed income	▸ Sovereign, municipal, corporate; and ▸ investment vs. non-investment grade (high yield).	▸ Sensitive to interest rates; and ▸ typically less volatile returns.	▸ Sensitive to fiscal policy related to climate challenges; ▸ sensitive to climate-related impacts on issuers' creditworthiness; and ▸ many climate impacts fall within the tenor of long-term debt.
Alternative investments	▸ Real estate investment trusts (REITs); ▸ commodities; ▸ currencies; ▸ private equity, venture capital (VC) funds; and ▸ derivatives, hedge funds.	▸ Attractive for diversification and for low or inverse correlation to market returns; and ▸ heterogeneous and wide-ranging risk/return profiles.	▸ Diversification offered by alternative assets may allow for greater hedging of climate risk; and ▸ climate risk exposure may be concentrated, opaque, or difficult to assess.

Source: Climate Finance Advisors and Ortec Finance (2019).[12]

It is also clear that climate change represents different risks across asset classes. Accordingly, portfolio managers must recognize that a company's capital structure will naturally reflect risk. For example, carbon-intensive companies like coal-powered utilities without an adaptation strategy will be at risk in the transition to a low-carbon economy. In such a scenario, equity shareholders (who are subordinate to creditors and bondholders in the capital structure) will be disproportionately impacted. Hence, asset allocation strategies must recognize asset class sensitivity alongside systemic and company-specific risks.

As well as being one of the key recommendations of the **Task Force on Climate-related Financial Disclosures (TCFD)** framework, climate scenario analysis is as important in the wider asset allocation process as it is in understanding the micro, macro, and ESG sensitivities within a single investment portfolio. What might that look like in an asset allocation context? The asset allocator would work to sensitize the portfolio against different warming scenarios using the 1.5°C (2.7°F) as promoted in the Paris Agreement of 2015 as a baseline.[13] Different scenarios should stress test different asset classes across regions, sectors, time periods, and temperature assumptions to understand risks that are now formally characterized as:

▸ **Physical risks.** These represent the physical risks manifested by climate change that may impact businesses' operations, strategy, infrastructure, workforce, or markets; they may carry wider implications across the investment value chain and to the financial system.

---
12 Climate Finance Advisors and Ortec Finance. 2019. *Scenario Analysis for Systemic Climate Risk.* Available at: https://climatefinanceadvisors.com/wp-content/uploads/2019/09/310-002-Climate-Risk-Report_V5.pdf
13 Task Force on Climate-related Financial Disclosures. 2019. *2019 Status Report.* Available at: www.fsb-tcfd.org/wp-content/uploads/2019/06/2019-TCFD-Status-Report-FINAL-053119.pdf

▶ **Transition risks**. These are the risks represented by legal, regulatory, policy, technology, and market change in the transition to a low carbon economy. Stranded asset risk, for example, would qualify as a transition risk for a portfolio.

Investors will inherently be exposed to varying degrees of both physical and transition risks in their investment portfolios. Strategic asset allocation is particularly useful in determining where these risks lie across different asset classes and strategy types over a multi-decade period. Depending on the extent of asset reallocation, some of these choices may require near-term versus long-term trade-offs. For example, reducing (or outright divesting) portfolio concentration to highly carbon-intensive investments in the energy sector will decrease exposure to long-term transition risk. However, this decision may in turn reduce the portfolio income yield as the energy sector is generally associated with an above market cashflow profile and dividend income stream unless capital is redeployed in another sector with similar yield characteristics.[14]

> ### CASE STUDIES
>
> ### The Path towards Net Zero
>
> The urgency to respond to the growing climate crisis is driving both national and corporate commitments towards Paris-aligned net zero carbon emissions targets. Greater emphasis on targets, timetables, and disclosure — particularly with regard to forward-looking data to describe the shape of the transition — is leading to an improved understanding for portfolio management analysis.
>
> The following initiatives can be seen to operate as epistemic communities[15] as they are vital in developing, advancing, and disseminating methodologies and tools to support efforts to decarbonize and Paris-align portfolios over the next several decades.
>
> ### Paris Aligned Investment Initiative (PAII)[16]
>
> Launched in 2019 by the Institutional Investors Group on Climate Change (IIGCC), PAII is a European asset owner-coordinated and led initiative working to develop methodologies and assessment tools related to aligning investment portfolios to the Paris Agreement. PAII's work includes the *Net Zero Investment Framework*, which defines element of a net zero strategy and offers recommended approaches and actions for investors to take in order to measure and align portfolios towards net zero carbon emissions.
>
> ### Transition Pathway Initiative (TPI)[17]
>
> Established in 2017, TPI is a global, asset-owner driven, asset-manager supported initiative developed in partnership with the Grantham Research Institute on Climate Change and the Environment at the London School of Economics. Supporting the transition towards a low-carbon economy, the TPI dataset and

---

14 Litterman, R. 2015. "David Swensen on the Fossil Fuel Divestment Debate." *Financial Analysts Journal* 71 (3): 11. Available at: www.cfainstitute.org/research/financial-analysts-journal/2015/david-swensen-on-the-fossil-fuel-divestment-debate
15 An epistemic community is a network of knowledge-based experts who help decision makers define the problems they face, identify various policy solutions, and assess the policy outcomes.
16 IIGCC. 2021. *Paris Aligned Investment Initiative*. Available at: www.iigcc.org/our-work/paris-aligned-investment-initiative/
17 Transition Pathway Initiative (TPI). 2021. *The TPI Tool*. Available at: www.transitionpathwayinitiative.org

tool utilize forward-looking carbon metrics to measure and determine companies' pathways relative to three benchmark scenarios defined by the Paris Agreement. Under TPI, companies are measured in two ways:

1. the quality of companies' governance and management of their greenhouse gas (GHG) emissions; and
2. carbon emissions relative to international targets and national commitments as defined by the Paris Agreement.

Net Zero Asset Owner Alliance[18]

Launched in 2019, the United Nations-convened Net Zero Asset Owner Alliance is a group of international asset owners who have committed to achieving emissions neutral investment portfolios by 2050 or sooner, supporting global efforts to limit temperature rises to 1.5°C (2.7°F). The Alliance recently finalized its 2025 Target Setting Protocol, which outlines how asset owners calculate and establish climate targets within portfolios and allocate capital towards decarbonization efforts.

Net Zero Asset Managers Initiative[19]

Launched in 2020, the Net Zero Asset Managers Initiative is a group of international asset managers who support the goal of net zero GHG emissions by 2050 or sooner, in line with efforts under the Paris Agreement to limit temperature rises to 1.5°C (2.7°F). Asset manager signatories also commit to support investing aligned with net zero emissions by 2050 or sooner.[20]

Net Zero Company Benchmark

The Net Zero Company Benchmark was developed and launched in 2020 by Climate Action 100+, an investor-led initiative that engages with the world's largest corporate greenhouse gas emitters to drive action. The Benchmark assesses corporate climate commitments based on publicly-available information to understand alignment to climate priorities (strong governance, reduced greenhouse gas emissions, and improved corporate disclosure) and to support investor engagement action.[21]

It is worth highlighting new literature that introduces the notion of the **Inevitable Policy Response (IPR)**.[22] IPR assumes that, in the current environment where the policy response to climate change is inadequate — perhaps best characterized as 'business as usual' — governments may potentially respond to increasing climate-borne damage in a sudden reflex reaction.

IPR may take shape through the introduction of economic incentives, such as a carbon tax or the formation of national carbon markets. It may also include other measures, including more stringent environmental regulations requiring greater levels of mitigation-associated capital investment for highly exposed companies. The nature and magnitude of IPR may carry considerable implications for an investment

---

18 PRI. 2020. *UN-Convened Net-Zero Asset Owner Alliance.* Available at: www.unpri.org/climate-change/un-convened-net-zero-asset-owner-alliance/5370.article
19 Net Zero Asset Managers Initiative. 2021. *Net Zero Asset Managers Initiative.* Available at: www.netzeroassetmanagers.org
20 Net Zero Asset Managers Initiative. 2021. *Inaugural 2025 Target Setting Protocol.* Available at: www.unepfi.org/wordpress/wp-content/uploads/2021/01/Alliance-Target-Setting-Protocol-2021.pdf
21 Climate Action 100+. 2021. *Net-Zero Company Benchmark.* Available at: www.climateaction100.org/progress/net-zero-company-benchmark
22 PRI. 2021. *What Is the Inevitable Policy Response?* Available at: www.unpri.org/inevitable-policy-response/what-is-the-inevitable-policy-response/4787.article

portfolio, particularly in the speed and scope of transition risk. Hence, more sophisticated approaches designed to understand the sensitivity of an investment portfolio to climate policy-related shocks and simulations are warranted as risk measures.

Climate-related portfolio analysis is nascent enough that it is worth highlighting the approaches of two practitioners, Mercer and Ortec Finance. Mercer has continued to refine its climate scenario model, now integrating it into a long-term, strategic asset allocation methodology that extends to 2100. Mercer's report *Investing in a Time of Climate Change* also addresses the need to enlarge asset allocation models beyond equities. This Mercer report formally extends its climate-informed asset allocation process to sustainability-themed equity, private equity, and real assets, including natural resources and infrastructure.

Exhibit 3: Illustrative Approach for Modeling the Investment Impacts of Climate Change

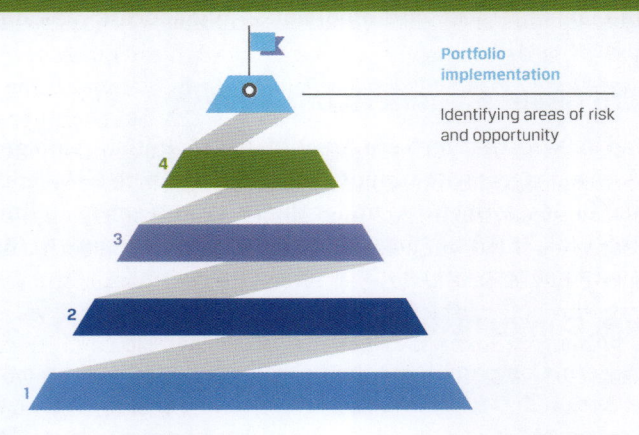

Portfolio implementation — Identifying areas of risk and opportunity

Climate change modelling and literature review
The modelling foundations are provided by a third-party macroeconomic model, E3ME, which draws upon the "GENIE" integrated assessment model (IAM). IAMs combine climate science and economic data to estimate the costs of mitigation, adaptation and physical damages.

Risk factors and scenarios
Three climate change scenarios provide a framework for the relative impacts for identified climate change risk factors over time.

Asset sensitivity
The sensitivity to the climate change risk factors is determined for different asset classes and industry sectors.

Portfolio implications
The sensitivity and scenarios are integrated into Mercer's investment modelling tool to estimate the impact of climate change on investment portfolio returns.

Source: Mercer.[23]

Ortec Finance's approach integrates climate risks into financial scenarios, which include transition, physical and extreme weather impacts, and pricing dynamics to cover all asset classes. For example, Exhibit 4 illustrates the impact on a representative UK pension fund portfolio over two different investment horizons and against three simulations — Orderly, Disorderly, and Failed — calibrated against the Paris Agreement.

---

23 Mercer. 2019. *Investing in a Time of Climate Change: The Sequel.* Available at: www.mercer.com.au/our-thinking/wealth/climate-change-the-sequel.html

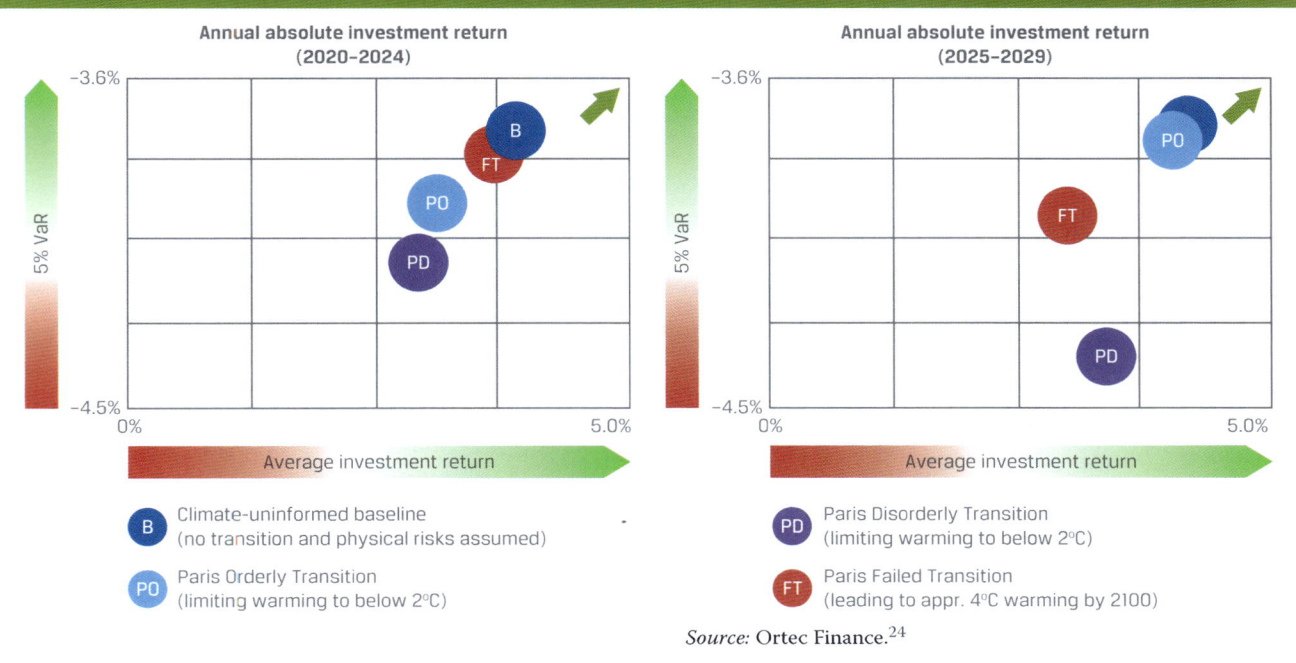

Integrating ESG: Strategic Asset Allocation Models

Exhibit 4: Investment Return of a Representative Pension Fund's Portfolio in Different Climate Pathways and Time Buckets (Stylized Risk–Return Projections)

Source: Ortec Finance.[24]

In the **nearer-term simulation (2020–2024)**, climate transition risks point to lower expected investment returns relative to the Paris-aligned pathways (Orderly and Disorderly). While a **Paris Orderly Transition** gradually prices in lower earnings expectations across the 2020–2024 period, a **Paris Disorderly Transition** represents an earnings correction that produces a shock in 2024 and higher subsequent volatility.

In the **later-term simulation (2025–2029)**, the average investment return in an orderly transition is similar to the climate-uninformed baseline where transition risk and physical risks are not modeled. In contrast, both the Paris Disorderly and Failed Transitions point to lower expected investment returns.

- In the **Paris Disorderly Transition pathway**, the sentiment shock occurring in 2025 and subsequent increase in volatility remain until 2026.
- The **Paris Failed Transition pathway** — characterizing a business-as-usual-scenario that brings about a 4°C (5.4°F) temperature increase by 2100 — leads to diminishing investment returns as the impact of physical risk increases.

---

24 Ortec Finance. 2019. *Scenario Analysis for Systemic Climate Risk: The Case for Assessing the Impacts of Climate Change on Macro-Economic Indicators Used by Institutional Investors.* Available at: https://climatefinanceadvisors.com/wp-content/uploads/2019/09/310-002-Climate-Risk-Report_V5.pdf

3 INTEGRATING ESG: ASSET MANAGER SELECTION

8.1.1 explain the impact of ESG factors on strategic asset allocation

Within the wider asset allocation process, it is also worth highlighting that allocators are increasingly integrating ESG factors and expectations into their manager selection process. Indeed, the PRI recently published a resource guide for asset owners who allocate to ESG investment managers.[25]

Allocators range from traditional asset owners, such as pension funds, to fund of funds (FoF) and multi-manager investment strategies. Rather than investing directly into securities and issuers, multi-manager strategies focus on building a platform of strong individual fund managers. These platforms may either focus on internally-managed funds from the same investment firm or funds managed by external managers as well.

Due diligence in regard to manager selection combines qualitative and quantitative metrics that, within a framework, track the development, performance, and improvement of managers. Many of the larger multi-manager and fund of funds platforms typically track, monitor, and assess between a hundred and several hundred individual portfolio managers. These multi-manager platforms then review this long list of tracked managers in order to reduce this list to a short list or watch list, ultimately tightening this to a final focus list of managers to allocate capital. In this respect, due diligence focuses on establishing baseline metrics to evaluate and compare managers. Metrics may include:

- the existence of an ESG policy;
- affiliation with investor initiatives, such as the Principles for Responsible Investment (PRI);
- accountability in the form of dedicated personnel and committee oversight;
- the manner and degree in which ESG is integrated in the investment process;
- ownership and stewardship activities; and
- client reporting capabilities.

Exhibit 5 depicts an example of a high-level manager selection process, in this case developed by BlackRock Alternative Advisors (BAA).

---

25 PRI. 2020. *Asset Owner Technical Guide – Investment Manager Selection*. Available at: https://www.unpri.org/manager-selection/asset-owner-technical-guide-investment-manager-selection-guide/6573.article

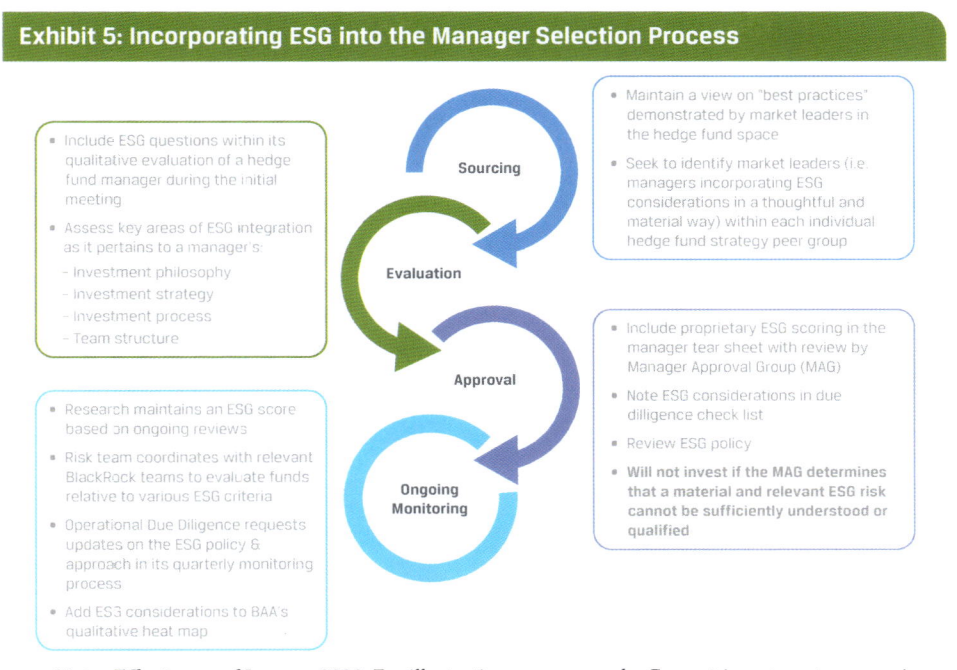

Integrating ESG: Asset Manager Selection

Exhibit 5: Incorporating ESG into the Manager Selection Process

Sourcing
- Maintain a view on "best practices" demonstrated by market leaders in the hedge fund space
- Seek to identify market leaders (i.e. managers incorporating ESG considerations in a thoughtful and material way) within each individual hedge fund strategy peer group

Evaluation
- Include ESG questions within its qualitative evaluation of a hedge fund manager during the initial meeting
- Assess key areas of ESG integration as it pertains to a manager's:
  - Investment philosophy
  - Investment strategy
  - Investment process
  - Team structure

Approval
- Include proprietary ESG scoring in the manager tear sheet with review by Manager Approval Group (MAG)
- Note ESG considerations in due diligence check list
- Review ESG policy
- Will not invest if the MAG determines that a material and relevant ESG risk cannot be sufficiently understood or qualified

Ongoing Monitoring
- Research maintains an ESG score based on ongoing reviews
- Risk team coordinates with relevant BlackRock teams to evaluate funds relative to various ESG criteria
- Operational Due Diligence requests updates on the ESG policy & approach in its quarterly monitoring process
- Add ESG considerations to BAA's qualitative heat map

Notes: Effective as of January 2020. For illustrative purposes only. Current investment process is subject to change and based on market conditions, managers' opinions, and other factors.

Source: BlackRock Alternative Advisors.

As a whole, the due diligence process offers a more nuanced perspective into the degree of ESG integration and the investment approach adopted. A formal monitoring and reporting framework also provides a picture into the progress and evolution of a manager's ESG capabilities and resourcing. While much of this process naturally focuses on investment facing capabilities, from ESG data integration to dedicated investment strategies, due diligence also commonly assesses operational risk of the investment manager itself. The operational risk portion of manager due diligence may examine what organizational framework and oversight exist at the firm level to support ESG activities at the fund level:

- Has the manager instituted ESG and/or stewardship policies?
- What compliance measures are in place to ensure that exclusion-oriented and/or ESG constraint-based investment mandates and strategies are observed?

Furthermore, because of growing regulatory requirements, they may also examine the sophistication of ESG and climate risk reporting.

Accordingly, multi-manager and fund of funds platforms are increasingly integrating their own ESG capabilities into more formal scoring frameworks. For some platforms, these frameworks represent a spectrum of capabilities across different strategies. For more sophisticated platforms, these frameworks have gone beyond simply informing the manager selection process to now acting as a formal factor or weight in the overall manager selection and allocation process.

Exhibit 6 shows how LGT Capital Partners has tracked the development of ESG capabilities among its managers for seven years, with the data illustrating the progress among the hedge fund managers it monitors.

Exhibit 6: ESG Ratings by the Number of Managers

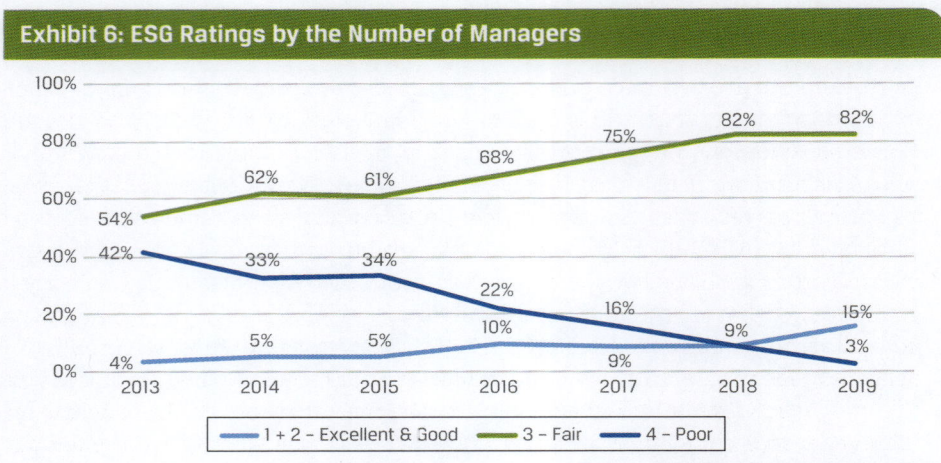

Year	1 + 2 – Excellent & Good	3 – Fair	4 – Poor
2013	4%	54%	42%
2014	5%	62%	33%
2015	5%	61%	34%
2016	10%	68%	22%
2017	9%	75%	16%
2018	9%	82%	9%
2019	15%	82%	3%

Source: LGT Capital Partners (2020).[26]

Exhibit 7 illustrates an example of a more complex fund of funds manager's approach, assessing the ESG capabilities among its underlying alternative managers. This stylized ranking summarizes due diligence performance at the operational (firm) level and at the investment (fund) level. What makes this exercise difficult is that it seeks to understand and score ESG capabilities across a range of strategy types, including arbitrage, credit, long/short, and macro investing. As we will later discuss, the nature of the underlying instruments or investment horizon or timeframe mean that ESG is more relevant and easily-applied for some portfolios than other strategies. The assessment also normalizes for firm size across funds, as smaller firms are generally less resourced and less able to absorb the financial costs of ESG compliance, research, data, and personnel requirements.

---

26 LGT Capital Partners. 2020. *ESG Report 2019*. Available at: www.lgtcp.com/shared/.content/publikationen/cp/esg_download/LGT-CP-ESG-Report-2019_en.pdf

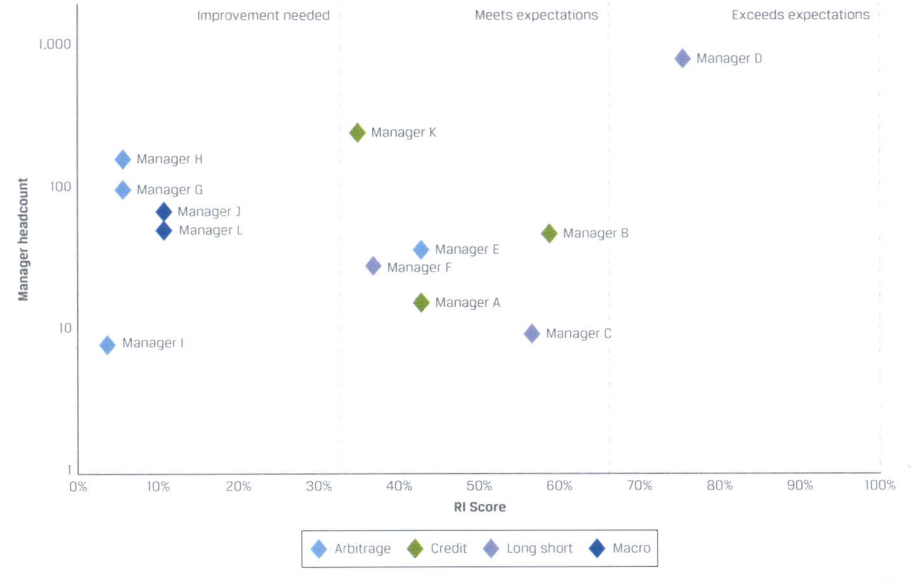

Exhibit 7: Assessing ESG Capabilities among a Platform of Alternative Managers

Source: Man FRM (2021).[27]

APPROACHES TO INTEGRATING ESG: PORTFOLIO LEVEL FRAMEWORK

4

- 8.1.2 describe approaches for integrating ESG into the portfolio management process
- 8.1.3 explain approaches for how internal and external ESG research and analysis is used by portfolio managers to make investment decisions

As earlier chapters demonstrate, there is a rich diversity of approaches for integrating ESG at the individual securities level. This heterogeneity is now carrying over to portfolio construction and management, where new methodologies and frameworks are leveraging ESG datasets with innovations that drive fundamental and quantitative, as well as active and passive, investment strategies.

The endgame for ESG integration at the portfolio level is the combination of top-down analytics and underlying ESG analysis to produce a more complete picture of ESG exposure and risk at the portfolio construction and management levels. In this respect, ESG integration within portfolio management requires a different manner of explanatory power than integration at the individual security level: It should embed ESG considerations into:

▶ the highest level, asset allocation decisions;

---

27 Man Group. 2021. *The Wheat from the Chaff – A Guide to Rating an RI Fund Manager*. Available at: www.man.com/maninstitute/wheat-and-chaff

- portfolio exposure to non-financial factors;
- risk management measures; and
- performance attribution.

Statistics published by the PRI are often used to frame investor activities in ESG integration. But what do these statistics really reveal about ESG integration at the portfolio level?[28]

Data compiled by Mercer Consulting (see Exhibit 8), one of the largest global institutional investment advisers, suggests that progress in ESG integration is marked by a high degree of variation depending on asset class and investment strategy type. What is perhaps more interesting, though, is that these data reinforce the notion that integration is broadly more advanced across managers despite being slower to manifest itself through formal- and dedicated sustainability-themed strategies.

Exhibit 8: Mercer Consulting's View on ESG Integration and Availability of Strategies by Asset Class

Asset Class	Manager Progress on ESG Integration*	Availability of Sustainability-Themed Strategies**
Public equity (active)	Medium/high	Low/medium
Fixed income	Low/medium	Low
Real estate	Medium/high	Low
Private equity and debt	Medium	Low/medium
Infrastructure	High	Medium/high
Natural resources***	Medium	Medium/high
Hedge funds	Low	Low

Explanatory notes:

* *Refers to the percent distribution of ESG1- and ESG2-rated strategies in the Mercer Global Investment Manager Database (GIMD), where available.*

** *Refers to the percent distribution of sustainability-themed strategies compared to the asset class universe — noting equities is a large universe, so the low relative number is not actually a low absolute number.*

*** *Conservative view – research updates in this asset class may result in a more favorable view than is currently held.*

- *Low: below 5%*
- *Low/medium: 5% to 10%*
- *Medium: 11% to 20%*
- *Medium/high: 21% to 40%*
- *High: above 40% (as of December 2018)*

Source: Mercer.[29]

What Exhibit 8 does not illustrate, though, is the breadth and diversity of approaches within each of these categories. Earlier chapters have discussed some of these ESG methodologies as applied to individual securities. Examining these at the portfolio level draws important distinctions and also highlights the challenges that many approaches face in the path towards a credible form of ESG integration.

---

28 PRI. 2020. *About the PRI.* Available at: www.unpri.org/pri/about-the-pri
29 PRI. 2021. *What Is the Inevitable Policy Response?* Available at: www.unpri.org/inevitable-policy-response/what-is-the-inevitable-policy-response/4787.article

Approaches to Integrating ESG: Portfolio Level Framework

This ESG process is detailed in Chapter 7.

It is worth revisiting the CFA Institute ESG integration framework (see Exhibit 9). This forms the foundation of integration. More importantly, it demonstrates the expanding, sequenced degrees of analysis at different levels. At its core, the framework represents the process of 'classical ESG research and analysis,' which focuses on the individual security level.

The framework then expands outward, assuming more layers of analysis across a greater number of dimensions — including asset classes and investment strategy types — within portfolio and ultimately asset allocation decision making.

Exhibit 9: ESG Integration Framework

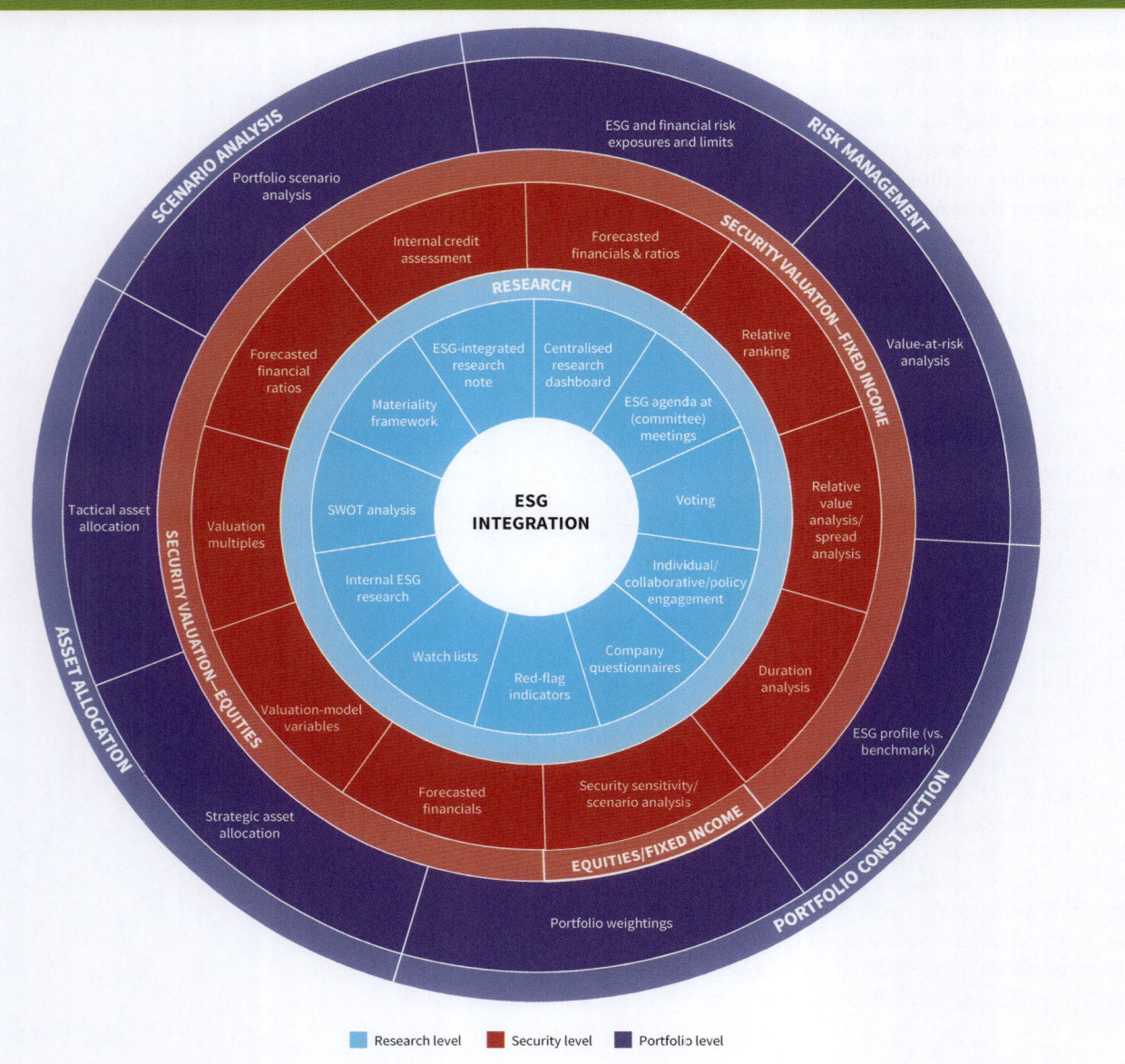

Source: CFA Institute (2018) in collaboration with PRI.[30]

It is important to emphasize that this illustration of ESG integration depicts roles that are distinct from one another, just as the role of portfolio manager is distinct from that of an investment research analyst.

---

30 CFA Institute and PRI. 2018. *Guidance and Case Studies for ESG Integration: Equities and Fixed Income.* Available at: www.unpri.org/investor-tools/guidance-and-case-studies-for-esg-integration-equities-and-fixed-income/3622.article

APPROACHES TO INTEGRATING ESG: ROLE OF ANALYSTS, PORTFOLIO MANAGERS, AND INTERNAL AND EXTERNAL RESEARCH

5

☐ 8.1.2 describe approaches for integrating ESG into the portfolio management process

☐ 8.1.3 explain approaches for how internal and external ESG research and analysis is used by portfolio managers to make investment decisions

Role of Analysts

Analysts (particularly fundamental analysts) present and justify their views in 'a story' or 'investment thesis' of a security, which generally entails incorporating different factors. These factors often include:

- the intrinsic value of the security;
- credit analysis;
- the potential for a re-rating or de-rating in valuation;
- potential risks;
- short-term and long-term catalysts; and
- an expectation on the security's earnings growth and cash flow profile.

ESG is an increasingly recognized element within securities analysis and, if material enough, may likely carry meaningful implications that help the investment thesis.

Role of Portfolio Managers

The role of portfolio managers, on the other hand, is of much broader scope. A portfolio manager constructs and manages a portfolio through a careful process that aggregates all of the individual, underlying risks. And while portfolio managers often form their own views for a given security, their primary role is to weigh security-specific conviction against:

- macro- and micro-economic data;
- portfolio financial and non-financial exposure; and
- sensitivities to potential shocks.

The treatment of ESG in a portfolio context — if properly and systematically integrated, regardless of whether in active or passive portfolio management — should be considered in the same light as these other factors.

The challenge that portfolio managers face is how to widen the focus of research and datasets largely optimized for security analysis into tools that can better inform portfolio and asset allocation analysis and decision making, particularly in understanding where and how ESG contributes to risk-adjusted returns.

To this end, the ESG framework should illustrate a continuity from micro- to macro-forms of analysis, including:

- the organizing principles and methodologies for ESG analysis;

- the identification and analysis of financial and non-financial (ESG) materiality at the individual security level;
- the approaches to build a composite picture of risks and exposure at a single portfolio level; and
- the representation of ESG risks and exposure that informs a mixed asset strategy, which may include many different, underlying strategies.

In addition, ESG integration should be considered in light of two different investment strategies:

- **Discretionary** ESG investment strategies most commonly take the form of a fundamental portfolio approach. A portfolio manager would work to complement bottom-up financial analysis alongside the consideration of ESG factors to reinforce the investment thesis of a particular holding. The portfolio manager would then work to understand the aggregate risk at the portfolio level across all factors to understand correlation and event risks and potential shocks to the portfolio.
- **Quantitative** investment strategies are, broadly speaking, rules-based approaches employing the statistical application of financial and/or non-financial factors to drive securities selection. Quantitative strategies generally seek to minimize the higher costs associated with discretionary active management. Where discretionary strategies often focus on depth within a portfolio, manifested through a portfolio of few, more concentrated holdings, quantitative strategies focus on breadth, using a much larger portfolio of holdings to target risk and volatility-adjusted returns.

Approaches may assume several forms when integrating ESG. Traditionally, passive or index-based strategies have been the most popular investment vehicles. These impose a custom index, typically with exclusion criteria. However, quantitative approaches are now becoming more sophisticated and rigorous when integrated into ESG, from beta-plus funds to single and multi-factor ESG models.

ESG integration can focus on risks as well as opportunities. A bias towards either of these can lead to different return profiles at the portfolio level as the emphasis can shift from downside protection to upside participation.

Developing a Policy that Reflects ESG-Integrated Portfolio Management

As a matter of definition — to the market, clients, and stakeholders — an ESG policy should formally outline the investment approach and degree of ESG integration within a firm. Particularly, asset managers should have ESG policies for asset classes and the approach used. The PRI provides guidance and templates to develop ESG policies.

There are well-established resources for developing a comprehensive ESG policy, though these have traditionally catered to the long-only equities and fixed-income strategies.[31] It is worth noting that investor organizations are now addressing policy development in alternative investment areas, including hedge funds.[32]

Further information on how ESG can be embedded in investment mandates and ESG policy can be found in Chapter 9.

---

31 PRI. 2018. *An Introduction to Responsible Investment: Policy, Structure and Process*. Available at: www.unpri.org/pri/an-introduction-to-responsible-investment/policy-structure-and-process
32 AIMA. 2021. *Responsible Investment*. Available at: www.aima.org/regulation/responsible-investment.html

Complementing Internal Research with External ESG Resources

Broadly speaking, ESG external research and analysis can be categorized between academic research and practitioner research. Each of these resources offers their own unique advantages and disadvantages for investors. While meta-analyses surveying more than 2,000 academic studies indicate an overall positive bias in the linkage between ESG and investment returns (see Exhibit 10), academic studies on an individual basis often end up disconnected from practice and are not widely or generally applicable. While certainly additive to the overall discussion, these are often unhelpful for practitioners who tend to search for cross-regional and cross-temporal factors or frameworks that can be universally or generally applied to portfolios. Practitioner research, on the other hand, is often less rigorous than academic work and tends to be less conservative in its assertion to correlate ESG with investment returns, sometimes ignoring other causal factors at play.

As the ESG industry matures, institutional investors are finding an increasingly diverse universe of external research resources. These resources now include not only ESG-specific research content but also new quantitative techniques, such as natural language processing, machine learning, and even artificial intelligence to organize ESG data. Indeed, the market for ESG content and indexes is expected to grow from USD300 million (GBP216 mn) in 2016 to almost USD1 billion (GBP0.7 bn) by 2021.[33] These resources complement internal investment research as well as provide internal quantitative and performance analytics teams the opportunity to refine methodologies for managing ESG risk. Just as external providers are innovating ESG datasets and producing research, so too are investors developing in-house capabilities to differentiate themselves across asset classes and investment strategy types.

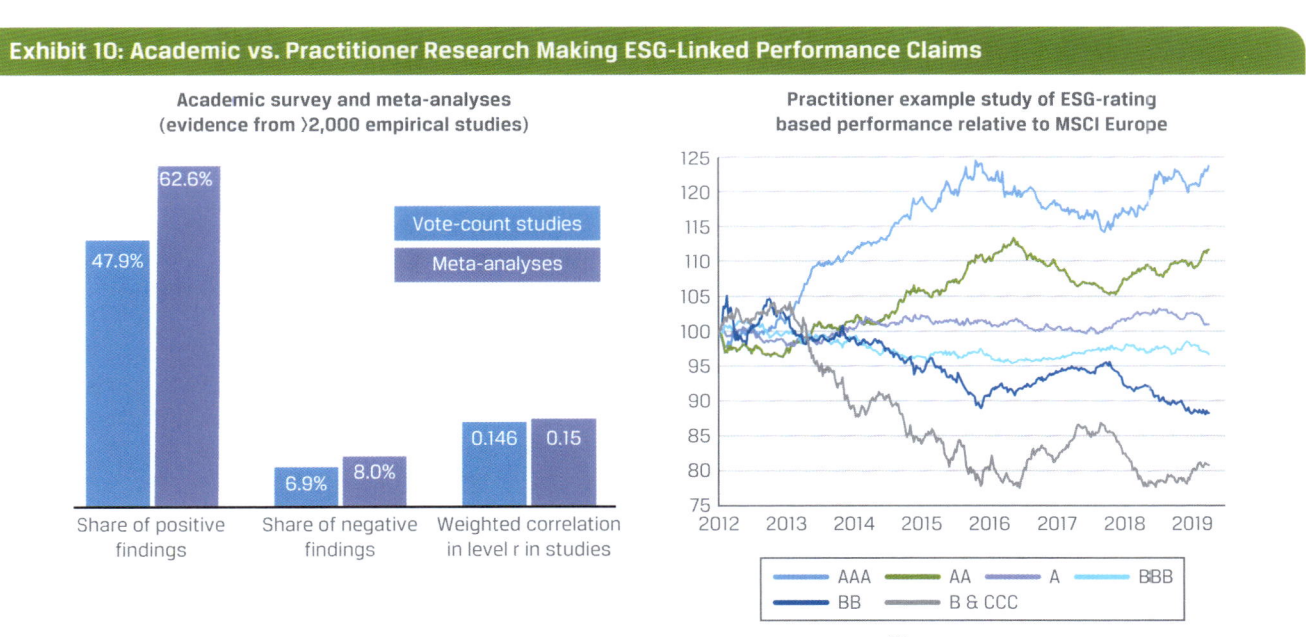

Exhibit 10: Academic vs. Practitioner Research Making ESG-Linked Performance Claims

Academic survey and meta-analyses (evidence from >2,000 empirical studies):
- Share of positive findings: Vote-count studies 47.9%, Meta-analyses 62.6%
- Share of negative findings: Vote-count studies 6.9%, Meta-analyses 8.0%
- Weighted correlation in level r in studies: Vote-count studies 0.146, Meta-analyses 0.15

Practitioner example study of ESG-rating based performance relative to MSCI Europe (2012–2019), by rating: AAA, AA, A, BBB, BB, B & CCC.

Source: MSCI ESG Research, FactSet, and Nordea Markets (2018).[34]

---

33 Pierron, A. 2020. *ESG Data Market: No Stopping Its Rise Now. Opimas.* Available at: www.opimas.com/research/548/detail/
34 MSCI ESG Research, FactSet, and Nordea Markets. 2018. *Research Insights: ESG.* Available at: https://nordeamarkets.com/wp-content/uploads/2018/09/ESG_140918.pdf

For most investors, the sheer breadth and diversity of external ESG research represents a difficult resource to replicate by internal research analysts. While research (such as ESG ratings from third-party data providers) comes at a cost, many of these other resources are freely available.

The list of practitioner resources, though by no means exhaustive, includes:

- sell-side research and analysis;
- academic studies;
- investment consultant research;
- third-party ESG data provider research;
- ESG-integrated fund distribution platforms;
- asset owner and asset manager white papers;
- investor initiative research;
- non-governmental organizations (NGOs) research;
- governmental agencies and central banks; and
- multilateral institutions and agencies.

Given the wide array of research resources available, portfolio managers should reflect on their research requirements. The profundity of research, from ESG integration at the individual security level to the portfolio level, continues to mature and provide investors with several ways to assess and report exposure. In fact, it is important to note that this spectrum ranges from reporting a static or backwards-looking picture of a portfolio's position-weighted ESG rating towards a more advanced quantification of underlying ESG risk and exposure in the manner applied by traditional quantitative finance measures.

Recommendations by the TCFD provide an important model for both a move towards ESG standards convergence and in elevating risk exposure metrics to the portfolio level from the underlying asset level. Where carbon intensity was previously determined in the form of carbon footprint on a per company or per asset basis, for example, portfolio managers may now treat carbon exposure on a portfolio-weighted basis. Weighted-average carbon intensity measures a portfolio's exposure to carbon-intensive companies on a position-weighted carbon exposure. Calculated as the carbon intensity (Scope 1 + 2 Emissions ÷ USD million revenues) weighted for each position within a portfolio, this metric can be employed by investors to tilt or overlay portfolios towards lower carbon exposure.

It is important to note that TCFD is a principles-based framework providing recommendations for assessing climate risk and exposure. Because TCFD is not prescriptive, different approaches to measure carbon intensity have developed. For example, while the European Union's (EU) Sustainable Finance Disclosure Regulation (SFDR) accounts for Scopes 1, 2, and 3 emissions, UK TCFD practice currently focuses on only Scope 1 and Scope 2 emissions. Scope 3 emissions, which represent indirect emissions that occur within a company's value chain, are particularly difficult to measure because of the potential lack of data, transparency, and disclosure within layers of a supply chain. As data and supply chain visibility improve, it is expected that emissions analysis will normalize to cover Scope 1, 2, and 3.

Exhibit 11: Weighted-Average Carbon Intensity at the Portfolio Level

$$\sum_{n}^{i} \left(\frac{\text{current value of investment}_i}{\text{current portfolio value}} \times \frac{\text{issuer's Scope 1 and Scope 2 GHG emissions}_i}{\text{issuer's US\$m revenue}_i} \right)$$

Source: Implementing the Recommendations of the TCFD.[35]

Investors should recognize the need to differentiate themselves irrespective of their approach to ESG integration. Asset owners continue to rebase their expectations for the quality of proprietary ESG research that asset managers and consultants can provide to them. In turn, investors complement external, off-the-shelf research and data analytics with internal, proprietary ESG research.

One of the less developed areas where investors are able to both innovate and differentiate themselves is in the demonstration of how ESG is embedded in their portfolio construction and management process. In this respect, the Sustainability Accounting Standards Board (SASB) has much to offer as their framework and materiality map spans issuer-specific materiality as well as overall portfolio exposure. Covering equities, fixed income, private equity, and real assets, SASB's *Materiality Map* is capable of assessing portfolio exposure to sustainability risks and opportunities across each issue.[36]

Another development is SASB work around the Sustainable Industry Classification System (SICS). Modeled after the Global Industry Classification Standard (GICS), SICS offers an improved industry classification standard that speaks directly to ESG materiality. The SICS system organizes companies according to their sustainability attributes, such as resource intensity, sustainability risks, and innovation opportunities.[37]

For more on SASB's materiality map, see Chapter 7.

The starting point that many portfolio managers employ is to upload their portfolios onto third-party ESG data provider online platforms. While these platforms vary in sophistication, they do offer the first composite picture of a portfolio's stock-specific risks on a number of potential ESG metrics. Many of these platforms are capable of:

- illustrating a portfolio's mean exposure and weighting towards low-, mid-, or high-scoring companies on ESG metrics;
- producing a picture of the portfolio's environmental and carbon exposure on an absolute-value basis, for instance, expressed as weighted-average carbon intensity; and
- approximating an overall controversy or risk score for the portfolio.

Asset owners and managers increasingly recognize the limitations of third-party ESG platforms and the need to develop more sophisticated ESG analytics platforms that combine third-party and proprietary capabilities. The rationale stems not only from the interest in safeguarding portfolio holdings — particularly with regard to clients' segregated investment mandates — but also in demonstrating a differentiated approach to understanding and reporting portfolio data. Given the subjectivity and divergence among ESG ratings providers, developing an approach that incorporates both third party and proprietary ESG data lowers an overreliance on a single provider and creates greater context for discussion when reviewing the risk profile of a portfolio.

---

35 Task Force on Climate-related Financial Disclosures. 2017. *Implementing the Recommendations of the Task Force on Climate-related Financial Disclosures.* Available at: www.fsb-tcfd.org/wp-content/uploads/2017/12/FINAL-TCFD-Annex-Amended-121517.pdf
36 Sustainability Accounting Standards Board (SASB). 2018. *SASB Materiality Map.* Available at: https://materiality.sasb.org/
37 Nascimento, D., and S. Payal. 2018. "Industry Classification & Environmental, Social and Governance (ESG) Standards" (September). Available at: www.norburypartners.com/industry-classification-esg-standards

For example, a portfolio ESG analytics tool employed by an asset manager may aggregate a number of different data streams from ESG providers to produce a picture of 'consensus,' rankings-oriented ESG scores and their variance alongside an internally-produced 'proprietary' ESG score, in addition to a view of absolute values-based environmental fund metrics and exposures.

These analytics tools enable investment teams to decompose both their portfolios and benchmark indexes, sort by ratings, and understand the distribution curves across a number of ESG metrics. They often provide drill-down capabilities that illustrate a more detailed picture of ESG characteristics on an underlying basis for positions.

Portfolio tools provide investors with the ability to stress test a portfolio against different ESG criteria (such as a sudden, hypothetical increase in the price of carbon emissions) to understand the sensitivity of the portfolio. This exercise is no different to how current portfolio tools provide the means to stress test portfolios against simulations, such as interest rate or oil shocks.

6. APPROACHES TO INTEGRATING ESG: QUANTITATIVE RESEARCH DEVELOPMENTS IN ESG INVESTING

- ☐ 8.1.2 describe approaches for integrating ESG into the portfolio management process
- ☐ 8.1.3 explain approaches for how internal and external ESG research and analysis is used by portfolio managers to make investment decisions

One of the most exciting areas of research development in portfolio management focuses on quantitatively understanding the risk properties of ESG. As Chapter 7 notes on the challenges to ESG integration at the individual security level, there is widespread disagreement about what an ESG factor represents. The fundamental manager's focus on bottom-up research elevates the ESG integration process as the primary means to drive price discovery, or understand the value of an asset or security. This process is often described in case study form.

Generally speaking, these case studies illustrate the long-term price appreciation of an issuer against the portfolio's investment position to demonstrate the investor's long-term holding period. Moreover, they are often annotated by interactions and engagements with the issuer's management as evidence that ESG integration is contributing to the fund's investment returns. But while single-security case studies often frame the investment process with a powerful engagement story, their anecdotal nature does not describe performance attribution from ESG exposure at a portfolio level. Portfolio analytics typically provide performance analytics that describe regional, sectoral, and stock-specific performance attribution over a given time period. In the same way, the assumption or contention that ESG is alpha generating in its own right must also be tested on the same attributional basis.

Hence, it is worth reflecting briefly on ESG research, ESG ratings and scores, and the signal or input they provide for active and passive strategies. Describing ESG performance attribution at a portfolio level requires quantifying ESG as a factor or risk premium in its own right. Third-party data providers are developing increasingly sophisticated ESG ratings and scoring methodologies, but many fall short in describing ESG as an uncorrelated, statistically independent factor. In fact, the ratings from many providers reveal a significant, underlying correlation to existing factors, such as value, quality, size, and momentum. In one respect, this should not be surprising. Transparency bias generally accrues to larger, more mature companies with higher ESG ratings. Nonetheless, the correlation to other factors effectively undermines the effort to define ESG as uniquely singular enough to be included in risk factor attribution analyses.

One of the most popular areas for research is the development and application of ESG ratings and scoring in the context of portfolio construction and management. In fact, the influence of ESG ratings within the investment community should not be underestimated, and its growing popularity presents a combination of positives and negatives that investors should consider. Supported by a growing number of academic and practitioner studies that demonstrate a correlation between corporate ESG operational metrics and financial returns, many investors have embraced ESG scoring methodologies.

In turn, ESG rating and scoring methodologies are evolving as institutionalized features both in retail and institutional investor platforms. For example, Morningstar, the popular investment and research platform catering to both retail and institutional investors, first introduced its sustainability rating to complement its core fund rating in 2016.[38] Updated in 2019 to incorporate the new Sustainalytics company-level *ESG Risk Rating*, the Morningstar methodology now reflects a company's ESG risks measured on the same scale across industries, and the overall fund rating shows the ESG risk embedded in the fund's portfolio.

For more on the Sustainalytics and Morningstar risk ratings, see Appendix to Chapter 7.

Exhibit 12: ESG Rating Correlation among Six Third-Party Data Providers

	N (1)	Mean (2)	Median (3)	Standard deviation (4)	Asset4 (5)	Sust. (6)	Inrate (7)	FTSE (8)	KLD (9)
Panel A: Total rating									
Asset4	31424	0.501	0.501	0.289					
Sustainalytics	32703	0.501	0.499	0.289	0.762				
Inrate	25945	0.501	0.534	0.284	0.233	0.303			
Bloomberg	32410	0.501	0.501	0.289	0.749	0.708	0.122		
KLD	32485	0.501	0.507	0.288	0.584	0.619	0.29	0.538	
MSCI IVA	32450	0.501	0.502	0.289	0.418	0.46	0.319	0.308	0.452
Average correlation								0.458	
Panel B: Environmental pillar									
Asset4	31261	0.501	0.501	0.289					
Sustainalytics	32532	0.501	0.501	0.289	0.71				
Inrate	25880	0.501	0.518	0.286	0.305	0.488			
Bloomberg	28258	0.501	0.501	0.289	0.651	0.566	0.206		
KLD	32403	0.501	0.498	0.281	0.629	0.654	0.422	0.472	
MSCI IVA	32361	0.501	0.502	0.289	0.174	0.325	0.403	0.14	0.284

Pearson Correlations

---

38 Morningstar. 2016. *The Morningstar Sustainability Rating*. Available at: www.morningstar.co.uk/uk/news/148119/the-morningstar-sustainability-rating.aspx

| | N (1) | Mean (2) | Median (3) | Standard deviation (4) | Pearson Correlations |||||
					Asset4(5)	Sust. (6)	Inrate (7)	FTSE (8)	KLD (9)
Average correlation								0.429	
Panel C: Social pillar									
Asset4	31424	0.501	0.501	0.289					
Sustainalytics	32703	0.501	0.504	0.289	0.617				
Inrate	25945	0.501	0.522	0.288	0.133	0.143			
Bloomberg	32322	0.501	0.507	0.288	0.682	0.53	0.061		
KLD	32485	0.501	0.505	0.288	0.397	0.423	0.128	0.302	
MSCI IVA	32450	0.501	0.5	0.289	0.282	0.323	0.236	0.207	0.351
Average correlation								0.321	
Panel D: Governance pillar									
Asset4	31424	0.501	0.501	0.289					
Sustainalytics	32703	0.501	0.504	0.289	0.312				
Inrate	25945	0.501	0.502	0.283	0.297	0.401			
Bloomberg	32410	0.501	0.487	0.283	0.421	0.34	0.343		
KLD	32485	0.501	0.489	0.237	0.059	0.034	0.083	0.095	
MSCI IVA	32450	0.501	0.501	0.288	0.141	0.129	0.144	0.045	0.152
Average correlation								0.2	

Source: Brandon, Krueger, and Schmidt.[39]

Readers may ask what common risk factors explain ESG ratings. One means of answering this question is to examine the underlying factor exposure of the highest-rated ESG companies versus the lowest-rated companies. This exercise reveals that what is purportedly marketed as an 'ESG signal' with quasi-predictive signaling power is instead driven largely by existing factors.

---

39 Brandon, R. G., P. Krueger, and P. S. Schmidt. 2021. "ESG Rating Disagreement and Stock Returns." *Financial Analysts Journal* 77 (4). Available at: https://www.cfainstitute.org/en/research/financial-analysts-journal/2021/1963186

Approaches to Integrating ESG: Quantitative Research Developments in ESG Investing

Exhibit 13: Underlying Factor Exposure among Existing Third-Party Data Providers (Arabesque S-Ray and RepRisk ESG)

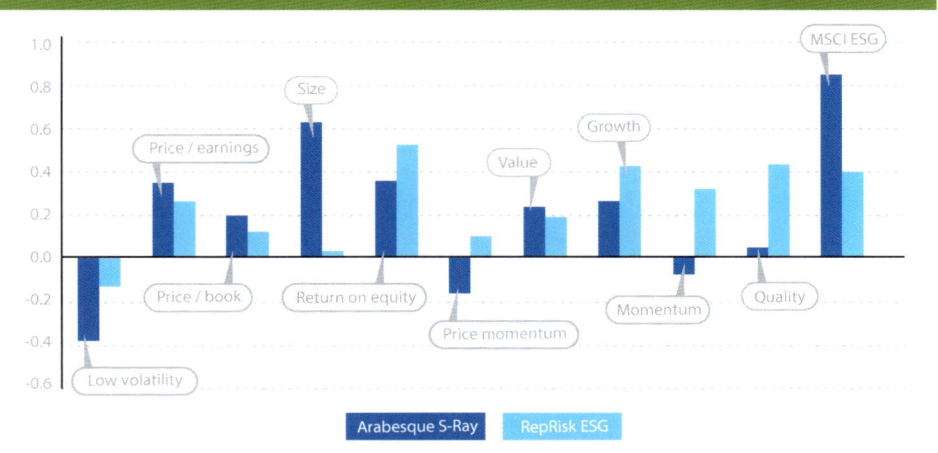

Source: J.P. Morgan, Arabesque, and RepRisk ESG.[40]

Exhibit 14: Underlying Factor Exposure among Existing Third-Party Data Providers (Sustainalytics and MSCI)

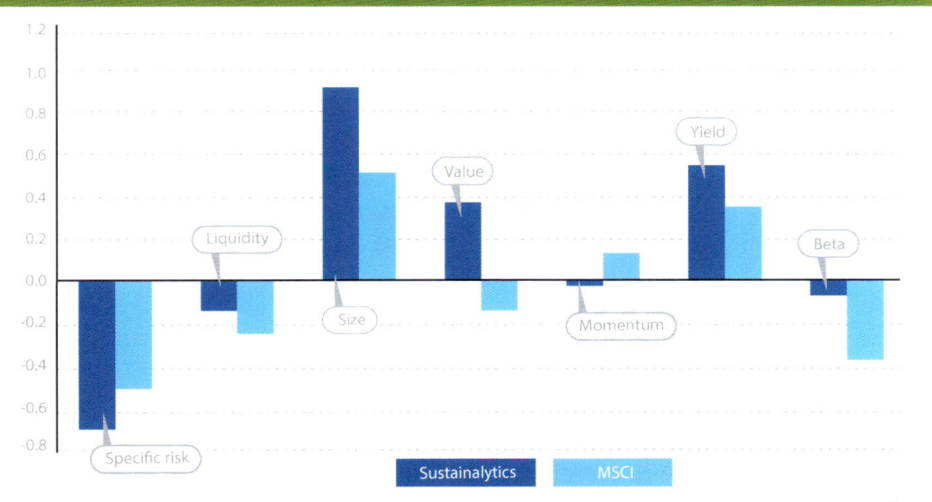

Source: Man Numeric, Sustainalytics, and MSCI.[41]

This represents, in effect, a causality problem for ESG. In other words:

- What exactly is ESG?
- If it can be quantified or measured, is it simply an amalgam of other established factors, like size and quality?

---

[40] J.P. Morgan. 2016. *ESG – Environmental, Social and Governance Investing: A Quantitative Perspective of How ESG Can Enhance Your Portfolio.* Available at: https://yoursri.com/media-new/download/jpm-esg-how-esg-can-enhance-your-portfolio.pdf

[41] Man Numeric, MSCI, and Sustainalytics. 2019. *ESG Data: Building a Solid Foundation.* Available at: www.man.com/maninstitute/esg-data-building-a-solid-foundation

The practitioner argument for causality is that a transparency bias towards large companies favors ESG because a common characteristic of high-ranking ESG companies is strong transparency and disclosure. Large companies, not surprisingly, are better equipped and staffed to address these issues, resulting in higher ESG scores. The linkage between quality and ESG as factors stems from the intuition that the governance of higher ESG-rated companies drives stronger decision making around capital allocation and shareholder returns.

If ESG does not represent a mix of existing factors like quality and value, then how can academics and practitioners begin to define it in its own right — as an uncorrelated factor? This is a fundamental question for investors because the potential development of ESG as an uncorrelated factor opens up powerful significant opportunities to better embed it within portfolio management.

7. THE EVOLUTION OF ESG INTEGRATION: EXCLUSIONARY PREFERENCES AND THEIR APPLICATION

- 8.1.4 explain the different approaches to screening and the benefits and limitations of the main approaches
- 8.1.5 explain the main indexes and benchmarking approaches applicable to sustainable and ESG investing, noting potential limitations

Screening represents the oldest, simplest approach to ESG investing. Negative screening imposes a set of exclusions based on ethical preferences or around a normative worldview to shape the investable universe of a portfolio. Indeed, its first formal use was aligned to religious values, when the Methodists avoided investing in businesses that dealt in alcohol, tobacco, and gambling. In the 18th century, the Quakers aligned their investment approach to their stance against slavery, choosing to screen out investments and boycott business interests that supported the slave trade. In a similar manner, Islamic approaches to investment apply hard or soft interpretations of Shariah principles to filter out companies that are not Shariah-compliant.[42]

Many investors apply exclusions to restrict exposure to certain sectors or securities that conflict with their worldview. Exclusions typically take the form of sectors or industries commonly known as 'sin sectors' that include tobacco, pornography, gaming, and alcohol. But exclusions can just as easily target specific companies or even countries. Exclusions have traditionally represented ethical and normative restrictions. For example, a church pension plan may exclude gambling, alcohol, and pornography while a pension fund that represents healthcare workers may exclude investment in the tobacco sector.

According to statistics maintained by the Global Sustainable Investment Alliance (GSIA), exclusions-based approaches remain the largest portion of dedicated, ESG-screened assets under management (AUM).[43] Their size and growth points to

---

[42] Shariah-compliant investment funds are a type of responsible investment governed by Islamic law. Like other faith-based screening approaches, Shariah-compliant funds operate on exclusionary screening that typically excludes: conventional banking and insurance; pork and non-Halal foods; alcohol; gambling; tobacco; adult entertainment; synthetic instruments like derivatives and swaps; and weapons. The Shariah Supervisory Board applies and arbitrates exclusionary criteria.

[43] For a detailed breakdown, please see: GSIA. 2018. *2018 Global Sustainable Investment Review*. Available at: www.gsi-alliance.org/wp-content/uploads/2019/06/GSIR_Review2018F.pdf

the expansion from traditional areas of exclusion, such as controversial arms and munitions, into other areas, such as tobacco, thermal, coal, and nuclear weapons. Because of their subjective nature and their regional, faith-based and normative specificity, exclusions are often treated as irreconcilable. For instance, it would be rare to find two pension funds with perfectly overlapping worldviews and normative expectations.

Nonetheless, it is possible to organize exclusions across four basic categories:

1. universal;
2. conduct-related;
3. faith-based; and
4. idiosyncratic exclusions.

Universal Exclusions

Universal exclusions represent exclusions supported by global norms and conventions, like those from the United Nations (UN) and the World Health Organization (WHO). It could be argued that controversial arms and munitions (cluster munitions and anti-personnel mines), nuclear weapons, tobacco, and varying degrees of exposure to coal-based power generation or extraction all qualify as universally accepted given normative support and the growing asset owner AUM they represent.

EXAMPLE 1

Arms and Munitions and Tobacco Exclusions

Arms and Munitions Exclusions

Exclusions governing investment in controversial arms and munitions are supported by multilateral treaties, conventions, and national legislation.

- **Ottawa Treaty (1997)** prohibits the use, stockpiling, production, and transfer of anti-personnel mines.
- **UN Convention on Cluster Munitions (2008)** prohibits the use, stockpiling, production, and transfer of cluster munitions.
- **UN Chemical Weapons Convention (1997)** prohibits the use, stockpiling, production, and transfer of chemical weapons.
- **UN Biological Weapons Convention (1975)** prohibits the use, stockpiling, production, and transfer of biological weapons.
- **Treaty on the Non-Proliferation of Nuclear Weapons (1968)** limits the spread of nuclear weapons to the group of so-called Nuclear-Weapons States (USA, Russia, UK, France, and China).
- **Belgium (2009)** bans investments in depleted uranium weapons.
- **UN Global Compact announced the decision (2017)** to exclude controversial weapons sectors from participating in the initiative.

> **Tobacco Exclusions**
>
> Although tobacco does not exhibit the same degree of universal acceptance that the exclusion over controversial arms and munitions does, it provides another example that can be said to be supported by the following:
>
> - **WHO Framework Convention (2003) on Tobacco Control,** with 181 parties committing to implementing a broad range of tobacco control measures.
> - **UN Global Compact (UNGC)** announced the decision (2017) to exclude tobacco companies from participating in the initiative as tobacco products are fundamentally misaligned with UNGC's commitment to advancing business action towards Sustainable Development Goal (SDG) 3 and are in direct conflict with the right to public health.
> - **UN SDGs (2015)** drive a collection of 17 global goals to eradicate poverty, protect the planet, and improve prosperity; many of the goals touch on tobacco as an impediment to improved social and environmental outcomes.

Conduct-Related Exclusions

Conduct-related exclusions are generally company or country-specific and often not a statement against the nature of the business itself. Labor infractions in the form of violations against the International Labour Organization (ILO) principles are often cited.

Faith-Based Exclusions

Faith-based exclusions are specific to religious institutional or individual investors. For more on faith-based exclusions, see Chapter 1.

Idiosyncratic Exclusions

Idiosyncratic exclusions are exclusions that are not supported by global consensus. For example, New Zealand's pension funds are singularly bound by statutory law to exclude companies involved in the processing of whale meat products.[44]

Applying Exclusionary Preferences

Exclusionary preferences are most commonly adopted and applied by asset owners rather than asset managers. While there are certainly asset managers who have formally instituted some form of values-based exclusionary screens, they currently represent a small minority. This is often because of their global reach and the subjective nature of negative screens. Hence, pooled or commingled investments and listed funds (such as undertakings for the collective investment in transferable securities [UCITS] funds) generally do not have exclusionary screens implemented, unless noted within their investment mandate. That said, asset managers do manage dedicated mandates for asset owners that commonly impose some form of an exclusionary screen.

---

44 NZ SuperFund. 2019. *Exclusions*. Available at: https://nzsuperfund.nz/how-we-invest-responsible-investment/exclusions

Among global asset owners, Norges Bank, in its Norwegian sovereign wealth fund (SWF), constructs and implements the most visible of these asset owner exclusion lists. Because of the size of its AUM, Norges Bank's exclusion list has been adopted by other Norwegian asset owners and continues to influence the construction of exclusions lists among other Nordic asset owners.[45]

Because of its relative ease of implementation, screening is the most universal approach within ESG investing. While the simplicity of exclusions means that they are often widely applied in both traditional asset classes as well as private markets and alternatives, the extent of exclusions may carry implications for a portfolio.

It is important to highlight that some issues continue to remain difficult to reconcile from a screening perspective, which means that investors often assume a best efforts approach in these cases. The degree of exclusions may carry significant implications from a portfolio management perspective, not just in terms of higher tracking error and active share, but also unintended factor exposure. Tracking error and active share are measures that represent the degree to which a portfolio deviates from its benchmark. A portfolio that imposes a broad set of exclusions (particularly sector exclusions, which represent a significant weight of their benchmark), will likely produce high active share and tracking error. This magnitude of difference may lead the portfolio manager to adopt a more appropriate ESG benchmark rather than a broad market benchmark.

On the other hand, a portfolio that applies a narrow exclusion list that doesn't by itself produce higher active share or tracking error may leave the benchmark index unchanged unless the exclusions represent a meaningful change to the risk–return profile to the investment fund. In addition, the list of excluded companies may not apply to index derivatives or proprietary index construction. This compromise is generally done to reflect the burden of repeatedly decomposing indexes. In some cases — particularly for smaller, more obscure indexes — investors make this compromise because of the prohibitive cost of purchasing the underlying constituent weights.[46]

EXERCISE

Construct an equities-only portfolio that aligns with your worldview. Consult the Global Industry Classification Standard (GICS)[47] to view its hierarchy of 11 sectors and underlying 24 industry groups. Discuss your construction:

- ▶ What sectors would you exclude? Are these normative (universally supported) or more idiosyncratic?
- ▶ How do your choices change the size of your investable universe?
- ▶ What implications would your chosen exclusions have for the overall portfolio's exposure?
- ▶ Would they make the portfolio more pro-cyclical or more defensive?
- ▶ How would it change its yield profile? What ways could you compensate for the effects of your exclusions?

---

45 Norges Bank. 2019. *Observation and Exclusion of Companies.* Available at: www.nbim.no/en/the-fund/responsible-investment/exclusion-of-companies/
46 For an example, see: Robeco Institutional Asset Management. 2019. *Exclusion Policy Robeco.* Available at: www.robeco.com/docm/docu-exclusion-policy-and-list.pdf
47 MSCI. 2020. *The Global Industry Classification Standard (GICS).* Available at: www.msci.com/gics

Another challenge is the treatment of asset classes and securities that fall outside of the traditional spectrum of responsible investment, which has generally been focused on:

- listed equities;
- listed corporate debt; and
- real assets.

Indeed, the PRI itself acknowledges this limitation in the language of its signatory commitment, which recognizes that ESG may impact the performance of portfolios to "varying degrees across companies, sectors, regions, asset classes and through time."[48]

As discussed earlier, ESG integration has a natural bias towards company-related assets, manifested in capital markets through equities and fixed income. With oversight of these assets, management teams and boards of directors drive decision making and long-term corporate strategy with feedback loops to shareholders and other stakeholders.

However, other assets classes that lack the directed actions of a management team or board of directors prove more problematic. For instance, synthetic assets (currencies, interest rate derivatives, broad-based equity indexes, and commodity futures) are not single-operated assets and fall outside the conventional framework of ESG analysis. For some security types, it is possible to draw tenuous linkages between, say, currency forward contracts and the ESG profile of the underlying sovereign issuer, but other instruments are more difficult. For example, an interest rate swap represents a derivative contract that exchanges the floating interest rate payment of, say, a sovereign bond or loan for a fixed interest rate. Investors should certainly be aware of the underlying risks to that sovereign payment, but simply netting out the ESG risk profile of the same sovereign on both sides of the contract effectively creates a wash or cancellation.

In addition, investment strategies, particularly at the multi-asset level, commonly invest in indexes for various reasons, including for cash management to cover potential redemptions by investors. Within this context, it is complicated and often can become expensive to frequently break down indexes from a screening perspective. Widely traded, liquid indexes are generally easier and less costly to decompose into their constituent or member weights, while the opposite is true for less popular, thinly-traded indexes. Hence, while an investor may maintain a formal exclusion list, they may also include a specific policy in their exclusion policy that omits indexes in the interest of efficient portfolio management.

8 ESG SCREENING WITHIN PORTFOLIOS AND ACROSS ASSET CLASSES: FIXED INCOME, CORPORATE DEBT, AND ESG BONDS

☐ 8.1.6 apply ESG screens to the main asset classes and their sub-sectors: fixed income; equities; and alternative investments

---

[48] PRI. 2020. *Signatories' Commitment*. Available at: https://www.unpri.org/pri/what-are-the-principles-for-responsible-investment

Exhibit 15: Examples of ESG Indexes, Benchmarks, and Their Methodologies (January 2021)

ESG Indexes	Asset class	Indexes ESG	Indexes E	Indexes S	Indexes G	Ratings ESG	Ratings E	Ratings S	Ratings G	Description
FTSE Russell	Equities	X	X	X	X	X	X	X	X	Rates above 4,000 securities in developed and emerging countries on 300 ESG indicators. Measures companies' revenue exposure and management to green and brown (fossil fuel) exposure.
FTSE4Good	Equities	X	X	X	X	X	X	X	X	Applies FTSE Russell ESG ratings data to select companies with at least a 3.1 (developed) and 2.5 (emerging) rating out of 5. Companies exposed to "significant controversies" and certain business activities (tobacco, weapons and coal) are also excluded.
JP Morgan ESG EMD	Fixed income	X				X				Designed for both corporate and sovereign emerging market debt. Combines exclusionary screening against worst offenders alongside ESG ratings integration. Adjusts constituent weights based on composite ESG score for each issuer which overweights green bonds, and companies with better scoring ESG profiles.
MSCI ESG	Equities	X	X	X	X	X	X	X	X	Offers more than 1,000 ESG indexes. Methodology is based on ESG ratings with screening criteria available (tobacco, weapons, coal, fossil fuel, Catholic, and Islamic values). Governance factor measures UN Global Compact compliance only.
S&P (DJSI) ESG	Equities, fixed income	X	X	X	X	X	X	X	X	Best-in-class indexes based on an ESG assessment of 4,500 corporates. Rules-based selection of top 10% to 30% (global or regional) of sustainable market cap based on ESG score. DJSI also offers indices with exclusions screens (weapons, alcohol, tobacco, gambling and pornography).
Sustainalytics	Equities	X	X	X	X	X	X	X	X	Supports partner index and passive strategies (such as STOXX, SGX, S&P, iShares, and Nifty) that employ different approaches (including negative screening, ESG ratings, low carbon and gender diversity).
Intercontinental exchange (ICE) ESG	Equities, fixed income	X	X	X	X		X	X		ICE manages roughly 40 ESG-related indexes. Driven on MSCI ESG data, ICE indexes – covering equities, fixed income, and real estate – include: thematic (environmental, water, energy); ESG best practices; and factors (such as diversity and inclusion).
Global Real Estate Standards Board (GRESB) ESG Benchmark	Real assets – infrastructure and real estate	X	X	X	X	X	X	X	X	GRESB ESG benchmark leverages GRESB's position as the leading investor initiative focused on real assets and infrastructure with a focus on commercial and residential real estate.

Source: Adapted from the *Journal of Environmental Investing.* Douglas, E., T. Van Holt, and T. Whelan. 2017. "Responsible Investing: Guide to ESG Data Providers and Relevant Trends." *Journal of Environmental Investing* 9 (1): 92–114. Available at: www.thejei.com/wp-content/uploads/2017/11/Journal-of-Environmental-Investing-8-No.-1.rev_-1.pdf

Fixed Income (Government, Sovereign, Corporate, and Other)

Generally speaking, ESG integration in fixed income has experienced a good deal of catch up relative to listed equities. However, there is still significant differentiation across the sub-asset classes. In Exhibit 16, Mercer's ratings for ESG integration within credit subclasses reveal a greater number of higher ratings — ESG1 and ESG2 — in investment-grade credit, emerging markets debt, and buy-and-maintain strategies, while government debt and high-yield credit experience lower degrees of integration. As we will discuss, lower levels of ESG integration in areas like sovereign debt and high-yield credit often reflect a scarcity in ESG ratings and datasets and ratings, particularly in the unlisted credit markets.

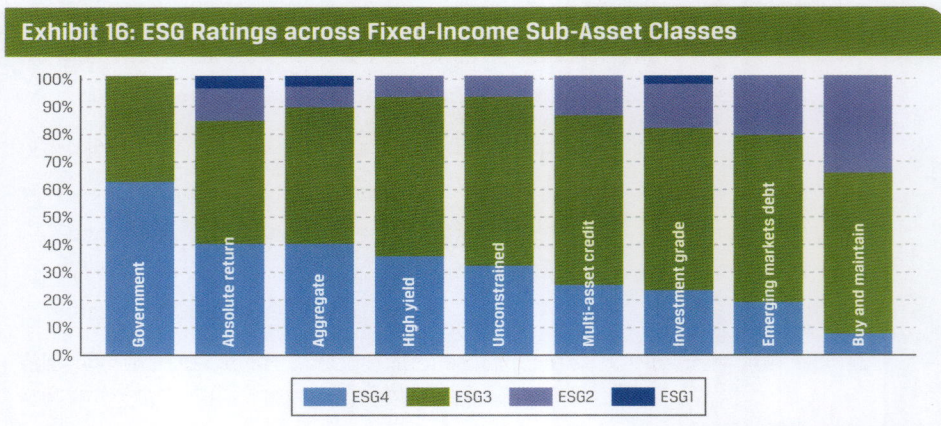

Exhibit 16: ESG Ratings across Fixed-Income Sub-Asset Classes

Source: MercerInsight (2020).[49]

Corporate Debt

Corporate debt is now enjoying greater levels of ESG integration. In some regards, this should not be surprising. Issuers of equity also tend to issue debt. Indeed, there is growing evidence of ESG-incorporated methodologies yielding meaningful performance differentials.

First, it is worth briefly highlighting why debt is distinct from equities. The debt issued by a single corporate — or sovereign, for that matter — often represents multiple credit risk profiles across bond issuances. These bond issuances represent different maturities, which refer to the payment date of a loan.

In contrast, companies issuing equity generally issue one common share class.[50] The temporal dimension across multiple debt maturities and credit risk profiles arguably lends itself to a more granular comprehension of ESG issues and their materiality.

---

49 MercerInsight. 2020. *Responsible Investment in Fixed Income*. Information on the aggregation methodology can be found in Appendix 2 of the report. All data as of 1 December 2019. Available at: www.mercer.com/our-thinking/wealth/responsible-investment-in-fixed-income.html

50 While most corporations maintain one common share class, there are companies — notably, Alphabet and Facebook — that operate multiple share classes. Different share classes may contain different shareholder rights, such as voting rights, dividend payouts, and rights to capital and special rights. MSCI ESG Research, Bloomberg Barclays Indexes, Barclays Research. Sustainalytics corporate ESG data are based on *ESG Rating* methodology, which has now been replaced with the *ESG Risk Rating Methodology*. Sustainalytics ESG Research, Bloomberg Barclays Indexes, Barclays Research. Sustainalytics corporate ESG data are based on *ESG Rating* methodology, which has now been replaced with the *ESG Risk Rating Methodology*.

ESG Screening within Portfolios and across Asset Classes: Fixed Income, Corporate Debt, and ESG Bonds 481

For example, one method available to a credit portfolio manager seeking to manage the long-term climate risk effects of an issuer is to invest in the issuer's shorter-dated maturing debt.

Exhibit 17 illustrates examples of two investment-grade bond portfolios with an ESG tilt applied. Although the short times (August 2009 to April 2016) limit the ability to make a strong performance claim across multiple economic cycles, both bond portfolios suggest that high ESG portfolios outperform low ESG portfolios despite being driven by different ESG methodologies. However, it is important to bear in mind that after the global financial crisis of 2008-09, 'quality' as a factor outperformed while 'value' largely underperformed. Given the strong correlation between high ESG and 'quality' among ESG vendors, it is important to note that the ESG-driven performance returns are not necessarily causal.

Exhibit 17: Investment-Grade Bond Portfolio Performance (High ESG over Low ESG)

Cumulate performance % of a high-ESG portfolio over a low-ESG portfolio using MSCI ESG data[33]

Cumulate performance % of a high-ESG portfolio over a low-ESG portfolio using Sustainalytics ESG data[34]

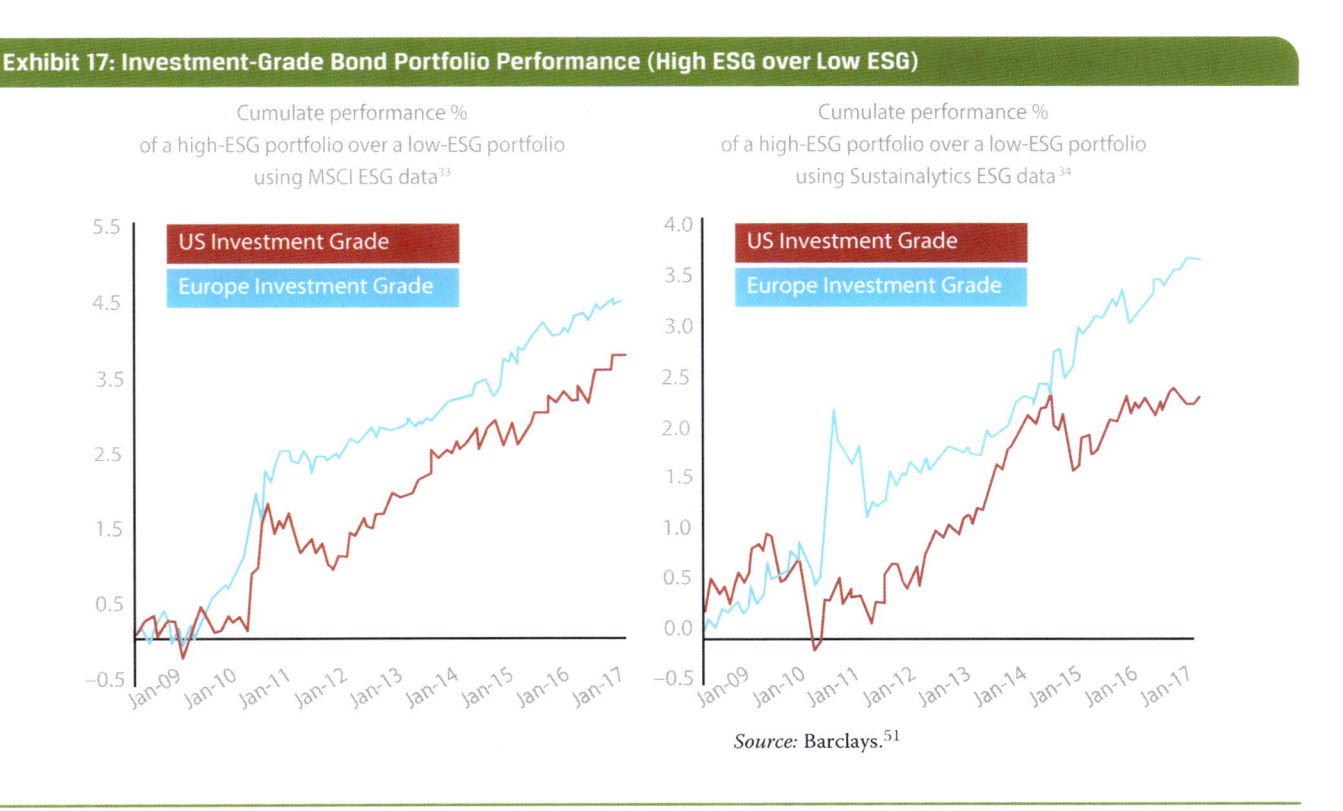

Source: Barclays.[51]

Exhibit 18 illustrates an ESG evaluation framework developed by BlueBay Asset Management, a fixed-income specialist asset manager. Based on an ESG integration approach, the framework leverages third-party ESG data to produce proprietary issuer ESG metrics:

▶ The Fundamental ESG Risk Metric examines fundamental ESG risk at the issuer level.

---

51 Barclays. 2018. *The Case for Sustainable Bond Investing Strengthens.* Sustainalytics data based on the firm's legacy ESG ratings. Available at: www.investmentbank.barclays.com/content/dam/barclaysmicrosites/ibpublic/documents/our-insights/ESG2/BarclaysIB-ImpactSeries4-ESG-in-credit-5MB.pdf

▶ The Investment ESG Score operates at the bond security level. The ESG score takes into account varying credit risk sensitivities, which result from the exposure to ESG risk factors. These ESG risk factors are inherently present as a function of the bond's features (or characteristics).

The ESG Score is unique in that it examines ESG both as risk and as opportunity within the overall score. While useful at the issuer level, its value and differentiation for both its internal investment teams and investors lies in elevating the picture of ESG risk from the individual bond to the single issuer level — and ultimately understanding ESG risk within a given credit portfolio.

Exhibit 18: Credit Investment-Grade Corporates Portfolio – Issuer ESG Metrics Summary

	Very Low ESG Risks	Low ESG Risks	Medium ESG Risks	High ESG Risks	Very High ESG Risks	+2	+1	0	-1	-2
Long	0.009	0.135	0.509	0.182	0.019	0.013	0.078	0.347	0.333	0.083
Short	0	-0.0013	-0.0016	-0.0005	0	0	-0.001	-0.0007	-0.0017	0

Note: The Fundamental ESG (Risk) Rating, assigned at the issuer level, relates to how well the borrower is managing the material ESG risks it faces, capturing current performance as well as trajectory of travel. The Investment ESG Score, assigned at the security level, relates to the extent to which the ESG risks are considered investment relevant and material, and if so, the direction and extent of that potential credit risk.
Source: BlueBay Asset Management (2020)

ESG Bond Types

New forms of credit issuance have emerged, designed to raise funding to deliver social and environmental objectives alongside a financial return. With the World Bank often playing a leading role in developing these markets and advising bond issuers, ESG-oriented bonds are typically organized around a few sustainable themes. What distinguishes these from conventional bonds is their underlying use of proceeds and the greater transparency they provide towards their use of proceeds. Investors include both asset managers and asset owners who may see these bonds as a way to advance sustainable finance as well as a means to diversify their asset mix.

Despite the development of ESG in fixed income, the absence of a universally recognized standards certification system for sustainable bonds should be acknowledged. A number of standards have emerged, notably the EU's proposal for an *EU Green Bond Standard*.[52,53] However, the absence of a universal standard is particularly urgent given the emergence of bond issues geared towards underlying sustainable themes, as shown in Exhibit 19. For instance, despite the green bond market emerging little more than a decade ago, labeled green bond issuance has increased by roughly 50% in the first half of 2019 to USD118 bn (GBP84.8 bn), of which 19% represented certified climate bonds.[54]

---

52 European Commission. 2019. *EU Green Bond Standard*. Available at: https://ec.europa.eu/info/publications/sustainable-finance-teg-green-bond-standard_en
53 ICMA. 2018. *Green Bond Principles (GBP)*. Available at: www.icmagroup.org/green-social-and-sustainability-bonds/green-bond-principles-gbp/
54 Climate Bonds Initiative. 2019. *Green Bonds Market Summary – H1 2019*. Available at: www.climatebonds.net/files/reports/h1_2019_highlights_final.pdf

Exhibit 19: Types of ESG Investing Bonds

Bond Type	Features
Green bonds	Green bonds, sometimes referred to as climate bonds, are any type of bond instrument that funds projects that provide a clear benefit to the environment, such as renewable energy projects. Originating in 2007 with the issuance of the first green bonds from the European Investment Bank (EIB) and the World Bank, some green bond indexes now track the development of issuance and offer investors a passive means of investing in green bonds. More information can be found on bonds in the International Capital Markets Association's (ICMA) *Green Bond Principles*.[55] Benchmark indexes include: ▶ S&P Green Bond Select Index; ▶ Bank of America Merrill Lynch Green Bond Index; and ▶ the Bloomberg Barclays MSCI Green Bond Index.
Social bonds	Social bonds fund projects that provide access to essential services, infrastructure, and social programs to underserved people and communities. Examples include projects providing: ▶ affordable housing; ▶ microfinance lending; ▶ healthcare; and ▶ education. The Spanish Instituto de Credito issued the first social bond in 2015. More information can be found on bonds in the ICMA's *Social Bond Principles*.[55]
Sustainability bonds	Sustainability bonds allow issuers to offer more broadly defined bonds that still create a positive social or environmental impact. In 2016, Starbucks issued the first US corporate sustainability bond of USD500 mn (GBP359 mn) that directly links the company's coffee sourcing supply chain to ESG criteria. More information can be found on bonds at the ICMA's *Sustainability Bond Guidelines*.[56]
Sustainability-linked bonds	Not to be confused with sustainability bonds, sustainability-linked bonds (SLBs) provide financing to issuers who commit to specific improvements in sustainability outcomes. These outcomes may be defined as environmental, social, and/or governance-related. More information can be found in the ICMA's *Sustainability-Linked Bond Principles*.[57]
Transition bonds	Transition bonds provide financing to 'brown' industries with high GHG emissions (such as mining, utilities, and heavy industry). Because of this fossil fuel exposure, these sectors are generally excluded from raising capital in sustainable finance markets. Transition bonds allow companies in these sectors to raise capital designated to the transition towards greener industries.
SDG-linked bonds	Though there is common overlap with green and social bonds, SDG-linked bonds enable issuers to raise capital by specifically committing and advancing to SDG-related targets. Issuers are generally required to provide evidence and assurance for business alignment to the targeted SDGs.
Blue bonds	Blue bonds fund projects with clear marine and ocean-based benefits, such as sustainable fishing projects. The Seychelles and the World Bank jointly issued the first blue bond in 2018.

Source: Mitchell, J. (2021).

---

[55] ICMA. 2020. *Social Bond Principles – Voluntary Process Guidelines for Issuing Social Bonds*. Available at: www.icmagroup.org/assets/documents/Regulatory/Green-Bonds/June-2020/Social-Bond-PrinciplesJune-2020-090620.pdf
[56] ICMA. 2018. *Sustainability Bond Guidelines*. Available at: www.icmagroup.org/assets/documents/Regulatory/Green-Bonds/Sustainability-Bonds-Guidelines-June-2018-270520.pdf
[57] ICMA. 2020. *Sustainability-Linked Bond Principles – Voluntary Process Guidelines*. Available at: www.icmagroup.org/assets/documents/Regulatory/Green-Bonds/June-2020/Sustainability-Linked-Bond-Principles-June-2020-171120.pdf

9 ESG SCREENING WITHIN PORTFOLIOS AND ACROSS ASSET CLASSES: GREEN SECURITIZATION AND SOVEREIGN DEBT

☐ 8.1.6 apply ESG screens to the main asset classes and their sub-sectors: fixed income; equities; and alternative investments

Green Securitization

An emerging area within credit, driven by several central banks including the Bank of England, leverages the momentum and research behind the green bond market to expand the conversation into green securitization.

Green securitization represents the mutualization of illiquid, 'green' assets or a series of assets into a security. Green collateralized loan obligations (CLOs), for which data that can be easily quantified and screened exists, constitute one such mutualized form of green securitization. This requires a common understanding of what 'sustainable assets' represent in a fixed-income context. The Green Finance Study Group (GFSG) defines sustainable assets as the following:

> *Sustainable loans, sustainable debt and sustainable bonds as specific financial products or debt linked to assets or investments that target environment and social sustainability; however, the more general consideration of financial sustainability is also contemplated.*[58]

Sovereign Debt

ESG integration approaches that lend themselves well to equities and corporate debt run into a number of difficulties when applied to sovereign debt. The number of governments issuing bonds, or sovereign debt, represent a much smaller investable universe than the number of corporates that issue corporate debt. Should their credit profile be strong enough, any listed corporate could issue some form of credit, from investment grade to high yield. While there is no limit to the creation of new corporate entities that issue fixed income, the pool of governments that issue debt is small by comparison and essentially finite.

By extension, the exclusion of countries (whether in the form of multilateral sanctions or economic sanctions limiting foreign direct investment [FDI]) will further reduce this pool and diversification potential. Here are some examples:

▶ US sanctions on Russia following its 2014 annexation of Crimea extended to Russian sovereign debt. US sanctions effectively limited any participant in the US financial system from financing or dealing in debt of longer than 90 days maturity.[59] Similarly, the Russian invasion of Ukraine in 2022 led to global sanctions that effectively restricted trading in Russian sovereigns.

---

58 G20 Sustainable Finance Study Group. 2018. *Towards a Sustainable Infrastructure Securitisation Market: The Role of Collateralised Loan Obligations (CLO).* Available at: https://g20sfwg.org/wp-content/uploads/2021/07/Towards_a_sustainable_infrastructure_securitisation_market.pdf
59 US Department of Treasury Resource Center. 2017. *Ukraine-/Russia-Related Sanctions.* Available at: https://home.treasury.gov/policy-issues/financial-sanctions/sanctions-programs-and-country-information/ukraine-russia-related-sanctions

- In 2019, the US government imposed sanctions on transactions tied to Venezuela, severely diminishing the trading liquidity of Venezuela's secondary sovereign debt.[60]

Credit rating agencies (CRAs) represent an important component for sovereign debt investors thus should be leveraged at both the issuer and the portfolio levels. Research already points to a high correlation among CRA ratings, as well as between CRA ratings and sovereign yields. This is quite different relative to the ESG ratings, which suffer with low correlation among ratings providers.

Fortunately, investors benefit from a growing pool of sovereign investment research resources. Not surprisingly, many of these resources focus on governance. Many ESG-focused sovereign debt investors begin by building and integrating an ESG framework based on the World Bank's Worldwide Governance Indicators (WGI). This dataset considers:

- a country's governance score; and
- its rankings on:
  - political stability;
  - voice and accountability;
  - government effectiveness;
  - rule of law;
  - regulatory quality; and
  - control of corruption.

Although this World Bank dataset is slow-moving, it offers a near 20-year time series and a means for investors to identify improving or deteriorating trends across these metrics. Investors can, in turn, examine either on a per sovereign basis or, as illustrated in Exhibit 20 with four of the six World Bank indicators, reflect on the change in momentum in the context of a portfolio holding many sovereign debt positions.

---

60 US Department of the Treasury. 2019. *Venezuela-Related Sanctions*. Available at: https://home.treasury.gov/policy-issues/financial-sanctions/sanctions-programs-and-country-information/venezuela-related-sanctions

Exhibit 20: Integrating World Bank World Governance Indicators to Screen for Change in Governance

Political stability and absence of violence or terrorism

Voice and accountability

Government effectiveness

Rule of law

Brazil | Indonesia | Phillipines | Russian Federation | Turkey | Columbia | Mexico | Poland | Thailand | South Africa

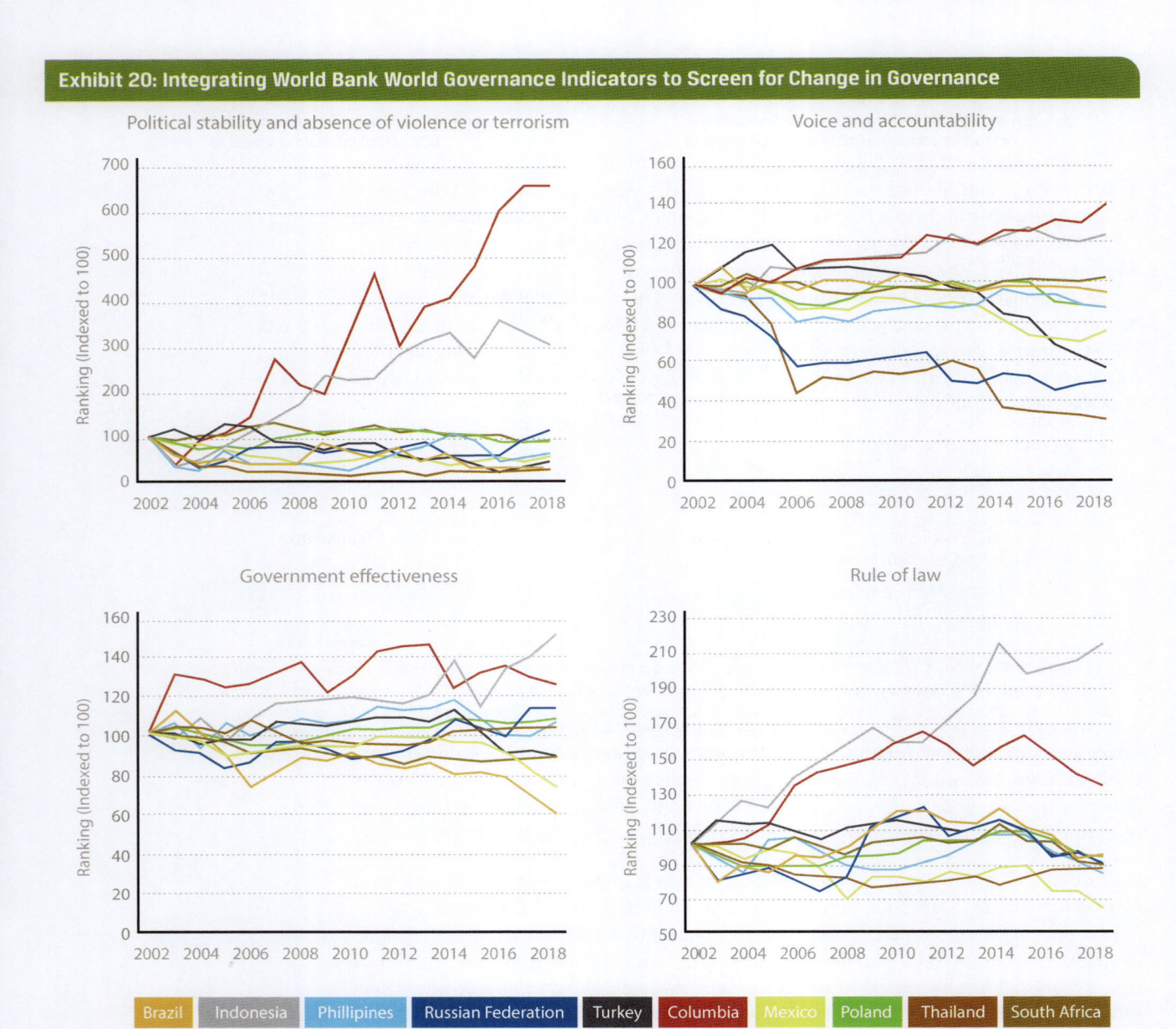

Note: The Worldwide Governance Indicators (WGI) project reports aggregated and individual governance indicators for over 200 countries and territories over the period 1996–2017 for six dimensions of governance. These aggregate indicators combine the views of a large number of enterprise, citizen, and expert survey respondents in industrial and developing countries. They are based on over 30 individual data sources produced by a variety of survey institutes, think tanks, non-governmental organizations, international organizations, and private sector firms.

Source: World Bank WGI.[61]

ESG tools are increasingly more sophisticated in leveraging datasets like the World Bank's WGI to draw out correlations between economic data. Exhibit 21 shows a significant correlation between country ESG risk and credit ratings, supporting the theory that ESG may be a leading indicator or at the very least a supporting factor for stable economies.

---

61 World Bank. 2019. *Worldwide Governance Indicators.* Available at: www.govindicators.org

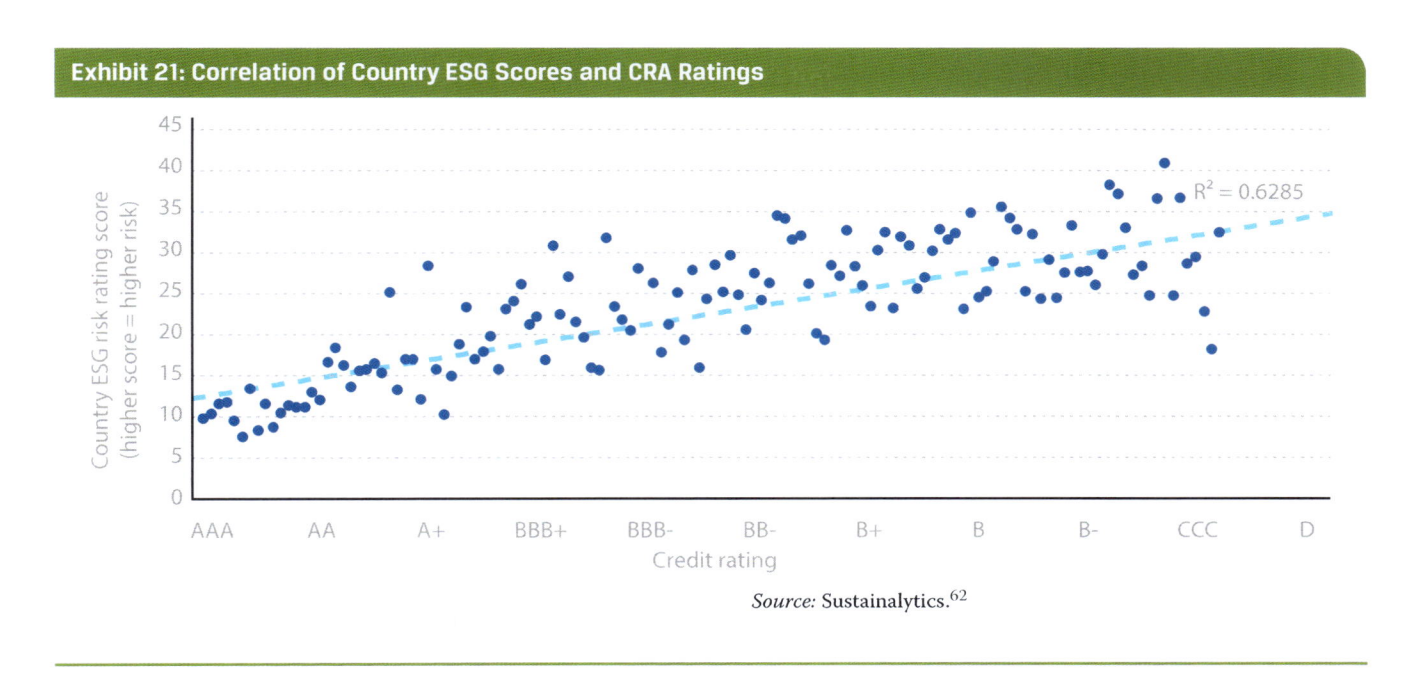

Exhibit 21: Correlation of Country ESG Scores and CRA Ratings

Source: Sustainalytics.[62]

Ultimately, though, investors should aim to embed ESG within their overall process, effectively normalizing it alongside other risk factor criteria. Exhibit 22 shows an example where a Z-scored ESG indicator, reflecting a composite of World Bank governance data and JP Morgan ESG data, sits as one of the active inputs with a portfolio's sovereign scoring tool.

---

62 Sustainalytics. 2017. *ESG Spotlight: Game of Bonds – Reassessing Sovereign Credit Ratings*. Available at: https://connect.sustainalytics.com/game-of-bonds-reassessing-sovereign-credit-ratings

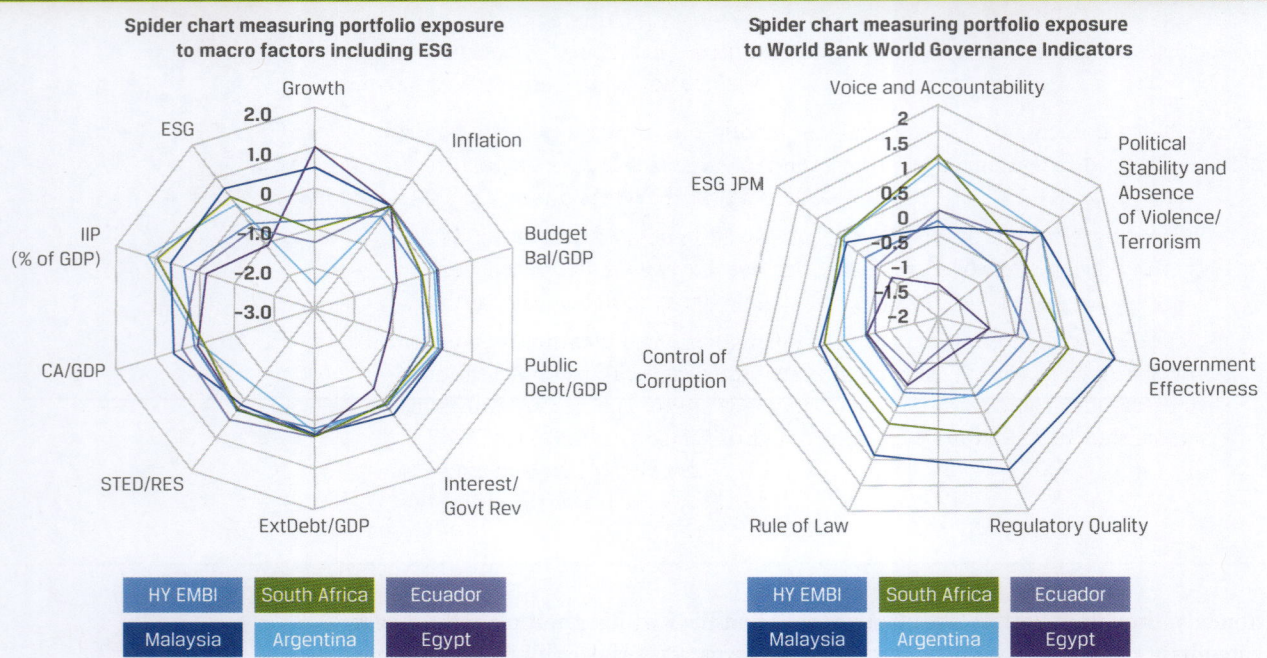

Exhibit 22: Portfolio Sovereign Scoring Tool – Illustrative Example

Spider chart measuring portfolio exposure to macro factors including ESG

Spider chart measuring portfolio exposure to World Bank World Governance Indicators

Legend: HY EMBI, South Africa, Ecuador, Malaysia, Argentina, Egypt

Note: Z-scores measure by standard deviations the distance between a single data point and the mean. They offer a way to test a raw score result against the normal population. The JP Morgan ESG suite of indexes is a global fixed-income index family that integrates ESG factors in a composite benchmark. The ESG JPM Index applies a multi-dimensional approach to ESG investing for fixed-income investors. It incorporates ESG score integration, positive screening, as well as exclusions of controversial sectors and UN Global Compact violators. ESG JPM Index scores are calculated daily, using data from RepRisk, Sustainalytics, and Climate Bonds Initiative (CBI) as inputs.

Sources: Man Group, JP Morgan, and World Bank.[63]

Like equities, sovereign debt is just as susceptible to distortion effects based on ESG ratings. These will be most notable in strategies that trade in both developed and emerging economies. ESG ratings and indicators like those of the World Bank tend to be structurally lower for emerging countries relative to developed economies, which enjoy higher standards of transparency, rule of law, regulatory authority, and anti-corruption. For instance, an emerging markets debt portfolio will benefit from a higher ESG score if it is underweight with emerging markets and overweight with defensive positions, like US treasuries or German bunds. Hence, it is critical to understand that this developed-emerging weighting is driving the overall ESG score.

10 ESG SCREENING WITHIN PORTFOLIOS AND ACROSS ASSET CLASSES: LISTED AND PRIVATE EQUITY

☐ 8.1.6 apply ESG screens to the main asset classes and their sub-sectors: fixed income; equities; and alternative investments

---

63 Osses, G., and M. Cal. 2019. *GEMD Strategies' Approach to Responsible Investing.*

Listed Equity

Listed equities represent the most developed asset class in terms of ESG integration. Equities have various advantages relative to other asset classes — notably, the greatest amount of transparency owing to its capital structure where creditors and shareholders coexist, albeit in a relationship that subordinates shareholders. The listed nature of equities and their ownership structure provide shareholders with the ability to exercise their view through their voting rights on many aspects of operational and strategic direction of the company, including its board of directors. Shareholder rights and voting are one of the most prominent manifestations of stewardship, where investors increasingly address non-financial objectives alongside financial issues.

Because of the enhanced nature of ESG disclosure among listed equities, all of the responsible investment strategies discussed in this chapter lend themselves to the asset class. This ranges not only from passive to active investment strategies, but from long-only to hedge funds as well. For that reason, this section will not restate the nature and mechanics of those investment strategies in a long-only context.

That said, hedge fund or long–short strategies are increasingly embedding ESG into portfolio construction and management. Hedge funds are alternative investment vehicles that employ leverage to enhance returns and hedging strategies to manage net risk and produce alpha. Shorting or short selling involves borrowing a security generally on margin, hence the leverage component in hedge funds, and then selling it into the market to be bought later. A successful short sale means that the investor is able to cover or buy back the security at a lower price than that which they initially paid to borrow it.

Indeed, the PRI now provides resources and formally includes a hedge fund module within its *Reporting Framework*.[64] In addition, organizations representing the interests of the hedge fund community (which include the Alternative Investment Managers Association [AIMA], the Managed Funds Association [MFA], and the Standards Board for Alternative Investments [SBAI], not to mention the PRI itself) now all convene working groups focused on ESG and regularly produce research, surveys, policy papers, and recommendations on practices.

Exhibit 23 and Exhibit 24 provide examples of an approach that a quantitative ESG long–short equity strategy might assume. As a sector-neutral portfolio, the long exposure represents the top or best decile of ESG-rated companies, while the short exposure represents the bottom or worst decile of ESG-rated stocks.[65] It operates across a number of data provider scores that include a proprietary, factor neutral one (Man Numeric), carbon intensity metrics, and even an event-driven sentiment strategy operating on ESG news using natural language processing (NLP).

Although exposure and returns vary across data and metrics, the long–short example provides empirical support for the logic that better-scoring ESG and carbon-efficient companies are capable of not only enhancing ESG exposure but also of potentially outperforming their poorer-scoring peers. In effect, the simulation finds betting against poorly-rated companies has the potential to reduce risk exposure and add resilience through lower drawdown.

Note, though, that in Exhibit 23 and Exhibit 24, all model spread performance shown is gross-of-fees and does not represent the performance of any portfolio or product. To calculate long-only model spreads, Man Numeric invests long in the top 10% ranked names within each sector and displays the gross of fees return. To calculate long–short model spreads, Man Numeric invests long in the top 10% ranked names

---

[64] PRI. 2018. *ESG Monitoring, Reporting and Dialogue in Private Equity*. Available at: www.unpri.org/private-equity/esg-monitoring-reporting-and-dialogue-in-private-equity/3295.article
[65] Market- and sector-neutral strategies are used to reduce portfolio exposure to overall risks while optimizing for investment return potential. These strategies focus on producing returns that are independent in market and sector volatility.

within each sector and short the bottom 10% ranked names within each sector and displays the gross of fees return. These spread returns are instantaneously rebalanced and do not reflect transaction costs. Rankings are based on Man Numeric's internal Alpha model scores.

Exhibit 23: Simulative Implications of Shorting Poor ESG Companies to Performance Exposure and Performance — Shorting Doubles Portfolio's ESG Exposure

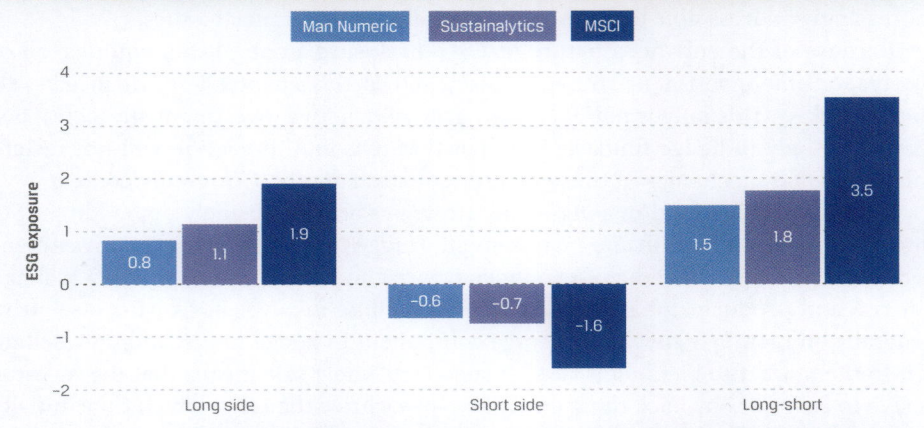

	Man Numeric	Sustainalytics	MSCI
Long side	0.8	1.1	1.9
Short side	−0.6	−0.7	−1.6
Long-short	1.5	1.8	3.5

Sources: MSCI ESG score; Sustainalytics ESG score; and Man Numeric proprietary ESG score as of 31 December 2019.[66]

Exhibit 24: Simulative Implications of Shorting Poor ESG Companies to Performance Exposure and Performance — Poor ESG Companies Have Underperformed

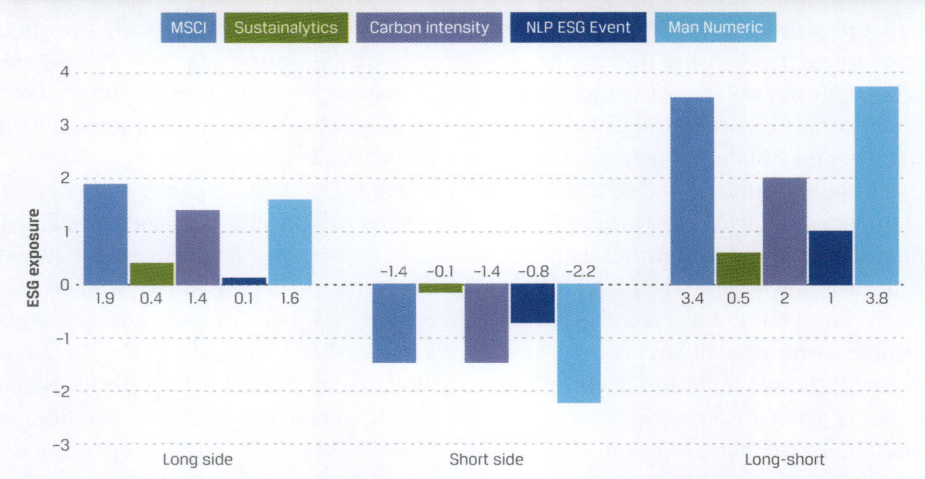

	MSCI	Sustainalytics	Carbon intensity	NLP ESG Event	Man Numeric
Long side	1.9	0.4	1.4	0.1	1.6
Short side	−1.4	−0.1	−1.4	−0.8	−2.2
Long-short	3.4	0.5	2	1	3.8

Sources: MSCI ESG score, Sustainalytics ESG score, Trucost carbon data, and Man Numeric proprietary ESG score as of 31 December 2019.[67]

---

66 Man Group. 2020. *The Big Green Short*. Available at: www.man.com/maninstitute/big-green-short

Private Equity

Like unlisted credit and real asset private markets, ESG integration in private equity faces several challenges, foremost being the lack of public transparency, established reporting standards, regulatory oversight, and public market expectations around ESG. The lack of compulsory non-financial reporting regulations like the EU's Non-Financial Reporting Directive (NFRD) for large European companies severely limits a private equity portfolio manager's ability to leverage ESG data for relative ranking and scoring comparability.[67]

In addition, smaller private companies are often capacity-challenged by ESG reporting requirements. The quality, consistency, and continuity of strong integrated reports published by many public companies represent a high hurdle to achieve for smaller companies. Early-stage companies also tend to operate with a much greater degree of freedom than more mature, listed companies. As a consequence, the portfolio manager will have to weigh the company's ESG trajectory (it may have established, but not yet met, ESG objectives) against the trajectories of more mature companies. This extends not only to the way the business or asset operates but also to the board level-devised strategy.

In some cases, private equity investors must negotiate against a strong founder or founder team, which, while a powerful internal motivator, may present long-term governance concerns. At the same time, early investors and significant shareholders are often strategic and long-term oriented, creating a powerful incentive to establish a strong set of ESG key performance indicators (KPIs) early in the company's life cycle. It may be in the interest of the general partners (GPs), investment professionals charged with investing and managing the fund's committed capital in companies, to establish specific, portfolio-wide metrics (obviously recognizing geographic and sectoral differences) as a means to support the overall portfolio strategy and communicate portfolio alignment to the fund's limited partner (LP) investors who invested in the overall private equity fund.

Exhibit 25 illustrates several ESG metrics tracked across different industries for several funds to gain a static, high-level picture of exposure.

Like other investor types, private equity investors may certainly impose exclusionary screening on any number of criteria to restrict investment in certain sectors, either normatively or ethically defined. However, private equity investors do not have the benefit of the breadth and diversity of indexes and benchmarks of the listed equities space, limiting opportunities for peer comparability analysis or portfolio optimization efforts around ESG criteria. However, portfolio managers can benchmark segments of the portfolio against smaller investment universes, even including public companies, if data comparability exists.

Hence, it is more likely that the GPs may apply some form of positive screening or thematic focus within their respective investment charter. In fact, because of the non-public nature of the private equity industry, LPs are increasing their expectations for GPs to integrate ESG analysis beyond screening in more robust forms. In addition, portfolio managers may establish minimum threshold ESG scoring for portfolio inclusion. Portfolio managers may address these challenges by formally establishing an ESG program that institutes in-depth, pre-deal ESG due diligence and ESG review for portfolio companies. Since ESG data for private equity firms may be more localized or regional, quantitative and systematic capabilities applied within the listed equities space will be of much less use.

---

67 European Commission. 2020. *Non-Financial Reporting.* Available at: https://ec.europa.eu/info/business-economy-euro/company-reporting-and-auditing/company-reporting/non-financial-reporting_en

Exhibit 25: Private Equity ESG Performance Data by Fund (Apax Partners) – Illustrative Example

Company	Sector	ENVIRONMENTAL CO$_2$ Emissions (tonnes)	Electricity (kwh)	Business Travel by Air (miles)	SOCIAL Sick Days (FTEs)	Voluntary Turnover	Workers Council	GOVERNANCE Anti-corruption policy	Cyber Security Function
Apex Europe VI									
Company A	Healthcare	47,451	59,402,437	0	70,072	1,280	Yes	Yes	Yes
Company B	Healthcare	—	—	—	32,675	301	No	Yes	No
Apex Europe VI									
Company A	Consumer	56,723	108,346,559	1,364,303	58,389	1,440	No	Yes	No
Company B	Healthcare	46,857	41,368,783	66,493,839	366	882	Yes	Yes	Yes
Company C	Services	2,400	1,394,000	115,000	2,717	254	Yes	Yes	Yes
Company D	Tech and telecom	468	272	3,882,723	-	114	No	Yes	No
Company E	Tech and telcom	13,275	85,682,875	10,779,548	70,497	3,993	Yes	Yes	Yes

Source: Adapted from PRI article

PRI. 2018. *ESG Monitoring, Reporting and Dialogue in Private Equity.* Available at: www.unpri.org/private-equity/esg-monitoring-reporting-and-dialogue-in-private-equity/3295.

ESG SCREENING WITHIN PORTFOLIOS AND ACROSS ASSET CLASSES: REAL ASSETS – REAL ESTATE AND INFRASTRUCTURE

☐ | 8.1.6 apply ESG screens to the main asset classes and their sub-sectors: fixed income; equities; and alternative investments

Real assets like real estate and infrastructure carry certain advantages and challenges compared to the equities and corporate fixed-income investment universe. In many cases, investors are majority owners or own the asset outright. Majority or full ownership stakes offer investors much greater control over the definition, application, and reporting of ESG data alongside or outside existing reporting standards like that of the Global Reporting Initiative (GRI).

Much like corporate unlisted fixed income, managing a portfolio of real assets requires building a picture of what the aggregate risk looks like as well as the correlation risk among all the underlying assets. GRESB's full benchmark[68] report provides a composite of:

- peer group information;
- overall portfolio KPI performance;
- aggregate environmental data in terms of usage and efficiency gains;
- a GRESB score that weights management, policy, and disclosure;
- risks and opportunities, monitoring, and environmental management system (EMS);
- environmental impact reduction targets; and
- data validation and assurance.

Nonetheless, this report depends heavily on companies, funds, and assets participating in the GRESB reporting assessment process. For portfolios where a significant percentage of the fund's holdings do not participate in the GRESB assessment, portfolio managers will need to supplement with their own ESG scoring.

As reporting data and standards improve for real assets, investors should work towards a stronger link between ESG considerations and their financial implications. One of the counterparts to the idea of an ESG risk premium conversation discussed in this chapter for the real asset investment universe is the potential for the existence of a green risk premium in real estate. Exhibit 26 demonstrates the increasing studies pointing to the existence of a green building premium across regions and for both commercial and residential real estate markets. This green building premium may help to more accurately price and understand the risks and implications of ESG in the real estate market.

---

68 GRESB. 2018. *GRESB Benchmark Report 2018*. Available at: https://gresb.com/benchmark-report/

Exhibit 26: Real Estate Studies and the Potential for a Green Building Premium

Author/Source	Year	Sample Period	Location	Segment	Sample Size (Number of Projects)	Scheme	Sales or Rental Yields	Price Increase/Decrease	Magnitude Sales	Magnitude Rents
Fuerst, McAllister, Nanda, Wyatt	2013	1995–2011	UK	Residential	325,950	EPC	Sales	Positive	6% to 14%	–
Kok, Kahn	2012	2007–2012	USA	Residential	1,604,879	Energy Star, GreenPoint Rated, LEED	Sales	Positive	9%	–
Deng, Li, Quigley	2012	2000–2010	Singapore	Residential	74,278	Green Mark	Sales	Positive	4% to 11%	–
Yoshida, Sugiura	2014	2002–2010	Japan	Residential	41,560	Tokyo Green Building Program	Sales	Mixed	–5% to +17%	–
Fuerst, McAllister	2011	1999–2008	USA	Office	24,479	Energy Star, LEED	Both	Positive	25% to 26%	4% to 5%
Kok, Jennen	2012	2005–2010	Netherlands	Office	1,072	EPC	Rents	Positive	–	6.5% to 12%
Newell, MacFarlane, Walker	2014	2011	Australia	Office	366	NABERS	Both	Mixed	–1% to 9%	–1% to 7%

Source: AllianzGI Global Solutions.[69]

Traditional residential housing model delivery had little regard for ESG factors. The primary model of delivery was concrete based, with inefficiencies among other building materials. Not surprisingly, the sector had a significant carbon footprint focused primarily on environmental criteria on a short-term, new build, and construction basis. ESG and impact-oriented residential strategies now focus on much broader criteria, actively integrating all components — particularly social considerations — within their portfolio.

Besides reducing the carbon footprint of their housing stock through more efficient building materials, community housing strategies now make efforts to deliver affordable mixed tenure housing solutions that provide greater social segmentation to meet the needs of the community — young people, first-time buyers, key workers, and seniors.

Investors with significant real estate exposure are increasingly leveraging the analytical modeling capabilities and historical datasets of insurance companies to understand weather risk generally and climate risk more specifically. Munich Re, one of the world's largest reinsurers, produces climate risk assessments that model potential property impact scenarios based on a broader set of twelve natural hazard types, including:

- earthquakes;
- volcanic eruptions,

---

[69] AllianzGI Global Solutions. 2015. *ESG in Real Estate.* Available at: www.risklab.com/media/151208_esg_in_real_estate.pdf

- tsunamis;
- tropical cyclones;
- extratropical storms;
- hail;
- tornadoes;
- lightning;
- wildfires;
- river floods;
- flash floods; and
- storm surges.

A joint study by Munich Re and PGGM (the Dutch pension fund) applies these analytics on PGGM's private real estate portfolio.[70]

A climate risk profile based on over 100 years of meteorological, weather, and hazardous-event data is capable of examining the climate risk of a diversified, global property portfolio across different dimensions — from overall hazard risk factor exposure to country and city (Exhibit 27) to individual property level risk. Capabilities now enable an extremely nuanced understanding of exact longitudinal and latitudinal data.

Exhibit 27: Climate Risk Overview for the Portfolio at the City Level

City/Metropolitan Statistical Area (MSA), country	Extratropical Storm	Flash Flood	River Flood	Storm Surge	Tornado	Tropical Cyclone	Wildfire
Marrero, USA	1.67	3.33	5.00	5.00	5.00	4.00	1.25
Savannah, USA	1.67	3.33	5.00	5.00	3.33	3.00	2.50
Palm Harbor, USA	1.67	3.33	1.00	5.00	5.00	4.00	3.75
Metairie, USA	1.49	3.33	5.00	5.00	5.00	3.11	0.00
Newark, USA	1.67	3.33	5.00	5.00	5.00	1.00	1.25
Amagasaki, Japan	1.67	3.33	5.00	5.00	1.67	4.00	1.25
Quanzhou, China	0.00	4.17	5.00	5.00	3.33	3.00	0.00
Miami, USA	1.49	3.58	0.60	3.14	5.00	4.00	0.98
Dalian Shi, China	1.67	4.91	4.43	4.43	3.33	0.00	0.00
Philadelphia, USA	1.67	3.33	0.00	5.00	5.00	1.00	2.50

Note: The numbers are based on PGGM portfolio weights of assets in each country and PGGM's rebasing of underlying hazard and risk scores.
Sources: PGGM and Munich Re.[71]

With growing evidence of sea-level rises capable of impacting population-dense coastal areas and communities, investors may also enhance the climate rate analysis of their portfolios by profiling a portfolio's exposure to elevation and coastline proximity (Exhibit 28). The effects of coastal erosion and flooding ultimately leading to managed retreats could carry meaningful consequences to property values and insurance

---

70 Munich Re and PGGM. 2019. *Climate Risk Assessment in Global Real Estate Investing.* Available at: www.pggm.nl/media/3ouenmff/pggm-position-paper-climate-risk-assessment-in-global-real-investing_september_2019.pdf

premiums. Indeed, a study already indicates that residential properties in the United States located in areas exposed to sea level rises already reflect a 7% discount relative to unexposed nearby homes.[71]

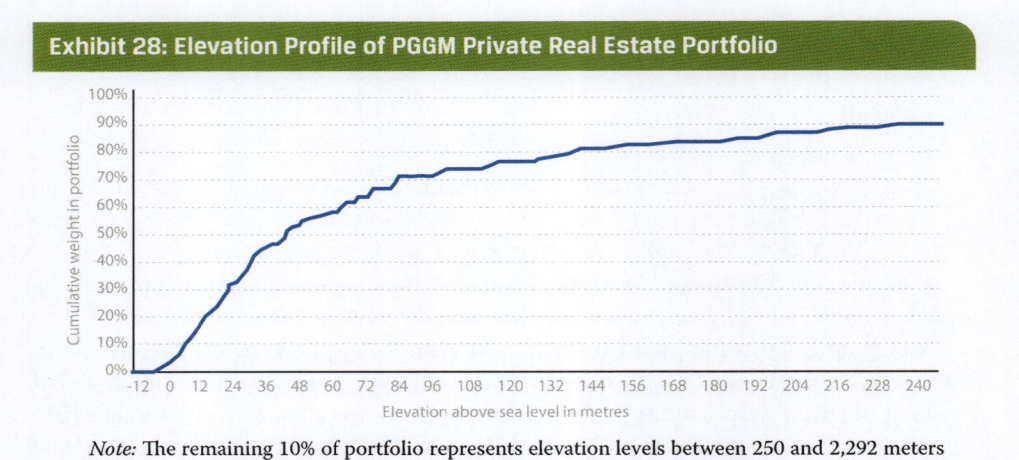

Exhibit 28: Elevation Profile of PGGM Private Real Estate Portfolio

Note: The remaining 10% of portfolio represents elevation levels between 250 and 2,292 meters above sea level.[71]

12 INTEGRATING ESG SCREENS WITHIN PORTFOLIOS TO MANAGE RISK AND GENERATE RETURNS

☐ 8.1.6 apply ESG screens to the main asset classes and their sub-sectors: fixed income; equities; and alternative investments

The effects and benefits of integrating ESG into portfolio management are an increasingly wide area of study. Investors typically address the effects to risk-adjusted returns of ESG integration in portfolio management through two dimensions:

▶ risk mitigation; and
▶ alpha generation.

Integrating ESG to Manage Portfolio Risk

Risk mitigation is the exercise of assessing and minimizing the exposure of a portfolio to ESG risks. Sometimes these risks are referred to as tail risks. In an ESG context, tail risks are generally long term in nature and describe a significant change or move by several standard deviations in the risk profile of an asset. Depending on the position size in a portfolio, the potential volatility of such an asset may carry significant implications for the portfolio's overall risk profile and to its potential risk-adjusted returns.

---

71 Bernstein, A., M. Gustafson, and R. Lewis. 2019. "Disaster on the Horizon: The Price Effect of Sea Level Rise." *Journal of Financial Economics* 134 (2): 253–272. Available at: https://doi.org/10.1016/j.jfineco.2019.03.013

For example, a real estate portfolio that is heavily invested in beachfront property at risk of coastal retreat should actively assess the potential impact to the portfolio's risk-adjusted returns and consider mitigating or minimizing its exposure.

In another example, a portfolio with significant holdings in the European utilities sector should routinely assess its exposure to understand its short-term risk to carbon price volatility and, in the long term, to a potential stranded asset write-down risk.

Much scrutiny is required when linking the correlation between ESG integration and investment returns. Fundamentally, any strong claim regarding ESG-driven performance requires a robust means to measure ESG. While firms may have certainly developed proprietary approaches to this problem, the ability to measure performance attribution for ESG does not commercially exist.

To this end, it is worth a short review of some general theory about risk within portfolio management and where ESG fits into the discussion. Financial risk in the traditional sense is generally expressed as a number. This number could assume many different forms:

- a variance;
- volatility; or
- value-at-risk (VAR).

Over the last half decade, numerous approaches have emerged to measure and price risk. The capital asset pricing model (CAPM) measures the proportional risk of a security or portfolio relative to market risk in the form of a premium.

More recently, Eugene Fama and Kenneth French introduced three-factor and, subsequently, five-factor models that both describe how certain risk premiums (investment risk, market risk, size risk, profitability risk, and value risk) are able to explain the probability distribution of investment returns.[72] Well-established evidence for these risk premiums — the differential between market returns and the risk-free rate, or the differential between high- and low-valued companies on a price-to-book basis — exists not only to drive factor-oriented investment strategies, but also to enhance risk factor portfolio attribution. In short, these efforts have contributed to the manner in which financial markets can identify, assign, and manage risk for single assets as well as portfolios.

Risk also appears as either idiosyncratic or systematic risk:

- Idiosyncratic risk describes firm- or stock-specific risk. In an ESG context, idiosyncratic risk could be posed by a company's staggered board of directors or a mining company that is repeatedly fined for its untreated mine tailings. In order to reduce or mitigate this kind of idiosyncratic risk, a portfolio manager may diversify the portfolio, diluting the exposure to the mining company. The portfolio manager may instead simply exit the poor-performing company outright, eliminating the risk.
- Systematic risk represents market risk, such as economic recession, that cannot be resolved through portfolio diversification alone.

These two perspectives on risk within financial markets are important for the expectations that we set for how we think about risk in an ESG context and for the questions they necessarily provoke. For instance:

- What evidence exists to demonstrate that ESG represents a risk premium?
- Broadly speaking, does ESG represent systematic risk or idiosyncratic risk?

---

[72] Fama, E., and K. French. 2014. "A Five-Factor Asset Pricing Model." *Journal of Financial Economics* 116 (1): 1–22. Available at: www.sciencedirect.com/science/article/abs/pii/S0304405X14002323

- Or does it, in a narrower form like climate risk, represent systematic risk to the financial system and wider global economy?
- If it does not represent a factor similar to those presented by Fama–French, does that mean that ESG integration is essentially process-oriented?

Studies demonstrating that almost 80% of alpha (returns in excess of market performance) can be attributed to portfolio factor risk rather than stock-specific risk would seem to support research efforts to identify and define ESG as a standalone factor.[73]

Needless to say, these are incredibly difficult questions that continue to raise significant debate among academics and practitioners alike. However, they are particularly important in the context of the often cited maxim 'what is measurable is manageable' for those trying to understand the implications of allocation to ESG-oriented assets and strategies. Furthermore, if the objective is to measure ESG, how is it defined relative to other factors, and how can it better inform investors' ability to manage a portfolio?

Despite the growing sophistication in ESG analysis across different asset classes and investment strategies, ESG is still largely characterized by its process-oriented approach for much of the investment management industry. This remains distinct from traditional approaches to risk, which, although reductive in nature, are also quantitative and generalizable. Moreover, treating ESG within portfolio management solely as a process turns it into a qualitative exercise that is subjective and difficult to measure.

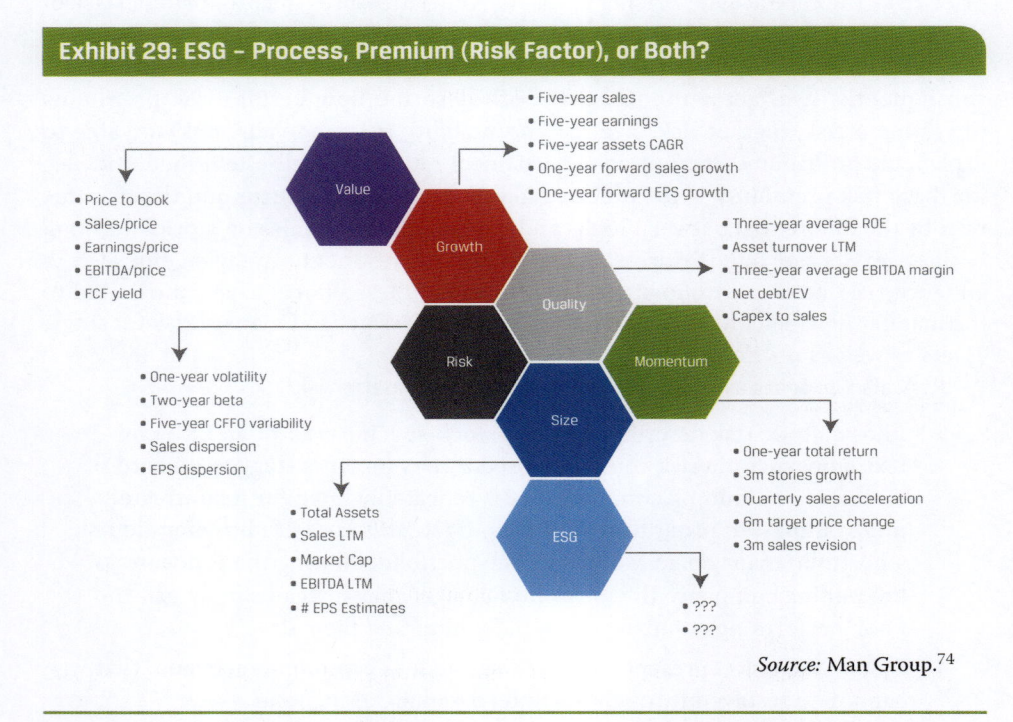

Exhibit 29: ESG – Process, Premium (Risk Factor), or Both?

Value:
- Price to book
- Sales/price
- Earnings/price
- EBITDA/price
- FCF yield

Growth:
- Five-year sales
- Five-year earnings
- Five-year assets CAGR
- One-year forward sales growth
- One-year forward EPS growth

Quality:
- Three-year average ROE
- Asset turnover LTM
- Three-year average EBITDA margin
- Net debt/EV
- Capex to sales

Risk:
- One-year volatility
- Two-year beta
- Five-year CFFO variability
- Sales dispersion
- EPS dispersion

Momentum:
- One-year total return
- 3m stories growth
- Quarterly sales acceleration
- 6m target price change
- 3m sales revision

Size:
- Total Assets
- Sales LTM
- Market Cap
- EBITDA LTM
- # EPS Estimates

ESG:
- ???
- ???

Source: Man Group.[74]

This not only increases the potential risk of greenwashing, but it also deprives asset allocators of the power of attributional analysis. It also means that outside of absolute value-based metrics like weighted-average carbon intensity, subjective ESG scores and rankings will continue to represent the prevailing means to approximate ESG risk in a portfolio.

---

73 Bender, J., P.B. Hammond, and W. Mok. 2013. "Can Alpha Be Captured by Risk Premia?" *Journal of Portfolio Management* 40 (2): 18–29. Available at: https://jpm.pm-research.com/content/40/2/18
74 Man Group. 2019. *ESG: Bringing Order to Uncertainty*. Available at: www.cfauk.org/-/media/files/pdf/pdf/3-events/jason_mitchell_slides.pdf

Integrating ESG to Generate Investment Returns

Although investors have traditionally employed ESG analysis for risk mitigation, many are growing more comfortable with framing ESG as a means to generate alpha. Indeed, many investors would intuitively agree with the broad assertion that a portfolio of better-managed, better-governed companies and assets would likely outperform a portfolio of poorly managed and governed peers — and potentially the market over the long term.

Yet, one of the challenges that remains is how to measure ESG-attributed performance, not just risk, at a portfolio level. Current evidence for ESG as performance enhancing often comes in the form of single-security or single-asset case studies. In many respects, these are incredibly useful. They may highlight innovative approaches for embedding ESG in valuation techniques or demonstrate new stewardship tactics when engaging company management on ESG issues. However, while a case study may convincingly explain, even causally, the linkage between investment returns and ESG operational performance, it represents a single anecdote and was most likely chosen because of selection bias. A case study does not explain ESG returns in formal attribution terms for the overall portfolio.

Generally speaking, institutional investors apply two popular approaches towards decomposing performance attribution: Brinson attribution and risk factor attribution. Attribution models serve to quantify and demonstrate the effects of asset allocation and selection decisions on investment returns. Brinson attribution decomposes performance returns based on a portfolio's active weights. For a given time series, this generally represents performance returns attributed to regional, sector, and stock-specific exposure.

There are efforts to embed ESG within risk factor analysis. A risk-based performance approach measures investment returns based on a portfolio's active factor exposures. These can be well-established Fama–French style factors or less-established factors like liquidity, low volatility, and currency carry.[75] Where the Brinson model emphasizes stock-specific attribution, which generally makes it popular for discretionary managers, risk factor attribution emphasizes both factor and security-specific exposures. Currently, neither model includes the capability to decompose factor risk exposure or performance attribution returns on an ESG basis.

QUANTITATIVE APPROACHES THAT EMBED ESG FACTORS — 13

☐ 8.1.6 apply ESG screens to the main asset classes and their sub-sectors: fixed income; equities; and alternative investments

We have reviewed quantitative strategies that apply a tilt or overlay through a screening methodology to drive greater portfolio exposure to some element of ESG. Quantitative strategies shape and direct the portfolio in aggregate or on a top-down basis rather than an individual issuer or asset basis. A more sophisticated approach directly embeds ESG into the algorithmic model, driving the stock selection for the portfolio. In effect, ESG operates much like any other factor within a multi-factor algorithmic investment strategy.

---

75 Fama, E., and K. French. 1993. "Common Risk Factors in the Returns on Stocks and Bonds." *Journal of Financial Economics* 33 (1): 3–56. Available at: https://doi.org/10.1016/0304-405X(93)90023-5

Quantitative managers build proprietary multi-factor models often based on a combination of well-established factors and more idiosyncratic factors. Each factor is prescribed an individual weight that, in turn, proportionally drives the multi-factor signal.

One of the advantages of a multi-factor model over a smart beta or beta plus strategy is diversification. Smart beta and beta plus investment strategies represent the compromise between passive, index-oriented investment and active investing at a lower cost than a traditional actively-managed strategy. The active element within these strategies generally emphasizes a single or dominant investment factor, such as value, quality, growth, or momentum.

A multi-factor strategy, on the other hand, seeks to maximize the benefits of diversification through the combination of a number of different factors. This is generally accomplished by allocating to factors on a top-down basis, or on a bottom-up basis, by allocating to individual securities that share certain common factor attributes. Factors that are negatively correlated to one another are combined to produce greater portfolio protection against a potential reversal by any one given factor.

Exhibit 30 and Exhibit 31 are examples that depict stylized multi-factor frameworks. Exhibit 31 includes an additional ESG factor within its equally-weighted, multi-factor algorithm.

Exhibit 30: Multi-Factor Combined Framework (Stylized)

	Alpha models				
Company	Value	Momentum	Quality	Combo	Rank
A	0.90	0.90	0.90	0.90	1
B	0.80	0.90	0.50	0.73	2
C	0.60	0.60	0.60	0.60	3
D	0.60	0.60	0.60	0.60	4
E	0.00	0.00	0.00	0.00	5

Source: Man Group.[76]

Exhibit 31: Multi-Factor Framework Integrating an ESG Factor (Stylized)

	Alpha models				Combo	
Company	Value	Momentum	Quality	ESG	ESG Combo	Rank
C	0.60	0.60	0.60	1.00	0.70	1
A	0.90	0.90	0.90	0.00	0.68	2
B	0.80	0.90	0.50	0.10	0.58	3
D	0.60	0.60	0.60	0.00	0.45	4
E	0.00	0.00	0.00	1.00	0.25	5

Source: Man Group.[77]

---

76 Man Group. 2019. *ESG Integration – No Silver Bullet*. Available at: www.man.com/maninstitute/esg-integration-no-silver-bullet

Beyond the fundamental question of how to measure ESG performance and risk exposure, investors must also consider the practical and operational issues when seeking to integrate ESG screens into portfolios and mandates. More specifically, the asset class and regional exposure of a portfolio may have significant implications on the coverage and integration of the ESG screen. Equities strategies, particularly those in developed markets with a focus on mid- to large-capitalization companies, generally benefit from greater, more mature ESG research coverage by third-party data vendors. More recently, corporate fixed-income portfolios are benefiting from more expansive ESG coverage as well as from a commitment by the CRAs to better integrate ESG factors into their credit analysis.[77]

Exhibit 32 illustrates the ESG ratings coverage gap of a high-yield credit portfolio where roughly 25% of the strategy's positions are unrated. Again, this coverage gap may be due to a number of reasons:

- the corporate bond issuer may be too small for ESG ratings providers to score;
- the bond may be a new issuer that has not yet been scored; or
- it may be unlisted debt.

Regardless of the reason, it is an important example for why and how multiple ESG data sources should be considered when assessing the ESG exposure profile of a portfolio. Noting coverage gaps when reporting to the investors of a portfolio is not only informationally helpful, but it also preserves the integrity of the ESG screening process.

That said, no best practice currently exists in terms of how to treat ESG coverage gaps within a portfolio. However, there are two potential approaches to address this issue:

- The simplest approach is to simply rescale the scoreable portion of the portfolio to 100% by proportionally resizing each scoreable position.
- The second approach is to apply Bayesian inference to the coverage ratio, effectively grossing it up to 100% by probabilistic inference.

Note that both approaches are reasonable with coverage gaps of up to 25%. Although no hard rule or best practice exists, normalizing for a gap in excess of 25% should be reviewed for whether it over- or under-represents a portfolio's true ESG exposure. This potentially undermines the integrity of ESG analysis at the portfolio level for the manager and may misrepresent the ESG exposure of the portfolio to the fund's investors.

---

77 PRI. 2021. *Statement on ESG in Credit Risk and Ratings*. Available at: www.unpri.org/credit-ratings/statement-on-esg-in-credit-ratings/77.article

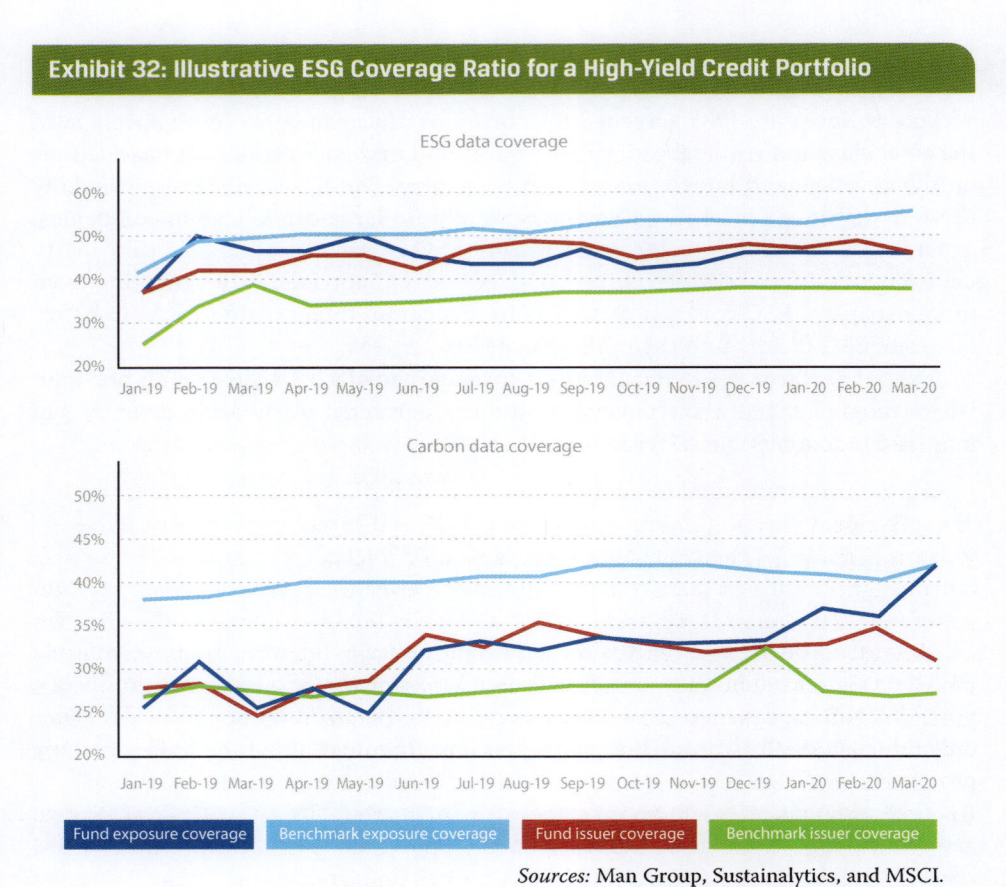

Exhibit 32: Illustrative ESG Coverage Ratio for a High-Yield Credit Portfolio

ESG data coverage

Carbon data coverage

Fund exposure coverage | Benchmark exposure coverage | Fund issuer coverage | Benchmark issuer coverage

Sources: Man Group, Sustainalytics, and MSCI.

Efforts to Develop Standards for ESG Investing: EU Regulatory Implications

The finance industry is currently undergoing a period of significant regulatory change in terms of ESG investing. Indeed, they represent the broadest, most comprehensive set of legislative action in sustainable finance. The EU Sustainable Finance Action Plan, which includes the EU Taxonomy and the Sustainable Finance Disclosure Regulation (SFDR), promises to carry profound implications for the investment management industry.[78,79]

The EU Taxonomy is a classification system organizing economic activities into environmentally sustainable activities. Policymakers see it as vital in steering the private sector participating in the funding of the European Green Deal. It provides a definitional baseline for ESG investing as a protection against greenwashing. Investors stand to benefit as the quality, prevalence, and comparability of non-financial data improve through other pieces of EU legislation like the Non-Financial Reporting Directive (NFRD), which is designed to improve European corporate disclosure.

---

78 European Commission. 2019. *EU Taxonomy for Sustainable Activities.* Available at: https://ec.europa.eu/info/business-economy-euro/banking-and-finance/sustainable-finance/eu-taxonomy-sustainable-activities_en

79 European Commission. 2019. *Regulation on Sustainability-Related Disclosures in the Financial Services Sector.* Available at: https://eur-lex.europa.eu/legal-content/EN/TXT/PDF/?uri=CELEX:32019R2088&from=EN

The EU SFDR focuses on disclosure at the entity (manager) and the product (investment strategy) levels. Notably, the EU SFDR also makes tremendous effort to normalize sustainability risk within all in-scope products. It organizes in-scope sustainability investment products into three major groups:

1. Article 9 or 'dark green' funds are products that have sustainable investment as their objective. As defined under the SFDR, sustainable investment may either contribute an environmental or social objective. However, they must "do no significant harm" (DNSH) to either of these objectives. Generally speaking, Article 9 funds will tend to be more impact-oriented.

2. Article 8 or 'light green' funds are products that more broadly promote environmental and/or social characteristics. While taking ESG criteria into consideration as one factor among many, they do not have to make sustainable investment the defining objective. It is expected that the majority of ESG investment products — particularly in the listed space — designate as Article 8.

3. Article 6 or 'Other' funds describes those funds that do not actively promote sustainable investment objectives or integrate sustainability criteria in ways that can be overtly marketed as such. That said, Article 6 funds may in fact integrate sustainability purely as a means to manage risk. In other words, SFDR assumes that all investors treat sustainability risks as part of their larger, ongoing risk management framework. If in-scope funds do not consider sustainability, they are required to provide a clear explanation for reasons in the fund's pre-contractual disclosures.

A summary of SFDR classification is as follows:

Article 6 – All Funds	Article 8 – All ESG	Article 9 - Sustainable
All managed products	'Light green' funds	'Dark green' funds
No integration of sustainability	Promotes, among other characteristics, environmental or social characteristics, or a combination but is not a main focus	Investment in economic activity that contributes to environmental objective
Can include stocks that are excluded from ESG funds, such as tobacco and coal producers, and should be clearly labelled as non-sustainable		Fund manager may be required to track an EU climate transition benchmark
		"Do no significant harm"

Increasing Level of Disclosure →

Source: Davy Group.[80]

---

[80] See https://www.davy.ie/market-and-insights/insights/capital-markets/horizons/sustainable-financial-disclosure-regulation-means-for-plcs.html.

Because this legislation will reshape much of EU sustainable finance within the EU and influence other regional regulatory approaches, it is worth including some of the seminal legislative elements.

EU legislation marks a distinct shift away from self-regulation towards a top-down, EU-driven organization of economic activities defined as sustainable investments. Broadly speaking, the policy objectives of these legislative pieces are to:

- provide protections against greenwashing for investment products sold into the EU;
- further embed sustainability within risk management for all investment products; and
- direct capital towards sustainable investment activities and away from unstable investment activities to support the EU's commitment towards a 2050 climate neutral economy.[81]

SFDR is a cornerstone of the EU Commission's ambitious Sustainable Finance Strategy. It applies to so-called "Financial Market Participants" ("FMPs"), notably fund and asset managers, insurers, pension funds, banks, and investment firms, that offer "Financial Products" subject to SFDR. Financial Products include funds, investment-based insurance products ("IBIPs"), and certain pension products and also extend to the portfolio management of segregated accounts. Under the SFDR, FMPs must make pre-contractual, periodic, and website disclosures on sustainability risks and factors and on certain environmental and social aspects of their Financial Products.

The European Commission has published Regulatory Technical Standards (RTS) under the SFDR. The RTS complement the provisions of SFDR applying from 10 March 2021 by providing detailed guidance on disclosures relating to principal adverse impacts ("PAIs") on sustainability factors at the FMP level and pre-contractual, periodic, and website disclosures of Financial Products promoting environmental or social characteristics (called "Art. 8 SFDR Products") or having sustainable investment as their objective (called "Art. 9 SFDR Products").

While the text of the RTS is now final, the RTS are not yet formally in force since the EU Council and the EU Parliament are granted a three-month scrutiny period (extendable by another three months) in which they can approve or reject the RTS as a whole. Since the RTS are technical and have been subject to a long consultation and redrafting process since February 2021, it is not expected that the Council or Parliament will object. If no objection is made, the RTS will apply from 1 January 2023.

Structure of the RTS

The RTS are composed of the RTS text and five separate annexes that contain the standardized disclosure templates, which FMPs must use to make the disclosures under Art. 4 SFDR and Art. 8 to 11 SFDR ("Templates").

The RTS text (and annexes 1, 2, 3, 4, 5) specify the exact content, methodology, and presentation of the information to be disclosed with the aim to improve the quality and comparability of reporting, as well as to address greenwashing. Specifically, the RTS define the details needed to meet disclosure obligations for manufacturers of financial products and financial advisers toward end-investors and disclosure obligations regarding adverse impacts on sustainability matters at entity and financial product levels.

---

81 European Commission. 2020. *Committing to Climate-Neutrality by 2050: Commission Proposes European Climate Law and Consults on the European Climate Pact.* Available at: https://ec.europa.eu/commission/presscorner/detail/en/ip_20_335

Quantitative Approaches That Embed ESG Factors

In five chapters, the RTS text deals with general disclosure rules (Chapter I), PAI reporting at the FMP level (Chapter II), pre-contractual disclosures for Art. 8 SFDR Products and Art. 9 SFDR Products (Chapter III), website disclosures for such products (Chapter IV), and periodic disclosures for such products (Chapter V). Different from the previous draft RTS, the requirements for pre-contractual and periodic disclosure of Art. 8 SFDR Products and Art. 9 SFDR Products are now set out directly in the respective Templates and, aside from the more complex Taxonomy disclosures, there are no additional provisions in the text of the RTS repeating the content of the Templates. This will facilitate working with the Templates because FMPs will no longer have to scrutinize both RTS text and Templates, which in some instances contained diverging guidance.

The first detailed disclosure on PAI for FMPs complying with Art. 4 SFDR based on the RTS is only due by 30 June 2023. Annex I to the RTS contains pre-defined mandatory and voluntary PAI indicators that FMPs must integrate into their data collection processes, down to the ultimate asset. Several mandatory PAI indicators for investee companies (equity and debt) are particularly challenging for investments in private companies. Data need to be collected at least on a quarterly basis.

Data Collection

FMPs must apply "best efforts" to obtain PAI indicator data for all investments from available sources, including investee companies, their own research, third-party data providers, or reasonable assumptions of the FMPs. The collection of PAI indicator data is also one of the main elements of the "do no significant harm" (DNSH) analysis for sustainable investments, and it may be difficult to qualify investments as "sustainable investments" if no data on PAI indicators (not even proxies or assumptions) are available.

Challenges in Integrating Taxonomy Disclosures into SFDR

- **Language:** FMPs will have to learn new vocabulary as the easily understandable term "Taxonomy-aligned investments" has been replaced by the much longer "investments in environmentally sustainable economic activities." This is in line with the wording in the Taxonomy Regulation, and the divergence in the draft RTS has led to some questions in the market. However, the concept has not been followed through for the Templates, which are now using both the old and the new term, potentially causing even more confusion for customers/investors.

- **Taxonomy KPIs:** FMPs are required to disclose the share of their investments in environmentally sustainable economic activities on the basis of all three Taxonomy KPIs (turnover, CapEx, and OpEx). While the pre-contractual disclosure can be based on only one single KPI (usually turnover), the period disclosures will have to be more detailed and use all three KPIs. This is due to the methodology used in the Art. 8 Taxonomy Delegated Act. Some of the environmentally sustainable economic activities will only show when using CapEx or OpEx as relevant KPI (e.g., expenditures to improve energy efficiency of buildings).

- **Taxonomy disclosure templates:** An additional issue to consider has been whether Art. 8 SFDR Products promoting environmental characteristics but not committing to make sustainable investments must also do the full Taxonomy disclosures. While the wording of Art. 6 Taxonomy Regulation seems to imply this, the ESAs have in the past mentioned on several occasions that such Art. 8 SFDR products would not have to disclose on Taxonomy. This issue has not been resolved by the RTS. The RTS and the Templates merely refer to Art. 6 Taxonomy Regulation. However, the

Taxonomy disclosures in the Templates are part of the section dealing with sustainable investments, which according to the Template guidance notice should only be filled out by Art. 8 SFDR Products making sustainable investments. For periodic disclosures of Art. 8 SFDR Products, there is a clear statement in the RTS that Taxonomy only needs to be included if the Art. 8 SFDR Product had committed to making sustainable investments contributing to an environmental objective. This has, however, not been picked up in the respective Template, and the EU Commission has yet to resolve.

▶ **Website disclosure:** FMPs have already been obliged under the SFDR to make certain disclosures on their websites. These included disclosures on the FMPs (notably, sustainability risk policies, consideration of PAI, and remuneration policies) as well as on Art. 8 SFDR Products and Art. 9 SFDR Products. The RTS now provide significantly more detailed website disclosures for PAI consideration and for Art. 8 SFDR Products and Art. 9 SFDR Products. In relation to PAI consideration, the detailed Template in Annex I will have to be used from 1 January 2023, including the collected PAI indicator data as well as actions taken, actions planned, and targets to address and mitigate the respective impacts. There are no Templates for the website disclosure of Art. 8 SFDR Products and Art. 9 SFDR Products, but the RTS require that FMPs disclose according to specific sections and contain guidance on the content of each of these sections.

These website disclosures are designed to complement the pre-contractual and periodic disclosures and must contain additional information on the continuous monitoring of sustainability indicators during the product lifecycle, methodologies, data sources and processing, possible limitations to methodologies and data, as well as a description of the investment due diligence and the FMPs engagement policies.

Another important feature of the new website disclosure requirements relates to language. The summary sections for the PAI consideration and for the product-related website disclosures need to be provided in multiple languages, including:

- In an official language of the FMP's or Financial Product's home member state;
- If different, in an additional language customary in the sphere of international finance (usually English); and
- If the FMP offers Financial Products in other EU member states or the respective Financial Product is marketed in other EU member states, in an official language of all of these host member states. For example, for a Luxembourg fund with English documentation marketed in Germany, France, and Spain, the summaries need to be provided in English, German, French, and Spanish.

Key elements of SFDR

▶ **Entity-level principal adverse impact (PAI) reporting:** The RTS (Chap 2) defines the content, methodology, and presentation of information for the sustainability indicators on adverse impacts on the climate and other environment-related adverse impacts and adverse impacts in the field of social and employee matters, respect for human rights, anti-corruption, and anti-bribery matters.

- **Indicators:** Annex 1 details a mandatory reporting template for the statement on the consideration of principal adverse impacts of investment decisions on sustainability factors. The indicators are divided into a core set of universal mandatory indicators as well as additional opt-in indicators for both environmental and social factors. Indicators are included for adverse impacts on sustainability factors from investment in investee companies, sovereigns, and real estate assets.
    - **Investment in investee companies mandatory indicators include:** GHG emissions (Scope 1,2,3), carbon footprint, GHG intensity of investee companies, exposure to companies active in the fossil fuel sector, share of non-renewable energy consumption and production, energy consumption intensity per high impact climate sector, activities negatively affecting biodiversity-sensitive areas, emission to water, hazardous waste and radioactive waste ratio, violation of UN global Compact principles and OECD Guidelines for Multinational Enterprises, lack of processes and compliance mechanisms to monitor compliance with the aforementioned, unadjusted pay gap, board gender diversity, and exposure to controversial weapons.
- **Information:** Alongside disclosure for the indicators, financial market participants should also include narrative elements on a summary, policies on the identification of principal adverse impacts, actions taken and planned to mitigate the principal adverse impacts, and adherence to international standards and historical comparison covering at least five previous reference periods.
- **Reporting schedule:** Reporting should be carried out by 30 June each year, with the previous year as a reference period.
- **Comply or explain:** Market participants that do not consider principal adverse impacts of investment decisions must disclose a statement and explanation on their website.

▶ **Pre-contractual product disclosures:** The RTS (Chap 3) set out the content and presentation of information to be disclosed at the pre-contractual level in sectoral documentation. Annexes 2 and 3 outline the templates to be used to specify how environmental or social characteristics or sustainable investment objectives are achieved.
- For financial products making sustainable investment, requirements are laid out for the compliance of the "do no significant harm" principle in relation to the principle adverse impact indicators. In order to connect the SFDR "do no significant harm" principle and the Taxonomy minimum safeguards, the report must also cover information on whether the investments are aligned with the OECD Guidelines for Multinational Enterprises and the UN Guiding Principles on Business and Human Rights, including the principles and rights set out in the eight fundamental conventions identified in the Declaration of the International Labour Organisation on Fundamental Principles and Rights at Work and the International Bill of Human Rights.

▶ **Articles 5 and 6 Products under the Taxonomy Regulation:**
- The RTS (Chap 3) include specific requirements for financial products under Art. 5 and Art. 6 of the Taxonomy Regulation related to identification of the environmental objective(s) the financial product contributes

to. The extent to which economic activities invested in qualify as environmentally sustainable must be shown in graphical representations of KPIs.
- The RTS (Chap 5) also lay out requirements for periodic disclosures by financial products where they are captured under Art 5 and 6 of the Taxonomy Regulation concerning the identification of environmental objective(s) the product contributes to and the extent to which the economic activities the product is invested in qualify as environmentally sustainable (shown in graphical representation of KPIs).

▶ **Product disclosures on website:** The RTS (Chap 4) detail the content and presentation of the information that financial market participants must publicly disclose on their website for these financial products. Disclosure must include a focus on the methodology and any screening criteria and data sources used, where and how information should be reported online, and a requirement to publish a two-page summary.

▶ **Periodic product-level disclosures:** Requirements for product-level periodic disclosure are laid out in Chap 5 of the RTS and use mandatory templates from Annexes 4 and 5:
- Reporting should include how the financial product succeeded in meeting its environmental or social characteristics (Art. 8 Products) or attained its sustainable investment objective (Art. 9 Products). The disclosures require a historical comparison covering up to five reference periods and the disclosure of the top 15 investments made during a particular reference period.
- Financial products that have sustainable investments must include information on how they have complied with the "do no significant harm" (DNSH) principle.

▶ **The principle of DNSH** was introduced in the Technical Expert Group Final Report of the EU Sustainable Finance Taxonomy:

- Under the DNSH principle, economic activities that make a substantial environmental contribution to the climate change mitigation or adaptation must not cause significant harm to the other designated environmental objectives. These include:
  - sustainable use and protection of water and marine resources;
  - transition to a circular economy, waste prevention, and recycling;
  - pollution prevention and control; and
  - protection of healthy ecosystems.[82]

The PRI has produced a number of case studies applying the DNSH principles and examining its implications.[83] Private equity and real estate investors appear to have constructed the most robust DNSH analysis, given their oversight on building-specific projects and construction. However, many of the case studies point to a number of challenges, from sourcing available and comparable data to identifying and verifying DNSH activities to isolating the specific share of revenue affected by a controversy.

---

82 European Commission. 2020. *TEG Final Report on the EU Taxonomy*. Available at: https://ec.europa.eu/info/files/200309-sustainable-finance-teg-final-report-taxonomy_en
83 PRI. 2021. *EU Taxonomy Alignment Case Studies*. Available at: www.unpri.org/policy/eu-sustainable-finance-taxonomy/eu-taxonomy-alignment-case-studies

Listed investors recognized that DNSH can be applied in either quantitative or qualitative manners, potentially leading to inconsistent approaches when compared to cross-sections of investors. In addition, investors are applying myriad proxy data, ranging from systematically examining controversy incidents to individually reviewing company filings, sustainability reports, product brochures, and minimum safety standards submission to the Statistical Classification of Economic Activities in the European Community (NACE) to verify whether activities, products, or services qualify.[84] While data providers offer controversy datasets, these controversies should be considered in terms of materiality, whether they remain outstanding, and how they relate to specific NACE DNSH.

Last, because DNSH-related thresholds are ultimately self-determined, there is a diverse set of metrics and thresholds to apply either at the underlying investment or at the portfolio level.

Other Efforts to Develop Standards for ESG Investing

In addition to EU regulatory change, a number of other initiatives and organizations are also working towards developing ESG standards for different use cases aimed at different stakeholder groups.

CFA Institute has published the Global ESG Disclosure Standards for Investment Products.[85] These standards specify the type of information that investment managers should provide to clients and investors about how ESG information or ESG issues are incorporated into a fund's or strategy's objectives, investment process, and stewardship activities. They include disclosure requirements related to the:

1. systematic consideration of financially material ESG information in investment decisions;
2. use of an ESG index as an investment universe;
3. use of an ESG screening criteria;
4. use of ESG targets and constraints in portfolio construction;
5. benchmarking of ESG characteristics or performance;
6. incorporation of ESG information or ESG issues into stewardship activities; and
7. incorporation of specific environmental and social impact objectives alongside risk and return objectives.

The standards' disclosure-oriented approach was informed by current ESG regulatory trends, but the standards are not anchored by any one regionally-specific regulation or prescriptive standard. Hence, they have the advantage of being truly global standards for all markets and all types of asset classes, investment strategies, and ESG approaches. The standardization of investment product ESG disclosures is important because it helps to set common expectations about the type of information that investment managers should provide. Standardization also helps protect investors by helping them to better understand, evaluate, and compare investment products.

---

84 The EU uses NACE, derived from the French *Nomenclature statistique des activités économiques dans la Communauté européenne*, as its statistical classification of economic activities. For more information, visit: https://ec.europa.eu/eurostat/documents/3859598/5902521/KS-RA-07-015-EN.PDF
85 See https://www.cfainstitute.org/en/ethics-standards/codes/esg-standards.

The European Commission-supported European Financial Reporting Advisory Group (EFRAG) has set out recommendations to the European Commission for possible EU sustainability reporting standards that would complement the EU's corporate Non-Financial Reporting Directive (NFRD) with a multi-stakeholder reporting framework.[86]

The International Organization of Securities Commissions (IOSCO) is the international body that brings together the world's securities regulators and is recognized as the global standard setter for the securities sector. At COP 26, in collaboration with IOSCO, the International Financial Reporting Standards (IFRS) Foundation established a new International Sustainability Standards Board (ISSB) to develop globally adopted sustainability disclosure standards, incorporating the Value Reporting Foundation and the Climate Disclosure Standards Board within its structure.

This new body will facilitate the development of a comprehensive global baseline of high-quality sustainability disclosure standards. ISSB will have a multi-location structure to ensure that the differing needs of the various regions are reflected as the standards are developed. Similar to the role of the IFRS Accounting Standards in setting out how a company prepares its financial statements, IFRS Sustainability Disclosure Standards will set out how a company discloses information about sustainability-related factors.

14 APPLYING ESG SCREENINGS TO INDIVIDUAL LISTED AND UNLISTED COMPANIES AND COLLECTIVE INVESTMENT FUNDS

> 8.1.7 distinguish between ESG screening of individual companies and collective investment funds: on an absolute basis; relative to sector/peer group data

Listed Companies and Collective Investment Funds

Screening for ESG or other criteria, whether among individual securities or across collective investments funds, will yield different results depending on the methodology. Moreover, the emergence of dedicated or branded ESG investment funds has now made it necessary to examine how these funds differ in terms of ESG characteristics.

Broadly speaking, the PRI recognizes three main approaches to screening:

1. **Negative screening** represents the avoidance of the worst performers. Functionally speaking, an investor might apply screening towards:
   - sectors;
   - regions;
   - issuers;
   - business activities and practices;
   - product and services; and
   - even security types, such as certain commodities.

---

86 European Financial Reporting Advisory Group (EFRAG). 2021. *Proposals for a Relevant and Dynamic EU Sustainability Reporting Standard-Setting*. Available at: www.efrag.org/Lab2

2. **Positive screening** is investment into the best ESG performers relative to industry peers across, as in point 1, different criteria.
3. **Norms-based screening** applies existing normative frameworks in order to screen issuers against internationally-recognized minimum standards of business practice. Screening generally applies globally-recognized frameworks like treaties, protocols, declarations, and conventions, including:
   - the *UN Global Compact*;
   - the UN Human Rights Declaration;
   - the ILO's *Declaration on Fundamental Principles and Rights at Work*;
   - the Kyoto Protocol; and
   - the Organisation for Economic Co-operation and Development (OECD) *Guidelines for Multinational Enterprises*.

In addition, the PRI has outlined a sequence of six steps for when investors implement screening as an investment approach:[87]

1. **Identify client priorities**: Investors should clearly disclose the objectives of screening within fund documentation.
2. **Publicize clear screening criteria**: Investors should disclose screening approaches in contractual agreements, such as the investment management agreement (IMA).
3. **Introduce oversight**: Investors should establish an internal control or compliance function that:
   - oversees screening;
   - conducts reviews; and
   - considers any changes in screening criteria.
4. **Adapt investment process**: Investors may want to consider refining the screening approach with greater sophistication and/or flexibility consistent with the fund documentation. Depending on the desired portfolio exposure, investors may choose to employ absolute, threshold, or relative exclusion methodologies.
5. **Review portfolio implications**: Investors should regularly assess and review the implications of screening on the portfolio, including changes in exposure to volatility, tracking error, and common risk factors.
6. **Monitor, report, and audit**: Investors should implement process and data assurance control functions that are either internally or even externally (third party) assured.

Screening generally requires a quantitative lens as well as an ESG dataset that offers wide coverage of global securities. Morningstar, the retail fund distributor, now includes a sustainability rating for funds alongside its core fund evaluation. Its sustainability rating is based on ESG risk metrics derived from Sustainalytics company-level data,

---

[87] PRI. 2020. *An Introduction to Responsible Investment: Screening.* Available at: www.unpri.org/an-introduction-to-responsible-investment/an-introduction-to-responsible-investment-screening/5834.article

applying the scoring methodology. Indeed, several other platforms have introduced ESG analytics aimed at measuring and grading both equities and fixed-income funds based on ESG criteria for end investors.[88,89]

For individual companies, screening on an absolute basis will automatically attribute low scores to certain industries and sectors depending on the criteria. Asset-heavy industries (and by association, companies within that industry or sector) that happen to be carbon emissions-intensive will likely score poorly on environmental metrics. This is useful for an investor to understand and quantify the exposure at risk within a portfolio of companies that produce high GHG emissions. For instance, if the price of carbon on the EU's Emissions Trading System (ETS) suddenly appreciates, a portfolio's exposure to such companies as utilities with a high dependency on coal-fired power generation will be at risk. This approach allows an investor to run simultaneous sensitivity analyses against ESG-related shocks, like the carbon price, to test the resilience and correlation of a portfolio.

However, this approach potentially sacrifices the benefit of a balanced portfolio relative to the market or benchmarks to which it is indexed to. In other words, an absolute values approach has the potential to not provide the context necessary to manage a diversified portfolio.

On the other hand, ESG screening premised on relative and peer-group datasets provides better context for building and maintaining a balanced, diversified portfolio. This approach potentially prevents wholesale exclusions of poorly-rated industries like mining on absolute value-based data, which may represent not only a meaningful driver of the economic cycle but also a significant weighting within main indexes. As we have discussed before, exclusions of this nature contribute to lower diversification and, consequently, higher active risk within a portfolio.

Despite the clear organizational benefits of ESG screening, whether on an absolute or relative basis, its approach does carry several challenges. One common criticism is its reductive approach. In other words, its quantitative measure does not consider softer forms of ESG, such as stewardship and engagement activities. In fact, an investor whose portfolio focuses on long-term stewardship opportunities in poorly rated ESG companies in order to improve performance will likely suffer from the poor optics of these companies at the portfolio level.

Exhibit 33 and Exhibit 34 depict two screens of global equities funds.

Exhibit 33 captures the top ten performing funds on a one-year basis, which are classified as being a 'sustainable investment' by Morningstar. The sustainable investment label indicates if the fund has prospectus language that explicitly calls out its focus on:

- sustainability;
- impact; or
- specific environmental, social, and/or governance factors in its investment process.

A sustainable investment-tagged fund may take a pro-active stance by selectively stating that they invest in, for example, low carbon or fossil fuel-free companies or firms that seek to address gender and diversity disparities in their workforce.

---

[88] Benjamin, J. 2019. "Lipper Plans ESG Scoring System for Mutual Funds." *Investment News* (12 March). Available at: www.investmentnews.com/lipper-plans-esg-scoring-system-for-mutual-funds-78547

[89] Iacurci, G. 2018. "UBS Global Wealth Management Will Give ESG Scores to Funds." *Investment News* (3 December). Available at: www.investmentnews.com/ubs-global-wealth-management-will-give-esg-scores-to-funds-77223

Despite the sustainable investment label, note the variability in the funds' respective sustainability ratings, which are based on ESG risk, as scored independently and quantitatively by Morningstar. Star ratings are a measure of a fund's risk-adjusted return against its peer group.

Exhibit 33: Morningstar-Ranked Global Equities Funds (by Sustainable Fund by Prospectus and One-Year Performance)

Rank	Fund Standard Name	AUM USD (mn)	One Year	Three Years	Five Years	Sustainable Fund by prospectus	Star Rating	Sustainability Rating
1	NEI Global Dividend	393	51.1	9.0	9.7	Yes	★★★★	Above average
2	Berenberg Sustainable World Equities	31	44.4	--	--	Yes	--	Average
3	Artisan Global Discovery	3	42.9	--	--	Yes	--	Below average
4	DNB Fund Global ESG	16	42.3	14.4	12.7	Yes	★★★	Average
5	Kames Global Sustainable Equity	130	41.0	16.3		Yes	★★★★★	Below average
6	Janus Henderson Horizon Global Sustainable Equity	199	39.6	14.1	11.3	Yes	★★★★★	High
7	Morgan Stanley INVF Global Opportunity	9,492	38.7	21.5	19.9	Yes	★★★★★	Above average
8	NN Duurzaam Aandelen Fonds	2,196	38.2	12.1	10.8	Yes	★★★	Above average
9	NN (L) Smart Connectivity	182	37.7	18.9	14.1	Yes	★★★	High
10	Öhman Global Marknad Hållbar	4,597	37.6	--	--	Yes	--	High

Source: Morningstar, 31 December 2019; Sustainable Fund by Prospectus as of 31 March 2020.[90]

Another issue that may exist is the award of a high sustainability rating for a fund that may in fact not have any of the essential ingredients to ESG integration — such as an ESG policy or systematic process — embedded within its process. This fund may be highly ranked on a coincidental basis by the fact its portfolio reflects low exposure to carbon-intensive industries or high ESG-rated companies purely by chance. This is not an explicit example of greenwashing as the investment manager is not intentionally over-representing their ESG credentials. But this misalignment or mischaracterization does have the potential to confuse the market, particularly for retail.

Exhibit 34 captures the top ten-performing funds on a one-year basis that have received a five-star rating by Morningstar. Note the coincidental ratings between several five-star-rated funds with correspondingly high sustainability ratings, corresponding to low ESG risk.

---

90 These are examples of fund searches within Morningstar, which is the largest platform. It is a database of funds that you can search according to different criteria. The link to this database is: www.morningstar.co.uk/uk/screener/fund.aspx#?filtersSelectedValue=%7B%22sustainabilityRating%22:%7B%22id%22:%225%22%7D%7D&page=1&perPage=10&sortField=legalName&sortOrder=asc

Exhibit 34: Morningstar-Ranked Global Equities Funds (by Star Rating and One-Year Performance)

Rank	Fund Standard Name	AUM USD (mn)	One Year	Three Years	Five Years	Sustainable Fund by prospectus	Star Rating	Sustainability Rating
1	Robeco QI Global Developed Conservative Equities Fund	373	17.1	10.6	12	Yes	★★★★★	Average
2	Nordea 1 – Global Portfolio Fund	160	15.3	17.1	14.9	No	★★★★★	Average
3	Nordea 1 – Global Opportunity Fund	261	15.3	15.5	13	No	★★★★★	Average
4	Double Dividend Equity Fund	--	15.2	11.4	11.2	Yes	★★★★★	High
5	SPP Global Solutions	290	15.1	15.9	14.3	Yes	★★★★★	High
6	Ethos Fund – Ethos Global Equities	177	14.9	16.6	14.5	--	★★★★★	High
7	Lindsell Train Global Equity Fund	11,043	14.7	20.1	21.9	--	★★★★★	High
8	Davy Global Brands Equity Fund	--	14.4	10.2	11	--	★★★★★	Above average
9	Mirova Global Sustainable Equity Fund	764	14.3	13.7	13.4	Yes	★★★★★	High
10	Amundi Funds Global Equity Conservative	251	14.3	10.2	10.5	No	★★★★★	Below average

Total Return Base Annualised (%)

Source: Morningstar, 8 October 2019; Sustainable Fund by Prospectus as of 31 March 2020.[91]

Unlisted Companies and Collective Investment Funds

Despite its widespread use in listed markets, screening can also be employed in the unlisted or private markets with many of the same principles and approaches applied. However, private markets and companies bring with them unique challenges. Chief among these is data: The capability to compare an investee company against cross-sectional competitor data or wider industry and sector data is often less robust because of lower degrees of disclosure and reporting.

MANAGING THE RISK AND RETURN DYNAMICS OF AN ESG INTEGRATED PORTFOLIO: OPTIMIZING PORTFOLIOS FOR ESG CRITERIA, STRATEGIES, OBJECTIVES, INVESTMENT CONSIDERATIONS, AND RISKS

☐ 8.1.8 explain how ESG integration impacts the risk–return dynamic of portfolio optimization

Practitioners in finance are increasingly benefiting from recent research that examines the relationship between ESG integration and its effects on risk–return dynamics. However, much of it focuses on the correlation between a particular ESG criterion and individual securities rather than the effects of ESG across an entire portfolio.[91] Some research has emerged, suggesting a correlation between ESG integration and greater diversification benefits,[92] but this is largely focused on equities strategies; there is little to point at how to optimize portfolios for ESG and measure the risk–return compromise.

ESG integration should not be seen as detrimental to the risk–return dynamic of portfolio optimization. Rather, it should be understood as simply another factor that potentially may enhance the risk and return profile. Like other ESG considerations, its construction and weighting in the context of the overall portfolio ultimately rests on how high a priority the investor assigns it, relative to other factors. Because of this, portfolio optimization is an increasingly important means to apply ESG criteria. Nonetheless, investors must weigh the trade-offs when quantitatively applying constraints to optimize for ESG outcomes within a portfolio. The process of portfolio optimization requires defining an upper and lower bound for a given variable and then applying it on an absolute or benchmark relative basis.

ESG optimization via constraints distinguishes itself from exclusionary screening in that it does not apply a fixed decision on specific securities. Rather, it is organizing the securities by their individual ESG profile to solve a specific ESG optimization at the overall portfolio level.

Exhibit 35 illustrates an example of a portfolio optimized for any given carbon emissions level below the fund's benchmark (BM). Because of the absolute nature of the data and more standardized reporting metrics, environmental data are generally easier to optimize in portfolios. Applied as a linear constraint in optimization, it demonstrates how the holdings overlap measured against an optimal portfolio that does not have any carbon restriction decreases as constraints become increasingly stringent across the x-axis.

---

[91] Bouslah, K., L. Kryzanowski, and B. M'Zali. 2011. *Relationship between Firm Risk and Individual Dimensions of Social Performance*. Proc. of the Annual Conf. of the Administrative Science Association of Canada, Montreal, Canada.

[92] Hoepner, A. G. F. 2010. "Portfolio Diversification and Environmental, Social or Governance criteria: Must Responsible Investments Really Be Poorly Diversified?" *Social Science Research Network Electronic Journal* (May). Available at: www.researchgate.net/publication/228231974_Portfolio_Diversification_and _Environmental_Social_or_Governance_Criteria_Must_Responsible_Investments_Really_Be_Poorly _Diversified \

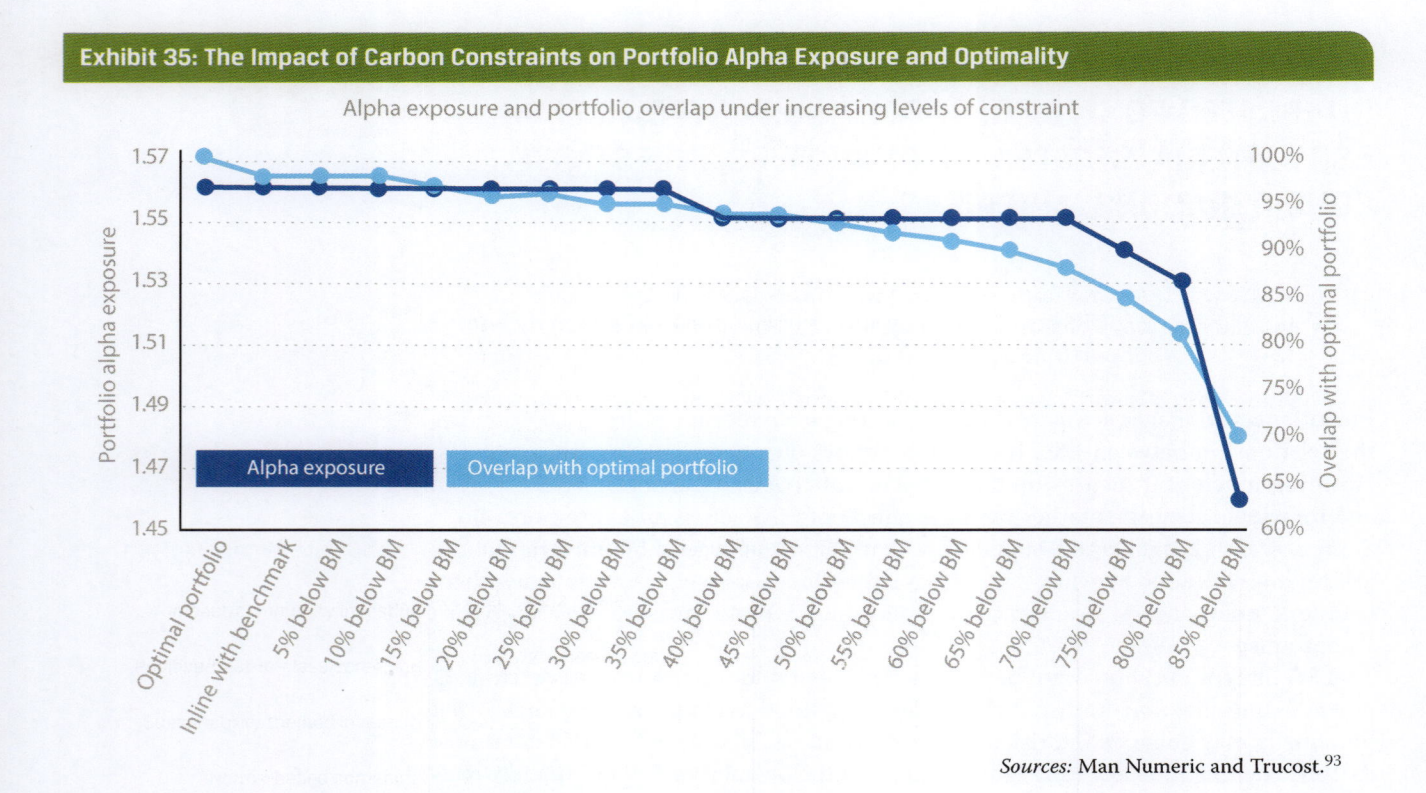

Exhibit 35: The Impact of Carbon Constraints on Portfolio Alpha Exposure and Optimality

Alpha exposure and portfolio overlap under increasing levels of constraint

Sources: Man Numeric and Trucost.[93]

Optimization is by no means confined to carbon data. Portfolios may seek to optimize broader ESG datasets taken from third-party vendors relative to active risk. Again, though, it is important to understand that targeted exposure that requires tighter constraints may likely result in an increase in deviation from an optimal portfolio. However, greater or lesser degrees of skewness in a particular ESG dataset may provide multiple paths to realizing the investor's targeted exposure. To this end, optimization strategies can design a fund to target either end of the distribution of a given ESG dataset. That might produce a strategy that solely invests in the top quartile of funds, or it may mean excluding the bottom quartile of companies based on ESG performance while understanding the impact of the constraint relative to portfolio optimality. It is worth highlighting that CFA Institute recently published *Climate Change Analysis in the Investment Process*, which includes a collection of case studies applying climate analysis to different asset classes and strategies.[94]

Indexes are increasingly optimized for a given degree of ESG improvement while solving a targeted tracking error relative to its core benchmark. It should be noted that optimizing for broader, more subjective ESG data — which commonly operate on a sector-relative ratings basis — may introduce higher active risk depending on the dataset used. For example, a company in the oil and gas sector may achieve a high environmental rating because of lower carbon emissions intensity relative to its sector peers. However, environmental data by itself — measured as tons of carbon emissions — will produce a greater absolute carbon exposure risk to a portfolio in the context

---

93 Man Group. 2019. *ESG Integration – No Silver Bullet*. Available at: www.man.com/maninstitute/esg-integration-no-silver-bullet

94 CFA Institute. 2020. *Climate Change Analysis in the Investment Process*. Available at: www.cfainstitute.org/en/research/industry-research/climate-change-analysis

of the market overall. Equally, a company — for example, an asset light company in the financial services sector — might have a poor ESG rating within its sector while simultaneously producing a low absolute carbon intensity in the context of the market.

Not surprisingly, portfolios that optimize for multiple factors — particularly a combination of absolute data and subjective rankings — may have to accept higher active risk to achieve both targets. Under this simulation, a portfolio manager may choose to optimize the portfolio to achieve the highest MSCI ESG ratings while reducing carbon emissions (100 to 150 basis points [bps]) with an associated increase to tracking error of 220 to 300 bps. A more conservative approach that seeks to minimize tracking error might instead target a tracking error of 150 to 200 bps, which achieves top ESG scores and a higher carbon emissions reduction.

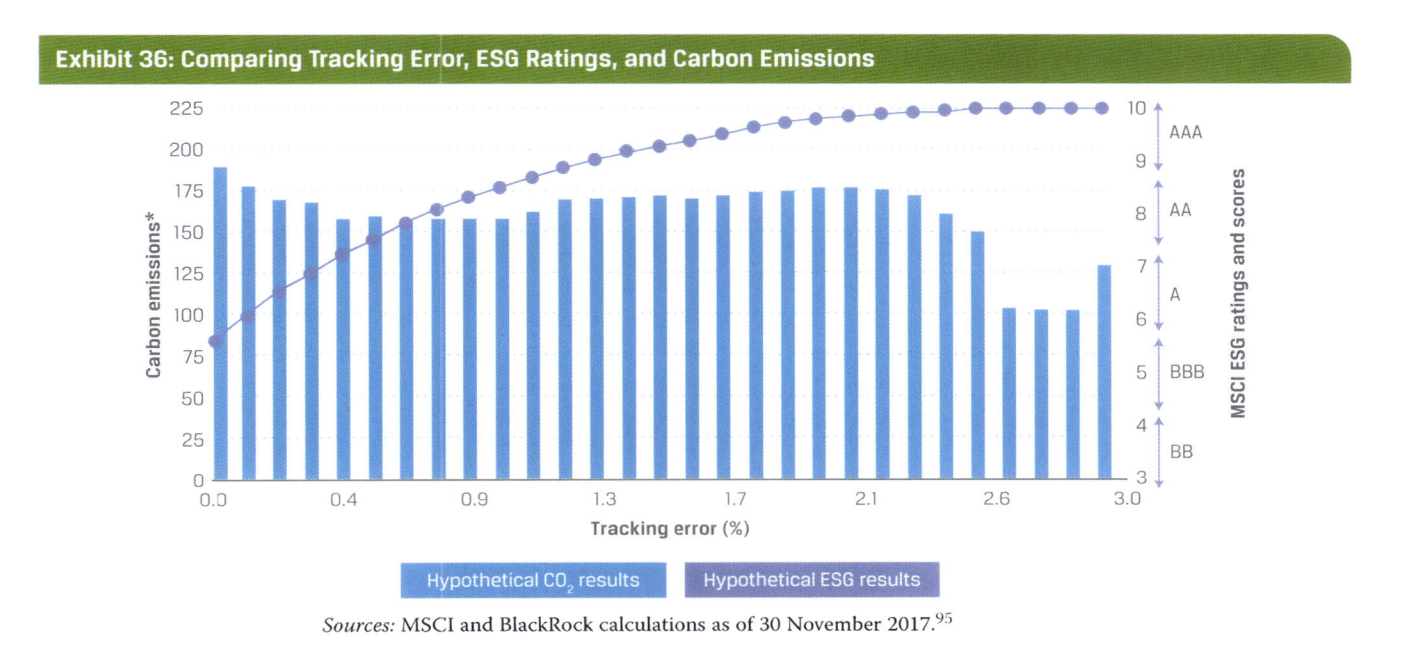

Exhibit 36: Comparing Tracking Error, ESG Ratings, and Carbon Emissions

Sources: MSCI and BlackRock calculations as of 30 November 2017.[95]

Where Exhibit 35 depicts a portfolio optimized solely around carbon constraint, and Exhibit 36 shows an ESG-optimized portfolio and its hypothetical effects on both ESG ratings and carbon emissions/tons against tracking error to the MSCI World. The trajectory suggests some correlation between incrementally higher ESG scores and lower emissions, but this is more pronounced over the first 100 bps of tracking error. This correlation gradually diminishes as an ESG-optimized portfolio rebalances to underweight the tail of companies that are both lower ESG scoring and higher carbon-emissions intensive. While an ESG-optimized portfolio can carry early, advantageous effects when taking into account a combination of absolute carbon emissions data and subjective ESG rankings, investors should recognize the trade-offs against drift in tracking error.

---

95 BlackRock. 2019. *Creating a Sustainable Core: Balancing ESG and Risk in Index Portfolios.* Available at: www.blackrock.com/institutions/en-gb/insights/investment-actions/balancing-esg-and-risk-in-index-portfolios

16 ESG STRATEGIES, OBJECTIVES, INVESTMENT CONSIDERATIONS, AND RISKS: FULL ESG INTEGRATION, EXCLUSIONARY SCREENING, AND POSITIVE ALIGNMENT

☐ 8.1.9 evaluate the different types of ESG analysis/SRI investment in terms of key objectives, investment considerations, and risks: full ESG integration; exclusionary screening; positive alignment/best-in-class; active ownership; thematic investing; impact investing; other

ESG integration focuses on measurability and comparability, often applying those tools in an iterative engagement with corporate management. PRI defines ESG integration as:

> *The systematic and explicit inclusion of material ESG factors into investment analysis and investment decisions.*[96]

While this definition is aimed at equity investors, its fundamental principle can be applied across most asset classes and strategies. In other words, ESG integration should be systematic in nature within the portfolio management process rather than applied as an ad-hoc exercise. This means that ESG, both as an investment framework and as an embedded process, should govern portfolio construction and management alongside other investment selection and risk management evaluation processes (such as financial, valuation, and factor-exposure analytics). This enables investors to better identify, assess, and quantify the materiality of ESG risks and ultimately understand the sensitivities and potential shocks within their portfolio.

The traditional argument for integrating ESG analysis has centered on its risk mitigation ability. Towards this end, negative screening seeks to avoid or minimize exposure to sectors that are more prone to risks, such as regulatory risks within the tobacco sector or economic risks like fossil fuel-related stranded assets.

Full ESG Integration

Full ESG integration enlarges the scope of ESG analysis beyond the focus of risk mitigation. It recognizes that ESG analysis will produce a better understanding of both risk and opportunity of both losers and winners.

Full ESG integration represents the systematic process of fully embedding financial and ESG analysis into investment decision making and portfolio management. It examines the materiality of ESG information across different investment horizons in order to identify portfolio risks as well as investment opportunities.

As defined by Robert Eccles and Mirtha Kastrapeli, full ESG integration is:

> *Investing with a systematic and explicit inclusion of ESG risks and opportunities in investment analysis.*[97]

Full ESG integration distinguishes itself by creating a circular process of financial and ESG analysis and iterative engagement activities with company management, concluding with these effects ultimately integrated into the valuation of a company.

---

[96] PRI. 2019. *A Practical Guide to ESG Integration for Equity Investing.* Available at: www.unpri.org/listed-equity/a-practical-guide-to-esg-integration-for-equity-investing/10.article

[97] BlackRock. 2019. *Creating a Sustainable Core: Balancing ESG and Risk in Index Portfolios.* Available at: www.blackrock.com/institutions/en-gb/insights/investment-actions/balancing-esg-and-risk-in-index-portfolios

Specialist investors often differentiate full ESG integration from the more general practice of ESG incorporation, which encompasses varying and often less formal degrees of ESG.

Fully integrated ESG strategies often combine quantitative approaches in order to exploit ESG datasets alongside fundamental tactics, like active engagement with company management at a securities level. At a portfolio level, the combination of quantitative and fundamental ESG integration provides an objective means to overlay ESG considerations with underlying, engagement-oriented interactions that help to reinforce and communicate both the stock selection and portfolio management process to end investors.

These ESG investment strategies often face fewer constraints than other ESG strategies impose. They tend not to be rules-based or box-ticking exercises. If external ESG ratings are used, they inform or complement the investment decision-making process rather than drive securities selection themselves as, say, a best-in-class strategy would do. Moreover, they carry an expectation that their ESG research and integration is far more rigorous and systematic, particularly their level of active engagement with corporate management. For these reasons, their portfolios tend to be more concentrated and composed of high-conviction holdings based primarily on internal investment research.

The following (Exhibit 37) provides an example of a holistic approach that combines negative screening and a more rigorous, ESG-driven approach that distinguishes both the financial and ESG profiles.

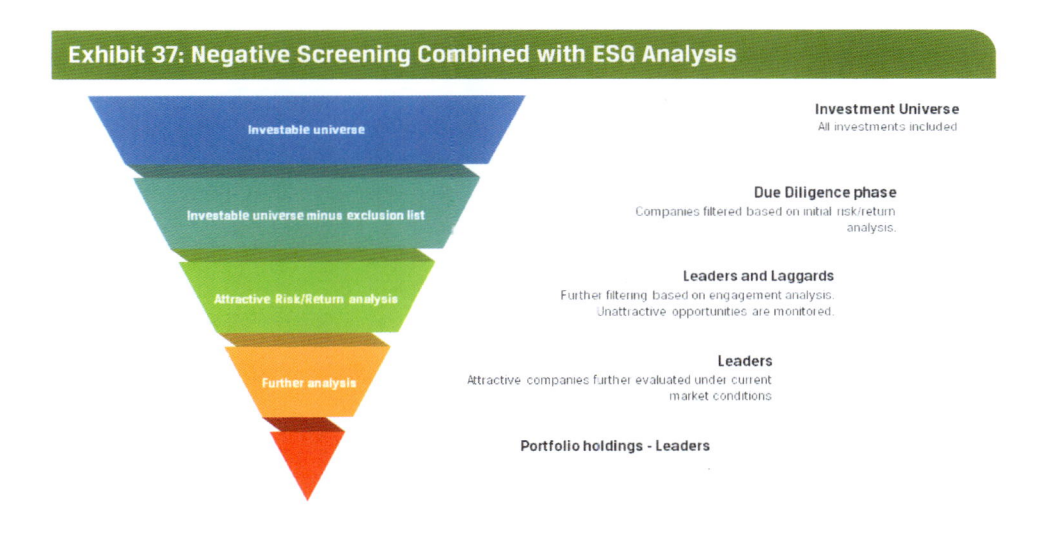

Exhibit 37: Negative Screening Combined with ESG Analysis

- Investable universe
- Investable universe minus exclusion list
- Attractive Risk/Return analysis
- Further analysis

Investment Universe — All investments included

Due Diligence phase — Companies filtered based on initial risk/return analysis.

Leaders and Laggards — Further filtering based on engagement analysis. Unattractive opportunities are monitored.

Leaders — Attractive companies further evaluated under current market conditions

Portfolio holdings - Leaders

However, full ESG integration does face its own challenges. Because it depends on deep-rooted, often proprietary ESG research, it often lacks the easily understandable optics — for instance, a high blended ESG portfolio score or low carbon exposure — that screened and best-in-class approaches provide. For these reasons, full ESG integration strategies often take greater efforts to:

- ▶ evidence internal and external research resources;
- ▶ document how ESG is embedded, typically in a process slide;
- ▶ track and report on engagement activities with company management;

- include portfolio exposure and weightings into sustainability themes like the SDGs;
- provide positive impact measurements of the portfolio against metrics like resource efficiency, water, and energy consumption; and
- support the process with investment case studies.

> **LOW BLENDED ESG SCORE**
>
> If a full ESG integration strategy produces a low blended ESG score or higher than average carbon exposure, the investment team should be fully prepared to explain the logic for this circumstance. They may demonstrate, through their engagement with company management, why the market has mischaracterized a company's ESG profile or why the market has misjudged the underlying rate of improvement based on their proprietary ESG data.

Exclusionary Screening

Exclusionary screening is the oldest and simplest approach within responsible investment. Emerging under the moniker of **socially responsible investment (SRI)**, the original objective was to impose a set of values or preferences to screen through an ethical or normative framework a portfolio's exposure to specific sectors. For example, a 'sin stocks' screen would typically exclude exposure in a portfolio to corporate issuers — stocks and bonds — in sectors like tobacco, pornography, gambling, and weapons.

For example, a pension plan belonging to a religious order will often exclude investment in gambling-, alcohol-, and pornography-related securities, while a pension fund that represents healthcare workers may exclude investment in the tobacco sector.

This approach has evolved from values-based screening to increasingly sophisticated approaches that now negatively screen across a much larger set of ESG criteria. Exclusions-based approaches continue to represent the large portion of dedicated AUM. This growth in exclusions reflects an expansion from traditionally screened areas (such as controversial arms and munitions) to more recently adopted areas that include tobacco and much of the energy extraction complex (including thermal coal, oil sands, and unconventional oil and gas).

It is important to understand that the degree of exclusions may carry significant implications from a portfolio management perspective — not just in terms of higher tracking error and active share, but also in unintended factor exposure. Investors (particularly asset managers) are generally more reluctant to adopt exclusions. With no beneficiaries directing a specific worldview and often a very diverse base of investors with exclusion preferences that may conflict, asset managers tend to default to as unconstrained an investment universe as possible.

Several other historical and structural drivers are behind this tendency towards sector- and market-neutrality. Within this approach, they will often manage segregated investment mandates for asset owners that prescribe exclusions. Within the alternative, specifically hedge fund, space, managers will generally have a preference for as unconstrained an investment universe as possible in the interest of potential available alpha generation, both on the long and the short side. The argument most often used for shorting stocks that would otherwise be on exclusions lists is a classical academic argument: that shorting securities potentially raises the cost of capital for firms in areas commonly excluded.[98]

Positive Alignment or Best-in-Class

Positive alignment or best-in-class represents, to some degree, the inverse of exclusionary screening. It employs a given ESG rating methodology to identify companies with better ESG performance relative to its industry peers. This approach is typically expressed by investing in the top decile, quintile, or quartile based on prescribed ESG criteria. The consistency of the ranking methodology and the portfolio's position-weighted exposure to higher-ranked companies are vital for this class of ESG strategies.

The diversity of ESG ratings methodologies and lack of ratings convergence are a key challenge these strategies face. They may score highly based on the portfolio manager's methodology but more poorly on another set of ESG metrics used by the fund's investor or, for instance, a fund distribution platform like Morningstar. Hence, best-in-class portfolios will be tested on transparency as well as consistency.

Because of this rating or score-imposed constraint, best-in-class strategies will generally have much less latitude to perform and apply proprietary research on lower-scoring companies that happen to exhibit positive momentum or improvement in their ESG metrics. For example, recent research has begun to demonstrate a correlation between positive momentum in ESG scores and financial returns.[99]

Finally, a common criticism for best-in-class ESG strategies is that their focus yields diminishing ESG returns with little opportunity to demonstrate incremental gains via active ownership efforts.

ESG STRATEGIES, OBJECTIVES, INVESTMENT CONSIDERATIONS, AND RISKS: THEMATIC AND IMPACT INVESTING

17

8.1.9 evaluate the different types of ESG analysis/SRI investment in terms of key objectives, investment considerations, and risks: full ESG integration; exclusionary screening; positive alignment/best-in-class; active ownership; thematic investing; impact investing; other

Thematic Investing

Thematic investing targets sustainability-aligned themes as a means to construct a portfolio. While often designed around long-term, resource scarcity-oriented themes, such as water or clean energy, thematic funds may also focus on sustainable sectors

---

98 Hvidkjær, S. 2017. *ESG Investing: A Literature Review*. Available at: https://dansif.dk/wp-content/uploads/2019/01/Litterature-review-UK-Sep-2017.pdf
99 Dunn, J., S. Fitzgibbons, and L. Pomorski. 2018. "Assessing Risk through Environmental, Social and Governance Exposures." *Journal of Investment Management* 16 (1). Available at: www.aqr.com/Insights/Research/Journal-Article/Assessing-Risk-through-Environmental-Social-and-Governance-Exposures

like healthcare. This approach may be expressed both fundamentally and quantitatively through active quant strategies or more passive vehicles, such as exchange-traded funds (ETFs).

Common sustainable themes are:

- clean energy;
- water;
- demographic change; and
- healthcare.

Addressed in the impact investing section that follows, frameworks like the SDGs increasingly provide a way to simultaneously invest across various sustainable themes for greater diversification.

The concentrated nature of thematic investing — particularly if it is based around a single theme like clean energy — sacrifices the benefits of portfolio diversification. The sectoral bias of the portfolio will drive the underlying factor exposure of the fund, potentially carrying relative performance and tracking error implications. Investors in thematic funds should be aware of the potential volatility and higher or lower associated risk.

Historically, clean energy thematic funds experienced greater volatility due to a number of factors, including:

- exposure to changing regulatory incentives (subsidies);
- a scarcity premium that reflected capital flows into and out of the sector; and
- poor cash flow profiles.

Hence, clean energy tends to be a pro-cyclical growth sector that underperforms when capital spending and the economic cycle contract. As an opposite example, water funds have a much more stable, regulatory outlook generally underpinned by strong cash flow and cash conversion. Often used as hedges against inflation, they will underperform during expansions in economic cycles when investors rotate towards growth.

Impact Investing

Although **impact investing** is attracting strong AUM flows and enjoying greater visibility due to the SDGs framework, impact investment has a long legacy. As discussed in Chapter 1, impact investing describes investments made with the intention of producing positive, measurable socio-environmental impacts without sacrificing financial returns.

Impact investors represent diverse interests and expectations for financial returns. More narrowly, mission investments are made by foundations and endowment funds to fulfill charitable objectives. They have commonly employed impact strategies with the aim of improving living standards while delivering market returns or even sub-market, concessional returns.

Impact strategies may include the development of low-cost community housing or critical waste and water infrastructure. Because of the prioritization of socio-economic objectives alongside, or above, financial returns, it is vital for impact strategies to build out and review reporting frameworks. The emergence of frameworks like the SDGs has popularized and broadened impact investing beyond its historical roots to different assets, including listed securities. Within this mandate, investment strategies align themselves to some portion of the SDG's 17 themes (see Exhibit 38) by providing portfolio exposure to individual themes and reporting on the fund's SDG impacts and improvement in any underlying KPI, as defined by the SDG text.

ESG Strategies, Objectives, Investment Considerations, and Risks: Thematic and Impact Investing

Exhibit 38: United Nations SDGs

SUSTAINABLE DEVELOPMENT GOALS

1. NO POVERTY
2. ZERO HUNGER
3. GOOD HEALTH AND WELL-BEING
4. QUALITY EDUCATION
5. GENDER EQUALITY
6. CLEAN WATER AND SANITATION
7. AFFORDABLE AND CLEAN ENERGY
8. DECENT WORK AND ECONOMIC GROWTH
9. INDUSTRY, INNOVATION AND INFRASTRUCTURE
10. REDUCED INEQUALITIES
11. SUSTAINABLE CITIES AND COMMUNITIES
12. RESPONSIBLE CONSUMPTION AND PRODUCTION
13. CLIMATE ACTION
14. LIFE BELOW WATER
15. LIFE ON LAND
16. PEACE, JUSTICE AND STRONG INSTITUTIONS
17. PARTNERSHIPS FOR THE GOALS

Source: United Nations.[100]

However, it should be noted that reporting and measuring SDG methodologies vary widely among data providers. For instance, some providers measure SDG impact based on alignment to a firm's products as well as the operational aspect, while other data measures align more broadly as a percentage of revenue exposure.

As an example, one form of portfolio analysis and reporting against the SDGs compares:

- fund exposure relative to benchmark exposure;
- overall, sectoral, and thematic contribution by the SDGs;
- performance metrics by underlying security; and
- a more detailed breakdown of how the provider classifies SDG contribution.

In this case, the data provider, Vigeo Eiris[101], an affiliate of Moody's, recognizes the individual alignment of the product and of issuer behavior alongside controversies.

Again, though, this form of reporting is generally designed for portfolio managers of investment mandates where the SDGs are either an explicit or implicit feature. Reporting in a listed context will generally lack the granularity and depth of reporting of conventional, unlisted impact portfolios. Nonetheless, it serves to support thematically consistent portfolio exposure and to signal commitment to reporting transparency. Its purpose is not to attribute investment returns in any causal form nor to add to the portfolio's risk exposure in any quantitative manner.

It is worth noting that applied approaches of the SDGs in certain asset classes, listed equities, for example, are more challenged in evidencing the presence of additionality and intentionality. A portfolio of listed securities should take efforts to clarify how

---

100 United Nations. 2020. *Sustainable Development Goals Knowledge Platform.* Available at: https://sustainabledevelopment.un.org (Please note that the content of this publication has not been approved by the United Nations and does not reflect the views of the United Nations or its officials or Member States.)

101 Vigeo Eiris. 2019. *Portfolio Analysis: Summary Report – SDGs* (March). Available at: http://vigeo-eiris.com/

the SDGs come into play regarding fund exposure in developed markets. Investors may choose to emphasize such areas as the portfolio's exposure across various metrics that are aligned with the SDGs. This would include exposure to:

- relevant product and services (revenue) exposure;
- regions, notably developing economies that the SDGs were originally designed for;
- sectors, such as water utilities, renewable energy, and healthcare;
- the relevance of supply chains;
- the additionality benefits of one or more of the SDGs, which may manifest in KPIs, such as job formation, renewable energy power generation, and potable water production; and
- additional sustainable forms of agriculture and aquaculture.

It is worth highlighting that new analytical approaches of the SDGs are emerging because of its tremendous adoption as an investment framework. For example, the Sustainable Development Investments Asset Owner Platform (SDI AOP) — a collective of asset owners including APG, AustralianSuper, British Columbia Investment Management Corporation (BCI), and PGGM — have established an artificial intelligence-driven platform that synthesizes SDG-related contribution information for investors. The AOP dataset is unique in that it covers more than 12,000 assets across all asset classes.

Active ownership "is the use of the rights and position of ownership to influence the activities or behaviour of investee companies."[102] Its investment approaches employ a number of different shareholder strategies aimed at driving positive change in the way a company is governed and managed. In effect, it takes the opposite approach of negative screening, as it views the act of divestment alone as incapable of collectivizing and directing investor preferences towards change.

Active ownership may leverage direct engagement between investor and company management, collaborative engagement where investors collectively drive for change, filing shareholder proposals and resolutions as well as a proxy voting strategy that is driven by a clear agenda to:

- encourage greater disclosure;
- improve transparency; and
- increase stronger awareness around ESG issues.

Companies that trade at meaningful discounts to their peer group or whose debt is distressed often have poor ESG metrics. Through influencing companies' behavior, the strategy is based on the theory that a linkage exists between improvements in corporate ESG metrics and the re-rating in equity value or credit through tighter spreads.

Academic support for the efficacy of active ownership is relatively sparse. While there are numerous case studies around company-specific engagements, there is more limited data measuring prolonged engagements and outcomes on their effects across dedicated active ownership strategies.

EXERCISE

Place yourself in the position of a large UK pension fund that is re-evaluating its pension strategy and looking to better integrate ESG investing.

---

102 PRI. 2016. *A Practical Guide to Active Ownership in Listed Equity*. Available at: www.unpri.org/listed-equity/a-practical-guide-to-active-ownership-in-listed-equity/2717.article

Exhibit 39: SDG Intensity Profile of Portfolio and Benchmark

	No Poverty	Zero Hunger	Good Health and well-being	Quality Education	Clean Water and Sanitation	Affordable and Clean Energy	Industry, Innovation, and Infrastructure	Sustainable Cities and Communities	Responsible Consumption and Production	Climate Action	Life Below Water	Life on Land
Communication Services				0.09%		0.00%	0.24%					
Consumer Discretionary			0.11%	-0.01%		1.11%	0.02%	0.00%				
Consumer Staples		-0.04%	0.02%			0.00%						
Energy												
Financials						0.04%	0.04%					
Health Care	0.27%		12.80%	-0.39%	0.09%		-0.40%	-0.02%	0.16%		-0.48%	
Industrials		-0.05%	-0.23%	0.08%	-0.11%	1.44%	-0.46%	-0.01%	0.02%	-0.08%	0.08%	-0.01%
Information Technology		-0.01%	-0.06%	-0.02%	-0.01%	-0.24%	-0.01%	-1.00%			-0.03%	
Materials		-0.10%	-0.06%		0.02%	0.14%		0.02%	0.04%		0.00%	0.05%
Real Estate						-0.11%						
Utilities					0.31%	-0.06%			0.00%		0.00%	

SDG Active Intensity by Sector

*Simulation equal-weighted portfolio across all assets under coverage versus the STOXX Global 1800 as a benchmark.
Source: Entis – SDI Asset Owner Platform. 2021. Available at: www.qontigo.com

For UK defined contribution (DC) plans, annual manager fees are capped at 75 bps, which pays for:

- management;
- performance; and
- the administration costs.

This fee is often too low to attract alternative active fund managers or alternative managers in areas like real estate, hedge funds, and infrastructure.

Considering these problems, how would you begin building out the ESG capabilities into the pension fund's process, given the fee limitations?

- What ESG strategies discussed in this chapter will likely not be suitable?
- What ESG analytics can be embedded in the pension fund's overall risk management process?
- What is the best way for the pension fund to build a comprehensive understanding of manager ESG capabilities?
- What area of ESG risk should the pension fund focus on developing?
- What ambitions should the pension set for engagement and stewardship by its underlying managers?

18 INTEGRATING ESG IN PASSIVE PORTFOLIOS AND ESTABLISHED DATASETS

8.1.10 describe approaches to managing passive ESG portfolios

The shift from active to passive investment strategies represents a substantial change in the allocation and composition of overall AUM. Indeed, passively managed assets have more than doubled as a percentage of total global AUM in the last decade.[103] The shift is even more pronounced in the United States, where assets in passively managed ETFs and mutual funds have increased from USD220 bn (GBP158 bn) to USD7 tn (GBP5 tn),[104] representing roughly 43% of the value of the S&P 500.[104]

Passive investment differentiates itself from actively managed strategies by the nature of its low costs and the simplicity of a determined, rules-based approach. Likewise, passive ESG approaches also seek to provide low cost alternatives to more expensive, actively managed investment funds. However, the relative nascent state of ESG and its data costs potentially mean that ESG passive strategies may run at a slightly higher fee structure relative to traditional passive strategies, although still significantly lower than actively managed ESG funds.[105]

---

103 Sushko, V., and G. Turner. 2018. "The Implications of Passive Investing for Securities Markets." *BIS Quarterly Review* (11 March). Available at: www.bis.org/publ/qtrpdf/r_qt1803j.htm

104 McCabe, P. 2018. "The Shift from Active to Passive Investing: Potential Risks to Financial Stability? Harvard Law School Forum on Corporate Governance and Financial Regulation." *Harvard Law School Forum on Corporate Governance* (29 November). Available at: https://corpgov.law.harvard.edu/2018/11/29/the-shift-from-active-to-passive-investing-potential-risks-to-financial-stability

105 PRI. 2022. "How Can a Passive Investor Be a Responsible Investor?" Available at: https://www.unpri.org/passive-investments/how-can-a-passive-investor-be-a-responsible-investor/4649.article

Integrating ESG in Passive Portfolios and Established Datasets

Noteworthy examples of asset owners circumventing actively-managed ESG strategies and directly investing or independently creating passive ESG strategies include the following:

- **California State Teachers' Retirement System (CalSTRS)** employs indexes to meet ESG objectives and achieve lower cost and efficiency for its beneficiaries, including the MSCI ACWI Low-Carbon Target Index.[106]
- Taiwan's **Bureau of Labour Funds (BLF)** pension scheme selected the FTSE4Good TIP Taiwan ESG Index for a five-year passive mandate.[107]
- Japan's **Government Pension Investment Fund (GPIF)**, the world's largest pension fund, is well known for its use of ESG-dedicated indexes. This follows the creation of the Nikkei 400, which linked corporate governance reforms under Prime Minister Shinzo Abe to improved capital efficiency metrics like return on equity (ROE). GPIF's indexes include global and domestic environmental strategies, which overweight carbon-efficient companies, as well as a socially-oriented index, the MSCI Japan Empowering Women Index. Exhibit 40 illustrates the diversity of approaches and sources that GPIF has employed within its passive investment strategy.

Exhibit 40: Indexes Adopted by Japan's GPIF

	FTSE Blossom Japan Index	MSCI Japan ESG Select Leaders Index	MSCI Japan Empowering Women Index (WIN)	S&P/JPX Carbon Efficient Index	S&P Global Ex-Japan LargeMidcap Carbon Efficient Index
Index concept	This uses the ESG assessment scheme used in the FTSE4Good Japan Index Series, which has one of the longest track records globally for ESG indexes. As a broad ESG index, it selects stocks with high absolute ESG scores and adjusts industry weights to neutral.	This is a broad ESG index that integrates various ESG risks into today's portfolio. It is based on MSCI ESG Research used globally by more than 1,000 clients. The index is comprised of stocks with relatively high ESG scores in each industry.	MSCI calculates the gender-diversity scores based on information disclosed under the Act on Promotion of Women's Participation and Advancement in the Workplace and selects companies with higher gender diversity scores from each sector. The first index designed to cover a broad range of factors related to gender diversity.	Based on carbon data provided by Trucost. S&P Dow Jones develops the index methodologies. The indexes are designed to increase index weights of the companies that have low carbon-to-revenue footprints (annual GHG emissions divided by annual revenues) and actively disclose carbon emission information.	
Subject of investment	Domestic equity	Domestic equity	Domestic equity	Domestic equity	Foreign equity
Parent index (number of stocks)	FTSE JAPAN INDEX (513 stocks)	MSCI JAPAN IMI TOP 700 (694 stocks)	MSCI JAPAN IMI TOP 500 (496 stocks)	TOPIX (2,124 stocks)	S&P Global ex-Japan Large-Mid Index (2,556 stocks)

---

106 Mussuto, M. 2018. *CalSTRS Green Initiative Task Force Report Evaluates ESG Risks*. Available at: www.calstrs.com/news-release/calstrs-green-initiative-task-force-report-evaluates-esg-risks
107 FTSE Russell. 2018. *Taiwan Bureau of Labor Funds Selects FTSE4Good TIP Taiwan ESG Index for $1.4 Billion Mandate*. Available at: www.ftserussell.com/press/taiwan-bureau-labor-funds-selects-ftse4good-tip-taiwan-esg-index-14-billion-mandate

	FTSE Blossom Japan Index	MSCI Japan ESG Select Leaders Index	MSCI Japan Empowering Women Index (WIN)	S&P/JPX Carbon Efficient Index	S&P Global Ex-Japan LargeMidcap Carbon Efficient Index
Index constituents	152	268	213	1,738	2,199
AUM (JPY bn)	642.8 (GBP 4.4 bn)	804.3 (GBP 5.5 bn)	474.6 (GBP 3.2 bn)	387.8 (GBP 2.6 bn)	1,205.2 (GBP8.2 bn)

Sources: GPIF and based on data from each index provider.[108]

Passive investing approaches have evolved from the replication of established indexes, like the S&P 500 or FTSE, to more sophisticated strategies. Because of the ease of use and low cost, exclusions-oriented responsible investment approaches were early adopters of passive investing:

▶ beginning with the MSCI KLD 400 Social Index;

▶ graduating to more mainstream indexes like the Dow Jones Sustainability Index; and

▶ now expanding to other asset classes and strategy types.

Passive ESG approaches now range from exclusions-oriented strategies, such as the MSCI World Ex-Tobacco, to approaches that target minimized exposure to fossil fuel either by excluding carbon emission and GHG-intensive industries or by applying a carbon emissions cap relative to the main index. Investors' willingness to deviate from the core index based on ESG and sector or security exclusions criteria will determine the degree of differential in tracking error.

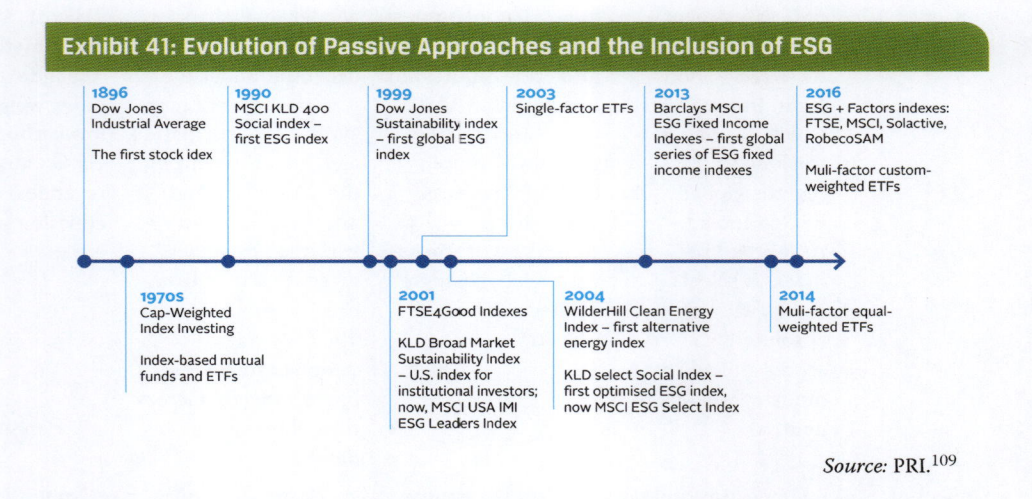

Exhibit 41: Evolution of Passive Approaches and the Inclusion of ESG

1896 Dow Jones Industrial Average — The first stock idex

1970s Cap-Weighted Index Investing — Index-based mutual funds and ETFs

1990 MSCI KLD 400 Social index – first ESG index

1999 Dow Jones Sustainability index – first global ESG index

2001 FTSE4Good Indexes — KLD Broad Market Sustainability Index – U.S. index for institutional investors; now, MSCI USA IMI ESG Leaders Index

2003 Single-factor ETFs

2004 WilderHill Clean Energy Index – first alternative energy index — KLD select Social Index – first optimised ESG index, now MSCI ESG Select Index

2013 Barclays MSCI ESG Fixed Income Indexes – first global series of ESG fixed income indexes

2014 Muli-factor equal-weighted ETFs

2016 ESG + Factors indexes: FTSE, MSCI, Solactive, RoboecoSAM — Muli-factor custom-weighted ETFs

Source: PRI.[109]

The wider availability of ESG data and greater investor interest in responsible investment has also led to the development of new, alternative approaches within passive investing. Single-factor ESG strategies (smart-beta and beta-plus) provide investors a passive means to weight an index towards a style factor while also screening for companies that perform better on ESG metrics. This is highly dependent on the

---

108 Japanese Government Pension Investment Fund. 2018. *ESG Report 2018 for All Generations*. Available at: www.gpif.go.jp/en/investment/190905_Esg_Report.pdf
109 PRI. 2022. "How Can a Passive Investor Be a Responsible Investor?" Available at: https://www.unpri.org/passive-investments/how-can-a-passive-investor-be-a-responsible-investor/4649.article

Integrating ESG in Passive Portfolios and Established Datasets

screening methodology and the ESG dataset employed. For example, the new MSCI Factor ESG Target Indexes target traditional style factors, like value and low volatility, while weighting the portfolio towards corporates with higher MSCI ESG ratings.[110]

Exhibit 42 illustrates the range and depth of ESG indexes developed by FTSE Russell. It addresses several investor motivations through a mix of indexes that prioritize:

- ESG on a holistic basis;
- subsets of ESG themes, such as climate and environmental markets;
- ethical and normative exclusions; and
- single ESG themes, like diversity as measured by female board representation.

It also includes investment styles, such as a minimum variance strategy with an ESG-screened overlay.

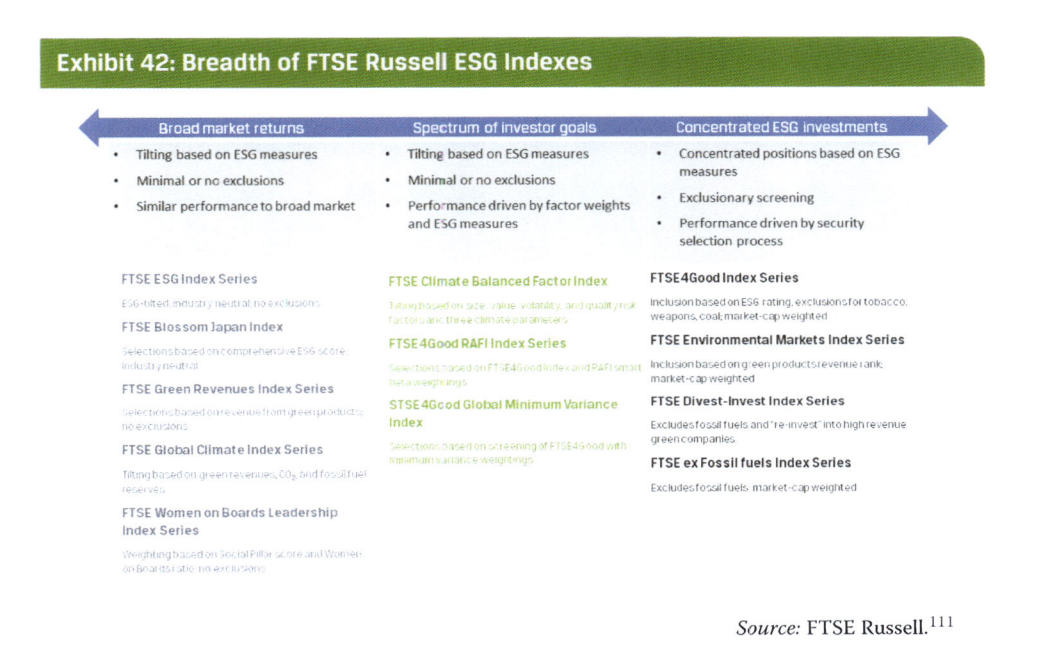

Exhibit 42: Breadth of FTSE Russell ESG Indexes

Broad market returns	Spectrum of investor goals	Concentrated ESG investments
• Tilting based on ESG measures • Minimal or no exclusions • Similar performance to broad market	• Tilting based on ESG measures • Minimal or no exclusions • Performance driven by factor weights and ESG measures	• Concentrated positions based on ESG measures • Exclusionary screening • Performance driven by security selection process
FTSE ESG Index Series ESG-tilted, industry neutral, no exclusions **FTSE Blossom Japan Index** Selections based on comprehensive ESG score, industry neutral **FTSE Green Revenues Index Series** Selections based on revenue from green products, no exclusions **FTSE Global Climate Index Series** Tilting based on green revenues, CO₂, and fossil fuel reserves **FTSE Women on Boards Leadership Index Series** Weighting based on Social Pillar score and Women on Boards ratio, no exclusions	**FTSE Climate Balanced Factor Index** Tilting based on size, value, volatility, and quality risk factors and three climate parameters **FTSE4Good RAFI Index Series** Selections based on FTSE4Good Index and RAFI smart beta weightings **FTSE4Good Global Minimum Variance Index** Selections based on screening of FTSE4Good with minimum variance weightings	**FTSE4Good Index Series** Inclusion based on ESG rating, exclusions for tobacco, weapons, coal; market-cap weighted **FTSE Environmental Markets Index Series** Inclusion based on green products revenue rank; market-cap weighted **FTSE Divest-Invest Index Series** Excludes fossil fuels and "re-invest" into high revenue green companies **FTSE ex Fossil fuels Index Series** Excludes fossil fuels; market-cap weighted

Source: FTSE Russell.[111]

Nonetheless, the inherent nature of passive investment strategies presents some challenges when integrating ESG.

Relying on Established Datasets

Traditional passive investment strategies rely on more established datasets for construction. These range from the uncontroversial, such as reconstituting indexes to apply style factors as overlays or tilts, for instance in smart beta strategies.

Though investors develop proprietary quantitative models, these models are often underpinned by both academic theory as well as supported by historical data to performance back tests. As an example, more than a century of US financial markets data exists to analyze business cycles and sensitivities to traditional factors like value and

---

110 Skypala, P. 2017. "ESG Investing and Smart Beta Combination Grows in Popularity." *Financial Times* (27 November). Available at: www.ft.com/content/3f236546-c9f8-11e7-ab18-7a9fb7d6163e
111 FTSE Russell. 2020. S*ustainability and ESG Indexes*. Available at: www.ftserussell.com/data/sustainability-and-esg-data/sustainability-esg-indexes

growth. And while the nuances of value continue to be debated and redefined, there is a general agreement for the fundamental identifiers of value, such as price-to-book and free cash flow multiples.

By comparison, ESG datasets are poor as they lack history, comparability, and regional breadth. For example, the most extensive ESG datasets provide little more than a decade of data.

ESG disclosure also remains largely voluntary, and there is still little global convergence around ESG accounting standards, such as the SASB. As a consequence, the methodology behind a passive ESG strategy is highly individualistic and interpretive. The construction of an ESG passive strategy is typically based around a third-party ESG dataset, which is premised on its own underlying selection methodology. While the diversity of available ESG datasets has helped drive the innovation and popularity of passive ESG strategies, it also creates the potential to confuse the market with differing and opaque integration approaches to ESG data.

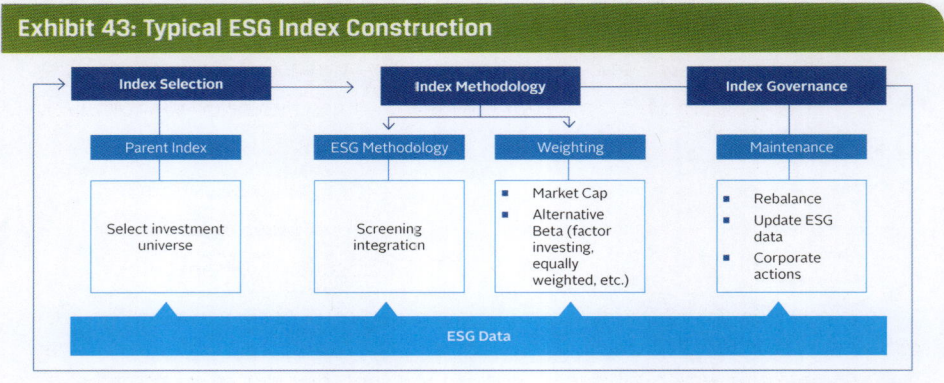

Exhibit 43: Typical ESG Index Construction

Index Selection	Index Methodology		Index Governance
Parent Index	ESG Methodology	Weighting	Maintenance
Select investment universe	Screening integration	• Market Cap • Alternative Beta (factor investing, equally weighted, etc.)	• Rebalance • Update ESG data • Corporate actions

ESG Data

Source: PRI.[110]

It is often said that, casually speaking, the only free lunch in investment is diversification. Hence, incorporating any given set of exclusions or ESG datasets into a passive investment strategy potentially carries unintended consequences, notably by limiting one's ability to diversify. This may result from portfolio distortion to unwanted factor and market exposure.

Despite their weight within a given broader index, reducing or eliminating exposure to certain sectors represents a natural re-weight to the remaining sectors and index constituents. Commonly excluded sectors, like tobacco and fossil fuels, represent a specific profile. Generally speaking, companies in these sectors are more mature and face less pressure to reinvest cash flow into growth-related, capital expenditure programs. As a result, stable operating margins equate to consistent cash flows and dividend pay-out ratios, which provide defensive, counter-cyclical exposure within portfolios. Indexes that exclude or minimize exposure to these sectors will naturally tilt portfolios towards a more cyclical, growth-oriented profile.

Excluding meaningful sectors or industries within an index, such as fossil fuels, will generate a higher tracking error. To be sure, targeting high tracking error is a commonly used tactic by active portfolio managers in an effort to beat their benchmark index, but this is generally employed by deviating from the index through idiosyncratic portfolio positioning and concentration.[112] The wholesale exclusion of sectors like fossil fuels represents an altogether different magnitude of tracking error that may dramatically alter the diversification and factor exposure of a portfolio. As discussed in the section titled "Optimizing Portfolios for ESG Criteria", portfolio optimization offers the means by which to mitigate these effects.

Active engagement and stewardship are key ESG ingredients. While passive investment strategies are capable of proxy voting, the nature of their strategies innately limits their ability to engage with portfolio companies unless coordinated by an established stewardship team. One implication of this is that passive investing may translate into shallower forms of stewardship activities with companies rather than more focused, often sustained, active engagement opportunities that are typical of actively managed ESG strategies. In fact, recent academic work increasingly yields evidence that active ESG shareholder engagement activities have the potential to manage down risk.

Despite the growth in passive investing AUM, academic research examining the performance considerations and trade-offs of ESG integration into passive portfolio management remains relatively scarce. Of the work that does exist, there is evidence of regional disparities in performance and risk-adjusted returns showing little difference between Europe and the United States.

---

112 For more information on tracking error and active share: Cremers, K. J. M., and A. Petajisto. 2009. *How Active Is Your Fund Manager? A New Measure That Predicts Performance.* AFA 2007 Chicago Meetings Paper; EFA 2007 Ljubljana Meetings Paper; Yale ICF Working Paper No. 06-14. Available at: https://ssrn.com/abstract=891719

KEY FACTS

1. Investment approaches can be characterized as discretionary and quantitative. ESG integration in discretionary approaches is process-oriented, while quantitative approaches, whether active or passive, are generally rules-based and factor-oriented.
2. Dynamic asset allocation tactically rebalances relative to its long-term allocation target mix. Strategic asset allocation, which only intermittently rebalances relative to its target mix, is more aligned to ESG integration, but investors will have to consider the diversification trade-offs by allocating more to an ESG or sustainability risk budget.
3. The Task Force on Climate-related Financial Disclosures (TCFD) includes a specific recommendation for climate scenario analysis. Asset allocation strategies can stress test their overall portfolios to understand the implications of physical climate risks (operational and strategic dislocations to business) and transition climate risks (regulatory, legal, policy, technology, and market-related) by simulating a number of scenarios with a baseline of 1.5 to 2°C (2.7 to 5.4°F).
4. Exclusionary screening can be organized into four basic categories:
    - universal;
    - conduct-related;
    - faith-based; and
    - idiosyncratic exclusions.
5. The exclusionary preferences are generally specified by the asset owners, not asset managers. As a rules-based investment approach, exclusionary screening is reductive by nature and does not generally consider softer, more qualitative forms of responsible investment, such as stewardship and engagement activities.
6. Imposing an exclusion screen or targeting an ESG score may introduce unintended factor exposure or skewness to a portfolio.
7. ESG data and ratings methodologies are still nascent. With correlations among ESG data providers relatively low, at 0.35 to 0.40, investors should recognize the lack of convergence. One way investors can differentiate themselves is by building ESG analytics platforms that combine off-the-shelf ESG data with proprietary approaches.
8. Portfolio managers should recognize the challenges within ESG datasets and methodologies. These include short historical data, lack of comparability, and coverage gaps within some asset classes and regions.
9. Simply put, passive ESG investing describes rules-based strategies to produce low cost indexes and benchmarks.
10. Portfolio optimization allows portfolio managers to target a specific ESG rating or environmental objective, such as carbon emissions reduction, while simultaneously managing the portfolio to tracking error range.
11. Full ESG integration involves the systematic and explicit inclusion of ESG risks and opportunities within stock selection and portfolio management.
12. Exclusionary screening imposes ethical or normative criteria to a portfolio investment universe.
13. Positive alignment introduces an inclusionary bias to a portfolio as it invests generally in better-performing companies on ESG metrics.

Key Facts

14. Thematic investing focuses on sustainability-related areas, such as water or renewable energy, with which to build a portfolio of companies.
15. Impact investing is unique relative to traditional ESG investing in elevating expectations of intentionality and additionality alongside (or in the case of concessional impact, below) market returns. Intentionality describes the primary motivation for investment. Additionality is the improvement in social value beyond what would have otherwise occurred without the impact investment.
16. Active ownership strategies employ ownership and voting rights to drive positive change in a company, generally through direct or collaborative engagement between management and investors.

FURTHER READING

The United Nations (UN) Principles for Responsible Investment (PRI) website contains many papers and collections of external parties' studies on the implementation of ESG in portfolio construction: www.unpri.org.

G20 Sustainable Finance Study Group 2018. *Towards a Sustainable Infrastructure Securitisation Market: The Role of Collateralised Loan Obligations*.http://unepinquiry.org/wp-content/uploads/2018/12/Towards_a_sustainable_infrastructure_securitisation_market.pdf

AIMA 2020. Short Selling and Responsible Investment. Available at: www.aima.org/sound-practices/industry-guides/short-selling-and-responsible-investment.html

Amundi Asset Management 2020. *ESG Investing in Recent Years: New Insights from Old Challenges*. DP-42-2019. Available at: https://research-center.amundi.com/page/Publications/Discussion-Paper/2020/ESG-Investing-in-Recent-Years-New-Insights-from-Old-Challenges?search=true

Andersson, M., P. Bolton, F. Samama. 2016. "Hedging Climate Risk." Financial Analysts Journal 72 (3). Available at https://papers.ssrn.com/sol3/papers.cfm?abstract_id=249962810.2469/faj.v72.n3.4

Bender, J., T. A. Bridges, C. He, A. Lester, X. Sun. 2018. "A Blueprint for Integrating ESG into Equity Portfolios." Journal of Investment Management 16 (1). Available at https://papers.ssrn.com/sol3/papers.cfm?abstract_id=3080381

Benedetti, D., E. Biffis, F. Chatzimichalakis, L. L. Fedele, I. Simm. 2019. *Climate Change Investment Risk: Optimal Portfolio Construction Ahead of the Transition to a Lower-Carbon Economy*. Available at: https://link.springer.com/article/10.1007%2Fs10479-019-03458-x

Buckle, M., S. Thomas. 2020. The Investment Environment: Official Training Manual. 18th ed.vol. 1. London: CFA Society of the United Kingdom.

Buckle, M., S. Thomas. 2020. The Investment Practice: Official Training Manual. 18th ed.vol. 2. London: CFA Society of the United Kingdom.

CFA Institute 2017. *Climate Change Analysis in the Investment Process*. Available at: www.cfainstitute.org/-/media/documents/article/industry-research/climate-change-analyis.ashx

CFA Institute and Swiss Sustainable Finance 2017. "Handbook on Sustainable Investments: Background Information and Practical Examples for Institutional Asset Owners." *Research Foundation Books* 2017 (5). Available at: www.cfainstitute.org/en/research/foundation/2017/handbook-on-sustainable-investments

Chatterji, A., R. Durand, D. Levine, S. Touboul. 2015. "Do Ratings of Firms Converge? Implications for Managers, Investors and Strategy Researchers." Strategic Management Journal 37 (8): 1597–614. Available at https://papers.ssrn.com/sol3/papers.cfm?abstract_id=252486110.1002/smj.2407

Climate Disclosure Standards Board and the Sustainability Accounting Standards Board 2019. *TCFD: Good Practice Handbook*. Available at: www.cdsb.net/sites/default/files/tcfd_good_practice_handbook_web_a4.pdf

Climate Finance Advisors and Ortec Finance 2019. *Scenario Analysis for Systemic Climate Risk: The Case for Assessing the Impacts of Climate Change on Macro-Economic Indicators Used by Institutional Investors*. Available at: https://climatefinanceadvisors.com/wp-content/uploads/2019/09/310-002-Climate-Risk-Report_V5.pdf

Commonwealth Development Corporation 2019. *ESG Toolkit for Fund Managers*. Available at: https://toolkit.cdcgroup.com/

Daniel, K. D., R. B. Litterman, G. Wagner. 2019. "Applying Asset Pricing Theory to Calibrate the Price of Climate Risk." NBER Working Paper No. 22795. Available at: www.nber.org/papers/w22795

Further Reading

DWS Research Institute 2020. *ESG in Strategic Asset Allocation (SAA): A Practical Implementation Framework.* Available at: www.dws.com/en-gb/insights/global-research-institute/esg-in-strategic-asset-allocation-saa-a-practical-implementation-framework/

European Financial Reporting Advisory Group (EFRAG) Project Task Force on Climate-Related Reporting (PTF-CRR). 2020. *How to Improve Climate-Related Reporting: A Summary of Good Practices from Europe and Beyond.* Available at: www.efrag.org/Assets/Download?assetUrl=/sites/webpublishing/SiteAssets/European%20Lab%20PTF-CRR%20%28Main%20Report%29.pdf

Friede, G., T. Busch, A. Bassen. 2015. "ESG and Financial Performance: Aggregated Evidence from More than 2,000 Empirical Studies." Journal of Sustainable Finance & Investment 5 (4): 210–33. 10.1080/20430795.2015.1118917

Furdak, R. E., E. Gao, J. Wee, E. Wu. 2019. *ESG Data: Building a Solid Foundation.* Available at: www.man.com/maninstitute/esg-data-building-a-solid-foundation

Furdak, R. E., V. Xiang, D. Zheng. 2020. *The Big Green Short.* Available at: www.man.com/maninstitute/big-green-short

Giglio, S., B. Kelly, J. Stroebel. 2020. "Climate Finance." Available at: https://papers.ssrn.com/sol3/papers.cfm?abstract_id=371913910.3386/w28226

Global Sustainable Investment Alliance (GSIA) 2018. *2018 Global Sustainable Investment Review.* Available at: www.gsi-alliance.org/wp-content/uploads/2019/06/GSIR_Review2018F.pdf

Institutional Investors Group on Climate Change (IIGCC) 2019. *Consultation: Net Zero Investment Framework.* Available at: www.iigcc.org/our-work/paris-aligned-investment-initiative/

International Capital Market Association (ICMA) 2018. *Green Bond Principles (GBP).* Available at: www.icmagroup.org/green-social-and-sustainability-bonds/green-bond-principles-gbp

KPMG 2020. *Sustainable Investing: Fast-Forwarding Its Evolution.* Available at: https://assets.kpmg/content/dam/kpmg/xx/pdf/2020/02/sustainable-investing.pdf

Lundström, E., C. Svensson. 2014. *Including ESG Concerns in the Portfolio Selection Process: An MCDM Approach.* KTH Royal Institute of Technology SCI School of Engineering Sciences. Available at: https://pdfs.semanticscholar.org/5666/0111dba181b5d3282f7f363acd08e5ea0828.pdf

Man Group 2019. *A Sustainable Future Podcast.* Available at: www.man.com/maninstitute/a-sustainable-future-podcast

Mercer. 2019. *Investing in a Time of Climate Change: The Sequel* 2019. Available at: https://info.mercer.com/rs/521-DEV-513/images/Climate-change-the-sequel-2019-full-report.pdf

Mercer. 2020. *Responsible Investment in Fixed Income.* Available at: www.mercer.com/our-thinking/wealth/responsible-investment-in-fixed-income.html

PIMCO 2020. *Bonds: ESG into Action.* Available at: www.pimco.co.uk/en-gb/investments/esg-investing

Pollard, J. L., M. W. Sherwood, R. G. Klobus. 2018. "Establishing ESG as Risk Premia." Journal of Investment Management 16 (1). Available at www.joim.com/establishing-esg-as-risk-premia/

PRI 2014. *Integrating ESG in Private Equity: A Guide for General Partners.* Available at: www.unpri.org/download?ac=252

PRI 2016. *A Practical Guide to ESG Integration for Equity Investing.* Available at: www.unpri.org/download?ac=10

PRI 2016. *Asset Owner Strategy Guide: How to Craft an Investment Strategy.* Available at: www.unpri.org/download?ac=4336

PRI 2018. *ESG Monitoring, Reporting and Dialogue in Private Equity.* Available at: www.unpri.org/private-equity/esg-monitoring-reporting-and-dialogue-in-private-equity/3295.article

PRI 2019. *A Practical Guide to ESG Integration in Sovereign Debt.* Available at: www.unpri.org/fixed-income/a-practical-guide-to-esg-integration-in-sovereign-debt/4781.article

PRI 2019. "Embedding ESG Issues into Strategic Asset Allocation Frameworks." Discussion paper. Available at: www.unpri.org/embedding-esg-issues-into-strategic-asset-allocation-frameworks-discussion-paper/4815.article

PRI 2020. *ESG Engagement for Sovereign Debt Investors*. Available at: www.unpri.org/sovereign-debt/esg-engagement-for-sovereign-debt-investors/6687.article

PRI 2020. *Reporting Framework Glossary*. Available at: www.unpri.org/reporting-and-assessment/reporting-framework-glossary/6937.article

PRI 2020. *Technical Guide: ESG Incorporation in Hedge Funds*. Available at: www.unpri.org/hedge-funds/technical-guide-esg-incorporation-in-hedge-funds/5729.article

Sherwood, M. W., J. L. Pollard. 2018. Responsible Investing: An Introduction to Environmental, Social and Governance Investments. London: Routledge. 10.4324/9780203712078

van Duuren, E., A. Plantinga, B. Scholtens. 2016. "ESG Integration and the Investment Management Process: Fundamental Investing Reinvented." Journal of Business Ethics 138:525–33. Available at https://link.springer.com/content/pdf/10.1007%2Fs10551-015-2610-8.pdf10.1007/s10551-015-2610-8

World Wildlife Fund (WWF) and Investec Asset Management 2019. *Sustainability & Satellites: New Frontiers in Sovereign Debt Investing*. Available at: www.wwf.org.uk/sites/default/files/2019-06/Investec_Sustainability_and_satellites_June_2019.pdf

SELF PRACTICE AND SELF ASSESSMENT

1. Which is one of the most material ESG factors institutional investors need to address within strategic asset allocation strategies?
   a. Climate risk
   b. Exclusionary screening
   c. Ownership and stewardship

2. Which of the following statements *best* describes discretionary ESG investment strategies?
   a. Discretionary investment strategies impose a custom index with ESG exclusion criteria
   b. Discretionary investment strategies complement bottom-up financial analysis with consideration of ESG factors
   c. Discretionary investment strategies are rules-based approaches to drive securities selection in ESG integrated portfolio construction

3. A bond that connects an issuer's raw material sourcing supply chain to ESG criteria is a:
   a. transition bond.
   b. sustainability bond.
   c. sustainability-linked bond.

4. Which type of ESG investing bond provides financing for sustainable fishing projects?
   a. Blue bond
   b. Green bond
   c. Sustainability bonds

5. Which of the following is a World Bank indicator for country governance?
   a. Control of corruption
   b. Affiliation with investor initiatives
   c. Non-governmental organization research

6. Investors typically address the effects to risk-adjusted returns of ESG integration in portfolio management through:
   a. risk mitigation and alpha generation.
   b. risk mitigation and dynamic asset allocation.
   c. factor risk allocation and dynamic asset allocation.

7. What is an advantage of a multi-factor model over a smart beta or beta plus strategy for ESG integration in portfolios?
   a. Lower cost
   b. Diversification
   c. Risk mitigation

8. Which of the following is a form of idiosyncratic exclusionary screening?
   a. Avoidance of investments in firms that sell tobacco products
   b. Exclusion of companies involved in the processing of whale meat products

c. Prohibition of the use, stockpiling, production, and transfer of cluster munitions

9. Which of the following statements about exclusionary screening is true?
    a. Imposing an exclusion screen may introduce unintended factor exposure
    b. Exclusionary screening imposes sustainability-related themes to a portfolio investment universe
    c. Exclusionary screening considers more qualitative forms of responsible investment, such as stewardship and engagement activities

10. Which of the following about thematic investing is true?
    a. It sacrifices the diversification benefits of portfolio investing
    b. It imposes normative criteria to a portfolio investment universe
    c. It describes investments made with the intention of producing positive, measurable socio-environmental impacts without sacrificing financial returns

The following information relates to questions 11-25
Self Assessment Questions

These questions are provided only to enable you to test your understanding of the chapter content. They are not indicative of the types and standard of questions you may see in the examination. The Self-Assessment questions do not include an explanation of the correct answer.

11. Which of the following is NOT a challenge surrounding ESG?
    a. Data availability and credibility
    b. Diversification of portfolio
    c. Characterization of risk–return profile of ESG funds
    d. Standardization of cross-industry ESG definition and measurability metrics

12. Which of the following is NOT a macro-economic climate consideration?
    a. Asset class sensitivity to interest rates
    b. Heterogeneity and wide-ranging risk/return profile
    c. Weighted-average carbon intensity for a single issuer position
    d. Ability to add low or inverse correlation relative to market returns

13. Which of these topics is not generally expected to be addressed by the portfolio management-related section of an ESG policy?
    a. Stewardship and active engagement efforts
    b. Corporate social responsibility activities, such as community volunteering
    c. ESG risk within the risk management function
    d. All of the above

14. Classes of ESG-oriented fixed-income debt issuance include:
    a. green bonds.
    b. blue bonds.
    c. green collateralized loan obligations (CLOs).
    d. all of the above.

Self Practice and Self Assessment 539

15. Which of the following statements is true?
    a. Sovereign debt is susceptible to distortion effects based on ESG ratings.
    b. ESG is a standalone component within the entire investment process.
    c. It is well understood that the long-term returns on equities outweigh the short-term risks associated with the adoption of ESG by companies as well as funds.
    d. Proprietary ESG data are often a real differentiator for investment firms.

16. Which of the following statements is false?
    a. ESG integration at the equity selection level automatically ensures ESG compliance at portfolio and asset-allocation levels.
    b. Lack of standardization of ESG measurability methods negatively impacts unified investor consensus.
    c. There is little academic proof of positive correlations between ESG integration in the portfolio and positive returns.
    d. Sub-components of ESG are uncorrelated, orthogonal factors.

17. Amongst 1) the Black-Litterman model, 2) the Brinson attribution model, 3) risk factor attribution, which is/are metric(s) to measure the effectiveness of ESG integration?
    a. 1 and 3
    b. 2 and 3
    c. None
    d. 1, 2, and 3

18. Which of the following is an active quantitative approach to embed ESG within a portfolio?
    a. Weighting ESG as an idiosyncratic factor in a multi-factor stock selection algorithm
    b. Consideration of ESG scoring and relevant metrics in security-specific investment decisions
    c. Minimizing tracking error against benchmark indexes
    d. Solving the mean–variance optimization problem to arrive at the best sectors for asset allocation

19. Which of these does NOT describe an approach within ESG portfolio integration?
    a. Impact investing
    b. Positive screening
    c. Green securitization
    d. Negative screening

20. What ESG feature is often overlooked in screening approaches for collective investment funds?
    a. Exclusions, such as those that are 'socially conscious'
    b. Position-weighted ESG portfolio score
    c. Portfolio carbon exposure
    d. Stewardship

21. A portfolio manager would optimize their portfolio for ESG considerations for

the purpose of:

   a. enhancing the risk–return profile.
   b. eliminating correlations between risk premiums.
   c. benchmarking.
   d. tackling skewness in ESG datasets.

22. Which of the following is NOT a reason for an asset owner to implement an exclusionary screening approach?

   a. It reflects a fundamental value of the asset owner's beneficiaries.
   b. It reflects a global or regional norm.
   c. It improves the portfolio's diversification benefits.
   d. It is the simplest approach.

23. Which of the following by itself is the LEAST naturally-suited investment strategy to accommodate the United Nations' Sustainable Development Goals (SDGs)?

   a. Thematic investment fund
   b. Impact fund
   c. Negative screening
   d. Positive screening

24. Which of the following does NOT represent the function(s) of ESG indexes?

   a. Investing to facilitate cash management at the multi-asset level
   b. To measure the sustainability of non-conventional ESG companies
   c. To allow seamless deconstruction and reconstruction of benchmarking tools to include ESG screening
   d. All of the above

25. Why have passive ESG index funds been criticized as being more active than they are presented?

   a. They have higher costs than traditional passive indexes
   b. The opaque methodology and construction of ESG indexes may include space for human judgment and bias
   c. Index inclusion may create crowding and overvaluation in specific securities
   d. Carbon constraints represent a higher tracking error than ESG score constraints

SOLUTIONS

1. A is correct. Climate change – and climate risk – has emerged as the most material ESG factor for institutional investors to address within asset allocation strategies. Climate risk is both systemic and local. It threatens the financial system and the global means of production as much as it poses risk on a more localized level for specific regions, sectors, and companies.

2. B is correct. Discretionary ESG investment strategies most commonly take the form of a fundamental portfolio approach. A portfolio manager would work to complement bottom-up financial analysis alongside the consideration of ESG factors to reinforce the investment thesis of a particular holding.

3. B is correct. Sustainability bonds allow issuers to offer more broadly defined bonds that still create a positive social or environmental impact. In 2016, Starbucks issued the first US corporate sustainability bond of USD500 mn (GPB359 mn) that directly links the company's coffee sourcing supply chain to ESG criteria.

4. A is correct. ESG-oriented bonds are typically organized around a few sustainable themes. What distinguishes these from conventional bonds is their underlying use of proceeds and the greater transparency they provide towards their use of proceeds. Blue bonds fund projects with clear marine and ocean-based benefits, such as sustainable fishing projects.

5. A is correct. The Worldwide Governance Indicators project reports aggregated and individual governance indicators for over 200 countries for six dimensions of governance, which include: political stability, voice and accountability, government effectiveness, rule of law, regulatory quality, and control of corruption.

6. A is correct. The effects and benefits of integrating ESG into portfolio management are an increasingly wide area of study. Investors typically address the effects to risk-adjusted returns of ESG integration in portfolio management through risk mitigation and alpha generation. Although investors have traditionally employed ESG analysis for risk mitigation, many are growing more comfortable with framing ESG as a means to generate alpha.

7. B is correct. One of the advantages of a multi-factor model over a smart beta or beta plus strategy is diversification. Smart beta and beta plus investment strategies represent the compromise between passive, index-oriented investment and active investing at a lower cost than a traditional actively-managed strategy. The active element within these strategies generally emphasizes a single or dominant investment factor, such as value, quality, growth, or momentum. A multi-factor strategy, on the other hand, seeks to maximize the benefits of diversification through the combination of a number of different factors.

8. B is correct. Idiosyncratic exclusions are exclusions that are not supported by global consensus. For example, New Zealand's pension funds are singularly bound by statutory law to exclude companies involved in the processing of whale meat products.

9. A is correct. The degree of exclusions may carry significant implications from a portfolio management perspective — not just in terms of higher tracking error and active share, but also in unintended factor exposure. Hence, imposing an exclusion screen may introduce unintended factor exposure.

10. A is correct. Thematic investing targets sustainability-aligned themes as a means to construct a portfolio. The concentrated nature of thematic investing — particularly if it is based around a single theme like clean energy — sacrifices the benefits of portfolio diversification. The sectoral bias of the portfolio will drive the underlying factor exposure of the fund, potentially carrying relative performance and tracking error implications.

11. B is correct.

12. C is correct.

13. B is correct.

14. D is correct.

15. A is correct.

16. A is correct.

17. B is correct.

18. A is correct.

19. C is correct.

20. D is correct.

21. A is correct.

22. C is correct.

23. C is correct.

24. D is correct.

25. B is correct.

CHAPTER 9

Investment Mandates, Portfolio Analytics, and Client Reporting

LEARNING OUTCOMES

Mastery	The candidate should be able to:
☐	**9.1.1** explain why mandate construction is of particular relevance and importance to the effective delivery of ESG investing: linking sustainable investing to the mandate; defining the sustainable investment strategy
☐	**9.1.2** explain how ESG screens can be embedded within investment mandates/portfolio guidelines to generate investment returns and manage portfolio risk
☐	**9.1.3** explain the most common features of ESG investing that asset owners and intermediaries, including pension consultants and fund selectors, are seeking to identify through request for proposal (RFP) and selection processes: voting, engagement, examples of decision making, and screening process
☐	**9.1.4** explain the different client types and their objectives which influence the type of ESG investing strategy selected
☐	**9.1.5** explain the key mechanisms for reporting on and monitoring performance and mandate alignment with client objectives
☐	**9.1.6** explain the key challenges in measuring and reporting ESG-related investment performance: active, passive, and smart beta approaches; performance attribution; sensitivity analysis; risk measurement; engagement activity/impact; and integrated reporting and investment review

1. INTRODUCTION: ACCOUNTABILITY TO CLIENTS AND ALIGNMENT WITH THEM

This chapter attempts to draw the threads of the earlier ones together in the ways that these topics are given effect in practice

- through the mandates and expectations set by clients and

- how fund managers communicate their environmental, social, and governance (ESG) work to their clients.

We will discuss how the challenges of the agency problem can occur within the investment chain and between investors and corporate management, as well as how the core corporate governance precepts of accountability and alignment can also be used to derive appropriate answers to these challenges in the investment sphere. Designing mandates to deliver investment processes focused on the long-term horizons typically sought by asset owners is key, though delivering this in practice is complex.

The chapter also discusses requests for proposals (RFPs), which are evaluation documents for consultants and asset allocators to conduct initial due diligence on prospective asset managers and an important mechanism for identifying potential providers of fund management services. If done well, the RFP process enables asset managers to provide useful information to consultants and asset allocators, by which they can be compared and evaluated. More broadly, the chapter considers the assessments that clients and their advisers use to identify appropriate fund managers and gain assurance that they are continuing to deliver the agreed-upon investment processes.

Finally, this chapter covers the screening and portfolio analytics tools that are emerging to assist asset owners and their advisers to assess ESG factors or to provide them with an appropriate basis for raising questions about fund manager approaches to ESG investing.

Accountability to Clients and Alignment with Them

The veteran founder of Vanguard, John Bogle, called our society a "double-agency" one—namely, a society in which corporate agents (as a practical matter, corporate CEOs) "who are duty-bound to represent their shareholders face money manager/agents who are themselves duty-bound to represent their mutual fund shareholders and their other clients, often pension funds."[1]

According to Bogle, there is a similarity between the agency problem that corporate governance is designed to address and the agency problems that occur in the investment chain. As with corporate governance, these investment chain agency problems can be addressed (though not completely solved) by careful alignment and accountability:

- Alignment should be designed such that the time frames and structures of portfolio manager assessment and remuneration closely reflect both the performance experienced by the clients they serve and the time frames over which they need performance to be delivered.
- Accountability should mean that portfolio managers respond to the clearly expressed intentions of their clients and report as fully as required.

Client mandates can deliver these two elements if they are designed well. There are a number of steps in properly designing mandates and in the oversight and monitoring process that assesses whether the mandates have, in fact, been delivered in practice. These steps can be characterized as shown in the following subsections.

Clarifying Client Needs: Defining the ESG Investment Strategy

The first step in the effective design of a mandate is that clients should be clear about their needs and set them out in a clear statement of ESG investment beliefs. Doing so will require them to define their investment goals and beliefs. Institutional clients will typically be keenly aware of the goals that they are trying to achieve (their risk-adjusted return target over the appropriate time horizon) but may find it harder to define their

---

1 See page 9 of J. C. Bogle, "The Modern Corporation and the Public Interest," *Financial Analysts Journal* 74 (Third Quarter 2018): 8–17. https://doi.org/10.2469/faj.v74.n3.1.

Introduction: Accountability to Clients and Alignment with Them

investment beliefs. Nevertheless, it is these beliefs that will help them to define how they believe they will create value and to set their investment approach. The investment beliefs—which might be expressed in a statement of investment principles—ought to guide the overall approach toward ESG investment (and investment more generally) and will help frame any mandate agreed on with an investment manager.

Fully Aligning Investment with Client ESG Beliefs

Once the client's investment beliefs are clarified, the next challenge is to ensure that they are reflected operationally in the fund manager's investment approach. Doing so can require a clear framing of basic expectations, including such issues as appropriate ESG screening approaches.

As suggested by a Principles for Responsible Investment (PRI) report, asset owners should ensure that mandates align investment across asset classes with their beliefs and strategies (while the text implies an equity mandate, the intent of its ambition is to expect integration and engagement, as appropriate, across all asset classes):

> *Attention should be paid to aligning timeframes through fees and pay structures, ensuring that ESG issues are fully integrated into investment decision-making, and ensuring that the investment manager engages with companies and issuers, and votes shareholdings."* [2]

Developing Client-Relevant ESG-Aware Investment Mandates

Ensuring that the mandate is fully operational is typically done through a detailed RFP process. Typically, this takes the form of a detailed questionnaire sent to a longlist of potential managers. Reports suggest that there are now always at least some ESG questions included in these questionnaires, though for the least ESG-aware clients, these are likely to be few and somewhat superficial. For those asset owners that take ESG investing more seriously, the questions will be detailed and challenging and form a significant element of the RFP decision-making process. The questionnaire is used to sift providers to develop a shortlist of potential managers, and then there is usually a so-called beauty-parade series of meetings between appropriate representatives of the asset owner (sometimes the investment committee of the board, executive team members, or just an investment consultant, depending on the scale of the mandate or the asset owner and its internal resources) and a number of potential fund managers (typically there are around three managers included at this stage of the process).

Tailoring ESG Investment Approach to Client Expectations

Different types of clients have very different expectations regarding ESG issues and the rest of their investment approach. Responding to those different expectations may require entirely different investment approaches and, indeed, different fund types. It is vital to find ways to ensure that the client and fund manager are aligned in their approach and have a full understanding of their appropriate expectations. This may be done outside the legal mandate as well as within it.

Holding Managers to Account

Once the mandate is agreed upon, the client will wish to ensure that the fund manager is indeed delivering in accordance with the mandate. This is unlikely just to be narrowly in terms of delivering financial performance in line with expectations, though if performance differs notably from what might be expected in given markets, then questions certainly should be asked just as often about striking outperformance of

---

2 PRI, "Aligning Expectations: Guidance for Asset Owners on Incorporating ESG Factors into Manager Selection, Appointment and Monitoring" (February 2013). www.unpri.org/download?ac=1614.

expectations as happens in relation to notable underperformance. However, this is not often the case. And for ESG mandates in particular, the assessment is likely to be across a broader range of issues. There are two forms that this work will take:

- monitoring meetings between the client and the fund manager and
- the manager's measurement and reporting of its ESG performance.

Each of these areas is explored in more depth later in this chapter.

2. CLARIFYING CLIENT NEEDS: DEFINING THE ESG INVESTMENT STRATEGY

9.1.1 explain why mandate construction is of particular relevance and importance to the effective delivery of ESG investing: linking sustainable investing to the mandate; defining the sustainable investment strategy

In order to incorporate the longer-term perspective discussed in Section 1 and an ESG mindset into the mandates that asset owners give fund managers, asset owners need to have a clear understanding of their own views on ESG investment and investment more generally. Today, it is common for asset owners to set out their investment beliefs—namely, a philosophy of what the institution believes will drive returns and deliver value over the relevant time horizon. Most asset owners these days incorporate a perspective on ESG factors.

The Pensions and Lifetime Savings Association (PLSA) produces a Stewardship Checklist for its members, which encourages just such a development of a broader philosophical approach.[3]

EXAMPLE 1

PLSA Stewardship Checklist

In this checklist (which is useful not just to pension schemes but for all asset owners), there are three key requirements.

To ensure an effective and meaningful stewardship strategy, investors should do the following:

- Be clear about how stewardship fits in their investment strategy and policy and how it helps meet their investment objectives. This should include
  - a clear and agreed understanding of the trustee board and relevant organizations' (e.g., the employer's) overall mission, purpose, and objectives;
  - a defined set of agreed investment beliefs—including on ESG issues—at a level that ensures everyone is comfortable but that is also sufficiently granular to meaningfully inform and guide the investment strategy and objectives;

---

3 PLSA, "PLSA Stewardship Guide and Voting Guidelines 2020" (2020). https://hsfnotes.com/corporate/2020/03/06/plsa-stewardship-guide-and-voting-guidelines-2020/.

- a robust framework for deciding and monitoring a scheme's investment policies—including on ESG issues—and the role that acting as an engaged steward of members' assets plays in this (this can be either a stand-alone policy or fully integrated into a scheme's investment policies); and
- a strategy for how stewardship fits into the manager selection process and ongoing relationship monitoring.

▶ Seek to ensure that fund managers and other service providers deliver effective integration of long-term ESG factors into their investment approach. Using due diligence and the fund manager appointment process, pension schemes will gain a clear understanding of the ESG integration and stewardship approaches of prospective fund managers. Schemes should ensure that these approaches are fully consistent with the scheme's investment strategy, policy, and objectives over the appropriate time horizon.

▶ Work with their advisers to consider the level of resources available for stewardship activities, which assets are covered, and what the appropriate structure is. Some schemes will have the resources for an in-house stewardship team. Others will need to outsource stewardship to either their existing asset manager or a specialist stewardship "overlay" provider. Note that delegating stewardship activities does not absolve schemes of responsibility. Instead, they should take ownership of the stewardship approach and ensure they have a clear understanding of work carried out on their behalf.

As the PLSA indicates, the investment philosophy is often shaped by the overall purpose of the organization, set by its founding documents. For many asset owners today, it is vital that ESG factors are integrated into that purpose—not least because, since October 2019, changes to the United Kingdom's Occupational Pension Scheme (Investment) Regulations 2005 have required pension schemes to set out in their statement of investment principles (SIP) their policies on how they consider financially material ESG factors in their investment approach, as well as the extent to which they undertake stewardship, including engagement and voting. New reporting requirements, in line with the European Union's Shareholder Rights Directive II, will reinforce the same sort of approach across the EU. Many other markets around the world have established similar expectations. The starting point for the investment process is often how ESG factors are viewed in the context of an overall investment philosophy or purpose.

The following are two representative examples of how such purposes are articulated by major global asset owners.

From CPP Investment Board (Canada):

> *CPP Investments invests the assets of the CPP with a singular objective—to maximize returns without undue risk of loss taking into account the factors that may affect the funding of the CPP. Our investment strategy is designed to capitalize on our comparative advantages while ensuring we maintain our commitment to responsible investing.*[4]

From AustralianSuper:

---

4 CPP Investments, "How We Invest" (2020). www.cppib.com/en/how-we-invest.

We work hard to maximise investment returns over the long term, so members can enjoy a better future. As long-term investors, we focus on investing in a mix of quality assets that can grow members' savings over time. We balance this with an understanding of the risks we need to take to achieve this objective and deliver competitive returns against our peers.

Our four core investment beliefs are the foundation of our investment approach. A rigorous governance framework and disciplined investment process help us allocate and manage members' savings and maintain our position as one of Australia's leading super funds.

Our four investment beliefs:

1. *We return all profits to members.*
2. *We believe in active management – both asset allocation and stock selection.*
3. *We use our scale to reduce costs and better structure investments.*
4. *We're aware of our responsibility to the broader community, consistent with our obligations to maximise benefits to members.*[5]

How the purpose and investment beliefs and philosophy see ESG factors impacting investment performance—whether as risk factors or value creators—will shape how ESG investing is integrated into mandates and what the asset owner will expect of its fund managers. This is well articulated in a McKinsey article from October 2017.[6] The article provides a framework for considering how to develop a policy and philosophy and then how it can practically be implemented. The authors state that "a sustainable investment strategy consists of building blocks familiar to institutional investors: a balance between risk and return and a thesis about which factors strongly influence corporate financial performance."

Responding to these two building blocks, the authors suggest that there are two fundamental questions that asset owners need to ask in developing their ESG investment philosophy. The first question is,

"Are ESG factors more important for risk management or value creation?" . . . If the mandate focuses on risk management, then the strategy might be designed to exclude companies, sectors, or geographies that investors see as particularly risky with respect to ESG factors, or to engage in dialogue with corporate managers about how to mitigate ESG risks. If value creation is the focus, on the other hand, investors might overweight their portfolios with companies or sectors that exhibit strong performance on ESG-related factors they believe are linked to value creation.

The second question is, "What ESG factors are material?" The authors note that this is much less straightforward than the simple statement of the issue might make it seem and that there are substantial reporting projects dedicated to identifying what is material at a sector level, let alone at an individual company level. The nature of the investment portfolio also adds a layer of complexity. The authors argue that "the selection of material factors is often influenced to some extent by exposure to asset classes, geographies, and specific companies. For example, governance factors tend to be especially important for private equity investments, since these investments are typically characterized by large ownership shares and limited regulatory oversight."

---

5 AustralianSuper, "How We Invest Members' Super: Our Long-Term Vision" (2020). www.australiansuper.com/investments/how-we-invest.

6 S. Bernow, B. Klempner, and C. Magnin, "From 'Why' to 'Why Not': Sustainable Investing as the New Normal," McKinsey & Company (October 2017). www.mckinsey.com/industries/private-equity-and-principal-investors/our-insights/from-why-to-why-not-sustainable-investing-as-the-new-normal.

FULLY ALIGNING INVESTMENT WITH CLIENT ESG BELIEFS

9.1.2 explain how ESG screens can be embedded within investment mandates/portfolio guidelines to generate investment returns and manage portfolio risk

Once the asset owner client has developed its investment philosophy and beliefs, these need to be translated into the specifics of the mandates that it awards to its fund managers. As a report from McKinsey indicates, there are two key questions that will frame how this is delivered in practice:

- Is ESG a risk management tool or a source of investment advantage?
- Which aspects of ESG most matter from the perspective of the asset owner?[7]

Determining the answers to these questions will be the starting point for shaping the mandates awarded. Furthermore, in shaping the detailed expectations, the answers will need to be reflected in the terms of the individual mandates themselves.

The answers will also help shape the overall **strategic asset allocation (SAA)** of the asset owner—the long-term exposures that it chooses to have in terms of asset classes and geographies. They may also inform decisions around the asset owner's **tactical asset allocation (TAA)**, or the short-term variations around the SAA to respond to nearer-term market and other circumstances.

EXAMPLE 2

Pension Fund Concerned about Climate Change

A pension fund has strong beliefs regarding the impending impacts of climate change, whereby:

- The fund might establish multiple mandates investing in new technologies, including renewable energy generation.
- The fund's mainstream equity and debt mandates may well include screens that exclude fossil fuel investments.
- The fund may require that any sovereign bond mandate include an active ESG overlay that seeks to limit exposure in countries where the physical impacts of climate change are likely to be most acute.

EXAMPLE 3

Foundation Investment Portfolio Concerned about Human Rights Abuses

A foundation investment portfolio, where the investment beliefs feature major concerns regarding human rights abuses, might be more likely to:

- apply a screening approach across portfolios requiring the exclusion of any investment facing significant allegations and

---

7 Bernow, Klempner, and Magnin, "From 'Why' to 'Why Not.'"

> ▶ screen out exposures to certain countries where human rights abuses are perceived to be a frequent occurrence or where human rights standards are deteriorating at a rapid rate.

Naturally in practice, the investment beliefs and the mandates that are created to reflect them are rarely as one dimensional as the two previous examples might imply. Furthermore, the client will always have an expectation of investment returns being generated alongside delivery of whatever broader expectations it places on the investment approach.

The report from McKinsey also provides a helpful framework for understanding the different ways in which ESG considerations can be reflected in an asset owner's investment approach and thus be fully operationalized in the work of its fund managers. This is shown in Exhibit 1.

Exhibit 1: Leading Institutions Apply Sustainable Investing Practices across Six Dimensions of Their Investment Process and Operations

Dimension of Investing	Elements of Sustainable Investing
Investment mandate	• Consideration of ESG factors, including prioritization • Targets
Investment beliefs and strategy	• Rationale for ESG integration • Material ESG factors
Investment operations enablers:	
✓ Tools and processes	• Negative screening • Positive screening • Proactive engagement
✓ Resources and organization	• ESG expertise and capabilities • Integration with investment teams • Collaborations and partnerships
✓ Performance management	• Review of external managers (screening and follow-up) • Follow-up on internal managers (including incentives)
✓ Public reporting	• Accountability • Transparency

Source: S. Bernow, B. Klempner, and C. Magnin, "From 'Why' to 'Why Not': Sustainable Investing as the New Normal," McKinsey & Company (October 2017). www.mckinsey.com/industries/private-equity-and-principal-investors/our-insights/from-why-to-why-not-sustainable-investing-as-the-new-normal.

Fund managers themselves, hoping to win mandates that reflect ESG considerations, will seek to develop their own policies that fully integrate ESG approaches into their portfolio management. This is an element of both marketing their approach and differentiating themselves in a crowded investment marketplace. An overarching policy also helps train and shape the mindset of the investment teams themselves. An ESG policy should formally outline the investment approach and degree of ESG integration within a firm.

Such an ESG policy is an opportunity for a fund manager to highlight the relevance or, in some cases, the lack of relevance of responsible investment norms and principles (such as those issued by the PRI) to a firm's investment strategy or strategies. A number of investment strategies face inherent challenges, some of which may be due to

▶ the lack of ESG data within their scope or

Fully Aligning Investment with Client ESG Beliefs

▸ a relative scarcity of methodologies and best practices to apply ESG integration in an asset class.

In each case, it is worth noting that the ESG market is developing very rapidly and new offerings are being brought to the market all the time, meaning that there are increasingly fewer gaps in supply. Whether these new offerings meet their needs will be for the asset owners to decide.

EXAMPLE 4

Multi-Strategy Investment Firm

It is in the interests of a multi-strategy investment firm that manages both fundamental and quantitative ESG strategies to highlight the fact that active ownership activities (such as engagement) are more relevant to more concentrated, fundamental strategies, rather than more diverse quantitative portfolios. The application of ESG strategies to certain asset classes—such as commodities or money market funds—is in its infancy.

The following are two examples of ESG philosophies from leading fund management firms.

RBC Global Asset Management:

> We invest in sustainable great companies at attractive valuations and steward them for the long term. We use intangible, ESG and business assessment combined with strong risk analysis to achieve this. Financial analysis and ESG assessment are intertwined in judging a business. Businesses thrive over the long term when they invest in ESG intangible factors that lead to stronger more sustainable financials.
>
> We consider ESG factors as non-traditional sources of risk and opportunity which we believe should form part of every company assessment. . . . The relevance of particular ESG issues varies from industry to industry, which is why we believe it is important to integrate ESG into the company assessment . . . rather than as a pre-screen or overlay. It facilitates engagement and ensures ESG risks and opportunities are incorporated into the fundamental valuation analysis driving financials.[8]

Generation Investment Management:

> Our investment process underpins our differentiated thinking about the dynamics that drive and influence the performance of companies. We construct portfolios of sustainable companies with the confidence derived from our deep research and analysis.
>
> A sustainable company is:
>
> 1. one whose current earnings do not borrow from its future earnings;
> 2. one whose sustainability practices, products and services drive revenues, profitability and competitive positioning; and
> 3. one that provides goods and services consistent with a low-carbon, prosperous, equitable, healthy and safe society.[9]

---

8 RBC Global Asset Management, "RBC Global Equity" (2019). http://global.rbcgam.com/global-equities/default.fs.
9 Generation Investment Management, "Generation Philosophy" (2019).

These philosophical statements then need to be operationalized into ESG policies that cover a range of practical issues. Regardless of the investment strategy or asset class, such an ESG policy needs to address the manner in which the portfolio manager

- addresses ESG issues at portfolio reviews,
- establishes the rationale and methodology for ESG portfolio-level assessment,
- assesses exposure to ESG risk within the risk management function,
- determines ESG impacts to the portfolio,
- responds in the investment decision-making process to ESG implications, and
- discloses ESG exposure to the fund's investors.

Portfolio managers should also find ways to embed ESG information in annual or interim reports alongside financial information and manager commentary to fund investors. Annual reports may include

- ESG activities across the portfolio,
- the frequency of engagement, and
- highlighted activities and their outcomes.

Portfolios with private or unlisted security exposure may choose to report portfolio performance against key performance indicators (KPIs) over a given investment period and relative to peers.

4. DEVELOPING CLIENT-RELEVANT ESG-AWARE INVESTMENT MANDATES

9.1.3 explain the most common features of ESG investing that asset owners and intermediaries, including pension consultants and fund selectors, are seeking to identify through request for proposal (RFP) and selection processes: voting, engagement, examples of decision making, and screening process

The International Corporate Governance Network's (ICGN's) "ICGN Model Contract Terms between Asset Owners and Managers" provides a helpful framework and proposes best practices for ESG-aware investment mandates around

- the monitoring and use of ESG factors,
- the integration of ESG factors into investment decision making,
- adherence to good practice around stewardship, and
- voting and reporting requirements.

The document states, "As important as setting standards within fund management contracts is how clients can effectively call their fund managers to account in respect of these mandates. The intended standards will most effectively be delivered where managers are made accountable on a regular basis for their delivery against them."[10]

---

10 ICGN, "ICGN Model Contract Terms between Asset Owners and Managers" (2015). www.icgn.org/sites/default/files/2021-06/ICGN_Model-Contract-Terms_2015_0.pdf.

Developing Client-Relevant ESG-Aware Investment Mandates

According to a 2016 PRI report, "How Asset Owners Can Drive Responsible Investment," investment mandates should require investment managers to do the following:

- "implement the asset owner's investment beliefs and relevant investment policies;
- integrate ESG issues into their investment research, analysis and decision-making processes.
- invest in a manner consistent with the asset owner's time horizons, understanding the key risks that must be managed to achieve the asset owner's portfolio goals;
- implement effective stewardship processes, including engagement with companies and issuers on ESG issues and, for listed equities, voting all shareholdings—this engagement should align with the asset owner's responsible investment and related policies;
- engage constructively and proactively with policymakers on responsible investment and ESG-related issues—this engagement should align with the asset owner's responsible investment and related policies;
- report on the actions taken and outcomes achieved—the reporting should enable the asset owner to assess the manner in which the investment manager has implemented the asset owner's investment beliefs and policies, and to understand how this has affected investment performance and ESG outcomes and impacts."[11]

Different asset managers adopt different responsible investment strategies because their investment philosophy and investment processes may fundamentally differ. For instance,

- some active investors focus on fundamental company-specific research, while others may emphasize quant models;
- some will be more event driven, while others will be more focused on identifying companies with a long-term track record of delivering superior financial performance; and
- passive investment approaches need to build ESG priorities into the design of the mandate and the way in which investment assets are selected; typically, this is by either
  - excluding certain investments (e.g., the fossil fuel sector or particularly carbon-intensive aspects of it) or
  - applying a "tilt" to a broad index (so that, to pursue the climate change example, the least carbon-intensive companies are chosen in each sector meaning that the overall portfolio has a reduced intensity).

As a result, different managers will integrate ESG factors in different ways:

- as a threshold requirement before investment can be considered,
- as factors that inform the valuation or provide a quant basis for adjusting (or tilting) exposures,
- as a risk assessment that offers a level of confidence in the valuation,
- as a basis for stewardship engagement, or

---

[11] PRI, "How Asset Owners Can Drive Responsible Investment: Beliefs, Strategies and Mandates" (2016). www.unpri.org/download?ac=1398.

- as a combination of two or more of these methods, which is very often the case.

An alternative form of classification has been developed by CFA Institute, in its "ESG Disclosure Standards for Investment Products" issued on 1 November 2021. Please see the appendix of this chapter for more information.[12]

Exhibit 2 highlights six ESG investment approaches (not all of them are mutually exclusive, so they might be offered in combination by some providers).

Exhibit 2: ESG Investment Approaches

ESG Investment Approach	Brief Description of Investment Approach
✓ ESG integration	Explicitly considers ESG-related factors that are material to the risk and return of the investment, alongside traditional financial factors, when making investment decisions
✓ ESG-related exclusions	Excludes securities, issuers, or companies from the investment product based on certain ESG-related activities, business practices, or business segments
✓ Best-in-class	Aims to invest in companies and issuers that perform better than peers on one or more performance metrics related to ESG matters
✓ ESG-related thematic focus	Aims to invest in sectors, industries, or companies that are expected to benefit from long-term macro or structural ESG-related trends
✓ Impact objective	Seeks to generate a positive, measurable social or environmental impact alongside a financial return
✓ Proxy voting, engagement, and stewardship	Uses rights and position of ownership to influence issuers' or companies' activities or behaviors

These variations in style should be readily apparent to asset owners (and the investment consultants that advise them). Therefore, they should help determine which is the most appropriate provider of services to fulfill the client's needs, consistent with their investment beliefs and philosophy. Exhibit 3 shows an example of a questionnaire an asset owner might use in determining what investment approach a fund manager uses:

Exhibit 3: Sample RFP Checklist of ESG Approaches

- ☐ Systematically considers financially material ESG information in investment decisions.
- ☐ Tracks an ESG index and/or uses an ESG index as an investment universe.
- ☐ Systematically applies ESG criteria to exclude certain investments and/or to determine if an investment is eligible for inclusion in the fund's portfolio.
- ☐ Sets allocation targets and/or constraints based on the ESG characteristics of investments.
- ☐ Sets targets and/or constraints for fund-level ESG characteristics.
- ☐ Considers ESG issues when exercising the rights and position associated with the ownership, management, and oversight of the fund's assets.

---

12 CFA Institute, "ESG Disclosure Standards for Investment Products Consultation Paper" (2020). www.cfainstitute.org/en/ethics-standards/codes/esg-standards.

☐   Has an explicit objective to generate a positive, measurable ESG outcome alongside a financial return.

The usual way that consultants and clients seek to understand and test fund managers' capabilities and approaches is through an RFP process (an invitation to pitch for potential business; see the following section for more details), usually followed by interviews of short-listed candidates. Naturally, the client wants to gain confidence that the fund manager can deliver satisfactory financial returns while staying within relevant risk parameters. In addition, with regard to ESG considerations, the client wants to know

- whether the approach to integration is sufficiently robust to deliver an appropriate portfolio structure,
- that the fund manager is capable of delivering with certainty any hard constraints on the portfolio (such as negative screens),
- that the manager can deliver appropriately effective engagement to preserve and enhance value, and
- that the manager actually delivers in practice what it sets out as its approach in these respects in its policy documents and other assertions.

There is often an overarching concern that the client is seeking confidence that the fund management firm genuinely has a solid ESG philosophy underpinning its actions, because that gives greatest confidence that the ESG activity is genuine and robust and will be delivered consistently over time.

Unless the fund manager can deliver all these necessary requirements, it is unlikely to make it through the due diligence process.

The RFP Process

The RFP process is a formalized one and partly formulaic in most cases. The questions asked are generally high level, and although they sometimes ask for examples of delivery to ensure that the fund manager can demonstrate the truth behind its assertions, the resulting information will rarely reveal much of the substance of what is going on. The questioning now typically goes deeper than the basic question of whether the fund manager is a signatory to PRI (which for a period of time in many RFPs was the sole ESG question), but this is often still the starting point.

The larger fund managers have RFP teams that deal with the flow of questions and hold a bank of answers, which builds and extends over time with input from practitioners, but this may occasionally come at the detriment of tailoring of responses. The result is that clients will be able to ask only the second- and third-level questions that actually get closer to the truth of the underlying processes in the face-to-face interviews of the short-listed candidates, which are typically the second part of a manager due diligence process. The RFP questioning process does at least have the benefit of narrowing the field to a shortlist of potential providers.

Exhibit 4 (marginally adapted from the original from PLSA) sets out what might be the major ESG considerations for a pension fund or other asset owner when seeking to allocate a new mandate across the full range of potential asset classes. These are elements that may need to be reflected in the RFP process to ensure that ESG issues are appropriately considered by the relevant mandate.

Exhibit 4: Possible Routes to Incorporating ESG Factors by Asset Class

	Mandate Choice	Investment Integration	Engagement
Passive/index tracking	Trustees should consider the index benchmark and any ESG tilts.	No or limited manager discretion in stock selection	Managers can exert influence on companies through engagement and voting. There is also scope for influence on market- and system-wide issues.
Active equity	Trustees could invest in ESG-oriented mandates, such as sustainable equity.	Managers should consider financially material ESG factors and their impact on future profitability in company evaluation. Traditionally, data availability and quality have limited the ability to do this in quantitative analysis, though this is changing.	Managers can exert influence on companies through engagement and voting.
Active fixed income	Some assets (such as green bonds) could be considered by trustees, but probably only as part of a broader fixed-income mandate.	Managers should consider the potential for ESG risks to impact credit ratings and borrowers' future ability to make repayments.	It is possible for managers to have engagement with borrowers on material ESG risks, particularly at the time of initial issuance.
Real estate	Some real estate strategies could have E and/or S objectives, and appropriate assets may be targeted to achieve these.	Managers should consider material environmental and social risks during acquisition and development and manage resource use during occupation.	Managers can engage with tenants and the local community to address potential issues and drive change.
Infrastructure	Trustees can consider portfolios biased toward infrastructure that supports a sustainable future.	Managers should assess the physical and societal risks arising from infrastructure assets. Longevity of investment means that systemic issues need to be considered.	Managers can exert influence on underlying companies or asset management through governance arrangements (e.g., board seats).
Private debt	Trustees could consider mandates that target lending at certain sustainable activities.	Managers should identify and seek mitigation of potential ESG risks during due diligence on loans.	Managers should have ongoing dialogue with borrowers to ensure that emerging and identified ESG risks are managed.
Private equity	Trustees can assess which companies the manager may target and the potential for unwanted or desired ESG exposures to arise.	The longevity of the investment means that systemic risks need to be considered. Managers should assess potential ESG risks during due diligence and ongoing ownership.	Managers would be expected to have a high level of influence over company management and ensure that governance structures are effective.

Source: Based on PLSA and Investor Forum, "Engaging the Engagers: A Practical Toolkit for Schemes to Achieve Effective Stewardship through Their Managers" (2020). www.investorforum.org.uk/wp-content/uploads/securepdfs/2020/07/Engaging-the-Engagers-stewardship-toolkit.pdf.

Developing Client-Relevant ESG-Aware Investment Mandates

As the PLSA and Investor Forum explain in their "Engaging the Engagers" report (the text refers just to pension schemes, but the same is true for all asset owners; similarly, the focus of the report is on engagement but the thinking extends to ESG issues more generally),

> *The appointment process for a new asset manager offers a key opportunity for pension schemes to thoroughly assess the market for a manager whose approach to stewardship, engagement and (where relevant) voting aligns with the scheme's own. Where a pension scheme is looking to hire a new asset manager through a tender and due diligence process, the statement of expectations with regard to stewardship should form a part of the contractual relationship with the manager. The due diligence process is likely to include some assessment of whether the manager can fulfil the pension scheme's expectations in the asset classes and geographies in question.*[13]

The document goes on to offer a series of potential questions to ask a fund manager as part of the due diligence process before appointment of a manager. As it states, not all questions will be suitable to every situation (for example, different asset classes or natures of mandate will demand different assessment criteria), and all will need to be tailored to the circumstances of the specific mandate. Nonetheless, the following list from the "Engaging the Engagers" report provides a good basis for asset owners to seek to test potential service providers and for fund managers to demonstrate the value that they can bring through their ESG work:

- "Understanding how the manager sees stewardship and engagement and what its main drivers for action are. This includes how consistently that philosophy is applied across asset classes and geographies.
  - How long term is the fund management firm's investment mindset? Is this reflected in the portfolio exposures, turnover and approach to engagement? How do these approaches vary across different teams and portfolios?
  - How does the manager decide on the resourcing given to stewardship? How is this overall resource shared across the firm's portfolios, asset classes and geographies? What plans are there for changing the resourcing of stewardship?
  - For which portfolios and asset classes does the manager believe it most needs to improve its approach to stewardship and engagement currently? What is being done to bring those up to the standards in the wider organisation?
- Seeking confidence in the processes by which the manager's objectives are set and progress against them is monitored.
  - What systems does the fund manager have in place to capture engagement objectives systematically and to measure progress against those objectives?
  - What differences do those systems reveal about the nature and effectiveness of engagement between different asset classes, portfolios or geographies?

---

13 PLSA and Investor Forum, "Engaging the Engagers: A Practical Toolkit for Schemes to Achieve Effective Stewardship through Their Managers" (2020). www.investorforum.org.uk/wp-content/uploads/securepdfs/2020/07/Engaging-the-Engagers-stewardship-toolkit.pdf.

- If different teams within the fund management firm have investment exposure to the same company or asset, how does the firm seek to have a concerted approach to stewardship and engagement? How does it leverage different perspectives and understandings of a business from those different teams?

▶ Understanding how the manager allocates its engagement efforts between the different forms of engagement.

- What form of engagement takes the majority of the manager's engagement resource? Why?
- Are different forms of engagement more relevant in different asset classes, portfolios or geographies? Explain how.
- What is the process for agreeing to escalate an engagement? What are the range of escalation tools available?
- How does the application of escalation vary between different asset classes, portfolios or geographies? Are these differences appropriate?"[14]

The aim of these questions is to provide a basis for assessing how robust each fund manager's approach to the area of stewardship and engagement is and, thus, a framework for effective differentiation between providers. The focus of the PLSA and Investor Forum report is largely on engagement, and so the focus of these questions is also. It is, however, relatively straightforward to broaden the coverage of the questions to encompass ESG integration as well (or instead).

Investment Integration

Asset owners have their own investment philosophies and preferred investment styles, so as clients, they will seek to test whether the responsible investment strategy adopted by the fund manager is coherent with their broader investment strategy and aligned with their preferences:

▶ Some clients might be more interested in investing with a quant-fund manager running a smart beta product.

▶ Others might prefer a fundamental stock-picking fund manager with a concentrated portfolio of companies.

The important thing is that both strategies integrate ESG issues in a relevant and value-adding way, given the specificities of their respective investment processes.

Therefore, clients' key questions in this regard will always be around the investment decision-making process. Typically this operates on two levels:

▶ An analysis of the formal process and, in particular, how ESG factors are integrated. This will usually also incorporate an assessment of the portfolio as it stands (perhaps using some of the available analytical tools) to take a view as to whether it is consistent with the assertions regarding ESG integration.

▶ A discussion of the process as it has been applied to individual assets, usually framed by the client identifying one or more assets that are questionable from an ESG perspective and testing how it was that the assets in question were deemed to be appropriate to be included in the portfolio.

---

14 PLSA and Investor Forum, "Engaging the Engagers."

Developing Client-Relevant ESG-Aware Investment Mandates

It is this systematic approach of assessing the overall portfolio and testing hard cases that usually reveals whether there is any real substance to the ESG element of the investment process.

The client is attempting to get under the surface of the fund manager's decision-making processes, to understand what actually determines whether an asset will be included in a portfolio or not and the decisions that lead to different weightings in the portfolio. It is only through highlighting the factors that may lead to these concrete investment decisions that the fund manager can genuinely demonstrate that its ESG integration approach

- is real and robust and
- can be replicated effectively over time.

Furthermore, it is only through understanding how these factors drive concrete investment decisions that the client will begin to have confidence in the robustness of the way ESG factors are integrated in practice. If the fund manager is appointed, future dialogue (the regular review meetings, typically annual, though sometimes more frequent) will again focus on assessing the overall portfolio for consistency with the asserted ESG integration and testing individual investment decisions to assess whether the investment process remains as promised and continues to robustly integrate ESG factors into decision making. It is consistency of investment approach that an asset owner tends to be seeking.

See Section 6 of this chapter for sample questions that a client might ask a fund manager as part of ongoing monitoring; some of these might also be useful or could be adapted for due diligence discussions.

As well as testing the investment process with hard cases, clients will usually look at metrics—notably portfolio turnover and Sharpe and other ratios—to see if these are consistent with what they understand of the investment process.

Increasingly, there are now also ESG portfolio assessment tools to facilitate the assessment of the portfolio as a whole. These look at the overall ESG assessment of the portfolio constituents (typically an overview of the portfolio assessed against each category of E, S, and G) and identify outliers in the portfolio, comparing these to the benchmark. While these assessments are subject to the challenges around ESG analysis (most notably, they are typically highly dependent on the disclosures made by individual companies, which are of variable quality and detail), they at least offer a basis for clients to test and challenge the effectiveness of ESG integration.

For further detail on challenges in ESG analysis, see Chapter 7.

Clients might also request that the fund manager provide them with an ESG performance attribution analysis, providing some insights into the value added by ESG factors on stock selection.

Clients can use these insights to test and challenge whether portfolio managers continue to invest in line with the method that they were hired to deliver.

This topic is discussed in more depth in Section 6.

Engagement and Voting

The other key area of client expectation is effective stewardship delivery. Clients will probe and test the effectiveness of fund manager voting and engagement approaches—both policy and delivery.

There are two crucial bases of assessment for any asset owner:

- Who does the stewardship work? Specifically, is it outsourced—delivered by a specialist stewardship team—or is it the portfolio managers (or how do these individuals successfully work together)?

- The closely connected issue of how significant the resources assigned to stewardship are

It should be no surprise that resourcing poses a real challenge to the effectiveness of engagement. As a recent study by the Institute of Chartered Secretaries & Administrators (ICSA, now the Chartered Governance Institute) states, "One factor mentioned by both issuers and investors [was] investors' resource constraints. With many major investors often holding thousands of firms in their portfolios, it is only natural that their resources are stretched to engage meaningfully with all companies."[15]

While teams are being expanded, this challenge remains; certainly, company chairs believe that limited investor resources are a major limitation for effective engagement, and it is a repeated frustration for them. The ICSA study suggests that there has been an increase in the quantity of engagement but companies perceive that this growth in activity was "not always accompanied by an increase in the quality of engagement."[16]

As discussed in depth in Chapter 6, prioritization of engagements is a key way for fund managers to respond to resource constraints. Asset owners will want to understand how the fund manager prioritizes engagements, both in terms of focusing on individual assets and in terms of prioritization of particular issues for engagement. Part of a responsive fund manager's approach to prioritization will be to understand what are clients' key priorities and how these might best be reflected in the fund manager's program of activity. An asset owner will seek to understand through the due diligence process how they can best influence their fund manager and how responsive to their priorities the chosen fund manager is likely to be.

Concentrated portfolios are more easily resourced from a stewardship perspective, and those firms that most pride themselves on being active stewards tend to be genuinely concentrated and so can commit significant resources to these activities. This leads to one way of addressing the resourcing issue: portfolio managers themselves becoming more actively involved in stewardship. This is natural for fundamental active equity managers who hold concentrated portfolios of stocks and would typically maintain a constant dialogue with management. This is particularly true in markets with low liquidity (such as small caps or emerging markets), where the option for larger investors to exit is less available, but stewardship becomes challenging with larger portfolios of many stocks where managers may not have a direct dialogue with all the companies. Fund management firms with more diversified portfolios are more likely to develop larger, more stand-alone stewardship teams.

The alternatives to building specialist stewardship resources internally are outsourcing and collective action.

Outsourcing

Outsourcing is done by almost all investors in the area of voting, where proxy advisers are hired to provide

- a voting platform and the pipework and
- advice on how to vote.

Different investors lean to different extents on such advice, but few ignore it entirely—not least because of the issue of the breadth of portfolios and the difficulty of addressing all votes in a concentrated period, especially for a potentially long tail of small investments. Voting service providers are somewhat controversial because

---

15 Institute of Chartered Secretaries & Administrators, "Shareholder Engagement: The State of Play" (July 2018). www.amecbrasil.org.br/wp-content/uploads/2018/07/ICSA_Shareholder_Engagement_July_2018.pdf.
16 Institute of Chartered Secretaries & Administrators, "Shareholder Engagement."

companies tend to believe that they have too much influence on voting decisions and thus press for higher standards of conduct; increasingly, investors ask these providers to apply their own voting templates, but few investors reveal the extent to which their voting differs in practice from the voting recommendations of their advisers. In turn, investors may express frustration that companies often seek more dialogue with the proxy advisory firms than they do with investors themselves.

Some asset owners take control of voting directly; others ask their fund managers to reflect their policies. But the majority tend to leave voting decisions entirely in the hands of their fund managers. They tend to do this having assessed the alignment between the fund manager's voting policies and approaches and their own as part of the due diligence process, with this alignment playing a part in their choice of manager. They will also seek to assess the quality of voting decision making over time as part of the ongoing monitoring process. As with monitoring of the investment process and investment decision making, this is best done by talking about hard cases that the client itself identifies.

Collective Action

The other way in which investors can share resources is through collective engagement approaches.

See Chapter 6 for details on collective vehicles—and engagement and voting more generally.

Assessing the Quality of Engagement and Voting

Since resources are always limited, clients should always ask how the fund manager ensures that the use of its resources is most effective. Fund managers should be able to set out a thought-through, structured approach to targeting engagement and delivering change for the benefit of clients.

> **EXAMPLE 5**
>
> **Fund Manager and Direct Engagement**
>
> A fund manager might undertake direct engagement with a few of the larger holdings in the portfolio where concerns on material ESG issues have been identified. This might be complemented with broader engagement on a number of issues with a larger number of companies through specialist providers.
>
> Also, the fund manager might identify one key issue (e.g., climate risk disclosure) where systemic change is required and that might best be addressed through collaborative engagement initiatives.

It is likely that any structured approach to resource efficiency will need to encompass some form of collective body, because such organizations assist in terms of both effectiveness and efficiency.

Voting is also considered by clients as a key aspect of stewardship. Voting often gets more attention in client assessments because the datapoints on voting are clearer. For example:

- How does the fund manager vote in general?
- By what process does the manager reach its decisions?
- How did the manager vote on specific controversial matters?

The most sophisticated clients seek to discuss specific votes at individual companies as the basis for testing whether the policy and process actually lead to justifiable results in practice. This enables more granular discussion, which reveals more of the substance of the fund manager's approach and prevents the fund manager from selecting individual cases that put its work in the best light.

Assessing engagement is harder. Because engagement is nuanced and long term, it is hard to have a clear view of its effectiveness. It occurs in private meetings, so the visibility of even the activity itself is low, but the difficulty goes further than this: Effectiveness is largely invisible even for the engager. Any investor that asserts with certainty that he has made a change happen at a company is most likely overstating his case: In almost every case, this simply cannot be known. There may be a correlation between what an investor sought and what happened, but correlation is not the same as causation. After all, it is not shareholders who make decisions about the strategies of companies but company boards; shareholders can influence and persuade, but it will always be the board that actually decides.

This is reflected in the performance measurements that investors themselves place around engagement. Mostly developed by the stewardship overlay providers, these tend to be schemes to reflect the changes made by companies as engagement progresses. Expressed as either milestones or objectives, the engagers measure progress toward concrete change or better practice over the three or more years typical of the engagement process. It is these metrics that clients can assess and challenge, in addition to having direct dialogue with the engagement team to gain some confidence in the robustness and sense that lies behind the measurements.

5. TAILORING THE ESG INVESTMENT APPROACH TO CLIENT EXPECTATIONS

9.1.4 explain the different client types and their objectives which influence the type of ESG investing strategy selected

Different clients (institutional, retail, or private) have different investment objectives, risk/return profiles, and drivers. These will influence the type of ESG investing strategies they will consider most attractive.

Exhibit 5 provides (highly) simplified and generalized insights into the likely primary drivers toward ESG investing and thus the relevant risk/return profiles and implied favored ESG approach for broad groupings of investors. As with all generalizations, there will be many individual exceptions to these indicative and broad-brush characteristics.

Exhibit 5: Overview of Investor Drivers

Investor	Defined benefit (DB) pension scheme	Defined contribution (DC) pension scheme	General insurer	Life insurer	Sovereign wealth fund	Foundation	Individual investor
Investment time horizon	10–70 years	10–70 years	1–2 years	10–50 years	30–150+ years	50–250+ years	1–50 years

Primary driver for ESG investment	Fiduciary duty	Fiduciary duty, personal perspectives of beneficiaries	Awareness of financial impacts of climate change	Recognition of implications of lengthy investment time horizons	Reputational risk	Reputational risk, investment consistent with founding or charitable aims	Personal ethics and perspectives
Risk mindset	Long-term perspective should permit higher risk tolerance	Where individual beneficiaries are permitted to switch providers, greater risk aversion than time horizon might otherwise imply	Loss aversion	Long-term perspective typically permits higher risk tolerance	High tolerance for illiquidity and short-term under-performance	High tolerance for illiquidity and short-term under-performance	Loss aversion
Implied favored ESG approach	ESG integration	Some exclusions, ESG integration	ESG integration	ESG integration	Some exclusions, ESG engagement approach often most important	Exclusions likely, to ensure investment is consistent with founding or charitable aims	Screened funds, strong ESG integration

In the institutional investment community, clients generally expect that ESG principles will be genuinely applied across the approach so that the asset owner can invest among asset classes and benefit across all of them from the integration of ESG factors and effective stewardship engagement. This expectation is increasingly true whatever asset class the asset owner is investing in (the scale of the membership of PRI emphasizes the scale of the commitment to ESG investing overall), and questions about the overall ESG philosophy and approach of the investment firm are usually built into the discussions.

As discussed earlier, often these expectations are written into the mandate—the contract between the fund manager and the client. On occasion, however, the specific ESG (or other) requirements of a client are included not in the contractual mandate itself but in a side letter, which also has contractual status. An insight into this model is provided by the Brunel Asset Management Accord.[17] This document sets out a pension manager's approach to long-term investment and ESG factors but in language that Brunel Pension Partnership believes is less suited to the hard legal language of a specific contract but more to a softer form of agreement whereby the fund managers are enabled to more clearly understand the client's perspective and thus align to it. For the purposes of this chapter, we discuss mandates in a way that encompasses side letters or any other legal documents that frame the agreement between a client and a fund manager.

The issue of time horizons of the asset owner and the overall investment philosophy, incorporating the institution's understanding of ESG factors and their impact on value over those time horizons, goes to the core of delivering mandates that actually encourage fund managers to respond appropriately to ESG risks and opportunities. As the ICGN's Model Mandate puts it,

---

17 Brunel Pension Partnership, "Brunel Asset Management Accord" (2018). www.brunelpensionpartnership.org/wp-content/uploads/2018/11/Brunel-Asset-Management-Accord-2018.pdf.

The time horizon of most asset owners is considerably longer than that of fund managers. Thus for long-term portfolios, the factors and risks which matter to the asset owner are somewhat different from those typically considered within fund management processes. But as these factors and risks will impact their long-term returns, many asset owners are keen to see more effective integration of these longer-term factors into investment processes.[18]

Even where an asset owner is seeking to invest in a particular ESG fund (for example, a bond fund tilted away from CO_2-intensive industries and toward businesses less likely to be disrupted by carbon taxes and constraints), asset owners are unlikely to simply ask about the approach in that specific fund. Rather, the overall mindset and philosophy of the fund manager are important because they provide a context of confidence that the specific fund has backing and will be resourced long term. Engagement is often an integrated activity across the investment firm, meaning that there may be an opportunity to leverage off activity on behalf of other portfolios and asset classes.

To take the example of a carbon-tilted bond fund, there might be direct stewardship in relation to the fixed-income investments, but the fund could also benefit from the investor's broader engagement approach. This means that the fund could be informed by engagement on equity portfolios. Thus, the bond fund could benefit from the changes that equity engagement can deliver at holdings in the bond portfolio also.

Fund managers that integrate ESG factors across their funds and genuinely join up their activities find that engaging with firms with the perspective of equity and bond investment (and potentially other exposures also—for example, through property portfolios) is often the most productive route of all. The investment house's overall approach to ESG investing thus matters to large asset owners, which will tend to probe whether this collaboration across the investment firm happens effectively.

The same is true for retail investors as well, but often these investors are looking more for a product. Inevitably, they are constrained by the investment vehicles that they can invest in, but also, they are more likely to be seeking out an investment fund that suits their personal ethics and perspective on the world. Therefore, they may seek out funds that exclude "sin stocks" or avoid particularly carbon-intensive businesses. In fact, this approach is often mirrored by some institutional investors (such as foundations or religion-linked asset owners) if they have a moral constraint on their freedom to invest. For these investors, the ability to deliver exclusions and effectively screened portfolios is often more important than the broader philosophical approach of the investment firm. Stewardship engagement is typically important to these investors but may also get less challenge and focus in discussions.

Growing fields (such as impact investing) have developed from offerings to high-net-worth individuals and foundations into more mainstream investment vehicles. They are at times offered to mainstream asset owners, although there are issues around the scalability of such investments. In many cases, it is difficult for large asset owners to take an interest in such opportunities because they may not be available in large enough pools for it to be worth the attention of the asset owner.

Liquidity is also an issue for this form of investment: Traditionally a private market form of investing, money is often locked up for lengthy periods, and exiting a position may be difficult for an institutional or retail investor in need of liquidity. One response to this from the investment community may be rebranding broader investment approaches as "impact"; the wise client will never buy on the basis of the brand but will always look to understand what the underlying investment philosophy and process is for any product and select accordingly. Nonetheless, fund managers'

---

18 ICGN, "ICGN Model Contract Terms between Asset Owners and Managers."

consideration of their portfolios' broader real-world impacts—and reporting on them—is a useful innovation in bringing home the reality of investment as part of the real world rather than in some way divorced from it.

HOLDING MANAGERS TO ACCOUNT: MONITORING DELIVERY

☐ 9.1.5 explain the key mechanisms for reporting on and monitoring performance and mandate alignment with client objectives

There will typically be annual performance discussions with fund managers once appointed; however, some clients may

- insist on more frequent dialogue (this likely is particularly the case if financial or other performance has given rise to concerns) or
- choose to send a message that they care only about the longer term by waiting longer for any such discussions.

Performance (at least for assets that are freely traded or otherwise regularly valued) is likely to be assessed or at least seen more frequently than this. One of the challenges for clients is always to ensure that their fund managers do not become more short term in their approach because they are aware the client is considering performance on a regular basis.

The Brunel Asset Management Accord highlights one way in which clients can do this. The document emphasizes that short-term underperformance is not in itself likely to give rise to undue concern for the client: "Investment performance, particularly in the short term, will be of limited significance in evaluating the manager."[19] Rather, the list of issues that it identifies as likely to give rise to concerns are much more about culture and a failure to adhere to the expected investment process or style:

- "Persistent failure to adhere to Brunel's investment principles and the spirit of the accord.
- A change in investment style, or investments that do not fit into the expected style.
- Lack of understanding of reasons for any underperformance, and/or a reluctance to learn lessons from mistakes. Conversely, complacency after good performance should be avoided.
- Failure to follow the investment restrictions or manage risk appropriately, including taking too little risk.
- Organisation instability or the loss of key personnel."

This focus on culture and conflicts—and an investment approach that is not consistent with the expected investment style—is consistent with the thinking of the ICGN Model Mandate.[20] Among other things, it asks for early reporting of the following:

- "the turnover in the portfolio for the reporting period and an explanation if the turnover is outside the expected turnover range for that period; . . .
- any changes to governance, ownership or structure of the manager, or in its investment approach or risk appetite; . . .

---
19 Brunel Pension Partnership, "Brunel Asset Management Accord."
20 ICGN, "ICGN Model Contract Terms between Asset Owners and Managers."

- any regulatory investigation or legal proceedings against the manager, any key staff or the fund; . . .
- any changes in staff ownership in the fund or any equivalent vehicle managed by the manager or changes in staff ownership in the manager itself; . . .
- regular financial accounts of the manager; . . .
- any changes in or waivers of the manager's conflicts of interest policy; and
- any additional conflicts that have arisen over the reporting period."

Moving away from market benchmarking helps change the mindset about performance and the particular focus on any underperformance. For example, for a client to seek absolute returns or performance of a certain number of percentage points above base rates is very different from seeking performance ahead of the standard equity benchmarks. Nonetheless, fund managers may be easily tempted to act in a more short-term way if they perform poorly against a general market performance, and clients who are concerned for long-term performance need to guard against this temptation.

As both Brunel Pension Partnership and the ICGN have shown, the crucial assessment in terms of ESG factors is whether the investment approach has been consistent with the process promised in the mandate and witnessed through the due diligence process. In many ways, the annual or other performance assessment is likely in practice to reflect the style of a due diligence process, seeking to confirm that the approach has remained consistent or to assess what may have changed.

To provide insights into what these processes are likely to involve, the following case study includes a sample set of probing questions of the sort that an asset owner might ask in discussions with a fund manager in ongoing regular conversations to assess whether the manager is performing in accordance with expectations. These are indicative only and are intended to provide an idea of the nature of insight and discussion that an actively engaged asset owner will be seeking (note that a few of these questions are developed from examples published in Engaging the Engagers).[21]

CASE STUDIES

Sample Questions an Asset Owner Might Ask to Gauge a Fund Manager's ESG Approach

Structural and Cultural

You place great emphasis on the size and experience of your firm's investment team.

- How do you ensure that you get a consistent level of quality in terms of ESG analysis from such a disparate group of analysts?
- Are there sectors or geographies where you currently worry that the analysis may be weaker?
- What do you do to address any weaknesses?

You highlight your interaction with other investment teams.

- What does this amount to in practice?
- Please provide concrete examples of how this has worked in the recent past, one with your ESG team and one with one of the other teams.
- How has interaction changed in recent years?

---

[21] PLSA and Investor Forum, "Engaging the Engagers."

How are your holdings in XX and YY consistent with your stated approach to stewardship and long-term investment? Aren't there clear risks associated with these businesses? How have your investment teams factored those risks into their decision making?

You have carried out a lengthy dialogue and engagement with ZZ.

- ▶ What impact has that had on the investment decision and the relative weighting in portfolios?

Property/Infrastructure Investments, Direct and Indirect

- ▶ In your estimate, which of your various property and infrastructure business holdings is best positioned in terms of preparedness for climate change and the physical disruptions, which seem increasingly frequent from extreme weather events?
- ▶ Which of your holdings is the least ready given the differences in geographical exposure to disruption?
- ▶ What does that mean for your portfolio positioning?

Financial Sector Investments

Bank X has recently made a commitment on coal project financing.

- ▶ Do you believe that undertaking is strong enough to ensure its risk profile on carbon-intensive assets?
- ▶ Not least given the bank's ongoing lending to oil- and gas-related projects, do you believe that it has a clear understanding of climate risk and potentially stranded assets in its lending portfolio?
- ▶ How have you assessed the lending practices of non-bank lenders in your portfolio relative to their peers? Please describe how you have analyzed their risk management in light of the significant failures in the sector and tightening regulatory environment.

You are interested in Insurance Company AA.

- ▶ Have you discussed with Insurance Company AA its approach to the risk of exposure to disruptions arising from climate change?
- ▶ How have you assessed its overall transition risk exposure?
- ▶ Are you confident that the company understands its exposures fully and is equipped and skilled enough to manage them appropriately?

Industrial Sector Investments

You are liaising with Industrial Business Y.

- Are you concerned by the allegations regarding worker treatment at Industrial Business Y?
- Have you built into your model any expectation of fines or substantial damage claims, and are you confident that the dividend remains secure in most realistic scenarios?
- Can you be sure that the business is sustainable when it relies on such employment practices to maintain profitability?
- Do you have concerns about the costs of any changes in facilities or working practices to avoid such exposures in the future?
- Do you believe the company will retain staff and continue to be able to recruit appropriately skilled individuals?

You have a sizable aggregate position in Company GG. The governance of the company is particularly weak.

- What makes you comfortable that the business is run and overseen effectively and will appropriately address emerging challenges?
- Is the complexity of the corporate structure more about financial structuring and tax minimization than anything else?
- In which case, is there a risk that the management and board (which suffers from poor independence and weak governance) may miss signals from the underlying businesses because information flow is weak through the complex corporate structure?
- How are you engaging with the company on these issues, and what progress have you made so far?

You are liaising with Company BB.

- What do you think about Company BB's exposure to corruption risks?
- Does it have satisfactory management structures to mitigate and manage such exposures?
- Are you confident in the company's approach to money-laundering protections and in knowing the full backgrounds of its business partners?

Extractives Sector Investments

You have some significant holdings in oil and gas businesses.

- What is your reflection on the risks that they face in terms of stranded assets?
- Which of these companies best understands the risks of climate change for their business models?
- How are they considering transitioning their businesses to a more carbon-constrained world?

State-linked extractives company Z is also highly politicized.

- Are you content that its investments are commercial and will give economic returns, rather than more based in geopolitics on behalf of the government?

Holding Managers to Account: Monitoring Delivery

You hold a number of mining businesses. Their business models are inherently unsustainable.

- ▶ Which of these companies manages its E&S risks best, and which retains the greatest downside exposures?
- ▶ Which has a better handle on health and safety issues, and which better considers the implications of climate change (including the physical risks of extreme weather events) for their business?
- ▶ What has that analysis meant for your investment allocations?

Debt Investments

The fund has a number of sovereign debt holdings, in particular exposures to the CC and DD governments.

- ▶ Do you believe those countries have appropriate and effective national responses to the challenge of climate change?
- ▶ Aren't their nations and economies particularly exposed to extreme weather events and also to water shortages already—factors that will only intensify as climate change progresses over the time horizon of your bond holdings?
- ▶ Will they be able to respond robustly and effectively to these challenges, without affecting economic activity and their ability to finance existing debt?
- ▶ What is your exposure to green bonds in the portfolio? Why is there only minimal exposure?

Engagement

- ▶ Is there clear disclosure of the processes by which objectives are set and progress against them monitored?
- ▶ Who on the team sets engagement objectives? What is the oversight process to ensure that these objectives are robust and material and remain consistently so across the organization?
- ▶ How is progress against objectives assessed and captured for reporting? How do you gain confidence that material change has indeed been delivered?
- ▶ How do you decide to escalate an engagement if it has not been effective initially? What is the decision-making process, and how do teams decide between different forms of escalation (such as collaborative engagement or going public with concerns)?
- ▶ Can you give examples of cases where you have chosen to exit investments rather than continue to pursue engagement?

Test the quality, materiality, and bespoke nature of the objectives for an appropriate sample of engagements.

- Asset EE is a significant holding and faces some key risks. Can you demonstrate objectives that are in place for engagement with the investment, what actions have been taken to deliver those objectives, and what progress has been made in delivery?
- You have sold out of Asset FF over the period. Can you outline the engagement experience with its management over the last two years? What would have needed to change for you to be comfortable continuing to hold the asset?
- Are headline market-wide announcements reinforced by robust and tailored asset-specific activity?
- You have made substantial public statements in the last period. How do these get translated to concrete actions on the ground? How have the dialogues with individual assets changed as a result? Please give examples, including of the relevant objectives set for engagement.

The other form of ongoing assessment of ESG delivery that clients are likely to perform is some form of portfolio-wide assessment. Inevitably, because this covers portfolios as a whole, it is on a more statistical basis as opposed to the more anecdotal basis of the questions in the previous case study. The main ESG research firms (the market is currently dominated by MSCI and Morningstar Sustainalytics) now provide standard tools for asset owners to assess the ESG factors in their portfolios and also ESG-linked performance attribution. Typically, an asset owner that signs up for these tools will receive an analysis of all its portfolios; alternatively, a fund manager might choose to use the service in order to test its own approach and prepare for client questioning.

Inevitably, because some of these tools are based on the research firms' data, they will be subject to the issues that arise around the quality and consistency of that data, and some fund managers may raise concerns that these are not fair representations of the portfolios that they construct and of the quality of their ESG integration. Such a fund manager should be prepared to demonstrate how its own analysis of the ESG exposure of assets in the portfolio is a more accurate representation than those provided by external research firms. Even though there are limits to the quality of the external research, these analyses offer a basis for a conversation. As long as all parties take into account the limitations of the third-party approach (rather than assuming that the analysis provides some perfect insight), the conversation can be a challenging and useful one. In particular, the questioning can help the fund manager reveal once again the quality of its ESG integration and the depth of thought that goes into its investment decision making.

The following case study provides insight into the sort of data and analysis that might be provided in one of these standard ESG portfolio analysis tools. It also discusses ways in which a client might use that information to probe the quality of delivery by a fund manager.

CASE STUDIES

ESG Attribution

This case study highlights the style of reporting that a client might receive from a fund manager or a third-party ESG research provider about the portfolio and the questions that might arise as a result. Of course, some fund managers carry out this form of research themselves so they can, at least in part, pre-empt these

Holding Managers to Account: Monitoring Delivery

questions or at least be ready for them when they do come. It would be possible, of course, for the client to look at the data and comparisons for aggregate ESG figures, but the use of individual E, S, and G factors seems most common.

Portfolio New Deal: Overall Portfolio Analysis

	Portfolio New Deal (%)	Benchmark (%)	Positioning above or below Benchmark (%)
E score	79.2	83.4	−4.2
S score	81.7	80.3	1.4
G score	84.2	84.6	−0.4

This analysis suggests that the portfolio is placed

- better than the benchmark on S factors,
- almost at benchmark on G factors, and
- significantly below benchmark on E factors.

Client interest is therefore likely to focus particularly on E exposures in the portfolio.

Naturally, there would be scope for a discussion about whether the benchmark is an appropriate comparison for the portfolio (in the same way that this is frequently a discussion in relation to investment performance analysis). There is also scope for debate and discussion about the ESG research provider's analysis, although this is probably best done on an individual company basis. Most clients recognize that there are flaws in any firm's ESG analysis and are likely to view discussions on individual ratings as an opportunity to test and understand the quality of the fund manager's own ESG analysis and integration.

Individual Company Analysis from an ESG Research Provider

There are usually separate tables for each E, S, and G score in these forms of analysis; we provide a sample of only one here. For the purposes of this case study, the table below focuses on the E score in the context of the overall portfolio positioning.

Bottom Five E Detractors

Company	E Score (%)	Portfolio E Score (%)	Benchmark E Score (%)	Detraction Level (%)
Digger Mining		79.2	83.4	50.2
Smoky Power Generation	39.7	79.2	83.4	43.7
Flaring Oil Producer	48.1	79.2	83.4	35.3
Leaky Manufacturing	56.7	79.2	83.4	26.7
Sullen Motors	62.1	79.2	83.4	21.3

Very often the client will also see a group of outperformers for each of the ESG categories but naturally will tend to focus on the detractors. They will concentrate on the individual cases and the investment decisions that have led to their inclusion in the portfolio (taking particular interest in whether their inclusion is consistent with the mandate that has been agreed on) and are likely also to use these specific cases to seek to understand

- what the relevant investment decisions reveal about the investment process overall,
- whether that overall process is consistent with their understanding of what the fund manager had undertaken to do in the due diligence discussions and in the agreed mandate, and
- whether they remain comfortable with the investment process given their clearer understanding of it.

It is likely, therefore, that an asset owner will ask some of the sorts of probing questions highlighted in the previous case study to assess whether

- the companies are indeed a sensible part of the portfolio or
- they are evidence that the manager is not in fact delivering the investment process (integrating ESG factors) that has been contracted for.

Very often a fund manager will explain that the rating provided by the agency is based on historical data and the fund manager's own engagement with the company indicates that it has already changed or is in the process of change. The client is likely then to explore

1. what engagement the fund manager has carried out,
2. its level of confidence in the company's approach as a result of that engagement, and
3. over what time horizon that change is likely to be more visible to external parties.

Prudent clients return to these cases after an appropriate amount of time has passed to see what has indeed changed over that period. Changes that reflect the fund manager's explanation will clearly reinforce client confidence; a lack of concrete change and no real prospect of such change may undermine it. Time often enables clearer determination of superior analysis.

Frequently, analyses include the carbon intensity of companies in the portfolio, often in comparison to a suitable index. We do not provide an example of this in this chapter, but for many clients, it will be an issue for close attention. It is also likely to be an area for close questioning, particularly if a fund manager's purported focus on climate change issues does not seem to be reflected in a less carbon-intensive portfolio. Again, if the fund manager asserts that this is a timing issue with the service provider's analysis, the client is likely to want to explore that further at future meetings once the manager's alternative analysis has had a chance to be delivered in practice.

HOLDING MANAGERS TO ACCOUNT: MEASUREMENT AND REPORTING

9.1.6 explain the key challenges in measuring and reporting ESG-related investment performance: active, passive, and smart beta approaches; performance attribution; sensitivity analysis; risk measurement; engagement activity/impact; and integrated reporting and investment review

ESG reporting by investment managers is widespread but varies in the quality of disclosure. It ranges from

- general discussions of current debates and themes with no clear linkage to the work of the fund manager, sometimes associated with generalized aspirations or assertions, to
- much more concrete discussions of the work actually done by fund managers and delivered in practice, to the shape of portfolios and change through engagement.

As discussed in detail in Chapter 6, the new UK Stewardship Code calls for more reporting on outcomes from stewardship and ESG activity, rather than just discussions about broader events or the policies and activities of signatories. This pressure for discussion of what has concretely been delivered to the benefit of clients (which some managers call "impact") should improve the quality of fund manager reporting, reducing generalized reporting and increasing the focus on concrete activity. We will see how fund managers have risen to this challenge from March 2021 and what impact it has had on reporting on stewardship and ESG activity elsewhere in the world.

Investment firms typically produce annual (and often quarterly) reports describing

- their investment processes,
- the themes that they have worked on, and
- case studies on ESG investing or stewardship (or both).

Investment firms that are signatories to the PRI are also required to submit an annual report on their activities. According to the PRI, the reporting process allows signatories to

- evaluate their responsible investment progress against an industry-standard framework,
- receive ongoing feedback and tools for improvement,
- benchmark their performance against peers,
- see the big picture by understanding the state of the market,
- strengthen internal processes and build ESG capacity, and
- summarize activities for staff, clients, shareholders, and regulators.[22]

A public version of the PRI report, as well as the headline scores, is made available to others. Naturally, those fund managers that perform particularly well on the PRI assessment will tend to highlight and publicize this—emphasizing in particular those asset classes where the fund manager performs best.

---

22 PRI, "The Reporting Process" (2020). www.unpri.org/reporting-and-assessment-resources/reporting-for-signatories/3057.article.

Alongside these reports, there are now multiple tools available to deliver information on the ESG characteristics of a portfolio and to measure those relative to relevant benchmarks. As a 2016 report by the Pensions and Lifetime Savings Association (PLSA) pointed out,

> *By applying ESG data to existing standard benchmarks, the pension fund can measure its portfolios against the same standard market benchmarks currently used to measure performance. For example, if the pension fund measures equity performance against the MSCI World, it can continue to use this same benchmark, but this time containing an ESG data set, to facilitate a comparison of the portfolio's ESG score with the MSCI World. Conversely, a pension fund could choose customised ESG indices for a more effective comparison. For example, if a pension fund has excluded fossil fuel stocks from its portfolio, it may wish to measure ESG performance against an index that has been optimised to exclude fossil fuel stocks.*[23]

Another form of reporting that some fund managers provide on the ESG characteristics of their portfolios is to report on real-world impacts or at least on the equivalent real-world impacts. Such measures as the tree-planting equivalent of a carbon-tilted fund (or the equivalent of the number of cars taken off the road) are somewhat theoretical and clearly rely on multiple assumptions; nonetheless, they relate the investment process to the real world and may prove especially powerful for retail investors in particular. Such reporting is still in its early stages and may well need further assurance and consistency for it to have real power.

There are also numerous performance attribution service providers, disaggregating the drivers of investment performance and identifying where performance comes from. Investors will be used to identifying the five leading stock performers and detractors from performance over their client's defined reporting period. This is usually accompanied by factor analysis and measurement of risk exposures as well.

Some of these factors and risk measurements are now likely to be attributed to ESG performance metrics. A form of ESG attribution that a client might be presented with, either by the fund manager or by a third-party provider, is outlined and discussed in the previous case study on ESG attribution.

The attribution of returns to ESG factors is challenging, not least because of the significant range of investment approaches that are included in the broad realm of ESG investing. It is relatively easy to assess the performance drag or enhancement that comes from excluding an industrial sector (such as tobacco), but it is hard to demonstrate the value added by a program of engagement, particularly given the timescales usually required for engagement programs to reach positive outcomes. Furthermore, the more fully integrated ESG factors become in the investment process, the harder it is to disaggregate a particular ESG driver from the broader investment decision.

In 2015, the PLSA published a disclosure guide for public equities developed by a group of pension schemes, setting out some pared-down expectations for manager-reporting on both ESG integration and stewardship activities.[24] The disclosure on ESG integration asks for separate disclosure on both

- identification of ESG risk and
- the management and monitoring of ESG risks and opportunities, with suggested possible disclosures in respect of each.

---

23 PLSA, "Environmental, Social and Corporate Governance (ESG) Made Simple Guide" (2016). www.plsa.co.uk/portals/0/Documents/0585-Environmental-Social-and-Corporate-Governance-ESG-Made-Simple.pdf.
24 PLSA, "A Guide to Responsible Investment Reporting in Public Equity" (2015). www.sustainablefinance.ch/upload/cms/user/2015_01_26_guide_to_responsible_investment_reporting_in_public_equity_published_NAPF1.pdf.

Holding Managers to Account: Measurement and Reporting

The following are the first three possible points offered as ways to demonstrate the identification of ESG risk and opportunity:

- "Examples of where and why the manager is prepared to take either stock or sector ESG risks or where it sees opportunities.
- Quantitative or qualitative examples of material ESG factors identified in fundamental analysis and stock valuation.
- Identification of long-term ESG secular trends and themes (as potential determinants of future growth or valuation, etc.) and the extent to which they have influenced portfolio construction decisions."

The proposed possible disclosures to demonstrate the management and monitoring of ESG risks and opportunities include the following:

> *"Stock level ESG analysis for top risk and performance detractors/contributors in the reporting period.*
> *Any material changes to portfolio companies' ESG performance. Examples may include where the manager's view of ESG risk and opportunity differs from the market/rating agencies."*

Similarly, the ICGN Model Mandate requests two areas of disclosure that are ESG-specific:

- *The manager's assessment of ESG risks that are embedded in the portfolio.* This should include both what these risks are and what the manager has done to identify, monitor, and manage them. This can readily be compared against the external tools used to assess ESG risk in the portfolio or the ESG element of the performance factorial analysis. This should prove to be a core element of the portfolio manager demonstrating genuine ESG investment credentials.
- *A detailed disclosure of stewardship engagement and voting activity.* The mandate is clear that these need to be two separate disclosures—that is, mere disclosure of voting activity is not sufficient to satisfy the requirement for engagement disclosure.

The PRI's 2016 "Practical Guide to ESG Integration for Equity Investing"[25] (which builds on the organization's 2013 publication on aligning expectations)[26] includes multiple case studies from fund managers outlining their approach to ESG integration and highlighting their assessments of how their ESG work has added value.

It is apparent that there are as many approaches to the integration of ESG factors as there are underlying investment approaches themselves. What the asset owner will want to know is whether the ESG approach is

- genuinely aligned with the fund manager's investment style,
- delivered effectively in practice, and
- aligned with her own investment needs and beliefs.

To guard against fund managers selecting individual cases that put their work in the best light, some clients seek to identify outliers so that they can test whether the asserted method for ESG integration is genuinely delivered in practice, consistently across the portfolio as a whole.

---

25 PRI, "Practical Guide to ESG Integration for Equity Investing: Executive Summary" (2016). www.unpri.org/listed-equity/a-practical-guide-to-esg-integration-for-equity-investing/10.article.
26 PRI, "Aligning Expectations: Guidance for Asset Owners on Incorporating ESG Factors into Manager Selection, Appointment and Monitoring."

There is no set or agreed format for engagement disclosure, so each fund manager has its own model. Typically, this includes statistics on activity at a greater or lesser level of granularity. It is no longer acceptable to provide statistics at the organization level that are not specifically tailored to the fund in question. In addition, the typical disclosure includes a sample of written descriptions of individual engagement meetings; again, these should be tailored to the fund, but many fund managers reveal more about the focus of their activities than they intend by the imbalance in their reporting toward their home market and region.

Many fund managers and, particularly, the specialist stewardship providers disclose their form of analysis of what has been delivered in the period through their engagement activities. Most use some measure of either milestones or progress against KPIs to provide their assessment of progress. These are proprietary models and inevitably are somewhat prone to some bias in the analysis; however, clients are able to test these in detail. At a minimum, these disclosures provide some transparency into deliverables from engagement.

KEY FACTS

1. Agency problems exist in the investment chain just as they exist between companies and their owners. This agency problem also extends to aligning ESG beliefs.
2. Accountability and alignment can be delivered in large part through aligning the time horizons of fund managers with their clients. This helps ensure that fund managers will work to accomplish their fiduciary duties.
3. This can be reinforced through a focus on longer-term factors rather than short-term performance assessment.
4. ESG integration will vary between different fund management firms and individual portfolio managers, tailored to the established investment style and approach.
5. Increasing numbers of advisory services are available to help clients assess the ESG delivery of their fund managers and attribute performance and E, S, and G characteristics of the portfolio. These are perhaps best used in dialogue with managers to test whether they are delivering their expected investment style in practice.
6. Asset owners will seek to challenge and debate hard cases of individual assets in portfolios so that they can understand how effective ESG integration is in practice and how well the portfolio reflects that integration.
7. Inadequate resourcing of ESG work is always a constraint on effectiveness and the application of the integration and engagement approach across portfolios. Collective engagement is one key way to bolster resources.
8. The ESG expectations of clients have a range of drivers and therefore manifest in different forms.

FURTHER READING

The Investor Forum. 2017. Review of 2017 Activities. www.investorforum.org.uk/wp-content/uploads/2018/07/Annual-review-2017.pdf

International Corporate Governance Network 2012. "ICGN Model Mandate Initiative." https://d3n8a8pro7vhmx.cloudfront.net/intentionalendowments/pages/27/attachments/original/1420777456/ICGN_Model_Mandate_Initiative.pdf?1420777456.

Lee, P. 2008. "Long-Term Low Friction: An Investment Framework Which Works for the Beneficiaries Rather Than Their Agents." *Tomorrow's Investor* (September). www.thersa.org/globalassets/pdfs/blogs/rsa-paul-lee.pdf.

PRI 2016. "Attributing Performance to ESG Factors" (4 September). www.unpri.org/listed-equity/attributing-performance-to-esg-factors/742.article.

Appendix: SFDR Disclosures and CFA Institute Disclosure Standards

APPENDIX: SFDR DISCLOSURES AND CFA INSTITUTE DISCLOSURE STANDARDS

The following sections provide some background information on SFDR disclosures and CFA Institute Disclosure Standards.

Global ESG Disclosure Standards for Investment Products

On 1 November 2021, CFA Institute issued the Global ESG Disclosure Standards for Investment Products, the first global voluntary standards for disclosing how an investment product considers ESG issues in its objectives, investment process, and stewardship activities.

The purpose of the Global ESG Disclosure Standards for Investment Products is to facilitate fair representation and full disclosure of an investment product's consideration of ESG issues in its objectives, investment process, or stewardship activities. When investment products' ESG approaches are fairly represented and fully disclosed, investors, consultants, advisers, and distributors can better understand, evaluate, and compare investment products, and the potential for greenwashing diminishes.

The Global ESG Disclosure Standards for Investment Products are compatible with

- all types of investment vehicles, including but not limited to pooled funds, exchange-traded funds (ETFs), strategies for separately managed accounts, limited partnerships, and insurance-based investment products;
- all asset classes, including but not limited to listed equities, fixed income, private equity, private debt, infrastructure, and real estate;
- all ESG approaches, including but not limited to ESG integration, exclusion, screening, best-in-class, thematic and sustainability-themed investing, impact investing, and stewardship;
- active and passive strategies; and
- national and regional investment product ESG disclosure regulations.

Compliance with the Global ESG Disclosure Standards for Investment Products is voluntary. An investment manager may choose the investment products to which it applies the standards. An investment manager may also choose to have an independent third party provide assurance for one or more of its ESG disclosure statements. All requirements and recommendations for both investment managers and firms conducting assurance engagements will be contained in the Examination Procedures for the Global ESG Disclosure Standards for Investment Products, which are expected to be issued in Fall 2022.

The Global ESG Disclosure Standards for Investment Products were developed and are maintained with extensive input from the volunteer investment professionals who have served and continue to serve on the CFA Institute ESG Technical Committee, ESG Verification Subcommittee, and ESG Working Group.

Global ESG Disclosure Standards for Investment Products

www.cfainstitute.org/-/media/documents/ESG-standards/Global-ESG-Disclosure-Standards-for-Investment-Products.pdf

Handbook

www.cfainstitute.org/-/media/documents/ESG-standards/Global-ESG-Disclosure-Standards-for-Investment-Products-Handbook.pdf

ESG Disclosure Statement Template

www.cfainstitute.org/-/media/documents/ESG-standards/eds-template.docx

SFDR Disclosures

On 6 April 2022, the European Commission adopted a set of technical standards to be used by financial market participants when disclosing sustainability-related information under the SFDR. The derived Delegated Regulation specifies the exact content, methodology, and presentation of the information to be disclosed, thereby improving its quality and comparability. Under these rules, financial market participants will provide detailed information about how they tackle and reduce any possible negative impacts that their investments may have on the environment and society in general.

These new requirements are expected to help assess the sustainability performance of financial products. Compliance with sustainability-related disclosures will contribute to strengthening investor protection and reduce greenwashing. This will ultimately support the financial system's transition toward a more sustainable economy.

The requirements are subject to scrutiny by the European Parliament and the European Council and are scheduled to take effect on 1 January 2023. Financial products need to start disclosing Taxonomy KPIs 18 months before companies are required to do so.

Delegated Regulation

https://ec.europa.eu/finance/docs/level-2-measures/C_2022_1931_1_EN_annexe_acte_autonome_part1_v6.pdf

Template: Principal Adverse Sustainability Impacts Statement

https://ec.europa.eu/finance/docs/level-2-measures/C_2022_1931_1_EN_annexe_acte_autonome_part1_v6.pdf

Template: Pre-Contractual Disclosure for the Financial Products Referred to in Article 8, Paragraphs 1, 2, and 2a, of Regulation (EU) 2019/2088 and Article 6, First Paragraph, of Regulation (EU) 2020/852

https://ec.europa.eu/finance/docs/level-2-measures/C_2022_1931_2_EN_annexe_acte_autonome_cp_part1_v5.pdf

Template: Pre-Contractual Disclosure for the Financial Products Referred to in Article 9, Paragraphs 1 to 4a, of Regulation (EU) 2019/2088 and Article 5, First Paragraph, of Regulation (EU) 2020/852

https://ec.europa.eu/finance/docs/level-2-measures/C_2022_1931_3_EN_annexe_acte_autonome_cp_part1_v5.pdf

Template: Periodic Disclosure for the Financial Products Referred to in Article 8, Paragraphs 1, 2, and 2a, of Regulation (EU) 2019/2088 and Article 6, First Paragraph, of Regulation (EU) 2020/852

https://ec.europa.eu/finance/docs/level-2-measures/C_2022_1931_4_EN_annexe_acte_autonome_cp_part1_v5.pdf

Template: Periodic Disclosure for the Financial Products Referred to in Article 9, Paragraphs 1 to 4a, of Regulation (EU) 2019/2088 and Article 5, First Paragraph, of Regulation (EU) 2020/852

https://ec.europa.eu/finance/docs/level-2-measures/C_2022_1931_5_EN_annexe_acte_autonome_cp_part1_v5.pdf

Alternatives: To date, SFDR disclosures have been silent on how to deal with short positions. In the context of taxonomy alignment, the RTS states that the calculation of taxonomy alignment should be netted by applying the methodology used to calculate net short positions in the EU short-selling regulation. Although this only explicitly refers to the calculation of taxonomy alignments, firms using short positions in their products may find this useful in determining how to approach shorting techniques/strategies in the context of the SFDR disclosures more broadly.

SELF PRACTICE AND SELF ASSESSMENT

1. What is the first step in the effective design of a client ESG investment mandate?
   a. Tailor ESG investment approach to client expectations.
   b. Develop client-relevant ESG-aware investment mandates.
   c. Clarify client needs and set them out in a clear statement of ESG investment beliefs.

2. An ESG policy of a fund management firm needs to address the manner in which the portfolio manager establishes:
   a. engagement with companies and issuers on ESG issues.
   b. rationale and methodology for ESG portfolio-level assessment.
   c. engagement with policymakers on responsible investment and ESG-related issues.

3. Which of the following best describes an ESG-related thematic focus? It:
   a. seeks to generate a positive, measurable social or environmental impact alongside a financial return.
   b. aims to invest in sectors, industries, or companies that are expected to benefit from long-term macro or structural ESG-related trends.
   c. excludes securities, issuers, or companies from the investment product based on certain ESG-related activities, business practices, or business segments.

4. To incorporate ESG factors in index tracking, managers can exert influence on companies through:
   a. engagement and voting.
   b. governance arrangements.
   c. representation on board seats.

5. Which of the following is the *most likely* primary driver of ESG investment for a sovereign wealth fund?
   a. Fiduciary duty
   b. Reputational risk
   c. Awareness of financial impacts of climate change

6. Which of the following describes the risk mindset of a general insurer?
   a. Loss aversion
   b. High risk tolerance
   c. High tolerance for illiquidity

7. Exclusions is the implied favored ESG approach of a:
   a. general insurer.
   b. charitable foundation.
   c. defined benefit pension scheme.

8. The Brunel Asset Management Accord:
   a. emphasizes that short-term underperformance is not in itself likely to give rise to undue concern.

Self Practice and Self Assessment

    b. provides a helpful framework and proposes best practices for ESG-aware investment mandates.

    c. produces a Stewardship Checklist for asset owners to ensure an effective and meaningful stewardship strategy.

9. The PLSA's guide on ESG integration requires disclosure on:

    a. elimination of ESG risks.

    b. short-term ESG secular trends.

    c. management and monitoring of ESG risks and opportunities.

10. The ICGN Model Mandate requires ESG-specific disclosure on:

    a. an ESG risk materiality map.

    b. ESG-aware investment mandates.

    c. stewardship engagement and voting activity.

The following information relates to questions 11-23

Self Assessment Questions

These questions are provided only to enable you to test your understanding of the chapter content. They are not indicative of the types and standard of questions you may see in the examination. The Self-Assessment questions do not include an explanation of the correct answer.

11. Reporting ESG information with consistency and continuity helps ensure compliance with the portfolio's ESG policy, responsiveness to ESG-related portfolio issues, and effective portfolio oversight. Which of the following is *not* one of McKinsey's proposed dimensions of investing for the purposes of applying sustainable investing practices?

    a. Investment beliefs and strategy

    b. Regulatory and policy environment

    c. Performance management

    d. Public reporting

12. Which of these forms of asset owner is most likely to apply an exclusion policy barring investment in all assets exposed to a particular business area?

    a. Defined benefit pension scheme

    b. General insurance business

    c. Charitable foundation

    d. Sovereign wealth fund

13. How might a fund manager demonstrate to clients that it is addressing the challenge of resourcing stewardship activities?

    a. Details the processes by which it prioritizes engagements

    b. Sets out how it is adding stewardship staff and building expertise among its fund managers

    c. Demonstrates its active participation in one or more formal collective engagement vehicles

    d. All of the above

14. What is the clearest risk for an asset owner of leaving voting decision making in the hands of its fund managers?

- a. Fund managers will fail to align the votes with their investment thesis.
- b. If a company is held by more than one fund manager, the asset owner's shares may be voted differently.
- c. Votes are more likely to be lost in the voting system.
- d. This reduces fund manager accountability for their decisions.

15. Which of the following is *not* a driver for clients to seek ESG investment, at least for one class of client?

- a. Fiduciary duty
- b. Reputational risk
- c. Personal ethics
- d. A belief that social issues are unimportant

16. Which of the following is *not* a typical way in which asset managers integrate ESG factors?

- a. Use ESG as a threshold requirement before investment can be considered.
- b. Use ESG as a factor that informs the valuation.
- c. Use ESG as a risk assessment that offers a level of confidence in the valuation.
- d. Use ESG as a basis for explaining investment holdings to clients.

17. Why might a client concentrate her attention on ESG outliers in her active monitoring and assessment of fund manager performance?

- a. Because companies with weak ESG performance will test how effective fund manager ESG integration is in practice
- b. Because allowing the fund manager to choose which case studies are focused on in discussions may lead to less insight
- c. Because the client can focus on ESG factors of most concern to her at a given time
- d. All of the above

18. Which two ESG-specific areas of disclosure are requested by the International Corporate Governance Network (ICGN) Model Mandate?

- a. A breakdown of the return on investment for each stakeholder group and details of how each form of ESG risk has been hedged by the portfolio manager
- b. A materiality map identifying the ESG impact of all investments and a detailed disclosure of the voting record of all executive and non-executive directors
- c. A detailed disclosure of stewardship engagement and voting activity must be made, and the manager's assessment of ESG risks must be embedded in the portfolio.
- d. A pro-rata environmental footprint of all investments must be estimated, and the impact of all externalities from investments must be identified.

19. Which of the following, according to the Brunel Asset Management Accord, is *not* in itself a likely cause for concern?

- a. Failure to manage risk appropriately
- b. A change in the expected investment style

Self Practice and Self Assessment

    c. Short-term underperformance

    d. Lack of understanding of reasons for underperformance

20. What behavioral step should clients take to ensure that fund managers invest in alignment with the investment horizons as agreed in ESG-focused client mandates?

    a. Clients assess investment performance *less* frequently and predictably.

    b. Clients assess investment performance *more* frequently and unpredictably.

    c. Clients raise questions about the ESG characteristics of each company newly purchased by a fund manager.

    d. Clients raise questions about the ESG characteristics of each company that is sold by a fund manager.

21. Which of the following are expected to be reported by the Pensions and Lifetime Savings Association (PLSA) disclosure guide for public equities?

    a. ESG integration and stewardship

    b. Social impact and stakeholder engagement

    c. ESG risk and carbon footprint

    d. Social risk and board engagement

22. Which of the following is *not* a way of assessing whether a fund manager effectively integrates ESG factors, according to the PLSA?

    a. Examples of where and why the manager is prepared to take either stock or sector ESG risks or where it sees opportunities

    b. Evaluation of how much financial return is directly attributable to ESG factors

    c. Quantitative or qualitative examples of material ESG factors identified in fundamental analysis and stock valuation

    d. Identification of long-term ESG secular trends and themes and the extent to which they have influenced portfolio construction decisions

23. Which of the following is likely to be a primary ESG driver for a European defined benefit pension scheme?

    a. Reputational risk

    b. Fiduciary duty

    c. Personal ethics

    d. Founding aims

SOLUTIONS

1. C is correct. The first step in the effective design of a mandate is that clients should be clear about their needs and set them out in a clear statement of ESG investment beliefs. Doing so will require them to define their investment goals and beliefs, which will help them define how they plan to create value and how they will orient their investment approach. The investment beliefs—which might be expressed in a statement of investment principles—ought to guide the overall approach toward ESG investment (and investment more generally) and will help frame any mandate agreed with an investment manager.

2. B is correct. An ESG policy should formally outline the investment approach and degree of ESG integration in a firm. An ESG policy needs to address the manner in which the portfolio manager

   - addresses ESG issues at portfolio reviews,
   - establishes the rationale and methodology for ESG portfolio-level assessment,
   - assesses exposure to ESG risk in the risk management function,
   - determines ESG impacts to the portfolio,
   - responds in the investment decision-making process to ESG implications, and
   - discloses ESG exposure to the fund's investors.

3. B is correct. The ESG Disclosure Standards for Investment Products proposed by CFA Institute highlight six main categories of products. An ESG-related thematic focus aims to invest in sectors, industries, or companies that are expected to benefit from long-term macro or structural ESG-related trends.

4. A is correct. There are major ESG considerations for a pension fund or other asset owner when seeking to allocate a new mandate across the full range of potential asset classes. The elements to ensure that ESG issues are appropriately delivered by the relevant mandate include mandate choice, investment integration, and engagement. In the case of passive/index tracking, managers can exert influence on companies through engagement and voting. There is also scope for influence on market- and system-wide issues.

5. B is correct. Different clients (institutional, retail, or private) have different investment objectives, risk/return profiles, and drivers. These will influence the type of ESG investing strategies they will consider most attractive. In the case of a sovereign wealth fund, the primary driver for ESG investment is reputational risk.

6. A is correct. Different clients (institutional, retail, or private) have different investment objectives, risk/return profiles, and drivers. The risk mindset of a general insurer is loss aversion, compared to a defined benefit pension scheme, which has a higher risk tolerance, and a sovereign wealth fund, which has high tolerance for illiquidity.

7. B is correct. Different clients (institutional, retail, or private) have different investment objectives, risk/return profiles, and drivers. These will influence the type of ESG investing strategies they will consider most attractive. The implied favored ESG approach of a charitable foundation is exclusions, to ensure investment is consistent with founding or charitable aims.

Solutions

8. A is correct. The Brunel Asset Management Accord sets out a pension manager's approach to long-term investment and ESG factors. It emphasizes that short-term underperformance is not in itself likely to give rise to undue concern for the client: "Investment performance, particularly in the short term, will be of limited significance in evaluating the manager."

9. C is correct. The PLSA published a disclosure guide for public equities developed by a group of pension schemes, setting out some pared-down expectations for manager reporting on both ESG integration and stewardship activities. The disclosure on ESG integration asks for separate disclosure on both identification of ESG risk and the management and monitoring of ESG risks and opportunities.

10. C is correct. The ICGN Model Mandate requests two areas of disclosure that are ESG specific:

    the manager's assessment of ESG risks that are embedded in the portfolio
    a detailed disclosure of stewardship engagement and voting activity

11. B is correct.

12. C is correct.

13. D is correct.

14. B is correct.

15. D is correct.

16. D is correct.

17. D is correct.

18. C is correct.

19. C is correct.

20. A is correct.

21. A is correct.

22. B is correct.

23. B is correct.

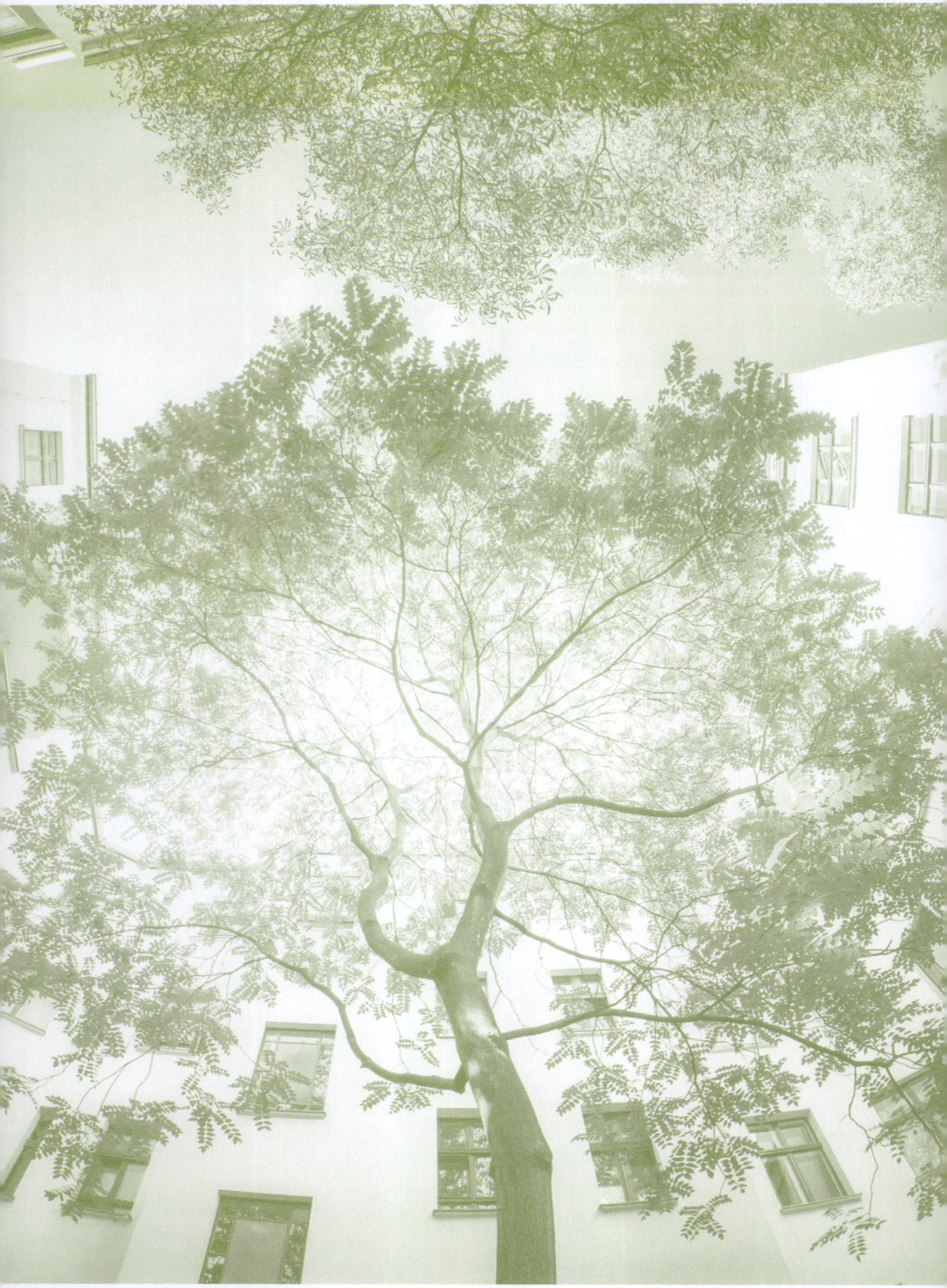

Printed in Great Britain
by Amazon